Rosa M. Manchón and Paul Kei Matsuda
Handbook of Second and Foreign Language Writing

Handbooks of Applied Linguistics

—

Communication Competence
Language and Communication Problems
Practical Solutions

Edited by
Karlfried Knapp
Gerd Antos
Daniel Perrin
Marjolijn Verspoor

Volume 11

Handbook of Second and Foreign Language Writing

Edited by
Rosa M. Manchón and Paul Kei Matsuda

DE GRUYTER

ISBN 978-1-61451-180-9
e-ISBN (PDF) 978-1-61451-133-5
e-ISBN (EPUB) 978-1-5015-0028-2

Library of Congress Cataloging-in-Publication Data
A CIP catalog record for this book has been applied for at the Library of Congress.

Bibliographic information published by the Deutsche Nationalbibliothek
The Deutsche Nationalbibliothek lists this publication in the Deutsche Nationalbibliografie;
detailed bibliographic data are available on the Internet at http://dnb.dnb.de.

© 2016 Walter de Gruyter Inc., Boston/Berlin
Typesetting: Meta Systems Publishing & Printservices GmbH, Wustermark
Printing and binding: CPI books GmbH, Leck
♾ Printed on acid-free paper
Printed in Germany

www.degruyter.com

Preface

The present volume constitutes another addition to the De Gruyter Mouton *Handbooks of Applied Linguistics*. As the reader can see from our subsequent *Introduction to the Handbook Series* on the next pages, the founding editors originally intended to comprise nine books only. However, various developments led us to abandon this self-imposed restriction, the most important ones being those in Applied Linguistics itself.

When we began planning this series in the late 1990s, the disciplinary status and scope of Applied Linguistics was less clear than it appears to be today. At that time, intensive debates were going on as to whether Applied Linguistics should be restricted to applying methods and findings from linguistics only, whether it should be regarded as a field of interdisciplinary synthesis drawing on psychology, sociology, ethnology and similar disciplines that are also dealing with aspects of language and communication, whether it should be regarded as an independent discipline in its own right, whether it was restricted to foreign language teaching, etc. Thus, what "Applied Linguistics" is and what an Applied Linguist does was highly controversial.

Against that backdrop, we felt that a series of Handbooks of Applied Linguistics could not simply be an accidental selection of descriptions of research findings and practical activities that were or could be published in books and articles labeled as "applied linguistic". Rather, for us such a series had to be based on an epistemological concept that frames the status and scope of our concept of Applied Linguistics. Departing from contemporary Philosophy of Science which sees academic disciplines under the pressure to successfully solve practical everyday problems encountered by the societies which aliment them, we emphasized the view that was at that time only emerging – the programmatic view that Applied Linguistics means the solving of real-world problems with language and communication. This concept appears to have become mainstream since.

In line with our conviction that Applied Linguistics is for problem solving, we decided to compile a series of books which aimed at giving representative descriptions of the ability of this field of academic inquiry of providing accounts, analyses, explanations and, where possible, solutions of everyday problems with language and communication. To delimit the range of topics to be dealt with, we planned a set of nine volumes which were intended to present findings and applications of Applied Linguistics in concentric circles, as it were, departing from aspects of the communication competence of the individual via those of interpersonal, intergroup, organizational, public, multilingual, foreign language, intercultural, and technical communication ultimately to the level of society at large.

From the reception this series received in the academic community, among practitioners and on the market, the underlying concept was a complete success. In fact, this success even triggered competitive handbook series by other publishers.

It has to be admitted, though, that the selection of topic areas for these nine volumes more than ten years ago was guided by what were key issues in Applied Linguistics at that time. Meanwhile, however, further problems with language and communication have come to the fore, and also some topics which were dealt with in individual chapters of the previous nine volumes meanwhile have attracted so much attention, generating so much new insights, that they merit an in-depth treatment in individual volumes devoted solely to these. This development, the fact that repeatedly distinguished colleagues approached us with proposals to edit further volumes in this handbook series and the market success convinced both De Gruyter Mouton publishers and the series editors to continue the *Handbooks of Applied Linguistics* beyond the initial nine.

Meanwhile, this is an open-ended series. It will publish individual, self-contained volumes that depart from the view that Applied Linguistics is problem solving and that give a coherent and representative account of how the respective area of practical problems with language and communication is dealt with in this field of inquiry.

The present volume is an example of this. It also marks a change in the series editorship, with Daniel Perrin and Marjolijn Verspoor succeeding the founding editors.

Karlfried Knapp (Erfurt)
Gerd Antos (Halle/Saale)
Daniel Perrin (Zürich)
Marjolijn Verspoor (Groningen)

Karlfried Knapp and Gert Antos

Introduction to the handbook series

Linguistics for problem solving

1 Science and application at the turn of the millennium

The distinction between "pure" and "applied" sciences is an old one. According to Meinel (2000), it was introduced by the Swedish chemist Wallerius in 1751 as part of the dispute of that time between the scholastic disciplines and the then emerging epistemic sciences. However, although the concept of "Applied Science" gained currency rapidly since that time, it has remained problematic.

Until recently, the distinction between "pure" and "applied" mirrored the distinction between "theory" and "practice". The latter ran all the way through Western history of science since its beginnings in antique times. At first, it was only philosophy that was regarded as a scholarly and, hence, theoretical discipline. Later it was followed by other leading disciplines, as e.g., the sciences. However, as academic disciplines, all of them remained theoretical. In fact, the process of achieving independence of theory was essential for the academic disciplines to become independent from political, religious or other contingencies and to establish themselves at universities and academies. This also implied a process of emancipation from practical concerns – an at times painful development which manifested (and occasionally still manifests) itself in the discrediting of and disdain for practice and practitioners. To some, already the very meaning of the notion "applied" carries a negative connotation, as is suggested by the contrast between the widely used synonym for "theoretical", i.e. "pure" (as used, e.g., in the distinction between "Pure" and "Applied Mathematics") and its natural antonym "impure". On a different level, a lower academic status sometimes is attributed to applied disciplines because of their alleged lack of originality – they are perceived as simply and one-directionally applying insights gained in basic research and watering them down by neglecting the limiting conditions under which these insights were achieved.

Today, however, the academic system is confronted with a new understanding of science. In politics, in society and, above all, in economy a new concept of science has gained acceptance which questions traditional views. In recent philosophy of science, this is labelled as "science under the pressure to succeed" – i.e. as science whose theoretical structure and criteria of evaluation are increasingly conditioned by the pressure of application (Carrier, Stöltzner, and Wette 2004):

> Whenever the public is interested in a particular subject, e.g., when a new disease develops that cannot be cured by conventional medication, the public requests science to provide new

insights in this area as quickly as possible. In doing so, the public is less interested in whether these new insights fit seamlessly into an existing theoretical framework, but rather whether they make new methods of treatment and curing possible. (Institut für Wirtschafts- und Technikforschung 2004, our translation).

With most of the practical problems like these, sciences cannot rely on knowledge that is already available, simply because such knowledge does not yet exist. Very often, the problems at hand do not fit neatly into the theoretical framework of one particular "pure science", and there is competition among disciplines with respect to which one provides the best theoretical and methodological resources for potential solutions. And more often than not the problems can be tackled only by adopting an interdisciplinary approach.

As a result, the traditional "Cascade Model", where insights were applied top-down from basic research to practice, no longer works in many cases. Instead, a kind of "application oriented basic research" is needed, where disciplines – conditioned by the pressure of application – take up a certain still diffuse practical issue, define it as a problem against the background of their respective theoretical and methodological paradigms, study this problem and finally develop various application oriented suggestions for solutions. In this sense, applied science, on the one hand, has to be conceived of as a scientific strategy for problem solving – a strategy that starts from mundane practical problems and ultimately aims at solving them. On the other hand, despite the dominance of application that applied sciences are subjected to, as sciences they can do nothing but develop such solutions in a theoretically reflected and methodologically well founded manner. The latter, of course, may lead to the well-known fact that even applied sciences often tend to concentrate on "application oriented basic research" only and thus appear to lose sight of the original practical problem. But despite such shifts in focus both the boundaries between disciplines and between pure and applied research are getting more and more blurred.

Today it is obvious that sciences are requested to provide more and something different than just theory, basic research or pure knowledge. Rather, sciences are increasingly being regarded as partners in a more comprehensive social and economic context of problem solving and are evaluated against expectations to be practically relevant. This also implies that sciences are expected to be critical, reflecting their impact on society. This new "applied" type of science is confronted with the question: Which role can the sciences play in solving individual, interpersonal, social, intercultural, political or technical problems? This question is typical of a conception of science that was especially developed and propagated by the influential philosopher Sir Karl Popper – a conception that also this handbook series is based on.

2 "Applied Linguistics": Concepts and controversies

The concept of "Applied Linguistics" is not as old as the notion of "Applied Science", but it has also been problematical in its relation to theoretical linguistics since its beginning. There seems to be a widespread consensus that the notion "Applied Linguistics" emerged in 1948 with the first issue of the journal *Language Learning* which used this compound in its subtitle *A Quarterly Journal of Applied Linguistics*. This history of its origin certainly explains why even today "Applied Linguistics" still tends to be predominantly associated with foreign language teaching and learning in the Anglophone literature in particular, as can bee seen e.g., from Johnson and Johnson (1998), whose *Encyclopedic Dictionary of Applied Linguistics* is explicitly subtitled *A Handbook for Language Teaching*. However, this theory of origin is historically wrong. As is pointed out by Back (1970), the concept of applying linguistics can be traced back to the early 19th century in Europe, and the very notion "Applied Linguistics" was used in the early 20th already.

2.1 Theoretically applied vs. practically Applied Linguistics

As with the relation between "Pure" and "Applied" sciences pointed out above, also with "Applied Linguistics" the first question to be asked is what makes it different from "Pure" or "Theoretical Linguistics". It is not surprising, then, that the terminologist Back takes this difference as the point of departure for his discussion of what constitutes "Applied Linguistics". In the light of recent controversies about this concept it is no doubt useful to remind us of his terminological distinctions.

Back (1970) distinguishes between "Theoretical Linguistics" – which aims at achieving knowledge for its own sake, without considering any other value –, "Practice" – i.e. any kind of activity that serves to achieve any purpose in life in the widest sense, apart from the striving for knowledge for its own sake – and "Applied Linguistics", as being based on "Theoretical Linguistics" on the one hand and as aiming at usability in "Practice" on the other. In addition, he makes a difference between "Theoretical Applied Linguistics" and "Practical Applied Linguistics", which is of particular interest here. The former is defined as the use of insights and methods of "Theoretical Linguistics" for gaining knowledge in another, non-linguistic discipline, such as ethnology, sociology, law or literary studies, the latter as the application of insights from linguistics in a practical field related to language, such as language teaching, translation, and the like. For Back, the contribution of applied linguistics is to be seen in the planning of practical action. Language teaching, for example, is practical action done by practitioners, and what applied linguistics can contribute to this is, e.g., to provide contrastive descriptions of the languages involved as a foundation for teaching methods. These contrastive descriptions in turn have to be based on the descriptive methods developed in theoretical linguistics.

However, in the light of the recent epistemological developments outlined above, it may be useful to reinterpret Back's notion of "Theoretically Applied Linguistics". As he himself points out, dealing with practical problems can have repercussions on the development of the theoretical field. Often new approaches, new theoretical concepts and new methods are a prerequisite for dealing with a particular type of practical problems, which may lead to an – at least in the beginning – "application oriented basic research" in applied linguistics itself, which with some justification could also be labelled "theoretically applied", as many such problems require the transgression of disciplinary boundaries. It is not rare that a domain of "Theoretically Applied Linguistics" or "application oriented basic research" takes on a life of its own, and that also something which is labelled as "Applied Linguistics" might in fact be rather remote from the mundane practical problems that originally initiated the respective subject area. But as long as a relation to the original practical problem can be established, it may be justified to count a particular field or discussion as belonging to applied linguistics, even if only "theoretically applied".

2.2 Applied linguistics as a response to structuralism and generativism

As mentioned before, in the Anglophone world in particular the view still appears to be widespread that the primary concerns of the subject area of applied linguistics should be restricted to second language acquisition and language instruction in the first place (see, e.g., Davies 1999 or Schmitt and Celce-Murcia 2002). However, in other parts of the world, and above all in Europe, there has been a development away from aspects of language learning to a wider focus on more general issues of language and communication.

This broadening of scope was in part a reaction to the narrowing down of the focus in linguistics that resulted from self-imposed methodological constraints which, as Ehlich (1999) points out, began with Saussurean structuralism and culminated in generative linguistics. For almost three decades since the late 1950s, these developments made "language" in a comprehensive sense, as related to the everyday experience of its users, vanish in favour of an idealised and basically artificial entity. This led in "Core" or theoretical linguistics to a neglect of almost all everyday problems with language and communication encountered by individuals and societies and made it necessary for those interested in socially accountable research into language and communication to draw on a wider range of disciplines, thus giving rise to a flourishing of interdisciplinary areas that have come to be referred to as hyphenated variants of linguistics, such as sociolinguistics, ethnolinguistics, psycholinguistics, conversation analysis, pragmatics, and so on (Davies and Elder 2004).

That these hyphenated variants of linguistics can be said to have originated from dealing with problems may lead to the impression that they fall completely into the scope of Applied Linguistics. This the more so as their original thematic focus is in line with a frequently quoted definition of applied linguistics as "the theoretical and empirical investigation of real world problems in which language is a central issue" (Brumfit 1997: 93). However, in the recent past much of the work done in these fields has itself been rather "theoretically applied" in the sense introduced above and ultimately even become mainstream in linguistics. Also, in view of the current epistemological developments that see all sciences under the pressure of application, one might even wonder if there is anything distinctive about applied linguistics at all.

Indeed it would be difficult if not impossible to delimit applied linguistics with respect to the practical problems studied and the disciplinary approaches used: Real-world problems with language (to which, for greater clarity, should be added: "with communication") are unlimited in principle. Also, many problems of this kind are unique and require quite different approaches. Some might be tackled successfully by applying already available linguistic theories and methods. Others might require for their solution the development of new methods and even new theories. Following a frequently used distinction first proposed by Widdowson (1980), one might label these approaches as "Linguistics Applied" or "Applied Linguistics". In addition, language is a trans-disciplinary subject par excellence, with the result that problems do not come labelled and may require for their solution the cooperation of various disciplines.

2.3 Conceptualisations and communities

The questions of what should be its reference discipline and which themes, areas of research and sub-disciplines it should deal with, have been discussed constantly and were also the subject of an intensive debate (e.g., Seidlhofer 2003). In the recent past, a number of edited volumes on applied linguistics have appeared which in their respective introductory chapters attempt at giving a definition of "Applied Linguistics". As can be seen from the existence of the Association Internationale de Linguistique Appliquée (AILA) and its numerous national affiliates, from the number of congresses held or books and journals published with the label "Applied Linguistics", applied linguistics appears to be a well-established and flourishing enterprise. Therefore, the collective need felt by authors and editors to introduce their publication with a definition of the subject area it is supposed to be about is astonishing at first sight. Quite obviously, what Ehlich (2006) has termed "the struggle for the object of inquiry" appears to be characteristic of linguistics – both of linguistics at large and applied linguistics. Its seems then, that the meaning and scope of "Applied Linguistics" cannot be taken for granted, and this is why a wide variety of controversial conceptualisations exist.

For example, in addition to the dichotomy mentioned above with respect to whether approaches to applied linguistics should in their theoretical foundations and methods be autonomous from theoretical linguistics or not, and apart from other controversies, there are diverging views on whether applied linguistics is an independent academic discipline (e.g., Kaplan and Grabe 2000) or not (e.g., Davies and Elder 2004), whether its scope should be mainly restricted to language teaching related topics (e.g., Schmitt and Celce-Murcia 2002) or not (e.g., Knapp 2006), or whether applied linguistics is a field of interdisciplinary synthesis where theories with their own integrity develop in close interaction with language users and professionals (e.g., Rampton 1997 [2003]) or whether this view should be rejected, as a true interdisciplinary approach is ultimately impossible (e.g., Widdowson 2005).

In contrast to such controversies Candlin and Sarangi (2004) point out that applied linguistics should be defined in the first place by the actions of those who practically *do* applied linguistics:

> [...] we see no especial purpose in reopening what has become a somewhat sterile debate on what applied linguistics is, or whether it is a distinctive and coherent discipline. [...] we see applied linguistics as a many centered and interdisciplinary endeavour whose coherence is achieved in purposeful, mediated action by its practitioners. [...] What we want to ask of applied linguistics is less what it is and more what it does, or rather what its practitioners do. (Candlin and Sarangi 2004: 1–2)

Against this background, they see applied linguistics as less characterised by its thematic scope – which indeed is hard to delimit – but rather by the two aspects of "relevance" and "reflexivity". Relevance refers to the purpose applied linguistic activities have for the targeted audience and to the degree that these activities in their collaborative practices meet the background and needs of those addressed – which, as matter of comprehensibility, also includes taking their conceptual and language level into account. Reflexivity means the contextualisation of the intellectual principles and practices, which is at the core of what characterises a professional community, and which is achieved by asking leading questions like "What kinds of purposes underlie what is done?", "Who is involved in their determination?", "By whom, and in what ways, is their achievement appraised?", "Who owns the outcomes?"

We agree with these authors that applied linguistics, in dealing with real world problems, is determined by disciplinary givens – such as e.g., theories, methods or standards of linguistics or any other discipline – but that it is determined at least as much by the social and situational givens of the practices of life. These do not only include the concrete practical problems themselves but also the theoretical and methodological standards of cooperating experts from other disciplines, as well as the conceptual and practical standards of the practitioners who are confronted with the practical problems in the first place. Thus, as Sarangi and van Leeuwen (2003) point out, applied linguists have to become part of the respective "community of practice".

If, however, applied linguists have to regard themselves as part of a community of practice, it is obvious that it is the entire community which determines what the respective subject matter is that the applied linguist deals with and how. In particular, it is the respective community of practice which determines which problems of the practitioners have to be considered. The consequence of this is that applied linguistics can be understood from very comprehensive to very specific, depending on what kind of problems are considered relevant by the respective community. Of course, following this participative understanding of applied linguistics also has consequences for the Handbooks of Applied Linguistics both with respect to the subjects covered and the way they are theoretically and practically treated.

3 Applied Linguistics for problem solving

Against this background, it seems reasonable not to define Applied Linguistics as an autonomous discipline or even only to delimit it by specifying a set of subjects it is supposed to study and typical disciplinary approaches it should use. Rather, in line with the collaborative and participatory perspective of the communities of practice applied linguists are involved in, this handbook series is based on the assumption that applied linguistics is a specific, problem-oriented way of "doing linguistics" related to the real-life world. In other words applied linguistics is conceived of here as "linguistics for problem solving".

To outline what we think is distinctive about this area of inquiry: Entirely in line with Popper's conception of science, we take it that applied linguistics starts from the assumption of an imperfect world in the areas of language and communication. This means, firstly, that linguistic and communicative competence in individuals, like other forms of human knowledge, is fragmentary and defective – if it exists at all. To express it more pointedly: Human linguistic and communicative behaviour is not "perfect". And on a different level, this imperfection also applies to the use and status of language and communication in and among groups or societies.

Secondly, we take it that Applied Linguists are convinced that the imperfection both of individual linguistic and communicative behaviour and language based relations between groups and societies can be clarified, understood and to some extent resolved by their intervention, e.g., by means of education, training or consultancy. Thirdly, we take it that applied linguistics proceeds by a specific mode of inquiry in that it mediates between the way language and communication is expertly studied in the linguistic disciplines and the way it is directly experienced in different domains of use. This implies that applied linguists are able to demonstrate that their findings – be they of a "Linguistics Applied" or "Applied Linguistics" nature – are not just "application oriented basic research" but can be made relevant to the real-life world.

Fourthly, we take it that applied linguistics is socially accountable. To the extent that the imperfections initiating applied linguistic activity involve both social actors and social structures, we take it that applied linguistics has to be critical and reflexive with respect to the results of its suggestions and solutions.

These assumptions yield the following questions which at the same time define objectives for Applied Linguistics:

1. Which linguistic problems are typical of which areas of language competence and language use?
2. How can linguistics define and describe these problems?
3. How can linguistics suggest, develop, or achieve solutions of these problems?
4. Which solutions result in which improvements in speakers' linguistic and communicative abilities or in the use and status of languages in and between groups?
5. What are additional effects of the linguistic intervention?

4 Objectives of this handbook series

These questions also determine the objectives of this book series. However, in view of the present boom in handbooks of linguistics and applied linguistics, one should ask what is specific about this series of thematically different volumes.

To begin with, it is important to emphasise what it is not aiming at:

– The handbook series does not want to take a snapshot view or even a "hit list" of fashionable topics, theories, debates or fields of study.
– Nor does it aim at a comprehensive coverage of linguistics because some selectivity with regard to the subject areas is both inevitable in a book series of this kind and part of its specific profile.

Instead, the book series will try

– to show that Applied Linguistics can offer a comprehensive, trustworthy and scientifically well-founded understanding of a wide range of problems,
– to show that Applied Linguistics can provide or develop instruments for solving new, still unpredictable problems,
– to show that Applied Linguistics is not confined to a restricted number of topics such as, e.g., foreign language learning, but that it successfully deals with a wide range of both everyday problems and areas of linguistics,
– to provide a state-of-the-art description of Applied Linguistics against the background of the ability of this area of academic inquiry to provide descriptions, analyses, explanations and, if possible, solutions of everyday problems. On the

one hand, this criterion is the link to trans-disciplinary co-operation. On the other, it is crucial in assessing to what extent linguistics can in fact be made relevant.

In short, it is by no means the intention of this series to duplicate the present state of knowledge about linguistics as represented in other publications with the supposed aim of providing a comprehensive survey. Rather, the intention is to present the knowledge available in applied linguistics today firstly from an explicitly problem solving perspective and secondly, in a non-technical, easily comprehensible way. Also it is intended with this publication to build bridges to neighbouring disciplines and to critically discuss which impact the solutions discussed do in fact have on practice. This is particularly necessary in areas like language teaching and learning – where for years there has been a tendency to adopt fashionable solutions without sufficient consideration of their actual impact on the reality in schools.

5 Criteria for the selection of topics

Based on the arguments outlined above, the handbook series has the following structure: Findings and applications of linguistics will be presented in concentric circles, as it were, starting out from the communication competence of the individual, proceeding via aspects of interpersonal and inter-group communication to technical communication and, ultimately, to the more general level of society. Thus, the topics of the first nine volumes are as follows:
1. Handbook of Individual Communication Competence
2. Handbook of Interpersonal Communication
3. Handbook of Communication in Organisations and Professions
4. Handbook of Communication in the Public Sphere
5. Handbook of Multilingualism and Multilingual Communication
6. Handbook of Foreign Language Communication and Learning
7. Handbook of Intercultural Communication
8. Handbook of Technical Communication
9. Handbook of Language and Communication: Diversity and Change

This thematic structure can be said to follow the sequence of experience with problems related to language and communication a human passes through in the course of his or her personal biographical development. This is why the topic areas of applied linguistics are structured here in ever-increasing concentric circles: in line with biographical development, the first circle starts with the communicative competence of the individual and also includes interpersonal communication as belonging to a person's private sphere. The second circle proceeds to the everyday environment and includes the professional and public sphere. The third circle extends to the experience of foreign languages and cultures, which at least in officially monolingual societies, is not made by everybody and if so, only later in life. Technical communication as the fourth circle is even more exclusive and restricted to a more special professional clientele. The ninth volume extends this process to focus on more general, supra-individual national and international issues.

For almost all of these topics, there already exist introductions, handbooks or other types of survey literature. However, what makes the present volumes unique is their explicit claim to focus on topics in language and communication as areas of everyday problems and their emphasis on pointing out the relevance of Applied Linguistics in dealing with them.

6 References

Back, Otto. 1970. Was bedeutet und was bezeichnet der Begriff ‚angewandte Sprachwissenschaft'? *Die Sprache* 16. 21–53.

Brumfit, Christopher. 1997. How applied linguistics is the same as any other science. *International Journal of Applied Linguistics* 7(1). 86–94.

Candlin, Chris N. and Srikant Sarangi. 2004. Making applied linguistics matter. *Journal of Applied Linguistics* 1(1). 1–8.

Carrier, Michael, Martin Stöltzner, and Jeanette Wette. 2004. *Theorienstruktur und Beurteilungsmaßstäbe unter den Bedingungen der Anwendungsdominanz.* Universitat Bielefeld: Institut fur Wissenschafts- und Technikforschung, http://www.uni-bielefeld.de/iwt/projekte/wissen/anwendungsdominanz.html (accessed 5 January 2007).

Davies, Alan. 1999. *An Introduction to Applied Linguistics. From Practice to Theory.* Edinburgh: Edinburgh University Press.

Davies, Alan and Catherine Elder. 2004. General introduction – Applied linguistics: Subject to discipline? In Alan Davies and Catherine Elder (eds.), *The Handbook of Applied Linguistics*, 1–16. Malden: Blackwell.

Ehlich, Konrad. 1999. Vom Nutzen der „Funktionalen Pragmatik" für die angewandte Linguistik. In Michael Becker-Mrotzek and Christine Doppler (eds.), *Medium Sprache im Beruf. Eine Aufgabe für die Linguistik*, 23–36. Tubingen: Narr.

Ehlich, Konrad. 2006. Mehrsprachigkeit für Europa – öffentliches Schweigen, linguistische Distanzen. In Sergio Cigada, Jean-Francois de Pietro, Daniel Elmiger, and Markus Nussbaumer (eds.), *Öffentliche Sprachdebatten – linguistische Positionen. Bulletin Suisse de Linguistique Appliquée/VALS-ASLA-Bulletin* 83(1). 11–28.

Johnson, Keith and Helen Johnson (eds.). 1998. *Encyclopedic Dictionary of Applied Linguistics. A Handbook for Language Teaching.* Oxford: Blackwell.

Kaplan, Robert B. and William Grabe. 2000. Applied linguistics and the *Annual Review of Applied Linguistics*. In William Grabe (ed.), *Applied Linguistics as an Emerging Discipline. Annual Review of Applied Linguistics* 20. 3–17.

Knapp, Karlfried. 2006. Vorwort. In Karlfried Knapp, Gerd Antos, Michael Becker-Mrotzek, Arnulf Deppermann, Susanne Göpferich, Joachim Gabowski, Michael Klemm, and Claudia Villiger (eds.), *Angewandte Linguistik. Ein Lehrbuch.* 2nd ed., xix–xxiii. Tübingen: Francke UTB.

Meinel, Christoph. 2000. Reine und angewandte Wissenschaft. *Das Magazin.* Ed. Wissenschaftszentrum Nordrhein-Westfalen 11(1). 10–11.

Rampton, Ben. 1997 [2003]. Retuning in applied linguistics. *International Journal of Applied Linguistics* 7(1). 3–25.

Sarangi, Srikant and Theo van Leeuwen. 2003. Applied linguistics and communities of practice: Gaining communality or losing disciplinary autonomy? In Srikant Sarangi and Theo van Leeuwen (eds.), *Applied Linguistics and Communities of Practice*, 1–8. London: Continuum.

Schmitt, Norbert and Marianne Celce-Murcia. 2002. An overview of applied linguistics. In Norbert Schmitt (ed.), *An Introduction to Applied Linguistics*. London: Arnold.

Seidlhofer, Barbara (ed.). 2003. *Controversies in Applied Linguistics*. Oxford, UK: Oxford University Press.

Widdowson, Henry. 1984 [1980]. Model and fictions. In Henry Widdowson (ed.), *Explorations in Applied Linguistics* 2. 21–27. Oxford, UK: Oxford University Press.

Widdowson, Henry. 2005. Applied linguistics, interdisciplinarity, and disparate realities. In Paul Bruthiaux, Dwight Atkinson, William G. Egginton, William Grabe, and Vaidehi Ramanathan (eds.), *Directions in Applied Linguistics. Essays in Honor of Robert B. Kaplan*, 12–25. Clevedon: Multilingual Matters.

Contents

I. Mapping the terrain

II. Populations and contexts

Rosa M. Manchón

Introduction: Past and future of L2 writing research

A substantial number of handbooks and encyclopedias have been published in the general field of Applied Linguistics in recent years. Some of them cover Applied Linguistics in general, including general collections such as the *Encyclopedia of Applied Linguistics* (Chapelle 2013), the *Handbooks of Applied Linguistics* – HAL – published by De Gruyter, or the *Routledge Handbooks of Applied Linguistics*. Others focus on specific subareas within the discipline, including (but not limited to): language learning and teaching (Doughty and Long 2003; Gass and Mackey 2012; Herschensohn and Young-Scholten 2013; Hinkel 2005, 2011; Long and Doughty 2009; Ritchie and Bhatia 2009), multilingualism (Martin-Jones, Blackledge, and Creese 2014), or educational linguistics (Spolsky and Hult 2008).

Conspicuously absent in this proliferation of disciplinary compendia is a handbook of second or foreign language (L2) writing, although it should be acknowledged that L2 writing has featured regularly in many of the above mentioned handbooks and encyclopedias. As a telling example, the 10 volume *Encyclopedia of Applied Linguistics* (Chapelle 2013) includes the following L2 writing-related entries across its different volumes: assessment of writing; corpus analysis of written English for academic purposes; grammar in academic writing; narrative development in second language acquisition: oral and written; peer response in second language writing; process and post-process approaches to writing; reading-writing connections; teaching writing; writing and content area learning; writing and genre studies; writing and language for specific purposes; and writing development in second language acquisition.

The absence of a comprehensive handbook of L2 writing is not justified when we consider that over the past three decades L2 writing has evolved into a well-established interdisciplinary field of inquiry characterized by well-defined areas of interest, distinct methods of inquiry, and the existence of identifiable professional networks for the dissemination of knowledge among practitioners. Thus, there is an academic forum totally devoted to L2 writing, the Symposium of Second Language Writing (SSLW), co-founded by Tony Silva and Paul Kei Matsuda. Originally envisaged as a biannual event based in the US, the SSLW, in consonance with the growth and gradual internationalization of research and practice in the field, has eventually turned into a well-attended annual academic gathering hosted by institutions across the world. Additionally, L2 writing research has also gradually made its way into major Applied Linguistics and composition conferences, including those of the American Association for Applied Linguistics, EUROSLA, or AILA conferences. In terms of publication venues, the *Journal Second Language Writing* is a well-established, prestigious international journal devoted to L2 writing scholarship. Articles on L2 writing have also been and continue to be published in most flagship Applied Linguistics journals, such as *Applied Linguistics, Language Learning*, the *Modern Language Journal, Studies in Second Language Acquisition*, and *TESOL Quarterly*. Studies of L2 writing also feature prominently in the *Journal of English for Academic Purposes* and, of course, *Assessing Writing*. Furthermore, there are book series monographically devoted to L2 writing, published by Parlor Press (edited by Paul Kei Matsuda) and the University of Michigan Press (edited by Diane Belcher and Jun Liu). Numerous monographs and edited collections on L2 writing have also been part of book series by major publishers in the area of language learning studies in the last decade, including Cambridge University Press (cf. Hyland 2012; Hyland and Hyland 2006), Continuum (cf. Hyland 2005, 2009; Tang 2012), de Gruyter Mouton (Manchón 2012), John Benjamins (cf. Byrnes and Manchón 2014; Manchón 2011), Lawrence Erlbaum (cf. Matsuda and Silva 2005), Multilingual Matters (cf. Bitchener and Storch 2016; Manchón 2009; Storch 2013; Thesen and Cooper 2014), or Routledge (cf. Bitchener and Ferris 2012; Leki, Cumming, and Silva 2008).

These disciplinary developments justify why a handbook of L2 writing should find its niche among the existing and ever growing body of Applied Linguistics handbooks and encyclopedias. The development of the field, together with the very nature of the phenomenon in focus in L2 writing scholarship, also explain why the current *Handbook of Second and Foreign Language Writing* finds its place in the de Gruyter *Handbooks of Applied Linguistics* (HAL). As noted by the HAL series editors, the HAL cover strands of research collectively concerned with real-world problems in which language is involved, thus adhering to a conception of Applied Linguistics in which application is one of its most distinctive characteristics. Coincidentally, an applied dimension has been crucially linked to the emergence and development of L2 writing scholarship, a "pedagogically-motivated area" (Belcher 2012: 131) and, hence, a rather practical enterprise in its origin essentially concerned with applying knowledge and insights from diverse linguistic, psychological, and educational disciplines in the practical endeavour of developing teaching approaches aimed at helping those who needed to acquire writing skills in an additional language mainly for diverse academic or work-related purposes. This applied dimension of L2 writing research and practice makes L2 writing attuned with some current conceptions of the nature of scientific endeavours, including Applied Linguistics research. Thus, in their Introduction to the *Handbook of Multilingualism and Multilingual Education* (Auer and Wei 2009. See also their introduction to this volume), Knapp and Antos (2009: vi) contended:

> Today, after the turn of the millennium, it is obvious that sciences are requested to provide more and something different than just theory, basic research or pure knowledge. Rather, sciences are increasingly being regarded as partners in a more social and economic context of problem solving and are evaluated against expectations to be practically relevant.

The practical relevance of L2 scholarly work is closely linked to the acknowledge-ment of and commitment towards the many and varied domains in the real world in which writing in an additional language is involved, domains in which the real-world problems in need of attention require or can benefit from the specialized knowledge that may derive from theoretical and empirical efforts by L2 writing specialists. Viewed in this way, a substantial part of L2 writing scholarship has been and will continue being very much in line with those visions of future work in Applied Linguistics according to which items in research agendas come from the world outside academia and back into the world again. In this respect, Bygate convincingly argues (Bygate 2015: xiii):

> The focus on 'real world problems' suggests that we should seek to start from the problems of the real world, of non-applied linguists rather than the 'researched problems', 'theoretical problems' or methodological problems and instead focus on problems identified and ratified by non-academics. This means defining our research agendas by reference to the wider com-munity rather than to the research community.

This attempt to define research agendas in part by reference to L2 writers and L2 writing contexts rather than by sole reference to the research community is well exemplified in many contributions to the present *Handbook* and readers are re-ferred to the chapters on writers in higher education (Chapter 6, Ferris), workplace literacy (Chapter 10, Parks) or the writing center (Chapter 21, Severino and Cogie) for telling examples of this orientation in Applied Linguistics work. Additionally, the present *Handbook* as a whole distinctively shows that, as is the case in the field of Applied Linguistics at large, there has been and there will be both theory and application in L2 writing past, present and future work.

In short, although still a developing field, L2 writing theory, research, and ped-agogical thinking have matured sufficiently for the field to engage in a retrospec-tive critical reflection of past achievements and in an equally critical prospective, look-forward analysis on what lies ahead in terms of theory, research, and applica-tions. This is the ultimate aim of the present *Handbook*. In order to fulfil this overall aim, the option taken was to invite contributors who are themselves renowned experts on their topics, attempting at the same time to incorporate new voices in the field. These L2 writing specialists represent diverse disciplinary positions, theo-retical approaches, and research traditions from different parts of the world, in-cluding Asia, Europe, and North America, hence exemplifying the gradual interna-tionalization of L2 writing research preoccupations and researchers, another dis-tinctive characteristic of the disciplinary field of second and foreign language writing.

1 Aims, scope, and structure

In line with the preceding observations, the *Handbook of Second and Foreign Lan-guage Writing* is conceptualized as an authoritative reference compendium of key developments in theory and research on second and foreign language writing that can be of value to researchers, professionals, and graduate students. It intends to contribute a retrospective critical reflection that can situate L2 writing research in its historical context and provide a state of the art view of past achievements, as well as a prospective critical analysis of what lies ahead in terms of theory, research, and applications. Accordingly, the *Handbook* aims to provide (i) foundational information on the emergence and subsequent evolution of this field of inquiry, (ii) state-of-the-art surveys of available theoretical and research (basic and applied) insights, (iii) overviews of research methods and approaches in L2 writing research, (iv) critical reflections on future developments, and (iv) explorations of existing and emerging disciplinary interfaces and intellectual bridges with other fields of inquiry.

The choice of areas to be covered in any handbook is necessarily selective and ultimately a reflection of the editors' own vision and interpretation of developments and disciplinary conversations in a given field of inquiry. The *Handbook of Second and Foreign Language Writing* is no exception to this rule. It is therefore acknowledged from the outset that only minimal attention or no attention at all is paid to otherwise relevant issues in research on L2 writing globally understood. Thus, some readers might miss a more comprehensive treatment of research on writing in languages other than English, which is nevertheless monographically covered in Chapter 8, by Melinda Reichelt. In addition, although not the central area of concern, research in a variety of languages is referred to in many other contributions to the *Handbook*, both when reviewing past achievements and when suggesting future developments, as noted in the final section of this chapter. Following with omissions, key concerns in some contexts with specific groups of L2 writers receive no coverage at all. Such is the case of the role of writing systems in learning to write, a most crucial concern in cases in which the writer's L1 and L2 do not share the same writing system.

These omissions and limitations are fully acknowledged. Yet, as with any other comprehensive publishing project, editorial decisions were taken regarding the criteria guiding the thematic selection. In this respect, rather than aiming at inclusiveness, the selection criteria sought to achieve comprehensiveness: the original intention was for the *Handbook* to reflect the collective knowledge and expertise built by what the *Handbook* Editors consider a disciplinary community (a concept itself open to interpretation), the community of a group of scholars across the globe who have united their efforts to uncover the idiosyncrasies of a multi-faceted and rather complex phenomenon, namely: the many facets of learning, teaching and researching writing in an additional language. The chapters in the *Handbook* are a reflection of those "facets" of the phenomenon that have attracted the most of scholarly attention, and the research on learning and teaching the "additional language", i.e. English, that has featured most prominently in empirical research and pedagogical thinking. Importantly, the *Handbook* also seeks to point to theoretical developments to be pursued, research and applications to be explored, research methods to be applied, and disciplinary boundaries to be crossed in L2 writing scholarship.

In terms of structure, the *Handbook* is divided into six parts. Part I (*Introduction: Mapping the Terrain*) includes 3 chapters in which the development of the field is traced (Chapter 1, by Tony Silva), key dimensions in L2 writing theory and research are synthesized (Chapter 2, by Alan Hirvela, Ken Hyland, and Rosa M. Manchón), and the most prominent theories and models informing developments in the field are critically discussed (Chapter 3, by Alister Cumming).

The next three parts in the Handbook provide syntheses of L2 writing empirical work. Part II (*Populations and Contexts*) includes seven chapters, each one offering an authoritative state-of-the-art account of research developments in the following domains: ESL writing in schools (Christina Ortmeier-Hooper, Shauna Wright, and Corey McCullough), EFL writing in schools (Icy Lee), L2 writers in higher education (Dana Ferris), L2 writers in study-abroad stays (Miyuki Sasaki), L2 writing in languages other than English (Melinda Reichelt), academic L2 literacy for graduate students and publishing scholars (Theresa Lillis and Mary Jane Curry) and, finally, workplace L2 literacy (Susan Parks). Collectively, and in attempt to document developments in the field, Part II includes analyses of areas of research that have attracted considerable attention in the development of the field, as well as others that have motivated more recent thinking and the posing of empirical questions, as is the case, for instance, of L2 writing instruction and practice in study abroad contexts.

Part III (*Learning Writing*) comprises 9 chapters that are equally intended as comprehensive syntheses of theoretical and empirical achievements in central areas of interest in L2 writing scholarship together with emerging preoccupations in the field. These syntheses cover trends and developments in the consideration of the linguistic and rhetorical features of L2 texts ("Focus on Texts and Readers: Linguistic and Rhetorical Features", by William Grabe and Cui Zhang), the abundant research in the study of L2 writers' processes and strategies (Julio Roca de Larios, Florentina Nicolás-Conesa and Yvette Coyle), the way in which L2 writing and L2 development interact (Charlene Polio and Ji-Hyun Park), what is known and remains to be explored about the development of electronic literacies (Paige Ware, Richard Kern and Mark Warschauer), about writing from sources, plagiarism and textual borrowing (Diane Pecorari), or about making use of feedback (Lynn Goldstein). This part of the *Handbook* also accounts for three more recent welcome additions to L2 writing research agendas, namely, voice and identity in L2 writing (Christine Tardy), multicompetence, multilingualism and L2 writing (Carol Rinnert and Hiroe Kobayashi), and collaborative L2 writing (Neomy Storch).

In Part IV we move to the areas of *Teaching and Assessing Writing*, two dimensions of L2 writing that have resulted in a fairly substantive body of available research. The 3 chapters in this section of the *Handbook* review previous research and point to future developments in three areas of crucial pedagogical relevance, namely: a comprehensive overview of theoretical and practical considerations of teachers' response to L2 students' writing (Fiona Hyland, Florentina Nicolás-Conesa and Lourdes Cerezo), an equally comprehensive backward glance and forward-looking exploration of scholarly debates around the writing center (Carol Severino and Jane Cogie) and, finally, a comprehensive analysis of essential theoretical and practical disciplinary preoccupations in the area of writing assessment (Sarah Weigle).

The analysis of academic preoccupations with learning and teaching writing leads to research methodology considerations in Part V (*Researching Writing*). The two contributions by Christine Pearson Casanave and Rosa M. Manchón offer critical explorations of qualitative and quantitative methods of disciplinary inquiry in the field paying special attention to methodological concerns that merit attention in future L2 writing empirical work.

The last part of the *Handbook* (Part VI) is devoted to *Interdisciplinary Relations* between L2 writing and culture (Dwight Atkinson), L2 writing and SLA studies (Rosa M. Manchón and Jessica Williams) and, finally, reading/writing and speaking/writing connections (Alan Hirvela and Diane Belcher). Collectively, these three chapters provide compelling evidence of the manner in which the field has grown and the gradual interdisciplinary and multidisciplinary nature of such development.

To guarantee consistency across the entire *Handbook*, all chapters in Parts II to VI follow an identical structure. Thus, they all start with a brief historical overview of the origins and development of research in the area covered in the chapter, which is followed by a critical interpretation of the existing theory and/or research in focus. In the case of chapters in Parts II, III, and IV, i.e. those devoted to synthesizing previous empirical research findings, the critical interpretation covers three central domains: main theories informing research (how disciplinary conversations in the area of research covered in the chapter have been framed), main methods of research (how the field has come to know what we know in a given research strand), main research insights, including major tenets and findings (what is known about the research strand under the spotlight) and, when appropriate, practical/applied implications and applications of available research insights. Finally, and in line with the overall aims of the *Handbook*, all chapters finish with critical reflections on future developments, i.e. what we need to know, and how researchers should go about (i) finding answers to open questions; (ii) applying new research methods; (iii) applying research insights to the solution of practical problems; and/or (iv) crossing disciplinary boundaries.

2 Looking into the future

The chapters in the present *Handbook* offer a mine of insights on the many and varied dimensions of learning, teaching, and researching writing that have attracted disciplinary attention. It would be a futile task to even attempt to summarize what the comprehensive syntheses that make up the *Handbook* uncover about the wealth of theoretical perspectives informing research and practice in the field, methodological approaches adopted in empirical work, and research insights obtained. Rather, it makes more sense to let the authors tell the story.

Instead, I finish this introductory chapter with a prospective analysis on the future of second and foreign language writing on the basis of a summary account of the reflections, claims, and suggestions put forward in the contributions that make up this *Handbook*.

2.1 Future theoretical developments

In his comprehensive account of theories and models in L2 writing scholarship, Cumming (Chapter 3) notes that the challenge for L2 writing is to develop theoretical approaches that can successfully "account for the multi-faceted complexity of L2 writing comprehensively" (p. 79). Interestingly, and in the absence of a comprehensive theory of L2 writing, several contributions point to **multidisciplinarity and theoretical diversity** as the norm in future research endeavours. It is argued that adopting and combining diverse theoretical approaches would benefit empirical explorations of different facets of one and the same phenomenon, be it writing development in study abroad contexts (Sasaki, Chapter 7), hitherto unexplored areas of writing in additional languages other than English (Reichelt, Chapter 8), or new items in research agendas on L2 writing processes and strategies (Roca et al., Chapter 12).

Embracing theoretical diversity can equally result in adopting distinct theoretical frameworks for the analysis of seemingly distinct facets of the multi-faceted phenomenon of L2 writing. Accordingly, as convincingly argued in several chapters, it will still be relevant to adopt cognitive approaches when the phenomenon in focus is to ascertain the manner in which writing in an additional language may contribute to language learning, a concern present in the analysis of such diverse areas as writing activity in the writing centre (Severino and Cogie, Chapter 21), writing in schools (Chapter 5, Lee), collaborative writing (Chapter 18, Storch), or pedagogical concerns in exploiting and processing feedback (Goldstein, Chapter 19, and Hyland et al., Chapter 20). In contrast, more sociocultural approaches are advocated when other facets of writing to learn are in focal attention, including identity issues (Tardy, Chapter 16), workplace writing (Parks, Chapter 10) or the socially-situated dimension of writing development (Polio and Park, Chapter 13).

Closely linked to theoretical diversity as a distinctive feature of future research agendas, a plea for inter- and cross-disciplinarity in future L2 writing work is another common thread across the *Handbook*. For instance, Cumming (Chapter 3), Hyland, Nicolás-Conesa and Cerezo (Chapter 19) and Manchón and Williams (Chapter 26) demand closer links between theories of L2 writing and theories of second language acquisition. Along similar lines, Lee (Chapter 5) argues in favour of the benefits that may derive from closer alignment between L2 writing research on EFL writing in schools and studies on L2 writing in "other fields of inquiry, such as SLA, psycholinguistics, cognitive psychology, sociolinguistics, text linguistics, computer-mediated language learning, and teacher education". Closer links between SLA and L2 writing are also expected to happen in future writing center research, a domain in which Severino and Cogie (Chapter 21) foresee a gradual increase of attention to "tutoring as a vehicle for language learning" (p. 466) and, accordingly, a progressive look to "Applied Linguistics and Second Language Acquisition for theoretical and research guidance" (p. 466). Additionally, crosspollination between L1 and L2 writing research is purported to be of the utmost importance in areas that have attracted continued empirical attention in both domains, as would be the case, for instance, of writing from sources (Pecorari, Chapter 15), or feedback provision and processing (F. Hyland et al., Chapter 20).

In short, the message from the contributions to the *Handbook* is that future research agendas ought to embrace theoretical diversity, and be characterised by multidisciplinarity and interdisciplinarity.

2.2 Future research developments

The contributions to the *Handbook* also include a wealth of suggestions as to the what and how of future empirical efforts. These prospective analyses include well-founded recommendations regarding relevant issues to be investigated, populations and contexts to be prioritized and methodological approaches be adopted.

First, several contributions argue in favour of more **context-embedded and socially-situated research initiatives** (cf. Lee in Chapter 5, Rinnert and Kobayashi in Chapter 17, Casanave in Chapter 23) pointing at the same time to the benefits that may result from collaboration among scholars working with diverse groups of L2 writers in different contexts. This is the suggestion put forward, for instance, by Ortmeier-Hooper et al. (Chapter 3), who point to the benefits of establishing "wider networks of collaboration" among L2 writing specialists working with primary and secondary L2 writers, by Lillis and Curry (Chapter 9), who argue in favour of exploring academic production practices across diverse contexts, or by Ware et al. (Chapter 14), who suggest pursuing "collaborative research designs" given that "such collaborative efforts are of increasing importance in light of greater global connectivity, as researchers work to capture not just the particulars of local contexts and uses, but also to gain an understanding of how such activities are nested in and influenced by diverse social and economic conditions" (p. 321). An extension of the interest in socially-situated research concerns the expansion and increase of classroom-based studies in areas as distinct as voice and identity (Tardy, Chapter 16), collaborative writing (Storch, Chapter 18) or feedback (Goldstein, Chapter 19, F. Hyland et al., Chapter 20).

Second, parallel to the theoretical diversity referred to above, reading through the *Handbook* distinctively leads to the identification of a collective future trend towards **methodological diversity** and **expansion of repertoires of research methods and approaches**. For instance, Weigle (Chapter 22) argues in favour of combining quantitative and qualitative research methods as an important move in "validating and improving assessment" (p. 486). In addition, together with suggestions for more qualitative, in-depth, grounded ethnographic approaches and ethnographic case studies and narratives (Casanave, Chapter 23) in areas such as writing in schools (Lee, Chapter 5), collaborative writing (Storch, Chapter 18), workplace literacy (Parks, Chapter 11), or multilingual writing (Rinnert and Kobayashi, Chapter 17), other contributors espouse the benefits of continuing the more cognitively-oriented, quantitative tradition when approaching the study of some facets of writing in study abroad contexts (Sasaki, Chapter 7) or the many open questions that exist on the purported language learning potential of L2 writing (as discussed, for instance, in chapters 18, 21 and 26). Closely linked to these suggestions for methodological diversity are recommendations for future research to opt for **triangulating data sources and research methods**, as suggested, among others, by Rinnert and Kobayashi (Chapter 17) or F. Hyland et al. (Chapter 20).

Third, many contributors articulate concerns about the predominance of short-term, one-shot studies in the field. To redress this situation, a collective plea for **methodologies that can capture development** emerges from the *Handbook*. In addition to the recommendations in this respect offered in the two chapters entirely devoted to research methodology (i.e. Chapter 23 by Casanave, and Chapter 24 by Manchón), telling examples are Polio and Parks' (Chapter 13) arguments in favour of "longitudinal intervention studies" in future investigations on language development and L2 writing, or Tardy's (Chapter 16) recommendation to expand available identity studies with longitudinal investigations, a research path that she argues would be valuable in providing more insightful visions of identity construction as it would permit "looking not just at how identities change over time and across spaces but also how such changes interact more specifically with L2 writing development" (p. 359). Longitudinal approaches that can shed light on development would also be welcome in the area of feedback studies, a domain in which Goldstein (Chapter 19) categorically states that "we know virtually nothing about the long-term effects of feedback and revision" (p. 424), a suggestion also echoed in F. Hyland et al.'s contribution (Chapter 20). The chorus of voices that distinctively argue in favour of methodologies that can capture development also include those of Sasaki's (Chapter 7) with respect to the relevance of looking into developmental trajectories in study abroad contexts, or Storch's (Chapter 18) regarding the analysis of potential long-term language-learning effects that may be fostered by collaborative writing. Importantly, along the lines of similar developments in various domains of SLA research, several contributions to the *Handbook* point to Complex Dynamic Systems as a suitable theoretical framework to inform future research on diverse facets of development of L2 writers and their texts: this is the case of Roca et al. (Chapter 12), Polio and Park (Chapter 13) and Rinnert and Kobayashi (Chapter 17).

In addition to how research should be conducted and what kind of methodological approaches ought to be adopted, the future of L2 writing is crucially linked to attempts to **answer remaining empirical questions**. In this respect, the contributions to the *Handbook* collectively offer a wealth of observations and suggestions of largely unexplored areas that need to be addressed, together with clear indications of how and why research foci need to be enlarged to make room for a wider diversity of writers and contexts of writing in future research preoccupations.

There are numerous suggestions in the *Handbook* regarding **new domains, populations and contexts** in need of more sustained empirical attention in future research agendas. In what follows I refer to those recommendations that more distinctively point to new, hitherto unexplored or only partially explored domains. But, of course, the *Handbook* also signals needed future developments in many other relevant facets of L2 writing that have already sparked considerable interest in the field, including policy issues (cf. Lillis and Curry, Chapter 9), the study of writing processes (cf. Roca et al., Chapter 12), the role of individual differences (cf. Roca et al., Chapter 12, Storch, Chapter 18, or F. Hyland et al., Chapter 20), or the relevance of making multimodality more central in future research preoccupations (as discussed, for instance, by Casanave, Chapter 23, or Hirvela and Belcher, Chapter 27).

Some of the most promising avenues to be explored in future research agendas include the following:

A. Future research efforts ought to pay attention to the various **dimensions of L2 writing** covered in Chapter 2: learning to write, and writing to learn, both content and language. As argued by Hirvela, Hyland and Manchón, "closer links and more cross-fertilization" (p. 59) among these orientations to the study of writing are to be expected. Although the writing-to-learn language (WLL) dimension is the most recent addition to theoretical, research and practical preoccupations in the field, it is here to stay. The WLL dimension of L2 writing transverses the whole *Handbook* and many voices distinctively point to the need to increase its presence in future research preoccupations, as clearly summarized by Lee (Chapter 5) when she observes that "Future research should investigate the teaching, learning ad assessment processes conductive to writing-to-learn as a whole in order to maximize the language learning potential of L2 writing". Severino and Cogie (Chapter 21) emphasize the relevance of "further emphasize writing centers as sites for continued second language learning", F. Hyland et al. (Chapter 20) elaborate on the role of feedback in promoting language development, and Hirvela and Belcher (Chapter 27) talk about the potential for writing and language learning that may be integral to multimodal (speaking and writing) instructional strategies. Therefore, we should expect a growing body of SLA-oriented L2 writing work exploring the language learning potential of writing in additional languages to be an integral part of future developments in the field.

B. **Technology and writing** is another area of future research interests. As examples of these trends, Ferris (Chapter 6) provides detailed suggestions as to how to go about studying the "affordances of technology", F. Hyland et al. (Chapter 20) point to the need to look into the role of technology in the domain of feedback studies, and Parks (Chapter 10) convincingly argues in favour of exploring how technological advances are influencing and transforming workplace practices. In her own words (p. 237):

> As the use of digital technologies continues to expand and diversify, much more attention needs to be given to how both asynchronous (e.g., email) and real-time synchronous tools (e.g., cell phones, Skype or platforms allowing for online conferencing such as Elluminate) are transforming workplace practices and more specifically, how the affordances may mediate text production by second/foreign language writers.

C. Many chapters in the Handbook converge in emphasizing the **poliphony of languages** that has become a distinctive feature of L2 writing, L2 writers, and L2 writing scholars. For example, Rinnert and Kobayashi (Chapter 17) draw our attention to the importance of considering the multi-lingual repertoire at the disposal of the L2 writer, hence acknowledging the relevance of looking into their multilingual practices and adding that:

> More research is needed to elucidate the different roles of L1/L2/L3 in composing processes and also how linguistic, cognitive, and social factors are likely to affect interactions among languages in multilingual writing [...]. In addition, studies of multilingual text construction [...] could be expanded to other languages and extended from two languages to three or more by the same multicompetent writer (p. 378).

Tardy (Chapter 16) adds the suggestion of a welcome examination of identity and voice in the multiple languages in which writers compose and claims that "Additional studies that explore how multilinguals draw on multiple linguistic and cultural resources for identity construction, and the extent to which they may draw on resources *across* languages, could better inform our understanding of the relationships between identity and language" (p. 359). Severnino and Cogie (Chapter 21) emphasize, perhaps for the first time ever, the multilingual nature of writing centers and writing center agents and, accordingly, pose questions for future research such as the following (p. 467):

> In terms of the tutoring dynamics that have preoccupied writing center researchers, how does a session between two international students compare to one between a native speaker and a non-native speaker? To a session between two resident bilinguals? To one between an international tutor and a resident bilingual student? To one between a resident bilingual tutor and

an international student? When tutors are from the majority of the world's population that speaks English as an additional rather than as a native language, how is the global/local balance of issues affected?

Another important reference to this polyphony of languages is provided by Casanave (Chapter 23), this time with respect to L2 writing researchers. Importantly, given the disciplinary position to reject monolingual and monocultural assumptions when exploring L2 writing, writers and contexts, Casanave cogently argues that L2 writing researchers "will increasingly need to be bilingual or to work on multilingual teams and to be active multiliterates who can conduct in-depth interviews, observations, and text-analyses in more than one language" (p. 509).

D. The underlying message of many contributions to the *Handbook* is that, despite the considerable body of accumulated empirical knowledge and pedagogical thinking, the field needs to expand research foci to make room for the study of **new additional languages, new contexts** in which L2 writing is learned, taught and practised, and **new L2 writers and agents** in these contexts. Accordingly, several chapters emphasize the relevance of exploring new questions about teachers, their professional development, and key concerns in writing teacher education, (see, for instance, future directions pointed to by Lee in Chapter 5, Reichelt in Chapter 8, Severino and Cogie in Chapter 21, or Hirvela and Belcher in Chapter 27). Equally worthy of attention would be the investigation of teachers' role in promoting pedagogical practices related to a shift toward digital literacies (Ware, Kern, and Warschauer, Chapter 14) or to feedback-related practices (Goldstein, Chapter 19, and Hyland et al., Chapter 20). In addition to putting teachers center stage, important contributions to the field are expected from a collective attempt to expand research to younger and less proficient writers, of different ages and backgrounds, as noted by Lee, Reichelt, Rinnert and Hiroe Kobayashi, or Roca and colleagues in their respective chapters.

Suggestions for the expansion of the range of writers is parallel to claims for an equal expansion of the range of contexts under the spotlight. Tardy (Chapter 16) suggests moving in the direction of investigating multilingual writers in an attempt to shed light on "how identities and voices are constructed in the transnational contexts that are increasingly common in today's globalized world" (p. 360). In Casanave's (Chapter 23) view, new contexts worthy of attention include "non-school contexts, professional writing, and issues that have political import beyond the US context", to which Ferris (Chapter 6: 155) adds:

> Settings around the world in which writers compose in L2s other than English [...] as well as those in which English is not an official or primary language. They also include contexts outside of the traditional research sites – language and writing classes – and increased considerations of how L2 writers function in their disciplinary coursework, as graduate students, and in their professional lives.

E. It was mentioned in an earlier section that the almost sole focus on English as the default additional language in L2 writing scholarship is a limitation of past research, which is consequently reflected in the limited coverage that writing in languages other than English receives in the *Handbook*. It comes as no surprise, therefore, that another loud message stemming from the collective work reported in the chapters that follow is the need to redress this situation in future research endeavours for both research-related and more ideological reasons. As telling examples, Reichelt (Chapter 8) offers a comprehensive research agenda, Lillis and Curry point to the need to explore academic writing in a range of languages, and Casanave (Chapter 23) crucially draws our attention to the need to reflect critically "on the relevance and ideological implications of English language scholarship world wide" and, accordingly, to the need to find "ways to encourage studies of writing in languages other than English" (p. 508).

F. A final area worthy of comment relates to the many and varied recommendations put forward with respect to worthy **real-world applications of future L2 writing research**. This applies, for instance, to potential applications of (i) text analysis to the improvement of "student writing outcomes", as suggested by Grabe and Zhang (Chapter 11); (ii) research on source use and plagiarism (Pecorari, Chapter 15), on feedback practices (Goldstein, Chapter 19), or on the potential of L2 writing for language learning (Manchón and Williams, Chapter 26) for language pedagogy, (iii) new research insights developed in studies of workplace literacy for effective practices and training programmes in workplace settings; (iv) action research on identity and voice for practitioners (Tardy, Chapter 16); or (v) research on assessment for a wide variety of applications in the real world, which are neatly summarized by Weigle (Chapter 22: 488) as follows:

> The increased importance of writing in an era of globalization, and the rising number of second language learners in writing courses, from beginning language learners in monolingual settings to advanced graduate students in multilingual settings, makes it imperative to continue seeking ways to assess writing that are authentic, fair, and feasible. The consequences of assessment may be far-reaching, and thus teachers, researchers, and policy makers must be cognizant of the factors that enhance or detract from test validity and fairness as they seek to assess student writing accurately.

To conclude, the retrospective critical reflection of past achievements, together with the critical, prospective, look-forward analyses on what lies ahead distinctively evidences that L2 writing will continue to grow as a vibrant field of research in which important developments in theory, research, and applications will be part of future preoccupations in research agendas. The chapters that follow offer authoritative, comprehensive analyses of these past achievements and of worthy avenues to explore in future research endeavours. I very much hope readers enjoy their reading journey into the past and on to the future of studies on second and foreign language writing.

3 References

Auer, Peter and Li Wei (eds.). 2009. *Handbook of multilingualism and multilingual communication*. Berlin: De Gruyter Mouton.

Belcher, Diane. 2012. Considering what we know and need to know about second language writing. *Applied Linguistics Review* 3. 131–150

Bitchener, John and Dana Ferris. 2012. *Written corrective feedback in second language acquisition and writing*. London: Routledge.

Bitchener, John and Neomy Storch. 2016. *Written corrective feedback for L2 development*. Bristol, UK: Multilingual Matters.

Bygate, Martin. 2015. Foreword. In Lubie Grujicic-Alatriste (ed.), *Linking discourse studies to professional practice*, xi–xiv. Bristol, UK: Multilingual Matters.

Byrnes, Heidi and Rosa M. Manchón (eds.). 2014. *Task-based language learning: Insights to and from writing*. Amsterdam: John Benjamins.

Chapelle, Carol (General Editor). 2013. *The encyclopedia of applied linguistics*. Malden, MA: Wiley-Blackwell.

Davies, Alan and Catherine Elder (eds.). 2004. *The handbook of applied linguistics*. Malden, MA: Wiley-Blackwell.

Doughty, Catherine and Michael Long (eds.). 2003. *The handbook of second language acquisition*. Malden, MA: Blackwell.

Gass, Susan and Alison Mackey (eds.). 2012. *The Routledge handbook of second language acquisition*. New York: Routledge.

Herschensohn, Julia and Martha Young-Scholten (eds.). 2013. *The Cambridge handbook of second language acquisition*. Cambridge: CUP.

Hinkel, Eli (ed.). 2005. *Handbook of research in second language teaching and learning*. Mahwah, NJ: Lawrence Erlbaum.

Hinkel, Eli (ed.). 2011. *Handbook of research in second language teaching and learning*. Mahwah, NJ: Lawrence Erlbaum.

Hyland, Ken. 2005. *Metadiscourse: Exploring interaction in writing*. London: Continuum.

Hyland, Ken. 2009. *Academic discourse*. London: Continuum.

Hyland, Ken. 2012. *Disciplinary identities. Individuality and community in academic discourse.* Cambridge: CUP

Hyland, Ken and Fiona Hyland (eds.). 2006. *Feedback in second language writing: Contexts and issues*. Cambridge: CUP.

Knapp, Karlfried and Gerd Antos. 2009. Introduction to the handbook series. Linguistics for problem solving. In Peter Auer and Li Wei (eds.), *Handbook of multilingualism and multilingual communication*, v–xv. Berlin: De Gruyter Mouton.

Leki, Ilona, Alister Cumming, and Tony Silva. 2008. *A synthesis of research on second language writing in English*. London: Routledge.

Long, Michael and Catherine Doughty (eds.). 2009. *The handbook of language teaching*. Malden, MA: Blackwell.

Manchón, Rosa M. (ed.). 2009. *Writing in foreign language contexts: Learning, teaching and research*. Bristol, UK: Multilingual Matters.

Manchón, Rosa M. (ed.). 2011. *Learning-to-write and writing-to-learn in an additional language*. Amsterdam: John Benjamins.

Manchón, Rosa M. (ed.). 2012. *L2 writing development: Multiple perspectives*. Berlin: De Gruyter Mouton.

Martin-Jones, Marilyn, Adrian Blackledge, and Angela Creese (eds.). 2014. *Handbook of multilingualism*. London: Routledge.

Matsuda, Paul and Tony Silva (eds.). 2005. *Second language writing research: Perspectives on the process of knowledge construction*. Mahwah, NJ: Lawrence Erlbaum

Ritchie, William and Tej Bhatia (eds.). 2009. *The new handbook of second language acquisition.* Bingley, UK: Emerald.

Spolsky, Bernard and Francis M. Hult (eds.). 2008. *The handbook of educational linguistics.* Malden, MA: Blackwell.

Storch, Neomy. 2013. *Collaborative writing in L2 classrooms.* Bristol: Multilingual Matters.

Tang, Ramona (ed.). 2012. *Academic writing in a second or foreign language. Issues and challenges facing ESL/EFL academic writers in higher education contexts.* London: Continuum

Thessen, Llucia and Linda Cooper (eds.). 2014. *Risk in academic writing. Postgraduate students, their teachers and the making of knowledge.* Bristol, UK: Multilingual Matters.

I. Mapping the terrain

Tony Silva

1 An overview of the development of the infrastructure of second language writing studies

The purpose of this chapter is not to provide a grand narrative or an all-encompassing description of the field of second language writing (L2W) studies. This is not possible to do in a single chapter; indeed, providing a comprehensive picture of the field is the purpose of this handbook as a whole. This chapter is primarily an overview of the infrastructure of the field of second language writing studies from an archeological perspective; that is, looking at the evolution of the field based on a study of its artifacts (material, intellectual, and institutional) and those who produce them. This orientation thus determines the topics addressed here and the extent to which they are elaborated. Consequently, this chapter will (1) stipulate a definition of L2W, (2) address some of the limitations of this chapter, (3) describe the methodology used in developing this chapter, (4) examine the infrastructure development of L2W decade by decade from 1950 to 2010 and some other, concurrent historical trends, (5) assess the condition of L2W studies around the globe, (6) provide a description of the current status of the field as a whole, (7) speculate on the future of L2W studies, and (8) provide a list of resources for further inquiry.

1 Introduction

The phenomenon of L2W will be defined here as writing done in a language other than the writer's native language(s)/mother tongue(s). Writing done in a native dialect or in a nativized variety of a language will *not* be considered L2W. The research area known as L2W will be understood as including the study of writing done in both second language contexts (where the language being learned is dominant, e.g., by a student from Warsaw learning Mandarin in Beijing) and foreign language contexts (where the language being learned is not dominant, e.g., the same student learning Mandarin in Rio de Janeiro).

While I have tried to be as inclusive as possible, I recognize that this overview disproportionally reflects scholarship done in the West, and more specifically, scholarship done in North America with adults in the context of higher education settings on writing in English as a second language. This situation, unfortunately, reflects the state of affairs in L2W studies at this moment and is the result, for better or for worse, of the fact that English is dominant in the academic world, that required courses exclusively devoted to writing (i.e., introductory composition) are idiosyncratically characteristic of the higher education system of the United States, and that it is easier to access and get permission to study adults rather than children. However, it should also be recognized that scholarship conducted and published in North America is produced by scholars from all over the world[1], that the L2W research is increasingly taking place outside North America (as in shown later in this chapter), and that interest in and publication on L2W in elementary and secondary schools is on the rise[2].

2 Methodology

The primary tool I used to inform this chapter is a relatively large and comprehensive database containing information on roughly 5,500 publications on second language writing. While I began to develop this database nearly thirty years ago as a resource for myself, I have also used it to create an annotated bibliography feature that has appeared in each issue of the *Journal of Second Language Writing* since 1993 and to produce an annual overview of current scholarship on L2W studies in *SLW News*, a publication of the Second Language Writing Interest Section of the TESOL International Association, since 2011.

I access items for this database by regularly reviewing other, relevant databases, including the Education Resources Information Center (ERIC) database, Linguistics and Language Behavior Abstracts (LLBA), ProQuest Dissertations and Theses, WorldCat (an online catalogue that allows access to the collections of 72,000 libraries in 170 countries and territories), and, of course, Amazon.com. I also regularly peruse more than 50 journals (see Appendix A for some of these) that, to a greater or lesser extent, typically publish articles on L2W.

The publications indexed in these databases are predominantly written in English; however, publications written in other languages are increasingly included – sometimes with titles and abstracts translated into English and sometimes not. I am fortunate to have graduate students and colleagues from around the world who are willing to help me with publications written in languages that I cannot read and also to help me identify and locate the growing number of studies focusing on L2W done in languages other than English.[3]

---

1 I base this claim on a recent exploratory study I did in which I examined all the dissertations on L2W completed in US universities in 2010. I found that about two thirds of these dissertations were done by individuals from outside the United States. I suspect that this pattern is similar for publications, students in graduate programs, memberships in professional organizations, and participants in professional conferences.

2 For examples of recent work on L2W in the K-12 context, see Leki, Cumming, and Silva (2008) – especially chapters 1 and 2, – de Oliveira and Silva (2013), de Oliveira, Silva, (2016), and Ortmeier-Hooper (2013)

3 While writing in second languages other than English is still a neglected area in the field, there are promising initiatives; for example, as a consequence of the ERASMUS Program in Europe, many

The types of publications selected for the database used to produce much of this chapter are journal articles, monographs, chapters in edited books and proceedings, doctoral dissertations, and ERIC documents[4]. The general criteria for inclusion of a publication in the bibliography is whether or not its focus is primarily or exclusively on L2W; publications only tangentially connected to L2W, for example, a second language acquisition study which merely uses the written texts of L2 writers, would not normally be included. A judgment about a publication's focus is made after a close reading of its title and abstract and by skimming its text if necessary.

Another source of information used for this chapter are responses from a number of L2W professionals to a query about the development of L2W studies in their countries and/or regions. A third source of information is my own personal experience gained as a L2W professional over the past thirty years.

3 The infrastructure L2W studies

3.1 Publication, focus of scholarship, and prominent scholars

This section will provide an account of published scholarship in L2W, supplemented by brief characterizations of the focus of this scholarship[5] and a listing of some of the prominent scholars producing this work[6]. Table 1.1 below provides a comprehensive overview of L2W publication; a decade by decade description will follow.

---

universities have set up language programs to prepare students for a stay abroad, including learning to write in the host language.

4 ERIC documents are typically conference papers or government publications located in an online database, called Education Resources Information Services, which is supported by the US Department of Education.

5 The research foci were chosen on the basis of counts, that is, how many times they appeared in the publications (contained in my database) during a particular period of time. As you will see, some foci appear in more than one period, reflecting a high level of interest over a long period of time.

6 As with the research foci, the prominent scholars were chosen on the basis of counts, that is, on the number of substantial publications (contained in my database) produced in a particular period of time. Unlike the research foci, the names of these scholars do not appear in more than one period – even though some of them published frequently in more than one period. The idea here was to showcase new/upcoming scholars. I would also like to acknowledge that some productive scholars may not appear in these lists – and I apologize to them in advance. I have tried to be as accurate as possible here, but I have no doubt that some individuals may have slipped through the cracks.

Tab. 1.1: Publications (1950–2010)[7].

Publication/Decade	1950s	1960s	1970s	1980s	1990s	2000s	*Total*
Journal Articles	8	34	143	631	962	1,028	2,806
Journals	4	7	44	134	186	198	411
Monographs	0	0	5	15	23	35	78
Collections/Proceedings	0	6	18	73	60	31	188
Chapters	0	7	26	172	322	221	748
Dissertations	0	5	28	189	339	378	939
ERIC Documents	0	7	37	198	198	34	474
Total Publications	8	53	239	1,205	1,844	1,696	5,083
Publications per Year	0.8	5.3	23.9	120.5	184.4	169.6	84.7

The 1950s. Scholarship on L2W done in the 1950s was very scarce. I could find only eight publications – all very short journal articles. The eight articles all appeared in journals based in the US and focused on applied linguistics (*Language Learning* and the *Modern Language Journal*) or English studies (*College Composition and Communication* and *College English*). During some years in the 1950s there was no published work on L2W; the average number of publications per year was less than one.

The focus of inquiry in the literature was on instruction, specifically, how to provide writing support for the relatively small number of nonnative English speaking international students (primarily Europeans) enrolled in college composition courses in universities in the USA. The authors of this literature were not, in any sense, specialists in L2W studies, and none of them continued to publish in the area – as far as I can tell.

The 1960s. The 1960s saw a modest increase in scholarship in L2W. 34 journal articles were published in a total of 7 different journals. The journals included, in order of numbers of articles on L2W, were *TESOL Quarterly* (published by the Teachers of English to Speakers of Other Languages organization – now known as the TESOL International Association), *English Language Teaching Journal* (a UK based journal published by Oxford University Press), *Language Learning*, *English Teaching Forum* (a journal produced and disseminated worldwide by the US Department of State), the *Journal of English as a Second Language* (now defunct), *College Composition and Communication* (published by the Conference on College

---

7 Note that (1) the numbers here should be seen as approximate; however, I believe that they do provide for a fairly accurate representation of the development of work in L2W studies to which I have access; (2) the total number of journals is not equal to the sum of the numbers from the six decades; this is due to the fact that there is substantial overlap across the decades, i.e., a substantial number of journals have published L2W focused articles in more than one decade; and (3) in the table, the numbers of journals and collections are not counted in the total numbers of publications, while the number of articles and chapters therein are.

Composition and Communication – part of the National Council of Teachers of English), and *TESL Reporter* (published by Brigham Young University in the US). In addition to journal articles, 1 edited collection of papers and 5 proceedings (from the TESOL and NAFSA [National Association for Foreign Student Affairs] conferences) were produced. However, typically only 1 chapter or paper on L2W was included in each of these works. Also produced were 5 L2W focused dissertations and 7 ERIC documents. The average number of publications on L2W issues per year was 5.3.

The foci of inquiry primarily included approaches to teaching writing, contrastive rhetoric, controlled and guided composition, error analysis, and writing assessment. The first generation of L2W specialists arose in the 1960s; this generation includes such figures as Robert Kaplan and Christina Bratt Paulston.

The 1970s. The 1970s saw a substantial increase in publications on L2W and some internationalization. 143 journal articles were published in a total of 44 different journals. The journals that account for most of the articles, in order of number of articles on L2W, included *TESOL Quarterly, English Language Teaching Journal, TESL Reporter, RELC Journal* (published by the Southeast Asian Ministers of Education Organisation [SEAMEO] Regional Language Centre [RELC] in Singapore), TESOL Newsletter (the newsletter of the Association of Teachers of English to Speakers of Other Languages, published from 1966 to 1990), *CIEFL Bulletin* (published by the Central Institute of English and Foreign Languages in India), *TESL Talk* (published in Ontario by the Canadian Ministry of Citizenship), *BELC Journal* (Bulletin of the English Language Center in Thailand), *College Composition and Communication*, and the *Journal of Basic Writing* (primarily a first language writing focused journal). In addition to journal articles, 5 monographs and 18 collections or proceedings, which included a total of 26 chapters focused on L2W, were produced. Again, the numbers of chapters specifically addressing L2W issues were relatively small. Also published were 28 L2W focused dissertations and 37 ERIC documents. The average number of publications on L2W issues per year was 23.9.

Some of the most common foci of this period included assessment, comparison of ESL and native English speaker writers, composing processes, contrastive (grammatical) analysis, contrastive rhetoric, language errors (the analysis and correction thereof), L1 interference, methodological/pedagogical issues (writing assignments; controlled, guided, and free writing; creative writing, and sentence combining), and textual features/elements (cohesion, paragraph structure, syntax/syntactic maturity, and T-units). Some authors beginning to publish frequently on L2W in the 1970s include Nancy Arapoff, Nancy Lay, Sandra McKay, Ann Raimes, Barry Taylor, Robert Weissberg, and Vivian Zamel.

The 1980s. The 1980s saw a very sizeable increase in the number of publications on L2W. 631 journal articles were published in a total of 134 different journals. The ten journals with the most articles on L2W, in order of number of articles on L2W, included *TESOL Quarterly, English Teaching Forum, TESOL Newsletter, ELT*

Journal, TECFORS (Teachers of English Composition to Foreign Students, a short lived journal published by the University of Houston, Texas), *TESL Reporter; English for Specific Purposes* (a UK based journal that commenced publication in 1980), *System* (a journal based in Sweden, first published in 1979); *TESL Canada Journal* (a Canadian journal first published in 1984), and Le *Français dans le monde* (the journal of the International Federation of Teachers of French). In addition to journal articles, 15 monographs and 73 collections or proceedings, which included a total of 172 chapters focusing on L2W, were produced.

Some of these collections were devoted exclusively to second language writing studies issues, e.g., Johnson and Roen's, *Richness in writing: Empowering ESL students* (1989), with 19 L2W focused chapters, and Robinson's, *Academic writing: Process and product* (1988), with 16 chapters devoted to L2W. However, again, the numbers of chapters specifically addressing L2W issues in most of these collections were relatively small. Also published were 189 L2W focused dissertations and 198 ERIC Documents. The average number of publications on second language writing issues per year was 120.5.

Some of the most common foci during this period include assessment (direct and indirect, holistic and analytic, and writing prompts,) comparisons of L1 and L2 writing and writers, composing (cognitive dimensions of L2 writing, L1 use in L2 writing, processes and subprocesses), contrastive rhetoric, discourse communities, error (analysis, correction, and gravity), L2W by children/K-12 students, modes of writing (narration, argumentation, and exposition), needs analysis, pedagogy (assignments, controlled/guided composition, dialogue journals, free writing, models, peer and teacher response, sentence combining, and student text reformulation), reading and writing connections, textual analysis, (contrastive, grammatical, syntactic), textual elements (coherence, cohesion), writer characteristics/variables (L2 proficiency, perceptions, writing apprehension, writer's block, identity), and writing labs/centers.

Some authors beginning to publish frequently in L2W studies in the 1980s include Chris Hall, Carol Edelsky, Joy Reid, Andrew Cohen, Kyle Perkins, Sarah Hudelson, Ruth Spack, Ulla Connor, Alister Cumming, Liz Hamp-Lyons, Daniel Horowitz, Ann Johns, Joy Kreeft Peyton, Charles Stansfield, and John Swales.

The 1990s. The 1990s saw an even greater increase in the number of publications on L2W. 962 journal articles were published in a total of 186 different journals. The ten journals with the most articles on L2W, in order of number of articles on L2W, included the *Journal of Second Language Writing* (first published in 1992 – the first journal devoted exclusively to second language writing studies), *TESOL Quarterly, English Teaching Forum, TESOL Journal,* (another TESOL publication, which first appeared in 1991, ceased publication in 2003, and was resurrected in 2010), *English for Specific Purposes, Foreign Language Annals* (the official journal of the American Council on the Teaching of Foreign Languages), *ELT Journal, College ESL,* (published by the City University of New York from 1991–2003), the *Modern Language Journal,* and *TESL Canada Journal.*

However, there were quite a few additional journals (many from outside the USA and some focused on second languages other than English) that published a substantial number of articles on L2W studies. These include *RELC Journal*, the *Canadian Modern Language Review* (published by the University of Toronto Press), *Journal of Asian Pacific Communication* (first published in 1990), *Hispania* (the flagship journal of Spanish Studies in the US), *Teaching English in the Two Year College* (an L1 composition studies journal), *TESL-EJ* (an early exclusively online journal), *TESOL Matters* (the sequel of *TESOL Newsletter*, published from 1991–2003), *Written Communication* (a primarily L1 writing based journal), *Language Learning, Applied Linguistics* (a second language acquisition oriented journal first appearing in 1980), *College English, Le Français dans le monde, Journal of Basic Writing, TESOL Newsletter*, and *Unterrichtspraxis* (the flagship journal for German Studies in the US).

In addition to journal articles, 23 monographs and 60 collections or proceedings, which included a total of 322 chapters focused on L2W, were produced. There were quite a few collections that were devoted exclusively to L2W studies issues, e.g. Carson and Leki's, *Reading in the composition classroom* (1993), with 20 chapters, and Belcher and Braine's, *Academic writing in a second language* (1995), with 18. However, again, the numbers of chapters specifically addressing L2W issues in most of the remaining collections were relatively small. Also published were 339 L2W focused dissertations and 198 ERIC documents. The average number of publications on L2W issues per year was 184.4.

Common foci during this period included academic and technical writing, argumentation, assessment, coherence, composing (processes and subprocesses, writing development, and writing strategies), connections between writing and reading and writing and speaking, contrastive rhetoric, critical thinking, culture, differences between L1 and L2 writing, error, genre, grammatical analysis, ideology and politics, pedagogy (dialogue journals, peer response, teacher and student response to student writing, and writing tasks and assignments), and writer perceptions.

Some authors beginning to publish frequently in the 1990s in L2W studies included Desmond Allison, Dwight Atkinson, Diane Belcher, Sarah Benesch, Linda Blanton, George Braine, Mark Brock, Joan Carson, Christine Casanave, Yu Ren Dong, Dana Ferris, Hugh Gosden, William Grabe, John Hedgcock, Ken Hyland, Michael Janopoulous, Loretta Kaspar, Hiroe Kobayashi, Barbara Kroll, Ryuko Kubota, Ilona Leki, Paul Kei Matsuda, Gayle Nelson, Kyoko Oi, Charlene Polio, Martha Pennington, Vaidehi Ramanathan, Melinda Reichelt, Abdolmehdi Riazi, Carol Rinnert, Sima Sengupta, Carol Severino, and Tony Silva.

The 2000s. In the 2000s, 1,028 journal articles were published in a total of 198 different journals. The journals that published more than ten articles during this period, in order of number of articles on L2W, included the *Journal of Second Language Writing, English Language Teaching Journal, System, Assessing Writing* (founded in 1994), *Journal of English for Academic Purposes* (first appearing in 2002 and addressing the use of English in academic contexts), *English for Specific Purposes, Foreign Language Annals, English Teaching Forum, Teaching English in the Two Year College, TESOL Quarterly, Computers and Composition* (primarily an L1 journal), *Written Communication, Computer Assisted Language Learning* (first appearing in 1990), *Canadian Modern Language Review,* and *Language Testing* (founded in 1984).

In addition to journal articles, 35 monographs and 31 collections or proceedings, which included a total of 221 chapters focused on L2W, were produced. There were quite a few collections devoted exclusively to L2W studies issues, e.g. Belcher and Hirvela's *Linking literacies: Perspectives on L2 reading-writing connections* (2001) with 17 chapters and Matsuda and Silva's *Second language writing research: Perspectives on the process of knowledge construction* (2005) with 16.

Also published were 378 L2W focused dissertations and 34 ERIC Documents. The total number of publications in the 2000s was 1,696; the average number of publications on L2W issues per year was 169.6.

Some of the most frequent topics addressed in this period included academic writing, argumentation, assessment and rating of texts, coherence and cohesion, composing (processes, revision, and strategies), connections between reading and writing, corpora of written L2 text and their analysis, development of writing ability, differences between first and second language writing, gender, genre, error, grammar correction, grammatical analysis, ideology and politics, narrative, pedagogy (peer response, tasks and assignments, teacher response/feedback), plagiarism, tutoring, writer variables (attitudes, beliefs, identity, perspectives), writing across the curriculum and within disciplines, and writing with computers.

Some authors who began to publish frequently in the 2000s in L2W studies include Khaled Barkaoui, John Bitchener, Joel Bloch, Gerd Bräuer, Anthony Bruton, Suresh Canagarajah, An Cheng, Deborah Crusan, John Flowerdew, Danielle Guénette, Linda Harklau, Eli Hinkel, Keiko Hirose, Alan Hirvela, Icy Lee, Jun Liu, Yichun Liu, Rosa Manchón, Liz Murphy, Lourdes Ortega, Christina Ortmeier-Hooper, Brian Paltridge, Diane Pecorari, Lia Plakans, Dudley Reynolds, Julio Roca de Larios, Miyuki Sasaki, Ling Shi, Steve Simposon, Paul Stapleton, Neomy Storch, Christine Tardy, John Truscott, Wenyu Wang, Sara Weigle, Siew-Mei Wu, Yongyan Yi, Xiaoye You, and Wei Zhu.

3.2 Trends in publication

As can be seen in Table 1.1 above, the numbers of publications have generally increased greatly since the 1950's in almost all categories. This is true of journal articles, the number of journals in which L2W focused articles have been published, monographs, collections/proceedings, chapters in collections, dissertations, ERIC documents, total publications, and publications per year. However, the increases in some categories from the 1990s to the 2000s are less dramatic than earlier increases. This is the case for journal articles, journals, and dissertations. Monographs continued to increase substantially. The number of collections/proceedings has actually decreased since the 1980's. There seems to have been a shift here from many collections with small numbers of chapters on L2W to fewer collections/proceedings, each with a larger number of L2W focused chapters and more collections/proceedings devoted exclusively to L2W. With regard to the chapters in these books, the large number for the 1990s is greatly inflated by one collection (White 1995), which is comprised of more than one hundred very short accounts of classroom activities. So actually it seems that the number of chapters has remained static. The number of ERIC documents has fallen sharply from the 1990s to the 2000s[8]. Overall, the total of publications has dipped slightly from the 1990s to the 2000s, perhaps reflecting a leveling off process. With regard to foci of these publications, there has been growth overall and a mix of continuing concerns and new topics in each period. In terms of prominent L2W scholars, each decade has brought with it larger numbers and greater diversity in nationality and geographic location.

3.3 Concurrent trends

In addition to trends in publication, there are some other important trends that deserve some attention. L2W studies has continued to absorb ideas from different fields: from linguistics (formal and functional), applied linguistics, psychology (behavioral and cognitive), rhetoric, composition studies, education, anthropology, sociology, the philosophy of science, and others[9]. It is also moving from a modernist, positivistic inquiry paradigm to a more postmodern, relativist perspective; from a view of knowledge as certain and unchanging to a view of knowledge as tentative and contingent. In terms of empirical research, L2W studies has moved from a sole focus on the designs and methods of quantitative empirical research to the inclusion of qualitative approaches and designs that incorporate both quantitative and qualitative elements, that is, mixed method studies. It has also become more open to hermeneutic (non-empirical interpretive) inquiry, for example, historical studies[10]. L2W studies has gone through a series of instructional approaches: controlled composition, current traditional and contrastive rhetoric, process approaches, English for academic purposes (EAP), and genre approaches and is now moving toward

---

8 The decrease in ERIC documents may be attributable to (1) the fact that in 2004 ERIC changed its procedure for acquiring literature and began to reengineer the database; while this was going on no new materials were received or accepted for the database, (2) the increase in venues for publication of scholarship on L2W, and (3) the growth of opportunities for personal online publication.
9 See Silva and Leki (2004) for more detailed information on influences on L2W studies.
10 See Silva (2005) for more on these paradigms and their elements.

an informed eclectic view, employing selected elements from the existing approaches and incorporating new theoretical and pedagogical ideas to address L2W instruction in particular contexts[11]. L2W studies has built an infrastructure involving professional journals, book series, conferences, groups within professional organizations, and academic programs in higher education and has expanded its reach from North America to throughout the world – these last two areas (infrastructure and globalization) will be discussed in more detail in the following sections.

4 The international context

In this section, the current state of L2W studies in the international context and the infrastructure of the field will be presented in terms of such entities as professional organizations, conferences, graduate programs, journals, book series, websites, and listservs[12].

4.1 North America

Canada. In Canada, L2W issues are taken up by such national organizations as TESL Canada and the Canadian Association of Applied Linguistics and by provincial organizations like TESL Ontario and British Columbia TEAL. These organizations also sponsor annual conferences where L2W issues are discussed. Journals addressing L2W issues include *TESL Canada Journal* and the *Canadian Modern Language Review*. There are also a number of universities in Canada where one can do graduate study on L2W. These include both English-medium (e.g., OISE/University of Toronto and the University of British Columbia) and French-medium (e.g., l'Université de Montreal, l'Université Laval) institutions.

   United States. In the US, there are several organizations that devote attention to L2W studies. These include the TESOL (Teaching English to Speakers of Other Languages) International Association, which has an L2W Interest Section with more than 2,200 members and CCCC (Conference College Composition and Communication) – primarily a first language writing organization – that has both a standing committee and a special interest group devoted to L2W issues.

   Each of these organizations has an annual conference at which a substantial number of sessions address L2W studies. In addition, there is the Symposium on

---

11 See Silva (1990) for more on the history of L2W instructional approaches.
12 I have queried L2W specialists around the world to get this information. However, please note that this is a work in progress; therefore, not all areas will be represented – I take full responsibility for any omissions or misrepresentations.

Second Language Writing – a relatively small conference that focuses exclusively on L2W issues. This symposium, which was founded in 1998 in the United States as a biennial conference, has become an annual and international event. To date, it has met in the United States at Purdue University (1998, 2000, 2002, 2004, 2006, 2008, 2012), at Arizona State University (2009, 2014), in Japan at Nagoya Gakuin University (2007), in Spain at the University of Murcia (2010), in Taiwan (2011), and at Shandong University (2013). Another professional forum, The Conference on Contrastive Rhetoric and Written Discourse Analysis, founded in 2004 at Indiana University – Purdue University Indianapolis, has been devoted largely to L2W issues. It has met in Indianapolis (2004, 2005, 2008, 2012, 2014), at Ohio State University (2007), at the University of Michigan (2009), and at Georgia State University (2010).

There are several US based journals, e.g., *TESOL Quarterly* and the *Modern Language Journal,* that publish articles on L2W; but there is only one journal devoted exclusively to L2W – the *Journal of Second Language Writing,* which has actually become more of an international journal – both in terms of its editors and advisory board and its readership. There are two book series exclusively devoted to L2W studies. They are the University of Michigan's Series on Teaching Multilingual Writers and Parlor Press's Second Language Writing Series. There are also graduate programs at a number of universities where students have done and can do a PhD focused on L2W. These include (among others) Arizona State University, Georgia State University, Indiana University, Indiana University of Pennsylvania, New York University, Ohio State University, Purdue University, Columbia University, the University of Arizona, the University of California at Davis, the University of Illinois at Urbana-Champaign, and the University of Texas at Austin.

4.2 Europe

In the European Union, L2W concerns are addressed by organizations such as the European Association of Teachers of Academic Writing (EATAW), the European Association for Research in Learning and Instruction (EARLI), and the European Writing Centers Association (EWCA)

Great Britain. In Great Britain, organizations such as the British Association of Teachers of EAP (BALEAP) and the Academic Literacies Group in London (ACLITS) take on L2W issues, as does the annual BALEAP conference. A number of journals based in England, such as *English Language Teaching Journal,* regularly publish articles on L2W.

Poland. In Poland, L2W is addressed by the country's International Association of Teachers of English as a Foreign Language affiliate, IATEFL Poland. This organization sponsors an annual conference where papers on L2W are presented. Other such conferences include the Conference on Foreign/Second Language Acquisition organized by the University of Silesia in Katowice and Classroom-Oriented Research co-organized by the University of Lodz and Adam Mickiewicz University in Kalisz. Significantly, the University of Lodz also sponsors a conference on Foreign Language Opportunities in Writing (FLOW) that is dedicated exclusively to foreign language writing.

Spain. In Spain, L2W issues are addressed by such organizations as the Spanish Association for Applied Linguistics (AESLA), the European Association for Language for Special Purposes (AELFE – based in Spain and Portugal), and the Spanish Association for Angloamerican Studies (AEDEAN). Annual conferences where L2W is on the program include AESLA and AELFE; other relevant conferences are linked with university departments and research groups. These include the INTER-LAE (Interpersonality in Academic Writing) conference at the University of Zaragoza and the PPRISEAL (Publishing and Presenting Research Internationally: Issues for Speakers of English as an Additional Language) conference at the University of La Laguna in Tenerife. Journals that publish articles on L2W include the *Spanish Journal of Applied Linguistics* (RESLA) (AESLA's journal), *Iberia* (AELFE's journal), and *Atlantis* (AEDEAN's journal). Many university departments publish their own journals, which address L2W studies to a greater or lesser extent. There are graduate programs at the University of Murcia, the Universidad of Alicante, and the Autonomous University of Barcelona where one can focus on L2W issues.

Sweden. In Sweden, organizations addressing L2W issues include the Swedish Society for the Study of English (SWESSE), the Swedish Association of Applied Linguistics (ASLA) – the local AILA affiliate, and the Swedish Organization of Teachers of ESP. Research on L2W can be presented at the conferences of these organizations. Much L2W instruction is offered in English and Swedish departments at Swedish Universities. Graduate study on L2W issues can be done at several of these universities.

4.3 Middle East

Israel. In Israel there are several organizations that address L2W. They include ACROLT (the Academic Committee on Language Testing), ETAI, (the English Teachers Association of Israel), UTELI (University Teaching of English Language), and the Academic Writing Forum. Each of these organizations holds an annual conference where L2W issues are on the program. There are institutions, for example, Bar Ilan University and Beit Berl College, where one can study L2W at the graduate level.

Lebanon. In Lebanon, L2W concerns are addressed by the Association of Teachers of English in Lebanon (ATEL), the Lebanese Association for Educational Studies, TESOL Lebanon, the Middle East – North Africa Writing Center Alliance (MENAWCA), and the Association of Professors of English and Translation at Arab Universities (APETAU), which hold annual conferences where papers on second language issues are presented. Scholarly articles on L2W are published in the Lebanon-based *International Journal of Arabic-English Studies* and the *Journal of the Association of American International Colleges and Universities*. Graduate programs in English are offered by the American University of Beirut, the Lebanese University, Beirut Arab University, Balamand University, University of Notre Dame, the Lebanese American University, Middle East University, and Université Saint Joseph.

Qatar. In Qatar, a number of organizations deal with L2W issues. These include TESOL Arabia (a regional organization), Qatar TESOL (the organization of writing centers in North Africa and the Middle East), the Qatar Writing Centers Network, and a regional affiliate of the International Writing Centers Association. Conferences where L2W papers are presented include TESOL Arabia and Qatar TESOL.

4.4 Asia

China. In Mainland China, L2W is the exclusive focus of the National Association of EFL Writing Teaching and Research (NAEWTR), which was established in 2006. NAETWR sponsors the National Symposium on EFL Writing Teaching and Research, held in Guangzhou in 2003, Wuhan in 2004, Xi'an in 2005, Beijing in 2006, Guiyang in 2007, Beijing Normal University in 2008, Jilin University in 2010, Shandong University in 2012, and Northwest University for Nationalities in 2014. Published proceedings from these gatherings include *Improving learning through writing: Theory and practice of the English length approach* (2004), *English writing teaching and research: Proceedings of the 2nd ESL teaching and research international seminar* (2006); *EFL writing research: Chinese perspectives and practice* (2008) and English *Writing in socio-cultural contexts* (2012). NAEWTR, in 2012, also established the *Journal of EFL Writing Teaching and Research* – only the second journal devoted exclusively to L2W. Other journals that have substantially published on L2W include *Foreign Language Teaching, Foreign Languages and their Teaching and Research, and Foreign Languages World*.

Hong Kong. L2W in Hong Kong is addressed by the Hong Kong Association of Applied Linguistics, which holds an annual conference where papers on L2W are presented. Graduate study in L2W can be done at the Chinese University of Hong Kong, University of Hong Kong, Hong Kong Polytechnic, and the City University of Hong Kong. The *Hong Kong Journal of Applied Linguistics* and the *Asian Journal of English Language Teaching* publish articles addressing L2W.

Japan. In Japan, L2W is addressed by such organizations as the Japanese Association of Language Teachers (JALT), the Japan Association of College English Teachers (JACET), the Japan Society of English Language Education (JASELE), and the Writing Centers Association of Japan (WCAJ) – the number of writing centers (dealing with both L1W and L2W) is increasing at Japanese universities. JACET has regional chapters, of which two, Kansai and Chubu, have writing research groups. The members organize a L2W symposium at the national conference and publish a book or journal together; for example, the Writing Research Group of JACET Kansai Chapter publishes the *Bulletin of the Writing Research Group, JACET Kansai Chapter,* annually. Papers on L2W issues are presented at the annual JALT, JACET, JASELE, and WCAJ conferences. It is possible to do a doctoral dissertation on L2W at several Japanese universities.

Singapore. L2W in Singapore is addressed by the Regional English Language Center, which holds the annual RELC conference and publishes *RELC Journal*. L2W can be studied at the graduate level at such universities as the National University of Singapore, Singapore Management University, Nanyang Technological University, and the National Institute of Education.

Taiwan. In Taiwan, L2W issues are addressed by organizations such as the English Teaching Research Association (ETRA) and the English Teacher Association (ETA). Taiwan hosts a recurring conference at Tamkang University – the Tamkang International Conference on Second Language Writing, devoted exclusively to L2W. Articles on L2W are published by journals such as *English Teaching and Learning* – which did a special issue on L2W in 2012. Many universities in Taiwan have graduate programs in TESOL or TEFL, in which students can do research on L2W. And numerous universities host writing centers or online learning centers that assist students with L2W.

4.5 Oceana

Australia. In Australia, L2W is addressed primarily by the Applied Linguistics Association of Australia (ALAA), which holds an annual conference at which papers on L2W are presented and publishes the *Australian Review of Applied Linguistics*. There are also a number of small pedagogically-focused TESOL conferences and research focused colloquia run by universities, for example, the University of Sydney's annual TESOL Research Network Colloquium. Graduate courses can be taken and MA and PhD studies done on L2W at several Australian universities.

New Zealand. In New Zealand L2W is addressed by a number of organizations, including the Applied Linguistics Association of New Zealand (ALANZ), the Tertiary Writing Network (TWN), the TESOL Association of New Zealand (TESOLANZ), and the New Zealand Association of Language Teachers (NZALT). Each of these associations holds a biannual or annual conference where papers on L2W issues are presented. Publications on L2W can be found in several journals, including New Zealand Studies in Applied Linguistics (ALANZ), the TESOLANZ Journal (TESOLANZ), and New Zealand Language Teacher (NZALT). Master's and/or doctoral work on L2W can be done at most universities in New Zealand under the auspices of schools of languages or general or applied linguistics.

5 The current status of the field

The foregoing review of the infrastructure of L2W reflects remarkable growth in this area of inquiry since its humble beginnings in the 1950s. L2W now has an international profile and a substantial presence and level of credibility at a number of highly regarded universities worldwide. Over the last 20 years or so, L2W has amassed a relatively large, rapidly growing, and truly international group of academic professionals devoted to its study. While L2W does not have an international professional association, it plays an increasingly important role in a number of national and international professional organizations in related areas, such as general second language studies, applied linguistics, composition studies, and education. In any case, the stage is set for the development of an international organization devoted exclusively to L2W; that is, the L2W community possesses all the requisite elements to form such an organization.

The field currently supports four recurring professional meetings devoted exclusively to L2W: the Symposium on Second Language Writing (international), the International Symposium on EFL Writing Teaching and Research (China), the Tamkang International Conference on Second Language Writing (Taiwan), and Foreign Language Opportunities in Writing (Poland). In addition, a number of non-recurring conferences focused on L2W have taken place in recent years. There are currently two journals devoted exclusively to L2W: the *Journal of Second Language Writing* published by Elsevier (Amsterdam) and the *Journal of EFL Writing Teaching and Research* published by Higher Education Press (China). Additionally, a number of journals in a variety of fields have published special issues on L2W.

L2W has not at this point developed a particular conceptual or theoretical framework or methodological approach; it has embraced a largely eclectic orientation toward inquiry, primarily adopting and adapting frameworks and approaches from other areas and creating new ones to meet changing needs, blending work from disparate areas, e.g., cognitive psychology, anthropology, and literary studies. Given the complexity of the phenomenon of L2W, such a multi-disciplinary approach would seem quite appropriate and also salutary in that it could serve to keep L2W professionals' options open and work to prevent them from being limited by the rigidity of a single theoretical or methodological paradigm. As a multidisciplinary area (like medicine, robotics, nanotechnology, human factors in engineering, etc.), L2W studies is in good company.

6 Conclusion

It is clear that L2W studies is an area of inquiry with a rich and very interesting history, that it is currently a vibrant developing area of study, and that it has a bright future. With increasing globalization comes the need for more and better communication across languages. And due to the influence of the internet, much of that communication is and will continue to be in writing. This will mean more interest in and resources for the study and teaching of L2W, which will result in the preparation of more L2W professionals and foster development in theory, research, and instruction. L2W studies has come a long way and has a long way to go.

7 References

Belcher, Diane and George Braine (eds.). 1995. *Academic writing in a second language: Essays on research and pedagogy*. Norwood, NJ: Ablex.

Belcher, Diane and Alan Hirvela (eds.). 2001. *Linking literacies: Perspectives on L2 reading-writing connections*. Ann Arbor: University of Michigan Press.

Carson, Joan and Ilona Leki (eds.). 1993. *Reading in the composition classroom: Second language perspectives*. Boston: Heinle & Heinle.

de Oliveira, Luciana. C. and Tony Silva (eds.). 2013. *L2 writing in secondary classrooms: Student experiences, academic issues, and teacher education*. New York: Routledge.

de Oliveira, Luciana C. and Tony Silva (eds.). 2016. *Second language writing in elementary classrooms: Instructional issues, content area writing, and teacher education*. New York: Palgrave Macmillan.

Johnson, Donna and Duane Roen (eds.). 1989. *Richness in writing: Empowering ESL students*. New York: Longman.

Leki, Ilona, Alister Cumming, and Tony Silva. 2008. *A synthesis of research on second language writing in English: 1980–2005*. New York: Routledge.

Matsuda, Paul and Tony Silva (eds.). 2005. *Second language writing research: Perspectives on the process of knowledge construction*. Mahwah, NJ: Lawrence Erlbaum Associates.

Ortmeier-Hooper, Christina. 2013. *The ELL writer: Moving beyond basics in the secondary classroom*. New York: Teachers College Press, Teachers College, Columbia University.

Robinson, Pauline (ed.). 1988. *Academic writing: Process and product*. London: Macmillan.

Silva, Tony. 1990. Second language composition instruction: Developments, issues, and directions in ESL. In Barbara Kroll (ed.), *Second language writing: Research insights for the classroom*, 11–23. New York: Cambridge University Press.

Silva, Tony. 2005. On the philosophical bases of inquiry in a second language Writing: Metaphysics, inquiry paradigms, and the intellectual zeitgeist. In Paul Matsuda and Tony Silva (eds.), *Second language writing research: Perspectives on the process of knowledge creation*, 3–15. Mahwah, NJ: Lawrence Erlbaum Associates

Silva, Tony and Ilona Leki. 2004. Family matters: The influence of applied linguistics and composition studies on second language writing studies: Past, present, and future. *The Modern Language Journal* 88. 1–13.

White, Ronald (ed.). 1995. *New ways in teaching writing*. Alexandria, VA: TESOL.

Appendix: Selected resources for further inquiry

A selected list of readings (journal articles and book chapters) that, collectively, provide an overview of the development of second language studies (in chronological order).

Gibian, George. 1951. College English for foreign students. *College English*, 13(3). 157–160.

Ives, Sumner. 1953. Help for the foreign student. *College Composition and Communication* 4(4). 141–144.

Erazmus, Edward. 1960. Second language composition teaching at the intermediate level. *Language Learning* 10(1/2). 25–31.

Pincas, Anita. 1962. Structural linguistics and systematic composition teaching to students of English as a second language. *Language Learning* 12(3). 185–194.

Kaplan, Robert. 1966. Cultural thought patterns in intercultural education. *Language Learning* 16(1). 1–20.

Zamel, Vivian. 1976. Teaching composition in the ESL classroom: What can we learn from the research in the teaching of English. *TESOL Quarterly* 10(1). 67–76.

Reid, Joy. 1984. ESL Composition: The linear product of American thought. *College Composition and Communication* 35. 449–452.

Horowitz, Daniel. 1986a. Process, not product: Less than meets the eye. *TESOL Quarterly* 20(1). 141–144.

Lebman-Kleine, JoAnne. 1986. In defense of teaching process in ESL composition. *TESOL Quarterly* 20(4). 783–788.

Hamp-Lyons, Liz. 1986. No new lamps for old yet, please. *TESOL Quarterly* 20(4). 790–796.

Horowitz, Daniel. 1986c. The author responds to Hamp-Lyons. *TESOL Quarterly* 20(4). 796–797.

Spack, Ruth. 1988. Initiating ESL students into the academic discourse community: How far should we go? *TESOL Quarterly* 22(1). 29–51.

Horowitz, Daniel. 1990. Fiction and non-fiction in the ESL/EFL classroom: Does the differencemake a difference? *English for Specific Purposes* 9(2). 161–168.

Santos, Terry. 1992. Ideology in composition: L1 and ESL. *Journal of Second Language Writing* 1(1). 1–15.

Benesch, Sarah. 1993. ESL, ideology, and the politics of pragmatism. *TESOL Quarterly* 27(4). 705–717.

Severino, C. 1993. The sociopolitical implications of response to second language and second dialect writing. *Journal of Second Language Writing* 2(3). 181–201.

Silva, Tony. 1993. The distinct nature of second language writing: The ESL research and its implications. *TESOL Quarterly* 27(4). 657–677.

Reid, Joy. 1994. Responding to ESL students' texts: The myths of appropriation. *TESOL Quarterly* 28(2). 273–292.

Hyon, Sunny. 1996. Genre in three traditions: Implications for ESL. *TESOL Quarterly* 30(4). 693–722.

Harklau, Linda, Kay M. Losey, and Meryl M. Siegal. 1999. Linguistically diverse students and college writing: What is equitable and appropriate? In Linda Harklau, Meryl Siegal, and Kay M. Losey (eds.), *Generation 1.5 meets college composition*, 1–14. Mahwah, NJ: Lawrence Erlbaum Associates.

Matsuda, Paul Kei. 1999. Composition studies and ESL writing: A disciplinary division of labor. *College Composition and Communication* 50(4). 699–721.

Truscott, John. 1996. The case against grammar correction in L2 writing classes. *Language Learning* 46(2). 327–369.

Ferris, Dana. 1999. The case for grammar correction in L2 writing classes: A response to Truscott (1996). *Journal of Second Language Writing* 8(1). 1–11.

Truscott, John. 1999. The case for "The case against grammar correction in L2 writing classes": A response to Ferris. *Journal of Second Language Writing* 8(2). 111–122.

Ferris, Dana. 2012. Written corrective feedback in second language acquisition and writing studies. *Language Teaching* 45(4). 446–459.

Connor, Ulla. 2002. New directions in contrastive rhetoric. *TESOL Quarterly* 36(4). 493–510.

Atkinson, Dwight. 2003. Writing and culture in the post-process era. *Journal of Second Language Writing* 12(1). 49–63.

Casanave, Christine P. 2003. Looking ahead to more sociopolitically-oriented case study research in L2 writing scholarship (But should it be called "post-process"?). *Journal of Second Language Writing* 12(1). 85–102.

Silva, Tony and Ilona Leki. 2004. Family matters: The influence of applied linguistics and composition studies on second language writing studies – Past, present, and future. *The Modern Language Journal* 88(1). 1–13.

Canagarajah, A. Suresh. 2006. The place of world Englishes in composition: Pluralization continued. *College Composition and Communication* 57(4). 586–619.

Li, Xiaoming. 2005. Composing culture in a fragmented world: The issue of representation in cross-cultural research. In Paul K. Matsuda and Tony Silva (eds.), *Second language writing research: Perspectives on the process of knowledge creation*, 121–131. Mahwah, NJ: Lawrence Erlbaum Associates.

Costino, Kim and Sunny Hyon. 2007. "A class for students like me": Reconsidering relationships among identity labels, residency status, and students' preferences for mainstream or multilingual composition. *Journal of Second Language Writing* 16(2). 63–81.

Roberge, Mark. 2008. *A teacher's perspective on Generation 1.5*. In Mark. Roberge, Meryl Siegal, & Linda Harklau (eds.), *Generation 1.5 in College Composition: Teaching academic writingto US-educated learners of ESL*, 3–24. New York, NY: Routledge.

Conference on College Composition and Communication. 2009. *CCCC statement on second language writing and writers*. Available at http://www.ncte.org/cccc/resources/positions/secondlangwriting.

Ferris, Dana. 2009. *Teaching college writing to diverse student populations* (Chapter 1: Defining L2 student audiences, 3–24). Ann Arbor: University of Michigan Press.

Crusan, Deborah. 2011. The promise of directed self-placement for second language writers. *TESOL Quarterly* 45(4). 774–780.

Shapiro, Shawna. 2011. Stuck in the remedial rut: Confronting resistance to ESL curriculum reform. *Journal of Basic Writing* 30(2). 24–52.

Reichelt, Melinda. 2011. Foreign language writing: An overview. In Tony Cimasko and Melinda Reichelt (eds.), *Foreign language writing instruction: Principles and Practices*, 3–21. Anderson, SC: Parlor Press.

Schultz, Jean M. 2011. Foreign language writing in the era of globalization. In Tony Cimasko and Melinda Reichelt (eds.), *Foreign language writing instruction: Principles and practices*, 65–82. Anderson, SC: Parlor Press.

Lefcowitz, Natalie. 2011. The quest for grammatical accuracy: Writing instruction among foreign and heritage language educators. In Tony Cimasko and Melinda Reichelt (eds.), *Foreign language writing instruction: Principles and practices*, 225–254. Anderson, SC: Parlor Press.

Reichelt, Melinda, Natalie Lefcowitz, Carol C. Rinnert, and Jean Marie Schultz. 2012. Key issues in foreign language writing. *Foreign Language Annals* 45(1). 22–41.

Yoon, Choongil. 2011. Concordancing in L2 writing class: An overview of research and issues. *Journal of English for Academic Purposes* 10(3). 130–139.

Belcher, Diane. 2012. Considering what we know and need to know about second language writing. *Applied Linguistics Review* 3(1). 131–150.

Di Gennaro, Kristen. 2012. The heterogeneous second-language population in US colleges and the impact on writing program design. *TETYC* 40(1). 57–67.

Wang, Junju. 2012. A synthesis of studies on L2 writing in the Chinese context. *Journal of EFL Writing Teaching and Research* 1(1). 10–21.

Wang, Lifei. 2012. Current developments of L2 writing research in China and abroad and its application. *Journal of EFL Writing Teaching and Research* 1(1). 1–9.

Williams, Jessica. 2012. The potential role (s) of writing in second language development. *Journal of Second Language Writing* 21(4). 321–331.

Disciplinary Dialogues. 2013. *Journal of Second Language Writing* 22(4). 425–450.

Liu, Pei-Hsun Emma and Dan J. Tannacito. 2013. Resistance by L2 writers: The role of racial and language ideology in imagined community and identity investment. *Journal of Second Language Writing* 22(4). 355–373.

Matsuda, Paul Kei, Tanita Saenkhum, and Steven Accardi. 2013. Writing teachers' perceptions of the presence and needs of second language writers: An institutional case study. *Journal of Second Language Writing* 22(1). 68–86.

Horner, Bruce, Min-Zhan Lu, Jacqueline J. Royster, and John Trimbur, J. 2011. Opinion: Language difference in writing: Toward a translingual approach. *College English* 73(3). 303–321.

Canagarajah, A. Suresh. 2013. Negotiating translingual literacy: An enactment. *Research in the Teaching of English* 48(1). 40–67.

Matsuda, Paul Kei. 2014. The lure of translingual writing. *PMLA* 129(3). 478–483

Atkinson, Dwight, Deborah Crusan, Paul Kei Matsuda, Christina Ortmeier-Hooper, Todd Ruecker, Steve Simpson, and Chris Tardy. 2015. Clarifying the relationship between L2 writing and translingual writing: An open letter to writing studies editors and organization leaders. *College English* 77(4). 383–386.

Journals publishing L2W focused work (in order of frequency of publication of L2W focused articles)

Journal of Second Language Writing
TESOL Quarterly
English Teaching Forum
ELT Journal
English for Specific Purposes
System
TESOL Newsletter
Foreign Language Annals
RELC Journal
Modern Language Journal
TESOL Journal
TESL Canada Journal
Canadian Modern Language Review
Journal of English for Academic Purposes
TESL Reporter
Assessing Writing
College ESL
TECFORS
ITL Review of Applied Linguistic
Language Learning
Written Communication
Journal of Basic Writing
Teaching English is the Two Year College
College Composition and Communication
Applied Linguistics
Language Testing
Computer Assisted Language Learning
Computers & Composition
TESL-EJ
Francais dans le Monde
Hispania
French Review
World Englishes
College English
IRAL

Journal of Asian Pacific Communication
Language Learning and Technology
Research in the Teaching of English
TESL Talk
TESOL Matters

Books

Monographs (In order of date of publication)

Gaudiani, Claire. 1981. *Teaching writing in the EFL curriculum*. Washington, DC: Center for Applied Linguistics.
Jacobs, Holly, Stephen Zinkgraf, Deanna Wormuth, V. Faye Hartfield, and Jane Hughley. 1981. *Testing ESL composition: A practical approach*. Rowley, MA: Newbury House.
Hughey, Jane, Deanna Wormuth, V. Faye Hartfield, and Holly Jacobs. 1983. *Teaching ESL composition: Principles and techniques*. Rowley, MA: Newbury House.
Raimes, Ann. 1983. *Techniques in teaching writing*. New York: Oxford University Press.
Krashen, Stephen. 1984. *Writing: Research, theory, and applications*. Oxford: Pergamon.
Byrne, Don. 1988. *Teaching writing skills*. London: Longman.
Hedge, Tricia. 1988. *Writing*. Oxford: Oxford University Press.
Swales, John. 1990. *Genre analysis. English in academic and research settings*. New York: Cambridge University Press.
White, Ron and Valerie Arndt. 1991. *Process writing*. London: Longman.
Leki, Ilona. 1992. *Understanding ESL writers: A guide for teachers*. Portsmouth, NH: Boynton-Cook.
Rodby, Judith. 1992. *Appropriating literacy: Writing and reading in English as a second language*. Portsmouth, NH: Boynton-Cook/Heineman.
Bates, Linda, Janet Lane, and Ellen Lange. 1993. *Writing clearly: Responding to ESL compositions*. Boston: Heinle & Heinle.
Reid, Joy. 1993. *Teaching ESL writing*. Englewood Cliffs, NJ: Regents/Prentice Hall.
Fox, Helen. 1994. *Listening to the world: Cultural issues in academic writing*. Urbana, IL: NCTE.
Smith, Veronica. 1995. *Thinking in a foreign language: An investigation into essay writing and translation by L2 learners*. Tubingen: G. Narr.
Tucker, Amy. 1995. *Decoding ESL: International students in the American college classroom* (Rev. ed.). Portsmouth, NH: Boynton/Cook.
Connor, Ulla. 1996. *Contrastive rhetoric: Cross-cultural aspects of second language writing*. New York: Cambridge University Press.
Grabe, William and Robert Kaplan. 1996. *Theory and practice of writing: An applied linguistics perspective*. New York: Longman.
Li, Xiao Ming. 1996. *"Good writing" in cross cultural context*. Albany, NY: State University of New York Press.
Pennington, Martha. 1996. *The computer and the non-native writer: A natural partnership*. Cresskill, NJ: Hampton Press, Inc.
Scott, Virginia. 1996. *Rethinking foreign language writing*. Boston: Heinle & Heinle.
Sonomura, Marion. 1996. *Idiomaticity in the basic writing of American English: Formulas and idioms in the writing of multilingual and creole-speaking community college students in Hawaii*. New York: Peter Lang.
Tribble, Chris. 1996. *Writing*. Oxford, UK: Oxford University Press.
Johns, Ann. 1997. *Text, role, and context: Developing academic literacies*. New York: Cambridge University Press.

Losey, Kay. 1997. *Listen to the silences: Mexican American interaction in the composition classroom and the community*. Norwood, NJ: Ablex.

Blanton, Linda. 1998. *Varied voices: On language and literacy learning*. Boston: Heinle & Heinle.

Byrd, Patricia and Joy Reid. 1998. *Grammar in the composition classroom: Essays on teaching ESL for college-bound students*. Portsmouth, NH: Heinle & Heinle.

Campbell, Cherry. 1998. *Teaching second-language writing: Interacting with text*. Portsmouth, NH: Heinle & Heinle.

Mlynarczyk, Rebeca. 1998. *Conversations of the mind: The uses of journal writing for second-language learners*. Mahwah, NJ: Erlbaum.

Wolfe-Quintero, Kate, Shunki Inagaki, and Hae-Young Kim. 1998. *Second language development in writing Measures of fluency, accuracy, & complexity*. Honolulu: University of Hawai'i Press.

Pogner, Karl-Heinz. 1999. *Schreiben im Beruf als Hadeln im Fach. [Writing on the job as social laction]*. Tubingen: Gunter Narr Verlag.

Casanave, Christine. 2002. *Writing games: Multicultural case studies of academic literacy practices in higher education*. Mahwah, NJ: Lawrence Erlbaum.

Canagarajah, Suresh. 2002. *Critical academic writing and multilingual students*. Ann Arbor, MI: University of Michigan Press.

Ferris, Dana. 2002. *Treatment of error in second language student writing*. Ann Arbor, MI: University of Michigan Press.

Hinkel, Eli. 2002. *Second language writers' text: Linguistic and rhetorical features*. Mahwah, NJ: Lawrence Erlbaum.

Liu, Jun and Jette Hansen. 2002. *Peer response in second language writing classrooms*. Ann Arbor, MI: University of Michigan Press.

Casanave, Christine Pearson. 2003. *Controversies in second language writing: Dilemmas and decisions in research and instruction*. Ann Arbor, MI: University of Michigan Press.

Hyland, Ken. 2003. *Second Language Writing*. Cambridge, UK: Cambridge University Press.

Bruce, Shanti and Ben Rafoth. 2004. *ESL Writers: A guide for writing center tutors*. Portsmouth, NH: Boynton/Cook Publishers.

Hinkel, Eli. 2004. *Teaching Academic ESL Writing: Practical techniques in vocabulary and grammar*. Mahwah, NJ: Lawrence Erlbaum Associates.

Hirvela, Alan. 2004. *Connecting reading and writing in second language writing instruction*. Ann Arbor, MI: University of Michigan Press.

Goldstein, Lynn. 2005. *Teacher written commentary in second language writing classrooms*. Ann Arbor, MI: University of Michigan Press.

Hirose, Keiko. 2005. *Product and process in the L1 and L2 writing of Japanese students of English*. Hiroshima, Japan: Keisuisha Company Limited.

Panofsky, Carolyn, Maria Pacheco, Sara Smith, Janet Santos, and Chad Fogelman. 2005. *Approaches to writing instruction for adolescent English language learners: A discussion of recent research and practice literature in relation to nationwide standards on writing*. Providence, RI: Education Alliance at Brown University.

Weissberg, Rob. 2006. *Connecting speaking and writing in second language writing instruction*. Ann Arbor, MI: University of Michigan Press.

Bloch, Joel. 2007. *Technologies in the second language composition classroom*. Ann Arbor, MI: University of Michigan Press.

Leki, Ilona. 2007. *Undergraduates in a second language: Challenges and complexities of academic literacy development*. Mahwah, NJ: Lawrence Erlbaum Associates.

Myers Zawacki, Terry, Eiman Hajabbasi, Anna Habib, Alex Antram, and Alokparna Das. 2007. *Valuing written accents: Non-native studens talk about identity, academic writing, and meeting teachers' expectations*. Fairfax, VA: George Mason University Press.

Paltridge, Brian and Sue Starfield. 2007. *Thesis and dissertation writing in a second language: A handbook for supervisors*. London: Routledge.

Leki, Ilona, Alister Cumming, and Tony Silva. 2008. *A synthesis of research on second language writing in English: 1980–2005*. New York: Routledge.

Ferris, Dana. 2009. *Teaching college writing to diverse student populations*. Ann Arbor, MI: University of Michigan Press.

Tardy, Christine. 2009. *Building genre knowledge*. West Lafayette, IN: Parlor Press.

Crusan, Deborah. 2010. *Assessment in the second language writing classroom*. Ann Arbor, MI: University of Michigan Press.

Lenski, Susan and Frances Verbruggen. 2010. *Writing instruction and assessment for English Language learners K-8*. New York: Guilford Press.

Lillis, Theresa M. and Mary Jane Curry. 2010. *Academic writing in a global context: The politics and practices of publishing in English*. New York: Routledge.

You, Xiaoye. 2010. *Writing in the devil's tongue: A history of English composition in China*. Carbondale, IL: Southern Illinois University Press.

Bitchener, John and Dana R. Ferris. 2011. *Written corrective feedback in second language acquisition and writing*. New York, NY: Routledge.

Casanave, Christine P. 2011. *Journal writing in second language education*. Ann Arbor: University of Michigan Press.

Connor, Ulla. 2011. *Intercultural rhetoric in the writing classroom*. Ann Arbor: University of Michigan Press.

Agustín Llach, María Pilar. 2011. *Lexical errors and accuracy in foreign language writing*. Bristol, UK: Multilingual Matters.

Tang, Romona. 2011. *Academic writing in a second or foreign language: Issues and challenges facing ESL/EFL academic writers in higher education contexts*. London: Continuum.

Wang, Xiao-Lei. 2011. *Learning to read and write in the multilingual family*. Clevedon, UK: Multilingual Matters.

Andrade, Maureen S. and Norman W. Evans. 2012. *Principles and practices for response in second language writing: Developing self-regulated learners*. New York: Routledge.

Bloch, Joel. 2012. *Plagiarism, intellectual property and the teaching of L2 writing*. Bristol, UK: Multilingual Matters.

Kamimura, Taeko. 2012. *Teaching EFL composition in Japan*. Tokyo: Senshudaigakushuppankyoku

Macqueen, Susy. 2012. *The emergence of patterns in second language writing: A sociocognitive exploration of lexical trails*. New York: Peter Lang.

Matarese, Valerie. 2012. *Supporting research writing: Roles and challenges in multilingual settings*: Amsterdam: Elsevier.

Curry, Mary Jane and Theresa Lillis. 2013. *A scholar's guide to getting published in English: critical choices and practical strategies*. Bristol, UK: Multilingual Matters.

Ferris, Dana. R. and John Hedgcock. 2013. *Teaching L2 composition: Purpose, process, and practice, 3rd edition*. New York: Routledge.

Hanauer, David I. and Karen Englander. 2013. *Scientific writing in a second language*: Anderson, SC: Parlor Press.

Ortmeier-Hooper, Christina. 2013. *The ELL writer: Moving beyond basics in the secondary classroom*. New York: Teachers College Press, Teachers College, Columbia University.

Laman, Tasha Tropp. 2013. *From ideas to words: Writing strategies for English language learners*. Portsmouth, NH: Heinemann.

Pecorari, Diane. 2013. *Teaching to avoid plagiarism*. Maidenhead: Open University Press.

Storch, Neomy. 2013. *Collaborative writing in L2 classrooms*, Buffalo: Multilingual Matters.

Cotos, Elena. 2014. *Genre-based automated writing evaluation for L2 research writing: From design to evaluation and enhancement*. New York, NY: Palgrave Macmillan.

Salazar, Danica. 2014. *Lexical bundles in native and non-native scientific writing: Applying a corpus-based study to language teaching*. Philadelphia, PA John Benjamins.

Hyland, Ken. 2016. *Learning and teaching writing*. New York: Routledge.

Collections (In order of date of publication)

McKay, Sandra (ed.). 1984. *Composing in a second language.* Rowley, MA: Newbury House.
Connor, Ulla and Robert Kaplan (eds.) 1987. *Writing across languages: Analysis of L2 text.* Reading, MA: Addison-Wesley.
Purves, Alan (ed.). 1988. *Writing across languages and cultures: Issues in contrastive rhetoric.* Newbury Park, CA: Sage.
Johnson, Donna and Duane Roen. (eds.). 1989. *Richness in writing: Empowering ESL students.* New York: Longman.
Connor, Ulla and Ann Johns (eds.). 1990. *Coherence in writing: Research and pedagogical perspectives.* Washington, DC: TESOL.
Kroll, Barbara (ed.). 1990. *Second Language Writing: Research insights for the classroom.* New York: Cambridge University Press.
Hamp-Lyons, Liz (ed.). 1991. *Assessing L2W in academic contexts.* Norwood, NJ: Ablex.
Brock, Mark and Larry Walters (eds.). 1993. *Teaching composition around the Pacific Rim: Politics and pedagogy.* Clevedon, UK: Multilingual Matters.
Carson, Joan and Ilona Leki (eds.). 1993. *Reading in the composition classroom: Second language perspectives.* Boston: Heinle & Heinle.
Peyton, Joy Kreeft, Jana Staton, and Roger W. Shuy (eds.). 1993. *Dialogue journals in the multilingual classroom: Building language fluency and writing skills through written interaction.* Norwood, NJ: Ablex.
Cumming, Alister (ed.). 1994. *Bilingual performance in reading and writing.* Ann Arbor, MI: Research Club in Language Learning.
Belcher, Diane and George Braine (eds.). 1995. *Academic writing in a second language: Essays on research and pedagogy.* Norwood, NJ: Ablex.
Pogner, Karl-Heinz. (ed.) 1995. *Odense Working Papers in Language and Communication,* No. 6. Odense, Denmark: Odense University Institute of Language and Communication.
White, Ronald (ed.). 1995. *New ways in teaching writing.* Alexandria, VA: TESOL.
Leeds, Bruce (ed.). 1996. *Writing in a second language: Insights from first and second language teaching and research.* New York: Longman.
Archibald, Alasdair and Gaynor Jeffrey (eds.). 1997. *Second language acquisition and writing: A multidisciplinary approach.* Southampton, England: The University at Southampton.
Pogner, Karl-Heinz (ed.). 1997. Writing: Text and interaction. *Odense Working Papers in Language and Communication, No. 14.* Odense, Denmark: Odense University Institute of Language and Communication.
Severino, Carol, Juan Guerra, and Johnnella Butler (eds.). 1997. *Writing in multicultural settings.* New York, NY: Modern Language Association
Zamel, Vivian and Ruth Spack (eds.). 1998. *Negotiating academic literacies: Teaching and learning across languages and cultures.* Mahwah, NJ: Lawrence Erlbaum Associates.
Candlin, Chistopher and Ken Hyland (eds.). 1999. *Writing: Texts, processes and practices.* London: Longman.
Harklau, Linda, Kay M. Losey, and Meryl Siegal (eds.). 1999. *Generation 1.5 meets college composition.* Mahwah, NJ: Lawrence Erlbaum Associates.
Brauer, Gerd (ed.). 2000. *Writing across languages.* Stamford, CT.: Ablex.
Belcher, Diane and Ulla Connor (eds.). 2001. *Reflections on multiliterate lives.* Buffalo, NY: Multilingual Matters.
Belcher, Diane and Alan Hirvela (eds.). 2001. *Linking literacies: Perspectives on L2 reading-writing connections.* Ann Arbor: University of Michigan Press.
Peregoy, Suzanne F. and Owen F. Boyle (eds.). 2001. *Reading, writing, & learning in ESL: A resource book for K-12 teachers* (3rd ed.). New York: Longman.

Silva, Tony and Paul Matsuda (eds.). 2001. *Landmark essays on ESL writing.* Mahwah, NJ: Erlbaum.
Silva, Tony and Paul Matsuda (eds.). 2001. *On second language writing.* Mahwah, NJ: Erlbaum.
Blanton, Linda and Barbara Kroll (eds.). 2002. *ESL composition tales: Reflections on teaching.* Ann Arbor, MI: University of Michigan Press.
Ransdell, Sarah and Marie-Laure Barbier (eds.). 2002. *New directions for research in L2 writing.* Boston: Kluwer Academic Publishers.
Kroll, Barbara (ed.). 2003. *Exploring the dynamics of second language writing.* Cambridge, UK: Cambridge University Press.
Matsuda, Paul K. and Tony Silva (eds.). 2005. *Second language writing research: Perspectives on the process of knowledge construction.* Mahwah, NJ: Erlbaum.
Hyland, Ken and Fiona Hyland (eds.) 2006. *Feedback on second language students' writing: Contexts and issues.* Cambridge, UK: Cambridge University Press.
Matsuda, Paul Kei, Michelle Cox, Jay Jordan, and Christina Ortmeier-Hooper (eds.). 2006. *Second language writing in the composition classroom: A critical sourcebook.* Boston, MA: Bedford/St. Martin's Press.
Matsuda, Paul Kei, Christina Ortmeier-Hooper, and Xiaoye You (eds.). 2006. *The politics of second language writing: In search of the promised land.* West Lafayette, IN: Parlor Press.
August, Diane and Timothy Shanahan (eds.). 2007. *Developing reading and writing in second language learners: Lessons from the Report of the National Literacy Panel on Language-Minority Children and Youth.* Hillsdale, NJ: Lawrence Erlbaum.
Shaw, Stuart D. and Cyril J. Weir (eds.). 2007 *Examining writing: Research and practice in assessing second language writing.* Cambridge: Cambridge University Press.
Reid, Joy (ed.). 2008. *Writing myths: Applying second language research to classroom teaching.* Ann Arbor, MI: University of Michigan Press.
Manchón, Rosa M. (ed.). 2009. *Writing in foreign language contexts: Learning, teaching, and research.* Clevedon, UK: Multilingual Matters.
Kasten, Susan (ed.). 2010. *Effective second language writing.* Alexandria, VA, TESOL.
Silva, Tony and Paul Kei Matsuda (eds.). 2010. *Practicing theory in second language writing.* West Lafayette, IN: Parlor Press.
Cimasko, Tony and Melinda Reichelt (eds.). 2011. Foreign language writing instruction: Principles and practices. Anderson, SC: Parlor Press.
Manchón, Rosa, M. (ed.). 2011. *Learning-to-write and writing-to-learn in an additional language.* Amsterdam: John Benjamins.
Manchón, Rosa, M. (ed.). 2012. *L2 writing development: Multiple perspectives.* Boston, MA: De Gruyter Mouton.
Tang, Ramona (ed.). 2012. *Academic writing in a second or foreign language. Issues and challenges facing ESL/EFL academic writers in higher education contexts.* London: Continuum.
Belcher, Diane D. and Gayle Nelson (eds.). 2013. *Critical and corpus-based approaches to intercultural rhetoric.* Ann Arbor: University of Michigan Press.
de Oliveira, Luciana C. and Tony Silva (eds.). 2013. *L2 writing in secondary classrooms: Student experiences, academic issues, and teacher education.* New York: Routledge.
Zawacki, Terry Myers and Michelle Cox (eds.). 2014. *WAC and second language writing: Research towards linguistically and culturally inclusive programs and practices.* Anderson, SC: Parlor Press.
Thessen, Lucia and Linda Cooper (eds.). 2014. *Risk in academic writing. Postgraduate students, their teachers and the making of knowledge.* Bristol, UK: Multilingual Matters.
Byrnes, Heidi and Rosa M. Manchón (eds.), *Task-based language learning: Insights to and from writing*, 27–52. Amsterdam: John Benjamins.
Bitchener, John and Neomy Storch. 2016. *Written corrective feedback for L2 development.* Bristol, UK: Multilingual Matters.

Bibliographies

Silva, Tony et al. 1992–Present. Selected bibliography of recent scholarship in second language writing. *Journal of Second Language Writing* (at the end of each issue.)

Tannacito, Dan. 1995. *A guide to writing English as a second or foreign language: An annotated bibliography of research and pedagogy.* Alexandria, VA: TESOL.

Silva, Tony, Colleen Brice, and Melinda Reichelt. 1999. *Annotated bibliography of scholarship in second language writing: 1993–1997.* Stamford, CT: Ablex.

Silva, Tony, Crissy McMartin-Miller, and Tony Cimasko. 2012. Recent scholarship on technology and second language writing: An annotated bibliography. In G. Kessler, A. Oskoz, & I. Elola (eds.), *Technology across writing contexts and tasks* (pp. 317–338). CALICO Monograph Series, Volume 10.

Position Paper

CCCC Statement on Second Language Writing and Writers. 2009. Available at http://www.ncte.org/cccc/resources/positions/secondlangwriting

Databases

ProQuest Thesis and Dissertation Database: http://www.proquest.com/en-US/catalogs/databases/detail/pqdt.shtml

Education Resource Information Center (ERIC): http://www.eric.ed.gov/

Linguistics and Language Behavior Abstracts: http://www.proquest.com/en-US/catalogs/databases/detail/llba-set-c.shtml

WorldCat: http://www.worldcat.org/

Alan Hirvela, Ken Hyland, and Rosa M. Manchón

2 Dimensions in L2 writing theory and research: Learning to write and writing to learn

1 Introduction

As noted by Cumming in his contribution to this *Handbook* (Chapter 3), "L2 writing is inherently multi-faceted, involving multiple issues and orientations that may not even be commensurate with each other" (pag. 65). The present chapter explores the multi-faceted nature of L2 writing from the perspective of three complementary orientations to its study, which are referred to in the literature as "learning-to-write" (LW), "writing-to-learn-content" (WLC), and "writing-to-learn-language" (WLL), respectively (Manchón 2011a). Each of these three orientations is ultimately related to the variables of purposes of learning and teaching writing, on the one hand, and to the contexts where L2 writing is learned and taught, on the other. In addition, each one puts emphasis on a different facet of writing: writing itself and written texts in LW, readers and contexts of use in WLC, and language in WLL (see Ortega 2011).

The study of the LW dimension has been privileged in L2 writing theory, empirical research, and pedagogical thinking. This orientation encompasses theoretical and empirical efforts aimed at advancing disciplinary understandings of the various facets (personal, social, educational, socio-political, ideological, cognitive, and linguistic) of writing in an additional language. As a rule, the body of knowledge accumulated on the LW perspective derives from studies on L2 writing as practiced in a range of "second" language contexts, including mainly academic and workplace settings (see chapters in Part II, this volume).

L2 writing has also been approached from the perspective of the way in which the act of writing itself may be instrumental in learning something else. The WLC perspective investigates L2 writing as a vehicle for the learning of disciplinary subject-matter in the content areas, mainly (although not solely) in "second" instructional settings. At the heart of the WLC perspective on L2 writing is the assumption that students ultimately use writing to show mastery of content knowledge, as well as to maximize their learning through the resources that writing provides, a transfer effect that is more fully discussed in a later section. In contrast, the WLL orientation is a much more recent addition to L2 writing research preoccupations and it represents a crucial area of study in the research agenda on SLA-L2 writing interfaces, as elaborated in more detail in Chapter 26. This approach explores L2 writing as a site for language learning, mostly (though not solely) in "foreign" language instructional settings. It includes the analysis of the language learning benefits that may potentially result from the act of writing itself, as well as from the processing of written corrective feedback on one's own writing.

As noted in previous publications (cf. Manchón 2011a; Ortega 2011), these three orientations to the study of L2 writing have developed almost independently from each other, have been informed by different theoretical frameworks, and have resulted in different pedagogical approaches to the learning and teaching of L2 writing. Thus, the LW and some WLC perspectives, with their emphasis on the "writing" component of L2 writing, have been informed by L1 composition, English for Specific Purposes and English for Academic Purposes research, and are associated (especially in North America) with composition classes and WAC (Writing across the Curriculum) programmes. In contrast, theory and research on the WLL perspective, with its emphasis on the "language" component of L2 writing, is informed by second language acquisition (SLA) studies, including cognitive and, to a lesser extent, socio-cultural approaches, as well as by cognitive theories of L1 and L2 writing.

In the remaining sections of this chapter we provide a synthesis of key issues of debate in the study of the LW (Ken Hyland), WLC (Alan Hirvela) and WLL (Rosa Manchón) dimensions of L2 writing. This overview is complemented with the analysis of theory and research undertaken in many contributions to this Handbook, as noted in the cross-references included throughout the chapter.

2 Learning to write in an L2

The ability of second language students to express themselves in writing is at the heart of what it means to be literate in a language and students are often evaluated by their control of it. Yet the complex nature of learning to write constantly evades adequate explanation and many forms of enquiry have been summoned to help clarify it. In line with the treatment of the other dimensions of L2 writing covered in this chapter, here we offer a brief overview of the main frameworks for understanding LW in L2 adult contexts, making a broad distinction between approaches which focus on either writers, texts, or readers (see K. Hyland 2016 for a fuller elaboration). Under the first heading we look at theories which concentrate on the writer and the cognitive *processes* used to create texts; in the second at those which focus on the products of writing by examining *texts* themselves; and in the third approach those on how writers incorporate a sense of *audience* into their writing. Each approach responds to and draws on the others, but the distinction offers a useful way of discussing some key issues.

2.1 Focusing on writers

Writer-oriented approaches seek to model what good writers do when they write so that these strategies can be taught to L2 students. This was the dominant paradigm in North America for many years, evolving over 30 years from the early work of Flower and Hayes (1981). Process theorists originally explained writing using the tools and models of cognitive psychology and the core idea is that writing is informed by certain basic cognitive processes, originally emphasising writing as a problem solving (in terms of the demands imposed by the thinking, cognitive dimension of writing activity) rather than an act of communication. In these early formulations (Flower and Hayes 1981; Hayes 2006), writing was seen as a "non-linear, exploratory, and generative process whereby writers discover and reformulate their ideas as they attempt to approximate meaning" (Zamel 1983: 165). Accordingly, generating a text was said to entail a continuous dynamic, cyclical interaction and interplay of several processes (planning, formulating, evaluating, revising), as well as close interaction between what has already been written and the emerging text.

More recently, however, L1 writing models of writing have brought the text generation process much more into focus, a process thought to be automatic in L1 writing in the early L1 writing models. The accumulated empirical evidence on the cognitive demands of text generation processes in both adults and children has led researchers to suggest that "translation is the fundamental cognitive process of writing" (Fayol, Alamargot, and Berninger 2012: 10) because translation "is the goal for planning and provides the product on which the review and revision processes operate" (p. 12). Accordingly, the centrality of the process of transcription is emphasized in Hayes's (2012a, b) latest formulation of a model of writing.

The research into writing processes has been considerable (see Smagorinsky 2006 for review. See also Chapter 12, this *Handbook*) and methods have extended beyond early experimental techniques to describe writing from the perspective of writers themselves, making use of writers' verbal reports while composing, task observation, and retrospective interviews. Some of this research has been longitudinal, following a few students over an extended period of their writing development and used multiple techniques. But while this research has helped build a better understanding of how writers write, models of learning are hampered by small-scale, often contradictory, studies and the difficulties of accessing unconscious processing. Many cognitive processes, in fact, are routine and internalized operations performed without any conscious recognition and therefore difficult to access.

Despite these limitations, cognitively-oriented empirical L2 writing research has provided rich insights on the linguo-cognitive nature of the problem-solving associated with the act of composing, especially from the perspective of how linguistic concerns compete for attention with other writing processes in L2 writers' text-production activity (see Manchón, Roca de Larios, and Murphy 2009; and Schoonen et al. 2009, for overviews of two comprehensive programmes of research in Spain and the Netherlands, respectively).

In terms of writing pedagogy, process research has established the importance of learning how to write by writing. In this approach teachers attempt to develop their students' ability to reflect on the strategies they use to plan, generate, and revise their texts. The teacher's role is to guide students through the writing process, avoiding an emphasis on form to help them develop strategies for generating, drafting, and refining ideas, processes greatly facilitated by word processor. Process research has also meant that cooperative writing, teacher conferences, problem-based tasks, journal-writing, group discussions, and portfolio assessments are now all commonplace practices. Teacher response is potentially one of the most influential aspects of the process as it is the point at which the teacher intervenes most explicitly to give correction and language instruction (Hyland 2004). The effectiveness of feedback in assisting learners to improve their writing over time, however, remains controversial (e.g. Bitchener and Ferris 2012; Truscott and Hsu 2008. See also chapters 19, 20 and 26, this *Handbook*).

Process approaches have been criticized in L2 contexts for failing to make explicit the language students need to write effectively (e.g. Delpit 1988; Hyland 2004), trapping them in an invisible curriculum where the language they need to write is withheld from them until the final 'editing' stage of the process. A model of learning based on personal freedom, self-expression and learner responsibility fails to offer any clear perspective on the social nature of writing and does not provide leaners with clear guidelines on how to construct the different kinds of texts they have to write. The approach is resolutely asocial, regarding the learner almost wholly individualistically and the writing process as an abstract, internal process which leads to discoveries about the self as much as about learning to write (e.g., Kent 1999). Cognition, however, is only one element of the writing process and we also need to consider forces outside the individual which help guide the writer to define problems and frame solutions. Students not only need help in how to *compose*, but also in understanding how texts are shaped by topic, audience, purpose and cultural norms so they can activate schemata, genre awareness, grammar proofing, and responsiveness to a particular audience.

2.2 Focusing on texts

This second broad category of LW studies views writing as an outcome of activity rather than as an activity itself. These theories start with surface forms and have a common interest in the linguistic or rhetorical resources available to writers for producing texts (see Hyland 2010 for an overview).

One way to see writing in this way is to view texts as autonomous *objects* which can be analysed and described independently of particular contexts, writers, or readers. Texts are simply orderly arrangements of words, clauses and sentences, and by following grammatical rules writers can encode a full semantic representation of their intended meanings. Learning to write means learning to control grammar. A considerable amount of research, most recently based on corpus findings, has been valuable in revealing salient features of texts (see Chapter 11), but teaching is often founded on a behavioural, habit-formation theory where learning to write often means little more than learning to demonstrate grammatical accuracy with little awareness of a reader beyond the teacher. Guided composition, gap filling and substitution exercises are the main teaching methods and writing is removed from context and the personal experiences of writers and readers.

The claim that good writing is context-free and fully explicit is now largely discredited as it ignores how texts are a response to particular communicative settings. There is no convincing evidence that either syntactic complexity or grammatical accuracy are the best measures of good writing or of learning to write. Many students can construct syntactically accurate sentences and yet are unable to produce appropriate written texts, and an obsessive focus on accuracy may deter them from taking risks which move them beyond their current competence.

A second way of seeing writing as text looks beyond surface structures to see them as *discourse* – the way we use language to achieve purposes in particular situations. The linguistic patterns of texts point to contexts beyond the page, implying a range of social constraints and choices which operate on writers in a particular setting. In this way, genre approaches have been productive in writing instruction by showing leaners how the forms of a text are resources to accomplish goals and intentions. *Genre* is essentially a term for grouping texts together, representing how writers typically use language to respond to recurring situations (Christie and Martin 1997; Swales 2004). Research into academic (Swales 2004) and professional (Bhatia 2008) genres has helped to develop an authoritative pedagogy grounded in research of texts and contexts.

ESP (and LSP more generally) and functional approaches offer L2 students the most systematic explanations of the ways writing works to communicate. These replace the inductive methods of process approaches by shifting writing instruction from the implicit and exploratory to a conscious manipulation of language and choice (e.g. Hasan 1996). A knowledge of grammar and how students can codify meanings in distinct and recognisable ways, becomes central to learning to write. Teaching methods therefore generally work top-down, first exploring how a text is organised in relation to its purpose, audience and message, then examining how its language features contribute to these meanings (Knapp and Watkins 1994). Strategies such as modelling and teacher-learner joint construction of texts are common and many teachers follow the 'teaching-learning cycle' (Feez 2001) which supports the learner through stages of contextualisation, analysis, discussion and joint negotiation of texts. ESP has tended to adopt more eclectic pedagogies focusing on move descriptions and consciousness-raising. Johns (1997) recommends mixed-genre portfolios to add a reflective dimension to teaching by requiring students to write texts in a range of genres, collect them together in a folder and then to write a reflection on the texts and on what they learnt.

Genre approaches have not been uncritically adopted in L2 writing classrooms, however. Critical theorists have attacked genre teaching for accommodating learners to the ideologies of the dominant culture embodied in valued genres (e.g. Benesch 2009). Genre proponents, however, contend that this argument can be levelled at almost all teaching approaches and that learning about genres actually provides a basis for critical engagement with cultural and textual practices. Process adherents have argued that genre instruction inhibits writers' self-expression through conformity and prescriptivism. But while genres *do* have a constraining power by implying the use of certain patterns, this does not *dictate* the way we write but simply shows the choices that are available to facilitate expression in that context. Essentially, genre theories suggest that LW means understanding how texts are typically structured and meanings conventionally expressed.

2.3 Focusing on readers

This final orientation to LW expands the idea of context beyond the local writing situation to the context of use and what writers do to address the *reader*. It is based on the idea that writing is a practice based on expectations: the reader's chances of interpreting the writer's purpose are increased if the writer anticipates what the reader might be expecting based on previous texts they have read of the same kind. In this view LW involves creating a text that the writer assumes the reader will recognise and expect and the process of reading involves drawing on assumptions about what the writer is trying to do. It is the unfamiliarity of these expectations which makes LW in an L2 so difficult because what is seen as logical, humorous, engaging, relevant or well-organised in writing is likely to differ across cultures.

Questions of audience have encouraged teachers to develop a sense of *readership* among students by exposing them to examples of texts in target genres and in providing multiple audiences using peer and teacher feedback. Of central importance in LW is developing an understanding of context as a set of recognizable conventions through which a text achieves its force. The text is where readers and writers meet. More generally, however, considering readers means looking at the ways writers, texts, and readers are joined together in *discourse communities*. While this continues to be a problematic idea, often laying too much stress on what people share rather than the differences within them, 'community' is a way of foregrounding the conceptual schema that individuals use to organize their experience and get things done using language (Hyland 2009). The idea has therefore been very influential in showing us how, for example, the kinds of essays produced by biology students draw on very different forms of argument, interpersonal conventions and ways of presenting facts and theories than those written by business students.

Learning to write in this context involves discovering how texts are socially constructed in response to the common purposes of target communities. As Johns (1997) observes:

> Those who can successfully produce and process texts within certain genres are members of communities, for academic learning does not take place independent of these communities ... What I am advocating, then, is an approach in which literacy classes become laboratories for the study of texts, roles, and contexts, for research into evolving student literacies and developing awareness and critique of communities and their textual contracts (Johns 1997: 14–19).

Rather than modelling the practices of experts, this approach offers students a guiding framework by raising their awareness of the connections between forms, purposes and roles in specific contexts. Teaching methods vary, but generally seek to give students experience of authentic, purposeful tasks related to the kinds of writing they will need to do in their target communities. This often means encouraging students to undertake their own analyses of target texts (Swales and Feak 2004).

2.4 Conclusion

Modern conceptions of LW see writing as a social practice, embedded in the cultural and institutional contexts in which writing is produced and the particular uses that are made of it. So while every act of writing is in a sense both personal and individual, it is also interactional and social, expressing a culturally recognized purpose, reflecting a particular kind of relationship and acknowledging an engagement in a given community. We might see the research as advising us to reject a single formula for teaching writing and look at what the different models tell us, assisting our learners to become researchers of the texts they will need.

3 Writing to learn content: Transfer and writing to learn in content areas

L2 writing scholarship has, in recent years, seen an increased interest in transfer and in writing to learn. However, relatively little attention has been paid to links between the two. In this section of the chapter we shift the focus from the preceding exploration of learning to write (LW) to writing to learn, especially in content areas (WLC). We will argue for looking more overtly at the relationship between transfer and WLC in the belief that WLC is fundamentally an act of transfer, thus making it necessary to bring a stronger transfer lens to WLC scholarship. We will first look at transfer itself through a brief review of its history and of key definitions of it and we will then discuss reasons why it is valuable to approach WLC from a transfer perspective and fill what will be called the "space between" what students learn and how they apply that learning.

3.1 A brief review of transfer

There has long been an interest in the transfer of linguistic knowledge from the L1 to the L2 in SLA studies (see Odlin 2013 for a recent review). Interest in transfer and L2 writing has emerged over the past two decades in conjunction with the evolution of the field of EAP in the sense that a core principle of EAP writing instruction is the idea that writing skills acquired in a writing course are meant to be used in other writing contexts beyond the course. That is, students will transfer knowledge and skills from the writing course to other situations in which writing is required. Here EAP is accounting for LW as well as WLC, though the latter is rarely named directly. In each case there is some application of writing skills to another act of writing.

With this background in mind, let's now look at some well-known definitions of transfer. Detterman (1993: 4) says that "transfer is the degree to which a behavior will be repeated in a new situation", while Navarre Cleary (2013: 62) offers this definition: "Transfer occurs when people make use of prior experiences to address new challenges". Thus, say Perkins and Salomon (1988: 22), "Something learned in one context has helped in another." One other definition worth noting comes from Beach (1999: 101), who explains that transfer involves "carrying the product of learning from one task, problem, situation, or institution to another."

Transfer, then, involves the movement of knowledge and skills from one place to another, and, as Green (2015: 1) points out, "Transfer of learning – the application of previous learning to a new context – has long been proclaimed one of education's central aims." However, the actual process by which this occurs is not a simple or necessarily effective one. Indeed, as Brent (2011: 562) points out, "Many studies of transfer reveal a disturbingly uneven pattern of results. Frequently, learning acquired in one context seemingly evaporates when the learner is asked to apply it in another, even when the contexts seem relatively similar." In the context of L2 writing, the complexities associated with transfer are perhaps best captured in recent work by James (2006, 2008, 2009, 2010, 2012), who has identified various difficulties L2 writers experience as they attempt to transfer what they have learned in EAP writing courses, leading to his conclusion that "promoting learning transfer from EAP instruction poses a substantial challenge. Generally speaking, successful learning does not automatically lead to successful transfer" (James 2014: 1). Compounding the challenges associated with transfer in L2 writing is James' (2012) finding that L2 writers lack the motivation to engage in transfer, particularly because they fail to see relevance between writing tasks assigned in their EAP writing courses and what they do beyond those courses in disciplinary contexts.

Despite the less than encouraging results generally obtained in L2 writing research, transfer remains a vital construct in L2 writing pedagogy. In the context of WLC, there seems to be little reason to teach writing if students are not going to apply, or transfer, what they learned to other writing tasks they encounter, including WLC contexts. Although a "general theory of transfer remains elusive" (Green

2015: 1), transfer is too important to what we do as writing teachers to be ignored. Our challenge is to make it work, not make it disappear. WLC is one area where there is considerable value in taking on this challenge.

3.2 WLC as a transfer environment: Conquering the "space between"

As noted earlier, transfer is central to WLC. At the heart of WLC is the belief that students ultimately use writing not just to demonstrate what they have learned through a written product, but also to maximize their learning through the resources that writing provides. Here there is a natural and strong role for transfer. For example, synthesizing information from multiple sources is a commonly assigned task in L2 writing courses. Students learn to synthesize in part so that, when faced with content in another course, such as a history class, they can employ the synthesizing skills they acquired to better read and write about the source texts they encountered. In this way their knowledge of history has been enriched by their use of writing as a means of learning. Doing so involves the transfer of the writing skills obtained in the L2 writing course to the new course environment. This suggests that if WLC is to be successful, a concerted effort must be made to help students see WLC as an act of transfer.

Helpful to the WLC cause is what James (2010) calls a "transfer climate" in the L2 writing class, which he views as "the support for learning transfer from an EAP course that students perceive in mainstream academic courses" (p. 133). Generating this kind of climate is what is necessary if students are to develop not only the skills but also the attitude or outlook necessary to promote the kind of transfer that WLC depends upon. To do so will require what we call filling the "space between" what students learn about writing and how they apply that knowledge, particularly for WLC.

James (2009) notes that there is an important difference between "transferable" knowledge and "transfer" of that knowledge, that is, what *can* be transferred and what is actually transferred. In WLC instruction, we aim to provide students with transferable knowledge, although we may fail to recognize how much space exists between the acquisition of that transferable knowledge and opportunities for students to engage in meaningful transfer of it. Leki (2007) provides an in-depth look at this phenomenon in four longitudinal case studies she reported and she makes a similar point when looking at students' difficulties in transferring genre knowledge taught in a writing course (Leki 2011). A central point she makes is that there is often a significant gap in time between when students learn about L2 writing and when they actually need to use it. This is one type of "space between" that must be addressed.

One helpful dichotomy from the transfer literature for WLC is a distinction made by Perkins and Salomon (1988) between "near transfer," that is, the use of

writing knowledge in situations that closely resemble each other, and "far transfer," which refers to transferring writing knowledge to a more distant context, such
as a writing task in another course. In LW situations, "near transfer" is perhaps
the more immediate issue as students move from one writing course task to the
next. "Far transfer" is much better suited to WLC, and may provide a helpful tool
in conceptualizing the WLC dimension of learning to write. That is, writing instructors, as they consider how students may apply acquired knowledge of L2 writing, can take into serious consideration the challenges that would accompany "far
transfer" situations and applications. This is another "space between" that must
be addressed if WLC ability is to emerge.

A recent promising development with respect to both "near transfer" and "far
transfer", especially the latter, is a theory of what DePalma and Ringer (2011) call
"adaptive transfer", concerned with "the adaptation of learning writing in unfamiliar situations" (p. 134). In these 'unfamiliar situations' they speak of, uncritical or
mechanical reuse of L2 writing knowledge already acquired is likely doomed to
failure because of differences between the new situation and those tasks students
completed while learning to write. It is the 'unfamiliar situations' that are at the
heart of what WLC is about. For instance, to return to the synthesizing example
provided earlier, the synthesizing skills students acquire in the L2 writing course,
however helpful, may not be perfectly calibrated to the writing situation that appears in the history course. Thus, while students attempt to transfer synthesizing
skills to their WLC work in the new course, they cannot afford a simple reuse of
those skills from the past.

The notion of adaptive transfer is a means by which writing teachers can address the "space between" learning and application by helping students learn
about the complexities accompanying "far transfer" to WLC tasks. Adaptive transfer, say DePalma and Ringer (2011: 143), is "the conscious or intuitive process of
applying or reshaping learned writing knowledge in new and potentially unfamiliar writing situations." From the WLC perspective, this can involve helping students recognize and understand the various nuances that characterize differences
in writing tasks across different tasks and contexts, such as the history class example just discussed. Students need to be sensitized to these nuances so that they
can engage in the 'reshaping' rather than 'reuse' of writing knowledge that DePalma and Ringer speak of. This can be achieved by having them analyze writing
tasks assigned in various disciplinary contexts and then discussing how they can
adapt what they have already learned to what these other tasks require. This is
how filling the "space between" can occur in meaningful ways, thus paving the
way for students to use writing as a tool for learning content. The complexities of
"far transfer" in these new contexts can be minimized by helping students understand and practice methods of adaptive transfer that are suited to engaging in WLC.

In short, we now find ourselves in an exciting time in which we are broadening
our understanding of L2 writing instruction to account for WLC as well as the tradi-

tional focus on LW. As teachers of L2 writing, our ultimate goal is to help students use writing for important purposes, including learning about content in a specified area or deepening the learning of the target language itself. That is, we want students to see and apply writing as a tool for learning. In the midst of this wish is an imperative for students to learn to engage in meaningful transfer, that is, adaptive transfer, of what they have learned in a writing course. This will only occur if we attend, in serious and sustained ways, to the "space between" what we teach and what students eventually will do with writing. In the case of the "far transfer" discussed here, the "space between" must be significant, and so it would behoove us to now look for effective ways of better understanding as well as filling that "space between" which stands between students and "far transfer" as it must take place in WLC. This may look like a daunting task, but it is also an exciting one, and it must be completed.

4 Writing as a site for studying and promoting L2 development

In this last section of the chapter we look into a more recent, SLA-oriented strand in L2 writing studies concerned with the exploration of L2 writing as a site for L2 acquisition, i.e. with the writing-to-learn language (WLL) orientation in the study of L2 writing. Given that Chapter 26 contributes a detailed analysis of this WLL dimension as a key area of study in the research agenda on SLA-L2 writing interfaces, we will restrict our account here to a brief reference to the motivation behind this orientation in the study of L2 writing and to the main issues of debate in current research agendas. Readers can find a full elaboration of these issues, together with an analysis of the projected future research agendas, in Chapter 26.

4.1 Motivation and origin of research on WLL

The claim that writing in an L2 can promote the development of L2 linguistic knowledge was first advanced, along with an effort to provide empirical evidence for it, by Cumming (1990), notably, in a journal better known for research on writing than L2 acquisition – *Written Communication*. He opined that writing in the L2 might prompt learners to "analyze and consolidate second language knowledge that they have previously (but not fully) acquired" (p. 483). He went on to suggest that when they write, L2 users might need to "monitor their language production in a way that is not necessary or feasible under time constraints of comprehending or conversing in a second language" (p. 483). Empirical evidence for his claim was provided in Cumming's own study as well as in its replication in Qi and Lapkin's

(1995) investigation. Both studies looked into the language learning potential of the problem-solving activity that characterizes composition writing because it was assumed that "problems that arise while producing the second language can trigger cognitive processes that are involved in second language learning" (Swain and Lapkin 1995: 371). These pioneering studies therefore explored the nature and the variables that may mediate the L2 writers noticing, hypothesis-testing, metalinguistic, and monitoring activities implemented wh., and anile engaged in composition writing. Three years later, Polio, Fleck and Leder (1998) supported Cumming's predictions on the language learning potential of writing with their finding that learners could improve their own writing when simply given additional time and that the revision process afforded them an opportunity to focus on form.

Renewed theoretical and empirical interest in the WLL dimension of L2 writing was triggered by Linda Harklau's (2002) timely reflection on the crucial role played by literacy practices in foreign language instructional settings and, consequently, on the need to expand L2 writing research agendas. She claimed that "it is important to investigate how L2 learners learn how to write, but it is just as important to learn more about the instrumental role that writing can play in the acquisition of a second language in educational settings" (Harklau 2002:345). Harklau's call was taken up five years later in a position paper by Manchón and Roca de Larios (2007), which Ortega (2011) considers to be "the first formal appearance of WLL as a specific dimension for L2 writing research" (p. 240). Manchón and Roca de Larios offered the psycholinguistic rationale for the purported language learning potential of L2 writing in instructed SLA contexts, which, echoing arguments in the pioneering studies by Cumming and Qi and Lapkin, they envisaged as closely linked to the problem-solving nature of composing. Their arguments were backed up with a selective and synthetic review of the empirical evidence available at the time on L2 writers' problem solving behaviour.

Interest in exploring the LLP of writing of writing has grown exponentially in recent years, as attested by the publication of a special issue on the topic in the *Journal of Second Language Writing* in 2012, several books (cf. Bitchener and Ferris 2012; Byrnes and Manchón 2014a; Manchón 2011a), and various position papers (cf. Bitchener 2012; Manchón 2011c, 2014; Williams 2008, 2012) that have collectively explored the connection between L2 writing and L2 learning, including both the act of writing itself and the processing of feedback. Of special note is also the fact that, contrary to what was the case in past collective works on L2 writing, forthcoming publications contain chapters the WLL dimension of L2 writing for the first time. Thus, the *Handbook of English for Academic Purposes* (Hyland and Shaw 2016) includes a chapter on "Language and L2 writing: Learning to write and writing to learn in academic contexts", and the *TESOL Encyclopedia of English Language Teaching* has an entry on "Writing as language learning".

These theoretical developments have been coupled with empirical efforts within a developing WLL-oriented research agenda, as discussed in the next section.

4.2 Main issues of debate

4.2.1 Characteristics of writing and potential learning outcomes

Theoretical debates on the language learning potential of writing have evolved around two main axes. On the one hand, based on SLA theories (both cognitive and sociocultural), a number of publications (cf. Bitchener 2012; Byrnes and Manchón 2014b, 2014c; Manchón 2011a, 2014; Polio 2012; Wigglesworth and Storch 2012a, b; Williams 2012) have looked into the defining characteristics of writing that can potentially be advantageous for language learning, exploring at the same time which specific language learning benefits may derive. On the other hand, several reviews have provided accounts of the empirical evidence for the purported language learning benefits of L2 writing that derives from diverse strands of empirical research in the field of both SLA and L2 writing, regardless of whether or not this empirical research was originally framed in the WLL paradigm. The body of empirical knowledge explored (see, for instance, reviews in Manchón 2011c; Williams 2012) includes, inter alia, (i) studies on writing processes and what they uncover about the nature and depth of the linguistic processing L2 writers engage in while composing; (ii) cognitively-oriented SLA studies concerned with the effects of task-related variables on linguistic performance, including task-modality effects, input-oriented vs output oriented learning tasks, or the influence of individual vs. collaborative writing conditions on writing processes and products; and (iii) studies on feedback processing and what they uncover about the connection between types of feedback and attentional processes, on the one hand, and (short-term) learning of L2 forms and structures, on the other (see Bitchener 2012, for a review).

The general consensus in the field is that both writing and the processing of feedback can bring about language learning benefits. As detailed in Chapter 26 (see also Byrnes & Manchón 2014b; Manchón 2011a, 2014; Williams 2012), a basic assumption in the field is that L2 writing can be a privileged site of language learning as a result of the deeper linguistic processing that can be made possible by the time nature of writing (which in principle allows greater time availability while writing and while processing feedback than what is the norm in oral communication) as well as by the permanent nature of the written text and the feedback on it (in contrast to the ephemeral nature of speech and or oral interactions). In addition, as discussed in Byrnes and Manchón (2014b, c. See also Manchón 2014), the problem-solving nature of the meaning-making activity inherent to the act of writing, especially composition writing, makes writing an ideal scenario for language learning, hence "recognizing the textual nature of writing in and of itself and, by extension, the overwhelming textual qualities of writing tasks and the nature of language processing in the act of textual meaning-making (p. 6). And they add: "No matter what else composing is and does, it is about creating new textual worlds where language plays a constitutive role, even in an increasingly multimodal world: In the act of composing and with their compositions as products writers re-semioticize existing realities and create entirely new worlds of meaning" (p. 6). Finally, from a more sociocultural perspective, it has been posited that writing also constitutes a site for language learning as a result of the scaffolding provided in collaborative writing and collaborative processing of feedback

The language learning benefits that may derive from the criterial characteristics of writing activity mentioned above have been claimed to be both direct and indirect, as fully discussed in Chapter 26. For our present purposes let us simply mention that the indirect learning effects are related to the writer's engagement in a number of attentional (see Manchón 2011a; Williams 2012) and motivational learning processes (see Zhang 2013). In addition, writing can also have a more direct effect in terms of expansion and consolidation of L2 knowledge.

The language learning benefits that may result from writing activity also include the noticing and cognitive comparison processes associated with feedback processing, provided that, as noted by Bitchener (2012) in his review of this research, for these benefits to materialize a necessary condition is that L2 writers engage in explicit, intentional processing of the feedback received. However, many empirical questions still exist on whether the potential effects of feedback (especially in the form of error correction) apply to immediate accuracy improvement in subsequent drafts (i.e. uptake), or else contribute to longer-term acquisition (i.e. retention).

4.2.2 Empirical research on the language learning potential of writing

These theoretical debates on the language learning benefits that may derive from the very act of writing and from the processing of feedback have been accompanied by a growing number of empirical studies that have investigated a whole range of basic and applied concerns including the following: (i) L2 writers' perception of the language learning potential (LLP) of L2 writing (Manchón and Roca de Larios 2011); (ii) the LLP of feedback-related issues (cf. Bitchener and Knoch 2010; Hanaoka and Izumi 2012; F. Hyland 2011; Shinani and Ellis 2013; Wigglesworth and Storch 2012a, b), (iii) the language learning that may derive from various task-related and task implementation conditions, including task complexity factors (cf. Ong 2014; Ong and Zhang 2010, 2014), individual and/or collaborative writing conditions (cf. Fernández-Dobao 2012; Niu 2009; Shehadeh 2011; Storch & Wigglesworth 2007; Wiggesworth & Storch 2012a, b) or task-modality effects (cf. Adams 2006; Adams and Ross-Feldman 2006; Kormos 2014; Kuiken and Vedder 2012; Tavakoli 2014).

The outcomes of these collective explorations and empirical investigations are fully elaborated upon in Chapter 26.

5 Conclusion

As noted at the outset, this chapter is intended as a contribution to the analysis of the multi-faceted nature of L2 writing with a synthetic overview of theory and research on three complementary orientations to its study represented by the "learning-to-write", "writing-to-learn-content", and "writing-to-learn-language" orientations. This overview clearly shows that L2 writing is not a monolithic phenomenon. Rather, the recognition of the situated nature of learning, teaching, and performing writing necessarily entails an equal recognition of the many purposes and values that writing may have for individuals and groups in diverse settings and communities of practice. Although up to now these three perspectives "have developed almost independently from each other, have been informed by different theoretical frameworks, and have resulted in different pedagogical procedures" (Manchón 2011b: 3), it is hoped that future L2 writing research pursues closer links and more cross-fertilization among the three orientations to the study of writing outlined in the chapter and more fully explored in several contributions to the Handbook.

6 Additional sources

Belcher, Diane and Alan Hirvela (eds.). 2008. *The oral-literate connection*. Ann Arbor, MI: University of Michigan Press.

Hirvela, Alan. 2011. Writing to learn in content areas: Research insights. In Rosa M. Manchón (ed.), *Learning-to-write and writing-to-learn in an additional language*, 37–59. Amsterdam: John Benjamins.

Hyland, Ken. 2016. *Teaching and researching writing*. London: Routledge.

Hyland, Ken. 2004. *Disciplinary discourses: Social interactions in academic writing*. Ann Arbor: University of Michigan Press

Leki, Ilona, Alister Cumming, and Tony Silva. 2008. *A synthesis of research on second language writing in English*. New York: Routledge/Taylor & Francis.

Manchón, Rosa M. 2014. Learning and teaching writing in the FL classroom: Fostering writing-to-learn approaches. In Patricia Driscoll, Ernesto Macaro, and Ann Swarbrick (eds.), *Debates in modern language education*, 96–107. London: Routledge.

Newell, George. 2006. Writing to learn: How alternative theories of school writing account for student performance. In Charles MacArthur, Steve Graham, and Jill Fitzgerald (eds.), *Handbook of writing research*, 235–247. New York: The Guilford Press.

Polio, Charlene and Jessica Williams. 2009. Teaching and testing writing. In Michael Long, and Catherine Doughty (eds.), *The handbook of language teaching*, 476–517. Oxford: Blackwell.

Roca de Larios, Julio. 2013. Second language writing as a psycholinguistic locus for L2 production and learning. *Journal of Second Language Writing* 22(4). 444–445.

Tynjala, Päivi, Lucia Mason, and Kirsti Lonka (eds.). 2001. *Writing as a learning tool: Integrating theory and practice*. Dordrecht, The Netherlands: Kluwer.

7 References

Adams, Rebecca. 2006. L2 tasks and orientation to form: A role for modality? *International Journal of Applied Linguistics* 152. 7–34.

Adams, Rebecca and Lauren Ross-Feldman. 2006. Does writing influence learner attention to form? In Diane Belcher and Alan Hirvela (eds.), *The oral-literate connection*, 243–266. Ann Arbor, MI: The University of Michigan Press.

Beach, King. 1999. Consequential transitions: A sociocultural expedition beyond transfer in education. *Review of Research in Education* 69. 101–139.

Benesch, Sarah. 2009. Theorizing and practicing critical English for academic purposes. *Journal of English for Academic Purposes* 8(2). 81–85.

Bereiter, Carl and Marlene Scardamalia. 1987. *The psychology of written composition*. Hillsdale, NJ: Erlbaum.

Brent, Doug. 2011. Transfer, transformation, and rhetorical knowledge: Insights from transfer theory. *Journal of Business and Technical Communication* 25. 396–420.

Bhatia, Vijay K. 2008. Genre analysis, ESP and professional practice. *English for Specific Purposes* 27. 161–174.

Bitchener, John. 2012. A reflection on 'the language learning potential' of written CF. *Journal of Second Language Writing* 22. 348–363.

Bitchener, John and Dana Ferris. 2012. *Written corrective feedback in second language acquisition and writing*. New York: Routledge.

Bitchener, John and Ute Knoch. 2010. The contribution of written corrective feedback to language development: A ten-month investigation. *Applied Linguistics* 31. 193–214.

Byrnes, Heidi and Rosa M. Manchón. 2014a. *Task-based language learning: Insights from and for L2 writing*. Amsterdam: John Benjamins.

Byrnes, Heidi and Rosa M. Manchón. 2014b. Task-based language learning: Insights from and for L2 writing. An introduction. In Heidi Byrnes and Rosa M. Manchón (eds.), *Task-based language learning: Insights to and from writing*, 1–23. Amsterdam: John Benjamins.

Byrnes, Heidi and Rosa M. Manchón. 2014c. Task, task performance, and writing development: Advancing the constructs and the research agenda. In Heidi Byrnes and Rosa M. Manchón (eds.), *Task-based language learning: Insights to and from writing*, 267–299. Amsterdam: John Benjamins.

Christie, Frances and James Martin (eds.). 1997. *Genre and institutions: Social processes in the workplace and school*. London: Cassell.

Cumming, Alister. 1990. Metalinguistic and ideational thinking in second language composing. *Written Communication* 7. 482–511.

Delpit, Lisa. 1988. The silenced dialogue: Power and pedagogy in educating other people's children. *Harvard Educational Review* 58. 280–98.

DePalma, Michael-John and Jeffrey M. Ringer. 2011. Toward a theory of adaptive transfer: Expanding disciplinary discussions of "transfer" in second-language writing and composition studies. *Journal of Second Language Writing* 20. 134–147.

Detterman, Douglas K. 1993. The case for prosecution: Transfer as an epiphenomenon. In Douglas K. Detterman and Robert J. Sternberg (eds.), *Transfer on trial: Intelligence, cognition, and instruction*, 1–24. Norwood, NJ: Ablex.

Fayol, Michel, Denise Alamargot, and Virginia Berninger. 2012. From cave writers to elite scribes to professional writers to universal writers, translation is fundamental to writing. In Michel Fayol, Denise Alamargot, and Virginia Berninger (eds.), *Translation of thought to written text while composing. Advancing theory, knowledge, research, methods, tools, and applications*, 3–14. London: Psychology Press.

Feez, Susan. 2001. Heritage and innovation in second language education. In Ann M. Johns (ed.), *Genre in the classroom*, 47–68. Mahwah, NJ: Lawrence Erlbaum.

Fernández-Dobao, Ana. 2012. Collaborative writing tasks in the L2 classroom: Comparing group, pair, and individual work. *Journal of Second Language Writing* 21. 40–58.

Flower, Linda and John Hayes. 1981. A cognitive process theory of writing. *College Composition and Communication* 32. 365–387.

Green, Jonathan H. 2015. Teaching for transfer in EAP: Hugging and bridging revisited. *English for Specific Purposes* 37. 1–12.

Hanaoka, Osamu and Shinichi Izumi. 2012. Noticing and uptake: Addressing pre-articulated covert problems in L2 writing. *Journal of Second Language Writing* 21. 332–347

Harklau, Linda. 2002. The role of writing in classroom second language acquisition. *Journal of Second Language Writing* 11. 329–350.

Hasan, Ruqaiya. 1996. Literacy, everyday talk and society. In Ruqaiya Hasan and Geoffrey Williams (eds.), *Literacy in society*, 377–424. London: Longman.

Hayes, John. 1996. A new framework for understanding cognition and affect in writing. In Michael Levy and Sarah Ransdell (eds.), *The science of writing*, 1–27. Mahwah, NJ: Lawrence Erlbaum

Hayes, John. 2012a. Modelling and remodeling writing. *Written Communication* 29. 369–388.

Hayes, John. 2012b. Evidence from language bursts, revision, and transcription for translation and its relation to other writing processes. In Michel Fayol, Denise Alamargot and Virginia Berninger (eds.), *Translation of thought to written text while composing. Advancing theory, knowledge, research, methods, tools, and applications*, 15–25. London: Psychology Press.

Hyland, Fiona. 2011. The language learning potential of form-focused feedback on writing: Students' and teachers' perception. In Rosa M. Manchón (ed.), *Learning-to-write and writing-to-learn in an additional language*, 159–179. Amsterdam: John Benjamins.

Hyland, Ken. 2004. *Genre and second language writers*. Ann Arbor: University of Michigan Press.

Hyland, Ken. 2009. *Academic discourse*. London: Continuum

Hyland, Ken. 2011. Learning to write: Issues in theory, research, and pedagogy. In Rosa M. Manchón (ed.), *Learning-to-write and writing-to-learn in an additional language*, 17–35. Amsterdam: John Benjamins.

Hyland, Ken. 2016. *Teaching and researching writing*. London: Routledge.

James, Mark A. 2006. Transfer of learning from a university content-based EAP course. *TESOL Quarterly* 40. 783–806.

James, Mark A. 2008. Transfer of second language writing skills: The influence of perceptions of task similarity/difference. *Written Communication* 25. 76–103.

James, Mark A. 2009. "Far" transfer of learning outcomes from an ESL writing course: Can the gap be bridged? *Journal of Second Language Writing* 18. 69–84.

James, Mark A. 2010. Transfer climate and EAP education: Students' perceptions of challenges to learning to transfer. *English for Specific Purposes* 29. 133–147.

James, Mark A. 2012. An investigation of motivation to transfer second language learning. *The Modern Language Journal* 96. 51–69.

James, Mark A. 2014. Learning transfer in English-for academic-purposes contexts: A systematic review of research. *Journal of English for Academic Purposes* 14. 1–13.

Johns, Ann. M. 1997. *Text, role and context: Developing academic literacies*. Cambridge: Cambridge University Press.

Kent, Thomas (ed.). 1999. *Post-process theory: Beyond the writing process paradigm*. Carbondale, IL: Southern Illinois University Press.

Knapp, Peter and Megan Watkin. 1994. *Context – text – grammar: Teaching the genres and grammar of school writing in infants and primary classrooms*. Sydney: Text Productions.

Kormos, Judit. 2014. Differences across modalities of performance: An investigation of linguistic and discourse complexity in narrative tasks. In Heidi Byrnes and Rosa M. Manchón (eds.), *Task-based language learning: Insights to and from writing*, 193–216. Amsterdam: John Benjamins.

Kuiken, Folkert and Ineke Vedder. 2012. Speaking and writing tasks and their effects on second language performance. In Susan Gass and Alison Mackey (eds.), *The Routledge handbook of second language acquisition*, 364–377. London: Routledge.

Leki, Ilona. 2007. *Undergraduates in a second language: Challenges and complexities of academic literacy development.* New York: Lawrence Erlbaum/Taylor & Francis Group.

Leki, Ilona. 2011. Learning to write in a second language: Multilingual graduates and undergraduates expanding genre repertoires. In Rosa M. Manchón (ed.), *Learning-to-write and writing-to-learn in an additional language*, 85–109. Amsterdam: John Benjamins.

Manchón, Rosa M. (ed.). 2011. *Learning-to-write and writing-to-learn in an additional language.* Amsterdam: John Benjamins.

Manchón, Rosa M. 2011b. Writing to learn the language: Issues in theory and research. In Rosa M. Manchón (ed.), *Learning-to-write and writing-to-learn in an additional language*, 61–82. Amsterdam: John Benjamins.

Manchón, Rosa M. 2011c. Situating the learning-to-write and writing-to-learn dimensions of L2 writing. In Rosa M. Manchón (ed.), *Learning-to-write and writing-to-learn in an additional language*, 3–14. Amsterdam: John Benjamins.

Manchón, Rosa M. 2014. The internal dimension of tasks: The interaction between task factors and learner factors in bringing about learning through writing. In Heidi Byrnes and Rosa M. Manchón (eds.), *Task-based language learning: Insights to and from writing*, 27–52. Amsterdam: John Benjamins.

Manchón, Rosa M. and Julio Roca de Larios. 2007. Writing-to-learn in instructed language contexts. In Eva Alcón-Soler and Pilar Safont (eds.), *The intercultural speaker. Using and acquiring English in instructed language contexts*, 101–121. Dordrecht: Springer-Verlag.

Manchón, Rosa M., Julio Roca de Larios, and Liz Murphy. 2009. The temporal dimension and problem-solving nature of foreign language composing processes. Implications for theory. In Rosa M. Manchón (ed.), *Writing in foreign language contexts: Learning, teaching and research*, 102–124. Clevendon, UK: Multilingual Matters.

Navarre Cleary, Michelle. 2013. Flowing and freestyling: Learning from adult students about process knowledge transfer. *College Composition and Communication* 64. 661–687.

Odlin, Terence. 2013. Crosslinguistic infl uence in second language acquisition. In Carol Chapelle (ed.), *The encyclopedia of applied linguistics*. New York: Blackwell Publishing Ltd. DOI: 10.1002/9781405198431.wbeal0292

Ong, Justina. 2014. How do planning time and task conditions affect metacognitive processes of L2 writers? *Journal of Second Language Writing* 23. 17–30

Ong, Justina and Lawrence Zhang. 2010. Effects of task complexity on the fluency and lexical complexity in EFL students' argumentative writing. *Journal of Second Language Writing* 19(4). 218–233.

Ong, Justina and Lawrence Zhang. 2013. Effects of the manipulation of cognitive processes on EFL writers' text quality. *TESOL Quarterly* 47. 375–398

Ortega, Lourdes. 2011. Reflections on the learning-to-write and writing-to-learn dimensions of second language writing. In Rosa M. Manchón (ed.), *Learning-to-write and writing-to-learn in an additional language*, 237–250. Amsterdam: John Benjamins

Perkins, David N. and Gravriel Salomon. 1988. Teaching for transfer. *Educational Leadership.* 46. 22–32.

Polio, Charlene, Catherine Fleck, and Nevin Leder. 1998. "If I only had more time:" ESL learners' changes in linguistic accuracy on essay revisions. *Journal of Second Language Writing* 7. 43–68.

Qi, Donald and Sharon Lapkin 2001. Exploring the role of noticing in a three-stage second language writing task. *Journal of Second Language Writing* 10. 277–303.

Schoonen, Robert, Patrick Snellings, Marie Stevenson, and Amos Van Gelderen. 2009. Towards a blueprint of the foreign language writer: The linguistic and cognitive demands of foreign language writing. In Rosa M. Manchón (ed.), *Writing in foreign language contexts: Learning, teaching, and research*, 77–101. Clevedon, UK: Multilingual Matters.

Shehadeh, Ali. 2011. Effects and student perceptions of collaborative writing in L2. *Journal of Second Language Writing* 20. 286–305.

Shintani, Natsuko and Rod Ellis. 2013. The comparative effect of direct written corrective feedback and metalinguistic explanation on learners' explicit and implicit knowledge of the English indefinite article. *Journal of Second Language Writing* 22. 286–306.

Smagorinsky, Peter (ed.). 2006. *Research on composition: Multiple perspectives on two decades of change.* New York: Teachers College Press.

Storch, Neomy. 1999. Are two heads better than one? Pairwork and grammatical accuracy. *System* 27. 363–374.

Storch, Neomy. 2001. How collaborative is pair work? ESL tertiary students composing in pairs. *Language Teaching Research* 5. 29–53.

Storch, Neomy and Gillian Wigglesworth. 2007. Writing tasks: The effects of collaboration. In María Pilar García Mayo (Ed.), *Investigating tasks in formal language learning*, 157–177. Clevedon, UK: Multilingual Matters.

Swales, John. 2004. *Research genres.* Cambridge: CUP

Swales, John and Christine Feak. 2004. *Academic writing for graduate students: Essential tasks and skills* (2nd edition). Ann Arbor, MI: University of Michigan Press.

Tavakoli, Parvaneh. 2014. Storyline complexity and syntactic complexity in writing and speaking tasks. In Heidi Byrnes and Rosa M. Manchón (eds.), *Task-based language learning: Insights to and from writing*, 217–236. Amsterdam: John Benjamins.

Truscott, John and Angela Yi-ping Hsu. 2008. Error correction, revision, and learning. *Journal of Second Language Writing* 17(4). 292–305.

Wigglesworth, Gillian and Neomy Storch. 2012a. What role for pair work in writing and writing feedback? *Journal of Second Language Writing* 21. 364–374.

Wigglesworth, Gillian and Neomy Storch. 2012b. Feedback and writing development through collaboration: A sociocultural approach. In Rosa M. Manchón (ed.), L2 writing development: Multiple perspectives, 69–99. Boston/Berlin: De Gruyter Mouton

Williams, Jessica. 2012. The potential role(s) of writing in second language development. *Journal of Second Language Writing* 21. 321–331.

Zamel, Vivian. 1983 The composing processes of advanced ESL students: six case-studies. *TESOL Quarterly* 17. 165–87.

Zhang, Lawrence. 2013. Second language writing as and for second language learning. *Journal of Second Language Writing* 22. 446–447.

Alister Cumming

3 Theoretical orientations to L2 writing

Theories serve a heuristic purpose for educators, researchers, and policy makers interested in writing in second languages. That is, theories define a principled, focal set of concepts, terms, and references to identify, reason about, and evaluate fundamental aspects of L2 writing. This purpose resembles the role of theories in science (Hacking 1983), except that L2 writing is not, of course, a science (in the sense that biology, chemistry, or physics are) because L2 writing is profoundly interconnected with other human abilities (such as literacy, language proficiency, or knowledge), conventions of social practice, societal institutions, and interpersonal relationships. Rather, L2 writing is a complex, multifaceted, and variable phenomenon, realized in diverse ways by differing populations of learners producing differing kinds of texts in differing societal contexts and acted upon for differing purposes in particular educational, settlement, or workplace programs around the world (Cumming 2010; Grabe 2001; Hornberger 2003; Leki, Cumming, and Silva 2008). The multi-faceted nature, international diversity, and varied purposes for which people perform, study, teach, and assess L2 writing mean that no single theory could ever account for L2 writing comprehensively. For these reasons, theories about L2 writing are visibly constrained by characteristics for which the philosopher Feyerbrand (2011) criticized all scientific theories: being partial, influenced by divergent interests, relative to specific cultures and historical periods, and asserting claims that may easily become ideologies. But, as Feyerbrand also argued about scientific theories, these characteristics justify the existence and value of various, even competing, theories about L2 writing.

Four major theories have dominated most published research and professional discussions about L2 writing over recent decades: contrastive rhetoric, cognitive models of composing, genre theories, and sociocultural theory. The present chapter reviews and compares these four sets of theories. Numerous other theories have been related systematically to studies of L2 writing, including critical theory (Auerbach 1992; Benesch 2001; Canagarajah 2002), dynamic systems theory (Baba and Nitta 2014; Verspoor, Schmid, and Xu 2012), goal theory (Cumming 2006), language socialization (Duff 2010; Flowerdew 2000; Kong and Pearson 2003), biliteracy (Gentil 2011; Hornberger 2003), or identity theories (Cummins and Early 2011; Gentil 2005; Harklau 2007). Each theory makes important contributions to understanding and acting on L2 writing and presents promising directions for further inquiry and policies. Various theoretical perspectives on L2 writing will continue to emerge because L2 writing is inherently multi-faceted, involving multiple issues and orientations that may not even be commensurable with each other (Atkinson 2013).

1 Contrastive rhetoric

Contrastive rhetoric is the most longstanding, and also controversial, theory about L2 writing, influential to the point of virtually defining the emergence of the study of L2 writing in North America through the 1960s and 1970s, but then declining in acceptance after criticisms since the late 1980s. This cycle demonstrates Kuhn's (1962) claim that scientific theories go through paradigm shifts, wherein established theories are replaced over time by new conceptualizations, based on changing professional consensus. Contrastive rhetoric is unique among theories related to L2 writing in having been developed directly from observations about the compositions of English writing by international students attending American universities. Apart from certain approaches to genre theories and biliteracy, most other theories about L2 writing have adapted existing theories from other fields – such as psychology, linguistics, or education – and applied them to studies of L2 writing.

1.1 Historical and conceptual overview

Contrastive rhetoric was proposed by Kaplan in an oft-cited (1966) article and elaborated more fully in his (1972) book for English teachers. A guiding purpose of contrastive rhetoric was as an analytic framework for teachers of English language and composition to appreciate the origin of certain rhetorical and syntactic structures that Kaplan perceived to prevail in compositions written in English for university courses by students whose first languages, and prior education and literacy experiences, he grouped (1972: 38) as either Semitic (Arabic and Hebrew); Oriental (Mandarin Chinese, Japanese, Korean, Malay, Indochinese, Thai, Malay, and Vietnamese), or Romance (Spanish, Portuguese, French, and Italian). The second purpose (elaborated in Kaplan 1972 but not much in Kaplan 1966) was for teachers to organize pedagogical practices to help such students counter these tendencies to develop advanced levels of writing proficiency in English.

Contrastive rhetoric is widely known, and criticized, for the first set of claims. The second set of pedagogical practices outlined in Kaplan (1972), however, became conventions for ESL composition curricula at advanced levels of English proficiency in higher education in subsequent generations around the world. The argument central to both aspects of contrastive rhetoric was rooted in foundation theories of linguistics (i.e., Chomsky's transformational generative grammar and notion of communicative competence) and rhetoric (both classic and contemporary theories of composition) of the time. Moreover, contrastive rhetoric was presented as a radical, progressive challenge – informed theoretically and empirically – to prevailing audio-lingual, oral-based, and grammar-focused language teaching methods and behavioristic psychology of learning, which Kaplan (1972) repeatedly asserted were, unlike his proposal, inadequate to assist the increasing numbers of students from international backgrounds then appearing at universities in California to improve their writing abilities in English for academic purposes. The empirical bases for Kaplan's claims followed from his introspective, interpretive analysis of "some seven hundred compositions written by mature students whose native languages were not English" (1972: 38). The rhetorical structures of these compositions were contrasted with those deemed to be conventional according to a variety of rhetoric and composition scholars and texts cited. The psycholinguistic bases for Kaplan's (1972: 92–93) proposed pedagogy involved focusing students on "discourse units" through "three forces operant upon these rules: the available means of perception (the psychological mode), the intent of the generator (the rhetorical mode), and the available syntactic possibilities (the grammatical mode)."

Connor (1996, 2011) has progressively reoriented Kaplan's initial ideas into what she termed "intercultural rhetoric" – acknowledging numerous criticisms of and limitations in the original theory as well as influences from emerging inquiry and theories in corpus linguistics, genre analysis, literacy, cultural studies, and translation studies – but retaining the central focus on "the study of written discourse between and among individuals with different cultural backgrounds" (Connor 2011: 2). Thousands of articles and theses have been produced within this theoretical framework since the 1970s, mostly involving analyses of written texts in particular educational or other institutional contexts mostly by learners of English from specific language backgrounds. Research based on this theory has been best realized in studies of particular written genres by specific populations (e.g., Connor, Davis, and DeRycker 1995; Connor and Mauranen 1999). The international realization and impact of the theory was most profound in Purves' (1992) and colleagues' study of writing in secondary schools in 14 countries, which evaluated and compared systematically the writing abilities of representative samples of learners in each country. The scope of that research was unique, and not accomplished since; this international, comparative study is also notable for the researchers devising unique, rather than common, rating scales to evaluate students' compositions in each country and language because of cultural and educational differences (following from ideas of contrastive rhetoric as well as differences evident in educational systems). Purves and Purves (1986), however, were among the first to assert that the rhetorical structures of written texts varied greatly within, not just between, languages and societies according to the practices and norms of particular "interpretive communities".

1.2 Critical interpretation and research

Criticisms of the conceptualizations, research methods, and implications of contrastive rhetoric have appeared since the 1980s, centering on Kaplan's (1966) and other researchers' tendencies to conflate, confuse, or misrepresent fundamental aspects of languages, cultures, societies, educational systems and experiences, texts, genres, and literacy practices. Mohan and Lo (1985) offered an early critique, demonstrating that the problems in writing displayed by Chinese learners of English in Vancouver arose primarily from their previous educational, not cultural, backgrounds and their limited language resources and experiences using English. Around the same time, Heath (1983) produced her influential ethnography, which was extensively researched, ethnographically based, and nuanced in a way that contrasted with all that Kaplan had presented. Heath (1983) demonstrated vividly that literacy practices vary greatly by subcultural groups according to ethnicity, family norms, and socio-economic status within communities in one town sharing the same (English) language and attending the same school. Similarly, Li (1996), working within the framework of contrastive rhetoric, demonstrated compellingly in interviews with experienced teachers of writing in China and the US that their standards for "good writing" by students vary as much within these two societies and among skilled teachers as they do across the societies and languages.

By the 1990s, Leki (1991) produced an extensive review article that acknowledged the achievements of contrastive rhetoric in progressively focusing pedagogy and learning at the level of discourse, audience concerns, and expected standards within academic disciplines; attending systematically to differences across languages; offering a vehicle for students to develop meta-cognitive awareness about conventions in their own writing and in their second languages; and asserting professional interests distinct from those of English mother-tongue composition. But Leki (1991) also condemned the research related to contrastive rhetoric for its basis mostly on text analyses (rather than the processes of composing, which were then reaching prominence in research), mixing language varieties and rhetorical genres, privileging European and North American norms over those of other cultures, promoting cultural stereotyping, not defining key concepts such as transfer, relying on style manuals to define conventions of rhetoric, adopting inadequate methods of sampling texts across languages or their representativeness within cultures, approaching pedagogy in ways that were overly prescriptive and text-oriented, promoting curricula that exclude English language learners from interacting with the very populations needed to develop membership in academic discourse communities, and implementing so many different research designs as to defy syntheses that could establish generalizable results.

Elaborating on some of these faults, Kubota and Lehner (2004) have proposed reorienting contrastive rhetoric toward critical theories that prompt students and teachers to question, as means of personal empowerment, the conventional status, values, and implications of their first and second language writing. Recently, Belcher (2014) offered a comprehensive and personal perspective on the historical aspirations and conceptual failings of contrastive rhetoric. Belcher observed that Kaplan's original formulation of contrastive rhetoric, and particularly its conception of cultures and identities, now seems out of place in current discussions of postmodernism, post-colonialism, and digital literacies, anthropological research on languages; and historical re-interpretations of Asian traditions of rhetoric. In sum, the aims and interests of contrastive rhetoric have faded or transformed in recent decades into those taken up more specifically or profoundly by other theories about L2 writing, for example, genre, critical, or identity theories (Atkinson 2013).

2 Cognitive models of composing

Research into the cognitive processes of composing describes the mental activities and behaviors through which people produce writing – seeking indications of the relevant knowledge and skills they employ and sequence as a basis to account for qualities of their written texts. Writing is viewed as psychological problem-solving, akin to performing other complex tasks that involve concerted mental effort, such as solving mathematical problems or interpreting challenging texts. The focus on individuals' cognition during task performance has led some researchers to use the word model (rather than theory) to describe their investigations and findings, acknowledging the purpose of aspiring to predict (i.e., model) with precision a certain facet of L2 composing, such as planning or word choice, in explicit detail, and for some cognitive psychologists, with an operational precision sufficient that the cognitive processes could be "modeled" in a computer program (see Hayes 2012). This theoretical perspective was formulated initially by cognitive psychologists studying writing (and other complex abilities) by native speakers of English then later applied to L2 writing (see Chapter 12, this volume).

2.1 Historical and conceptual overview

Research on the cognitive processes of writing flourished in the early 1980s, offering new insights into people's performance and thinking while they write and providing an alternative framework to conventional methods of analyzing texts (as static objects after people had produced them). A proliferation of publications from extensive programs of scientific research reoriented what writing was considered to be. Two influential models appeared, following from Simon's theories of cognition as human problem solving (Ericsson and Simon 1980) and using principles of task analysis to trace and then later analyze the processes of composing as people performed defined writing tasks. The methods of process tracing have included people verbalizing what they attended to as they wrote, stimulating their recall in reference to explicit parts of their writing, video-taping their writing and revisions in progress, and/or in recent studies, logging keystrokes on computers or monitoring eye movements while composing (see Chapters 12 and 24, this volume).

Hayes and Flower (1980) put forward an influential model that specified subprocesses of generating and self-monitoring text through: planning, organizing, and goal setting; translating thoughts into text; and reviewing (by reading and editing), all in relation to a writer's long-term memory (based on knowledge of the topic, audience, and stored writing plans) and the task environment (topic, audience, and motivating cues, and considering a text produced so far). Hayes (2012) has revised the model subsequently to distinguish a control level (of motivation, goal setting, current plan, and writing schemata), a process level (of writing processes with a proposer, translator, transcriber, and evaluator and of task environment that involves transcribing technology, task materials, written plans, text written so far, and collaborators and critics), and a resource level (of attention, working memory, long-term memory, and reading). The other, related model was proposed by Bereiter and Scardamalia (1987) who specified a basic, knowledge-telling knowledge model, which young children use to tell serially in writing what they know about a topic, and a more expert knowledge-transforming model, in which skilled writers also tell their knowledge but adjust, shape, and revise it as they write to conform to their goals, audience concerns, knowledge of text and language conventions, and evaluations of text produced thus far. Bereiter and Scardamalia characterized the cognitive dimensions of writing as an ongoing mental dialectic between content and rhetorical concerns. Galbraith (2009) has proposed reconceptualizing cognitive processes as elements of the knowledge a person has available for writing.

Various researchers applied these models and process-tracing methods to L2 writing in the 1980s and 1990s (Krapels 1990). Initial studies described the writing processes of learners of second languages (Jones and Tetroe 1987; Raimes 1987). Others later compared cognitive strategies while writing in first and second languages (Arndt 1987; Whalen and Menard 1995) or between more and less skilled writers in their second languages (Cumming 1989; Sasaki 2000). Other researchers examined subprocesses of L2 writing such as revising (Hall 1990), fluency in generating text (Chenoweth and Hayes 2001), or restructuring (Roca de Larios, Murphy, and Manchón 1999). The upshot of these studies has been to confirm that people's strategic processes for composing are similar, and seemingly transfer, across first and second languages, but they are constrained in the L2 by limited vocabulary, grammar, and fluency, which correspondingly require extra attention and pose uncertainties during L2 writing (Fitzgerald 2006). Prior to these empirical studies, educators like Zamel (1982) and Hughey et al. (1983) advocated that L2 writing instructors should, like their counterparts in English L1 education, approach writing as a process, and the term became a standard element in curricula for L2 writing around the world, emphasizing how pedagogy should engage students purposefully in stages of planning, drafting, and revising their compositions.

2.2 Critical interpretation and research

Cognitive models continue to be a dominant focus of research in Europe, producing refinements, innovations in research and analytic methods, and tested specifications of models of L2 writing processes (Albrechtsen, Haartrup and Henriksen 2008; Galbraith 2009; Manchón and Roca de Larios 2007; Schoonen et al. 2011; Stevenson, Schoonen, and de Glopper 2006; van Weijen et al. 2009). Promising educational implications have come from experimental studies demonstrating the effects of training students in various cognitive strategies to improve their L2 writing (Baaijen, Galbraith, and de Glopper 2014; Fidalgo, Torrance, and García 2009; Galbraith 2009; Ojima 2006; Olson and Land 2007; Torrance, van Waes, and Galbraith 2007; van Gelderen, Oostdam, and van Schooten 2011; Yeh 1998). At a micro-level, the extended, frequent attention that L2 writers devote while composing to word choices – mixing and evaluating their languages and knowledge – shows particular potential for consolidating their lexical competence (Cumming 2013; Murphy and Roca de Larios 2010; Tullock and Fernández-Villanueva 2013; Wang and Wen 2002). At a macro-level, Sasaki (2009, 2012) and Nicolás-Conesa, Roca de Larios, and Coyle (2014) have established that the motivation for writing in English differs distinctly among students who have had, or not had, extended contact with users of English, because the former have an experiential basis on which to construct mental models and use strategies to imagine real audiences and contexts for their writing in that language.

Rijlaarsdam and Bergh (2006: 50–51) observed that models of L2 writing processes have advanced to a point of being able to predict some of the variance in written text quality, but they also acknowledged that such research, like most inquiry into human behavior (and all other theories discussed below), is constrained by uncertainties about (a) executive control over processes, (b) appropriate units of observation, (c) causal relations between composing processes and text qualities, and (d) reconciling the linearity of composing sequences with the multiple parallel processes of cognition. More broadly, constraints have long been acknowledged on the research methods of verbal reports and controlled, experimental-type conditions for writing associated with most (but certainly not all) research into cognitive aspects of L2 writing. Two major constraints are what Ericsson and Simon (1983) and Smagorinsky (1994) called veridicality and reactivity. That is, people cannot perceive or report on all of their own cognitive processes, and people may be inclined to state in verbal reports what they expect researchers want to hear. One approach to counter these problems is to triangulate multiple data sources, which Polio (2003) observed has seldom been done in L2 writing research. A second approach is to reject the information-processing metaphor of cognitive science in order to reconceive verbal reports about writing processes within an alternative theoretical framework such as sociocultural theory (Barkaoui 2011).

A third, related, and most prevalent approach has been to research L2 writing not in experimental- or exam-type conditions at all, but rather as it develops over time from an emic (insider, rather than etic, outsider) perspective in natural, social contexts of written communication. Rationales for adopting a socio-cognitive approach to study L2 writing in naturally occurring, rather than experimental, contexts were articulated in Parks and Maguire's study of learning to write nursing notes in a bilingual hospital (1999), Riazi's (1997) study of Iranian graduate students preparing theses at a Canadian university, and Sasaki's (2009) study of Japanese students writing papers for English university courses. Over the past decade, inquiry in natural contexts of written communication has prevailed in most published studies of L2 writing, highlighting people's potential to develop multi-competence in writing and in languages from an ethnographic and discourse-community, rather than a singularly cognitive, orientation to performance on experimental tasks (Leki 2007; Ortega and Carson 2010). Moreover, radical arguments have been made that current times are a "post-process era" (Atkinson 2003), so educators should strive "to understand specifically English L2 writing in critical, post-modernist, post-colonial terms" (Leki 2003: 104) and act critically on the complexity, variability, unpredictability, and social and ideological bases of L2 writing.

3 Genre theories

Genre theories applied to studies of L2 writing define the conventional organization of types of texts, the discourse practices and knowledge, and the sequences of development that L2 writers acquire and can be expected to perform in education, work, and social or technical communications. Conceptualizations of genre are implemented widely around the world but with differing realizations in particular educational systems and from several, interrelated disciplinary orientations. In addition to theoretical foundations in rhetoric, linguistics, and education the popularity of genre as an analytic unit for L2 writing arises from many educators perceiving, as Paltridge (2001: 4) remarked, the "notion of genre as being the 'right size' for a unit on which to base language learning programs". As with research on cognitive models of composing, theories about genres initially appeared in studies of English as a first language and were then later applied to studies of L2 writing.

3.1 Historical and conceptual overview

Rhetorical studies since ancient Greece have distinguished genres of drama, epic, and lyric and then in subsequent centuries, conventional literary forms established in prose fiction such as the novel, confession, anatomy, and romance (Frye 1957). Applying the term genre to describe distinct, recurrent, non-literary forms of communication was therefore perhaps inevitable as rhetoricians, linguists, anthropologists, and educators expanded their inquiries in the late 20th century to analyze ordinary as well as specialized conventions for communication. Inevitable too perhaps was that applications of the term genre to studies of L2 writing came from differing foundational orientations. As numerous analysts have documented (Hyland 2004: 24–53; Hyon 1996; Johns 2003), three distinct approaches to genre have evolved since the 1970s, based respectively on studies of systemic-functional linguistics, English for specific purposes, and new rhetoric.

Systemic-functional linguistics (SFL) is the comprehensive theory of Halliday (1994) and colleagues in Sydney, Australia, which has been applied extensively to analyses of written texts by Martin (1992; Martin and Rose 2008) and of oral and written language development in schools by Christie (2012). SFL describes how people use languages to create meanings in social contexts, making choices among possible linguistic resources to communicate and achieve functions in socially recognizable ways with texts and with each other. Genres are said to occur as conventionally sequenced, goal-oriented, and patterned ways of organizing and combining oral and written discourse for social interactions. Empirical research involves identifying prevalent genres, analyzing their common grammatical and lexical realizations, and documenting their sequencing, content, and logic as conventional discourse practices. Genre-based pedagogy derived explicitly from SFL has been an approach for teaching English to adult migrants and children in Australia since the 1980s (Feez and Joyce 1998; Gibbons 1993; Paltridge 2001). Genre-based pedagogy involves identifying samples of "elemental" genres suitable to the social context and learner population, and then series of cycles of teaching and learning relevant content and sociocultural knowledge, modeling and analyzing texts, students jointly and then independently scaffolding and constructing texts, and finally their linking related texts. Principled applications of SFL to L2 education and research have been made as well in the US (Byrnes, Maxim, and Norris 2010; Schleppegrell 2004), Canada (Mohan 1986, 2007), Hong Kong (Hyland 2004), and the UK (Coffin and Donohue 2014).

The two other approaches to genre developed mostly in North America then likewise have spread internationally since the 1980s. A distinctive approach to genre analysis emerged from applied linguistic research involving needs and discourse analysis to inform courses for teaching English for specific purposes (ESP), particularly academic, technical, or professional writing for international students in certain fields of higher education or work. Rather than elaborating a unifying theory (as in SFL), the ESP approach to genre has focused on empirical research – usually text, corpus, or discourse analyses, but also case studies, observations, and surveys – as a basis for teaching and curriculum design in specific contexts. Nonetheless, books by Swales (1990) and Johns (1997) and articles published in the journals *English for Specific Purposes* and *English for Academic Purposes* serve as focal points for articulating and exemplifying the concerns and research methods of this approach for identifying conventional patterns of text structures (e.g., of rhetorical moves in research articles) important to learn by, and to teach to, members of a specialized discourse community (e.g., students of engineering, law, or nursing). Most analyses from this approach occur on a small-scale as curriculum development or teacher-based inquiry so they are not reported beyond local educational settings (Hyland 2007).

While ESP approaches to genre research focused on issues mostly related to teaching L2 writing, a separate set of studies and differing theoretical orientations emerged among scholars of English L1 writing in North America, generally called New Rhetoric (NR). NR research involves analyses of texts but interprets their characteristics, development, and constantly changing nature as social actions in reference to the community of discourse, knowledge, power, status, and activity in which they appear and evolve (Bazerman 1988; Berkenkotter and Huckin 1995; Freeman and Medway 1994). The research concerns are as much institutional ethnography as discourse analysis, involving participant observation, interviews, and records of individual and group interactions and development along with text analyses. Genres are analyzed to be understood as phenomena of unique social contexts rather than to derive principles directly for teaching. NR theories of genres aspire to explain how individuals, groups, and subcultures acquire, use, and change written genres, particularly in workplaces or specialized academic or technical fields (rather than in composition or language courses) and to demonstrate and evaluate how certain genres privilege, exclude, oppress, or empower certain groups of people. Over recent decades, this orientation to genre has spread internationally and merged with or evolved into theories of multiliteracies or critical discourse analysis (Cope and Kalantzis 2000; Kress 2013; Wodak and Meyer 2009).

3.2 Critical interpretation and research

Continuing as the predominant approach in Australian education and in ESP courses, new research relating genre theories to L2 writing is currently active in the US, notably through programs of inquiry by Tardy (2011, 2012) on English for academic purposes in universities, by Schleppegrell and colleagues (2004, 2013; Schleppegrell and Colombi 2002; Schleppegrell and O'Hallaron 2011) on English language learners in schools, and by Byrnes (2012, 2014; Byrnes, Maxim, and Norris 2010) on German language programs at universities. Tardy has emphasized the long-term development of genre knowledge as a combination and interaction of rhetorical, formal, subject-matter, and process knowledge. Schleppegrell and colleagues have emphasized the value of teachers and children learning meta-linguistic terms to conceptualize, analyze, and perform their knowledge of genres central to educational success. Byrnes and colleagues have demonstrated the application of SFL principles for designing, implementing, and evaluating teaching, learning, and assessment activities in foreign-language university programs.

Corpus analysis techniques and powerful computer data bases have propelled text-based genre research (Hyland, Chau, and Handford 2012; Simpson and Swales

2001). Cross-linguistic studies of writers' texts in their first and second languages, based on SFL, have started to appear (Lindgren and Stevenson 2013), though notably later than studies based on cognitive or intercultural rhetorical theories. Most genre research has focused on specific kinds of academic, technical, or professional texts written by adults, but children and adolescents necessarily acquire, and need to be taught and practice, genre knowledge and related meta-linguistic concepts and terms, particularly in culturally diverse contexts (Christie 2012; Mohan 2007; Schleppegrell 2004). Numerous recent studies have investigated adolescents' L1 and L2 writing both inside and outside of schools, revealing a surprising variety of genres practiced even among learners not otherwise considered academically successful (Cumming 2012; de Oliveira and Silva 2013).

The appearance of differing versions of genre theories internationally and across differing educational contexts affirms Feyerbrand's (2011) claim that scientific theories are relative to particular societies and historical periods. Each of the three dominant genre theories address, but place greater or lesser emphasis on, written texts and social contexts. The greatest difference among them with implications for L2 writing, however, concerns whether or not genres and accompanying linguistic forms should be taught and studied explicitly in programs of language education (as SFL and ESP approaches recommend) or not (as NR approaches suggest). Freeman (1993), for example, argued that genre practices can only be acquired effectively within activities of writing by and for members of specialized communities and their unique knowledge and purposes, which composition classes cannot recreate and may even distort or misrepresent. Critical theorists such as Benesch (2001) likewise have charged that genre theories tend to define dogmatically, and force students into adopting, formulaic conventions of writing and learning, reinforcing unequal power relations for minority students. In contrast, SFL and ESP theorists such as Christie (2012) or Swales (1990) have argued that explicit awareness of genres and related language forms are exactly what minority or novice learners need to acquire and practice to become empowered and able in their writing. A final limitation of genre theories is that their primary focus on texts, language, and social contexts does not feature an explicitly psychological theory of learning. So to explain learning and development, researchers and educators have needed to draw upon related, sociocultural theories of learning, activity theory, or language socialization, as discussed in the next section (Russell 1997).

4 Sociocultural theory

Sociocultural theory is a broad-based, interrelated set of theories that aim to explain how human consciousness and abilities develop through the mediation of culturally organized activities, tools, and concepts. Languages and literacies are considered to be primary mediating tools through which people communicate, socialize, think, learn, and develop via ongoing, routine uses, and practices with other people via artifacts that are both symbolic (e.g., words, patterns of interaction) and material (e.g., printed texts or computers). People experience each language and its literate realizations uniquely through their interactions with others, appropriating from them culturally conventional modes of acting, thinking, and interacting through the technologies afforded by available media and tools. Unlike the focus of cognitive psychology on individuals' writing behaviors, skills, and knowledge – or the focus of contrastive rhetoric or genre theories on analyzing and acquiring text structures and functions – sociocultural theories focus on collaborations among people, either students interacting with teachers or with other students, to produce writing and learn from each other (see Chapter 18, this volume, and Storch 2013).

4.1 Historical and conceptual overview

Formulated initially in Soviet Russia in the 1920s, sociocultural theory came into the fore internationally in the 1980s and has advanced actively since across a broad range of fields, especially in North America and Australia. Centered on Vygotsky's (1978, 1987) principles of mediation, the zone of proximal development, dialectic processes, and the genetic method, sociocultural theory also includes activity theory (developed more fully by Leont'ev 1978, 1981 and Engeström, Miettinen, and Punamaki 1999) and related concepts from Marxist psychology, pragmatics of cultural practices, and phenomenological sociology (Prior 2006).

A central concept in sociocultural theory is mediation. All human knowledge, higher cognitive abilities, and activities are considered to be mediated culturally and historically by social practices for using symbolic and material tools. Learners internalize culturally appropriate ways of using language, literacy, and media through their observations, experiences, negotiations, and practices with other people's uses of them, gradually adopting abilities to use them independently. This process is said to occur in a zone of proximal development (ZPD), defined as the distance between what a learner can accomplish alone and what that person can achieve with the support of more capable experts, peers, and/or cultural artifacts (Vygotsky 1987). Specifically, the ZPD is conceived of as "the collaborative construction of opportunities for individuals to develop their mental ability" (Lantolf 2000: 17), following a general path from social interaction to independent functioning. Kinginger (2002) identified three interpretations of the ZPD in language education – as skills, metalinguistic knowledge, and scaffolding – each of which represents ways in which people transform, either explicitly or implicitly, others' uses of material and symbolic tools into self-controlled psychological abilities. Individual development involves ongoing tensions and changes that occur as dialectic processes that unify individual psychology with social practices, biological capacities, and material and symbolic resources. To observe the development of people's mental abilities closely over time, Vygotsky (1978) advocated a "genetic research method" involving longitudinal case studies. Activity theory has been elaborated since as a basis to describe and analyze the socially organized systems such as workplaces or classrooms in which people share, perform, negotiate, and think about specific tasks, achieving individual and group outcomes, and in the process acquiring complex abilities such as writing and languages.

Prior (2006: 54) remarked that "sociocultural theories represent the dominant paradigm for writing research today," and he went to observe the broad range of interdisciplinary traditions that have been researched from this perspective since the early 1980s, grouping their themes into studies of oral-literate development and cross-cultural differences, emerging school literacies and technologies, and writing in higher education, academic disciplines, and workplaces (which bear affinities with new rhetoric genre studies discussed above). Englert, Mariage and Dunsmore (2006) recounted how most applications of sociocultural theory to pedagogy for English L1 writing have promoted tenets of modeling, scaffolding, and practicing writing through sociocognitive apprenticeship, procedural facilitation and tools, and participation in communities of practice. Much research applying sociocultural theory to L2 learning and teaching has focused on defining and exemplifying concepts central to the theory, particularly in respect to the development of oral language abilities, but there have been distinct lines of inquiry into L2 writing as well (Lantolf and Thorne 2006; Lantolf and 2008a; Swain, Kinear and Steinman 2011).

Initial applications of sociocultural theory to L2 writing appeared in Moll (1989, 1990) and colleagues' action research, demonstrating the pedagogical benefits of teachers of Hispanic students in the Midwest US schools reorienting their teaching, classroom activities, and own knowledge to understand and build on, rather than ignore (as English curricula tended to previously), the evident "funds of knowledge" that students' had in their families, local communities, and cultural identities. Other early studies like Donato and McCormick (1994) emphasized the mediating roles of students writing journals as tools, both symbolic and material, to reflect on and develop their foreign language knowledge and abilities. Aljaafreh and Lantolf (1994) put forward a prototypical analysis of tutoring L2 writing that traced and evaluated individual students' development of abilities to write with gradually increasing independence and less reliance on support and feedback from the tutor (see also Chapter 18, this volume).

4.2 Critical interpretation and research

Most socioculturally-oriented research on L2 writing has focused on two types of learning contexts, each considered to be optimal sites to observe and document the qualities of interaction wherein L2 students progressively perform, appropriate, and develop language and writing abilities within their ZPDs from others: (a) tutors' one-on-one interactions with individual students or (b) collaborative or computer-mediated writing among student peers. This research has tended to follow the genetic method, involving detailed, longitudinal case-studies of a few people's talk, negotiations, writing, and development of certain language and literate abilities through specific interactions in one natural and/or instructional context. Gibbons (1993, and in subsequent publications), Ferreira and Lantolf (2008), and Parks, Huot, Hamers and Lemonnier (2005) have provided unique examples of sociocultural research analyzing L2 writing instruction and development among whole classes of students. The upshot of this inquiry is that a skilled teacher need not (indeed, probably cannot) attempt to construct a ZPD with all students at once, but rather can strategically organize students into groups performing long-term, sequenced writing tasks that are within – and which advance, when accompanied by additional individual dialogue with the teacher and other students – students' ZPDs.

Sociocultural studies of one-on-one tutoring have documented tutors' and their students' interactions over time as they negotiate a ZPD together to model, practice, and extend L2 writing tasks with increased mutual understanding, independence, and effectiveness (Aljaafreh and Lantolf 1994; Cumming 2012; Knouzi 2012). Rather than adopting a fixed instructional approach in these studies, tutors pitched tasks, scaffolded support, provided evaluative feedback, and sequenced activities individually to each learner's ZPDs based on reciprocal understandings and relationships evolving between tutor and student alike, following sociocultural principles of dynamic assessment (Lantolf and Poehner 2008b; Leung 2007). Nassaji and Cumming (2000) documented similar written interactions in the context of ongoing dialogue journals between a teacher and young ESL student. Suzuki (2012) extended this line of inquiry to analyze the effects of systematic corrective feedback on L2 students' writing. Macqueen (2012) provided an in-depth sociocognitive analysis of the long-term acquisition of academic lexico-grammatical patterns in the writing of four international students she had tutored.

The most prolific applications of sociocultural theories to studies of L2 writing have focused on collaborative writing among groups of student peers or in computer-mediated contexts, as reviewed in detail in Storch (2013) and Chapter 18 of the present volume. Swain and colleagues (2006; Brooks and Swain 2009; Swain and Lapkin 2002; Watanabe and Swain 2007) have proposed the concepts of collaborative dialogue and languaging to explain the value, on the basis of sociocultural theory, of L2 students talking, thinking about, and evaluating their language production with each other.

Applications of sociocultural theory to L2 writing have mostly been to detailed case studies and by a tendency to describe opportunities that exist for L2 learning or writing improvement in contexts of tutoring or collaboration rather than providing firm, large-scale evidence of students' achievements. Moreover, most of these studies have determined that a range of variables impact differentially on the effectiveness of group pairings in collaborative writing, including L2 proficiency, age, gender, students' L1s, and relationships established (or not) among learners – raising useful cautions for teachers but concerns about the variable nature of collaborative writing. Questions have been raised as well about the authenticity of controlled, fixed writing tasks, such as dictogloss, employed in many of these studies (Storch 2013). Harwood and Petric (2012) and Yang (2014), in contrast, are notable for illuminating interactions from a sociocultural perspective among L2 writers in writing tasks in real academic courses rather than in language courses or during tutoring. Most research on L2 writing lacks relevant, valid measures of L2 writing development (Polio 2003; see Chapter 13 this volume), and perhaps the detailed accounts of learners' development offered in sociocultural studies raise expectations for evidence of achievement greater or different than might be sought from research from other paradigms of inquiry (Norris and Manchón 2012). To address this concern, Poehner and Lantolf (2013) have been devising unique L2 diagnostic and achievement tests based on sociocultural principles. Nonetheless, the case-study evidence advanced thus far for the effectiveness of tutoring, collaborative writing, and dynamic assessment poses theoretically-informed challenges not only to the conventional organization of education for L2 writing in large classes that operate in a transmission, rather than transactional, mode of instruction but also to the increasing institutional separation of assessment from contexts of teaching and learning (Cumming 2014; Wells 1999).

5 Conclusion and future developments

What do current theories provide researchers, educators, assessors, and learners of L2 writing? At a minimum, they provide concepts, principles, and methods to analyze, organize, and evaluate curricula, instruction, and assessment for L2 learners of writing. As Belcher and Hirvela (2010) and Atkinson (2010) demonstrated, theories of various kinds provide doctoral students and teachers with a focal perspective from which to conceptualize, analyze, interpret, and report on their studies of and thinking about L2 writing. The same value holds for published research. The challenge for theories of L2 writing, however, is to account for the multi-faceted complexity of L2 writing comprehensively. As Silva (1990: 20) observed decades ago, a "comprehensive conceptualization of what L2 writing involves" must "meaningfully account for the contributions of the writer, reader, text, and context, as well as their interaction."

Current theories address some of these matters, but no one theory addresses them all sufficiently. Contrastive rhetoric provided principles for teaching L2 writing for decades but was overshadowed by more sophisticated and focused theories and research. Cognitive models have assisted L2 researchers and teachers to help learners to appreciate and develop ways of thinking strategically and effectively while composing. Genre theories have informed what types of texts and metalin-guistic awareness to teach L2 writers and expect in specialized written interactions, but they have done so from differing theoretical realizations and emphases. Socio-cultural theories have demonstrated how L2 writing develops and can be promoted in situations of tutoring and student peer collaborations, but their applications to conventional classroom instruction remain limited.

What other issues remain to be considered? No current theories about L2 writing comprehensively address macro-societal and institutional systems of power, as Dressman, Wilder, and Connor (2005) observed in analyzing theories of reading, though well-documented neo-Freirian programs of action research have demon-strated that inequities arising from systemic disadvantage can successfully be ad-dressed for and with L2 writers in specific multilingual contexts (Auerbach 1992; Cumming 2012; Cummins and Early 2011; Hornberger 2003; Moll 1989, 1990). Al-though sociocultural, cognitive, or genre theories may provide explanations gener-ally for how L2 writing abilities develop, there is the vexing problem for assessment and curricula that people can achieve comparable levels of proficiency in L2 writ-ing with distinctly different types of rhetorical, discourse, lexical, and syntactic performances, as illuminated in studies by Jarvis, Grant, Bikowski, and Ferris (2003) and Friginal, Li, and Weigle (2014). A broader dilemma for education was raised in Cumming's (2003) conclusion that differing theoretical emphases, within instructional programs locally as well as internationally, lead to differing realiza-tions and experiences of what and how L2 writing is taught, learned, and assessed. Theories of L2 writing also need to align more closely to and mutually inform theo-ries of second language acquisition (Ortega 2012; Polio 2012). A final challenge involves developing theoretical frames that are capable of synthesizing compre-hensively, to account for and make practical sense of, the ever-increasing prolifera-tion and eclectic diversity of empirical research on L2 writing (Hornberger 2003; Leki, Cumming, and Silva 2008; Norris and Manchón 2012).

6 Additional sources

Atkinson, Dwight (ed.). 2013. Disciplinary dialogues. *Journal of Second Language Writing* 4. 452–450.

Connor, Ulla. 1996. *Contrastive rhetoric: Cross-cultural aspects of second language writing*. New York: Cambridge University Press.

Hayes, John. 2012. Modeling and remodeling writing. *Written Communication* 29. 369–388.

Hornberger, Nancy (ed.). 2003. *Continua of biliteracy: An ecological framework for educational policy, research, and practice in multilingual settings*. Clevedon, UK: Multilingual Matters.

Leki, Ilona, Alister Cumming, and Tony Silva. 2008. *A synthesis of research on second language writing in English*. London: Routledge.

Manchón, Rosa M. (ed.). 2012. *L2 writing development: Multiple perspectives*. Berlin: Walter de Gruyter.

MacArthur, Charles, Steve Graham, and Jill Fitzgerald (eds.). 2016. *Handbook of writing research* (2nd ed.). New York: Guilford Press.

Prior, Paul. 2006. A sociocultural theory of writing. In Charles MacArthur, Steve Graham, and Jill Fitzgerald (eds.), *Handbook of writing research*, 54–66. New York: Guilford Press.

Silva, Tony and Paul Matsuda (eds.). 2010. *Practicing theory in second language writing*. West Lafayette, IN: Parlor Press.

Tardy, Christine. 2009. *Building genre knowledge*. West Lafayette, IN: Parlor Press.

7 References

Albrechtsen, Dorte, Kirsten Haastrup, and Brigit Henriksen. 2008. *Vocabulary and writing in first and second languages: Processes and development*. Houndmills, UK: Palgrave Macmillan.

Aljaafreh, Ali and James Lantolf. 1994. Negative feedback as regulation and second language learning in the Zone of Proximal Development. *The Modern Language Journal* 78. 465–483.

Arndt, Valerie. 1987. Six writers in search of texts: A protocol based study of L1 and L2 writing. *ELT Journal* 41. 257–267.

Atkinson, Dwight. 2003. L2 writing in the post-process era: Introduction. *Journal of Second Language Writing* 12. 3–15.

Atkinson, Dwight. 2010. Between theory with a big T and practice with a small p: Why theory matters. In Tony Silva and Paul Matsuda (eds.), *Practicing theory in second language writing*, 5–18. West Lafayette, IN: Parlor Press.

Auerbach, Elsa. 1992. *Making meaning, making change: Participatory curriculum development for adult ESL literacy*. Washington, DC: Center for Applied Linguistics and Delta Systems.

Baaijen, Veerle, David Galbraith, and Kees de Glopper. 2014. Effects of writing beliefs and planning on writing performance. *Learning and Instruction* 33. 81–91.

Baba, Kyoko and Ryo Nitta. 2014. Phase transitions in development of writing fluency from a complex dynamic systems perspective. *Language Learning* 64. 1–35.

Barkaoui, Khaled. 2011. Think-aloud protocols in research on essay rating: An empirical study of their veridicality and reactivity. *Language Testing* 28. 51–75.

Bazerman, Charles. 1988. *Shaping written knowledge: The genre and activity of the experimental article in science*. Madison, WI: University of Wisconsin Press.

Belcher, Diane. 2014. What we need and don't need intercultural rhetoric for: A retrospective and prospective look at an evolving research area. *Journal of Second Language Writing* 25. 59–67.

Belcher, Diane and Alan Hirvela. 2010. The role of theory in dissertations on L2 writing: Doctoral students' perspectives. In Tony Silva and Paul Matsuda (eds.), *Practicing theory in second language writing*, 263–284. West Lafayette, IN: Parlor Press.

Benesch, Sarah. 2001. *Critical English for academic purposes: Theory, politics, and practice*. Mahwah, N.J.: Erlbaum.

Bereiter, Carl and Marlene Scardamalia. 1987. *The psychology of written composition*. Hillsdale, NJ: Erlbaum.

Berkenkotter, Carol and Thomas Huckin. 1995. *Genre knowledge in disciplinary communication: Cognition/culture/power*. Hillsdale, NJ: Erlbaum.

Brooks, Lindsay and Merrill Swain. 2009. Languaging in CW: Creation of and response to expertise. In Alison Mackey and Charlene Polio (eds.), *Multiple perspectives on interaction*, 58–89. New York: Routledge.

Byrnes, Heidi. 2012. Conceptualizing FL writing development in collegiate settings: A genre-based systemic functional linguistic approach. In Rosa M. Manchón (ed.), *L2 Writing development: Multiple perspectives*, 191–219. Berlin: de Gruyter Mouton.

Byrnes, Heidi. 2014. Linking task and writing for language development: Evidence from a genre-based curricular approach. In Heidi Byrnes and Rosa M. Manchón (eds.) 2014. *Task-based language learning: Insights from and for L2 writing*, 237–263. Amsterdam: John Benjamins.

Byrnes, Heidi, Hiram Maxim, and John Norris. 2010. Realizing advanced foreign language writing development in collegiate education: Curricular design, pedagogy, assessment. *Modern Language Journal* 94 [Supplement].

Canagarajah, Suresh. 2002. *Critical academic writing and multilingual students*. Ann Arbor, MI: University of Michigan Press.

Chenoweth, Ann and John Hayes. 2001. Fluency in writing: Generating text in L1 and L2. *Written Communication* 18. 80–90.

Christie, Frances. 2012. Language education throughout the school years: A functional perspective. *Language Learning* 62 [Supplement 1].

Coffin, Caroline and Jim Donohue. 2014. A language as social semiotic-based approach to teaching and learning in higher education. *Language Learning* 64 [Supplement 1].

Connor, Ulla. 1996. *Contrastive rhetoric: Cross-cultural aspects of second language writing*. New York: Cambridge University Press.

Connor, Ulla. 2011. *Intercultural rhetoric in the writing classroom*. Ann Arbor, MI: University of Michigan Press.

Connor, Ulla, Kenneth Davis, and Teun D. Rycker. 1995. Correctness and clarity in applying for overseas jobs: A cross-cultural analysis of US and Flemish applications. *Text* 1. 457–475.

Connor, Ulla and Anna Mauranen. 1999. Linguistic analysis of grant proposals: European Union Research Grants. *English for Specific Purposes* 18. 47–62.

Cope, Bill and Mary Kalantzis (eds.). 2000. *Multiliteracies: Literacy learning and the design of social futures*. London: Routledge.

Cumming, Alister. 1989. Writing expertise and second language proficiency. *Language Learning* 39. 81–141.

Cumming, Alister. 2003. Experienced ESL/EFL writing instructors' conceptualization of their teaching: Curriculum options and implications. In Barbara Kroll (ed.), *Exploring the dynamics of second language writing*, 71–92. New York: Cambridge University Press.

Cumming, Alister (ed.). 2006. *Goals for academic writing: ESL students and their instructors*. Amsterdam: Benjamins.

Cumming, Alister. 2010. Theories, frameworks, and heuristics: Some reflections on inquiry and second-language writing. In Tony Silva and Paul Matsuda (eds.), *Practicing theory in second language writing*, 19–47. West Lafayette, IN: Parlor Press.

Cumming, Alister (ed.). 2012. *Adolescent literacies in a multicultural context*. New York: Routledge.

Cumming, Alister. 2013. Multiple dimensions of academic language and literacy development. In Lourdes Ortega, Alister Cumming, and Nick Ellis (eds.) *Agendas for language learning research. Language Learning* 63 [Supplement 1], 130–152.

Cumming, Alister. 2014. Linking assessment to curricula, teaching, and learning in language education. In David Qian and Liying Li (eds.), *Teaching and learning English in East Asian universities: Global visions and local practices*, 2–18. Newcastle, UK: Cambridge Scholars Publishing.

Cummins, James and Margaret Early (eds.). 2011. *Identity texts: The collaborative creation of power in multilingual schools*. London, UK: Trentham Books.

Donato, Richard and Dawn McCormick. 1994. A sociocultural perspective on language learning strategies: The role of mediation. *Modern Language Journal* 78. 453–464.

Dressman, Mark, Phillip Wilder, and Julia Connor. 2005. Theories of failure and the failure of theories: A cognitive/sociocultural/macrostructural study of eight struggling students. *Research in the Teaching of English* 40. 8–61.

Duff, Patricia. 2010. Language socialization into academic discourse communities. *Annual Review of Applied Linguistics* 30. 169–192.

Engeström, Yrjö, Reijo Miettinen, and Raija-Leena Punamaki (eds.). 1999. *Perspectives on Activity Theory*. Cambridge, UK: Cambridge University Press.

Englert, Carol, Troy Mariage, and Kailonnie Dunsmore. 2006. Tenets of sociocultural theory in writing instruction research. In Charles MacArthur, Steve Graham, and Jill Fitzgerald (eds.), *Handbook of writing research*, 208–221. New York: Guilford Press.

Ericsson, Anders and Herbert Simon. 1980. *Protocol analysis: Verbal reports as data*. Cambridge, MA: MIT Press.

Feez, Susan and Helen Joyce. 1998. *Text-based syllabus design*. Sydney, Australia: National Centre for English Language Teaching and Research, Macquarie University.

Ferreira, Marilia and James Lantolf. 2008. A concept-based approach to teaching writing through genre analysis. In James Lantolf and Mathew Poehner (eds.), *Sociocultural theory and the teaching of second languages*, 285–320. London: Equinox.

Feyerabend, Paul. 2011. *The tyranny of science*. Cambridge, UK: Polity Press.

Fidalgo, Raquel, Mark Torrance, and Jesús-Nicasio García 2009. The long-term effects of strategy-focussed writing instruction for grade six students. *Contemporary Educational Psychology* 33. 672–693.

Fitzgerald, Jill. 2006. Multilingual writing in preschool through 12th grade. In Charles MacArthur, Steve Graham, and Jill Fitzgerald (eds.), *Handbook of writing research*, 337–354. New York: Guilford Press.

Flowerdew, John. 2000. Discourse community, legitimate peripheral participation, and the non-native-English-speaking scholar. *TESOL Quarterly* 34. 127–150.

Freeman, Aviva. 1993. Show and tell? The role of explicit teaching in the learning of new genres. *Research in the Teaching of English* 27. 222–251.

Freeman, Aviva and Peter Medway (eds.). 1994. *Learning and teaching genre*. Portsmouth, NH: Boynton/Cook.

Friginal, Eric, Man Li, and Sara Weigle. 2014. Revisiting multiple profiles of learner compositions: A comparison of highly rated NS and NNS essays. *Journal of Second Language Writing* 23. 1–16.

Frye, Northrop. 1957. Rhetorical criticism: Theory of genres. In Northrop Frye, *The anatomy of criticism: Four essays*, 243–337. Princeton, NJ: Princeton University Press.

Galbraith, David. 2009. Writing about what we know: Generating ideas in writing. In Roger Beard, Debra Myhill, Jeni Riley, and Martin Nystand (eds.), *The SAGE handbook of writing development*, 48–64. London: Sage.

Gentil, Guillaume. 2005. Commitments to academic biliteracy: Case studies of francophone university writers. *Written Communication* 22. 421–471.

Gentil, Guillaume. 2011. A biliteracy agenda for genre research. *Journal of Second Language Writing* 20. 6–23.

van Gelderen, Amos, Ron Oostdam, and Erik Van Schooten. 2011. Does foreign language writing benefit from increased lexical fluency? Evidence from a classroom experiment. *Language Learning* 61. 281–321.

Gibbons, Pauline. 1993. *Learning to learn in a second language*. Portsmouth, NH: Heinemann.

Grabe, William. 2001. Notes toward a theory of second language writing. In Tony Silva and Paul Matsuda (eds.), *On second language writing*, 39–57. Mahwah, NJ: Erlbaum.

Hacking, Ian. 1983. *Representing and intervening: Introductory topics in the philosophy of natural science*. Cambridge, UK: Cambridge University Press.

Hall, Chris. 1990. Managing the complexity of revising across languages. *TESOL Quarterly* 24. 43–60.

Halliday, Michael. 1994. *An introduction to Functional Grammar*, 2nd edition. London: Edward Arnold.

Harklau, Linda. 2007. The adolescent English language learner: Identities lost and found. In James Cummins and Chris Davison (eds.), *The international handbook of English language teaching*, 639–654. New York: Springer.

Harwood, Nigel and Bojana Petric. 2012. Performance in the citing behavior of two student writers. *Written Communication*, 29. 55–103.

Hayes, John and Linda Flower. 1980. Identifying the organization of writing processes. In Lee Gregg and Erwin Steinberg (eds.), *Cognitive processes in writing*, 3–30. Hillsdale, NJ: Erlbaum.

Heath, Shirley Brice. 1983. *Ways with words: Language, life, and work in communities and classrooms*. New York: Cambridge University Press.

Hughey, Jane, Deanna Wormuth, Faye Hartfield, and Holly Jacobs. 1983. *Teaching ESL composition: Principles and techniques*. Rowley, MA: Newbury House.

Hyland, Ken. 2004. *Genre and second language writing*. Ann Arbor, MI: University of Michigan Press.

Hyland, Ken. 2007. English for specific purposes: Some influences and impacts. In James Cummins and Chris Davison (eds.), *International handbook of English language teaching*, 391–402. New York: Springer.

Hyland, Ken, Meng Huat Chau, and Michael Handford (eds.). 2012. *Corpus applications in Applied Linguistics*. London: Continuum.

Hyon, Sunny. 1996. Genre in three traditions: Implications for ESL. *TESOL Quarterly* 30. 693–722.

Jarvis, Scott, Leslie Grant, Dawn Bikowski, and Dana Ferris. 2003. Exploring multiple profiles of highly rated learner compositions. *Journal of Second Language Writing* 12. 377–403.

Johns, Ann. 1997. *Text, role, and context: Developing academic literacies*. New York: Cambridge University Press.

Johns, Ann. 2003. Genre and ESL/EFL composition instruction. In Barbara Kroll (ed.), *Exploring the dynamics of second language writing*, 195–217. New York: Cambridge University Press.

Jones, Stan and Jackie Tetroe. 1987. Composing in a second language. In Ann Matsuhashi (ed.), *Writing in real time: Modeling the production processes*, 34–57. Norwood, NJ: Ablex.

Kaplan, Robert. 1966. Cultural thought patterns in intercultural education. *Language Learning* 16. 1–20.

Kaplan, Robert. 1972. *The anatomy of rhetoric: Prolegomena to a functional theory of rhetoric*. Philadelphia, PA: Center for Curriculum Development, Inc.

Kinginger, Celeste. 2002. Defining the zone of proximal development in US foreign language education. *Applied Linguistics* 23. 240–261.

Kong, Ailing and David Pearson. 2003. The road to participation: The construction of a literacy practice in a learning community of linguistically diverse learners. *Research in the Teaching of English* 38. 85–124.

Knouzi, Ibtissem. 2012. Tutoring in the zone of proximal development. In Alister Cumming (ed.), *Adolescent literacies in a multicultural context*, 118–132. New York: Routledge.

Krapels, Alexandra. 1990. An overview of second language writing process research. In Barbara Kroll (ed.), *Second language writing: Research insights for the classroom*, 37–56. New York: Cambridge University Press.

Kress, Gunther. 2013. *Multimodality: A social semiotic approach to contemporary communication*. London: Routledge.

Kubota, Ryuko and Al Lehner. 2004. Toward critical contrastive rhetoric. *Journal of Second Language Writing* 13. 7–27.

Kuhn, Thomas. 1962. *The structure of scientific revolutions*. Chicago: University of Chicago Press.

Lantolf, James. 2000. Second language learning as a mediated process. *Language Teaching* 33. 79–96.

Lantolf, James and Mathew Poehner (eds.). 2008a. *Sociocultural theory and the teaching of second languages*. London: Equinox.

Lantolf, James and Mathew Poehner. 2008b. Dynamic assessment. In Elana Shohamy (vol. ed.) and Nancy Hornberger (series ed.), *Language testing and assessment*, vol. 7 of *Encyclopedia of language and education*, 2nd edition, 273–284. New York: Springer.

Lantolf, James and Steven Thorne. 2006. *Sociocultural theory and the genesis of second language development*. Oxford: Oxford University Press.

Leki, Ilona. 1991. Twenty five years of contrastive rhetoric: Text analysis and writing pedagogies. *TESOL Quarterly* 25. 123–143.

Leki, Ilona. 2003. Coda: Pushing L2 writing research. *Journal of Second Language Writing* 12. 103–105.

Leki, Ilona. 2007. *Undergraduates in a second language: Challenges and complexities of academic literacy development*. Mahwah, NJ: Erlbaum.

Leontťev, Alexei. 1978. *Activity, consciousness and personality*. Englewood Cliffs, NJ: Prentice Hall.

Leontťev, Alexei. 1981. The problem of activity in psychology. In James Wertsch (ed.), *The concept of activity in Soviet psychology*, 37–71. New York: Sharpe.

Leung, Constant. 2007. Dynamic assessment: Assessment *for* and *as* teaching. *Language Assessment Quarterly* 4. 257–278.

Li, Xiao-Ming. 1996. *"Good writing" in cross-cultural context*. Albany, NY: State University of New York Press.

Lindgren, Eva and Marie Stevenson. 2013. Interactional resources in the letters of young writers in Swedish and English. *Journal of Second Language Writing* 22. 390–405.

Macqueen, Susy. 2012. *The emergence of patterns in second language writing*. Bern: Peter Lang.

Manchón, Rosa M. and Julio Roca de Larios. 2007. On the temporal nature of planning in L1 and L2 composing. *Language Learning* 27. 549–593.

Martin, James. 1992. *English text: System and structure*. Amsterdam: John Benjamins.

Martin, James and David Rose. 2008. *Genre relations: Mapping culture*. London: Equinox.

Mohan, Bernard. 1986. *Language and content*. Reading, MA: Addison-Wesley.

Mohan, Bernard. 2007. Knowledge structures in social practices. In James Cummins and Chris Davison (eds.), *International handbook of English language teaching*, 303–315. New York: Springer.

Mohan, Bernard and Winnie Lo. 1985. Academic writing and Chinese students: Transfer and developmental factors. *TESOL Quarterly* 19. 515–534.

Moll, Luis. 1989. Teaching second language students: A Vygotskian perspective. In Donna Johnson and Duane Roen (eds.), *Richness in writing*, 55–69. New York: Longman.

Moll, Luis (ed.). 1990. *Vygotsky and education: Instructional implications and applications of sociohistorical psychology*. New York: Cambridge University Press.

Murphy, Liz and Julio Roca de Larios. 2010. Searching for words: One strategic use of the mother tongue by advanced Spanish EFL learners. *Journal of Second Language Writing* 19. 61–81.

Nassaji, Hossein and Alister Cumming. 2000. What's in a ZPD? A case study of a young ESL student and teacher interacting through dialogue journals. *Language Teaching Research* 4. 95–121.

Nicolás–Conesa, Florentina, Julio Roca de Larios, and Yvette Coyle. 2014. Development of EFL students' mental models of writing and their effects on performance. *Journal of Second Language Writing* 24. 1–19.

Norris, John and Rosa M. Manchón. 2012. Investigating L2 writing development from multiple perspectives: Issues in theory and research. In Rosa M. Manchón (ed.), *L2 writing development: Multiple perspectives*, 221–244. Berlin: De Gruyter Mouton.

de Oliveira, Luciana and Tony Silva (eds.). 2013. *L2 Writing in secondary classrooms. Student experiences, academic issues, and teacher education*. New York: Routledge.

Olson, Carol and Robert Land. 2007. A cognitive strategies approach to reading and writing instruction for English language learners in secondary school. *Research in the Teaching of English* 41. 269–303.

Ojima, Maki. 2006. Concept mapping as pre-task planning: A case study of three Japanese ESL writers. *System* 34. 566–585.

Ortega, L. 2012. Epilogue: Exploring L2 writing–SLA interfaces. *Journal of Second Language Writing,* 21. 401–415.

Ortega, Lourdes and Joan Carson. 2010. Multicompetence, social context, and L2 writing research praxis. In Tony Silva and Paul Matsuda (eds.), *Practicing theory in second language writing*, 48–71. West Lafayette, IN: Parlor Press.

Paltridge, Brian. 2001. *Genre and the language learning classroom*. Ann Arbor, MI: University of Michigan Press.

Parks, Susan, Diane Huot, Josiane Hamers, and France Lemonnier. 2005. "History of theatre" websites: A brief history of the writing process in a high school ESL language arts class. *Journal of Second Language Writing* 14. 233–258.

Parks, Susan and Mary Maguire. 1999. Coping with on-the-job writing in ESL: A constructivist-semiotic perspective. *Language Learning* 49. 143–175.

Poehner, Mathew and James Lantolf. 2013. Bringing the ZPD into the equation: Capturing L2 development during computerized Dynamic Assessment. *Language Teaching Research* 17. 323–342.

Polio, Charlene. 2003. Research on second language writing: An overview of what we investigate and how. In Barbara Kroll (ed.), *Exploring the dynamics of second language writing*, 35–65. New York: Cambridge University Press.

Polio, Charlene. 2012. The relevance of second language acquisition theory to the written error correction debate. *Journal of Second Language Writing* 21. 375–389.

Purves, Alan (ed.). 1992. *The IEA study of written composition II: Education and performance in fourteen countries*. Oxford, UK: Pergamon.

Purves, Alan and William Purves. 1986. Viewpoints: Cultures, text models, and the activity of writing. *Research in the Teaching of English* 20. 174–197.

Raimes, Ann. 1987. Language proficiency, writing ability, and composing strategies: A study of ESL college student writers. *Language Learning* 37. 439–468.

Riazi, Abdolmehdi. 1997. Acquiring disciplinary literacy: A social-cognitive analysis of text production and learning among Iranian graduate students of education. *Journal of Second Language Writing* 6. 105–137.

Rijlaarsdam, Gert and Huub van den Bergh. 2006. Writing process theory: A functional dynamic approach. In Charles MacArthur, Steve Graham, and Jill Fitzgerald (eds.), *Handbook of writing research*, 41–53. New York: Guilford Press.

Roca de Larios, Julio, Liz Murphy, and Rosa M. Manchón. 1999. The use of restructuring strategies in EFL writing: A study of Spanish learners of English as a foreign language. *Journal of Second Language Writing* 8. 13–44.

Russell, David. 1997. Rethinking genre in school and society: An activity theory analysis. *Written Communication* 14. 504–554.

Sasaki, Miyuki. 2000. Toward an empirical model of EFL writing processes: An exploratory study. *Journal of Second Language Writing* 9. 259–291.

Sasaki, Miyuki. 2009. Changes in English as a foreign language students' writing over 3.5 years: A sociocognitive account. In Rosa M. Manchón (ed.), *Writing in foreign language contexts: Learning, teaching, and research*, 49–76. Bristol, UK: Multilingual Matters.

Sasaki, Miyuki. 2012. Effects of varying lengths of study-abroad experiences on Japanese EFL students' L2 writing ability and motivation: A longitudinal study. *TESOL Quarterly* 45. 81–105.

Schoonen, Rob, Amos van Gelderen, Reinoud Stoel, Jan Hulstijn, and Kees de Glopper. 2011. Modeling the development of L1 and EFL writing proficiency of secondary-school students. *Language Learning* 61. 31–79.

Schleppegrell, Mary. 2004. *The language of schooling*. Mahwah, NJ: Erlbaum.

Schleppegrell, Mary. 2013. The role of metalanguage in supporting academic language development. In Lourdes Ortega, Alister Cumming, and Nick Ellis (eds.), *Agendas for language learning research. Language Learning* 63 [Supplement 1], 153–170.

Schleppegrell, Mary & Cecilia Colombi (eds.). 2002. *Developing advanced literacy in first and second languages*. Mahwah, NJ: Erlbaum.

Schleppegrell, Mary and Catherine O'Hallaron. 2011. Teaching academic language in L2 secondary settings. *Annual Review of Applied Linguistics* 31. 3–18.

Silva, Tony. 1990. Second language composition instruction: Developments, issues, and directions in ESL. In Barbara Kroll (ed.), *Second language writing: Research insights for the classroom*, 11–23. New York: Cambridge University Press.

Simpson, Rita and John Swales (eds.). 2001. *Corpus linguistics in North America*. Ann Arbor, MI: University of Michigan Press.

Smagorinsky, Peter (ed.). 1994. *Speaking about writing: Reflections on research methodology*. Thousand Oaks, CA: Sage.

Stevenson, Marie, Rob Schoonen, and Kees de Glopper. 2006. Revising in two languages: A multidimensional comparison of online writing revisions. *Journal of Second Language Writing* 15. 201–233.

Storch, Neomy. 2013. *Collaborative writing in L2 classrooms*. Bristol, UK: Multilingual Matters.

Suzuki, Wataru. 2012. Written languaging, direct correction, and second language writing revision. *Language Learning* 62. 1110–1133.

Swain, Merrill. 2006. Languaging, agency and collaboration in advanced second language proficiency. In Heidi Brynes (ed.), *Advanced language learning: The contribution of Halliday and Vygotsky*, 95–108. London: Continuum.

Swain, Merrill, Penny Kinnear, and Linda Steinman. 2011. *Sociocultural theory in second language education: An introduction through narratives*. Bristol, UK: Multingual Matters.

Swain, Merrill and Sharon Lapkin. 2002. Talking it through: Two French immersion learners' response to reformulation. *International Journal of Educational Research* 37. 285–304.

Swales, John. 1990. *Genre analysis: English in academic and research settings*. New York: Cambridge University Press.

Tardy, Christine (ed.). 2011. *The future of genre in second language writing: A North American perspective* [Special issue]. *Journal of Second Language Writing* 20.

Tardy, Christine. 2012. A rhetorical genre theory perspective on L2 writing development. In Rosa M. Manchón (ed.), *L2 writing development: Multiple perspectives*, 165–190. Berlin: De Gruyter Mouton.

Torrance, Mark, Luuk van Waes, and David Galbraith (eds.). 2007. *Writing and cognition: Research and applications*. Amsterdam: Elsevier.

Tullock, Brandon and Marta Fernández-Villanueva. 2013. The role of previously learned languages in the thought processes of multilingual writers at the Deutsche Schule Barcelona. *Research in the Teaching of English* 47. 420–441.

Verspoor, Marjolin, Monika Schmid, and Xiaoyan Xu. 2012. A dynamic usage based perspective on L2 writing. *Journal of Second Language Writing* 21. 239–263.

Vygotsky, Lev. 1978. *Mind in society: The development of higher psychological processes*. Cambridge, MA: Harvard University Press.

Vygotsky, Lev. 1987. *The collected works of L. S. Vygotsky*. Robert Rieber and Aaron Carton (eds. and trans.). New York: Plenum.

Wang, Wenyu and Qiufang Wen. 2002. L1 use in the L2 composing process: An exploratory study of 16 Chinese EFL writers. *Journal of Second Language Writing* 11. 225–246.

Watanabe, Yuko and Merrill Swain. 2007. Effects of proficiency differences and patterns of pair interaction on second language learning: Collaborative dialogue between adult ESL learners. *Language Teaching Research* 11. 121–142.

van Weijen, Daphne, Huub van den Bergh, Gert Rijlaarsdam, and Ted Sanders. 2009. L1 use during L2 writing: An empirical study of a complex phenomenon. *Journal of Second Language Writing* 18. 235–250.

Wells, Gordon. 1999. *Dialogic inquiry: Towards a sociocultural practice and theory of education*. New York: Cambridge University Press.

Whalen, Karen and Nathan Menard. 1995. L1 and L2 writers' strategic and linguistic knowledge: A model of multiple-level discourse processing. *Language Learning* 45. 381–418.

Wodak, Ruth and Michael Meyer. 2009. *Methods of critical discourse analysis*, 2nd edition, 62–86. London: Sage.

Yang, Luxin. 2014. Examining the mediational means in collaborative writing: Case studies of undergraduate ESL students in business courses. *Journal of Second Language Writing* 23. 74–89.

Yeh, Stuart. 1998. Empowering education: Teaching argumentative writing to cultural minority middle-school students. *Research in the Teaching of English* 33. 49–83.

Zamel, Vivian. 1982. Writing: The process of discovering meaning. *TESOL Quarterly* 16. 195–209.

II. Populations and contexts

Christina Ortmeier-Hooper, Shauna Wight, and Corey McCullough
4 ESL writing in schools

1 Introduction

In English-dominant contexts, the number of second-language (L2) writers in primary and secondary schools has risen exponentially over the past two decades. Currently, there are over 5 million English-language learners (ELLs) in US primary and secondary schools or K-12 schools (NCES 2012), and in Canada, the UK, and Australia, census data confirm the growing presence of school-age English learners in schools, particularly in metropolitan areas (Block 2008; Dooley 2003; Milnes and Cheng 2008; O'Bryne 2001). In Australia, for example, 25% of children speak a language other than English, including indigenous languages (Barratt-Pugh and Rohl 2001). Despite this demographic trend, published studies on school-age ESL writers have been infrequent (Matsuda and DePew 2002; Harklau and Pinnow 2009). Matsuda and DePew (2002) reported that 3% of studies published in the *Journal of Second Language Writing (JSLW)* in the prior decade focused on school-age writers, a marginalization that persists in the discipline. However, new research trends indicate increasing interest in school-age L2 writers (Cummings 2012; de Oliveira and Silva 2013; Ortmeier-Hooper and Enright 2011). This chapter provides an overview of published research on ESL writers in schools to enhance researchers' understanding of the complexities at play in this age group and the intricacies of L2 writing in schools. We begin by examining the historical place and theoretical perspectives of this research. We then explore the empirical methods and findings marking this body of work before exploring areas for future research and providing additional resources.

2 A disciplinary positioning of current research

Historically, the field of second-language writing has focused on the needs and experiences of international college-age and adult L2 writers, often paralleling work in L1 college composition studies (Leki 2006; Matsuda 2006). This limited scope has meant that research on resident and immigrant L2 writers in primary (ages 5–11) and secondary school (ages 12–18) has been underrepresented. However, our review suggests that studies on the literacy development of ESL writers have occurred in adjacent fields like bilingual education and literacy studies. Studies in these fields favor an integrated approach to literacy but rarely focus exclusively on writing. Accordingly, this research on younger L2 writers is not traditionally marked as "second-language writing" or "composition/writing studies." Instead, such research is labeled by the following key terms: "English language learner (ELL)," "English learners (EL)," "bilingual learners," "dual language learners (DLL)," "biliteracy," "multilingualism/multiliteracies," "academic literacy," and "literacy." Such studies have been published in academic presses and journals throughout these related fields, and thus may remain unknown to L2 writing specialists working exclusively in higher education. Much published research on ESL writers in schools can be traced to a first generation of scholars in the 1980s and 90s who established a research agenda and inspired subsequent scholars to expand this area of the field.

2.1 Contemporary research on ESL writing in schools: First-generation (1985–1999)

The first generation of contemporary studies on primary-level L2 writers in English-dominant contexts can be traced to the mid-1980s. Early studies examined students in bilingual education programs primarily in US contexts. Edelsky (1982, 1986) was one of the first researchers to examine the writing of young bilinguals in naturalistic settings, rather than through testing. Influenced by innovative trends in L1 writing research that sought broad, rich descriptions of how young students engaged with writing (Calkins 1980; Graves 1983), Edelsky argued that there was a lack of comparable research on writing in bilingual education. Studies by Edelsky (1986, 1989) and Ammon (1985) coincided with a burgeoning interest in the reading development and emergent literacy practices of bilingual writers in elementary schools (Freeman and Whitesell 1985; Freeman and Freeman 1992; Perez and Torres-Guzman 1992). Nonetheless, literacy and second language acquisition research often prioritized students' reading development over writing (Harklau 2002).

At the secondary level, research was also limited, though work by Hudelson (1986, 1989) began to document the writing experiences and challenges of adolescent L2 writers. In the 1990s, research by Valdés (1998, 1999), Harklau (1994a, 1994b) and Fu (1995) enriched our understanding of ESL writers' experiences in secondary schools. Harklau's ethnographic work compared US students' writing experiences in ESL and mainstream English language arts classrooms, while Fu's study of US-Laotian adolescents documented how ESL writers were often placed in low-level classrooms with few opportunities for writing practice.

2.2 Contemporary research on ESL writing in schools: Second-generation (2000–2012)

By the late 1990s, college-level L2 writing scholars expressed a growing interest in resident-ESL and immigrant writers studying in US colleges and universities (Harklau, Siegel, and Losey 1999). Since resident L2 students had experiences in US high schools before entering first-year college composition classrooms, some writing scholars began to research identity negotiations and experiences these students faced in transitioning from high school to college (Harklau 1999, 2000; Ortmeier-Hooper 2008; Matsuda and Matsuda 2009). The late 1990s also marked changes in national educational policies that would impact ESL students in primary and secondary schools, including the elimination of many bilingual and dual-language programs in the US, despite the documented literacy benefits of such programs (Fu and Matoush 2006; Moll, Saez, and Dworin 2001). In recent years, researchers have been responding to legislation, like the US No Child Left Behind Act and Common Core Standards, whose complexities (e.g. more testing, curricular mandates, and annual yearly reports on specific student populations) have far-reaching implications for the education of resident ESL and bilingual students in K-12 schools.

At the beginning of the new millennium, a second generation of scholarship on school-age writers emerged. These studies placed *writing* at the forefront of their research agendas and focused their work on young multilingual writers' experiences, texts/narratives, composing processes, instruction, and teachers (Campano 2007; Enright 2011; Gebhard 2004; Gebhard and Harman 2011; Kibler 2010, 2011a, 2011b; Ruecker 2015; Samway 2006; Villalva 2006a, 2006b; Yi 2007, 2008). Likewise, new studies from established voices, including Valdés (2003), Fu (2003, 2009), and Harklau (2001), continued to respond to the impact of educational policies on ESL writers in schools. Together, these studies highlight distinctions between the research settings of higher education and primary and secondary schools. The recognition of these differences, made more urgent by demographic shifts in schools, has prompted calls for further research and theory development on younger ESL writers (Harklau 2011; Leki, Cumming, and Silva 2008).

3 Theoretical trends

Most current researchers acknowledge the complexity and interplay of social and cultural influences upon young ESL writers in a given community. Accordingly, many employ sociocultural and sociolinguistic theories that examine how culturally and historically-constructed contexts shape learning and language development. Such perspectives allow researchers to consider how an individual's knowing, valuing, believing, being, and speaking/writing reflect participation in a particular group at a given moment of time. Even scholars who do research on the development of young ESL writers typically frame their work in social, not cognitive, terms, drawing on sociolinguistic paradigms and theories. Because these theories all examine the social and cultural contexts surrounding language and literacy, they overlap and are rarely used in isolation. Crossover interests across the theoretical landscape include a concern for scaffolding instruction (sociolinguistics, Systemic Functional Linguistics – SFL –, multiliteracies), a critical transformation of literacy practices (NLS, multiliteracies, sociocritical), a difference-as-resource model (sociolinguistics, New Literacy Studies – NLS –, multiliteracies, transnationalism, sociocritical), and an examination of the micro and macro-level influences surrounding students and classrooms (NLS, multiliteracies, transnationalism, ecological). In this section, we will elaborate on some of these theoretical paradigms, providing references to relevant scholars and studies that exemplify these frames. Findings from these studies and others are discussed in section 5 of this chapter.

3.1 Situated learning, community of practice, and genre theories

Several scholars have relied upon situated learning (Lave and Wenger 1991) and community of practice theories (Wenger 1998) to explain how ESL student writers gain knowledge and access to discourse by interacting with others in the group or community (Gebhard 2004; Yi 2010b). These theoretical frames have been particularly useful in considering how young ESL writers learn academic language and engage in literacy practices in various communities (Yi 2010b). Situated learning theories have also considered how instruction might help ESL writers understand how genres are used in a specific discourse community.

One result of this interest has been a move among some researchers to consider genre and rhetorical theories that are relevant to multilingual writing pedagogy. Some scholars, like Hirvela (2013), use theories of contrastive rhetoric and argumentation to consider how school-age ESL writers approach argumentative writing for academic purposes. Reynolds (2005) and Spycher (2007) examine how students' meta-linguistic understanding of available rhetorical choices impacts their acquisition of genre-specific conventions and moves. Drawing on Halliday (1978), Australian scholars (Christie and Derewianka 2008; Christie and Martin 2007) adapted systemic functional linguistics (SFL), another theoretical approach to genre, to the unique needs of non-dominant-language students in school settings. Using SFL, researchers consider students' developing understanding of a genre's field (content), mode (grammar, organization), and tenor (audience, context) (Achugar, Schleppegrell, and Oteiza 2007; Ajayi 2009; Fang, Schleppengrell, and Cox 2006; Gebhard and Harman 2011; Gebhard, Harman, and Seger 2007).

However, some scholars suggest that SFL presents an overly broad, stable conception of genre, while others question whether an overemphasis on school-based genres adequately prepares advanced multilinguals for writing in university, community, and professional settings (Gebhard and Harmon 2011). Gebhard and Harmon (2011) have argued that pairing SFL with theoretical frames from New Literacy Studies (Gee 1991; Street 1995) can alleviate this limitation. New Literacy Studies (NLS) theories introduce a more culturally-sensitive view of first- and second-language literacy, which encourages researchers to consider literacies' functions outside of school contexts. NLS theorists have argued that literacy events, practices, and instruction are rarely neutral or universal, varying from one culture and situation to the next.

3.2 Multiliteracies, transnational, and socio-critical approaches

As with NLS, multiliteracies theory, derived from the work of the New London Group (2000), acknowledges the kinds of literacies that students experience beyond the classroom in a globalized and technologically-interconnected society. Cope and Kalantzis (2000) and Lo Bianco (2000) have argued for literacy perspectives that acknowledge the multilingual and multimodal communication practices among today's youth. The use of these theories is particularly evident in studies of primary (Kenner, Kress, Al-Khatib, Kam, and Tsai 2004; Maguire and Graves 2001) and secondary (Ajayi 2009; Black 2005; Smythe and Neufeld 2010; Yi 2010b) ESL writers composing with new media and in digital, social networking spaces. By employing theoretical frames that consider writing practices in hybrid or digital spaces, L2 writing researchers highlight students' versatility across modalities, as well as their use of L1 literacies. Such frameworks are consistent with Canagarajah's (2002) call for a shift away from deficit models of ESL writers and towards a "difference-as-resource" perspective in our research and teaching (p. 13).

Biliteracy theory (Fu 2009) and transnational theory (Valdés 2003; Yi 2010a) likewise emphasize the benefits of students' linguistic diversity. For example, Fu (2003, 2009) provides a framework for studying young writers' transition from L1 to L2 writing, underscoring the importance of students' "funds of knowledge" and biliteracy backgrounds as building blocks for their L2 writing practices (Moll, Saez, and Dworin 2001). A similar approach, transnationalism helps researchers and teachers conceptualize how multilinguals use literacy to move between cultures. Transnationalism, defined by Basch, Glick-Schiller, and Szanton (1994) as "the process by which immigrants forge and sustain multi-stranded social relations that link together their societies of origin and settlement," shifts viewpoints away from deficit models of ESL writers (p. 8). Scholarship on transnational primary and secondary ESL students in the United States has indicated that they construct more positive self-images and experience greater academic success than those who don't maintain cross-cultural ties (Gibson 1988; Lam 2009; Lam and Rosario-Ramos 2009; Yi 2010a).

Socio-critical approaches move beyond recognizing the inherent value in multilingual and multimodal literacies to politicizing these abilities (Franquiz and Salinas 2011). Gutierrez (2008) has argued that research on immigrant students must acknowledge the "increasingly complex, transnational, and hybrid world" (p. 148), while considering issues of power and access inherent in such shifts. These trends parallel scholarship within the broader field of L2 writing that focuses on critical theories and pedagogies (Canagarajah 2013) as well as ESL writers' competencies in academic (Jordan 2012; Ortmeier-Hooper 2013) and self-sponsored (Yi 2010a, 2010b) writing.

3.3 Identity theories

Another theoretical area employed in the scholarship focuses on identity formation, particularly during ESL writers' adolescence. This research considers how
past and present interactions shape students' identities as literate individuals,
while acknowledging that adolescence is a developmental stage defined in part by
identity formation and negotiation (Erikson 1968). Studies employing this theoretical perspective often draw upon Ivanič's (1998) work connecting identity to writing, and Norton's (1997) research exploring how second language acquisition is
impacted both by issues of identity and interactions with the target language community. Others have drawn upon social identity theory to explore how adolescent
ESL students' identity allegiances may shift based on which groups that they wish
to affiliate with or distance themselves from. Such work is exemplified by Ibrahim
(1999), Ortmeier-Hooper (2010), Wilson (2013), and Yi (2010a), who have all examined how ESL adolescents' writing development is impacted by their identity construction. Identity theories highlight the complex and sometimes contradictory
choices that L2 adolescents make as they try to balance competing individual, academic, familial, and social pressures.

3.4 Ecological theories and future trends

Ecological theories examine learning and language acquisition within larger systems of activity while also considering the interdependence of contextual factors
in the data analysis. (Bronfenbrenner 1995; Leather and Dam 2003). Ecological
theories enable researchers to situate their data and analysis of student writing and
instruction alongside the challenges of assessment and other national education
policies. For example, Enright and Gilliland (2011) illustrated how national legislation, such as No Child Left Behind, socialize multilingual students into certain literacy practices. Kenner's (2004) examination of primary school ESL students' home
and school "literacy eco-systems" found that these systems were dynamic and fluid. Ortmeier-Hooper & Enright (2011) offer a conceptual structure that acknowledges how literacy development and maturation occur simultaneously with young
writers, and how a number of contextual factors – from home literacies to social
interactions to school curricular policies – impact the trajectories of young writers
within a given school environment (p. 170).

4 Research methods

Consistent with theoretical trends, methodological approaches to ESL writing research in schools are also characterized by an increasing focus on sociocultural
perspectives as well as the curricular demands of education policy. L2 writing

scholars note an ongoing shift from earlier, linguistics-based quantitative research on phenomena such as textual components and cognitive processes to studies that consider the social, cultural, and pedagogical factors that influence L2 writers (Edelsky 1986; Leki, Cumming, and Silva 2008). This shift is especially visible in the K-12 context, where contemporary research has favored qualitative methods such as case studies, ethnographies, interviews, narratives, and action research. The emphasis on qualitative methods began in the 1980s, when sociocultural and developmental theories led researchers to seek methods to move beyond decontextualized test scores and focus on the needs, identities, and contexts of the writers (Edelsky 1986). Recently, qualitative research methods have explored lesson delivery, writing and identity, curricular innovations and constraints, the influence of peers and teachers, and student composing processes. Even quantitative and statistical studies of L2 writers' texts in immigrant and bilingual contexts have paid increasing attention to the socio-cultural, -political and -economic circumstances surrounding students and their schools, resulting in more mixed-method approaches to research. This section reviews the methods employed by this current work.

4.1 Case studies and ethnographic methods

Case studies (Ajayi 2009; Edelsky 1986; Enright 2006b; Gebhard 2004, 2005; Kenner et al. 2004; Ortmeier-Hooper 2010) of individual students and groups of students are the most common qualitative approaches to K-12 ESL writing research. Case studies seek to explain facets of individual student writers and their experiences (Kibler 2013), school-based programs (Enright 2006b), and individual classroom practices (Brisk, Hodgson, and Connor 2010; Harklau 1994a). Longitudinal case studies on individual subjects have provided important insights into the identity development of L2 writers across multiple settings (Harklau 2000, 2001).

Ethnographic research methods have proved useful in K-12 L2 writing research because they describe multiple subjects within intact social, cultural, and/or educational contexts over longer periods of time (Black 2005; Duff 2001; Fu 1995; Harklau 1994a, 2000; Ibrahim 1999; Laman and Van Sluys 2008; Toohey 1998). For instance, Maguire and Graves (2001) used ethnographic methodology to examine the ways in which three eight-year-old Muslim girls in Montreal, Canada were able to mediate their discursive identities both in class and via journal entries. Longitudinal studies like those conducted by Fu (1995, 2003) have presented research on ESL writers as part of particular communities, like Chinatown in New York City, or compared the school experiences of siblings within a single family.

4.2 Text and discourse-based studies

Text and discourse-analysis studies have provided insight into the characteristics, composing processes, and textual features of L2 writers at differing stages of L2 writing development. These methods have helped researchers analyze L2 writers' accuracy, fluency, coherence, use of subordination, and evidence of metacognitive awareness (Tarone, Downing, Cohen, Gillette, Murie, and Dailey 1993; Reynolds 2002, 2005; Spycher 2007). For instance, Reynolds (2002, 2004) studied the texts of middle-school ESL writers to examine written fluency and to analyze their meta-cognitive understanding of language and genre. In addition, discourse analysis of the talk that often surrounds writing instruction has been important, as illustrated by Kibler's (2011a) study of teacher-student dialogue in writing conferences.

4.3 Action research and school-university collaborations

Kapper (2006) posited that K-12 teachers have much to contribute to discussions on ESL writers in schools but are often hindered by limited access to scholarly research, time, funding, and logistical support. The method of action research allows K-12 practitioners, often in collaboration with university scholars, to utilize classroom data to develop better understandings of student writing development and classroom instruction. Studies by Brisk, Hodgson, and Connor (2011), and Gebhard, Harman, and Seger (2007) provide models for collaborative research initiatives led by teams of teachers and university-based researchers. Other university-based scholars have employed methods that highlight "scholarship of engagement" models that encourage researchers to embrace collaboration and help schools improve instruction while simultaneously conducting research (Boyer 1996; Fu 2003).

5 Major research findings

The most significant findings emerging from our review of scholarship on ESL writers in schools are governed by two major conclusions. First, the contextual factors that impact primary and secondary schools are quite different from those in colleges and universities, and these factors must be taken into consideration when considering the writing development, processes, practices, and instruction of younger ESL writers. Since most K-12 schools are publicly funded and students are required to attend, they often serve a broader range of ESL students than post-secondary institutions. ESL writers in schools, particularly in English-dominant contexts, reflect a wider variety of backgrounds, linguistic profiles, English proficiency levels, ages, and educational trajectories than their college counterparts. This leads to the second conclusion that we can draw from the research: primary and secondary ESL writers are not a monolithic group and have highly variable school experiences. This variability is dependent upon a number of conditions, including socio-economic circumstances of students, school funding, teacher professional development, curricular constraints imposed by administrators and government officials, testing mandates, and the reception of immigrants and non-native English speakers, among other factors. To date, findings have documented these conditions and provided rich descriptions of the unique circumstances of ESL writers in schools, including L2 students' self-sponsored writing practices. Although we acknowledge contingent areas of overlap, we place these findings into five broad categories: (1) ESL students' writing development in schools; (2) teacher preparation and pedagogy; (3) multi-modal writing and out-of-school literacy practices; (4) identity-writing connections; and (5) the impact of educational policies on L2 writers, curriculum, and placement.

5.1 The writing development of ESL writers in schools

In studies of primary school ESL writers, findings suggest that writing instruction need not be delayed until students reach higher levels of English reading or oral proficiency (Edelsky 1986). Scholars have noted that writing-reading processes are often interdependent, meaning that reading and writing development support one another (Edelsky 1986; Hudelson 1989). Research also suggests that younger ESL writers' use of inverted spellings, drawings, and their first language when they write were not detrimental to students' overall English writing development (Hudelson 1989). Young ESL writers also proved able to critically examine texts and develop criteria for evaluating their effectiveness (Brisk 2015; Samway 2006).

Furthermore, studies have found that students' use of their L1 in the classroom enhances their writing development, motivation to learn, and sense of communicative competency. For example, Barratt-Pugh and Rohl (2001) examined the writing practices of bilingual Khmer-English students in a dual-language program in Western Australia, finding that, in terms of mechanical skills and use of conventions, students demonstrated parallel writing development across both languages. Students in the study used knowledge of one writing system to support the development of the other (p. 669). In a related developmental study, Fu (2009) identified four stages of transitions as students move from first-language to second-language writing competence, noting how they used mixed-language approaches in their writing to communicate meaning. Fu found that writing development was nonlinear, observing that students relied more heavily on their first language as they encountered new content or genres in their English writing activities.

At the secondary level, research on the writing development of adolescents has found that the lack of class time dedicated to writing instruction impedes students' progress, especially regarding response and revision strategies, genre exposure, understanding of academic conventions, and rhetorical awareness (Enright 2011; Harklau 1994a; Reynolds 2002, 2005; Spycher 2007). Comparative studies of ESL writers across grade levels have suggested that many secondary students show little growth in their writing at the 8th, 10th, and college grade levels (Tarone et al.

1993). Reynolds (2005) noted that native English writers in the middle grades had stronger associations between texts' rhetorical and social functions than ESL writers, suggesting that lack of fluency may come not only from grammatical limitations, but also from a lack of practice in writing for varying purposes and audiences. Other research has found that the development of writing skills is tied, in part, to home and New Literacy practices (Dooley and Thanaperumal 2011; Franquiz and Salinas 2011).

5.2 Teacher preparation and pedagogy

A significant body of work has been dedicated to investigating how teachers support writing development (Harklau 1999; Laman and Van Sluys 2008; Toohey 1998), but teacher preparation and L2 writing is still understudied (Hirvela and Belcher 2007). Most studies acknowledge that a lack of teacher training in L2 writing compounds challenges for ESL writers in schools (Larsen 2013; Seloni 2013; Yi 2013). Menken and Antunez' (2001) survey of 1075 US teacher education programs found that only 25 % had ESL programs, and only 48 % required mainstream teacher candidates to have coursework on teaching ELLs. Furthermore, coursework on second language writing is either unavailable or optional in many education programs. Teachers in many school districts may have limited knowledge of or experience with these students, particularly regarding their writing (Walker, Shafer, and Liams 2004). De Oliveira and Shoffner (2009) offered a model cross-disciplinary English teaching methods course for mainstream teachers and encouraged more programs to follow suit. Studies suggest that pre-service preparation is paramount since teachers have limited professional development opportunities in ESL once they enter the workforce (Athanases, Bennett, and Wahleithner 2013; McEachron and Bhatti 2005).

A number of studies have documented pedagogical approaches that have been especially effective in promoting primary and secondary L2 students' literacy development. Franquiz and Salinas (2011), for example, observed how newcomer students benefitted from the integration of content instruction and English writing development through a comprehensive curriculum intertwining historical thinking with digitalized primary sources. In the unit described in the study, newly-arrived adolescents progressed when writing instruction combined technical skills with genre awareness and opportunities to examine how texts make meaning within politicized writing contexts. In other studies, SFL-based pedagogies have successfully incorporated peer and teacher collaboration by combining scaffolding with genre theory (Christie and Derewianka 1998; Gebhard et al. 2007). The SFL approach emphasizes whole-class collaborations in which teachers and students deconstruct then reconstruct texts to decide which textual, rhetorical, and linguistic features are appropriate for a particular rhetorical situation (Gebhard and Harman 2011). Research suggests that multilingual students benefit from SFL because their inexperience with the written conventions of the new culture poses challenges in understanding the expectations of their content area teachers (Enright and Gilliand 2011; Kibler 2011b).

5.3 Technology, multi-modal writing, and literacy practices outside of school

While classroom collaboration provides support for both young and adolescent L2 writers, these learners' participation in a nexus of literacy practices outside school generates foundations upon which teachers can and should build. In countries where English serves as the dominant language, multilingual students often continue to study their L1 through community organizations, family interactions, and online spaces (Black 2005; Kenner et al. 2004; Lam 2000, 2009; Lam and Rosario-Ramos 2009; Maguire and Graves 2001; Yi 2010;). This literacy engagement in the L1 provides sustained cultural connections, improved self-concepts, flexible identities, and increased rhetorical sophistication (Smythe and Neufeld 2010; Yi 2010b). Everyday engagement with technology and mass media also makes dominant cultural materials more accessible to immigrants (Ajayi 2009; Duff 2001). By tapping these extracurricular literacies for academic use, teachers have successfully used personal (Maguire and Graves 2001; Fu 1995), bilingual (Edelsky 1989), and multimodal (Ajayi 2009) approaches to support school-aged ESL writers.

Research has underscored the importance of home literacy practices in the development of writing skills (Van Sluys 2006). While some ESL writers may have strong support in speaking and writing in both L1 and English at home (Moll et al. 2001; Reyes 2006), others may live in communities where English is rarely spoken outside the home, where exposure to L1 writing is limited, and where there are fewer opportunities for English literacy practices outside of school (Fu 2003; Qian and Pan 2006). In all cases, researchers point to the importance of building on home and common daily literacy practices in helping younger children develop their English writing. Laman and Van Sluys (2008) detailed how school-based writing practices can situate multilingual students as valued members of the classroom community and allow them to draw upon their linguistic and cultural resources to enhance their writing and learning. Studies also suggest that for young children, language learning is often bidirectional between parents and children, with children acting as informants and between L1 and L2 for their family members and communities (Fu 2009; Reyes 2006; Valdés 2003). Yet in schools, ESL writers often find few school-based writing opportunities to use or build upon their strengths.

5.4 Identity-writing connections

Some studies have examined the connections between writers' identities as "ESL" students and instruction, as well as how "ESL" identities shift as the students transition from high school to college. At the primary levels, research suggests that students' choices in their written texts are connected to interactions between identity and audience (Reyes 2006). At the secondary level, researchers suggest that adolescent students' identity negotiations and perceptions of institutional labels often play substantive roles in motivation and writing practices (Harklau 1999; Ortmeier-Hooper 2008, 2010). For instance, adolescents often express concern about how identity labels placed upon them result in their being tracked into lower-level academic programs (Fu 1995; Harklau 1994b; Ortmeier-Hooper 2010, 2013). While being labeled ESL positions many students as outsiders within their peer and academic communities, ESL associations and services can also increase teacher flexibility and provide a safe haven among students facing similar challenges (Enright 2011; Harklau 1994a, 2000; Kanno and Applebaum 1995; Ortmeier-Hooper 2010).

5.5 The impact of educational policies on L2 writers, curriculum, and placement

Researchers have also found that national education policies and mandates play a role in the kinds of educational trajectories that are available to L2 writers, particularly at the secondary level. In the US, for example, the No Child Left Behind Act and Common Core Standards have increased the level of standardization and testing for all learners. Consequently, teachers of ESL writers tend to emphasize genres that appear on exams, often at the expense of more advanced genres of writing (Enright and Gilliand 2011; Ortmeier-Hooper and Enright 2011). This finding is especially true at the secondary level where high stakes tests for school accountability, graduation, and college entrance become paramount (Harklau 2011).

Studies have documented how frequently ESL students, particularly in secondary schools, are tracked into lower-level courses (Enright and Gilliland 2011; Fu 1995; Harklau 1994b; Ortmeier-Hooper 2010; Villalva 2006b). Academic tracking is prevalent and problematic in countries like the US and often forecloses rich writing opportunities for ESL students. As a result, ESL writers may find it difficult to exit lower tracks and enter college-bound courses (Harklau 1994b). Writing assessments often serve as a tool for determining students' ability to enter college preparatory courses, and the rote, decontextualized approaches often found within remedial classes can restrict advancement (Enright and Gilliand 2011; Fu 1995; Harklau 1994b; NCES 2012; Ortmeier-Hooper 2010, 2013; Ortmeier-Hooper and Enright 2011).

6 New directions

The past decade of research on ESL writers in schools has opened up necessary lines of scholarship for the field, but this work must continue to broaden in scope and depth. We close this chapter by exploring directions for future research and development.

6.1 The need for effective response systems for K-12 ESL writers

Throughout English-dominant school contexts, ESL and many content-area teachers continue to seek suitable pedagogical strategies for teaching young and adolescent ESL writers. Promising initiatives like the National Writing Project in the US have brought attention to ESL writers in primary and secondary schools, but there continues to be a vital need for L2 writing scholars to be more involved in these conversations at the national and local levels. Often, school teachers interested in L2 writing can only find textbooks and materials for college-level students. There is a need to create more accessibility to L2 writing knowledge among researchers, teachers, policymakers, teacher educators, and other writing/literacy scholars. Shifts in research paradigms and methods geared toward engaging classroom teachers and researchers in collaborative pursuits are promising. Such models offer researchers a two-fold opportunity: first, they allow university-based scholars to engage in surrounding communities and broaden their understanding of school-age student writers; and second, school-university partnerships create ways to bridge conversations and expand the network of stakeholders interested in these students.

Areas for further research that can inform pedagogy include effective teacher response, error feedback, student revision, and peer review at the primary and secondary school levels. As noted above, the research on ESL writers in schools, particularly at the secondary level, has focused on the *lack* of effective teacher response and peer review. The natural progression would be to identify and examine effective teacher response techniques, students' responses to feedback, student revision practices, and peer review. Similarly, the writing assessment of ESL students in primary and secondary schools is understudied, and discussions on assessment have been driven by college-level findings or studies on native-English students. More research is needed to determine if these findings also hold true in primary and secondary school settings and with younger writers.

Overall, more studies are needed on innovative and effective writing programs for bilingual and ESL students in primary and secondary school contexts, such as SFL approaches. Specifically, longitudinal studies could help researchers to pinpoint how well the SFL method helps students analyze and adjust their writing as they move across disciplinary boundaries and grade levels.

6.2 Connections between out-of-school and in-school writing practices

Studies by Yi (2007, 2010a, 2010b) provide insight into how ESL writers compose in digital environments and the ways in which those writing experiences impact their identities as writers. While this current research enables us to understand how ESL writers may use technology and digital composing practices outside of school, the small scale of these recent accounts still leaves many questions unanswered. For one, while some ESL writers may have access to technology-rich school and home environments, many others do not. We are still unsure how issues of access to technology affects L2 writers' development. In light of the digital composing and technology-rich instructional trends in L1 composition across the grade levels, there is a need for more studies that examine the triumphs and challenges faced by younger multilingual writers based on their use of these resources.

Similarly, research has yet to examine the extra-curricular writing activities of ESL students. Most schools offer a number of literacy-rich extracurricular activities that promote reading and writing (e.g. school newspapers, literary journals, book clubs, school-to-work professional programs). Only a few studies have documented L2 students' participation and experiences in these settings as part of their growing identities as writers (Roozen and Herrerra 2010). Studies on the importance of heritage language (HL) writing opportunities for ESL writers are also necessary.

6.3 ESL writers' transitions across grade levels and educational institutions

In the late 1990s, Harklau, Losey, and Siegal (1999) and Harklau (2000) chronicled immigrant students' transitions from US secondary schools to college, but research on students' experiences as they move across grade levels and institutions continues to be neglected. For example, little attention has been paid to students' transitions from elementary to secondary schools. The gap in research on this transition is particularly surprising since such shifts affect larger numbers of students, who may feel alienated by frequent testing, a more rigid curriculum, intensified peer relationships, and an increasingly depersonalized institutional context. In the US, for example, the drop-out rate of immigrant students increases dramatically and disproportionately upon entering secondary school (Fine and Jaffe-Walter 2007), yet no studies to date have considered the role that writing may have in these outcomes. Similarly, studies on the writing experiences of secondary ESL students in alternative educational settings (e.g. General Education Diplomas [GEDs] or alternative diploma programs, vocational schools, charter schools, and on-line high school classes) are almost nonexistent. Researchers and educators must understand the unique needs and challenges these students face at each educational level in order to improve academic and vocational trajectories.

6.4 Multi-site projects and a challenge for the future

Finally, one of most challenging areas for future research is the need for multi-site research projects. The research reviewed in this chapter exemplifies the work of a few scholars conducting mostly smaller-scale case studies on classrooms or individual students, which may arise from a lack of funding and resources. Small-scale studies, which have contributed so much to our understanding of college-level L1 composition and L2 writing, often fail to resonate with policymakers and administrators. While current research enables L2 writing scholars to understand the depth of context and diversity of individual settings and students, it is difficult to advocate for instructional changes without a more comprehensive and cooperative research agenda. Likewise, researchers in countries with similar demographic shifts are often not in conversation with one another. Therefore, future research should begin building wider networks of collaboration among L2 writing researchers working with primary and secondary school populations in an effort to replicate studies and consider the regional similarities and differences among ESL students' writing experiences.

Leki, Cummings, and Silva (2008) surmised that the research on ESL writing in schools had been sparse due, in part, to the fact that researchers had been "overwhelmed by the more immediate and serious problems observed in the contexts where the writing takes place" (p. 26). However, the inherent complexity of studying L2 writing research in schools is one reason that these sites provide such rich opportunities for writing researchers to expand theories and develop a stronger understanding of the interplay between institutional challenges, the student writers, and their texts. The growing numbers of school-age ESL writers in K-12 institutions make the commitment for continued research and conversations into this population both significant and necessary.

7 Additional sources

Britain Department of Education. *English as an additional language.* Available at:
    http://www.education.gov.uk/schools/pupilsupport/inclusionandlearnersupport/eal
Cumming, Alister (ed.). 2012. *Adolescent literacies in a multicultural context.* New York: Routledge.
de Courcy, Michèle, Karen Doley, Robert Jackson, Jenny Miller, and Kathy Rushton. 2012.
    Teaching EAL/D learners in Australian classrooms. Newton, Australia: Primary English
    Teaching Association of Australia (PETAA). Available at: http//www.petaa.edu/au/resources/
    full-list-of-petaa-papers
de Oliveira, Luciana and Tony Silva. 2013. *L2 writing in secondary classrooms: Academic issues,
    student experiences, and teacher education.* New York: Routledge.
The National Commission on Writing. 2008. *Words have no borders: Student voices on
    immigration, language and culture.* Available at: http://www.host-collegeboard.com/
    advocacy/writing/Words_Have_No_Borders.pdf
National Council of Teachers of English. 2008. *English language learners: A policy research brief.*
    Available at: http://www.ncte.org/library/nctefiles/resources/policyresearch/ellresearchbrief.pdf
National Writing Project. *English language learners network.* Available at: http://www.nwp.org/cs/
    public/print/programs/ell
Ontario Ministry of Education. 2007. *English language learners: Policies and procedures for
    Ontario elementary and secondary Schools, kindergarten to grade 12.* Available at:
    http://www.edu.gov.on.ca/eng/document/esleldprograms/esleldprograms.pdf

8 References

Achugar, Mariana, Mary Schleppegrell, and Teresa Oteíza. 2007. Engaging teachers in language analysis: A functional linguistics approach to reflective literacy. *English teaching: practice and critique* 6(2). 8–24.

Ajayi, Lasisi. 2009. English as a second language learners' exploration of multimodal texts in a junior high school. *Journal of Adolescent and Adult Literacy* 52(7). 585–595.

Ammon, Paul. 1985. Helping children learn to write in English as a second language: Some observations and some hypotheses. In Sarah Warshauer Freedman (ed.), *The acquisition of written language*. Norwood, NJ: Ablex.

Athanases, Steven, Lisa Bennett, and Milchelsen Wahleithner. 2013. Responsive teacher inquiry for learning about adolescents English learners as developing writers. In Luciana de Oliveira and Tony Silva (eds.). *L2 writing in secondary classrooms. Academic issues, student experiences, and teacher education*, 149–165. New York: Routledge.

Barratt-Pugh, Caroline and Mary Rohl. 2001. Learning in two languages: A bilingual program in western Australia. *The Reading Teacher* 54(7). 664–676.

Basch Linda, Nina Glick-Schiller, and Cristina Szanton Blanc. 1994. *Nations unbound: Transnational projects, postcolonial predicaments, and deterritorialized nation-states*. Langhorne, PA: Gordon and Breach.

Black, Rebecca. 2005. Access and affiliation: The literacy and composition practices of English language learners in an online fanfiction community. *Journal of Adolescent & Adult Literacy* 49(2). 118–128.

Block, David. 2008. *Multilingual identities in a global city: London stories*. London: Palgrave Macmillan.

Boyer, Ernest. 1996. The scholarship of engagement. *Journal of Public Outreach* 1(1). 11–20.

Brisk, Maria Estela, Tracy Hodgson-Drysdale, and Cheryl O'Connor. 2011. A study of a collaborative instructional project informed by systemic functional linguistic theory: Report writing in elementary grades. *Journal of Education* 191. 1–12.

Brisk, Maria Estela. 2015. *Engaging students in academic literacies: Genre-based pedagogy for K-5 classrooms*. New York: Routledge.

Bronfenbrenner, Urie. 1995. Developmental ecology through space and time: A future perspective. In Phyllis Moen, Glen Elder Jr, and Kurt Lüscher (eds.) *Examining lives in the context: Perspectives on the ecology of human development*, 619–647. Washington, DC: American Psychological Association.

Cope, Bill and Mary Kalantzis (eds.). 2000. *Multiliteracies: Literacy learning and the design of social futures*. London & New York: Routledge.

Calkins, Lucy. 1980. When children want to punctuate. *Language Arts* 57. 567–573.

Campano, Gerald. 2007. *Immigrant students and literacy: Reading, writing and remembering*. New York: Teachers College Press.

Canagarajah, Suresh. 2013. *Translingual practice: Global Englishes and cosmopolitan relations*. New York: Routledge.

Canagarajah, Suresh. 2002. *Critical academic writing and multilingual students*. Ann Arbor: University of. Michigan Press.

Christie, F. and Derewianka, B. 2008. *School discourse: Learning to write across the years of schooling*. London: Continuum.

Christie, Frances and James Martin (eds.). 2007. *Language, knowledge, and pedagogy: Functional linguistic and sociological perspectives*. London: Continuum.

Cummings, Alister (ed.). 2012. *Adolescent literacies in a multicultural context*. New York: Routledge.

De Oliveira, Luciana and Melanie Shoffner. 2009. Addressing the needs of English language learners in an English methods course. *English Education* 42(1). 91–111.

De Oliveira, Luciana and Tony Silva. 2013. *L2 writing in secondary classrooms: Academic issues, student experiences, and teacher education.* New York: Routledge.

Dooley, Karen. 2003. Reconceptualising equity: Pedagogy for Chinese students in Australian schools. *Australian Educational Researcher* 30. 25–42.

Dooley, Karen and Pavithiran Thangaperumal. 2011. Pedagogy and participation: Literacy education for low-literate refugee students of African origin in a western school system. *Language and Education* 25(2). 385–297.

Duff, Patricia. 2001. Language, literacy, content, and (pop)culture: Challenges for ESL students in mainstream courses. *Canadian Modern Language Review* 58. 103–132.

Edelsky, Carole. 1982. Writing in a bilingual program: The relation of L1 and L2 texts. *TESOL Quarterly* 16. 211–228.

Edelsky, Carole. 1986. *Writing in a bilingual program: Había una vez.* Norwood, NJ: Ablex.

Edelsky, Carole. 1989. Bilingual children's writing: Fact and fiction. In Dona Johnson and Duane Roen (eds.), *Richness in writing: Empowering ESL students*, 165–176. White Plains, NY: Longman.

Enright, Kerry Anne. 2011. Language and literacy for a new mainstream. *American Educational Research Journal* 48(1). 80–118.

Enright, Kerry Anne. 2013. Adolescent writers and academic trajectories: Situating L2 writing in the content areas. In Luciana de Oliveira and Tony Silva (eds.), *L2 writing in the secondary classroom*, 27–43. New York: Routledge.

Enright, Kerry Anne and Betsy Gilliand. 2011. Multilingual writing in an age of accountability: From policy to practice in US high school classrooms. *Journal of Second Language Writing* 20. 182–195.

Erikson, Erik. 1968. *Identity: Youth and crisis.* New York: Norton.

Fang, Zhihui, Mary Schleppegrell, and Beverly Cox. 2006. Understanding the language demands of schooling: Nouns in academic registers. *Journal of Literacy Research* 38(3). 247–273.

Flower, Linda and John Hayes. 1981. A cognitive process theory of writing. *College Composition and Communication* 32. 365–387.

Fránquiz, Maria and Cinthia Salinas. 2011. Newcomers developing english literacy through historical thinking and digitized primary sources. *Journal of Second Language Writing* 20. 196–210.

Freeman, Yvonne. 1992. *Whole language for second language learners.* Portsmouth, NH: Heinemann.

Freeman, Yvonne and Lynne Whitesell. 1985. What preschoolers already know about print. *Educational Horizons* 64(1). 22–25.

Fu, Danling. 1995. *My trouble is my English: Asian students and the American dream.* Portsmouth, NH: Heinemann.

Fu, Danling. 2003. *An island of English: Teaching ESL in Chinatown.* Portsmouth, NH: Heinemann.

Fu, Danling. 2009. *Writing between languages: How English language learners make the transition to fluency, grades 4–12.* Portsmouth, NH: Heinemann.

Fu, Danling and Mary Matoush. 2006. Writing development and biliteracy. In Paul K. Matsuda, Christina Ortmeier-Hooper, and Xiaoye You (eds.), *The politics of second language writing*, 5–29. West Lafayette, IN: Parlor.

Gebhard, Meg. 2004. Fast capitalism, school reform, and second language literacy practices. *Modern Language Journal* 88(2). 245–265.

Gebhard, Meg and Ruth Harman. 2011. Reconsidering genre theory in K-12 schools. *Journal of Second Language Writing* 20. 45–55.

Gebhard, Meg, Ruth Harman, and Wendy Seger. 2007. Reclaiming recess: Learning the language of persuasion. *Language Arts* 84(5). 419–430.

Gee, James. 1991. Sociocultural approaches to literacy. *Annual Review of Applied Linguistics* 12. 31–48.

Gibson, Margaret. 1988. *Accommodation without assimilation: Sikh immigrants in an American high school*. Ithaca, NY: Cornell University Press.

Graves, Donald. 1983. *Writing: Teachers and children at work*. Portsmouth, NH: Heinemann.

Gutiérrez, Kris. 1992. A comparison of instructional contexts in writing process classrooms with Latino children. *Education and Urban Society* 24(2). 224–262.

Gutiérrez, Kris. 2008. Developing a sociocritical literacy in the third space. *Reading Research Quarterly* 43(2). 148–164.

Halliday, Michael. 1978. *Language as social semiotic: The social interpretation of language and meaning*. London: University Park Press.

Harklau, Linda. 1994a. ESL and mainstream classes: Contrasting second language learning contexts. *TESOL Quarterly* 28(2). 241–272.

Harklau, Linda. 1994b. Tracking and linguistic minority students: Consequences of ability grouping for second language learners. *Linguistics and Education* 6. 221–248.

Harklau, Linda. 1999. The ESL learning environment in secondary school. In Christian Faltis and Paula Wolfe (eds.), *So much to say: Adolescents, bilingualism, and ESL in the secondary school*, 42–61. New York, NY: Teachers College Press.

Harklau, Linda. 2000. From the "good kids" to the "worst:" Representations of English language learners across educational settings. *TESOL Quarterly* 34. 35–67.

Harklau, Linda. 2001. From high school to college: Student perspectives on literacy practices. *Journal of Literacy Research* 33. 33–70.

Harklau, Linda. 2002. The role of writing in classroom second language acquisition. *Journal of Second Language Writing* 11. 329–350.

Harklau, Linda. 2011. Commentary: Adolescent L2 writing research as an emerging field. *Journal of Second Language Writing* 20. 227–230.

Harklau, Linda, Kay Losey, and Mary Siegal. (eds.). 1999. *Generation 1.5 meets college composition: Issues in the teaching of writing to US-education learners of ESL*. Mahwah, NJ: Lawrence Erlbaum.

Harklau, Linda and Rachel Pinnow. 2009. Adolescent second-language writing. In Leila Christenbury, Randy Bomer, and Peter Smagorinsky (eds.), *Handbook of Adolescent Literacy Research*, 126–137. New York: Guilford.

Hirvela, Alan. 2013. Preparing English language learners for argumentative writing. In Luciana de Oliveira and Tony Silva (eds.), *L2 writing in the secondary classrooms*, 67–86. New York: Routledge.

Hirvela, Alan and Diane Belcher. 2007. Writing scholars as teacher educators: Exploring writing teacher education. *Journal of Second Language Writing* 16. 125–128.

Hudelson, Sarah. 1986. ESL children's writing: What we've learned, what we're learning. In Pat Rigg and D. Scott Enright (eds.), *Children and ESL: Integrating perspectives*. Washington D.C.: TESOL.

Hudelson, Sarah. 1989. *Write on: Children writing in ESL*. Englewood Cliffs, NJ: Prentice Hall Regents.

Ibrahim, Awad. 1999. Becoming black: Rap and hip-hop, race, gender, identity, and the politics of ESL learning. *TESOL Quarterly* 33(3). 349–369.

Ivanič, Roz. 1998. *Writing and identity: The discoursal construction of identity in academic writing*. Amsterdam: John Benjamins.

Jordan, Jay. 2012. *Redesigning composition for multilingual realities*. Urbana, IL: Southern Illinois UP/NCTE.

Kanno, Yasuko and Sheila Applebaum. 1995. ESL students speak up: Their stories of how we are doing. *TESL Canada Journal* 2. 32–49.

Kapper, Jessie Moore. 2006. Mapping post-secondary classifications and second language writing research in the United States. In Paul K. Matsuda, Christina Ortmeier-Hooper, and Xiaoye You (eds.), *Politics of second language writing: In search of the promised land*, 247–261. West Lafayette, IN: Parlor.

Kenner, Charmian. 2004. *Becoming biliterate*: Young children learning different writing systems. Stoke-on-Trent: Trentham Books.

Kenner, Charmian, Gunther Kress, Hayat Al-Khatib, Roy Kam, and Kuan-Chun Tsai. 2004. Finding the keys to biliteracy: How young children interpret different writing systems. *Language and Education* 18(2). 124–144.

Kibler, Amanda. 2010. Writing through two languages: First language expertise in a language minority classroom. *Journal of Second Language Writing* 19. 121–142.

Kibler, Amanda. 2011a. Understanding the "mmhm": Dilemmas in talk between teachers and adolescent emergent bilingual students. *Linguistics and Education* 22. 213–232.

Kibler, Amanda. 2011b. "I write it in a way that people can read it": How teachers and adolescent writers describe their content area writing. *Journal of Second Language Writing* 20. 211–226.

Krashen, Stephen. 1989. We acquire vocabulary and spelling by reading: Additional evidence for the input hypothesis. *The Modern Language Journal* 73. 440–464.

Lam, Wan Shun. 2000. L2 literacy and design of the self: A case study of a teenager writing on the internet. *TESOL Quarterly* 34(3). 457–483.

Lam, Wan Shun. 2009. Multiliteracies on instant messaging in negotiating local, translocal, and transnational affiliations: A case of an adolescent immigrant. *Reading Research Quarterly* 44(4). 377–97.

Lam, Wan Shun and Enid Rosario-Ramos. 2009. Multilingual literacies in transnational digitally-mediated contexts: An exploratory study of immigrant teens in the US *Language and Education* 23(2). 171–190.

Laman, Tasha and Katie Van Sluys. 2008. Being and becoming: Multilingual writers' practices. *Language Arts* 85(4). 265–274.

Larsen, Ditlev. 2013. Focus on pre-service preparation for ESL writing instruction: Secondary teacher perspectives. In Luciana de Oliveira and Tony Silva (eds.). *L2 Writing in the Secondary Classrooms*, 119–132. New York: Routledge.

Lave, Jean and Etienne Wenger. 1991. *Situated learning: Legitimate peripheral participation*. Cambridge, UK: Cambridge University Press.

Leather, Jonathan and Jet van Dam (eds.). 2003. *Ecology of language acquisition*. London: Kluwer.

Leki, Ilona. 2006. The legacy of freshman composition. In Paul K. Matsuda, Christina Ortmeier-Hooper, and Xiaoye You (eds.) *Politics of second language writing: In search of the promised land*, 59–74. Parlor Press.

Leki, Ilona, Alister Cumming, and Tony Silva. 2008e. *A synthesis of research on L2 writing in English*. Mahwah, NJ: Lawrence Erlbaum.

Lo Bianco, Joseph. 2000. Multiliteracies and multilingualism. In Bill Cope and Mary Kalantzis (eds.) *Multiliteracies: Literacy learning and the design of social futures*, 92–105. South Yarra: Macmillan.

Maguire, Mary and Barbara Graves. 2001. Speaking personalities in primary school children's L2 writing. *TESOL Quarterly* 35(4). 561–93.

Matsuda, Paul K. and Kevin D. Pew. 2002. Early second language writing: An introduction. *Journal of Second Language Writing* 11. 261–268.

Matsuda, Paul K. 2006. The myth of linguistic homogeneity in US college composition. *College English* 68(6). 637–651.

Matsuda, Paul K. and Aya Matsuda. 2009. The erasure of resident ESL writers. In Mark Roberge, Meryl Siegal, and Linda Harklau (eds.) *Generation 1.5 in college composition: Teaching academic writing to US-educated learners of ESL*, 50–64. London: Routledge.

McCarthey, Sarah, Georgia Garcia, Angela Lopez-Velasquez, Shumin Lin, and Yi-Huey Guo. 2004. Understanding writing contexts for English language learners. *Research in the Teaching of English* 38. 351–394.

McEachron, Gail and Ghazala Bhatti. 2005. Language support for immigrant children: A study of state schools in the UK and US. *Language and Curriculum* 18(2). 164–180.

Menken, Kate and Beth Antunez. 2001. An overview of the preparation and certification of teachers working with Limited English Proficient (LEP) students. *ERIC Publications*

Miller, Jennifer. 2000. Language use, identity, and social interaction: Migrant students in Australia. *Research on Language and Social Interaction* 33. 69–100.

Milnes, Terry and Liying Cheng. 2008. Teachers' assessment of ESL students in mainstream classes: Challenges, strategies, and decision-making. *TESL Canada Journal* 25(2). 40–65.

Moll, Luis, Ruth Sáez, and Joel Dworin. 2001. Exploring biliteracy: Two student case examples of writing as a social practice *Elementary School Journal* 101(4). 435–449.

National Center for Education Statistics (NCES). 2012. *English language learners in public schools*. Retrieved from: http://nces.ed.gov/programs/coe/indicator_ell.asp

New London Group. 1996. A pedagogy of multiliteracies: Designing social futures. Harvard Educational Review 6(6). 60–92.

Norton, Bonny. 1997. Language, identity, and the ownership of English. *TESOL Quarterly* 31(3). 409–429.

O'Byrne, Barbara. 2001. Needed: A compass to navigate the multilingual English classroom. *Journal of Adult and Adolescent Literacy* 44(5). 440–449.

Ortmeier-Hooper, Christina. 2008. English may be my second language, but I'm not 'ESL.' *College Composition and Communication* 59(3). 389–419.

Ortmeier-Hooper, Christina. 2010. The shifting nature of identity: Social identity, L2 writers, and high school. In Michelle Cox, Jay Jordan, Christina Ortmeier-Hooper, & Gwen Gray Schwartz (eds.). *Reinventing identities in second language writing*, 5–28. Urbana, IL: NCTE Press.

Ortmeier-Hooper, Christina. 2013. *The ELL writer: Moving beyond basics in the secondary classroom*. New York: Teachers College Press.

Ortmeier-Hooper, Christina and Enright, Kerry Anne. 2011. Mapping new territory: Toward an understanding of adolescent L2 writers and writing in US contexts. *Journal of Second Language Writing* 20(3). 167–181.

Perez, Bertha and Maria Torres-Guzman. 1992. *Learning in two worlds: An integrated. Spanish/ English biliteracy approach*. New York: Longman.

Qian, Gaoyin and Junlin Pan. 2006. Susanna's way of becoming literate: A case study of literacy acquisition by a young girl from a Chinese immigrant family. *Reading Horizons* 47(1). 75–96.

Reyes, Iliana. 2006. Exploring connections between emergent biliteracy and bilingualism. *Journal of Early Childhood Literacy* 6(3). 267–292.

Reynolds, Dudley. 2002. Learning to make things happen in different ways: Causality in the writing of middle-grade English language learners. *Journal of Second Language Writing* 11(4). 311–28.

Reynolds, Dudley. 2005. Linguistic correlates of second language literacy development: Evidence from middle-grade learner essays. *Journal of Second Language Writing* 14(1). 19–45.

Roozen, Kevin and Angelica Herrera. 2010. "Indigenous interests": Reconciling literate identities across extracurricular and curricular contexts. In Michelle Cox, Jay Jordan, Christina Ortmeier-Hooper, and Gwen Schwartz (eds.), *Reinventing identities in second language writing*, 139–162. Urbana, IL: NCTE Press.

Ruecker, Todd. 2015. *Transiciones: Pathways of Latinas and Latinos writing in high school and college*. Logan, Utah: Utah State University Press.

Samway, Katharine. 2006. *When English language learners write: Connecting research and practice*. Portsmouth, NH: Heinemann.

Seloni, Lisya. 2013. Understanding how pre-service teachers develop a working knowledge of L2 writing: Toward a socioculturally oriented postmethod pedagogy. In Luciana de Oliveira and Tony Silva (eds.). *L2 Writing in the Secondary Classrooms*, 166–189. New York: Routledge.

Smythe, Suzanne and Paul Neufeld. 2010. Podcast time: Negotiating digital literacies and communities of learning in a middle years ELL classroom. *Journal of Adolescent & Adult Literacy* 53. 488–496.

Spycher, Pamela. 2007. Academic writing of adolescent English learners: Learning to use "although." *Journal of Second Language Writing* 16. 238–254.

Street, Brian. 1995. *Social literacies: Critical approaches to literacy in development, ethnography and education*. London: Longman.

Suárez-Orozco, Carola and Marcelo Suárez-Orozco. 2001. *Children of immigration: The developing child*. Cambridge, MA: Harvard University Press.

Tarone, Elaine, Bruce Downing, Andrew Cohen, Susan Gillette, Robin Murie, and Bev Dailey. 1993. The writing of Southeast Asian-American students in secondary school and university. *Journal of Second Language Writing* 2(2). 149–172.

Toohey, Kelleen. 1998. "Breaking them up, taking them away": ESL students in grade 1. *TESOL Quarterly* 32(1). 61–84.

Valdés, Guadalupe. 1998. The world outside and inside schools: Language and immigrant children. *Educational Researcher* 27. 4–18.

Valdés, Guadalupe. 1999. Incipient bilingualism and the development of English language writing abilities in the secondary school. In Christian Faltis and Paula Wolfe (eds.), *So much to say: Adolescents, bilingualism, and ESL in the secondary school*, 138–176. New York, NY: Teachers College Press.

Valdés, Guadalupe. 2003. *Definitions of giftedness: Young interpreters of immigrant backgrounds*. Mahwah, NJ: Erlbaum.

Van Sluys, Katie. 2006. *What if and why?: Literacy invitations for multilingual classrooms*. Portsmouth, NH: Heinemann.

Villalva, Kerry. 2006a. Hidden literacies and inquiry approaches of bilingual high school writers. *Written Communication* 23(1). 91–129.

Villalva, Kerry. 2006b. Reforming high school writing: Opportunities and constraints for generation 1.5 writers. In Paul K. Matsuda, Christina Ortmeier-Hooper, and Xiaoye You (eds.), *Politics of second language writing: In search of the promised land*. West Lafayette, IN: Parlor Press.

Walker, Anne, Jill Shafer, and Michelle Liams. 2004. Not in my classroom: Teachers' attitudes towards English language learners in the mainstream classroom." *NABE Journal of Research and Practice* 2(1). 130–160.

Wenger, Etienne. 1998. *Communities of practice: Learning, meaning, and identity*. Cambridge: Cambridge University Press.

Wilson, Jennifer. 2013. The role of social relationships in the writing of multilingual adolescents. In Luciana de Oliveira and Tony Silva (eds.). *L2 Writing in the Secondary Classrooms*, 87–103. New York: Routledge.

Yi, Youngjoo. 2007. Engaging literacy: A biliterate student's composing practices beyond school. *Journal of Second Language Writing* 16(1). 23–39.

Yi, Youngjoo. 2008. Relay writing in an adolescent online community. *Journal of Adolescent and Adult Literacy* 51(6). 260–270.

Yi, Youngjoo. 2010a. Identity matters: Theories that help explore adolescent multilingual writers and their identities. In Michelle Cox, Jay Jordan, Christina Ortmeier-Hooper, and Gwen Schwartz (eds.) *Reinventing identities in second language*, 303–324. Urbana Champaign, IL: NCTE.

Yi, Youngjoo. 2010b. Adolescent multilingual writer's transitions between in- and out-of-school writing practices. *Journal of Second Language Writing* 19(1). 17–32.

Yi, Youngjoo. 2013. ESOL teachers as writing teachers: From the voices of high school pre-service teachers. In Luciana de Oliveira and Tony Silva (eds.). *L2 Writing in the Secondary Classrooms*, 133–148. New York: Routledge.

Icy Lee
5 EFL writing in schools

1 Introduction

To date, English is the most extensively studied foreign language (FL) around the world. As a result of the global spread of English and the increasing importance of written communications, ranging from informal writing for social networking to more formal writing for academic studies, writing in English as a FL has received more and more attention over the last few decades. This is evidenced by the increasing emphasis placed in EFL writing programs in different educational systems of the world, earlier starting ages for EFL education (Reichelt 2009), as well as the expanded "scope, substance and significance of writing" (Cumming 2009: 216) in EFL education. While research on EFL writing has been burgeoning from the turn of the century, there is an overall lack of primary and secondary school representation (Ortega 2009) (which holds true in the field of L2 writing in general – see Harklau 2011; Leki, Cumming, and Silva 2008; Matsuda and DePew 2002; Ortmeier-Hoope, and Enright 2011). Consequently, we have little knowledge about the theory, research, and pedagogy of EFL writing that affects younger students learning to write in primary and secondary schools. This chapter attempts to redress such an imbalance by focusing on EFL writing in schools. It starts by examining the origin and development of EFL writing in schools. It then provides a critical review of the research literature by examining the major theories, research methods, as well as findings and insights from current research. The chapter concludes by looking ahead to discuss the theory, research, pedagogy, and methodology that should continue to inform our knowledge of EFL writing in schools.

2 Origin and development of research on "EFL writing in schools"

Our current knowledge about L2/EFL school writing is rather limited, originating mostly from research on L1 early literacy development (e.g., Bereiter and Scardamalia 1987; Hunt 1965; Kress 1994) and bilingual education research (Valdes 1992). However, research on bilingualism has tended to put a stronger emphasis on the spoken language, whereas research on biliteracy has focused on the development of reading rather than writing skills. Although recent bilingual literacy research has addressed the issue of writing, it has little interaction with the mainstream L2 writing research (Matsuda and DePew 2002). In general, L2 writing is rarely discussed in relation to K-12 education (i.e. kindergarten, primary, and secondary education) but rather has affinities with composition studies, applied linguistics, second language acquisition, foreign language, as well as college L2 writing studies (Matsuda and DePew 2002). Matsuda and DePew (2002) outline a number of reasons to explain the scarcity of research on L2 school writing, including scholars' lack of familiarity with children's learning environments, the range of external and internal official conditions that have to be met when dealing with children (including access to research participants in school contexts), the difficulties teachers usually face in bringing research in line with their daily teaching routines, and the financial difficulties involved in doing research in school contexts.

Ortega reports that only 6% (10 out of 154) of the empirical studies published in the *Journal of Second Language Writing* (*JSLW*) from 1992–2007 focused on EFL school contexts. Such an under-representation of EFL school writing can be explained by similar reasons put forward by Matsuda and DePew (2002), specifically the general lack of systematic EFL writing instruction in schools and researchers' relative lack of familiarity with the contextual factors that govern the teaching and learning of EFL writing in school settings. In view of earlier starting ages of EFL writing instruction and the increased emphasis on FL writing instruction in general (Reichelt 2009; Reichelt et al. 2012), research into the distinct and unique features of EFL writers and writing in schools, as well as the contextual factors that influence EFL students' writing (such as school-based curricular constraints, educational policies, conditions of writing) will advance our theoretical and pedagogical understandings of L2 writing. EFL students spend a substantial amount of time learning how to write (i.e., learning to write) in schools before entering university. Research on this group of learners is of great significance because it can generate insights about factors that can best promote their writing development, so that they can be better prepared for the demands of high-stakes writing examinations in the FL, university-entrance examinations, as well as college/university writing. Research insights can also inform policy making for EFL writing programs in schools and teachers' instructional practices. Also, in many EFL school contexts, writing to learn (i.e., writing as a means to learn the language) is an important dimension of EFL writing instruction. Research on this can shed light on how the language learning potential of EFL writing can be exploited and maximized (Manchón 2011; Ortega 2012). By focusing on EFL writing research in schools, this book chapter contributes to the expanding scholarship on EFL writing and adds to our currently limited knowledge of EFL writing research in the school context, thus filling a significant void in the literature.

3 Critical interpretation of the existing research in "EFL writing in schools"

Following the footsteps of Ortega (2009), who provides a review of studies on EFL writing published in *JSLW* from 1992–2007, I extend her literature review and examine the publication patterns in *JSLW* in the last 20 years, i.e., from 1992 to 2011, paying specific attention to EFL writing research conducted in schools during the 20-year period 1992–2011. To complete my literature review[1], I also examine empirical studies about EFL writing in schools published in other L2 journals, yielding a total of 72 journal articles in the last 20 years (1992–2011) (including the 17 published in *JSLW*, marked with an asterisk) (see Table 5.1 for a summary). There has been a marked increase in published research on EFL writing in schools from the turn of the century (probably due to earlier starting age of EFL learning in many European and Asian countries and hence larger numbers of school age learners writing in English), with 61 (85%) being published since 2000. It is noteworthy that the bulk of the research is conducted in secondary contexts (i.e., grade 7 and above) as only 12 out of 72 (17%) studies addressed primary EFL learners.

Five major strands of research have emerged from my review of the literature on EFL writing in schools – (1) focus on students; (2) focus on student texts; (3) focus on teaching and learning; (4) focus on assessment and feedback; and (5) focus on writing teacher development. In this section, I provide a critical interpretation of these areas of research. For each strand of research, I identify the major theories that have framed the studies, examine the major methodologies adopted to investigate the key issues, and highlight salient findings of the studies. Where appropriate, I also discuss the implications of major research insights for teaching and learning EFL writing.

---

[1] During my review, I tried my best to include research on EFL writing in schools published in second language writing, second/foreign language learning, and applied linguistics journals in the last 20 years. As some studies about EFL writing may not use EFL as the keyword, and hence might not have appeared in my search of relevant electronic databases, I conducted an additional search through the key journals that have published empirical studies on EFL writing in schools so as to include as many relevant studies as possible. I have to acknowledge, however, that my review reflects my own resource availability (as well as limitations), and I cannot claim that it has exhausted all empirical studies on EFL writing published from 1992–2011.

Tab. 5.1: Studies on EFL writing in schools (1992–2011).

Country	Author (Year)	Participants	Age/Grade of students	Themes	Research type	Data sources	Total
Denmark	Lars Stenius Stæhr (2008)	Secondary students	15–16 / grade 9	Vocabulary size and listening, reading and writing skills	Experimental study	Reading test, listening test, writing test, and vocabulary size test.	1
Finland	Makinen (1992)	Pre-university students	18–19	Topical depth and writing quality in compositions	Descriptive study	Students' compositions	1
France, Korea, Spain, Thailand and Cyprus	Furneaux et al. (2007)	Secondary school teachers	NA	Teacher stance in feedback	Descriptive study	Teachers' comments on one student essay; questionnaire survey	1
Germany	*Reichelt (1997)	Secondary school teachers and students	19–20 / grade 13	Writing instruction at the German Gymnasium	Case study	Classroom observations; interviews; documents	1
Hong Kong	Woo et al. (2011)	Primary-five students and their English teacher	10–11 / grade 5	Wikis to scaffold collaborative writing	Case study	Questionnaires; interviews; students' editing information in wikis	29
	Lee (2011a)	Secondary school teachers	NA	Feedback revolution	Survey	Questionnaires	
	Lee (2011b)	Secondary students	12–13 / grade 7	Formative assessment in writing	Case study	Interviews;; question-naires; classroom observations; meeting notes, field notes	
	Lee (2011c)	Secondary school teachers	NA	Writing teacher education	Case study	Interviews and classroom research data	
	Lee (2011d)	Secondary school teachers	NA	Teacher feedback	Case study	Documents and interviews	
	Tsui & Ng (2010)	Secondary students	NA	Cultural contexts and situated possibilities in teaching writing	Case study	Interviews	

Study	Participants	Age/Grade	Focus	Method	Data sources
*Lee (2010)	Primary and secondary school teachers	NA	Writing teacher education and teacher learning	Case study	Interviews; classroom research reports
Mok (2009)	Secondary students	Grade 7	Critical thinking in English writing classes	Case study	Classroom observation
Lee (2009)	Secondary school teachers	NA	Teachers' beliefs and written feedback practice	Mixed methods	Students' texts; questionnaires; interviews
*Lee (2008a)	Secondary school teachers	NA	Teachers' written feedback practices	Case study	Feedback analysis; interviews
*Lee (2008b)	Secondary students	12–13 / grade 7	Student reactions to teacher feedback	Case study	Questionnaires, checklists. protocols; classroom observations; feedback analysis
Mak & Coniam (2008)	Secondary students	Grade 7	Using wikis to enhance and develop writing skills	Mixed methods	Students' texts; interviews
*Lo & Hyland (2007)	Primary students	NA	Students' engagement and motivation in writing	Case study	Reflective journals; interviews; students' log entries
Lee (2007)	Secondary students	NA	Feedback – Assessment for learning or assessment of learning?	Case study	Teachers' written feedback; interviews
Firkins et al. (2007)	Secondary students	11–18	Teaching writing to low proficiency EFL students	Action research	Interviews; teaching materials; classroom observations; students' texts
Ho (2006)	Primary students	7–9	Process approach	Experimental study	Questionnaires; interviews; writing tests; observations
Lee (2005)	Secondary students	12–18	Students' perceptions of error correction	Survey	Questionnaires; interviews
*Lee (2004)	Secondary students and teachers	Grade 7–13	Teachers' beliefs and performance in error correction	Case study	Questionnaires; interviews; error correction task

Tab. 5.1 (continued)

Country	Author (Year)	Participants	Age/Grade of students	Themes	Research type	Data sources	Total
	Lee (2003)	Secondary school teachers	NA	Teachers' perspectives, practices and problems regarding error feedback	Survey	Questionnaires; telephone interviews	
	Glenwright (2002)	Secondary students and teachers	NA	Effects of benchmarking on writing assessment	Case study	Teacher assessments of students' writing; interviews	
	Sengupta (2000)	Secondary students	15–16 / grade 10	Effects of revision strategy instruction	Experimental study	Writing tests; revision tasks; questionnaires; interviews	
	*Tusi & Ng (2000)	Secondary students	Grades 12 and 13	Peer feedback	Mixed methods	Questionnaire survey; students' texts; teacher and peer comments; interviews	
	Sengupta (1998a)	Secondary students	Grades 10 and 11	Text revision and text improvement	Case study	Students' texts	
	Sengupta (1998b)	Secondary students	NA	Peer feedback	Mixed methods	Self-revisions, peer revisions, students' texts, interviews	
	Lee (1998)	Secondary school teachers	NA	Writing teachers' beliefs and practices	Survey	Questionnaires; interviews;	
	Sengupta & Falvey (1998)	Secondary school teachers	NA	Role of teaching context in teachers' perceptions of L2 writing pedagogy	Case study	Questionnaires; interviews; classroom observations, written protocols; documentary analysis.	

	*Hyland & Milton (1997)	Secondary students	NA	Qualification and certainty in L1 and L2 students' writing	Corpus study	Corpora of essays	
	*Pennington et al. (1996)	Secondary students	NA	HK students' response to process writing	Case study	Classroom observations; questionnaires	
	Pennington et al. (1995)	Secondary school teachers	NA	Factors shaping the introduction of process writing in Hong Kong secondary schools	Case study	Questionnaires	
Hungary	*Kormos (2011)	Secondary students	17 and 18	Task complexity and linguistic and discourse features of narrative writing performance	Descriptive study	Documents: students writing	1
Iceland	Berman (1994)	Secondary students	17–18 / second year of upper-secondary school	Learners' transfer of writing skills between languages	Experimental study	Writing tests	1
India	*Ramanathan (2003)	Students at all levels	K-12	Written textual production and consumption in vernacular and English-medium settings	Ethnographic study	Interviews, classroom observations; documents	1
Iran	Ghahremani – Ghajar & Abdolhamid Mirhosseini (2005)	Secondary school students	16	Dialogue journal writing	Ethnographic study	Informal written interviews, journal entries	1
Israel	Argaman & Abu-Rabia (2002)	Secondary students	12–13 / Grade 7	Language anxiety and reading and writing	Experimental study	Questionnaires; reading; writing tests	1

Tab. 5.1 (continued)

Country	Author (Year)	Participants	Age/Grade of students	Themes	Research type	Data sources	Total
Japan	Kobayakawa (2011)	Secondary students	NA	Writing tasks in Japanese high school English textbooks	Descriptive study	Language textbooks	3
	*Kobayashi & Rinnert (2002)	Secondary students	18–20	Student perceptions of first language literacy instruction and implications for second language writing	Interview study	Interviews	
	Duppenthaler (2002)	Secondary students	Second year students	Effect of different types of written feedback on student motivation	Experimental study	Questionnaires	
Korea	Yi & Kellogg (2006)	Primary students	NA	Reported speech in primary EFL writing	Case study	Dialogic diary writing	1
Morocco	*Blanton (2002)	Primary students	6	L2 literacy acquisition in child–teacher interaction	Ethnographic study	Observations; notes; interviews; videotapes	1
Norway	Olsen (1999)	Secondary students	NA	Errors and compensatory strategies in EFL writing	Descriptive study	Students' texts	1
Poland	*Reichelt (2005)	Teachers and students at various secondary levels	NA	English-language writing instruction in Poland	Case study	Interviews; classroom observations	1
Spain	Whittaker et al. (2011)	Secondary students	15–17	Written discourse development	Experimental study	Writing tests; vocabulary tests	12
	Llach (2010)	Primary and secondary students	Grades 4 and 8	Lexical gap-filling mechanisms	Longitudinal descriptive study	Students' texts	

Study	Population	Age/Level	Focus	Study type	Data
Santos et al. (2010)	Secondary students	15–16	Effects of two types of direct written corrective feedback on noticing and uptake	Experimental study	Students' texts
Martínez Esteban & Roca de Larios (2010)	Secondary students	15 / 3rd year of secondary education	Models as a form of written feedback	Descriptive study	Students' texts
*Roca de Larios et al. (2008)	Secondary students	16–17	Strategic behaviour in the allocation of time to writing processes	Experimental study	Students' texts; think aloud protocols
Bruton (2007a)	Secondary students	NA	Vocabulary learning in collaborative EFL translational writing	Descriptive study	Students translations
Bruton (2007b)	Secondary students	4th year of secondary school	Vocabulary learning from dictionary referencing and language feedback in EFL translational writing	Experimental study	Students' translation tests
Manchón & Roca de Larios (2007)	Students of different proficiency levels	Level 1 secondary students	Planning process of L1 and L2 writing	Experimental study	Think-aloud protocols; retrospective questionnaires
Roca de Larios et al. (2006)	Secondary students	16–17	Generating text in native and foreign language writing	Experimental study	Think-aloud protocols; students' texts
Navés et al. (2005)	Primary and secondary students	Grade 5 – 12	Cross linguistic influence in relation to school grade and language dominance	Descriptive study	Students' texts; questionnaires
Torras & Celaya (2001)	School students	NA	Age-related differences in written production	Experimental study	Students' texts; written and oral tests

Tab. 5.1 (continued)

Country	Author (Year)	Participants	Age/Grade of students	Themes	Research type	Data sources	Total
	Roca de Larios et al. (2001)	Secondary and university students and university graduates	16–17 / 3rd year of secondary education	Formulation processes in L1 and L2 writing	Experimental study	Think-aloud protocols; questionnaires	
Switzerland	Miller & Sullivan (2008)	Secondary students	14 / Grade 7	Psycholinguistic dimension of EFL writing	Descriptive study	Computer logging; students' texts	2
	Lindgren & Sullivan (2003)	Swedish 13-year-olds female writers	13	Stimulated recall as a trigger for increasing noticing and language awareness	Case study	Stimulated recall; computer logging; students' texts	
Taiwan	Hwang et al. (2011)	Secondary students	Grade 3	Multimedia web annotation system and its effect on writing	Experimental study	Learning tests; students' annotations; question-naire survey; interviews	6
	Chien (2011)	Secondary students	Grade 12	Discourse organization in writing	Descriptive study	Students' texts; interviews	
	*He & Wang (2009)	Primary students	7 / Grade 1	Invented spelling and its relation with phonological awareness and grapheme-phoneme principles	Case study	Students' texts; interviews; students' read aloud	
	Chang et al., (2009)	Primary students	Grade 2	Self and peer proofreading in EFL writing	Descriptive study	Students' texts; revisions; questionnaires	
	Chang et al., (2008)	Primary students	Grade 1	Writing activities and four language skills	Case study	Field notes; classroom tapes; discussions with the instructor	
	Yang & Chen (2007)	Secondary students	Grade 10	Technology-enhanced language learning	Case study	Questionnaires; interviews; e-mails; document analysis	

Country	Study	Participants	Age/Grade	Focus	Design	Instruments	N
The Netherlands	*Stevenson et al. (2006)	Junior high school students	13–14	Online writing revisions in L1 and F1	Experimental study	Students' texts	6
	Snellings et al. (2004)	Secondary students	14–15 / Grade 9	Lexical retrieval on L2 writing	Experimental study	Vocabulary tests	
	Schoonen et al. (2011)	Secondary students	13–14 / Grade 8	Development of L1 and EFL writing proficiency	Experimental study	Writing tests; vocabulary test; grammatical knowledge tests	
	Gelderen et al. (2011)	Secondary students	Grade 10–11	Lexical fluency in writing	Experimental study	Writing tests	
	Schoonen et al. (2003)	Secondary students	Grade 8	The role of linguistic fluency, linguistic knowledge and metacognitive knowledge in writing	Experimental study	Writing tests; grammatical knowledge tests; other knowledge tests	
	Snellings et al. (2002)	Secondary students	14–15 / Grade 9	Lexical retrieval in writing	Experimental study	Vocabulary test; lexical decision and picture-naming tasks	
Vietnam	Hudson et al. (2009)	Pre-service teachers in upper secondary schools	NA	Mentoring EFL pre-service teachers in EFL writing	Survey	Questionnaires	1
Total							**72**

NA = not available;
* = Published in the *Journal of Second Language Writing*

3.1 Focus on students

The first line of research that focuses on the EFL school writers concerns the composing process, contributed primarily by the large-scale research programs conducted with secondary learners in Spain (e.g., Manchón and Roca de Larios 2007; Roca de Larios, Manchón, and Murphy 2006; Roca de Larios, Manchón, and Murphy 2008; Roca de Larios, Marín, and Murphy 2001) and the Netherlands (e.g., Schoonen et al. 2011; Snellings, van Gelderen, and de Glopper 2004; Stevenson, Schoonen, and de Glopper 2006). The research is primarily cognitively oriented, drawing upon the influential model of L1 writing process proposed by Flower and Hayes (1981), and mainly adopts experimental and longitudinal research to investigate different aspects of EFL students' composing processes (see Chapter 13, this *Handbook*).

Research conducted in Spain by Manchón and her colleagues (Manchón and Roca de Larios 2007; Roca de Larios, Manchón, and Murphy 2006; Roca de Larios, Manchón, and Murphy 2008) has focused on EFL writers' problem-solving strategies during composing, such as planning, formulation, and revising, as well as temporal analysis of the formulation process during composing. The findings suggest that in timed essay writing, EFL writers of all proficiency levels spend much more time on formulation than planning and revision, but less proficient EFL writers tend to spend even more time (over 80%) on formulation. As EFL writers reach a threshold level of writing competence, they are able to strike a balance among the three cognitive activities of planning, formulating, and revising. Proficiency appears to have an influence on the type of formulation problems the writers pose, with less proficient students being more preoccupied with using searching strategies to compensate for their interlanguage deficits than more proficient learners (Roca de Larios et al. 2006). Research in the Netherlands has investigated the relative importance of linguistic fluency, linguistic knowledge, and metacognitive knowledge in L1 and EFL writing (Schoonen et al. 2003; Schoonen et al. 2011), as well as lexical retrieval (Snellings, van Gelderen, and de Glopper 2002; Snellings, van Gelderen, and de Glopper 2004) among Dutch secondary students. The studies by the research team led by Schoonen show that linguistic processing plays an essential role in EFL writing because when students engage in writing, they have to look for the right expressions, and as a result, less attention is devoted to conceptual processing that focuses on content and text structure. Compared with L1 writing, FL writing is more strongly correlated to linguistic fluency and linguistic knowledge. While both L1 and FL writing depends on metacognitive and linguistic knowledge, metacognitive knowledge appears to play a more important role in L1 than FL writing. Several studies have focused specifically on lexical retrieval as a subprocess in L2 writing. The study by Snellings, van Gelderen, and de Glopper (2002), for instance, demonstrates that experimental intervention in the form of computerized training in lexical retrieval (using computer-assisted exercise where Dutch secondary students received immediate feedback on speed and correctness on words) can lead to improved lexical retrieval speed and greater frequency and accuracy in the use of trained words. However, there is no evidence to show that improving fluency on lexical retrieval impacts positively on overall writing quality (Snellings, van Gelderen, and de Glopper 2004). The Spain- and Netherlands-based research has made a significant contribution to EFL writing research, though more research is warranted to explore issues of cross-linguistic transfer – e.g., when dissimilar languages and cultures are involved. One important pedagogical implication is that EFL writing teachers can make school students become more aware of their own composing processes, help them with formulating ideas, and enhance their problem-solving strategies, so that composing can be made more effective and efficient for learners of different proficiency levels. Less proficient EFL learners in particular can be given more help with formulation and problem-solving strategies that deal with ideational or textual issues.

Another line of research on EFL writers addresses the issue of beginning age for learning EFL writing. The study by Torras and Celaya (2001), framed by psycholinguistic research on age factors in the development of bilingualism, investigates the writing performance of two groups of Catalonian students beginning to learn EFL at the age of 8 and 11 respectively. The results of the experimental study show that students who begin to learn English as a FL at an older age seem to write better than those who start learning English at a younger age. This could be explained by the fact that older learners are more mature cognitively and are better able to benefit from their L1 literacy skills and the learning strategies taught in school. However, two recent case studies conducted in Taiwan have demonstrated the benefits of introducing EFL writing to beginning EFL learners in the first and second grades. Chang, Chang, and Hsu (2008) show that an early introduction of writing (comprising mainly fun writing activities) to grade one students can change young primary students' attitudes to EFL writing, facilitate the development of their writing skills, and foster their reading, speaking and listening skills. In a similar vein, the same authors (Chang, Chang, and Hsu 2009) have demonstrated the benefits of early starting age for learning EFL writing, since the second graders in their study are able to benefit from self- and peer-proofreading, develop positive attitudes to these activities, and enhance their grammar awareness. As more and more EFL learners in the world are learning English at a younger age, and writing programs are being delivered to students at a younger age, such findings are valuable but need to be substantiated by more research, especially research with learners speaking different native languages, of different proficiency levels, and from different educational contexts.

3.2 Focus on student texts

The second major strand identified in the research literature focuses specifically on the written texts produced by EFL writers, including lexical, grammatical, and discourse features of EFL writers' texts. Such research mainly draws upon theories in vocabulary acquisition, contrastive rhetoric, and cross-linguistic influence, making use of textual analysis to investigate the characteristics of EFL students' writing. Overall, the studies demonstrate the important role vocabulary, grammar and discourse play in EFL writers' writing. In terms of vocabulary, Naves and Celaya (2005) have found that in multilingual contexts, older and more proficient EFL (Catalan-Spanish) learners use fewer lexical inventions and borrowings in FL writing than younger and less proficient learners, suggesting that with students' growth in language proficiency they are less reliant on L1 in writing. However, since the texts produced by L1 and EFL writers differ mostly in lexical variety, sophistication and range, as shown in the Hungary-based study by Kormos (2011), it is important for EFL writing classes to focus on lexical development even for higher-proficiency learners. Grammatical proficiency, as demonstrated in Olsen's (1999) study conducted in Norway, also plays an important role in EFL students' writing development. Due to cross-linguistic influence EFL learners of lower proficiency make more grammatical, orthographic and syntactical errors in writing, and they resort to their first language more often than their more proficient counterparts. As EFL learners' lack of exposure to the target language can impede their learning of FL writing, exposing less proficient EFL learners to the target language (e.g., through extensive reading) can help them reduce their grammatical, orthographic, and syntactic errors in writing. Also, grammatical proficiency in the target language is found to facilitate transfer of discourse skills from L1 to FL, as suggested in Berman's (1994) study where secondary EFL students in Iceland are able to transfer essay organization skills from L1 (Icelandic) to FL (English).

Research on EFL student texts shows that attention to the discourse level is important, too. Makinen's (1992) study with Finnish pre-university students has found that more proficient EFL learners are better at developing their topics in writing and there is a clear relationship between topical structure and overall coherence in writing, In Spain, research by Whittaker, Llinares, and McCabe (2011) based on a longitudinal textual analysis of secondary students' writing has shown that the development in EFL students' writing is evidenced by improvement in textual cohesion and overall coherence in their writing, which can be attributed to their continuing exposure to English and their cognitive maturity. Hyland and Milton's (1997) study about the use of doubt and certainty markers (as part of pragmatic competence) in writing has shown that Hong Kong EFL learners rely on a narrow range of items (mainly modal verbs and adverbs) in expressing doubt and certainty in their school writing. They tend to use simpler syntactical constructions and display more problems in expressing preciseness in certainty statements. To conclude, whereas an explicit focus on the development of topics in writing can help EFL students achieve better coherence in writing (Makinen 1992), explicit instruction in the textual features of writing (e.g., register and coherence) can lead to substantial gains in students' improvement in writing (Whittaker, Llinares, and McCabe 2011).

Explicit instruction can also be adopted to help EFL students become familiar with relevant discourse conventions and raise their awareness of ways to convey different degrees of doubt and certainty in writing (Hyland and Milton 1997).

3.3 Focus on teaching and learning

A number of studies have homed in on the EFL writing classroom, exploring different aspects of the teaching and learning of writing, drawing on process and genre theories of writing, collaborative learning theory, and sociocultural theory of learning. Such classroom-based research mainly relies on the case study and mixed method approach to shed light on the exigencies in the writing classroom.

A few studies have focused on the process-oriented classroom, specifically what happens in the process writing classroom when teachers attempt to bring innovation to traditional product-oriented practice (e.g., Pennington and Cheung 1995; Sengupta 1998a, 2000). While Ho's (2006) study in Hong Kong primary classrooms shows positive results of a process writing program in improving students' writing skills and attitude towards writing, the study by Pennington, Brock, and Brock (1996) has produced mixed results regarding Hong Kong secondary students' reactions to process pedagogy – due to factors such as students' proficiency level, teachers' attitude to process writing, and their pedagogical competence in implementing the innovation. Hong Kong students seem to hold entrenched beliefs about teacher and student roles in the writing classroom, as their experience with peer evaluation (as part of the writing process) has failed to alter their perception of the important role the teacher plays as reader and evaluator of student writing (Sengupta 1998b; Tsui and Ng 2000). To adopt process pedagogy and peer evaluation effectively in EFL classrooms, Tsui and Ng (2010) remind us of the importance for teachers to respond to situated possibilities of learning when engaging students in peer review during the writing process – e.g., by capitalizing on the Chinese cultural tradition that values the "self-group relationship" ("self" as the small self and "group" as the large self – based on the Chinese maxim "Sacrifice the small self for the sake of the large self"), of which group harmony is one essential aspect. Overall, these studies on process writing and peer evaluation suggest that applying Western methodologies to periphery communities can be problematic, and that it is crucial to take account of the sociocultural dimension of different EFL contexts to maximize the effectiveness of innovations.

Compared with process pedagogy, there is scant research on genre pedagogy in the EFL school context. Research by Firkins, Forey, and Sengupta (2007) with Hong Kong low-proficiency students shows that an instructional approach based on systemic functional linguistics (consisting of modeling, joint construction, and independent construction of texts) can help students organize their writing and is an effective way to teach low proficiency EFL students to write. More research on a genre approach or a process-genre approach is warranted.

As more and more educational systems in EFL contexts have become technology-driven, research on the use of technologies to enhance the teaching and learning of EFL writing has been growing in recent years. Most of such work has investigated the application of Web 2.0 technology (e.g., wikis) in the EFL writing classroom, its impact on learning, as well as teachers' and students' perceptions of the integration of technology in the writing classroom (Mak and Coniam 2008; Woo et al. 2011). Through working collaboratively with wikis in Hong Kong secondary classrooms, the writing experience is made more authentic and engaging, and students are able to produce longer and more coherent texts (Mak and Coniam 2008). Also conducted in Hong Kong, Woo et al. (2011) show that even grade 5 primary learners are receptive to the use of wikis to help them write and engage in online collaborative work. Students enjoy using the wiki and think it helps them write better and work better as a team, and more active students are willing to spend more time on the writing project and get better writing scores. Using learning activities supported by Virtual Pen, a multimedia web annotation system, the study conducted by Hwang, Shadiev, and Huang (2011) in Taiwan shows that the technology-enhanced writing classroom can facilitate secondary students' writing performance (also see Yang and Chen 2007). Students are able to practice writing in an asynchronous learning environment, which gives them enough time to engage with the learning material and develop content. Overall, the findings generated by these studies are promising, suggesting that EFL teachers can make better and further use of technology to promote elementary and secondary students' writing development.

There are studies that address other aspects of the teaching and learning of writing, like student motivation, engagement, and higher-order thinking. Such research has been conducted against the backdrop of traditional EFL writing classrooms, which are teacher-dominated, product-centered, quantity-driven, and examination-oriented. Lo and Hyland (2007) report on a new writing program developed for grade 5 primary students in Hong Kong, which takes into account students' interests and needs by strengthening pre-writing input, involving students in classroom discussion and sharing of ideas, and emphasizing post-writing activities and peers as audiences. The results show that the entire writing experience is perceived as more "collaborative, meaningful, purposeful, and motivating for the students" (Lo and Hyland 2007: 224). There are studies that attend to issues of voice, self-reflection and critical thinking in writing. Focusing on Iranian high school students' self-reflective writing ability, Ghahremani-Ghajar and Mirhosseini (2005) demonstrate that dialogue journal writing is a powerful language education activity that can empower EFL learners, provide them with opportunities to express their voice, and lead to gains in their self-reflective writing ability. Mok (2009), using classroom observation data in Hong Kong secondary writing classrooms, concludes that teachers fail to motivate students and create the space of learning that takes into consideration students' critical thinking. Causes include ineffective questioning techniques (that focus mainly on lower order questions), lack of attention to the writing process, as well as a teacher-dominated, product-centered, and quantity-driven approach that encourages a surface approach to learning. Together, these studies have demonstrated that apart from writing pedagogies, issues like students' motivation, engagement, critical thinking, and self-reflection are pertinent to the EFL writing classroom and merit attention.

3.4 Focus on assessment and feedback

Another line of research on EFL writing in schools has focused on assessment and feedback. Such research is framed by theories in SLA, L2 composition, and assessment for learning, using mainly the case study design involving questionnaires, interviews, and document analysis (e.g., analysis of teacher feedback), as well as the experimental design to look into various aspects of error correction.

In general, EFL classroom writing assessment is found to be predominantly language-focused. Furneaux, Paran, and Fairfax (2007) show that the majority of EFL secondary teachers' in Cyprus, France, Korea, Spain, and Thailand play the role of language teachers when they respond to student writing, paying much less attention to content and ideas. They focus inordinately on grammar in their feedback and largely assume the provider role, i.e., providing correct answers for students. Such findings are corroborated by Lee's (2004, 2005, 2008a, 2008b) research in Hong Kong secondary classrooms, where teachers are found to use a narrow range of error feedback strategies in responding to student writing. They rely mainly on direct error feedback (i.e., underlining errors and providing correct answers) and mark errors comprehensively. Students prefer teachers to mark all errors (Lee 2005), and their beliefs are shown to be in line with teachers' practices, suggesting that students' beliefs, preferences, and expectations are possibly shaped by teachers' practices. It is rather surprising to note that almost half of the teachers' corrections in Lee's (2004) study are inaccurate or unnecessary. As badly done corrections can harm students' writing development (Ferris 1999), teachers need to rethink their error-focused approach to feedback, involve students more actively in the error feedback process, and receive training in error correction.

While most L2 feedback research has focused on using feedback to facilitate students' learning of writing (i.e., learning-to-write), recent research conducted in Spain approaches the topic from a different perspective both theoretically and methodologically – focusing on the writing-to-learn potential of corrective feedback and using an experimental design. The study by Santos, Serrano, and Manchón (2010) compares the effects of error correction (correcting errors related to grammar, vocabulary and textual cohesion) and reformulation (rewriting student texts to make them sound as native-like as possible without changing original meaning) on noticing (amount of corrections noticed) and uptake (accurate revisions) among secondary students in Spain. While error correction has positive effects on both noticing and uptake, it appears to have a clear advantage over reformulation in terms of student uptake. Specifically, Martínez Esteban and Roca de Larios (2010) demonstrate that models as a form of written feedback could help secondary Spanish students notice their gaps in writing and facilitate their revision (also see Coyle and Roca de Larios 2014). The Spain-based research, which addresses the language learning potential of feedback, suggests that different forms of corrective feedback can have a role to play in aiding EFL students' interlanguage development, and further exploration along this line is needed.

Another emphasis emanating from research on assessment and feedback concerns the tensions and contradictions EFL writing teachers face in assessing and giving feedback to student writing. For example, there are huge discrepancies between teachers' beliefs and practices regarding feedback (Lee 2009a), as well as a gulf between their practices and recommended principles (Lee 2008a). Although teachers believe that they should be helping students become independent in self-editing, for instance, their feedback practices encourage a totally passive attitude among students, as they busy themselves with catching every single error for students. While teachers do not find their feedback practices effective and may ponder the possibility of change, they feel constrained by a host of contextual factors that make innovation difficult, if not impossible. Their feedback practices are deeply influenced by the sociocultural and sociopolitical contexts of their work, requiring them to mark all written errors in order to fulfill the school's internal appraisal system (Lee 2008a). It is equally difficult for teachers to implement assessment for learning (i.e., using assessment to promote learning and improve teaching) in EFL writing classrooms, which are mostly dominated by the examination culture. In Hong Kong, teachers' attempts to implement assessment for learning in classroom writing (Lee 2011a, 2011b) have yielded mixed results, uncovering a range of school (e.g., entrenched beliefs about the primacy of comprehensive error feedback) and systemic issues (e.g., examination-driven system) that have to be addressed (Lee and Coniam 2013). While assessment for learning has potential to improve student motivation and learning of writing, it is the contextual and sociocultural aspect of teachers' work that poses impediments to assessment innovation. As pointed out by Enright and Gilliland (2011) and Reichelt (1997, 2005), rich insights about L2/EFL school writing can be gained from an in-depth investigation into the broader educational and sociocultural contexts that govern writing teachers' work.

3.5 Focus on writing teacher development

More recently, informed by L2 writing and teacher education research, some studies have focused on the development of EFL writing teachers, though this is an under-developed area. In a special issue on writing teacher education in *JSLW*, Hirvela and Belcher (2007) call for more research on L2 writing teacher education to find out how teachers teach writing and what teacher education can do to cater for the needs of writing teachers. In their survey of Vietnamese pre-service teachers, Hudson, Nguyen, and Hudson (2009) have found that the large majority of pre-service teachers feel that mentoring for learning how to teach writing is inadequate. Lee's (2010b, 2011c) case studies reveal that even in-service teachers in Hong Kong are under-prepared to teach writing. Teachers are faced with problems and challenges in teaching writing, as they find it difficult to implement what they have learnt from teacher education programs. However, Lee's findings show that teacher education can have a positive impact on teacher learning. It is therefore important that teacher educators respond to the needs of teachers by helping them grapple with challenges arising from their work contexts.

4 Where do we go from here?

Having examined the key issues in the research literature on EFL writing in schools over the past two decades, the salient research findings, and practical implications, in this concluding section I look ahead by reflecting critically on some possible directions for future development, hopefully to build on current achievements and explore new frontiers and advance knowledge of EFL writing in schools. In this regard, I propose four areas that will continue to inform theory, research and pedagogy in EFL writing in schools, and I conclude this section with suggestions of alternative methodologies for research on EFL writing in schools.

4.1 Diversity and context

While the literature review in the preceding section has pointed to some commonalities in the needs of EFL learners and in the concerns of EFL teachers and researchers, it has also uncovered differences and diversity across cultural and educational contexts. Ortega (2009) rightly says that "each context comes with its own history and its own cultural and social values and constraints" and that good EFL writing research is built on our knowledge of writing that is "fully contextualized and capitalizes on diversity" (p. 250). Writing is not only an individual, cognitive process but also a socially situated activity that cannot be separated from its socio-cultural context. EFL school writing, for instance, is often affected by contextual constraints such as large class sizes and the examination-oriented culture (Leki 2001). Apart from approaching writing from cognitive and psycholinguistic perspectives, future research has to take cognizance of both context and diversity, as well as the interaction between cognitive, social and sociocultural factors (Riazi 1997). As such, sociocultural theory can have an increasingly important role to play in research on EFL writing in schools. Specifically, activity theory as a sub-theory of sociocultural theory originating from Vygotsky (1978, 1987) and further expanded by Leontťev (1978) and Engeström (1987), can be utilized to shed light on writing as an activity system, and how it is mediated by rules (i.e., norms and sanctions), community (i.e., participants), and division of labor (i.e., how teacher and student roles are distributed). Activity systems parallel Casanave's (2009) call for an ecological perspective (also originating from sociocultural theory) in future EFL writing research. An ecological framework can supplement the cognitive, linguistic, and technological approaches to EFL writing research and enable us to examine the "local conditions of learning and teaching" (Casanave 2009: 257).

4.2 Classroom practices

EFL teachers' continuing quest for suitable pedagogical approaches for school students has hitherto been influenced by center pedagogies, such as process writing and peer review. While research can continue to investigate the implementation of these center pedagogies in various EFL contexts and the tensions arising consequently, it is important to focus on the institutional and sociocultural contexts in which these pedagogies take place and to investigate how these pedagogies can be adapted to suit the needs of different learners in different contexts. Future EFL writing research will benefit from a focus on the ecological realities of teaching and learning in local contexts and provide insights into how EFL writing teachers can blend idealism and realism in their teaching contexts.

In terms of assessment and feedback, research has pointed to a missing link between assessment, teaching, and learning, where error-focused feedback approaches dominate the lives of teachers and learners and yet contribute little to the improvement of learning. Further and deeper understanding of issues about error correction and teacher feedback will require a more in-depth, ethnographic and ecological approach to gather insights into unresolved issues in relation to feedback and assessment for learning. Lee's studies (2008a, 2009a, 2011a, 2011b) point to a possible "culprit" that thwarts innovation in feedback and assessment for learning – namely, the need to respond to all written errors in student writing. Given this, and in spite of practical difficulties and possible ethical concerns, it would be helpful to conduct (quasi) experimental research on the effects of focused (i.e., selective error feedback) versus unfocused corrective feedback (i.e., comprehensive error feedback) (see Van Beuningen, De Jong, and Kuiken 2008; van Beuningen 2010). If it is found that comprehensive error feedback is unhelpful in EFL school contexts, such findings can provide useful information to guide teachers' decision making with regard to the extent of error feedback (Bitchener 2012). Future research could also investigate the use of alternative feedback techniques which are more textual in nature, such as the use of reformulations and model texts, and further explore the language learning potential of feedback, i.e., feedback for acquisition, in addition to feedback for accuracy (Bitchener 2012; Manchón 2009, 2011). More broadly, future research should investigate the teaching, learning and assessment processes conducive to writing-to-learn as a whole in order to maximize the language learning potential of EFL writing.

The growing importance of technology in the EFL writing classroom, as well as the rise of new literacies (Lankshear 1997; Lankshear and Knobel 2006), is another area that merits attention. The place of digital multimodal texts can be explored to find out how images, sound, and music can be combined with texts to create digital artifacts in the EFL writing classroom (Hull and Nelson 2005) – to enable students to practice integrated skills, provide opportunities for creative writing, encourage reflection and higher-order thinking, and above all, develop students' multimedia literacy. As suggested by Cumming (2009), the notion of literacy has to be expanded in future studies of EFL writing, and this is also true of research conducted in school contexts.

4.3 Writing teacher education

Research on writing teachers' professional development and writing teacher education is in its infancy. At least three areas are important for future studies of EFL writing teacher education. First, research can focus on how writing teacher education programs can be better designed to prepare teachers for teaching writing in EFL schools. Second, given the central role of assessment in promoting learning and teaching, future research on writing teacher education should place a stronger emphasis on EFL teachers' assessment capacity and literacy in writing, including how to prepare them to respond to writing more effectively. This line of research would be particularly fruitful in EFL contexts whose curricula are examination-driven. Third, the growing popularity of technology in writing and the rise of new literacies (e.g., blog writing, wikis, chat rooms, multimodal texts) has made it necessary for teachers to develop a broader perspective of the notion of literacy and enhance their preparedness to teach writing through technology (Cumming 2009), so that they can help students develop new kinds of literacies such as multimedia literacy.

4.4 Primary writing

While the abovementioned areas of further research can be applied to all levels in the school context, research with primary schoolchildren is an area that is in need of future development. Currently, EFL writing is introduced at an early age in many countries but the bulk of EFL school writing research is conducted with secondary learners. As a result, relatively little information has been gathered about younger EFL learners, their teachers and their learning contexts. There are indeed many areas which researchers can turn to in order to learn more about the host of issues posed in the preceding sections in 4.1 to 4.3, particularly how primary learners can be helped to write to learn and to learn to write in a FL.

4.5 Alternative methodologies

To better reflect issues of diversity and context and to explore the whole range of issues concerning classroom practice, future research of EFL writing in schools should make greater use of in-depth ethnographic studies and longitudinal research to investigate issues over longer periods of time, incorporating an ecological perspective and zeroing in on the conditions of learning and teaching specific to the contexts under investigation. More attention should be given to observational data (to supplement other data sources such as self-report data) to illuminate the teaching, learning, and assessment processes in the classroom. To gather in-depth data about the teaching and learning of EFL writing, narrative inquiry as a qualitative method can be used to investigate the lived experiences of EFL teachers and students, making use of data sources such as autobiographies, written reflections, interviews, and conversations. In spite of the constraints school teachers face in conducting classroom-based research, to generate knowledge useful for the practitioners themselves more teacher research and action research should be encouraged. The concept of "teacher as researcher" may be less familiar to school teachers than university teachers, but the insights garnered from teacher research is of particular value and relevance to frontline teachers, and as such, it should be promoted. Both emic and etic perspectives are useful and can continue to inform research on EFL school writing, particularly in primary contexts.

5 Conclusion

School is a special and unique context, and in order to yield rich and comprehensive knowledge about EFL writing in schools it is important to adopt a synthetic approach in research where both the parts and the whole are factored into the research design (Ortmeier-Hooper and Enright 2011). Given this, research can focus on the individual learner, the student text, the classroom, and the teacher, situated within the broader institutional, sociocultural, and sociopolitical contexts that frame the pertinent issues under investigation. As reminded by Leki, Cumming, and Silva (2008), cultural factors figure prominently in L2 writing research and such factors cannot be ignored in research on EFL writing in school contexts. Research on EFL writing in schools is also going to benefit from a cross-disciplinary approach, with EFL writing research conducted in other fields of inquiry, such as SLA, psycholinguistics, cognitive psychology, sociolinguistics, text linguistics, computer-mediated language learning, and teacher education. It is hoped that burgeoning research on EFL writing in schools, particularly in primary contexts, across disciplinary boundaries will further advance theories and practices in L2 writing and bring new knowledge and new insights to benefit the teaching and learning of writing in EFL schools.

6 Additional sources

Agustín-Llach, M. Pilar. 2010. Lexical gap-filling mechanisms in foreign language writing. *System* 38(4). 529–538.

Blanton, Linda. 2002. Seeing the invisible: Situating L2 literacy acquisition in child-teacher interaction. *Journal of Second Language Writing* 11. 295–310.

Bruton, Anthony. 2007. Vocabulary learning from dictionary referencing and language feedback in EFL translational writing. *Language Teaching Research* 11(4). 413–431.

Cimasko, Tony and Melinda Reichelt. 2011. *Foreign language writing instruction: Principles and practices*. West Lafayette, IN: Parlor Press.

He, Tung-hsien and Wen-lien Wang. 2009. Invented spelling of EFL young beginning writers and its relation with phonological awareness and grapheme-phoneme principles. *Journal of Second Language Writing* 18. 44–56.

Kobayashi, Hiroe and Carol Rinnert. 2002. High school student perception of first language literacy instruction: implications for second language writing. *Journal of Second Language Writing* 11(2). 91–116.

Lee, Icy. 2003. L2 writing teachers' perspectives, practices and problems regarding error feedback. *Assessing Writing* 8(3). 216–237.

Lindgren, Eva and Kirk P. H. Sullivan. 2003. Stimulated recall as a trigger for increasing noticing and language awareness in the L2 writing classroom: A case study of two young female writers. *Language Awareness* 12(3–4). 172–186.

Miller, Karen and Kirk P. H. Sullivan. 2008. The psycholinguistic dimension in second language writing: Opportunities for research and pedagogy using computer keystroke logging. *TESOL Quarterly* 42(3). 433–454.

Sengupta, Sima and Peter Falvey. 1998. The role of the teaching context in Hong Kong English teachers' perceptions of L2 writing pedagogy. *Evaluation and Research in Education* 12(2). 72–95.

7 References

Bereiter, Carl and Marlene Scardamalia. 1987. *The psychology of written composition*. Hillsdale, NJ: Lawrence Erlbaum Associates.

Berman, Robert. 1994. Learners' transfer of writing skills between languages. *TESL Canada Journal*. 12. 29–46.

Bitchener, John. 2012. A reflection on 'the language learning potential' of written CF. *Journal of Second Language Writing*. 21. 348–363.

Casanave, Christine Pearson. 2009. Training for writing or training for reality? Challenges facing EFL writing teachers and students in language teacher education programs. In Rosa M. Manchón (ed.), *Writing in foreign language contexts: Learning, teaching, and research*, 256–277. Bristol, UK: Multilingual Matters.

Chang, Fang-Chi, Shu Chang, and Hsiu-Fen Hsu. 2008. Writing activities as stimuli for integrating the four language skills in EFL grade-one classes in Taiwan. *English Teaching and Learning*. 32. 115–154.

Chang, Fang-Chi and Hsiu-Fen Hsu. 2009. Self- and peer-proofreading for EFL young beginning writers. *Taiwan Journal of TESOL*. 6(1). 1–29.

Coyle, Yvette and Julio Roca de Larios. 2014. Exploring the role played by error correction and models on children's reported noticing and output production in an L2 writing task. *Studies in Second Language Acquisition* 36. 451–485.

Cumming, Alister. 2009. The contribution of studies of foreign language writing to research, theory, and policies. In Rosa M. Manchón (ed.), *Writing in foreign language contexts: Learning, teaching, and researching*, 209–231. Clevedon, UK: Multilingual Matters.

Engeström, Yrjö. 1987. *Learning by expanding: An activity theoretical approach to developmental research*. Helsinki: Orienta-Konsultit.

Enright, Kerry Anne and Betsy Gilliland. 2011. Multilingual writing in an age of accountability: From policy to practice in US high school classrooms. *Journal of Second Language Writing* 20(3). 182–195.

Esteban Noelia and Julio Roca de Larios. 2010. The use of models as a form of written feedback to secondary school pupils of English. *International Journal of English Studies* 10. 143–170.

Ferris, Dana. 1999. The case of grammar correction in L2 writing classes: A response to Truscott (1996). *Journal of Second Language Writing* 8. 1–11.

Firkins, Arthur, Gail Forey, and Sima Sengupta. 2007. Teaching writing to low proficiency EFL students.
ELT Journal 64. 341–352.

Flower, Linda and John Hayes. 1981. A cognitive process theory of writing. *College Composition and Communication* 32. 365–387.

Furneaux, Clare, Amos Paran, and Beverly Fairfax. 2007. Teacher stance as reflected in feedback on student writing: An empirical study of secondary school teachers in five countries. *International Review of Applied Linguistics in Language Teaching* 45. 69–94.

Ghahremani-Ghajar, Sue-san and Seyyed Abdolhamid Mirhosseini. 2005. English class or speaking about everything class: Dialogue journal writing as a critical literacy practice in an Iranian High school. *Language, Culture and Curriculum* 18. 286–299.

Harklau, Linda. 2011. Commentary: Adolescent L2 writing research as an emerging field. *Journal of Second Language Writing* 20. 227–230.

Hirvela, Alan and Diane Belcher. 2007. Writing scholars as teacher educators: Exploring writing teacher education. *Journal of Second Language Writing* 16. 125–128.

Ho, Belinda. 2006. Using the process approach to teach writing in 6 Hong Kong primary classrooms. *New Horizons in Education* 53. 22–41.

Hudson, Peter, Hoa Thi Mai Nguyen, and Sue Hudson. 2009. Mentoring EFL pre-service teachers in EFL writing. *TESL Canada Journal* 27. 85–102.

Hull, Glynda and Mark Evan Nelson. 2005. Locating the semiotic power of multimodality. *Written Communication* 22. 224–260.

Hunt, Kellogg. 1965. *Grammatical structures written at three grade levels*. Champaign, IL: The National Council of Teachers of English.

Hwang, Wu-Yuin, Rustam Shadiev, and Szu-Min Huang. 2011. A study of a multimedia web annotation system and its effect on the EFL writing and speaking performance of junior high school students. *ReCALL* 23. 160–180.

Hyland, Ken and John Milton. 1997. Qualifications and certainty in L1 and L2 students' writing. *Journal of Second Language Writing* 6. 183–205.

Kormos, Judit. 2011. Task complexity and linguistic and discourse features of narrative writing performance. *Journal of Second Language Writing* 20. 148–161.

Kress, Gunther. 1994. *Learning to write* (2nd edition). London: Routledge.

Lankshear, Colin. 1997. *Changing literacies.* Buckingham: Open University Press.

Lankshear, Colin and Michele Knobel. 2006. *New literacies: Everyday practices and classroom learning* (2nd ed.). Buckingham: Open University Press.

Lee, Icy. 1998. Writing in the Hong Kong secondary classroom: Teachers' beliefs and practice. *Hong Kong Journal of Applied Linguistics* 3. 61–76.

Lee, Icy. 2004. Error correction in L2 secondary writing classrooms: The case of Hong Kong. *Journal of Second Language Writing* 13. 285–312.

Lee, Icy. 2005. Error correction in the L2 writing classroom: What do students think? *TESL Canada Journa.* 22. 1–16.

Lee, Icy. 2007. Feedback in Hong Kong secondary writing classrooms: Assessment for learning or assessment of learning? *Assessing Writing* 12. 180–198.

Lee, Icy. 2008a. Understanding teachers' written feedback practices in Hong Kong secondary classrooms. *Journal of Second Language Writing* 17. 69–85.

Lee, Icy. 2008b. Student reactions to teacher feedback in two Hong Kong secondary classrooms. *Journal of Second Language Writing* 17. 144–164.

Lee, Icy. 2009a. Ten mismatches between teachers' beliefs and written feedback practice. *ELT Journal* 63. 13–22.

Lee, Icy. 2009b. A new look at an old problem: How teachers can liberate themselves from the drudgery of marking student writing. *Prospect* 24. 34–41.

Lee, Icy. 2010b. Writing teacher education and teacher learning: Testimonies of four EFL teachers. *Journal of Second Language Writing* 19. 143–157.

Lee, Icy. 2011a. Feedback revolution: What gets in the way? *ELT Journal* 65. 1–12.

Lee, Icy. 2011b. Formative assessment in EFL writing: An exploratory case study. *Changing English: Studies in Culture and Education* 18. 99–111.

Lee, Icy. 2011c. L2 writing teacher education for in-service teachers: Opportunities and challenges. *English in Australia* 46. 31–39.

Lee, Icy and David Coniam. 2013. Introducing assessment for learning for EFL writing in an assessment of learning examination-driven system in Hong Kong. *Journal of Second Language Writing* 22. 34–50.

Leki, Ilona. 2001. Materials, educational, and ideological challenges of teaching EFL writing at the turn of the century. *International Journal of English Studies* 9(2). 197–209.

Leki, Ilona, Alister Cumming, and Tony Silva. 2008. *A synthesis of research on L2 writing in English.* Mahwah, NJ: Lawrence Erlbaum.

Leontťev, Alexei. 1978. *Problems of the development of mind.* Moscow: Progress.

Lo, Julia and Fiona Hyland. 2007. Enhancing students' engagement and motivation in writing: The case of primary students in Hong Kong. *Journal of Second Language Writing* 16. 219–237.

Mak, Barley and David Coniam. 2008. Using wikis to enhance and develop writing skills among secondary school students in Hong Kong. *System* 36. 437–455.

Makinen, Kaarina. 1992. Topical depth and writing quality in student EFL compositions. *Scandinavian Journal of Educational Research* 36. 237–247.

Manchón, Rosa M. 2009. Broadening the perspective of L2 writing scholarship: The contribution of research on foreign language writing. In Rosa M. Manchón (ed.), *Writing in foreign language contexts. Learning, teaching, and research*, 1–19. Clevedon, UK: Multilingual Matters.

Manchón, Rosa M. (ed.). 2011. *Learning-to-write and writing-to-learn in an additional language.* Amsterdam: John Benjamins.

Manchón, Rosa M. and Julio Roca de Larios. 2007. On the temporal nature of planning in L1 and L2 composing. *Language Learning* 57. 549–593.

Martínez-Esteban, Noelia and Julio Roca de Larios. 2010. The use of models as a form of written feedback to secondary school pupils of English. *International Journal of English Studies* 10. 143–170.

Matsuda, Paul K. and Kevin DePew. 2002. Early second language writing: An introduction. *Journal of Second Language Writing* 11. 261–268.

Mok, Jane. 2009. From policies to realities: developing students' critical thinking in Hong Kong secondary school English writing classes. *RELC Journal* 40. 262–279.

Navés, Teresa, Immaculada Miralpeix, and M. Luz Celaya. 2005. Who transfers more ... and what? Crosslinguistic influence in relation to school grade and language dominance in EFL. *International Journal of Multilingualism* 2. 113–134.

Olsen, S. 1999. Errors and compensatory strategies: A study of grammar and vocabulary in texts written by Norwegian learners of English. *System* 27. 191–205.

Ortega, Lourdes. 2009. Studying writing across EFL contexts: Looking back and moving forward. In Rosa M. Manchón (ed.), *Writing in foreign language contexts: Learning, teaching, and research*, 232–255. Clevedon, UK: Multilingual Matters.

Ortega, Lourdes. 2012. Epilogue: Exploring L2 writing–SLA interfaces. *Journal of Second Language Writing*. 21. 404–415.

Ortmeier-Hooper, Christina and Kerry Anne Enright. 2011. Mapping new territory: Toward an understanding of adolescent L2 writers and writing in US contexts. *Journal of Second Language Writing* 20(3). 167–181.

Pennington, Martha, Mark N. Brock, and Francis Yue Brock. 1996. Explaining Hong Kong students' response to process writing: An exploration of causes and outcomes. *Journal of Second Language Writing* 5. 227–252.

Pennington, Martha and Mark Cheung. 1995. Factors shaping the introduction of process writing in Hong Kong secondary schools. *Language, Culture and Curriculum* 8. 1–20.

Reichelt, Melinda. 1997. Writing instruction at the German Gymnasium: A 13th-grade English class writes the Abitur. *Journal of Second Language Writing* 6. 265–291.

Reichelt, Melinda. 2005. English-language writing instruction in Poland. *Journal of Second Language Writing* 14. 215–232.

Reichelt, Melinda. 2009. A critical evaluation of writing teaching programmes in different foreign language settings. In Rosa M. Manchón (ed.), *Writing in foreign language contexts: Learning, teaching, and research*, 183–206. Clevedon, UK: Multilingual Matters.

Reichelt, Melinda, Natalie Lefkowitz, Carol Rinnert, and Jean Marie Schultz. 2012. Key issues in foreign language writing. *Foreign Language Annals* 45. 22–41.

Riazi, Abdolmehdi. 1997. Acquiring disciplinary literacy: A social-cognitive analysis of text production and learning among Iranian graduate students of education. *Journal of Second Language Writing* 6. 105–137.

Roca de Larios, Julio, Rosa M. Manchón, and Liz Murphy. 2006. Generating text in native and foreign language writing: A temporal analysis of problem-solving formulation processes. *The Modern Language Journal* 90. 100–114.

Roca de Larios, Julio, Rosa M. Manchón and Liz Murphy. 2008. The foreign language writer's strategic behaviour in the allocation of time to writing processes. *Journal of Second Language Writing* 17. 30–47.

Roca de Larios, Julio, Javier Marín, and Liz Murphy. 2001. A temporal analysis of formulation processes in L1 and L2 writing. *Language Learning* 51. 497–538.

Santos, María, Sonia López-Serrano, and Rosa M. Manchón. 2010. The differential effect of two types of direct written corrective feedback on noticing and uptake: Reformulation vs. error correction. *International Journal of English Studies* 10. 131–154.

Schoonen, Rob, Amos van Gelderen, A., Kees de Glopper, Jan Hulstijn, Annegien Simis, Patrick Snellings, and Marie Stevenson, M. 2003. First language and second language writing: The role of linguistic knowledge, speed of processing, and metacognitive knowledge. *Language Learning* 53. 165–202.

Schoonen, Rob, Amos van Gelderen, Reinoud Stole, Jan Hulstijn, and Kees de Glopper. 2011. Modeling the development of L1 and EFL writing proficiency of secondary school students. *Language Learning* 61(1). 31–79.

Sengupta, Sima. 1998a. From text revision to text improvement: A story of secondary school composition. *RELC Journal* 29. 110–137.

Sengupta, Sima. 1998b. Peer evaluation: "I am not the teacher". *ELT Journal* 52. 19–28.

Sengupta, Sima. 2000. An investigation into the effects of revision strategy instruction on L2 secondary school learners. *System* 28. 97–113.

Snellings, Patrick, Amos van Gelderen, and Kees de Glopper. 2002. Lexical retrieval: An aspect of fluent second language production that can be enhanced. *Language Learning* 52. 723–754.

Snellings, Patrick, Amos Van Gelderen, and Kees de Glopper. 2004. The effect of enhanced lexical retrieval on L2 writing; A classroom experiment. *Applied Psycholinguistics* 25. 175–200.

Stevenson, Marie, Rob Schoonen, and Kees Glopper. 2006. Revising in two languages: A multidimensional comparison of online writing revisions in L1 and FL. *Journal of Second Language Writing* 15. 201–233.

Torras, Rosa M. and M. Luz Celaya. 2001. Age-related differences in the development of written production: An empirical study of EFL school learners. *International Journal of English Studies* 1. 103–126.

Tsui, Amy and Maria Ng. 2000. Do secondary L2 writers benefit from peer comments? *Journal of Second Language Writing* 9. 147–170.

Tsui, Amy and Maria Ng. 2010. Cultural contexts and situated possibilities in the teaching of second language writing. *Journal of Teacher Education* 61. 364–375.

Valdés, Guadalupe. 1992. Bilingual minorities and language issues in writing. *Written Communication* 9. 85–136.

Van Beuningen, Catherine. 2010. Corrective feedback in L2 writing: theoretical perspectives, empirical insights, and future directions. *International Journal of English Studies* 10. 1–27.

Van Beuningen, Catherine, Nijva D. Jong, and Folkert Kuiken. 2008. The effect of direct and indirect corrective feedback on L2 learners' written accuracy. *ITL International Journal of Applied Linguistics* 156. 279–296

Vygotsky, Lev. 1978. *Mind in society: The development of higher psychological processes.* Cambridge, MA: Harvard University Press.

Vygotsky, Lev. 1987. Thinking and speech. In R. W. Rieber and A. S. Carton (eds.), *The collected works of L. S. Vygotsky: Vol. 1: Problems of general psychology*, 39–285. New York: Plenum.

Whittaker, Rachel , Ana Llinares, and Ann McCabe. 2011. Written discourse development in CLIL at secondary school. *Language Teaching Research* 15. 343–362.

Woo, Matsuko, Samuel Chu, Andrew Ho, and Xuanxi Li. 2011. Using a wiki to scaffold primary-school students' collaborative writing. *Educational Technology and Society* 14. 43–54.

Yang, Shu Ching and Yi-Ju Chen. 2007. Technology-enhanced language learning: A case study. *Computers in Human Behavior* 23. 860–879.

Dana R. Ferris
6 L2 writers in higher education

1 Introduction

The vast majority of research on L2 writers over the past half-century has focused on students in higher education contexts, especially in the United States. Approaches to such work have changed over time, largely in response to changes in student populations and institutions' attempts to address the needs of diverse students. Further, research on L2 writers in higher education has shifted focus at points because of the divergent disciplinary traditions that influence it (Matsuda 2003; Silva and Leki 2004). In particular, approaches to teaching L2 writers have been driven by developments in second language acquisition theory and in mainstream (L1) composition theory.

Today, the population of multilingual writers in higher education settings is recognized by faculty and administrators as large and complex. In the US, the number of international students (both graduates and undergraduates) is higher than at any point in history, and it has grown by at least 10 % annually over the past six years. US-educated L2 writers, including both immigrants and the children of first-generation immigrants (Harklau, Losey, and Siegal 1999) are also enrolled in great numbers at all levels of higher education. Institutions are often not well equipped – or even always willing – to meet the students' range of needs for additional support as they pursue their studies and meet academic literacy expectations (see Kubota and Abels 2006). When they do offer courses for L2 writers, they may rely upon outdated models of instruction that fail to capture the complexity of academic literacy tasks. Similar complexities exist outside of the US, whether in English-medium contexts or in foreign language settings (Cimasko and Reichelt 2011; Thaiss, Bräuer, Carlino, Ganobcsik-Williams, and Sinha 2012). However, postsecondary institutions in the US tend to admit students from a broader range of backgrounds and language/literacy skills than do many other countries, making L2 writing a higher education issue with which institutions must grapple. Because of the size and urgency of the issues involved, it is important to both reflect upon the research that has already been completed and especially to expand its scope for the future.

In this chapter, I will survey the published research on L2 writers in higher education. I start by discussing the theoretical perspectives that influenced these studies. I describe the broad range of methods that led to the published empirical research. I then discuss the major themes, questions, and findings that have emerged from this body of work.[1] The chapter concludes with a brief discussion of future research areas.

---

[1] The discussion in this chapter focuses particularly on research with undergraduates. See Chapter 9 for an overview of research focused on graduate and professional L2 writers. See also Chapter 8 for a discussion on L2 writers employing languages other than English.

2 Main theories informing research

As described by Matsuda (2003) and Silva and Leki (2004), L2 writing in general (including considerations of students in higher education) is a field or a subfield with several intersecting disciplinary traditions. Most notably, L2 writing theory, research, and practice, stands at the intersection of two major fields, rhetoric/composition and linguistics/applied linguistics. Thus, L2 writing research has drawn from second language acquisition theory (on psycholinguistic and sociolinguistic processes through which L2 literacy develops), and on linguistic descriptions of discourse and especially of text structure (Beaugrande and Dressler 1981; Kinneavy 1971). Some of this theory in turn is derived from work in psychology, education, and anthropology, among other fields. L2 writing research has also been influenced by L1 composition theory regarding, for example, writers' cognitive processes as they compose (Bereiter and Scardamalia 1987; Flower and Hayes 1981) and sociocultural theories on expert-novice interaction and on contexts or activity systems (Leontiev 1981; Vygotsky 1986). As we will see in the next section, the eclectic mix of research methods in research on L2 writers reflects its diverse disciplinary and theoretical origins.

2.1 Main methods of research

2.1.1 Text analysis

As we have already noted, the vast majority of L2 writing research has focused on learners in higher education settings, often (but not always) in the US. Nearly every empirical paradigm one can imagine has been employed at one point or another (see Matsuda and Silva 2005). The earliest empirical work, inspired by Kaplan's (1966) article in which he articulated the "contrastive rhetoric hypothesis" (see Atkinson, Chapter 26), employed text analysis to examine L2 students' writing for various linguistic features. A collection edited by Connor and Kaplan (1987) provides a good example of these earlier studies. Text analysis methods have also been employed to study the effects of classroom response strategies, including teacher-student writing conferences (e.g., Ewert 2009; Goldstein and Conrad 1990), peer response interactions and their influence on student revision (e.g., Mendonça and Johnson 1994), and teacher commentary or error correction (e.g., Bitchener and Knoch 2010; Ferris 2006; Ferris, Pezone, Tade, and Tinti 1997). Text analysis has also been a key component in studies of writing assessment, for example, in examinations of textual features that appear to influence raters' scores (Hamp-Lyons 1991). Text analysis in the modern era is facilitated by methods of corpus linguistics, which allow large collections of texts (corpora) to be quickly and precisely analyzed using sophisticated computational and statistical techniques (Biber 1988; Biber, Conrad, and Reppen 1998).

2.1.2 Case study and ethnography

In the 1970s, several researchers, following models from L1 composition research, began investigating college-level L2 writers using case study methods. Rather than analyzing groups of students' texts, these researchers (e.g., Cohen and Robbins 1976; Raimes 1985; Zamel 1983) looked deeply into the "cases" (narratives) of individual student writers, using techniques such as observations, interviews, think-alouds, and analysis of focal students' texts to build a nuanced picture of how individual L2 writers function in academic settings. Other qualitative researchers added ethnographic methods to provide broad, rich descriptions of contexts in which L2 writers learn, including comparison of programs (e.g., Atkinson and Ramanathan 1995), in-depth studies of a specific class and its instructor (e.g., Tardy 2006), and examination of artifacts of L2 writing instruction (e.g., Ramanathan and Atkinson 1999; Ramanathan and Kaplan 1996).

2.1.3 Quasi-experimental research

L2 writing researchers also designed studies that examined specific pedagogical treatments (such as the presence or absence of error correction, e.g., Bitchener, Young, and Cameron 2005) or of training for peer review sessions, e.g., Stanley 1992). Though designs vary from study to study, they typically include a pretest-treatment-posttest sequence (and, in some cases, a delayed posttest) and either a control vs. treatment group or several different treatment groups. Such studies usually report their findings using descriptive and inferential statistics.

2.1.4 Survey research

Another heavily used method is survey research. Researchers have surveyed a range of informants about a variety of topics. For example, many researchers have elicited student perspectives on various pedagogical issues such as what type of feedback mode they prefer (written or oral, e.g., Arndt 1993) or feedback source (teacher or peers, e.g., Zhang 1995). Teachers have also been utilized as informants about their own pedagogical choices and strategies; in some of these studies, both teacher and student responses are collected and compared (e.g., Cohen and Cavalcanti 1990; Montgomery and Baker 2007). Finally, readers or consumers of student writing, such as faculty in the disciplines, have been surveyed about their reactions to errors made in texts by L2 writers (e.g., Santos 1988). Survey results are typically reported with minimal use of descriptive statistics (frequencies and percentages).

To summarize, over the past several decades, researchers have employed all empirical methods typically found in social science research to investigate various questions related to L2 writers in higher education. Though there have occasionally been some methodological wars – or at least skirmishes – between proponents of quantitative and qualitative methods, many L2 writing scholars have moved towards accepting the peaceful co-existence of methods at both ends of the spectrum, acknowledging that methods should be matched to research questions, not rigidly prescribed (or proscribed). Indeed, some researchers today design mixed-methods studies, combining, for example, case study interviews, surveys, and text analysis to look simultaneously at smaller and larger populations as they investigate several different research questions (see, e.g., Ferris, Brown, Liu, and Stine 2011).

3 Major research insights

3.1 Descriptions of L2 writers in higher education

Because the population of L2 writers in colleges and universities has grown and changed so rapidly, one foundational area of research has focused on describing student characteristics. Much of the historical work on L2 writers in higher education has examined demographic and educational trends in the United States over the second half of the 20th century and into the 21st. The US has a tradition of teaching "composition" to undergraduate students that dates back to the 1870s at Harvard University (Brereton 1995; Connors 1997).[2] Beginning in the 1940s, the numbers of international undergraduates studying in the US climbed rapidly, and university English departments began to consider the issues arising from an increasingly diverse student population in their first-year composition (FYC) courses (Matsuda 2003). L2 writers were taught in university intensive language programs (the first was the University of Michigan English Language Institute, founded in 1941) until they were deemed ready for college-level work and then, in some contexts, in specially designed sections of FYC.

A different group of L2 writers began appearing in US colleges and universities in the 1970s, resident immigrants (especially refugees from Southeast Asia) who had come to the US with their parents as children. These students often had interrupted language and literacy development in their L1s and a later start in L2 development, arriving in college with language and literacy needs distinct from those of both monolingual English peers and international students (Ferris 2009; Matsuda and Matsuda 2009). Later still, a new group of L2 writers described as "Generation 1.5" learners – the US-educated children of first-generation immigrants – be-

---

2 Due to space limitations, my choice of citations in this chapter is representative and illustrative rather than comprehensive.

gan to receive attention from researchers, administrators, and teachers (Ferris 2009; Harklau, Losey, and Siegal 1999; Roberge, Losey, and Siegal 2009). US colleges and universities today must consider the needs and characteristics of international students vs. US-resident students; furthermore, institutions must be sensitive to differences between recently arrived residents, longer-term residents, and US-born students when they explore the best ways to place, teach, assess, and support the large and complex group of students variously referred to as "L2" or "multilingual" or "ESL" writers.

In sum, US institutions of higher education, depending upon their location and scope (two-year colleges, four-year colleges/universities, universities that offer graduate programs) may now include growing numbers of international students, resident immigrants, and Generation 1.5 students, and these multilingual writers are found in a broad range of academic disciplines and degree programs. It can no longer be assumed, for example, that L2 students will cluster in programs in engineering, mathematics, or science. A final factor adding to the complexity is the rise of transfer students, meaning undergraduates who begin their studies at a two-year college and then transfer to a four-year college or university. Many writing programs and L2 transfer students find that the transition between writing requirements at two-year and four-year colleges is not always a smooth one.

Although much of the research on L2 writers in postsecondary institutions has come from the US and has been focused on English as the primary L2 (see Chapter 8 for a review focused on L2s other than English), students around the world writing in L2 in higher education face a range of challenges depending upon their specific context. Space does not permit a detailed description of the wide range of approaches to writing across different geographic regions and languages, but several recent collections have provided such surveys (Cimasko and Reichelt 2011; Thaiss et al. 2012).[3] Some generalizations and themes have emerged from studies of L2 writing across various contexts.

First, institutions must be aware that students in (or from) different contexts may have a range of prior experiences that they bring into writing in higher education. Countries and regions have widely divergent philosophies and approaches to the teaching of student writers (whether L1 or L2) in higher education. Though "composition" or "writing" as a stand-alone academic subject is rare outside the US, students in many contexts are expected to be proficient, sophisticated academic writers by the time they reach postsecondary education, and students engage in demanding writing-to-learn projects in both L1 and L2 at the secondary level (Reichelt 2011). In some countries, students do not write much at all in any language (even L1); when they do write in L2, writing tasks tend to be short and are designed either to practice other language skills or respond to something they

---

3 There also was a 2008 special issue of the *Journal of Second Language Writing*, edited by Rosa M. Manchón and Pieter De Haan, devoted to the topic of writing in a foreign language.

have read (e.g., a work of literature). Thus, they do not gain much fluency or confidence in their ability to compose longer L2 texts.

Second, L2 student populations vary widely across different contexts. In some settings, the only L2 students will be international students. In others, as in the US, there will be a mix of internationals and resident immigrants. The role, status, and even the structure of the L2 may also vary considerably across different contexts (Canagarajah 2006). In some countries, for example, studying English is highly valued, required of all students from an early age, and considered essential to an effective education. In other contexts, FL instruction is considered an optional extra. Student motivations and attitude toward L2 instruction in general and L2 writing in particular may also vary according to the prevailing value assigned to L2 learning as well as individual student characteristics.

Third, students may have experienced dramatic variation in the conditions under which writing was taught, with some teachers facing large classes and heavy teaching loads necessitating different strategies from what might be considered best practices in US college composition settings. Also, in many countries, curriculum is heavily constrained by local and national standards and regulations to which writing instruction must conform (see Lee 2009; You 2006). Finally, in some contexts, L2 students are treated with compassion and support in the form of remedial coursework and assigned writing tutors. In others, they are expected to be independent and self-sufficient as academic writers. It is assumed in the latter instance that if students are proficient enough to be in a postsecondary institution, they can manage their workload without extra consideration of their L2 status.

In short, writing, writers, and the teaching of writing are viewed and approached differently around the world (as well described in Thaiss et al. 2012). Thus, scholars studying L2 writers must avoid two-way overgeneralizations: (1) that student writers from other parts of the world will be similar to those in their own context; and (2) that all L2 writers, regardless of background, will be similar to each other.

3.2 Pedagogical approaches to the teaching of L2 writers

Historical research on the teaching of L2 writing has highlighted the various ways L2 writers have been taught in colleges and universities. Again, this discussion is US-focused, not only because the US has been the most studied but also because it is more common for US-based L2 writers to be in "writing" courses in higher education than it might be elsewhere. Several previous authors have summarized this history (Matsuda 2003, 2012; Silva 1990), which has gone through at least four different but overlapping phases:

1. Controlled or guided composition: In the 1940s and 1950s, L2 college writers were taught in English language programs that relied on the audio-lingual method of L2 instruction and were heavily influenced by structural linguistics

and behavioral psychology. Writing was seen primarily as a way to practice language learned from listening and reading, and it was tightly structured so that students would not be asked to compose texts beyond their proficiency level and to minimize production errors that might arise from more free-form writing.

2. Current-traditional or paragraph-pattern method: In this approach, adapted from L1 composition pedagogy in the 1960s–70s, students were taught to write well-structured paragraphs and essays with prescribed elements (thesis, topic statement, etc.) in carefully defined patterns or modes (narration, comparison/contrast, description, etc.). This approach was adopted for L2 writing because it was perceived to bridge the gap for intermediate learners between writing sentences and freely composing longer texts. In both of these early methods, error correction was also a prominent feature.

3. Process approach: Again adapted from L1 composition as well as prevailing L2 acquisition theory, students were taught to focus on their own writing processes (invention, revision, etc.) and to de-emphasize concern for the final product (focus on ideas, worry less about accuracy). This approach was appealing because it focused on building L2 writers' fluency, confidence, and enjoyment in writing rather than on whether every sentence and paragraph was perfectly formed.

4. English for academic purposes approach: Adapted from the English for specific purposes model of L2 instruction, which in turn is connected to genre theory and pedagogy (Swales 1990; Tardy 2009), this model focused on helping students understand the expectations of an academic audience and build the skills needed to successfully complete academic writing tasks (e.g., using sources, understanding writing prompts).

To summarize, L2 writers in higher education are (a) diverse not only culturally and linguistically but also in their backgrounds, especially their educational pathways and prior experiences with L2 writing (and L2 literacy in general); and (b) likely to have experienced a range of instructional approaches to L2 writing, both before and during their college/university studies.

3.3 Differences between writing in L1 and L2

One important issue in the literature on L2 writing is the nature, degree, and significance of differences between writing in L1 versus writing in L2 and, by extension, of observed distinctions between texts written by L1 writers and L2 college writers. This large issue can be divided into three related (and controversial) questions:

1. Is the process of acquiring writing skills different in L1 vs. L2?
2. If it is different, does it warrant a different teaching approach?

3. If L2 writing students are given a different teaching approach (and a different classroom context and different label) does the harm of distinguishing them in this way outweigh the benefits of doing so?

One group of scholars holds passionately that differences between L1 and L2 students are not important, that writing pedagogy should be essentially the same for both groups, and indeed that attaching labels such as "L2" or "ESL" or "multilingual" to a subgroup of student writers harms them by problematizing them or treating them as "other" (Spack 1997; Zamel 1997). More recently, L1 composition scholars have argued for a "translingual" view of writing instruction that moves beyond an "English-only ideology" (Horner 2010: 11) because "... attempting to teach students to reproduce a single, standardized English in their writing is both futile and inappropriate" (Horner 2010: 5).

Other scholars have argued that L2 writers are undertaking a fundamentally different task with the added challenge of ongoing second language acquisition occurring simultaneously with developing college-level writing competence (Conference on College Composition and Communication 2009; Ferris 2009; Matsuda 2012). While this latter group would agree with the former that L2 writers shouldn't be "othered" or treated as problems, they would also assert that L2 writers' distinct backgrounds and knowledge bases necessitate a re-examination of curricular, assessment, and instructional practices to ensure that programs and pedagogy are responsive to their unique needs.

Empirical research to some extent supports the arguments of both sides. There is little evidence, for example, that pedagogical practices imported from L1 composition, such as multiple-drafting, portfolio assessment, peer feedback, and teacher-student conferences, bring harm to L2 writers. It is also quite possible for advanced multilingual writers to be successful in mainstream writing courses and in their courses in the disciplines, especially if such courses employ enlightened "universal design" principles that support students from all backgrounds. Further, there is evidence in the literature that L2 writers from immigrant/Generation 1.5 backgrounds may resist or resent labeling practices in college/university settings that treat them as "other" and that place them in classes with traditional ESL students (Costino and Hyon 2007; Ferris, Liu, Sinha, and Senna 2013; Ortmeier-Hooper 2008).

On the other hand, there is ample evidence that L2 college writers may indeed produce texts with characteristics that are observable and distinct from those of their L1 peers (Hinkel 2002; Hyland 2016; Silva 1993) and make linguistic errors that are different in frequency and type than L1 writers exhibit (Bitchener and Ferris 2012). There is also evidence that these textual differences and errors may cause L2 writing to be judged more harshly by academic evaluators (Hamp-Lyons 1991; Santos 1988; Vann, Lorenz and Meyer 1991). Finally, research on the placement and assessment of L2 writers suggests that L2 college students are disproportionately placed in remedial writing courses and more likely to fail timed writing examinations (Crusan 2006, 2010; Hamp-Lyons 1991; Weigle 2006). In short, although L2 writing experts may wish, from a philosophical standpoint, that institutions would take a more broadminded view of L2 writers' differences – embracing them rather than trying to train L2 students to write like L1 students – the truth is that L2 writers *are* different, and sometimes these distinctions *do* matter in some highly practical and sometimes painful ways.

3.4 Placement, curriculum, and assessment

As just noted, the increased student diversity in colleges and universities has led to concerns about institutional placement practices – how (and by whom) incoming undergraduates are assessed and placed into entry-level writing coursework. Placement practices vary widely across institutions. Some universities use a system-wide or statewide placement instrument (e.g., the English Placement Test used by the 24-campus California State University system), many two-year colleges use a commercially developed instrument such as ACT's COMPASS®, and other colleges utilize in-house placement systems that might include a writing sample and a grammar or reading test. In a handful of contexts, programs have utilized directed self-placement (DSP) processes in which students respond to a questionnaire and/or take a test of some kind, receive counseling as to appropriate placement options, and then are allowed to make the final decision themselves about course enrollment. In some two-year college settings, the institutions are allowed to use placement scores for advising purposes, but students who desire to attempt courses at a different level than their placement score indicates must be allowed to do so.

L2 writing experts argue that large-scale placement mechanisms are not discriminating enough to appropriately place diverse student writers (see Crusan 2006, 2010). As a result, L2 writers fail such placement examinations in large numbers and are assigned to remedial coursework rather than college-level classes. Until recently, it was assumed that the mechanisms were accurate (or close enough) and that students placed in pre-college-level classes indeed needed to be in such classes. Experts have begun to wonder whether developmental writing classes are necessary and effective for all lower-scoring students and have begun to experiment with alternate models known as stretch courses (which combine developmental and FYC classes into one syllabus, usually with more hours of instruction). One important issue that arises from this placement concern is the discouragement and loss of motivation that can occur when students are forced into remedial classes that do not carry graduation credit. This reaction can become even stronger when multilingual US-educated students who were mainstreamed out of bilingual/ELL instruction in elementary or early secondary years are placed in college into an "ESL" writing class (Costino and Hyon 2007; Harklau 2000).

Even if one assumes that local placement processes are accurate and effective, questions arise as to which course models are most appropriate for L2 writers entering college. In some contexts, L2 students may be placed into specialized writing courses at the developmental level and then are mainstreamed with native speakers when they reach FYC courses. In others, there is a parallel sequence of L2 course equivalents that students can choose to take (or may even be required to take) in lieu of the courses for L1 students. Some programs even offer such specialized L2 writing courses at the sophomore and upper-division levels (see Holten 2009; Roberge 2009). There is debate among composition specialists as to the "best" curricular path for L2 writers in higher education settings. Some argue that it is important for L2 students to be mainstreamed as soon as possible so that they can interact with L1 peers around their writing and accustom themselves to expectations beyond the often-sheltered world of the ESL program. Others assert that some students have specialized needs for assistance with their writing that are quite distinct from those of L1 writers, and that such students would benefit greatly from smaller classes designed for their specific developmental stage (e.g., spending more time on fewer assignments or providing more language-focused classroom instruction that would be less appropriate for L1 students). In particular, it is argued, teachers who are trained to evaluate and address L2 writers' needs for classroom instruction and feedback can especially facilitate their development.

There is little empirical evidence as to whether one placement model is better than the other; indeed, given differences across local contexts and institutions, it is highly unlikely the one model could ever fit students in all higher education settings. However, L2 writing experts counsel that where possible, offering students a choice as to course options is optimal (CCCC 2009; Costino and Hyon 2007; Ferris 2009). Further, choice implies not only the existence of course placement alternatives but students' freedom to opt into or out of L2 writing courses rather than being forced onto a particular path because of their placement results.

A different and challenging set of placement and curriculum issues arises in open-access/open-enrollment community colleges. In some contexts, students who are barely literate in English – either because they are newcomers or because they found creative ways to get through their secondary programs – enroll in ESL or developmental courses at community colleges, which cannot by law turn them away and which face the daunting task of trying to remediate the language and literacy skills of these often highly motivated students (see Patthey, Thomas-Spiegel, and Dillon 2009). What can an institution do when it matriculates students whose language and literacy skills are far below even the bottom level of the developmental writing sequence – without the resources to serve such students? These troubling ethical and practical questions are made even more urgent by recent budget-driven remediation limits established by many college and university systems. Such time limits ignore the principles that second language acquisition takes time and that academic literacy skills are complex; student development cannot be compressed into a few months of remedial coursework.

Once students have been placed into a course or sequence of courses, a final question that arises is how best to assess their writing progress at the end of a specific course or at a particular point in their undergraduate studies. Many institutions, for example, require students to either pass an upper-division writing proficiency examination or take an advanced writing course in order to graduate. Available research suggests that such broadly based writing assessment procedures may disadvantage L2 writers (see Weigle 2006). Specifically, students struggle with writing under time pressure and sometimes with the topics and/or the wording of the prompts (Kroll 1990). There is evidence that raters – who typically are not trained L2 teachers – may be distracted by L2 features in texts and may thus give lower scores to L2 students (Hamp-Lyons 1991). These outcomes raise a number of philosophical issues as to (a) whether such writing assessments are optimal and necessary for anyone; and (b) whether such assessments are systemically unfair to L2 writers (Johns 1995; Leki 2003, 2006).

3.5 Instructional approaches

As described in 3.2 above, several general pedagogical models have been used to design instruction for L2 writers. Mismatches sometimes occur, unfortunately, when students make the transition from a developmental ESL curriculum into a mainstream writing program (and/or into general education programs). In 1995, Atkinson and Ramanathan published an ethnographic comparison of two writing programs at the same university, one an English language program for incoming international students deemed unready for college-level writing courses and the other a mainstream FYC program. The researchers found that despite serving the same students (at different points in time) and having ostensibly the same curricular goals, the two programs valued different writing processes and products. When L2 writers moved from ESL courses to FYC courses, they found that their five-paragraph "workpersonlike" essays brought them negative feedback and low grades. The authors suggested that administrators and instructors in both programs needed to do a better job of articulating their values and goals and especially facilitating smoother transitions for the students.

Though this study was published nearly 20 years ago, and I have for space considerations oversimplified the summary here, the gap still exists in many contexts between mainstream writing programs and developmental ESL writing programs at universities, stand-alone intensive English programs housed on college campuses, and community-college ESL programs. Textbooks published and used for those developmental course levels often stop with the paragraph-pattern model described above, and course syllabi and assignments follow the models in the textbooks. As a result, students are not taught to negotiate the gap between simpler, more formulaic essay styles and challenging college-level assignments that draw upon intertextual skills and require research and abstract thinking (Ferris 2009;

Harklau 2000). These critical transitions are better navigated in contexts where the developmental, ESL, and college-level writing programs are under one roof with a common faculty and the goals and expectations at each individual course level can be more easily articulated with the rest of the curriculum. (Holten 2009).

In addition to broader questions of how courses for L2 writers should be structured, many researchers over the years have examined specific classroom strategies to assess their effectiveness. For instance, several researchers have examined whether it is beneficial or harmful for L2 writers to use their L1 during the writing process (Jones and Tetroe 1987; Kobayashi and Rinnert 1992). While in general it is assumed that language switches happen frequently during writing and that they are mostly subconscious, in some instances, using the L1 to generate ideas (as a prewriting strategy) can reduce writers' anxiety over getting started.

By far the largest body of empirical work on classroom techniques for L2 writers in higher education has focused on various forms of feedback – teacher commentary, error correction, teacher-student writing conferences, and peer response. In addition, researchers have examined L2 writers' interactions with tutors in writing centers (see next section). This research base is too large to review thoroughly here, so I will instead offer several generalizations (see chapters 20 and 21 for more discussion and specific references).

1. L2 writers value teacher commentary and are not offended or demoralized by it. On the contrary, they prefer teacher feedback to any other kind of feedback (peer or self).

2. The formal characteristics of teachers' written commentary (e.g., length, syntactic form, directness or indirectness) may influence students' comprehension of the feedback and/or their ability to utilize it in revision or for future writing.

3. L2 students have mixed reactions to peer feedback, and studies have yielded varied results as to the benefits of peer commentary. However, when students are prepared or trained for peer feedback, the outcomes improve.

4. Students also value expert feedback on the language errors in their writing and prefer for it to be comprehensive and informative (teachers provide the corrections themselves or give clear indications about what the problem is). Such feedback appears to help students improve the accuracy of revised texts and future new texts when it is selective (focused on only a few features at a time); when it focuses on features that are rule-governed rather than idiosyncratic; and when some kind of explanation accompanies it (in the form of an error code, a brief verbal explanation of the rule, or in-person clarification during a writing conference). (For a recent comprehensive review of studies on error correction in L2 writing, see Bitchener and Ferris 2012; see also chapters 19–20 in this volume).

This summary of studies on feedback paints a fairly positive picture. However, it should be noted that this research base speaks far more to the *potential* for feedback to be facilitative for L2 writers than it does about the feedback student writers *typically* receive in college/university classes. I will return to this point in the next section and in the concluding section of the chapter.

3.6 Teacher preparation

As the above discussion suggests, the preparation and qualifications of those who teach L2 writers is an important concern for both researchers and writing program administrators. In its position statement on L2 writing and writers, the Conference on College Composition and Communication argues that "Any writing course ... that enrolls any second language writers should be taught by an instructor who is able to identify and is prepared to address the linguistic and cultural needs of second language writers" (CCCC 2009). More TESOL programs offer coursework in teaching L2 writing than in the past, but such classes are typically either not available or not required for instructors pursuing training in mainstream composition instruction.

As discussed in earlier sections, there are philosophical divisions between L1 and L2 composition and even among L2 writing specialists as to the best ways to approach placement, assessment, instruction, and feedback for L2 writers. Some instructors in a writing program feel that L2 writers are no different from other students and should not be "othered"; some believe that the only thing L2 writers need is intensive grammar instruction and error correction; and some believe that with a sensitive, nuanced approach to diverse student needs, L1 and L2 students can be taught together. Because of these divergent views, L2 writers will have different experiences in writing courses depending upon which instructor they happen to encounter. It is thus important that researchers and administrators work to identify what teachers need to know, the best models for pre-service and in-service teacher preparation, and the best ways to assess teacher performance and student progress in mixed/mainstream composition classes as well as in specialized L2 writing courses.

3.7 Beyond the writing classroom: Support services and writing in the disciplines

Most colleges and universities provide tutoring and study skills support for their students in the form of writing centers or learning skills centers. One area of research in L2 writing focuses on the experiences of L2 writers in writing centers where they receive one-on-one peer tutoring and/or expert tutoring from trained staff. It is clear from the work that has been done that there is great potential for such intensive, individualized assistance to help L2 writers be more successful in their studies, but it is equally apparent that these possibilities are not always fully realized (see Chapter 21). Problems include inadequate preparation for tutors and mismatches between mainstream writing center philosophy (which often explicitly proscribes sentence-level work or a focus on form) and student needs, leading to frustration on both sides of the interactions.

As colleges and universities matriculate a larger and more linguistically complex group of students, another area of concern is their progress in courses in the disciplines, beyond the language or writing class. In its first version of its position statement on Second Language Writing and Writers, the Conference on College Composition and Communication (CCCC) argued that " ... the acquisition of a second language and second-language literacy is a time-consuming process that will continue through students' academic careers and beyond" (CCCC 2001). Wolfe-Quintero and Segade (1999: 196) also noted that "writing ability is developed through an entire undergraduate education ... and L2 students have unique language needs that require assistance throughout their undergraduate career." Faculty teaching in other disciplines typically have little preparation for how to develop or assess student writing for any group of students, let alone L2 writers. Research on undergraduate L2 writers in the disciplines (and their instructors) has been minimal to date, with most relevant work having focused on graduate student writing. However, a recent (December 2011) special issue of the journal *Across the Disciplines* and the publication of a book designed to help faculty in the disciplines work effectively with multilingual students (Hafernik and Wiant 2012) are promising signs that specialists in L2 writing and in writing across the curriculum/in the disciplines (WAC/WID) are turning their attention to these increasingly pressing interests and concerns.

4 Future research directions

Although much research on L2 writers has focused on learners at the postsecondary level, more still remains to be done. The increases in *quantity* – more students attempting college than ever before, more international students, more resident immigrants – and in the *complexity* of student populations require us to keep examining questions surrounding whom we are serving and how well we are meeting their academic language and literacy needs. In the immediate future, L2 writing research and practice needs to go in at least three specific (interrelated) directions. First, we must use increasingly nuanced terms for the populations of writers whom we study. There are advantages and disadvantages to complicating our terminology. The benefit, of course, is precision and avoiding essentialization of L2 writers. The risk is that our work may become less accessible to those outside our somewhat narrow area of specialty. We must seek to describe the large and diverse L2 writer population and their needs in ways that are precise and clear to other faculty outside of our own specialty and to administrators.

Second, in future research we will consider L2 writers in a much broader range of contexts. These include, of course, settings around the world in which writers compose in L2s other than English (see Chapter 8) as well as those in which English is not an official or primary language. They also include contexts outside of the traditional research sites – language and writing classes – and increased considerations of how L2 writers function in their disciplinary coursework, as graduate students, and in their professional lives (see Chapter 9).

Finally, future research and teaching will be heavily influenced by the affordances of technology for work with L2 writers (and writers in general). For example, corpus linguistics work is rapidly advancing to the point where classroom teachers and researchers who are not highly trained specialists in computational linguistics can use widely available corpus tools to assemble corpora, examine them for a range of variables, and apply findings to classroom instruction (see Bennett 2010; Conrad 2008; Reppen 2010). Ongoing investigations of digital literacy, multimodal composing, and social media practices being conducted by various groups of researchers (education/literacy specialists, composition scholars, communications experts, etc.) will yield insights for teaching and raise questions for work specifically with L2 writers (see Chapter 14). Further, technology provides new and interesting ways for students to receive feedback on their texts and to study the nature and effects of response to student writing (see Kessler, Oskoz, and Elola 2012).

This examination of L2 writers in higher education comes at a time when many challenging questions are being asked about postsecondary institutions – by politicians, by journalists, and by stakeholders (students, parents, alumni donors, etc.). What is the real value of a college degree? What have students actually learned when they have completed four years (or more) of a university education? Are institutions of higher education focusing on the right things, and are they doing so in ways that are financially and ethically sound? These are difficult issues. It is important to consider how the processes of admission, placement, instruction, and assessment of L2 college/university writers intersect with this increased societal scrutiny of higher education – but it will not be easy.

5 Additional sources

Belcher, Diane and Braine, George (eds.). 1995. *Academic writing in a second language: Essays on research and pedagogy.* Norwood, NJ: Ablex.

Casanave, Christine Pearson. 2004. *Controversies in second language writing: Dilemmas and decisions in research and instruction.* Ann Arbor, MI: University of Michigan.

Cox, Michelle and Myers Zawacki, Terry (eds.). 2011. WAC and second language writing: Cross-field research, theory, and program development. *Across the Disciplines*, 8 (Special Issue, December 2011). Retrieved 7-9-2012 from http://wac.colostate.edu/atd/ell/index.cfm.

Leki, Ilona. 2007. *Undergraduates in a second language: Challenges and complexities of academic literacy development.* New York: Erlbaum/Taylor & Francis.

Manchón, Rosa M. and Pieter de Haan. 2008. Writing in foreign language contexts: An introduction. *Journal of Second Language Writing 17.* 1–6.

Reid, Joy M. (ed.). 2008. *Writing myths: Applying second language research to classroom teaching.* Ann Arbor, MI: University of Michigan.

Silva, Tony and Paul Kei Matsuda (eds.). 2010. *Practicing theory in second language writing.* West Lafayette, IN: Parlor Press.

Zamel, Vivian and Ruth Spack (eds.). 1998. *Negotiating academic literacies: Teaching and learning across languages and cultures.* Mahwah, NJ: Erlbaum.

6 References

Atkinson, Dwight and Vai Ramanathan. 1995. Cultures of writing: A ethnographic comparison of L1 and L2 university writing/language programs. *TESOL Quarterly* 29. 539–568.

Arndt, Valerie. 1993. Response to writing: Using feedback to inform the writing process. In Brock, Mark Newell and Larry Walters (eds.), *Teaching composition around the Pacific Rim: Politics & pedagogy*, 90–116. Clevedon, UK: Multilingual Matters.

Bereiter, Carl and Marlene Scardamalia. 1987. *The psychology of written composition.* Hillsdale, NJ: Lawrence Erlbaum Associates.

Beaugrande, Robert de and Wolfgang Dressler. 1981. *Introduction to text linguistics.* London: Longman.

Bennett, Gena. 2010. *Using corpora in the language learning classroom.* Ann Arbor, MI: University of Michigan Press.

Biber, Douglas. 1988. *Variation across speech and writing.* Cambridge: Cambridge University Press.

Biber, Douglas, Susan Conrad, and Randi Reppen. 1998. *Corpus linguistics: Investigating language structure and use.* Cambridge: Cambridge University Press.

Bitchener, John and Dana Ferris. 2012. *Written corrective feedback in second language acquisition and writing.* New York: Routledge.

Bitchener, John and Ute Knoch. 2010. The contribution of written corrective feedback to language development: A ten month investigation. *Applied Linguistics* 31. 193–214.

Bitchener, John, Stuart Young, and Denise Cameron. 2005. The effect of different types of corrective feedback on ESL student writing. *Journal of Second Language Writing* 9. 227–258.

Brereton, John C. 1995. *The origins of composition studies in the American college, 1875–1925.* Pittsburgh, PA: University of Pittsburgh Press.

Canagarajah, Suresh. 2006. The place of World Englishes in composition: pluralization continued. *College Composition and Communication* 57(4). 586–619.

Cimasko, Tony and Melinda Reichelt (eds.). 2011. *Foreign language writing instruction: Principles and practices.* Anderson, SC: Parlor Press.

Cohen, Andrew and Marilda Cavalcanti. 1990. Feedback on written compositions: Teacher and student verbal reports. In Barbara Kroll (ed.), *Second language writing: Research insights for the classroom*, 155–177. Cambridge, UK: Cambridge University Press.

Cohen, Andrew and Margaret Robbins. 1976. Toward assessing interlanguage performance: The relationship between selected errors, learners' characteristics, and learners' expectations. *Language Learning* 26. 45–66.

Conference on College Composition and Communication (CCCC). 2001/2009. Statement on second language writing and writers. http://www.ncte.org/cccc/resources/positions/secondlangwriting [Retrieved 2–11–13].

Connor, Ulla and Robert Kaplan (eds.). 1987. *Writing across languages: Analysis of L2 text.* Reading, MA: Addison-Wesley.

Connors, Robert. 1997. *Composition-Rhetoric: Backgrounds, theory, and pedagogy.* Pittsburgh, PA: University of Pittsburgh Press.

Conrad, Susan M. 2008. Myth 6: Corpus-based research is too complicated to be useful for writing teachers. In Joy Reid (ed.), *Writing myths: Applying second language research to classroom teaching*, 115–139. Ann Arbor, MI: University of Michigan Press.

Costino, Kimberly A. and Sunny Hyon. 2007. "A class for students like me": Reconsidering relationships among identity labels, residency status, and students' preferences for mainstream or multilingual composition. *Journal of Second Language Writing* 16(2). 63–81.

Crusan, Deborah. 2006. The politics of implementing online directed self-placement for second language writers. In Paul Kei Matsuda, Christina Ortmeier-Hooper, and Xiao You (eds.), *The politics of second language writing: In search of the Promised Land*, 205–221. West Lafayette, IN: Parlor Press.

Crusan, Deborah. 2010. *Assessment in the second language writing classroom.* Ann Arbor, MI: University of Michigan Press.

Emig, Janet. 1971. *The composing processes of twelfth graders.* Urbana, IL: NCTE.

Ewert, Doreen. 2009. L2 writing conferences: Investigating teacher talk. *Journal of Second Language Writing* 18. 251–269.

Ferris, Dana. 2006. Does error feedback help student writers? New evidence on the short- and long-term effects of written error correction. In Ken Hyland and Fiona Hyland (eds.), *Feedback in second language writing: Contexts and issues*, 81–104. Cambridge, UK: Cambridge University Press.

Ferris, Dana. 2009. *Teaching college writing to diverse student populations.* Ann Arbor, MI: University of Michigan Press.

Ferris, Dana, Jeffrey Brown, Hsiang Liu, and Maria Stine. 2011. Responding to L2 students in college writing classes: What teachers say and what they do. *TESOL Quarterly* 45. 207–234.

Ferris, Dana, Susan Pezone, Cathy Tade, and Sharee Tinti. 1997. Teacher commentary on student writing: Descriptions and implications. *Journal of Second Language Writing* 6. 155–182.

Flower, Linda and John Hayes. 1981. A cognitive process theory of writing. *College Composition and Communication* 32(4). 365–387.

Goldstein, Lynn and Susan Conrad. 1990. Student input and the negotiation of meaning in ESL writing conferences. *TESOL Quarterly* 24. 443–460.

Hafernik, Johnnie and Fredel Wiant. 2012. *Integrating multilingual students into college classrooms: Practical advice for faculty.* Bristol, UK: Multilingual Matters.

Harklau, Linda. 2000. From the "good kids" to the "worst": Representations of English language learners across educational settings. *TESOL Quarterly* 34. 35–67.

Harklau, Linda, Kay Losey, and Meryl Siegal (eds.). 1999. *Generation 1.5 meets college composition: Issues in the teaching of writing to US-educated learners of ESL.* Mahwah, New Jersey: Lawrence Erlbaum Associates.

Hamp-Lyons, Liz (ed.). 1991. *Assessing second language writing in academic contexts.* Norwood, NJ: Ablex.

Hinkel, Eli. 2002. *Second language writers' text.* Mahwah, NJ: Lawrence Erlbaum Associates.

Holten, Christine. 2009. Creating an inter-departmental course for Generation 1.5 ESL writers: Challenges faced and lessons learned. In Mark Roberge, Meryl Siegal, and Linda Harklau (eds.), *Generation 1.5 in college composition*, 170–184. New York: Routledge.

Horner, Bruce. 2010. Introduction: From "English only" to cross-language relations in composition. In Brue Horner, Min-Zhan Lu, and Paul Kei Matsuda (eds.), *Cross language relations in composition*, 1–17. Carbondale, IL: Southern Illinois University Press.

Hyland, Ken. 2016. *Teaching and researching writing.* London: Routledge.

Johns, Ann. 1995. Genre and pedagogical purposes. *Journal of Second Language Writing* 4. 181–190.

Jones, Stan and Jacqueline Tetroe. 1987. Composing in a second language. In Ann Matsuhashi (ed.), *Writing in real time: Modelling production processes*, 34–57. Norwood, NJ: Ablex.

Kessler, Greg, Ana Oskoz, and Idoia Elola (eds.). 2012. *Technology across writing contexts and tasks*. San Marcos, TX: CALICO.

Kinneavy, James L. 1971. *A theory of discourse*. Englewood Cliffs, NJ: Prentice-Hall.

Kobayashi, Hiroe and Carol Rinnert. 1992. Effects of first language on second language writing: Translation versus direct composition. *Language Learning* 42(2). 183–215.

Kroll, Barbara. 1990. What does time buy? ESL student performance on home versus class compositions. In Barbara Kroll (ed.), *Second language writing: Research insights for the classroom*, 140–154. Cambridge: Cambridge University Press.

Kubota, Ryuko and Kimberly Abels. 2006. Improving institutional ESL/EAP support for international students: Seeking the Promised Land. In Paul Kei Matsuda, Christina Ortmeier-Hooper, and Xiaoye You (eds.), *The politics of second language writing: In search of the Promised Land*, 75–93. West Lafayette, IN: Parlor Press.

Lee, Icy. 2009. Ten mismatches between teachers' beliefs and written feedback practice. *ELT Journal* 63(1). 13–22.

Leki, Ilona. 2003. A challenge to second language writing professionals: Is writing overrated? In Barbara Kroll (ed.), *Exploring the dynamics of second language writing*, 315–331. Cambridge, UK: Cambridge University Press.

Leki, Ilona. 2006. The legacy of first-year composition. In Paul Kei Matsuda, Christina Ortmeier-Hooper, and Xiaoye You (eds.), *The politics of second language writing: In search of the Promised Land*, 59–74. West Lafayette, IN: Parlor Press.

Leki, Ilona. 2009. Before the conversation: A sketch of some possible backgrounds, experiences, and attitudes among ESL students visiting a writing center. In Shanti Bruce and Ben Rafoth (eds.), *ESL writers: A guide for writing center tutors* (2nd Ed.), 1–17. Portsmouth, NH: Heinemann Boynton/Cook.

Leontiev, Alekseĭ Alekseevich. 1981. The problem of activity in psychology. In James V. Wertsch (ed.), *The concept of activity in Soviet psychology*, 37–71. Armonk, NY: Sharpe.

Matsuda, Paul Kei. 2003. Second-language writing in the twentieth century: A situated historical perspective. In Barbara Kroll (ed.), *Exploring the dynamics of second language writing*, 15–34. Cambridge, UK: Cambridge University Press.

Matsuda, Paul Kei. 2012. Teaching composition in the multilingual world: Second language writing in composition studies. In Kelly Ritter and Paul Kei Matsuda (eds.), *Exploring composition studies: Sites, issues, and perspectives*, 36–51. Logan, UT: Utah State University Press.

Matsuda, Paul Kei and Aya Matsuda. 2009. The erasure of resident ESL writers. In Mark Roberge, Meryl Siegal, and Linda Harklau (eds.), *Generation 1.5 in college composition: Teaching academic writing to US-educated learners of ESL*, 50–64. New York: Routledge.

Matsuda, Paul Kei and Tony Silva (eds.). 2005. *Second language writing research: Perspectives on the process of knowledge construction* Mahwah, NJ: Erlbaum.

Mendonça, Cássia and Karen Johnson. 1994. Peer review negotiations: Revision activities in ESL writing instruction. *TESOL Quarterly* 28. 745–769.

Montgomery, Julie and Wendy Baker. 2007. Teacher-written feedback: Student perceptions, teacher self-assessment, and actual teacher performance. *Journal of Second Language Writing* 16. 82–99.

Ortmeier-Hooper, Christina. 2008. English may be my second language – but I'm not "ESL." *College Composition and Communication* 59(3). 389–419.

Patthey, Genevieve, Joan Thomas-Spiegel, and Paul Dillon. 2009. Educational pathways of Generation 1.5 students in community college courses. In Mark Roberge, Meryl Siegal, and Linda Harklau (eds.), *Generation 1.5 in college composition*, 135–149. New York: Routledge.

Raimes, Ann. 1985. What unskilled ESL students do as they write: A classroom study of composing. *TESOL Quarterly* 19. 229–258.

Ramanathan, Vai and Dwight Atkinson. 1999. Individualism, academic writing, and ESL writers. *Journal of Second Language Writing* 8. 45–75.

Ramanathan, Vai and Robert Kaplan. 1996. Audience and voice in current L1 composition texts: Some implications for ESL student writers. *Journal of Second Language Writing* 5. 21–34.

Reichelt, Melinda. 2011. Foreign language writing: An overview. In Tony Cimasko and Melinda Reichelt (eds.), *Foreign language writing instruction: Principles & practices*, 3–21. Anderson, SC: Parlor Press.

Reppen, Randi. 2010. *Using corpora in the language classroom*. Cambridge, UK: Cambridge University Press.

Roberge, Mark. 2009. A teacher's perspective on Generation 1.5. In Mark Roberge, Meryl Siegal, and Linda Harklau (eds.), *Generation 1.5 in college composition*, 3–24. New York: Routledge.

Roberge, Mark, Meryl Siegal, and Linda Harklau (eds.). 2009. *Generation 1.5 in college composition*. New York: Routledge.

Santos, Terry. 1988. Professors' reactions to the academic writing of nonnative-speaking students. *TESOL Quarterly* 22. 69–90.

Silva, Tony. 1990. Second language composition instruction: Developments, issues, and directions in ESL. In Barbara Kroll (ed.), *Second language writing: Research insights for the classroom*, 11–23. Cambridge, UK: Cambridge University Press.

Silva, Tony. 1993. Toward an understanding of the distinct nature of L2 writing: The ESL research and its implications. *TESOL Quarterly* 27. 657–677.

Silva, Tony and Ilona Leki. 2004. Family matters: The influence of applied linguistics and composition studies on second language writing studies: Past, present, and future. *Modern Language Journal* 88. 1–13.

Spack, Ruth. 1997. The rhetorical construction of multilingual students. *TESOL Quarterly* 31. 765–774.

Swales, John. 1990. *Genre analysis: English in academic and research settings*. Cambridge, UK: Cambridge University Press.

Reppen, Randi. 2010. *Using corpora in the language classroom*. Cambridge, UK: Cambridge University Press.

Tardy, Christine. 2006. Appropriation, ownership, and agency: Negotiating teacher feedback in academic settings. In Ken Hyland and Fiona Hyland (eds.), *Feedback in second language writing: Contexts and issues*, 60–78. Cambridge, UK: Cambridge University Press.

Tardy, Christine. 2009. *Building genre knowledge*. West Lafayette, IN: Parlor Press.

Thaiss, Christopher, Gerd Bräuer, Paula Carlino, Lisa Ganobcsik-Williams, & Aparna Sinha (eds.). 2012. *Writing programs worldwide: Profiles of academic writing in many places*. Fort Collins, CO: The WAC Clearinghouse and Parlor Press.

Vann, Roberta, Frederick Lorenz, and Daisy Meyer. 1991. Error gravity: Faculty response to errors in written discourse of nonnative speakers of English. In Liz Hamp-Lyons (ed.), *Assessing second language writing in academic contexts*, 181–195. Norwood, NJ: Ablex.

Vygotsky, Lev. 1986. *Thought and language* (A. Kozulin, Trans.). Cambridge, MA: MIT Press. (Original work published 1934.)

Weigle, Sara. 2006. Investing in assessment: Designing tests to promote positive washback. In Paul Kei Matsuda, Christina Ortmeier-Hooper, and Xiaoye You (eds.), *The politics of second language writing: In search of the Promised Land*, 222–244. West Lafayette, IN: Parlor Press.

Wolfe-Quintero, Kate and Gabriela Segade. 1999. University support for second-language writers across the curriculum. In Linda Harklau, Kay Losey, and Meryl Siegal (eds.), *Generation 1.5 meets college composition*, 191–209. Mahwah, NJ: Erlbaum.

You, Xiaoye. 2006. Globalization and the politics of teaching EFL writing. In Paul Kei Matsuda, Christina Ortmeier-Hooper and Xiaoye You (eds.), *The politics of second language writing: In search of the Promised Land*, 188–202. West Lafayette, IN: Parlor Press.

Zamel, Vivian. 1983. The composing processes of advanced ESL students: Six case studies. *TESOL Quarterly* 17. 165–187.

Zamel, Vivian. 1997. Toward a model of transculturation. *TESOL Quarterly*, 31. 341–352.

Zhang, Shuqiang. 1995. Reexamining the affective advantage of peer feedback in the ESL writing class. *Journal of Second Language Writing* 4. 209–222.

Miyuki Sasaki
7 L2 writers in study-abroad contexts

1 Introduction

This chapter reviews studies that investigate how L2 writers develop in study-abroad (SA) contexts. I adopt a revised version of Kinginger's (2009: 18) definition of the term "study abroad," that is, "a temporary sojourn of pre-defined duration undertaken for acquiring a second language (L2) ability," excluding more permanent stays such as immigration.

L2 writers' growth overseas is a sub-category of L2 writing development dealt with in Polio and Park (Chapter 13) because studying abroad inevitably involves a period of time during which people cannot help changing, which may be called a form of "development." Although Polio and Park focus mainly on the linguistic aspects of such change, this chapter takes a broader view of L2 writing in that it looks at "multiple-language written literacy capacities" (Ortega 2012: 404), a perspective traditionally adopted in the field of L2 writing. In this chapter, therefore, L2 writing is based not only on traditional models of text construction (e.g., Grabe and Kaplan 1996), which require linguistic components such as vocabulary, syntax, cohesion, coherence, but also on more functional views, including knowledge of genre and a multi-competent "repertoire of knowledge" (Kobayashi and Rinnert 2013: 126), which is called for when a writer seeks the best way to write an effective text in a given situation (see below). This view seems more appropriate for this chapter especially because most current studies tend to treat L2 learning processes in SA contexts as part of language socialization, where the learner learns the target language as part of the process of becoming a member of a given society (e.g., Kinginger 2013).

With these assumptions in mind, I open this chapter with a brief historical overview of previous studies that have dealt with the effects of SA contexts on L2 learners in general, and then in particular with those that have focused on the development of L2 writers in study-abroad contests. Because there have been very few studies of the development of any aspect of L2 writing in SA contexts, especially before 2000, I synthesize studies targeting the development of other aspects of L2 development so that readers can derive a more comprehensive view of past SA-related studies in terms of framing theories, research targets, methods used, and major findings. When categorizing these past SA studies in terms of theory, I broadly adopt Atkinson's (2011: 18) distinction between "cognitive" and "alternative" approaches, where the latter refer to studies guided by the assumption that language development cannot (or should not) be confined to the learners' linguistic knowledge, skills, and systems. However, I exclude Atkinson's assumption underlying the cognitivists' approach whereby "knowledge exists separate from its context" (Ortega 2011: 168) from the classification in the present chapter because all SA studies assume that learning is affected by the SA environment. When categorizing each study, I thus use the following two questions as practical guides, drawing on Ortega's (2011) theorization of Atkinson's distinction:

1. Are explanations of SA effects psychological (i.e., learning occurs only inside the head; *cognitivism*) or socially oriented (*alternative*)?
2. Does the researcher focus on entities and objects such as language and communicative competence (*cognitivism*) as a static state or on actions and processes such as dynamism emerging in response to the given environment (*alternative*)?

As mentioned above, I first present a brief but overarching view of past SA studies targeting aspects of the participants' development other than L2 writing. I then focus on some of the existing empirical studies related to L2 writing development. This leads to the final stage, which suggests future directions for SA-related L2 writing studies. Having been encouraged by the enterprising spirit of various "alternative" types of studies such as those included in Manchón (2012), I suggest a number of directions for exploring the multiple-faceted and ever-changing nature of L2 writing in SA contexts, where the writers must adapt not only to a given foreign community but also to the accelerating globalization that follows these writers everywhere.

2 A Brief history of SA studies

The history of SA studies was marked by three main events: (1) the publication of Freed's (1995) first exclusive collection of SA studies, (2) the launching of the European Community Action Scheme for the Mobility of University Students (ERASMUS) Program in 1987, which promotes SA studies in Europe (e.g., Murphy-Lejeune 2002), and (3) the publication of Kinginger (2008), a more recent mixed-methods SA-study published in the *Modern Language Journal* monograph series. Roughly between Freed's (1995) and Kinginger's (2008) publications, SA-related studies were mainly cognitive in orientation, focusing on linguistic change measured through pre- and post-test designs. By contrast, Kinginger (2009) showed that the results of a well-documented cognitive study can benefit from a sociocultural (alternative) case study of six students selected from the 23 participants in the study. These students were American university students staying in France over a semester, and their linguistic gains were assessed through quantifiable measures such as a multiple choice test of grammatical knowledge, reading and listening abilities, and spoken role-plays. Moreover, the six students were carefully selected on the basis of their background, L2 proficiency, and motivation as well as of data drawn from their journal logs and interview narratives. The quantitative and qualitative data successfully complemented each other in explaining various individual differences observed in the quantitative results.

Starting around the time Kinginger's (2008) study was published, just as in other areas in applied linguistics (Atkinson 2011), SA studies with both cognitive and alternative epistemological orientations seem to become more diversified in terms of informing theories and consequent research targets. For example, recent SA studies with cognitive orientations do not simply investigate the students' linguistic gains through pre- and post-test designs but explore more complex interactions as part of the development of various cognitive abilities as well as the participants' profiles, including attitudes, beliefs, and experiences in the given SA contexts (e.g., Pérez-Vidal and Juan-Garau 2011). Meanwhile, other alternative studies have become either exclusively non-cognitive, focusing on non-linguistic aspects of SA students (e.g., Kinginger 2013), or have started to adopt mixed designs, as in Kinginger (2008), using both quantitative and qualitative data and epistemologies.

With these theoretical changes over time as background, I first summarize past SA studies in terms of participants, research questions, targets to be investigated, and major findings. In terms of participants, most SA studies tend to target students in mid- to higher-education in the USA, Europe, and Japan. These studies typically ask the following two questions:

1. Do SA experiences (usually about a semester-long but sometimes as long as one year) have any impact on the sojourners?
2. If so, what was (were) the most influential factor(s) that led to this outcome?

To answer these questions, many studies (especially those with a cognitive orientation) employed either inter-participant comparisons between SA and At-Home (AH) groups or between SA, AH, and Home-Immersion (HI) groups, or intra-participant comparisons using pre- and post-measures. Other characteristics (e.g., their theoretical orientations, targeted variables, and findings) shared by most past SA studies can be summarized as follows:

1. The most popular research targets were speaking skills and related knowledge, including oral proficiency, oral fluency, accuracy, and vocabulary (e.g., Collentine 2004; Segalowitz and Freed 2004) or pragmatic knowledge and processing both at the micro level (related to part of language use, e.g., Lafford 1995) or the macro level (related to overall language use, e.g., Matsumura 2007), in all of which SA experiences usually had positive impacts;
2. Very few studies targeted L2 listening (e.g., Cubillos, Chieffo, and Fan 2007), reading (e.g., Dewey 2004), or writing (see the next section). Among these, the effects of SA tended to be positive (e.g., Kaplan 1989 for listening) or mixed (e.g., Sasaki 2004 for writing);
3. The learners' knowledge and skills were often measured quantitatively through performance-based tests such as the Oral Proficiency Interview (OPI) or discourse completion tasks. Until around 2005, very few studies of the cognitive type included data on the students' affect or perceptions (see the next section);

4. Studies often reported mixed results, which may have been caused by differences in external factors such as learning contexts, amount and quality of contact time with the target language, or internal factors such the learners' personal attributes, including initial L2 proficiency, motivation, or identity. In general, highly motivated students with higher initial L2 proficiency who stayed abroad longer had previous L2-related experiences and had more contact with the L2 (especially outside of the classroom) in SA contexts tended to perform better than those who did not have these characteristics;

5. When the participants' language processing was examined, the findings suggested that SA students improved their strategic competence (the ability to cope with a situation using available resources) by becoming better at planning, monitoring, and evaluating their language use than their AH counterparts;

6. Although small in number before 2000, non-cognitive (alternative) studies (e.g., Siegal's 1995 ethnographic case study) and mixed-design studies (e.g., Huebner 1995) did exist, and these provided important insights (e.g., reasons for individual differences in improvement) for what could not have been explained by exclusively cognitive studies;

7. As mentioned earlier, more recent SA studies have become more epistemologically and methodologically diversified. "Cognitive" studies have tended to include both product and process variables (e.g., the function of managing strategies and other cognitive traits such as working memory) as well as their interactions with the learners' linguistic systems (e.g., Cubillos et al. 2007 for listening and Segalowitz and Freed 2004 for speaking, all of which I call "late-cognitive" in the section below). Furthermore, the number of alternative or mixed-method studies has become larger, with their theoretical framing becoming increasingly diversified (e.g., Jackson 2008).

3 Selected empirical studies of L2 writers in SA contexts

As mentioned in the previous section, L2 writing is one of the least investigated subfields in the empirical SA literature. Among the few studies conducted so far, I selected studies that appear to have sounder methodological foundations (e.g., having reasonably comparable AH or HI counterparts to the SA participants). I then categorized their theoretical orientations according to a revised version of Atkinson's (2011) distinction between "cognitive" and "alternative" approaches (see above). On the basis of the overarching survey presented in the previous section, I also divided the cognitive studies into earlier and later ones according to the complexity in their research design (see Item 7 in the previous section) and also added the new category of "mixed-data" approach. To turn these into useful resources for planning future studies of L2 writing, I describe them in some detail while including information about participants, methods, and major findings.

3.1 Cognitively-oriented studies

The following four studies were judged to be cognitive because their fundamental orientations were marked by the two typical characteristics of cognitive studies, which I operationally defined drawing on Ortega's (2011) characterization (see Section 1): (1) they mainly target cognitive aspects of the participants' development; and (2) they treat the participants' ability and knowledge as a static state rather than emerging in response to the given environment. However, among the four cognitive studies presented here, the last three are categorized as "later" because they used other non-linguistic traits (e.g., attitude, L2 contact hours, and learning strategies) that might influence individual differences in the participants' linguistic gains, whereas a lack attention to such features characterizes earlier cognitive studies. The inclusion of such data helps us understand how and why the ultimate results (linguistic gains, loss, or no gains) were obtained at the conclusion of SA stays, an outcome earlier cognitive studies could not explain.

3.1.1 Freed, So, and Lazar (2003): Earlier cognitive

This is one of the pioneering studies examining the effects of SA on literacy development. Freed et al. (2003) compared the L2 speaking and writing gains of four American AH university students with four SA counterparts who spent one semester in France. Six "non-teacher NS judges" (p. 6) subjectively assessed (i.e., without being given any evaluation criteria) the fluency of the two groups' Oral Proficiency Interview (OPI) production and found that the SA students were more fluent than the AH students following their stay abroad. This assessment was supported by quantifiable characteristics of the participants' oral production including quantity, speed, and absence of disfluency markers such as "unduly long pauses and groups of filled pauses" (p. 6). Similarly, "five non-teacher NS judges" (p. 7) subjectively evaluated the fluency of the compositions written by the same participants. Unlike their oral performance, the AH group's compositions were judged to be more fluent in both the pre- and post-SA periods, while the SA group made no significant improvement in terms of this subjective fluency evaluation.

3.1.2 Pérez-Vidal and Juan-Garau (2011): Late cognitive

Unlike Freed et al. (2003), Pérez-Vidal and Juan-Garau's (2011) study was a type of intra-participant comparison in which the researchers compared the development of oral and written production of 35 Catalan/Spanish bilingual university students over a six-month (80 hours) course of formal instruction in English with their development over their subsequent three-month SA experiences in English-speaking countries, especially the UK. Pérez-Vidal and Juan-Garau also used questionnaire data to capture the participants' individual profiles, including language use, attitude, beliefs, motivation, and experiences during their overseas stay. All participants wrote a 30-minute opinion composition, and 20 students role-played for seven minutes at three points: before receiving formal instruction (T1), after receiving formal instruction (T2), and at the conclusion of the SA program (T3).

The participants' oral production and compositions were rated equally in terms of fluency (measured in words per clause and words per minute), accuracy (measured as a ratio of grammatical, lexical, and pragmatic errors), grammatical complexity (measured in number of dependent clauses per clause, clauses per T-unit, number of coordinate clauses divided by number of combined subordinate clauses), lexical complexity (measured by word types divided by word tokens; see Pérez-Vidal and Juan-Garau for details), and ratios of formulaic expressions (e.g., "on the other hand"). The results show that the participants did not significantly improve in these aspects of oral production during the formal instruction period but that they significantly improved in terms of fluency, complexity, and use of formulaic expressions during the SA period.

The questionnaires revealed that among many factors examined, "opportunities for input and interaction an SA period provides" (p. 175) were significantly related to improvement in speaking. On the other hand, the participants' writing fluency (measured in terms of words per minute) and lexical complexity (see above) significantly decreased during formal instruction at home while these two variables significantly improved during the SA period. However, the number of areas showing improvement during the SA period was lower in the participants' writing than in their oral production. In terms of their experiences during the SA period, those who improved greatly in writing tended to do "extracurricular academic activities" (p. 179) and to be "eager to learn" and "emotionally aware" (p. 181), which was not a characteristic of those who achieved greater speaking improvement during their SA period. Overall, it appears that writing skills required more effort than speaking skills if they were to improve.

3.1.3 Llanes, Tragant, and Serrano (2012): Late cognitive

This study is similar to Pérez-Vidal and Juan-Garau (2011) in that the authors compared the effects of semester-long SA experiences in the UK by 24 Spanish-speaking participants on fluency, complexity, and accuracy (measured as in Pérez-Vidal and Juan-Garau 2011) in both spoken (narratives) and written (15-minute descriptive essays) English. However, Llanes et al. did not compare the effects of SA with those of formal instruction at home but instead used a pre- and post-test design. Furthermore, they included a greater number of individual difference variables, including attitude, orientation toward learning the L2, degree pursued, registration in English classes, degree of L2 interaction, and the participants' self-perceptions of linguistic progress in the L2. These variables were quantified through questionnaire item scores. Although they were measured on the assumption that respondents' perceptions and feelings are static and therefore can be captured through questionnaire items, the decision to include the students' own perspective is noteworthy because this was not usually the case in traditional cognitive analyses. The results of this study were similar to those of Pérez-Vidal and Juan-Garau in that the participants' writing significantly improved only in the area of fluency, whereas their speaking improved in more areas, including fluency and lexical complexity.

As regards the relationship between the participants' linguistic improvement and their individual characteristics and perceptions, I will focus only on significant results related to their written improvement. Humanities majors improved their writing fluency and syntactic complexity further than those who majored in translation or science. As regards SA environments, those who lived with a family improved their written accuracy further than those who lived in an apartment or a residence hall. Those who had less contact with L1 speakers at home improved their fluency, and those who had more contact with L2 speakers improved their accuracy. As regards the participants' perceptions, those who felt that their reading improved during the SA period also felt that their written syntactic complexity improved, while those who felt that their writing improved also reported that their fluency and syntactic complexity improved and that their perceptions of improvement in their accent were related to their perceived written fluency.

3.1.4 Llanes and Muñoz (2013): Late cognitive

This study introduced the variable of "age" in the comparison of the impact of SA experiences on oral and written abilities. Llanes and Muñoz thus compared four groups of: (1) children (M_{age} = 10.5, the average of the two children's groups; Groups 1 and 2) who spent two to three months abroad (SA children; n = 39); (2) children who stayed at home (AH children; n = 34); (3) adults (M_{age} = 20.9, the average of the two adult groups; Groups 3 and (4) adults who spent two to three months abroad (SA adults; n = 46); and (4) adults who stayed at home (AH adults; n = 20). All were Spanish-speaking, and their SA environment was English-speaking. The authors used a pre- and post-design to compare the participants' spoken and written output in terms of fluency, lexical and syntactic complexity, and accuracy measured as in other cognitive studies. The authors also collected data related to L2 language contact through a questionnaire. The within-participant comparison revealed that: (1) SA children improved in oral fluency, complexity, and accuracy as well as written complexity and accuracy, whereas AH children did not improve in any of these; (2) SA adults improved in speaking fluency, and AH adults improved in lexical complexity in writing. In contrast, the between-participant comparison revealed that the SA participants (adults and children) outperformed the AH participants in all aspects of oral skills as well as in syntactic complexity in writing. These results are similar to those of the cognitive studies reviewed above. In terms of comparison between children and adults, SA had stronger positive effects on adults in terms of oral lexical complexity in addition to all aspects of writing abilities. The results of a MANCOVA (multiple analyses of covariance) with age and contexts as the independent variables showed an interaction between age and context variables, indicating that "the SA setting seems to be more beneficial for children in terms of the improvement in oral skills, whereas the AH context seems to foster the development of writing skills, especially for adults" (p. 79). Overall, it appears that here again, writing skills take more time and more life experience to develop compared to speaking skills in SA contexts. Finally, this study is special in that the authors explain their results in terms of recent SLA perspectives such as DeKeyser's (2007) automatization theory and Ellis's (2005) distinction between implicit and explicit knowledge, which have rarely been employed in past SA studies.

3.2 Mixed-data studies

A series of SA studies was conducted by myself. These studies are different from the typical cognitive studies reviewed in Section 3.1 in that: (1) they observed changes in both product-oriented aspects (e.g., composition scores) and process-oriented aspects (e.g., writing strategies) of L2 writing; (2) two of them continued observing the participants over a relatively long period after their SA ended; and (3) they used interview data to investigate participants' own (emic) perspective to help explain quantifiable changes in their performance over time. However, these studies (along with other cognitive studies reviewed in the previous section) share a similar positivistic epistemology in that they were conducted under the assumption that there could exist patterns shared by a group of participants even though these patterns might contain outliers that belong to no pattern. My stance is thus close to what Denzin and Lincoln (2000) call "postpositivism" (p. 165) in that I believe in the co-existence of regularities and randomness resulting from historical and environmental factors. That is, my studies do not share the epistemological assumptions (e.g., constructivism) made by many of the alternative studies (e.g., the sociocognitive approach) exemplified by Atkinson (2011). Unlike the ethnographic part of Kinginger's study (2008), the part of these studies related to qualitative data simply supplemented the quantitative results obtained. I therefore call my three studies "mixed-data" studies instead of the more commonly used "mixed-methods" label (e.g., Cresswell 2002).

3.2.1 Sasaki (2004): Mixed data

This study was not originally intended to investigate the effects of SA experiences but to investigate the L2 writing behavior of 11 Japanese students between their first and fourth years in university. The data, including their argumentative compositions, were collected once a year over 3.5 years. In addition, the participants' emic accounts of the reasons for their development were collected at the end of the fourth year. When the study started in 1998, all were 18-year-old undergraduates majoring in British and American studies. Because six of the 11 students spent 2 to 8 months in English-speaking countries mainly in their third year in university, the study could also compare the six SA students with the five AH students who were similar in terms of L2 proficiency (measured as the sum of listening and grammar test scores), L2 writing ability (measured through 30-minute argumentative compositions), and strategy use (e.g., global planning, re-reading, and L1-to-L2 translation) at the start of the study. The results revealed that the SA and AH groups developed similarly over time in terms of L2 proficiency, composition quality, and fluency. They also learned to use global planning for the content to be written. The only differences between the two groups were that: (1) the SA students learned not to stop in order to translate their ideas into the L2 as often as in their first year; and (2) 67 % of the SA students became more motivated to write better in the L2 whereas none of the AH students mentioned such increased motivation.

3.2.2 Sasaki (2007): Mixed-data

This study was a follow-up to Sasaki (2004). Sasaki (2007) examined more immediate effects of SA experiences on students' L2 proficiency and L2 (argumentative) writing ability and strategy use by shortening the observation period to one year, which took place immediately before and after the SA students' experiences abroad. The SA group consisted of 7 students who spent 4 to 9 months in English-speaking countries, and the AH group consisted of 6 students. The results revealed that: (1) both SA and AH groups significantly improved in overall L2 proficiency; (2) unlike in Sasaki (2004), only the SA group significantly improved its L2 composition scores and writing fluency; and (3) as in Sasaki (2004), only the SA group became more motivated to write better in the L2, which was reflected in their changed use of L2 writing strategies.

3.2.3 Sasaki (2011): Mixed-data

After conducting Sasaki (2004) and (2007), I realized the importance of the relationship between students' L2 writing development, motivation, and relational changes over time. Furthermore, while I collected data for these two studies (between 1998 and 2003), SA became increasingly popular in Japan (Ministry of Education, Culture, Sports, Science, and Technology, Japan 2012), which made the value of a shorter (e.g., 2 months) stay abroad appear less substantial to the students than a longer stay (e.g., 8 months). Noticing these phenomena motivated me to conduct the most recent study (Sasaki 2011), in which I examined the effects of different lengths of SA experiences on the two variables of L2 writing ability and motivation to write in the L2. I subsequently divided the participants into four groups according to the lengths of the overseas stays they experienced during the 3.5-year observation period: AH group ($n = 9$) – zero months abroad; SA-1.5–2 group ($n = 9$) – 1.5 to 2 months abroad; SA-4 group ($n = 7$) – SA-4 months abroad; and SA-8-to-11 group ($n = 12$) – SA-8–11 months abroad. Once a year over the 3.5-year observation period, all 37 participants wrote argumentative compositions for about 30 minutes and provided 30- to 60-minute-interview data about their L2 learning experiences and motivation to study L2 writing. At the end of their fourth year in university (after the fourth data collection session), they were again interviewed about what they thought had led to changes in their L2 writing and motivation to write in the L2 over the 3.5-year observation period (15 to 30 minutes). The results revealed that: (1) as in Sasaki (2004), those who spent time abroad improved their L2 writing ability over the 3.5 years whereas the AH students did not; (2) the SA students were generally more motivated to study L2 writing even before their overseas stay, yet their motivation became stronger after coming home, and such motivational improvement seemed to be related to their formation of "L2-related imagined communities" (p. 81), where they could imagine themselves writing in the L2 for communicative purposes; and (3) those who spent more than 4 months abroad significantly improved their L2 writing ability compared to those who spent only 1.5 to 2 months abroad.

All three studies agree that SA had positive effects on L2 writing ability development in terms of both product and process. However, as mentioned above, the differences between the results of Sasaki (2004) and those of Sasaki (2011) suggest that when data were collected for Sasaki (2011) (10 years later than for Sasaki 2004), the effects of shorter stays (e.g., 1.5- to 2-months) may have become weaker. This suggests that the results of similar studies may be susceptible to the sociocultural value of SA experiences at a given time and in a given society (Sasaki 2012). Furthermore, the results of Sasaki (2011) indicate that the SA students' motivation was different from that of the AH students from the beginning of the study even though their L2 proficiency and writing ability were similar, and that the nature of the SA students' motivation further changed as a result of their overseas experience, a phenomenon indicating that the learners' initial condition may have produced unexpectedly powerful results, as dynamic systems theory (DST) predicts (e.g., Verspoor, de Bot, and Lowie 2011; see below for SA studies more clearly framed within a DST perspective). Finally, all three studies suggest that the participants' own explanations (emic data) were helpful in distinguishing the true effects of SA experiences (e.g., writing long texts) from those that were not (e.g., effective L2 writing strategies such as global planning were mainly learned in English classes at home), which could have been missed had I taken an exclusively etic cognitive perspective.

3.3 Alternative studies

Very few SA studies can be identified as "alternative" in that they satisfy the two litmus characteristics set up in the analysis undertaken in this chapter: (1) any explanation is socially oriented; and (2) the researchers focus on action and processes that dynamically emerge in response to a given environment. With these criteria in mind, I selected three recent studies: one was conducted within a pseudo-dynamic systems theory (DST) approach, and the other two were written by the same author, with the earlier version claimed to be framed by a sociocognitive approach (e.g., Riazi 1997) and the later version by Cook's (2007) multi-competence perspective, a more specific version of the earlier sociocognitive framing.

3.3.1 Serrano, Tragant, and Llanes (2012): DST interpretations of the results

I call the theoretical framing of this study "pseudo-DST" because the authors did not start with a DST approach through which to examine their research targets but in the end found that some of their findings matched the typical characteristics of a DST system. A DST approach treats language development as an emergent system sensitive to its initial state as well as to internal and external influences, expecting non-linear random developmental trajectories while constantly adapting to the given environment (Verspoor et al. 2011). In the event, Serrano et al. found that their L2 learners' developmental trajectories closely exemplified such systems.

Serrano et al.'s study is similar to Llanes et al. (2012), which was categorized above as a "late-cognitive" study in that the authors compared the effects on 14 Spanish-speaking university students of a 1-year long SA stay in the UK in terms of fluency, complexity, lexical richness, and accuracy (measured as in Llanes et al. 2012) in both speaking (narratives) and writing (15-minute descriptive essays). In addition to these linguistic variables, the authors also investigated the effects of individual differences related to their attitude toward British people as well as the manner and amount of L2 language contact. The differences between this study and Llanes et al. (2012) are that this study examined the effects of a longer period (1 year vs. 1 semester) and at more frequent intervals (three times vs. twice), and paid greater attention to how some aspects (e.g., fluency) of speaking and writing preceded others (e.g., syntactic accuracy) as well as how such sequences interacted with speaking and writing. To save space, I present the results below only if they are related to the participants' writing development.

These results reveal that: (1) speaking developed earlier than writing (if both abilities improved to any extent) and in a non-linear manner; (2) fluency development preceded the development of lexical richness and accuracy in both speaking and writing; (3) those who thought that British people were more "sociable" and "humble" improved their writing ability; and (4) having more experiences with non-Spanish-speaking friends and living with English-speaking people helped them improve their writing in terms of lexical richness. Although results (1) to (4) concur with those of previous SA studies, as mentioned earlier, the authors further argue that some of these results conform to DST characteristics. For example, Results 1 and 2 show representative characteristics of the DST system (non-linear development as well as the dependence of the present level of development on the last one; see, for example, Verspoor et al. 2011). Moreover, this finding was made possible by Serrano et al.'s complex research design, with many variables observed on several occasions over time. The authors therefore end the study suggesting that a DST approach might be a more suitable way for future studies investigating SA students' development, with more data collection points and greater focus on individual development rather than on group tendencies.

3.3.2 Kobayashi and Rinnert (2007): Sociocognitive

This study is unique both in the use of a sociocognitive approach and of composition structures as its target. Kobayashi and Rinnert used the term "sociocognitive approach" in the sense that it "conceives of writing as a primary mental activities by an individual writer within a particular social context and recognizes the importance of writers' previous experiences and perceptions in constructing their own writing abilities and practices" (p. 92). This stance resonates with the operational definition of L2 writing proposed earlier in this chapter, namely of L2 writing as multiple-language written literacy capacities.

In this study, Kobayashi and Rinnert compared three groups: an AH Group ($n = 10$), consisting of Japanese university students who received only L1 writing instruction mainly in high school; an SA Group ($n = 10$), consisting of university students who received L1 writing instruction mainly in high school and L2 (English) instruction during a 2-semester-long stay in an L2-speaking country; and a Long-SA Group ($n = 5$) consisting of graduate students and teachers who spent 3.5 to 14 years in English-speaking countries. All wrote explanatory/argumentative compositions in both the L1 and the L2 on one of two topics chosen by the researchers. In addition, they were also interviewed for 2 to 3 hours "about the construction of the texts and decisions made during the writing process as well as the writers' perceptions of L1 and L2 writing and possible background influences" (p. 95). The results related to effects of SA on L2 writing were as follows: (1) the SA and Long-SA groups (with overseas experience) used "counterargument with refutation" (p. 96) twice as often in the L1 as in the L2 (60 % in the L1, 33 % in the L2), whereas the AH Group used this strategy with the same frequency (30 %) in the L1 and the L2; (2) the SA and Long-SA groups' more frequent use of counterarguments was caused by its complex transfer from the L2 writing instruction they had previously received in and out of Japan and therefore by the value the participants attached to it, even if some were not confident in using it in the L2; (3) the Long-SA Group used specific contextualization (e.g., defining terms) in the introduction to both their L1 and L2 compositions much more frequently than AH and SA Groups, which can be attributed to the Long-SA group's extensive L2 writing training in their specialized field (e.g., social sciences) while overseas. These findings show that the participants did not simply apply the knowledge and skills they had acquired overseas. Instead, their final choice of the most appropriate rhetorical patterns was the result of complex decision-making based on their evaluation of the situation.

3.2.3 Kobayashi and Rinnert (2012): Multi-competence theory

My review of this paper focuses on the second half of the study because the first half overlaps with Kobayashi and Rinnert (2007) as the background to the second half. This study is unique in that on the basis of the results obtained in Kobayashi and Rinnert (2007), the case study forming the second half of the study is framed by Cook's (2007) multi-competence theory, which assumes that learning an additional language is not simply adding one language to the original but rather a "dynamic and fluid" system (Kobayashi and Rinnert 2012: 5) drawing on both L1 and L2, with the ever-changing system adapting to the given situation. Although their application of Cook's multi-competence theory can be interpreted as a specific version of the sociocognitive approach they used for their 2007 study, Cook's theory better suits the case of Natsu, the Japanese participant featured in the second half of the study. Although Natsu was in fact an SA participant in their 2007 study (she had spent 3 years in high school in Australia before their 2007 study), the authors followed her for an additional 2.5 years. During that time, Natsu experienced additional overseas stays in order to learn not only the L2 but also a third language (L3). In university, Natsu was a Chinese major. Over her first year in university (Time 1), Kobayashi and Rinnert collected Natsu's Japanese L1 and English L2 argumentative compositions as well as her L1, L2, and Chinese L3 argumentative compositions 2.5 years later (Time 2) after Natsu spent 1 year in China. Kobayashi and Rinnert also interviewed Natsu for a total of 80 hours and corresponded with her by email during the 2.5-year observation period.

In the case study of Natsu, Kobayashi and Rinnert found that: (1) the structure of her L2 composition at Time 1 was based on knowledge acquired in Australia, her first SA site, but was also influenced by her knowledge of L1 writing; (2) her Time 2 essays in the L1, L2, and L3 shared a common structure of "justification" (presenting a position and supporting it with clear reasons and evidence, p. 114) because she had by then come to believe that this type of argumentative construction was effective across languages; however, (3) she also added some "language-specific text features ... in order to appeal to the prospective audience" (p. 122), a strategy she had learned through formal instruction and self-training in the L2 and through her stay in China for the L3. For example, she ended her Time 3 Chinese compositions with a four-word idiom because she believed that it was an effective way to conclude. These findings again suggest that the effects of SA experiences become incorporated over time into the learners' multi-competent language ability system, which they use based on their assessment of each context.

4 Summary and suggestions for further research

On the basis of the 10 previous studies related to L2 writers in the SA contexts reviewed above, I now list the findings shared by many of them:

1. Although SA experiences are often effective in improving L2 writing skills, their development is slower than oral skill development for both adults and children;
2. Among the three L2 writing aspects of fluency, complexity and accuracy, fluency tends to develop earliest;
3. Compared with the development of speaking ability, the development of writing ability requires extra effort, motivation, a positive attitude toward English-speaking people, more contact time and life experiences, and stronger determination to learn;
4. SA experiences improve motivation to write better by using effective strategies;
5. The effects of SA experiences can be affected by the value given to them in the given society;
6. The students' L2 writing development trajectories fit some of the typical DST characteristics (e.g., non-linear development, potentially strong effect of the initial condition);
7. Through the acquisition of L1, L2, and even L3 writing systems, students learn to choose what they think is the most appealing way of writing from their existing knowledge and skills repertoire for the given situation.

On the basis of this summary of previous studies as well as the general history of SA studies reviewed earlier, I now suggest possible future research directions in terms of: (1) framing theory; (2) participants; (3) data collection methods; and (4) aspect(s) of L2 writing to be investigated.

4.1 Framing theories

We saw that most SA studies investigating L2 writing development are cognitive supported by a (post-)positivistic perspective. Among the 10 studies reviewed above, only three can be classified as "alternative" in terms of Atkinson's (2011) theorization. Moreover, three studies with mixed-data designs were also supported by quantitative data. Because SA studies of L2 writing are still few in number, my first suggestion is to further promote studies of the cognitive type and especially of the late-cognitive type. That is, further studies could investigate the interaction between the participants' linguistic gains and various other cognitive (e.g., learning strategies), affective (e.g., motivation), and environmental factors (e.g., L2 contact hours) in a more sophisticated manner (e.g., using structural equation modeling with a sufficiently large sample; see Miglietta and Tartaglia 2009, who applied a similar design to an immigrant population). The results of such studies will be useful to those who plan large-scale SA programs in terms of the participants' preparation, their living conditions, the curriculum, and the maintenance of the participants' linguistic abilities after they return home. The results would be also useful in explaining why and how the program in question can be more effective than AH programs to stakeholders who have invested in SA programs (Kinginger 2009). Yet, we now know that some learners cannot fit within such "cure-all" arrangements, and we must therefore uncover the reasons for their superficially random-looking deviation so that we can make programs more flexible for them. This is where I believe that the findings of alternative studies may have practical implications in addition to contributing pure knowledge to the field. I therefore recommend that studies of the alternative type be also conducted. For such purposes, ethnographic case studies can be promising, as in the case of Kinginger (2008), where the results of case studies reported in its second half were insightful in explaining the quantitative results reported in its first half. However, the validity of such case studies should of course be verified by means of appropriate methodology (e.g., "thick description and triangulation," as explained in Duff 2008: 43–44).

In addition, many other alternative theories can be applied to investigating L2 writers in SA contexts. For example, the theories used in the chapters in Manchón (2012) are all alternative, and we saw that only two of them (DST and multi-competence theories) have been applied to SA research. However, since all chapters deal with L2 writing development, I believe that the theories used in all the other chapters in that volume could also be applied to SA studies. For example, the sociocultural approach used by Wiggleworth and Storch (2012) would be useful in revealing what is happening inside the classroom. The results of applying such an approach to individuals' learning processes in SA contexts could further promote the idea of "writing to learn" rather than "learning to write" (Manchón 2011). Another example is the "goal theory" applied by Cumming (2012). Detailed analyses of micro-aspects of the participants' goals and of changes in their proficiency over time could be useful in explaining why some learners become more motivated to learn than others during and after their overseas stay (cf. Sasaki 2011).

4.2 Participants

Most of the participants in previous SA studies were university students from the US, Spain, or Japan. After the ERASMUS program was launched in 1987, an increasing number of European researchers undertook SA-related studies, especially of Spanish-speaking university students sent to English-speaking countries. Llanes and Muñoz (2013) was the one exception that compared children and adults, and their results are useful not only for teachers and researchers but also for program administrators who plan SA programs for students of different ages. In my view, there should be more studies investigating students of more diversified ages, L1s, and cultural backgrounds over longer periods of time.

4.3 Data

What is to be researched is the most crucial issue in any study. Looking back at what was examined in past SA studies (and not exclusively those related to L2 writing), we learn that they mainly focused on the participants' learning processes or their products but also that products appear to have generally been either academic types of writing (e.g., Kobayashi and Rinnert 2013) or narratives (e.g., Llanes and Muñoz 2013) for the sake of comparison with the same participants' speaking products on a similar basis (i.e., many studies focused on spoken narratives to be compared with written ones). In a conspicuously large number of studies, the prompts (e.g., "My life: past, present, and future expectations" given by Llanes and Muñoz 2013: 72) were given simply to collect data to examine the participants' development in fluency, complexity, and accuracy (with the participants sometimes having to write the text within 15 minutes). Having learned about the types of data used in these previous SA studies, I believe that studies of students' development in writing for other types of genres are needed, especially for those of a more specific nature than mere academic argumentation (e.g., business proposals) informed by the most current genre theory (e.g., Tardy 2013). Moreover, combining such studies with studies of changes in the participants' goals could contribute to the field by providing more realistic developmental trajectories of L2 learners in SA contexts.

Another type of data that has seldom been investigated is the nature and content of the classrooms in which SA students study abroad. All relevant factors, including the teachers' beliefs, background, training, and their relationship with the students as well as the methods and tasks used in the classroom should be considered if our aim is to investigate the true effects of SA experiences. For example, if the teacher uses collaborative writing (cf., Chapter 18, this volume) as part of

L2 writing activities, we need to examine the teacher's skill at using that particular method, how familiar the students are with the method, and how effective it is in improving the students' target writing skills, among other research targets.

As a possible future direction responding to such calls for further studies in terms of theoretical frameworks, participants, and types of data, part of a longitudinal study conducted by Taguchi (2012) might be suggestive. Drawing on DST theory, she observed the development in 48 students of pragmatic knowledge and processing in English in a home immersion (HI) program in a university in Japan. What may be most insightful among her findings was that some students could not develop polite forms of email writing because they had become too friendly with some of their English-speaking teachers, a practice that may not be desirable when they eventually went abroad. This kind of sociolinguistic knowledge is something students may not be able to learn unless they spend some time in the target culture and experience negative feedback caused by such conduct. This is because people's feelings toward acceptable formality in a new mode of L2 writing such as emailing might differ even among L2-speaking stakeholders such as professors as well as future employers and colleagues. Tracing such situated and individualistic developmental trajectories will probably require some type of "alternative" framework using various types of data (e.g., email texts, students' and teachers' interviews, and the scores of tests measuring the students' ability to process and produce the most appropriate ways of writing emails). Lastly, with the rapidly increasing popularity of various new types of writing modes using ICT technology (e.g., Facebook, Tweets, Webchat, etc.), the target genres to be pursued will become even more complex, adding factors such as conflicts between interlocutors from various non-L2 cultures, which was not such a serious issue in the field of L2 writing before. And yet, this may be one of the most essential as well as promising directions for SA studies of L2 writing (especially as regards English as a second language writing) in this globalized world.

5 Acknowledgments

I would like to thank Paul Bruthiaux and Hiroe Kobayashi for their valuable comments and suggestions. The preparation of this chapter was aided by Research Grant No. 20520533 for the 2012 to 2016 academic years from the Ministry of Education, Culture, Sports, Science, and Technology of Japan.

6 Additional sources

Aveni, Valerie. 2005. *Study abroad and second language use: Constructing the self.* Cambridge: Cambridge University Press.

Churchill, Eton and Margaret DuFon. 2006. Evolving threads in study abroad research.
    In Margaret DuFon and Eton Churchill (eds.), *Language learners in study abroad contexts*,
    1–27. Clevedon, UK: Multilingual Matters.
Collentine, Joseph. 2009. Study abroad research: Findings, implications, and future directions.
    In Michael H. Long and Catherine J. Doughty (eds.), *The handbook of language teaching*,
    218–233. New York: Blackwell.
Freed, Barbara F., Dan P. Dewey, Norman, Segalowitz, and Randall Halter. 2004. The language
    contact profile. *Studies in Second Language Acquisition* 26. 349–356.
Kinginger, Celeste. 2013. Language socialization in study abroad. In Carol A. Chapelle (ed.),
    The encyclopedia of applied linguistics. New York: Blackwell.
Larsen-Freeman, Diane and Lynn Cameron. 2008. *Complex systems and applied linguistics*.
    Oxford: Oxford University Press.
Magnan, Sally and Barbara Lafford. 2012. Learning through immersion during study abroad.
    In Susan Gass and Alison Mackey (eds.), *Handbook of second language acquisition*, 525–540.
    New York: Routledge.
Mairworm, Friedhelm, Wolfgang Staube, and Ulrich Teichler. 1991. *Learning in Europe: The
    ERASMUS experience: A survey of the 1988–89 ERASMUS Students*. London: Jessica Kingsley.
Ren, Wei. 2014. A longitudinal investigation into L2 learners' cognitive processes during study
    abroad. *Applied Linguistics* 35(5). 575–594.
Song, Juyoung. 2012. Imagined communities and language socialization practices in transnational
    space: A case study of two Korean "study abroad" families in the United States. *The Modern
    Language Journal* 96(4). 507–524.

7 References

Atkinson, Dwight (ed.). 2011. *Alternative approaches to second language acquisition*. London:
    Routledge.
Collentine, Joseph. 2004. The effects of learning contexts of morphosyntactic and lexical
    development. *Studies in Second Language Acquisition* 26. 227–248.
Cook, Vivian. 2007. Multi-competence: Black hole or wormhole for second language acquisition
    research? In Zhao-Hong Han (ed.), *Understanding second language process* [sic], 16–26.
    Clevedon: Multilingual Matters.
Cresswell, John W. 2002. *Research design: Qualitative, quantitative, and mixed methods
    approaches*, 2nd edn. Thousand Oaks, CA: Sage.
Cubillos, Jorge H., Lisa Chieffo, and Chunbo Fan. 2008. The impact of short-term study abroad
    programs on L2 listening comprehension skills. *Foreign Language Annals* 41. 157–185.
Cumming, Alister. 2012. Goal theory and second-language writing development: Two ways.
    In Rosa M. Manchón (ed.), *L2 writing development: Multiple perspectives*, 135–164. Bristol:
    Multilingual Matters.
DeKeyser, Robert. 2007. *Practice in a second language: Perspectives from applied linguistics and
    cognitive psychology*. New York: Cambridge University Press.
Denzin, Norman and Yvonna S. Lincoln (eds.) 2000. *Handbook of qualitative research*, 2nd edn.
    Thousand Oaks, CA: Sage.
Dewey, Dan P. 2004. A comparison of reading development by learners of Japanese in intensive
    domestic immersion and study abroad contexts. *Studies in Second Language Acquisition* 26.
    303–327.
Duff, Patricia A. 2008. *Case study research in applied linguistics*. New York: Lawrence Erlbaum.
Ellis, Rod. 2005. Measuring implicit and explicit knowledge of a second language: A psychometric
    study. *Studies in Second Language Acquisition* 27. 141–172.

Freed, Barbara F. (ed.). 1995. *Second language acquisition in a study abroad context*. Amsterdam: John Benjamins.

Freed, Barbara F., Sufumi So, and Nicole A. Lazar. 2003. Language learning abroad: How do gains in written fluency compare with gains in oral fluency in French as a second language? *ADFL Bulletin* 34(3). 34–40.

Grabe, William and Robert B. Kaplan. 1996. *Theory and practice of writing*. New York: Longman.

Huebner, Thom. 1995. The effects of overseas language programs: Report on a case study of an intensive Japanese course. In Barbara F. Freed (ed.), *Second language acquisition in a study abroad context*, 171–193. Amsterdam: John Benjamins.

Jackson, Jane. 2008. *Language identity and study abroad: Sociocultural perspectives*. London: Equinox.

Kaplan, Marsha A. 1989. French in the community: A survey of language use abroad. *The French Review* 63(2). 290–301.

Kinginger, Celeste. 2008. Language learning in study abroad: Case studies of Americans in France. *The Modern Language Journal, Supplement to Volume* 92. 1–124.

Kinginger, Celeste. 2009. *Language learning and study abroad: A critical reading of research*. New York: Palgrave Macmillan.

Kinginger, Celeste (ed.). 2013. *Social and cultural aspects of language learning in study abroad*. Amsterdam: John Benjamins.

Kobayashi, Hiroe and Carol Rinnert. 2007. Transferability of argumentative writing competence from L2 to L1: Effects of overseas experience. In Maeve Conrick and Martin Howard (eds.), *From applied linguistics to linguistics applied: Issues, practices, trends. British Studies in Applied Linguistics*, 91–110. London: British Association of Applied Linguistics.

Kobayashi, Hiroe and Carol Rinnert. 2012. Understanding L2 writing development from a multicompetence perspective: Dynamic repertoires of knowledge and text construction. In Rosa M. Manchón (ed.), *L2 writing development: Multiple perspectives*, 101–134. Boston, MA: De Gruyter Mouton.

Lafford, Barbara A. 1995. Getting into, through, and out of a survival situation: A comparison of communicative strategies used by students studying Spanish abroad and at home. In Barbara F. Freed (ed.), *Second language acquisition in a study abroad context*, 97–121. Amsterdam: John Benjamins.

Llanes, Àngels and Carmen Muñoz. 2013. Age effects in a study-abroad context: Children and adults studying abroad and at home. *Language Learning* 63. 63–90.

Llanes, Àngels, Elsa Tragant, and Raquel Serrano. 2012. The role of individual differences in a study abroad experience: The case of Erasmus students. *International Journal of Multilingualism* 9(3). 318–342.

Manchón, Rosa M. (ed.). 2011. *Learning-to-write and writing-to-learn in an additional language*. Amsterdam: John Benjamins.

Manchón, Rosa M. (ed.). 2012. *L2 writing development: Multiple perspectives*. Boston, MA: De Gruyter Mouton.

Matsumura, Shoichi. 2007. Exploring the after effects of study abroad on interlanguage pragmatic development. *Intercultural Pragmatics* 4(2). 167–192.

Miglietta, Anna and Stefano Tartaglia. 2009. The influence of length of stay, linguistic competence, and media exposure in immigrants' adaptation. *Cross-Cultural Research* 43(1). 46–61.

Ministry of Education, Culture, Sports, Science, and Technology, Japan. 2012. *Nihonjin no kaigai ryuugaku joukyou* [Trends among Japanese studying abroad]. Tokyo.

Murphy-Lejeune, Elizabeth. 2002. *Student mobility and narrative in Europe: The new strangers*. London: Routledge.

Ortega, Lourdes. 2011. SLA after the social turn: Where cognitivism and its alternatives stand. In Dwight Atkinson (ed.), *Alternative approaches to second language acquisition*, 167–180. London: Routledge.

Ortega, Lourdes. 2012. Epilogue: Exploring L2 writing-SLA interfaces. *Journal of Second Language Writing* 21. 404–415.

Pérez-Vidal, Carmen and María Juan-Garau. 2011. The effect of context and input conditions on oral and written development: A study abroad perspective. *International Review of Applied Linguistics* 49. 157–185.

Riazi, A. Mehdi. 1997. Acquiring disciplinary literacy: A social-cognitive analysis of text production and learning among Iranian graduate students of education. *Journal of Second Language Writing* 6(2). 105–137.

Sasaki, Miyuki. 2004. A multiple-data analysis of the 3.5-year development of EFL student writers. *Language Learning* 54. 525–582.

Sasaki, Miyuki. 2007. Effects of study-abroad experiences on EFL writers: A multiple-data analysis. *The Modern Language Journal* 91. 602–620.

Sasaki, Miyuki. 2011. Effects of varying lengths of study-abroad experiences on Japanese EFL students' L2 writing ability and motivation: A longitudinal study. *TESOL Quarterly* 45. 81–105.

Sasaki, Miyuki. 2012. An alternative approach to replication studies in language writing: An ecological perspective. *Journal of Second Language Writing* 21. 303–305.

Segalowitz, Norman and Barbara F. Freed. 2004. Learning Spanish in at home and study abroad contexts. *Studies in Second Language Acquisition* 26. 173–199.

Serrano, Raquel, Elsa Tragant, and Àngels Llanes 2012) A longitudinal analysis of the effects of one year abroad. *The Canadian Modern Language Review* 68(2). 138–163.

Siegal, Meryl. 1995. Individual differences and study abroad: Women learning Japanese in Japan. In Barbara F. Freed (ed.), *Second language acquisition in a study abroad context*, 225–244. Amsterdam: John Benjamins.

Taguchi, Naoko. 2012. *Context, individual differences, and pragmatic competence*. Bristol: Multilingual Matters.

Tardy, Christine M. 2013. *Building genre knowledge*. West Lafayette, IN: Parlor Press.

Verspoor, Marjolijn, Kees de Bot, and Wander Lowie (eds.). 2011. *A dynamic approach to second language development: Methods and techniques*. Amsterdam: John Benjamins.

Wigglesworth, Gillian and Neomy Storch. 2012. Feedback and writing development through collaboration: A socio-cultural approach. In Rosa M. Manchón (ed.), *L2 writing development: Multiple perspectives*. 69–99. Boston, MA: De Gruyter Mouton.

Melinda Reichelt
8 L2 writing in languages other than English

Although most of the L2 writing research has focused on writing in English, the study of L2 writing also includes writing done in any other language, as long as that language is not the mother tongue of the writer. However, the ways, reasons, and motivation levels for writing in non-English L2s may be different from those of writers composing in L2 English, mostly because of the special role that English plays in the world. Some research has indicated that EFL writers may perceive L2 writing as more useful than L2 writers of other languages do, primarily because they believe they will use it in their future work lives (Bruton, Marks, and Broca-Fernández 2010. But see Chapter 7). Because of differences between writing in L2 English and writing in other L2s, an understanding of writing in non-English L2s is necessary to make our knowledge of L2 writing more complete.

1 Brief historical overview of the origins and development of research in L2 (non-English) writing

Over the years, an increasing amount of research has been published about L2 writing in languages other than English. However, researchers working in this area may not see themselves as part of a group with a common focus, a clear research agenda, and a shared body of literature to draw on. Instead, those involved with this field may identify with the particular language they teach, considering themselves L2 specialists rather than writing specialists (Hubert and Bonzo 2010; Reichelt 1999). Until the last decade or so, publication of research on writing in non-English L2's has been quite limited, and the existing body of research is still relatively small. Until recently, most of the published research in this area was conducted in North America. While publications about non-English L2 writing appear in a broad range of venues, the majority of the published research on non-English L2 writing has appeared in publications addressing foreign language professionals rather than in journals addressing writing/composition specialists (Reichelt 1999). Especially in the 1980's and 1990's, those undertaking FL writing research sometimes exhibited little or no familiarity with other work on non-English L2 writing. This lack of a common framework has meant that a coherent conversation about issues of common concern has been somewhat slow to develop, and, until recently, discussion of non-English L2 writing did not become a significant part of the conversations about L2 writing, which have tended to focus on writing in English as an L2.

In 1999, I published a report of the literature on non-English writing in the US. I began with work from the 1970's, during which only 13 relevant sources were published, must of which provided pedagogical recommendations regarding writing to teachers of various foreign languages. In the 1980's and 1990's, the number of published works increased, and the literature began to include more research. Of the 233 sources I reviewed, 140 discussed pedagogical issues such as the overall writing curriculum for a foreign language program, specific writing assignments or teaching techniques, or approaches to feedback and assessment of writing. The remaining 93 sources were works of research focusing on topics such as writers' texts, attitudes, and processes, as well as the effects of various pedagogical practices. Over half (48) of the 93 research-oriented works were published as dissertations, very few of which were eventually published in another format. During this period, researchers began to investigate various topics, some of which would continue to be pursued in later years. These topics included the role and uses of feedback (Cohen 1987; Hedgcock and Lefkowitz 1994, 1996; Kepner 1991), students' processes of revision (Chavez 1996; Hedgcock and Lefkowitz 1992), features of student texts (Chastain 1990; Lantolt 1988), error and error correction (Frantzen 1995; Frantzen and Rissell 1987; Hendrickson 1980; LaLande 1982; Truscott 1996), and comparison of L1 and L2 writing (Pennington and So 1993).

Since 1999, the amount of published works in the area has increased substantially. In 2008, increasing interest in the field of non-English FL writing was evidenced by the fact that the theme of the 2008 Seventh Symposium on Second Language Writing (West Lafayette, Indiana, USA) was designated "Foreign Language Writing Instruction: Principles and Practices." In 2011, a volume of chapters based on conferences presentations from the 2008 Symposium on Second Language Writing was published (Cimasko and Reichelt 2011).

It is important to note that most of the literature published in English on non-English L2 writing still addresses FL writing in the US or Canada, with little research on non-English L2 writing stemming from other contexts. However, exceptions to this exist, including the following: Leblay's (2007) research on students writing in French as a foreign language in Finland, Li, and Akahori's (2008) research on students writing in Japanese as a foreign language in China, Luoma and Tarnanen's (2003) work on writing in Finnish as a second language (SL) in Finland; Pennington and So's (1993) work on writing in Japanese as a FL in Singapore; van Beuningen, de Jong, and Kuiken's (2008, 2012) work on SL writers writing in Dutch in the Netherlands, and de Haan and van Esch's (2005) and Nas and van Esch's (2011) work on writing in Spanish as an FL in the Netherlands.

Examination of the literature reveals a number of questions that have been taken up in the research and are now forming the beginnings of a research agenda for this blossoming field:

– What are the effects on writing of the conditions under which students write, the tasks they write, and the resources they draw on, including technology?

- What is the role of various individual and sociocultural factors, including language background and multilingualism?
- What is the nature of the development of students' writing ability, processes, and strategies?
- What is the role of feedback and assessment?
- What is the role of writing in L2 learning and in the overall L2 curriculum?

2 Disciplinary critical interpretation of the existing theory and research in L2 (non-English) writing

2.1 How disciplinary conversations in non-English L2 writing have been framed

Not surprisingly, many researchers frame their work by citing sources on L1 writing, ESL/EFL writing, second language acquisition, linguistics, L2 learning and teaching, and/or literacy. Additionally, some frame their work in terms of cognitive processes, such as Khaldieh (2000), who cites Flower and Hayes' (1981) model of cognitive processes in writing, or Manchón (2011), who draws on SLA theories of output (VanPatten and Williams 2007).

However, much of the work on non-English L2 writing, especially more recent work, has been influenced by the "social turn" in writing research (Matsuda 2003), which emphasizes the situated nature of writing. For example, Haneda (2005, 2007) and Eola and Oskoz (2010) frame their work in terms of Lave and Wenger's (1991) notions of situated learning and learners' degrees of participation in a community of practice, while Kern and Schultz (2005) frame their discussion of target language literacy in terms of Halliday's (1978) sociolinguistic concept of situated meaning making. On a related note, other authors examine non-English L2 writing from the perspective of multilingualism (Cenoz and Gorter 2011; De Angelis and Jessner 2012; Kobayashi and Rinnert 2013), drawing on, for example, Cook's (2008) notion of multicompetence.

Other researchers frame their work in terms of linguistic theories, typically ones that emphasize the social aspects of language as communication. For example, Byrnes (2009, 2011, 2012) frames her work by referring to Halliday's (1984) Systemic Functional Linguistics, and van Esch, de Haan, and Nas (2004) place their work in the context of Canale and Swain's (1980) notion of communicative competence. Even research that focuses on writers' texts, especially more recent works of this nature, have been influenced by the social turn. This is evident in the genre-focused work of authors such as Byrnes (2002), Byrnes, Maxim, and Norris (2010), and Yigitoglu and Reichelt, (2012), who draw on genre theory (Christie and Martin 1997; Swales 1990; Tardy 2011), which emphasizes that texts are the results of social practices.

2.2 Main methods of research

Empirical research into non-English L2 writing employs a range of methods and instruments.

2.2.1 Quantitative approaches

The quantitatively-oriented research in this area includes a relatively limited number of experimental or quasi-experimental studies, that is, studies that contain a treatment and a control group (e.g., van Beuningen, de Jong, and Kuiken 2008, 2012). Instead, some of the quantitatively-focused research focuses on relationships between the features of students' writing and other factors, such as the conditions under which texts were written, the pedagogical procedures employed before students wrote (Armstrong 2010; East 2006; Niño 2008), the type of writing task that was assigned (Kuiken and Vedder 2007, 2008; Way, Joiner, and Seaman 2000), or learner characteristics (Iwashita and Sekiguchi 2009; Liu 2009). Other text-focused research investigates within-text qualities of student writing, such as the work of Benevento and Storch (2011), who compare L2 French writers' achievements in discourse structure, linguistic complexity, and linguistic accuracy. Typical research procedures or instruments used in quantitatively-focused research include text analysis and questionnaires.

2.2.2 Qualitative and qualitative/quantitative approaches

Research into non-English L2 writing includes considerably more work that is primarily or partly qualitative in nature, including case studies and other research that relies on observation, interviews, questionnaires, and think-aloud and written protocols (see, e.g., Haneda 2005; Hedgcock and Lefkowitz 2011; Kennedy and Miceli 2010; Luoma and Tarnanen 2003). Additionally, some research in the field employs a combination of quantitative and qualitative approaches, typically involving both analysis of student texts as well as the gathering of supplemental data, e.g., through interviews, questionnaires, observations, and/or spoken or written protocols (see, e.g., Cohen and Brooks-Carson 2001; East 2007; Grainger 2005; Hedgcock and Lefkowitz 1996; Knutson 2006; New 1999).

2.3 Critique of research methods

In 2001, I reviewed 32 published works that investigated the outcomes of various writing-related pedagogical practices in FL teaching in the US (Reichelt 2001). I urged future researchers to adequately describe their research procedures to allow their work to be evaluated and replicated, and to avoid the flaws of some of the

already-existing research, including, in experimental and quasi-experimental research, the existence of confounding variables and the lack of control groups, necessary tests of statistical significance, and reliable measurement procedures. Since
this critique was published, the overall quality of the published research has improved. Most researchers provide thorough descriptions of their research procedures (e.g., Haneda 2005; Kennedy and Miceli 2010; Kobayashi and Rinnert 2013).
Additionally, experimental and quasi-experimental work typically exhibits principles of good design research, including use of control groups when practical, reliable measurement procedures, and necessary tests of statistical significance (e.g.,
Bonzo 2008; Kuiken and Vedder 2008; East 2007; van Beuningen, de Jong, and
Kuiken 2008, 2012). This improvement provides researchers a body of work on
which to base further inquiry as well as models of well-designed research.

3 Research insights

While researchers have investigated a broad range of sub-topics in the area, because the body of research published in English on non-English L2 writing is small,
there is no critical mass of findings that allows for strong claims about the nature
of writing in non-English L2s. This situation is exacerbated by the fact that the
findings of research on writing in any particular L2 by a group of writers from a
particular linguistic background, writing in a particular context, cannot necessarily
be generalized to writing in other L2s, nor to writing done by writers from other
linguistic backgrounds in other contexts. Additionally, studies have been done on
students of varying ages and levels, but most work has concentrated on tertiary-
level students, leaving us with little knowledge of younger writers. Nonetheless,
some broad, rather tentative assertions can be made about findings in the field.

3.1 Conditions, tasks, and resources

One prominent line of inquiry investigates the effects on writing of the conditions
under which students write, the tasks they write, and the resources they draw on,
including technology. Findings in this area indicate that the type of writing task
undertaken or the conditions under which texts are written can (but do not necessarily) affect some aspects of students' written products.

3.1.1 Technology

Research findings indicate that students generally have positive reactions to using
technology while writing, and that it can improve some aspects of students' writing
or writing processes. However, to date, results do not indicate that technology use
has a hugely transformative effect on students' non-English L2 writing.

In Lee's (2010b) investigation of advanced Spanish university students blogging done outside class, she reports increased motivation for writing and increased fluency over the course of the term. However, a non-blogging group control group was not included in the research, so it is possible that the writing experience in general, not the blogging aspect of it, accounted for these results. Lee (2010a) found that wiki use amongst her beginning-level university students of Spanish fostered collaboration and revision in her students' writing. She also reports that students indicated enjoyment of wiki use. Again, no control group was used.

Pérez-Sotelo and González-Bueno (2003) compared first-semester college L2 Spanish writers' dialog journal texts written via e-mail, on the one hand, with dialog journals written with pencil and paper. They found that texts written via paper and pencil were more grammatically accurate than e-mail texts, but that the two types of texts did not differ significantly in terms of lexical accuracy or fluency. They also report that students had positive attitudes toward dialog journaling via e-mail.

Kennedy and Miceli (2010) conducted case studies of three university-level intermediate learners writing in Italian, using a corpus and bilingual (English-Italian) dictionary as references. They found considerable variation among the three writers in frequency and purposes for using these resources, with two students employing the corpus as primarily a grammar, usage and lexical resource, and only one fully exploiting its unique potential for pattern-hunting. Kennedy and Miceli emphasize the importance they recognized, in hindsight, of training students to use the corpus by explaining all of its functions. O'Sullivan and Chambers (2006), who investigated university-level undergraduate and graduate students' use of a French-language corpus, also highlight the notion of training for corpus use. They report that their FL French writers had positive attitudes toward corpus use, with the intermediate students who received more training reporting more positive attitudes than their advanced counterparts, who received less training. They also report that a comparison of texts written with and without corpus consultation indicated that, with corpus use, grammatical as well as lexical errors decreased.

Niño (2008) investigated a controversial type of technology: machine translation of students' L1 texts into L2 Spanish. Niño compared texts that advanced learners of Spanish had translated, unassisted, into Spanish, with texts that had been machine-translated into Spanish and edited afterwards by a comparable group of L2 Spanish students. Lexical, grammatical, and discourse scores were similar for the two groups; not surprisingly, the machine-translation group performed considerably better on spelling.

3.1.2 Task type

Another vein of research has considered task type, investigating especially whether task type influences the characteristics of the writing produced. Results indicate that task type sometimes, but not always, affects some aspects of student writing. However, because of a lack of consistency from study to study in types of tasks assigned and rating criteria used, no strong conclusions can be drawn.

Kuiken and Vedder (2007, 2008) investigated the writing of Dutch university students in L2 Italian (beginners) and L2 French (with previous study). Students wrote tasks of differing degrees of cognitive complexity. Regarding the 2007 study, they report that greater task complexity resulted in more lexical variation and fewer errors. They attribute the increase in accuracy in large part to students' making a lower ratio of lexical errors on the more complex task. In the 2008 study, they found no differences between students' responses to the different task-types in terms of syntactic complexity or lexical variation, but the texts that students wrote for the more cognitively demanding text were more linguistically accurate.

Cohen and Brooks-Carson (2011) also examined the effect of task type in their study of university intermediate French learners, comparing writing done directly in L2 French with writing done in L1 and then translated into French. No significant differences were found in grammar scores, but students who wrote directly in French received better scores for expression and transitions. As a caveat, the authors note that the two task-types may not have been completely distinct: in retrospective reports, students indicated that they were often thinking in English, even during the writing-in-French task.

Way, Joiner, and Seaman (2000) examined the effects of task type and prompts on the writing of secondary-level novice learners of French, rating it holistically and for fluency, syntactic complexity, and grammatical accuracy. They found that of the three task types investigated (descriptive, narrative, and expository), the descriptive task produced the highest average scores, and the expository task the lowest. They also found that of the three prompt types – bare (asking students to write a letter to a pen pal), vocabulary (the bare prompt plus a list of relevant vocabulary) and prose model (an example letter from a pen pal, accompanied by the instruction to respond to the letter) – the bare prompt produced the lowest mean scores, and the prose model the highest.

Bonzo (2008) compared texts written by university-level L2 German learners under two conditions: one in which students had a choice of topic, and one in which topics were assigned. Students' fluency scores but not grammatical complexity scores were higher when they chose their own topics.

Ruiz-Funes (2001) investigated the effects of task type in a somewhat different way, analyzing students' interpretation of a task as represented by the texts they produced. Third-year university FL Spanish students read a literary selection and were given specific instructions about how to analyze it. Students interpreted the task in three different ways, some producing summaries only, some producing summary plus comment, and some producing an interpretation with a rhetorical purpose. She notes that students who wrote syntactically complex sentences and/or wrote with grammatically accuracy did not necessarily produce "elaborated ideas" (226).

3.1.3 Conditions under which texts were written

A small number of researchers have investigated the features of texts written under different conditions, finding minimal differences. For example, East (2006, 2007) compares texts written by intermediate-level secondary school L2 German learners, with and without bilingual dictionaries. No difference was seen in students' overall scores, but East (2006) reports that tests written with dictionaries exhibited both more lexical sophistication and more misuses of words that were looked up. East (2007) notes that dictionary use appeared to help lower-intermediate students but hinder more advanced students.

Some work has provided evidence of the usefulness of assigning ungraded writing. In a study of blog use, Armstrong and Retterer (2008) found that their university – level intermediate Spanish learners averaged more words in ungraded than in graded blog writing, and that students who wrote the most also increased their accuracy in verb usage and the complexity of their sentences. Armstrong (2010) also compared texts written under graded and ungraded conditions, analyzing the fluency, complexity, and accuracy of her university-level fourth-semester L2 Spanish students' writing. She concluded that providing grades had little impact on their texts.

3.2 Individual and sociocultural factors, including language

Another line of research investigates the role of various individual and sociocultural factors. Findings indicate, not surprisingly, that more advanced students generally outperform their less-advanced counterparts, and that students' backgrounds, including their linguistic backgrounds, affect their writing.

3.2.1 Texts by more- versus less-advanced students

Some researchers have undertaken comparisons of the texts written by more-advanced versus less-advanced students, typically as parts of broader studies. Not surprisingly, more-advanced students have performed better on some measures than their less advanced peers (van Esch, de Haan, and Nas 2004; de Haan and van Esch 2005). Ryshina-Pankova (2011), in her study of book reviews written by university-level German as a FL writers, found that more advanced writers "move[d] away from direct expression of authorial opinion ... and employ[ed] a more intersubjective and thus more persuasive reader-orientation in their texts" (243).

3.2.2 Texts by learners of various backgrounds

Researchers have found that, not surprisingly, learners' backgrounds affect the texts they produce. Iwashita and Sekiguchi (2009) studied the university L2 Japanese writing of students from a range of linguistic backgrounds who were studying in Australia. Students with previous study of Japanese at the university level and with character-based L1s performed best on use of kanji (the Chinese characters used as part of the Japanese writing system), as well as in several other areas. Liu (2009) also focuses on learner background in an investigation of the Chinese-language writing of third-year and fourth-year university-level heritage language learners of Chinese. Liu argues that, because their overall language skills have not reached a high enough level, these students "sacrifice textual structuring for orthographic and linguistic accuracy" (p. 66).

Several other works highlight the uniqueness of the writing development of heritage language and trilingual writers. Hedgcock and Lefkowitz (2011) focused on university-level heritage language learners (HLLs) of Spanish in the US Through surveys of monolingual students of Spanish and HLLs, interviews with professors, and examination of course materials, they found that the traditional writing-to-learn approach used was not appropriate for HL students, who needed to develop writing skills for use beyond the classroom. Haneda (2005) also examined issues related to HL learning in her case study of two L2 Japanese learners at a Canadian university. One was an Anglophone who had been immersed in Japanese for one year in a high school in Japan, and one spoke Japanese at home but rarely read Japanese and struggled with writing. Haneda found that the two students wrote in Japanese in very different ways that reflected their histories and identities.

Cenoz and Gorter (2011) report on their exploratory study of secondary-level multilingual writers in Spain composing in Basque, Spanish, and English. Essays were scored for content, organization, vocabulary, language use, and mechanics. The researchers found significant correlations across languages for all areas but organization, indicating that "the boundaries between their languages are permeable ... [and] there can be multidirectional patterns of interaction among the languages" (p. 367). Similarly, Kobayashi and Rinnert (2013) investigated the L1, L2 (English), and L3 (Chinese) writing of a Japanese student, gathering quantitative and qualitative data related to her essays, writing processes, attitude, and identity. They found that, not surprisingly, her personal and cultural identity affected her writing, and that, similar to Cenoz and Gorter's findings, some writing skills and processes were shared across languages.

3.3 The development of students' writing ability and processes

3.3.1 Text development over time

In investigating the development of students' texts over time, researchers have found improvement in some but not necessarily all aspects of student writing. Benevento and Storch (2011) examined the writing of learners of French over a period of six months during their last year of secondary school, investigating whether or not various aspects of students' writing developed uniformly over time. They found improvement at the discourse level and in linguistic complexity, but not in linguistic accuracy. They noted that students relied on "prefabricated chunks" (97), and that their ability to use these chunks creatively improved over time. Serrano and Howard (2007) also examined students' writing development over time, in their case focusing on the Spanish-language writing of an English-speaking child in a Spanish-English two-way immersion program in the US. Data was collected from the beginning of the student's third-grade year through the end of the student's fifth-grade year; the student improved in all three areas investigated: composition, grammar, and mechanics.

3.3.2 Writers' processes

Researchers have investigated a wide range of topics related to writers' processes. They have found that it is not uncommon for writers to employ their L1 while composing in L2, and that doing so is not necessarily detrimental to writing quality. Through think-aloud protocols, it was mentioned above that Cohen and Brooks-Carson (2011) found that the university-level intermediate French learners in their study, even when told to write directly in (L2) French, often thought in L1. In a study of the purposes of L1 use in L2 writing, Schwarzer (2004) found that students in their first semester of studying university Hebrew, writing dialog journals in Hebrew, used their L1 and code-switching for communicative and clarification purposes, and as a learning strategy. Knutson (2006) found that for her intermediate and advanced university FL French students, L1 use did not necessarily make the writing process more complex or influence the characteristics of the resulting text.

Using a case study approach, Ruiz-Funes (1999) investigated the reading-to-write process of a university third-year FL Spanish student. She identified the major processes the student used: synthesizing, monitoring, structuring, elaborating, planning, writing, revising, and editing.

Some researchers have investigated another aspect of the writing process: revision. Using a keystroke tracking device, New (1999) investigated university-level intermediate FL French writers' revision while word processing. Both (self-reported) good and poor writers undertook revisions, and they undertook more surface-level revisions than revisions of content. In a comparison of students' L1 (English) and FL German writing, Thorson (2000) found that her university students wrote less in German than in their L1, but revised more in German than in L1.

Researchers such as Khaldieh (2000) have investigated writers' use of strategies while composing. In his study of American university undergraduate and graduate learners of Arabic, Khaldieh found that both proficient and less-proficient learners "were active users of different learning strategies to varying degrees"

(p. 522). Grainger (2005) reports on possible difficulties in investigating strategy use. In his study, FL Japanese undergraduate university students of various proficiency levels completed a language learning strategy questionnaire not designed for Japanese. They scored highly on most items related to using reading and writing strategies, which did not reflect the typical struggles of L2 students with Japanese orthography. Grainger suggests that learners may have interpreted questions in terms of *hiragana,* in which each character represents a syllable, rather than in terms of the more difficult, Chinese-based logographic *kanji* system – since *hiriga-na* is typically used in materials for beginning L2 Japanese learners. Grainger argues researchers must adapt the use of strategy inventories to better fit specific languages. Grainger's work highlights the fact that writing in one L2 may not involve the same processes or challenges as writing in other L2s.

3.4 Feedback and assessment

3.4.1 Error correction

In research investigating error correction, results have been mixed, with more recent works showing positive effects. Truscott (1996) reviewed others' studies of grammar correction in L2 writing, including studies of non-English L2 writing such as Kepner (1991) and Semke (1984). In his review article, he argues that grammar correction in L2 writing should be abandoned because research, theoretical reasoning, and practical experience indicate that it is ineffective and can be harmful. In her 1999 response to Truscott, Ferris argues that abandoning grammar correction would be premature. In subsequent publications on this topic, Truscott (1999, 2004) and Ferris (2002, 2004) do not resolve the issue nor come to agreement on it.

In a study of SL Dutch secondary students in the Netherlands, van Beuningen, de Jong, and Kuiken (2008) compared the results of direct corrective feedback on errors, indirect corrective feedback, and no corrective feedback. Of the three, they found that only direct feedback had a significant long-term effect on accuracy, and the effect was positive. In a related study, van Beuningen, de Jong, and Kuiken (2012) investigated the impact of direct and indirect comprehensive feedback on writing. They found both types of comprehensive feedback to be more effective in increasing accuracy than was self-editing or practice writing, both in revision and in new pieces of writing, and that comprehensive feedback did not lead to simplified writing. Their research did not, however, include ratings of the overall quality of students' writing.

Li and Akahori (2008) investigated the effectiveness of supplementing handwritten correction on their students' FL Japanese writing with two different kinds of correction: audio and playback strokes. Students were enrolled at a language school in China. Low-level students' writing benefited from error feedback with audio while high-level students' writing benefited from error feedback with playback strokes; they suggest that for lower-level students, the error feedback with playback strokes created cognitive overload. Like van Beuningen, de Jong, and Kuiken (2008, 2012), they also did not include in their study ratings of the overall quality of students' writing.

3.4.2 Perceptions of feedback

Other researchers have examined students' perceptions of feedback on their writing. Hedgcock and Lefkowitz (1994, 1996) investigated perceptions regarding feedback and revision of university-level ESL learners as well as Anglophone FL learners of French, Spanish, and German. While the FL writers wanted teacher input on content, structure, and linguistic accuracy, they preferred written feedback over oral feedback, wanted feedback on lexical and grammatical features of their writing, and viewed grammar practice as the purpose of FL writing. Amores (1997) investigated not teacher feedback, but peer feedback. Students in a third-year university Spanish tended to define peer-editing in terms of social and emotional terms, but nonetheless, she found no evidence that audience awareness had shaped their writing.

3.4.3 Assessment of texts

Researchers have investigated expert, learner, and machine scoring of writers' texts. East (2009) examined the reliability of an analytic rubric for scoring FL German writing and found that it was highly reliable. East attributes at least some of the reliability to the fact that the rubric was developed with the specific features of German (e.g., a high degree of inflection) in mind. Chiang (1999) also examined an analytic scoring rubric, one designed for L2 French writing. Chiang determined that the rubric, which included evaluation of morphology, syntax, cohesion, and coherence, had strong content validity and reliability but lacked to some degree in construct validity. Chiang also compared raters' analytic scores with their holistic scores on a set of essays, finding that in their holistic scoring, raters relied largely on discourse features, especially cohesion. Brown, Solovieva, and Egget (2011) used both holistic rating (based on the ACTFL proficiency rating scale) and measures of writing complexity in analyzing the writing of university third-year FL Russian learners in the US, before and after a course of study designed to improve their writing. Findings pointed to the importance of using both holistic and quantitative scoring to measure students' writing progress. Frey and Heringer (2007) analyzed an automatic rating system developed for L2 German. The authors found a high correlation between the scores of human raters and automated scores. Finally, Luoma and Tarnanen (2003) describe the development and use of a self-rating instrument for writing by SL learners of Finnish. They argue that the tool is useful in helping learners reflect on their own writing.

3.5 Learning and curricular issues

Researchers have also explored the role of writing in second language acquisition and in the overall L2 curriculum. Manchón (2011) reviewed the potential of FL writing for fostering language learning and concludes that writing involves students in important learning-related processes such as noticing and metalinguistic reflection, but that it is still unclear whether these processes eventually lead to L2 learning. Learning outcomes, she writes, depend on whether writers are given enough time to write, participate in "explicit, deep processing learning conditions" (p. 58), engage in collaboration that fosters learning, and are involved in a process of output followed by input, reflection, and further output. Thorson (2011) investigated German-language students' perceptions of L2 writing as a tool for increasing oral proficiency. She found that students believed free writing and journal writing, with their focus on fluency rather than accuracy, were particularly helpful in advancing oral skills.

Others have explored the question of what role L2 writing should play in the overall L2 curriculum (Haneda 2007; Reichelt, Lefkowitz, Rinnert, and Schultz 2012), arguing that writing-related curricular decisions need to be grounded in theory and reflection. Various researchers advocate task-based/genre-based approaches (Byrnes 2002; Byrnes, Maxim, and Norris 2010; Yigitoglu and Reichelt 2012), and approaches based on Sociocultural Theory (Roebuck 2001) and Activity Theory (Haneda 2007). Kern and Schultz (2005) and Schultz (2011) argue for writing instruction that helps students develop their interpretive skills and multiple literacies to explore social, literary, and historical themes relevant to the L2. Additionally, Hedgcock and Lefkowitz (2011) argue for an approaches that take into consideration the needs of heritage language learners.

4 Critical reflections on future developments

4.1 Finding answers to open questions

While researchers have begun to investigate a broad range of topics within non-English L2 writing, much more work needs to be done. More research is needed on writers at the secondary level and below. Additionally, given the rapid development of technology, continued investigation is needed into how students put technology to use when writing, and into whether increased training allows students to put various technologies to better use. Researchers should also continue to investigate the impact of task type and topics, as well as the effect of the conditions under which writers compose. This research should focus especially on how students interpret tasks, since student interpretations of the same task can vary significantly. Researchers should also investigate the potential for learning of student writing without receiving a grade, especially given the labor-intensive nature of grading student writing.

Other topics that deserve further attention include the role of writers' backgrounds, including their L1(s) and previous language learning experiences. This includes further attention to the needs of heritage language learners and to the nature of writing in L3, L4, etc. Additionally, we need to learn more about how non-English L2 writing develops, including what areas tend to improve over time, and whether pedagogical intervention can affect this development. We also need to know more about students' writing processes, including L1 use, strategy use, revision processes, and reading-writing connections. Investigations into these areas need to account for the fact that these processes not only vary from writer to writer, but may vary from language to language, depending, for example, on the orthography of the language.

We are sure to see further research into error correction, given the current enthusiasm for this topic. Researchers should continue to investigate what kinds of errors (if any) are effectively addressed through error correction and what kinds of correction are most effective. Additionally, researchers should investigate the overall impact of error correction by rating essays holistically, not just for language features. Researchers should also look into students' perceptions of error feedback.

Another area deserving further attention is assessment: What kinds of rating instruments are most valid and reliable? In creating and researching assessment instruments, researchers should consider the purpose of writing instruction in the context they are investigating.

Beyond this, a special effort should be made to investigate the impact on writing instruction of the instructional context, including the sociolinguistic role and status of the target language in that context.

4.2 Applying new research methods

While researchers should continue to use time-tested research methods, they should also exploit methods that have more recently become available because of recently-developed technology. This includes the use of keystroke logging programs (van Waes, Leijten, van Weijen, and van Weijen 2009; Thorson 2000), which can provide detailed information about students' writing and revision processes. Computerized rating of student texts (Frey and Heringer 2007) has potential to provide researchers with another important tool for both assessment and for measuring certain aspects of the development of an individual's writing over time.

4.3 Applying research insights to the solution of practical problems

Further research is needed to evaluate different pedagogical approaches and their usefulness in various contexts. This includes further investigation of the role writing might play in development of other L2 skills as well as the needs students have for L2 writing beyond the classroom. Such research should involve needs analysis, reflection, and investigation of students' perspectives on the role and usefulness of writing in their lives (see Leki 2001).

A related practical problem concerns what role writing should play in the broader curriculum. Haneda (2007), in overviewing multiple perspectives on university-level non-English FL writing, outlines three distinct views of how writing should be used in FL classes: 1) the view that process-oriented, communicative writing tasks are only realistic for students at advanced levels 2) the contrasting view that that writing should always have a communicative purpose, even when assigned to lower-level FL students, and 3) the view that writing should focus on development of students' overall literacy, where literacy is seen as a social practice that allows students to express their ideas, work with teacher and peer support, transform content they have gained from reading into written form, and analyze texts critically (Byrnes, Maxim, and Norris 2010; Kern 2004; Kern and Schultz 2005). Research should investigate which of these views is most appropriate and effective for various contexts.

4.4 Crossing disciplinary boundaries

Since research into non-English L2 writing is just beginning to coalesce as an area of focused inquiry, it is important for researchers to familiarize themselves with the body of work in the area (including work published in languages other than English not covered in the chapter) and to develop their own research agenda, one distinct from research in writing in L2 English. On the other hand, the field should continue to draw on the related disciplines out of which it has developed.

5 Additional Sources

Allen, Joseph. 2008. Why learning to write in Chinese is a waste of time: A modest proposal. *Foreign Language Annals* 41. 237–249.

Fukushima, Tatsuya. 2007. Simulation in JFL: Business writing. *Simulation and Gaming* 38. 48–66.

Hatasa, Yukiko. 2011. L2 writing instruction in Japanese as a foreign language. In Tony Cimasko and Melinda Reichelt (eds.), *Foreign language writing instruction: Principles and practices*, 98–117, Anderson, South Carolina: Parlor Press.

Lefkowitz, Natalie. 2011. The quest for grammatical accuracy: Writing instruction among foreign and heritage language educators. In Tony Cimasko and Melinda Reichelt (eds.), *Foreign language writing instruction: Principles and practices*, 225–254. Anderson, South Carolina: Parlor Press.

Martínez-Gibson, Elizabeth. 1998. A study on cultural awareness through commercials and writing. *Foreign Language Annals* 31. 115–139.

Mills, Nicole and Mélanie Péron. 2008. Global simulation and writing self-beliefs of intermediate French students. *ITL International Journal of Applied Linguistics* 156. 239–273.

O'Brien, Teresa. 2004. Writing in a foreign language: Teaching and learning. *Language Teaching* 37. 1–28.

Reichelt, Melinda. 2009. Bibliography of sources on foreign language writing. In Rosa M. Manchón (ed.), *Writing in foreign language contexts: Learning, teaching, and research*, 281–296. Bristol: Multilingual Matters.

Reichelt, Melinda. 2009. A critical evaluation of writing teaching programmes in different foreign language settings. In Rosa M. Manchón (ed.), *Writing in foreign language contexts: Learning, teaching, and research*, 183–206. Bristol: Multilingual Matters.

Ruiz-Funes, Marcela. 2011. Reading to write in a foreign language: Cognition and task representation. In Tony Cimasko and Melinda Reichelt (eds.), *Foreign language writing instruction: Principles and practices*, 22–43. Anderson, South Carolina: Parlor Press.

6 References

Amores, María. 1997. A new perspective on peer-editing. *Foreign Language Annals*. 30. 513–522.

Armstrong, Kimberly. 2010. Fluency, accuracy, and complexity in graded and ungraded writing. *Foreign Language Annals* 43. 690–702.

Armstrong, Kimberly and Oscar Retterer. 2008. Blogging as L2 writing: A case study. *AACE Journal* 16. 233–251.

Benevento, Cathleen and Neomy Storch. 2011. Investigating writing development in secondary school learners of French. *Assessing Writing* 16. 97–110.

Bonzo, Joshua. 2008. To assign a topic or not: Observing fluency and complexity in intermediate foreign language writing. *Foreign Language Annals* 41. 722–735.

Brown, N. Anthony, Raissa Solovieva, and Dennis Eggett. 2011. Qualitative and quantitative measures of second language writing: Potential outcomes of informal target language learning abroad. *Foreign Language Annals* 44. 105–121.

Bruton, Anthony, Emilia Alonso-Marks, and Angeles Broca-Fernández. 2010. Perceived writing likes and needs in Spanish and English as foreign languages. *Hispania* 93. 471–89.

Byrnes, Heidi. 2002. The role of task and task-based assessment in a content-oriented collegiate foreign language curriculum. *Language Testing* 19. 419–437.

Byrnes, Heidi. 2009. Emergent L2 German writing ability in a curricular context: A longitudinal study of grammatical metaphor. *Linguistics and Education* 20. 50–66.

Byrnes, Heidi. 2011. Beyond writing as language learning or content learning: Construing foreign language writing as meaning-making. In Rosa M. Manchón (ed.), *Learning-to-write and writing-to-learn in an additional language*, 133–157. Amsterdam: John Benjamins.

Byrnes, Heidi. 2012. Conceptualizing FL writing development in collegiate settings: A genre-based systemic functional linguistics approach. In Rosa M. Manchón (ed.), *L2 writing development: Multiple perspectives*, 191–219. Boston/Berlin: De Gruyter Mouton.

Byrnes, Heidi, Hiram Maxim, and John Norris. 2010. Realizing advanced foreign language writing development in collegiate education: Curricular design, pedagogy, assessment. [Monograph.] *Modern Language Journal* 94. Supplement s-1. 203–221.

Canale, Michael and Merrill Swain. 1980. Theoretical bases of communicative approaches to second language teaching and testing. *Applied Linguistics* 1. 1–47.

Cenoz, Jasone and Durk Gorter. 2011. Focus on multilingualism: A study of trilingual writing. *The Modern Language Journal* 95. 356–369.

Chastain, Kenneth. 1990. Characteristics of graded and ungraded compositions. *Modern Language Journal* 74. 10–14.

Chavez, Monika. 1996. Non-revised writing, revised writing, and error detection by learner characteristics. *International Journal of Applied Linguistics* 6. 163–198.

Chiang, Steve. 1999. Assessing grammatical and textual features in L2 writing samples: The case of French as a foreign language. *Modern Language Journal* 83. 219–232.

Christie, Frances and James Martin (eds.). 1997. *Genre and Institutions: Social processes in the workplace and school.* London: Continuum.

Cimasko, Tony and Melinda Reichelt. 2011. *Foreign language writing instruction: Principles and practices.* Anderson, South Carolina: Parlor Press.

Cohen, Andrew. 1987. Student processing of feedback on their compositions. In Anita Wenden and Joan Rubin (eds.), *Learner strategies in language learning*, 57–69. Englewood Cliffs, NJ: Prentice-Hall.

Cohen, Andrew and Amanda Brooks-Carson. 2001. Research on direct versus translated writing: Students' strategies and their results. *The Modern Language Journal* 85. 169–188.

Cook, Vivian. 2008. Multicompetence: Black hole or wormhole for second language acquisition research? In Zhao Hong Han (ed.), *Understanding second language process*, 16–26. Clevedon, UK: Multilingual Matters.

De Angelis, Gessica and Ulrike Jessner. 2012. Writing across languages in a bilingual context: A dynamic systems theory approach. In Rosa M. Manchón (ed.), L2 writing development: Multiple perspectives, 47–68. Berlin/Boston: De Gruyter Mouton.

de Haan, Pieter and Kees van Esch. 2005. The development of writing in English and Spanish as foreign languages. *Assessing Writing* 10. 100–116.

East, Martin. 2006. The impact of bilingual dictionaries on lexical sophistication and lexical accuracy in tests of L2 writing proficiency: A quantitative analysis. *Assessing Writing* 11. 179–197.

East, Martin. 2007. Bilingual dictionaries in tests of L2 writing proficiency: Do they make a difference? *Language Testing* 24. 331–353.

East, Martin. 2009. Evaluating the reliability of a detailed analytic scoring rubric for foreign language writing. *Assessing Writing* 14. 88–115.

Eola, Idoia and Ana Oskoz. 2010. Collaborative writing: Fostering foreign language and writing conventions development. *Language Learning and Technology* 14. 51–71.

Ferris, Dana. 1999. The case for grammar correction in L2 writing classes: A response to Truscott. *Journal of Second Language Writing* 8. 1–11.

Ferris, Dana. 2002. *Treatment of error in second-language student writing.* Ann Arbor, MI: University of Michigan Press.

Ferris, Dana. 2004. The "grammar correction" debate in L2 writing: Where are we, and where do we go from here? (and what do we do in the meantime …?) *Journal of Second Language Writing* 13. 49–62.

Flower, Linda and John Hayes. 1981. A cognitive process theory of writing. *College Composition and Communication* 32. 365–87.

Frantzen, Diana. 1995. The effects of grammar supplementation on written accuracy in an intermediate Spanish course. *Modern Language Journal* 79. 329–344.

Frantzen, Diana and Rissel, Dorothy. 1987. Learner self-correction of written compositions: What does it show us? In Bill VanPatten, Trisha Dvorak, and James Lee (eds.), *Foreign language learning: A research perspective*, 92–107. Cambridge: Newbury House.

Frey, Evelyn and Hans Heringer. 2007. Automatische Bewertung schriftlicher Lernerproduktion. *Linguistische Berichte* 211. 319–335.

Grainger, Peter. 2005. Second language learning strategies and Japanese: Does orthography make a difference? *System* 33. 327–339.

Halliday, Michael A. K. 1978. *Language as social semiotic: The social interpretation of language and meaning*. Baltimore, MD: University Park Press.

Halliday, Michael A. K. 1994. *An introduction to functional grammar* (2nd edition). London: Arnold.

Haneda, Mari. 2005. Investing in foreign-language writing: A study of two multicultural learners. *Journal of Language, Identity, and Education* 4. 269–290.

Haneda, Mari. 2007. Modes of engagement in foreign language writing: An activity theoretical perspective. *Canadian Modern Language Review* 64. 297–327.

Hedgcock, John and Natalie Lefkowitz. 1992. Collaborative oral/aural revision in foreign language writing instruction. *Journal of Second Language Writing* 3. 255–276.

Hedgcock, John and Natalie Lefkowitz. 1994. Feedback on feedback: Assessing learner receptivity to teacher response in L2 Composing. *Journal of Second Language Writing* 3. 141–163.

Hedgcock, John and Natalie Lefkowitz. 1996. Some input on input: Two analyses of student response to expert feedback in L2 writing. *The Modern Language Journal* 80. 287–308.

Hedgcock, John and Natalie Lefkowitz. 2011. Exploring the learning potential of writing development in heritage language education. In Rosa M. Manchón (ed.), *Learning-to-write and writing-to-learn in an additional language*, 209–223. Amsterdam: John Benjamins.

Hendrickson, James. 1980. The treatment of error in written work. *Modern Language Journal* 64. 216–221.

Hubert, Michael and Joshua Bonzo. 2010. Does second language writing research impact US university foreign language instruction? *System* 38. 517–528.

Iwashita, Noriko and Sachiyo Sekiguchi. 2009. Effects of learner background on the development of writing skills in Japanese as a second language. *Australian Review of Applied Linguistics* 32. 03.1–03.20.

Kennedy, Claire and Tiziana Miceli. 2010. Corpus-assisted creative writing: Introducing intermediate Italian learners to corpus as a reference resource. *Language Learning and Technology* 14. 28–44.

Kepner, Christine. 1991. An experiment in the relationship of types of written feedback to the development of second-language writing skills. *Modern Language Journal* 27. 383–411.

Kern, Richard. 2004. Literacy and advanced foreign language learning: Rethinking the curriculum. In Heidi. Byrnes and Hiram H. Maxim (eds.), *Advanced foreign language learning: A challenge to college programs*, 2–18. Boston: Heinle.

Kern, Richard and Jean Marie Schultz. 2005. Beyond orality: Investigating literacy and the literary in second and foreign language instruction. *The Modern Language Journal* 89. 381–392.

Khaldieh, Salim. 2000. Learning strategies and writing processes of proficient vs. less-proficient learners of Arabic. *Foreign Language Annals* 33. 522–533.

Knutson, Elizabeth. 2006. Thinking in English, writing in French. *The French Review* 80. 88–111.

Kobayashi, Hiroe and Carol Rinnert. 2013. L1/L2/L3 writing development: Longitudinal case study of a Japanese multicompetent writer. *Journal of Second Language Writing* 22. 4–33.

Kuiken, Folkert and Ineke Vedder. 2007. Task complexity and measures of linguistic performance in L2 writing. *IRAL* 45. 261–284.

Kuiken, Folkert and Ineke Vedder. 2008. Cognitive task complexity and written output in Italian and French as a foreign language. *Journal of Second Language Writing* 17. 48–60.

LaLande, John. 1982. Reducing composition errors: An experiment. *Modern Language Journal* 66. 140–149.

Lantolf, James. 1988. The syntactic complexity of written texts in Spanish as a foreign language: A markedness perspective. *Hispania* 71. 933–940.

Lave, Jean and Etienne Wenger. 1991. *Situated learning: Legitimate peripheral participation.* Cambridge, England: Cambridge University Press.

Leblay, Christophe. 2007. L'avante-text comme text *sur le vif*: Analyse génétique d'opérations d'écriture en temps reel [Fore-texts as real life text: A text-genetic analysis of writing operations in real time]. *Langue Française* 155. 101–113.

Lee, Lina. 2010a. Exploring wiki-mediated collaborative writing: A case study in an elementary Spanish course. *CALICO Journal* 27. 260–276.

Lee, Lina. 2010b. Fostering reflective writing and interactive exchange through blogging in an advanced language course. *ReCALL* 22. 212–227.

Leki, Ilona. 2001. Material, educational, and ideological challenges of teaching EFL writing at the turn of the century. *International Journal of English Studies* 1. 197–209.

Li, Kai and Kanji Akahori. 2008. Development and evaluation of a feedback support system with audio and playback strokes. *CALICO Journal* 26. 91–107.

Liu, Haiyong. 2009. Learning to compose: Characteristics of advanced Chinese heritage writers. *Hong Kong Journal of Applied Linguistics* 12. 63–80.

Luoma, Sari and Mirja Tarnanen. 2003. Creating a self-rating instrument for second language writing: from idea to implementation. *Language Testing* 20. 440–465.

Manchón, Rosa M. 2011. The language learning potential of writing in foreign language contexts: Lessons from research. In Tony Cimasko and Melinda Reichelt (eds.), *Foreign language writing instruction: Principles and practices*, 44–64. Anderson, South Carolina: Parlor Press.

Matsuda, Paul K. 2003. Process and post-process: A discursive history. *Journal of second language writing*, 12(1). 65–83.

Matsuda, P. K. 2003. Process and post-process: A discursive history. *Journal of second language writing*, 12(1), 65–83. Process and post-process: A discursive history. *Journal of Second Language Writing* 12. 65–83.

Nas, Marly and Kees van Esch. 2011. Developing Spanish FL writing skills at a Netherlands university: In search of balance. In Tony Cimasko and Melinda Reichelt (eds.), *Foreign language writing instruction: Principles and practices*, 201–224. Anderson, South Carolina: Parlor Press.

New, Elizabeth. 1999. Computer-aided writing in French as a foreign language: A qualitative and quantitative look at the process of revision. *The Modern Language Journal* 83. 81–97.

Niño, Ana. 2008. Evaluating the use of machine translation post-editing in the foreign language class. *Computer Assisted Language Learning* 21. 29–49.

O'Sullivan, Íde and Angela Chambers. 2006. Learners' writing skills in French: Corpus consultation and learner evaluation. *Journal of Second Language Writing* 15. 49–68.

Pennington, Martha and Sufumi So. 1993. Comparing writing process and product across two languages: A study of six Singaporean university student writers. *Journal of Second Language Writing* 2. 41–63.

Pérez-Sotelo, Luisa and Manuela González-Bueno. 2003. IDEA: Electronic writing outcomes in L2: Accuracy vs. other outcomes. *Hispania* 86. 869–873.

Reichelt, Melinda. 1999. Toward a more comprehensive view of L2 writing: Foreign language writing in the US *Journal of Second Language Writing* 8. 181–204.

Reichelt, Melinda. 2001. A critical review of research on FL writing classroom practices. *Modern Language Journal* 85. 578–598.

Reichelt, Melinda, Natalie Lefkowitz, Carol Rinnert, and Jean Marie Schultz. 2012. Key issues in foreign language writing. *Foreign Language Annals* 45. 22–41.

Roebuck, Regina. 2001. Teaching composition in the college level foreign language class: Insights and activities from sociocultural theory. *Foreign Language Annals* 34. 206–215.

Ruiz-Funes, Marcela. 1999. The process of reading-to-write used by a skilled Spanish-as-a-foreign language student: A case study. *Foreign Language Annals* 32. 45–62.

Ruiz-Funes, Marcela. 2001. Task representation in foreign language reading-to-write. *Foreign Language Annals* 34. 226–34.

Ryshina-Pankova, Marianna. 2011. Developmental changes in the use of interactional resources: Persuading the reader in FL book reviews. *Journal of Second Language Writing* 20. 243–256.

Schultz, Jean Marie. 2011. Foreign language writing in the era of globalization. In Tony Cimasko and Melinda Reichelt (eds.), *Foreign language writing instruction: Principles and practices*, 65–82. Anderson, South Carolina: Parlor Press.

Schwarzer, David. 2004. Student and teacher strategies for communicating through dialogue journals in Hebrew: A teacher research project. *Foreign Language Annals* 37. 77–84.

Semke, Harriet. 1984. Effects of the red pen. *Foreign Language Annals,* 17. 195–202.

Serrano, Raquel and Elizabeth Howard 2007. Second language writing development in English and Spanish in a two-way immersion programme. *The International Journal of Bilingual Education and Bilingualism* 10. 152–170.

Swales, John 1990. *Genre analysis: English in academic and research settings*. Cambridge: Cambridge University Press.

Tardy, Christine. 2011. The history and future of genre in second language writing. *Journal of Second Language Writing* 20. 1–5.

Thorson, Helga. 2000. Using the computer to compare foreign and native language writing processes: A statistical and case study approach. *The Modern Language Journal* 84. 155–170.

Thorson, Helga. 2011. Student perceptions of writing as a tool for increasing oral proficiency in German. In Tony Cimasko and Melinda Reichelt (eds.), *Foreign language writing instruction: Principles and practices*, 255–284. Anderson, South Carolina: Parlor Press.

Truscott, John. 1996. The case against grammar correction in L2 writing classes. *Language Learning* 46. 327–369.

Truscott, John. 1999. The case for "The case against grammar correction in L2 writing classes": A response to Ferris. *Journal of Second Language Writing* 8. 111–122.

Truscott, John. 2004. Evidence and conjecture on the effects of correction: A response to Chandler. *Journal of Second Language Writing* 13. 337–343.

van Beuningen, Catherine, Nivja de Jong, and Folkert Kuiken. 2008. The effect of direct and indirect corrective feedback on L2 learners' written accuracy. *ITL: International Journal of Applied Linguistics* 156. 279–296.

van Beuningen, Catherine, Nivja de Jong, and Folkert Kuiken. 2012. Evidence on the effectiveness of comprehensive error correction in second language writing. *Language Learning* 62. 1–41.

van Esch, Kees, Pieter de Haan and Marly Nas. 2004. El desarollo de la escritura en inglés y español como lenguas extranjeras [The development of writing in English and Spanish as foreign languages]. *Estudios de Lingüística Aplicada* 39. 53–79.

VanPatten, Bill and Jessica Williams. 2007. Introduction: The nature of theories. In Bill VanPatten and Jessica Williams (eds.), *Theories in second language acquisition*, 1–16. Mahwah, NJ: Lawrence Erlbaum.

van Waes, Luuk, Mariëlle Leijten, and Daphne van Weijen. 2009. Keystroke logging in writing research: Observing writing processes with Inputlog. *GFL-German as a Foreign Language Journal* 2. 41–64.

Way, Denise, Elizabeth Joiner, and Michael Seaman. 2000. Writing in the secondary foreign language classroom: The effects of prompts and tasks on novice learners of French. *The Modern Language Journal* 84. 171–184.

Yigitoglu, Nur and Melinda Reichelt. 2014. Using a genre-based approach for writing instruction in a less-commonly-taught language. *Language Awareness* 23. 187–202.

Theresa Lillis and Mary Jane Curry

9 Academic writing for publication in a multilingual world

1 Introduction

A focus on academic writing for publication does not of itself demand a focus on writing in a *second* or *foreign* language: writing for academic publication is an essential aspect of the work of scholars globally, whether writing in one or more languages, and whether these are considered first or additional languages or as part of a multilingual repertoire. What is the case, however, is that whilst there is some research on writing for publication in scholars' 'first' languages, by far most work on writing for publication has focused on writing by scholars who are writing in a 'second' or 'additional' language. Furthermore, the field is characterised by a focus on writing in one particular 'second' language, English, because of its high status in academic publishing, notably journal articles. There is far less research on writing for publication in other second or additional languages and, where other languages are discussed, it is usually in the context of a comparison with the linguistic and rhetorical practices of English. The field of writing for publication therefore has to a large extent been forged in a context where English is the assumed linguistic medium of academic texts and where researchers are often driven by an interest in the issues faced by multilingual scholars writing in English in the contemporary context of the global dominance of English in academic publishing.

In offering an overview of this field, which has developed over the past 30 years, we have organised this chapter in the following ways. Firstly, in order to provide a working map of the intellectual traditions shaping this field of inquiry, we review what we see as four influential research traditions and summarise what we see as their key contributions to the study of academic writing for publication: English for academic purposes (EAP), Second Language Writing (SLW), Contrastive/Intercultural Rhetoric and New Literacy Studies. There is always a danger of reifying the complex disciplinary spaces which researchers inhabit, and we recognise: a) that the labelling of any tradition or locating a scholar within it risks oversimplifying the many strands of research and thinking that shape their/our work; and b) that what is understood by specific labelling varies considerably, historically and geographically. But we open with this simplified map in the hope that it will be useful to scholars wanting to get a grip on the range and types of research approaches and theoretical apparatus that populate this field. Secondly, we focus on a substantive issue, which is the extent to which disciplinarity has figured in research on academic writing for publication and the extent to which writing for publication differs according to the disciplines in which scholars work, notably between social sciences-arts-humanities and sciences, technology, engineering and mathematics (STEM). Thirdly, we explore key ideologies underpinning research and theory in this field, which we organise in terms of orientations towards writers, texts, practices and language(s)ing. We conclude by discussing ongoing debates within the field and directions for future research.

2 The growth of a field of inquiry

2.1 Research traditions in exploring academic writing for publication

Research on academic writing for publication draws on a number of disciplinary fields often dependent on the geohistorical location of researchers. Whilst our categorisation of core fields or subfields risks the danger of creating simplistic or too rigid boundaries[1] – we consider such categories useful for offering a working map of key approaches shaping the field of academic writing for publication: English for Academic Purposes (EAP), Second Language Writing (SLW), Contrastive/Intercultural Rhetoric (CR/IR), New Literacy Studies.

2.1.1 English for Academic Purposes (EAP)

For more than 30 years the field of English for Academic Purposes has involved researchers and practitioners exploring the nature of the types and forms of English considered necessary for academic communication. As a field it 'seeks to provide insights into the structures and meanings of texts, into the demands placed by academic contexts on communicative behaviours, and into the pedagogic practices by which these behaviours can be developed' (Hyland and Hamp-Lyons 2002:3; see also Hyland 2006). The predominant emphasis has been on identifying in detail the nature of the language, texts, and genres that *students* writing at university level need in order to be successful in their studies (see Jordan 2002), although a focus on writing for publication is a growing area of interest. Indeed, for some prominent EAP researchers, writing for publication has always been a key focus. Swales, for example, whilst centring his research and pedagogic attention on the analysis of the academic demands made of students, has always had an eye on the prestigious types of academic texts – such as journal articles – that graduates might be required to produce in their future careers (see Swales and Feak 2000, 2012). Swales' work on genre and 'move analysis' in the research article (1990,

---

[1] Depending on a researcher's positioning, all of these subfields might be categorised, for example, as Applied Linguistics or Writing Studies.

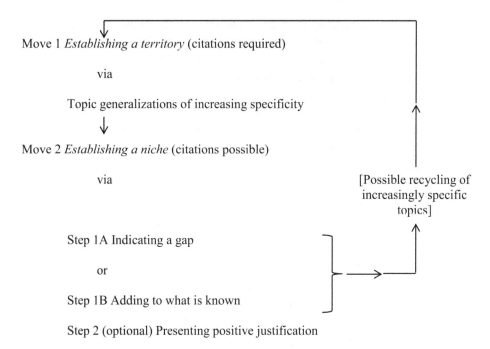

Move 1 *Establishing a territory* (citations required)

       via

       Topic generalizations of increasing specificity

Move 2 *Establishing a niche* (citations possible)

       via   [Possible recycling of increasingly specific topics]

       Step 1A Indicating a gap

       or

       Step 1B Adding to what is known

       Step 2 (optional) Presenting positive justification

Fig. 9.1: A revised CARS model for Moves 1 and 2 in research article introductions (Source: Swales 2004: 230).

2004) has been widely taken up for pedagogic purposes – to show writers how to structure their article abstracts and introductions – but also for research purposes, for example, as an analytic tool for tracking the rhetorical structure of discipline-specific articles (e.g. Kanoksilapatham 2005) and for identifying similarities between the rhetorical structure of articles in English and other languages (taken up in CR/IR studies, as we return to below); other examples of work on research articles using move analysis include Hopkins and Dudley-Evans (1988) on discussion sections, Ozturk (2007) on introductions, and Yang and Allison (2003) on conclusions.

The use of corpora is a key approach to the analysis of texts for academic publication, where large corpora of texts are built in order to enable the identification, quantification and analysis of patterns of textual features. Key contributions include the work of Harwood (2005 a, b) who analysed 'self-promotional I and we' in research articles in four disciplines and extensive work by Hyland, who has analysed metadiscoursal features across the sciences, engineering, social sciences, and humanities (e.g. 2000, 2004, 2005) and whose work is widely cited and used in cross-cultural and cross-disciplinary studies (see e.g. Lorés-Sanz, Mur-Dueñas, and Lafuente-Millán 2011 on interpersonality, discussed below).

In addition to identifying linguistic and rhetorical patterns across disciplinary fields, corpora have been used to compare the texts of 'expert' and 'novice' writers.

Hewings and Hewings (2002), for example, focused on the different uses of 'anticipatory 'it'' in published and student writing; Aktas and Cortes (2008) compared the use of 'shell nouns' as cohesive devices in published research articles and 'ESL' students' writing; Hyland (2002) in analyzing self-reference (e.g. *I, me, my, our, we*), compared patterns across one corpus of published articles from a range of disciplines with a corpus of academic reports written by students using English as an additional language. Making comparisons between 'expert' and 'novice' writers or between published academic texts and writing by students is of key interest in EAP given the potential pedagogic value of such findings. In addition to corpora approaches, work includes qualitative methods using smaller data sets: for example, Hopkins and Dudley-Evans (1988) analyzed discussions of results in master's level dissertations and published conference proceedings; Basturkmen (2009) compared the 'commenting on results move' in published journal articles and master dissertations.

With regard to reaching an understanding about academic writing for publication in an additional language, it is worth adding a cautionary point about the ways in which some corpora studies are built and results interpreted. 'Expert' corpora tend to be constituted by English-medium articles published in high status journals, often with little mention of the linguistic profile of writers (usually because such corpora are built from published texts with little information about authors): one consequence arising from this approach is to presume that such corpora are made of articles written by 'native' users of English. These corpora tend to be used as a point of comparison with corpora constituted by articles marked as being written by users of other languages. Some researchers do not mention linguistic profile and some use a proxy to signal linguistic profile of writers (e.g. geographical location of institutional affiliation, Lafuente-Millán et al. 2010; Lillis et al. 2010). Using text-based corpora for reaching conclusions about the phenomenon of writing for publication according to linguistic profile of writers may mask more complex linguistic repertoires and patterns of production (an issue we return to below).

EAP has established itself as an influential tradition internationally – with strong roots in the UK – in the analysis of academic texts and has influenced other traditions, notably contrastive/intercultural rhetoric (see 2.1.3). Some early researchers within the EAP tradition adopted approaches to academic writing for publication which prefigured the more recent interest in ethnographic approaches (see 2.1.4); for example, St. John (1987) explored the experiences of Spanish scientists writing for English-medium journals; Baldauf and Jernudd (1987) focused on Scandinavian psychologists' experiences in publishing in both English and their local languages and the challenges they faced. Swales (1987) emphasised the global context in which writing for publication was taking place and possible consequences for knowledge production: empirically he focused on the range of genres used for academic purposes (e.g. 1988) but also on what Canagarajah later (1996) called the "non discursive" challenges faced by "off-network" scholars (Swales 1987) when writing for publication in English; ideologically Swales raised questions about the impact of the status of English on knowledge exchange (e.g. 1997); methodologically he used a range of research tools including analysis of texts and ethnographically oriented approaches (i.e. 1990, 1998). Such methodological openness is evident in recent EAP research (see, e.g. *Journal of English for Academic Purposes* special issues on 'Advanced academic literacy', 2005, and 'Writing for publication in multilingual contexts', 2014).

A key contribution that EAP has made is the mapping of the textual aspects of academic writing for publication at the level of linguistic features, rhetorical organisation, genres or text types. This approach has: a) challenged *a priori* assumptions about what academic texts are/should be; b) facilitated analyses of different types of writing for publication, most clearly in relation to text types and genres; c) made visible patterns of textual features that can be used pedagogically. Some early work on writing for publication in EAP also contributed theoretical and methodological tools that are being taken up in more recent research, in particular, the use of ethnography.

2.1.2 Second language writing (SLW)

As the name indicates, 'writing' is the central focus of second language writing, a tradition whose geohistorical roots are firmly based in the United States. SLW emerged from the interests of teachers and researchers seeking to put student writing in a 'second' language on the institutional agenda of a higher education system where first language writing was already established (for overview, see Silva and Matsuda 2000; Matsuda, Ortmeier-Hooper, and You 2006; see also Manchón 2009 who draws on SLW but focusing on 'foreign' language writing). Whilst the focus in this field has largely been on exploring SLW from a 'classroom' or pedagogic perspective, there is growing interest in researching writing for publication. This latter work has mainly focused on "international" graduate students – who move to the United States to do postgraduate study – and the challenges they face in writing for publication (e.g. Cho 2004; Tardy 2004, 2005). Such challenges include: the use of specific rhetorical and linguistic conventions in writing academic articles; negotiating relationships with co-authors; and learning the practices of journal publishing, such as responding to reviews. Findings indicate that student writers gain confidence by seeing models of how successful scholars work, gaining experience from presenting work at conferences (Chang and Kanno 2010) and enlisting the help of advisors. Some contributors have focused on the experiences of scholars working in the United States (e.g. Liu 2004), while some research in SLW has focused on graduates writing for publication in English and other languages from the context and perspectives of graduates working outside the Anglophone centre (Flowerdew 1999b, 2000). Li (2006), for example, charts the challenges and decisions faced by a Chinese graduate computer scientist in a 'mainland' Chinese university in beginning to write for publication, pointing to 'layers' of communities (relating to discipline, linguistic medium, specific sub-disciplinary conversations). A recurring theme across SLW research is the considerable pressure writers experienced to write for publication in English (see Cho 2004).

Approaches within SLW tend to reflect a research interest in the perspectives of writers rather than in the analysis of texts, often using qualitative research methods such as interviews and focus groups and, in some instances, the examining of documents relating to submissions and revision multiple of texts written for publication (e.g. Artemeva 2000; Belcher 2007; Canagarajah 1996, 2002; Casanave 1998; Flowerdew and Li 2009). We return to the focus on production below.

A key contribution of SLW to the researching of academic writing for publication has been the documenting of the experiences of 'international' graduate students writing for publication and, increasingly, the documenting of the experiences and practices of graduates and scholars writing for publication in English and other languages. Such work has in general foregrounded writers' perspectives and in particular identified the challenges faced and potential solutions.

2.1.3 Contrastive/Intercultural Rhetoric (CR/IR)

Research in contrastive rhetoric (CR) and more recent work in intercultural rhetoric (IR) generally focuses on writing in one or more languages and/or writing by writers using one or more languages (see Chapter 3). 'Intercultural' is increasingly being used instead of 'contrastive' to signal a shift away from reified notions of language and culture – which were strongly critiqued in early CR studies – towards a recognition of the dynamism and complexity at the levels of language, 'culture' and disciplinarity in any instance of writing (for debates around these terms, see Connor 2004, 2011). As with all fields dealing with academic writing, CR/IR has focused predominantly on student writing but has expanded from an early concern with comparing student texts written in more than one language to comparing published texts, particularly the research article (for examples which consider 'academic discourse/styles' or include a focus on both student and professional writing, see Cmerjkova 1996; Duszak 1994, 1997; Mauranen 1993; Ventola and Mauranen 1996). According to Connor (2004), research in CR/IR has broadly taken one of three approaches to the comparison of writing in different languages: text analysis, genre analysis and corpus linguistics. Text-oriented research has sought to identify and (in some instances) quantify key linguistic features in published texts, such as reformulation markers in academic articles in English, Spanish and Catalan (Cuenca 2003), epistemic modality in English and Spanish (Martín 2002) and hedging by 'native speaker' and 'non-native speaker' writers based on text analysis (Hinkel

1997); or as mapped across languages and writer linguistic profiles, as in Yang's (2013) study of Chinese and English. Genre studies have compared the rhetorical structures of academic texts in different languages using Swales's (1990, 2004) model (discussed above): for example, Golebiowski (1998) and Duszak (1994) focused on Polish-medium articles in psychology and linguistics, respectively; Fakhri (2004) on Arabic article introductions in humanities and social sciences; ElMalik and Nesi (2008) on move structure in medical research articles written by British as compared with Sudanese authors; and Mur-Dueñas (2010) on the analysis of article introductions in English and Spanish. Conclusions reached about the stability of the generic move structure across journal articles in different languages vary. For example, considering Hungarian introductions to theoretical articles in linguistics, Árvay and Tanko (2004: 89) conclude that Swales' model fails to capture the 'wide variety of Hungarian introduction-structures'. Some research also signals the influence over time of English-medium rhetorical practices, for example, Salager-Meyer, Alcáraz Ariza and Zambrano (2003) compare 'academic conflict' in medical papers in three languages.

Corpus studies have enabled researchers to investigate specific features of academic discourse, as illustrated by Carrió-Pastor's (2013) study of 'sentence connectors' in English-medium published articles by Spanish and English writers, and Fløttum, Dahl and Kinn's (2006) analysis of multiple features (including metatextual expressions and bibliographical references) across English, French and Norwegian in the fields of linguistics, economics and medicine. Corpus approaches have also been used to explore genres other than research articles: for example, conference abstracts (Yakhontova 2006) and book reviews (Moreno and Suárez 2010). A driving force behind work in contrastive/intercultural rhetoric has been to identify patterns of discourse in order to help students or 'novices' and/or users of English as an additional language to produce successful texts.

A key contribution from CR/IR has been the tracking of linguistic, rhetorical and generic features in academic texts across languages. Recent work emphasises the multidimensionality to cultural-linguistic frameworks – to include factors such as disciplinarity – and explores the influence of rhetorical practices across languages, for example, the influence of English on linguistic and rhetorical patterns in other languages.

2.1.4 New Literacy Studies

Strongly influenced by work in New Literacy Studies (e.g. Gee 2000) and Academic Literacies (e.g. Lea and Street 1998; Lillis and Scott 2007) researchers are increasingly adopting ethnographic approaches to the study of academic writing for publication which involve not only adopting specific methodologies but also shifting the theoretical framing of the phenomenon. In broad terms, researchers using ethnographic methods start from a view of literacy as 'social practice' which involves:

1. A *theoretical position* on writing which states that writing cannot and should not be viewed as separate from contexts of use and users.
2. An *empirical position* which states that texts, uses and users need to be the subjects of empirical research rather than being driven by *a priori* assumptions and value positions. (Lillis 2013: 16)

Ethnographic methods used to explore literacy as a social practice – here, writing for publication – include the collection and analysis of a range of data such as texts, interviews, observations, photographs and documentary data. Particular importance is attached to securing an *emic* or insider perspective in addition to the *etic* perspective of researcher-analysts (although the complex relationship between these stances is acknowledged, Lillis 2008). Thus, for example, researchers use interview methods to gain insight into multilingual scholars' perspectives on what and why they write (e.g. Ammon 2001; Buckingham 2008; Cheung 2010; Flowerdew and Li 2009; Lillis 2008: Pérez-Llantada, Plo, and Ferguson 2011). Some scholars foreground the emic perspective through the use of autobiographical accounts: for example, Belcher and Connor (2001) provide 18 narratives by established multilingual scholars from a variety of disciplinary, linguistic and educational backgrounds from Austria, China, Taiwan, Finland, France, Ghana, Germany, India, Iran, Japan, Lebanon, Lithuania, Mexico, Sri Lanka and Puerto Rico. Some researchers draw on a combination of approaches to connect autobiographical experiences with contemporary text production practices to offer both empirical accounts and theoretical framings of what is involved in writing for publication in the current global context. For instance, Casanave (2002) interweaves autobiographical narratives of her experiences in academic writing with related theoretical discussions, followed by case studies of multilingual writers including novice researchers in Japan and established multilingual academics working in the United States. Canagarajah (1996, 2002) offers an auto-ethnographic account of his experiences as a Sri Lankan scholar along with accounts of other scholars' practices in order to situate and theorize these accounts in terms of centre/periphery relations around knowledge production. Working from 'a dialogical self-case study design', bilingual (French-English) scholars Gentil and Séror (2014) situate their own language choices for publishing in the larger context of Canada's official bilingualism – albeit with 'regional asymmetries' (p. 18) – including those in their location in Ottawa.

A growing focus of interest is the exploration of text production practices, by tracking text trajectories towards submission and publication: this involves collecting and analyzing a range of data including drafts, submitted and revised versions of texts, and editors' and reviewers' comments. Early work using this approach was by Flowerdew (2000) who tracked the publishing practices and experiences of a Hong Kong scholar, paying careful attention to reviewers' comments (2001). In our research involving a longitudinal text-oriented ethnographic study, we have for more than a decade explored the experiences and practices of writing for publi-

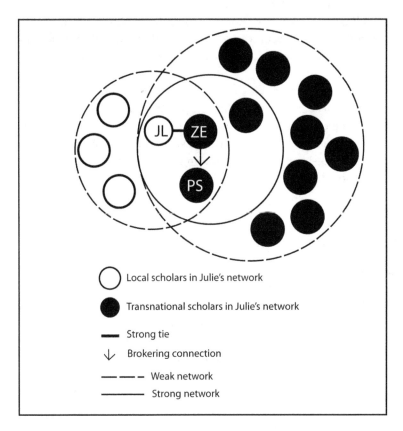

Local scholars in Julie's network

Transnational scholars in Julie's network

Strong tie

↓ Brokering connection

Weak network

Strong network

Fig. 9.2: Network diagram, Julie, associate professor of psychology, Central Europe (Source: Lillis and Curry 2010, Chapter 3, p. 81).

cation of 50 scholars from four national contexts, Hungary, Slovakia, Spain, and Portugal (Curry and Lillis 2004, 2014; Lillis and Curry 2010). We have constructed a substantial database including field notes made in more than 60 visits to 12 institutions; the collection of approximately 1200 texts written by scholars and 500 copies of correspondence about texts between participants and others (e.g. colleagues, reviewers, editors); some 250 text-based interviews with scholars; and documentary data from academic departments and institutions as well as policy documents. From this data set, we have tracked the production trajectories of texts – using 'text histories' as a key analytic framework (see Lillis and Curry 2010 pages 4–5) – and analysed networks of activity in the production of texts (Curry and Lillis 2010; Lillis and Curry 2006a, 2010; see Figure 9.2 for an example of a network diagram); categorised the range of 'literacy brokers' involved in mediating text production (Lillis and Curry 2006b, 2010); examined the use of citations across languages (Lillis et al. 2010) and analysed the imperatives driving the establishment of English-medium national journals in contexts where English is not the official language (Lillis 2012). We have paid attention to detailing empirically the phenomenon of writing for publication in a multilingual world and explored the ideological orientations – to language, English, and the politics of place – of key participants.

A key contribution of ethnographic approaches has been to make visible the nature of contemporary academic text production practices and how these are inflected through ideological orientations towards English, language, style and place. Research in this tradition has placed centre stage the experiences and perspectives of scholars, alongside debates surrounding the politics of text production and evaluation at national and transnational levels.

3 Disciplinarity in the study of academic writing for publication

A focus on disciplinarity occurs with greater or lesser emphasis in the literature across the research traditions mentioned above. As discussed, some researchers have investigated the features of texts within specific disciplines (e.g. Hewings and Hewings 2001, on geography, and 2002 on business; Hyland 2004, 2005 across broader fields such as sciences and social sciences). In many cases, however, the academic discipline of research participants is backgrounded in favour of concerns about individual proficiency, linguistic profile or geolinguistic location. Indeed, disciplinarity in some instances seems to be an artefact of researchers' disciplinary location or populations to which researchers have access (e.g. for applied linguistics/English teaching, see Basturkmen 2009; Cheung 2010; Liu 2004; Shi 2002; for biochemistry, Li 2012; for geography, Paasi 2005; for management, Tietze and Dick 2009). In other cases, the English proficiency level of participants is linked to the discipline chosen as the focus of study. For example, in a comparative study of the publishing records of Hong Kong scholars whose first language was Cantonese as compared with English, Braine (2005) examined texts by applied linguists because he thought their presumed 'better proficiency in English' (p. 708) as compared with scholars from other disciplines would facilitate their English-medium publishing efforts.

In contrast, some research attaches importance to considering both geographical and disciplinary location. For example, Peterson and Shaw (2002) used questionnaires, interviews and publishing records to explore the academic publishing genres and writing experiences of 70 Danish scholars in nine departments of one business school. They identified scholars' use of citations in multiple languages, which they believed signalled the linguistic medium of their academic reading and the languages of the genres in which scholars published. In a recent study, Gnutzmann and Rabe (2014) interviewed 24 German scholars in four 'disciplinary cultures' (biology, mechanical engineering, history and German linguistics). Their findings highlighted not only variations in textual demands but also how the data used in disciplinary research affect the ways that scholars write.

A key claim made by studies comparing the publishing experiences of scholars across disciplines is that there is a firm division between the natural and social sciences (and in some cases, humanities) in terms of the pressure to publish in English and multilingual scholars' responses to it. Tardy's (2004) survey of the literature on the role of English in publishing in the natural sciences identified historical and economic factors, including access to bibliometric and information technologies. She also noted studies which point to the preponderance of Anglophone journal editors and referees, a prevalence of English-medium citations in publications, and the influence of English discursive norms as key dynamics favouring the use of English.

Survey research on multilingual academics located in various disciplines and geolinguistic contexts also offers support for the claim of greater pressure to publish in the sciences than in other disciplines. In Poland, Duszak and Lewkowicz's (2008) survey showed that 97 % of responding medical researchers published in English compared with 68 % of scholars from psychology and 54 % of language scholars. Flowerdew's (1999a) survey of 717 Cantonese-speaking scholars in Hong Kong across disciplines documented their experience with English, attitudes about publishing in English, and challenges and strategies for publishing in English. He found that natural scientists 'were most prolific in terms of [publishing] international refereed journal articles in English' (p. 134). A comparable range of disciplines was represented in a survey of Swedish scholars conducted by Olsson and Sheridan (2012), who found that 75–100 % of scientists were publishing in English as compared with 10 % of scholars in the Faculty of Arts and Education.

Despite the apparently higher rates of publishing in English, researchers have determined that scientists' experiences of writing are not straightforward. To quantify whether more effort was expended – and anxiety induced – in writing for publication in English rather than in scholars' L1 and/or national language, Hanauer and Englander (2011) surveyed 141 Mexican scientists across a number of disciplines. As compared with using Spanish, scientists reported that they perceived writing in English as 24 % more difficult, inducing 21 % more anxiety and causing 11 % more dissatisfaction with the product than when writing Spanish-medium articles. Similarly, in an interview-based study of 10 senior natural and social scientists in Spain, Pérez-Llantada, Plo, and Ferguson (2011) documented scientists' feelings of resigned acceptance of the dominance of English and acknowledgment of the additional burden imposed by using English. Okamura (2006) identified differences in senior Japanese biologists' experiences of publishing in English with those of junior scholars. Among the 13 biologists she interviewed, the more established academics seemed better able to understand the expectations of their audience and had developed strategies that supported their publishing efforts.

Pressure to publish in English is also increasing in the social sciences and to some extent in the humanities (Flowerdew and Li 2009). Our research on the experiences of European scholars in education and psychology demonstrates that while the majority experience pressure to publish in English, many also maintain publishing agendas in local languages (Curry and Lillis 2004; Lillis and Curry 2010). The growing use of the Social Science Citation Index and the Arts and Humanities Citation Index in global reward systems appears to be putting increased pressure on scholars in these disciplines to publish not only in English-medium journals but also in journals included in these high status indexes (see Curry and Lillis 2013; see also Bocanegra-Valle 2014 on the European Reference for the Humanities).

Another key theme in the literature foregrounding scholars' disciplines in relation to writing is collaboration. As STEM fields tend generally to collaborate more than other disciplines in conducting and writing research, many studies of publishing in science have identified collaboration as a key aspect of success (e.g. Curry 2014; Gnutzmann and Rabe 2014; Ordóñez-Matamoros, Cozzens and García 2010)[2]. Collaboration has also been noted in social science disciplines such as business (Peterson and Shaw 2002). Likewise, we identify collaboration as a key dimension to the text production practices of psychology and education scholars in our study. This collaboration often includes the involvement of literacy brokers (Lillis and Curry 2006b) and academic research networks (Curry and Lillis 2010; Lillis and Curry 2006a) in both research activity and 'official' (i.e. as is evident in named authoring on published papers) and 'unofficial' co-authorship.

4 Theoretical and ideological orientations towards the study of academic writing for publication

In the different traditions of researching writing for publication, orientations towards the study of writing for publication vary, most obviously at the level of the *empirical object* under study (e.g. whether the focus is primarily on the text, the writer, or the context) and the *methodology* used (i.e. a range of linguistic or rhetorical approaches, a range of ethnographic approaches survey research). However, there is considerable overlap in the ideological orientations underpinning research, evidenced by the foundational categories and assumptions underpinning the study of writing for publication:

---

2 Bibliometric studies aim to map out publication activity through network and statistical analysis. Research analysing co-authoring and citation patterns in published journal articles has demonstrated the increase in international collaboration and development of academic research networks (e.g. Jonkers and Tijssen 2008).

1. Language is treated as a discrete and boundaried phenomenon. Thus 'English' (even where multiple Englishes are mentioned) tends to be treated as a discrete phenomenon which can be compared with other discrete and equally boundaried linguistic phenomena, such as 'Spanish' and 'Chinese'. This orientation reflects the core approach to 'language' in applied linguistics and studies of writing more generally and legitimises categories such as 'native', 'first', 'second', 'foreign', 'additional' language (even in works where these are critiqued). The underlying monolithic epistemological and ideological positions towards 'language' (and 'culture') continue to be powerful even in research where it is critiqued.
2. Research on writing for publication continues to be often premised on English – and English-medium texts – as a stable or fixed point for cross/inter linguistic comparison (for critical discussion see Kubota 2010; see discussion below on 'languaging'). There is a tendency to focus on identifying generalised patterns of prevailing norms and conventions, whether in terms of language or genre, rather than on difference or divergence (both intra-linguistically – within assumed single languages and interlinguistically – comparisons across languages).
3. Emphasis tends to be on the individual writer and an individualised notion of writer 'competence'. This reflects the approach to writing adopted across most western academic fields of study, where the individual – the 'writer' – is construed analytically as the producer of meanings and a focus on individual activity is privileged above group activity.
4. Following from an emphasis on writing as individual competence and language as a discrete phenomenon, there is a tendency to adopt a deficit position on writers and writing, that is, to focus on what writers apparently *don't* know or *can't* do, and to emphasize what they need to do in order to produce appropriate texts.
5. The nature of moving towards or achieving 'advanced academic literacy' (including writing for publication) tends to be construed in terms of a trajectory *from* novice *to* expert. This reflects the influence of sociocognitive approaches to learning, including neo-Vygotskyan theories and approaches which frame writing as participating in communities (of learning, of discourse, of practice, e.g. Swales 1990; Wenger 1998; see also Uzuner 2008 for a review of research on scholars' participation practices).

All five positions continue to be powerful but are being questioned: for example, notions such as 'languaging' (Møller and Jørgensen 2009), 'mixing', 'meshing' (Canagarajah 2013) and 'translinguality' (Horner et al. 2011) are increasingly on the agenda in studies of *student* writing and are beginning to be considered in studies of writing for publication. This is evident in the questioning of a centre variety or 'native' English as the norm in producing academic papers (e.g. Mauranen and

Metsa-Ketela 2006) and in studies exploring the nature of published English-medium texts written by scholars who also write in other languages (e.g. Burgess and Martin 2010).

The increasing recognition of writing involving multiple participants at different stages of the process (e.g. Englander 2006; Flowerdew 2000; Lillis and Curry 2010; Tardy and Matsuda 2009) including researching multilingual editors' rationales for publishing journals in English, instead of or alongside other languages (Lillis 2012), is challenging the dominant focus on individual production and leading to a consideration of networks of activity (e.g. Ferenz 2005; Curry and Lillis 2010) and the notion of English as a 'networked resource' (Lillis 2012; Lillis and Curry 2013). A focus on networks of activity including the range of literacy brokers involved in text production is also challenging any presumed linear trajectory from novice to expert, shifting the emphasis towards a focus on how scholars working in multiple communities are channeling resources to meet their wide-ranging commitments and institutional pressures (Belcher 2007; Canagarajah 2002; Li 2012; Lillis and Curry 2010; Swales 1987). Within a framing of academic writing for publication which foregrounds networks, brokers and resources, the meaningfulness of adopting a deficit approach becomes more questionable. Questions arise not only in terms of accuracy of representation – much research shows that 'competence' and expertise are shared or distributed across networks of activity – but also in terms of any assumed autonomous value being attached to 'linguistic competence' (Chang and Kanno 2010; Lillis and Curry 2010).

5 Current debates and future directions

One way of charting the current state of work on writing for publication is as two interlinked threads, with the first overlapping in some areas of empirical research with the second, and the second responding in some ways to the first, by raising questions about key assumptions.

Thread 1: The assumption is that English is the global language of academic knowledge production and a central goal of research is to identify the key features of English-medium texts to make such features visible. Making these features visible – sometimes through comparison with linguistic and rhetorical practices in a number of languages – is considered to be valuable for scholars who can be enabled to make conscious choices about which features and conventions to use. Possible areas of future research in this vein include the tracking of shifting rhetorical practices globally, not only according to genre and linguistic medium but also across new modes of production and redistribution, such as academic blogging (for example and discussion, see https://elfaproject.wordpress.com/category/anna-mauranen.)

Thread 2: More recently – although this thread of work is not new (e.g. Swales 1987) – critical discussions about the global status of English have articulated concerns about issues of equity and access, the nature of the kinds of English(es) that best suit academic knowledge exchange and questions about the directionality of knowledge exchange (i.e. from centre to periphery, from 'other' languages into English, rather than only from English into/alongside other languages). This phase has been brought about in large part by research exploring scholars' practices and perspectives on writing for publication as well as a concern with teasing out the drivers for *English*-medium knowledge production, including global evaluation systems nested within commercial enterprise (e.g. Thomson Reuters) and policy at national and international levels (see special issue of the journal *Language Policy*, 2013). Three developments in the field characterize Thread 2 and are opening up areas of future research:

1. Interest is growing in production practices. Whilst progress has been made, the empirical base is small and there is a need to continue exploring production and exchange practices across diverse contexts;
2. Research on writing for publication is increasingly being carried out by scholars from around the world, rather than principally from the Anglophone centre, which brings to bear a more complex perspective on the phenomenon being studied. For example, at the 2011 Symposium on Second Language Writing in Taipei, Taiwan, Hui-Tzu Min (2011) documented the critical response of Taiwanese academics to governmental pressure to publish in English-medium journals listed in high status journal indexes; Feng, Beckett, and Huang (2013), focusing on academic writing by Chinese scholars, challenge any straightforward notions of directionality in knowledge production and exchange; Salager-Meyer (2012) discusses the complexity of Open Access initiatives, arguing that the academic community globally needs to engage in such initiatives. Future research will need to foreground political and institutional policies and pressures to publish and explore how scholars' writing practices are refracted through policies at local and transnational levels;
3. There is a growing focus on writing for publication in languages other than English in ways which are not premised on English as the norm or framed as comparisons with English, but as semiotic and linguistic resources for knowledge making in their own right (see e.g. Castelló, Iñesta and Corcelles 2012; Donohue's talk at the 2013 conference of the European Association of Teachers of Academic Writing). Future research needs to explore academic writing in a range of languages, with the emphasis not solely on linguistic difference but on how the use of a range of semiotic resources serves to sustain local and transnational knowledge exchange practices. While there is much still to be done to develop research along these directions, current developments in the study of academic writing for publication signal that it is a vibrant field.

6 Additional sources

AILA Research Network on Academic Publishing and Presenting in a global context
http://www.aila.info/en/research/list-of-rens/academic-publishing-and-presenting-in-a-global-context.html
Blommaert, Jan. 2013. *Ethnography, superdiversity and linguistic landscapes. Chronicles of complexity.* Clevedon: Multilingual Matters
English for Specific Purposes
Journal of Advanced Composition
Journal of English for Academic Purposes
Journal of Second Language Writing
Bibliography on translanguaging *http://www.translingualwriting.com/translingual-writing-bibliography.php*
Hyland, Ken and Philip Shaw (eds.). 2016. *Handbook of English for academic purposes.* London: Routledge
Language Policy
Leki, Ilona, Alister Cumming, and Tony Silva. 2008. *A synthesis of research on second language writing in English.* New York: Routledge.

7 References

Aktas, Rahime Nur and Viviana Cortes. 2008. Shell nouns as cohesive devices in published and ESL student writing. *Journal of English for Academic Purposes* 7(1). 3–14.
Ammon, Ulrich (ed.). 2001. *The dominance of English as a language of science.* Berlin & New York: Mouton de Gruyter.
Artemeva, Natalia. 2000. Revising a research article: Dialogic negotiation. In Patrick Dias and Anthony Pare (eds.), *Transitions: writing in academic and workplace settings,* 183–197. Cresskill, NJ: Hampton Press.
Arvay, Anett and Gyula Tanko. 2004. A contrastive analysis of English and Hungarian theoretical research article introductions. *International Review of Applied Linguistics in Language Teaching* 42(1). 71–100.
Basturkmen, Helen. 2009. Commenting on results in published research articles and masters dissertations in language teaching. *Journal of English for Academic Purposes* 8(4). 241–251.
Baldauf, Richard and Bjørn Jernudd. 1987. Academic communication in a foreign language: The example of Scandinavian psychology. *Australian Review of Applied Linguistics* 10(1). 98–117.
Belcher, Diane. 2007. Seeking acceptance in an English-only research world. *Journal of Second Language Writing* 16(1). 1–22.
Belcher, Diane and Ulla Connor (eds.). 2001. *Reflections on multiliterate lives.* Clevedon, UK: Multilingual Matters.
Bocanegra-Valle, Ana. 2014. 'English is my default academic language': Voices from LSP scholars publishing in a multilingual journal. *Journal of English for Academic Purposes* 13. 65–77.
Braine, George. 2005. The challenge of academic publishing: A Hong Kong perspective. *TESOL Quarterly* 39(4). 707–716.
Buckingham, Louisa. 2008. Development of English academic writing competence by Turkish scholars. *International Journal of Doctoral Studies* 3. 1–18.
Burgess, Sally and Pedro Martín Martín. 2010. Interpersonal features of Spanish social sciences journal abstracts: a diachronic study. In Rosa Lorés-Sanz, Pilar Mur-Dueñas, and Enrique

Lafuente-Millán (eds.), *Constructing interpersonality: Multiple perspectives on written academic genres*, 99–115. Newcastle upon Tyne: Cambridge Scholars Publishing.

Canagarajah, A. Suresh. 1996. "Nondiscursive" requirements in academic publishing, material resources of periphery scholars, and the politics of knowledge production. *Written Communication* 13(4). 435–472.

Canagarajah, A. Suresh. 2002. *A geopolitics of academic writing*. Pittsburgh, PA: University of Pittsburgh Press.

Canagarajah, A. Suresh. 2013. *Translingual practice: Global Englishes and cosmopolitan relations*. London: Routledge.

Carrió-Pastor, María Luisa. 2013. A contrastive study of the variation of sentence connectors in academic English. *Journal of English for Academic Purposes* 12(3). 192–202.

Casanave, Christine. 1998. Transitions: The balancing act of bilingual academics. *Journal of Second Language Writing* 12(1). 175–203.

Casanave, Christine. 2002. *Writing games: Multicultural case studies of academic literacy practices in higher education*. Mahwah, NJ: Lawrence Erlbaum.

Castelló, Montserrat, Anna Iñesta and Mariona Corcelles. 2012. Learning to write a research article: PhD students' transitions toward disciplinary writing regulation. *Research in the Teaching of English* 47(4). 442–477.

Chang, Yu-Jung and Yasuko Kanno. 2010. NNES doctoral students in English-speaking academe: The nexus between language and discipline. *Applied Linguistics* 31(5). 671–692.

Cheung, Yin Ling. 2010. Challenges in writing refereed English journal papers and institutional support for research publication. *Asian Journal of English Language Teaching* 20(1). 207–224.

Cho, Seonhee. 2004. Challenges of entering discourse communities through publishing in English: Perspectives of non-native speaking doctoral students in the United States of America. *Journal of Language, Identity, and Education* 3(1). 47–72.

Cmejrkova, Svetla. 1996. Academic writing in Czech and English. In Eija Ventola and Anna Mauranen (eds.), *Academic writing: Intercultural and textual issues*, 137–152. Amsterdam: John Benjamins.

Connor, Ulla. 2004. Intercultural rhetoric research: beyond texts. *Journal of English for Academic Purposes* 3(4). 291–305.

Connor, Ulla. 2011. *Intercultural rhetoric in the writing classroom*. Ann Arbor: University of Michigan Press.

Cuenca, Maria-José. 2003. Two ways to reformulate: A contrastive analysis of reformulation markers. *Journal of Pragmatics* 35. 1069–1093.

Curry, Mary Jane. 2014. Graphics as invention heuristics in writing for publication by academic engineers. In Mary Jane Curry and David Ian Hanauer (eds.), *Language, literacy, and learning in STEM education: Research methods and perspectives from applied linguistics*, 87–106. Amsterdam: Benjamins.

Curry, Mary Jane and Theresa Lillis. 2004. Multilingual scholars and the imperative to publish in English: Negotiating interests, demands, and rewards. *TESOL Quarterly* 38(4). 663–688.

Curry, Mary Jane and Theresa Lillis. 2010. Academic research networks: Accessing resources for English-medium publishing. *English for Specific Purposes* 29(4). 281–295.

Curry, Mary Jane and Theresa Lillis. 2013. Introduction to the thematic issue: Participating in academic publishing – consequences of linguistic policies and practices. *Language Policy* 12(3). 209–213.

Curry, Mary Jane and Theresa Lillis. 2014. Strategies and tactics in academic knowledge production by multilingual scholars. *Education Policy Analysis Archives* 22(31). http://dx.doi.org/10.14507/epaa.v22n32.2014[dx.doi.org]

Donohue, Christiane. 2013. Challenging loss: Language, culture, and the future of academic writing research and teaching. Plenary workshop, European Association for Teachers of Academic Writing Conference, Budapest, Hungary, June 27–29.

Duszak, Anna. 1994. Academic discourse and intellectual styles. *Journal of Pragmatics* 21. 291–313.

Duszak, Anna. 1997. Cross-cultural academic communication: a discourse-community view. In Anna Duszak (ed.), *Culture and styles in academic discourse,* 11–39. Berlin & New York: Mouton de Gruyter.

Duszak, Anna and Jo Lewkowicz. 2008. Publishing academic texts in English: A Polish perspective. *Journal of English for Academic Purposes* 7(2). 108–120.

ElMalik, Abdullahi Tamul and Hilary Nesi. 2008. Publishing research in a second language: The case of Sudanese contributors to medical journals. *Journal of English for Academic Purposes* 7(2). 87–96.

Englander, Karen. 2006. Revision of scientific manuscripts by nonnative-English-speaking scientists in response to journal editors' criticism of the language. *Journal of Applied Linguistics* 3(2). 129–161.

Fakhri, Ahmed. 2004. Rhetorical properties of Arabic research article introductions. *Journal of Pragmatics* 36. 1119–1138.

Feng, Haiying, Gulbahar H. Beckett, and Dawang Huang. 2013. From 'import' to 'import – export' oriented internationalization: the impact of national policy on scholarly publication in China. *Language Policy* 12(3). 251–272.

Ferenz, Orna. 2005. EFL writers' social networks: impact on advanced academic literacy development. *Journal of English for Academic Purposes* 4(4). 339–351.

Fløttum, Kjersti, Trine Dahl, and Torodd Kinn. 2006. *Academic voices: Across languages and disciplines.* Amsterdam: Benjamins.

Flowerdew, John. 1999a. Writing for scholarly publication in English: The case of Hong Kong. *Journal of Second Language Writing* 8(2). 123–145.

Flowerdew, John. 1999b. Problems in writing for scholarly publication in English: The case of Hong Kong. *Journal of Second Language Writing* 8(3). 243–264.

Flowerdew, John. 2000. Discourse community, legitimate peripheral participation, and the nonnative-English-speaking scholar. *TESOL Quarterly* 34(1). 127–150.

Flowerdew, John. 2001. Attitudes of journal editors to nonnative speaker contributions. *TESOL Quarterly,* 35(1). 121–150.

Flowerdew, John and Yongyan Li. 2009. English or Chinese? The trade-off between local and international publication among Chinese academics in the humanities and social sciences. *Journal of Second Language Writing* 18. 1–16.

Gee, James. 2000. The New Literacy Studies. In David Barton, Mary Hamilton, and Roz Ivanič (eds.), *Situated literacies,* 180–196. London: Routledge.

Gentil, Guillaume and Jérémie Séror. 2014. Canada has two official languages – Or does it? Case studies of Canadian scholars' language choices and practices in disseminating knowledge. *Journal of English for Academic Purposes* 13. 17–30.

Gnutzmann, Claus and Frank Rabe. 2014. 'Theoretical subtleties' or 'text modules'? German researchers' language demands and attitude across disciplinary cultures. *Journal of English for Academic Purposes* 13. 31–40.

Golebiowski, Zofia. 1998. Rhetorical approaches to scientific writing: an English-Polish comparative study. *Text* 18(1). 67–102.

Hanauer, David and Karen Englander. 2011. Quantifying the burden of writing research articles in a second language: Data from Mexican scientists. *Written Communication* 28(4). 403–416

Harwood, Nigel. 2005a. "I hoped to counteract the memory problem, but I made no impact whatsoever": Discussing methods in computing science using *I*. *English for Specific Purposes* 24. 243–267.

Harwood, Nigel. 2005b. "Nowhere has anyone attempted ... In this article I do just that": A corpus-based study of self-promotional *I* and *we* in academic writing across four disciplines. *Journal of Pragmatics* 37. 1027–1231.

Hewings, Ann and Martin Hewings. 2001. Anticipatory 'it' in academic writing: an indicator of disciplinary difference and developing disciplinary knowledge. In Martin Hewings (ed.), *Academic writing in context: Implications and applications,* 199–214. Birmingham, UK: University of Birmingham Press.

Hewings, Martin and Ann Hewings. 2002. "It is interesting to note that..." A comparative study of anticipatory 'it' in student and published writing. *English for Specific Purposes* 21(4). 367–383.

Hinkel, Eli.1997. Indirectness in L1 and L2 academic writing. *Journal of Pragmatics.* 27. 361–386.

Hopkins, Andy and Tony Dudley-Evans. 1988. A genre-based investigation of the discussion sections in articles and dissertations. *English for Specific Purposes* 7. 113–121.

Horner, Bruce, Min-Zhan Lu, Jacqueline Jones Royster, and John Trimbur. 2011. Language difference in writing: Toward a translingual approach. *College English* 73(3). 302–321.

Hyland, Ken. 2000. *Disciplinary discourses: Social interactions in academic writing.* Harlow, Essex: Pearson Educational.

Hyland, Ken. 2002. Authority and invisibility: authorial identity in academic writing. *Journal of Pragmatics* 34. 1091–1112.

Hyland, Ken. 2004. *Genre and second language writing.* Ann Arbor: University of Michigan Press.

Hyland, Ken. 2005. *Metadiscourse: Exploring interaction in writing.* London: Continuum.

Hyland, Ken. 2006. *English for academic purposes: An advanced resource book.* London: Routledge.

Hyland, Ken and Liz Hamp Lyons. 2002. EAP: Issues and directions. *Journal of English for Academic Purposes* 1(1). 1–12.

Jonkers, Koen and Robert Tijssen. 2008. Chinese researchers returning home: impacts of international mobility on research collaboration and scientific productivity. *Scientometrics* 77(2). 309–333.

Jordan, Robert. 2002. The growth of EAP in Britain. *Journal of English for Academic Purposes* 1. 69–78.

Kanoksilapatham, Budsaba. 2005. Rhetorical structure of biochemistry research articles. *English for Specific Purposes* 24. 269–292.

Kubota, Ryuko. 2010. Cross-cultural perspectives on writing: contrastive rhetoric. In Nancy Hornberger and Sandra McKay (eds.), *Sociolinguistics and language education*, 265–89. Bristol, UK: Multilingual Matters.

Lafuente-Millán, Enrique, Pilar Mur-Dueñas, Rosa Lorés-Sanz, and Ignacio Vázquez-Orta. 2010. Interpersonality in written academic discourse: Three analytical perspectives. In Rosa Lorés-Sanz, Pilar Mur-Dueñas, and Enrique Lafuente-Millán (eds.), *Constructing interpersonality: Multiple perspectives on written academic genres*, 13–40. Newcastle upon Tyne: Cambridge Scholars Publishing.

Lea, Mary and Brian Street. 1998. Student writing in higher education: An academic literacies approach. *Studies in Higher Education* 23(2). 157–72.

Li, Yongyan. 2006. Negotiating knowledge contribution to multiple discourse communities: A doctoral student of computer science writing for publication. *Journal of Second Language Writing* 15. 159–178.

Li, Yongyan. 2012. "I have no time to find out where the sentences came from; I just rebuild them": A biochemistry professor eliminating novices' textual borrowing. *Journal of Second Language Writing* 21. 59–70.

Lillis, Theresa. 2008. Ethnography as method, methodology, and "deep theorizing": Closing the gap between text and context in academic writing research. *Written Communication* 25(3). 353–388.

Lillis, Theresa. 2012. Economies of signs in writing for academic publication: the case of English medium "national" journals. *Journal of Advanced Composition* 32(3–4). 695–722.

Lillis, Theresa. 2013. *The sociolinguistics of writing.* Edinburgh: Edinburgh University Press.

Lillis, Theresa and Mary Jane Curry. 2006a. Reframing notions of competence in scholarly writing: From individual to networked activity. *Revista Canaria de Estudios Ingleses* 53. 63–78.

Lillis, Theresa and Mary Jane Curry. 2006b. Professional academic writing by multilingual scholars: Interactions with literacy brokers in the production of English-medium texts. *Written Communication* 23(1). 3–35.

Lillis, Theresa and Mary Jane Curry. 2010. *Academic writing in a global context: The politics and practices of publishing in English.* London: Routledge.

Lillis, Theresa and Mary Jane Curry. 2013. English, academic publishing and international development: access and participation in the global knowledge economy. In Elizabeth Erling and Phillip Seargeant (eds.), *English and international development*, 220–242. Clevedon, UK: Multilingual Matters.

Lillis, Theresa, Ann Hewings, Dimitra Vladimirou, and Mary Jane Curry. 2010. The geolinguistics of English as an Academic lingua franca: Citation practices across English-medium national and English-medium international journals. *International Journal of Applied Linguistics* 20(1). 111–135.

Lillis, Theresa and Mary Scott. 2007. Defining academic literacies research: issues of epistemology, ideology and strategy. *Journal of Applied Linguistics* 4(1). 5–32.

Liu, Jun. 2004. Co-constructing academic discourse from the periphery: Chinese applied linguists' centripetal participation in scholarly publication. *Asian Journal of English Language Teaching* 14. 1–22.

Lorés-Sanz, Rosa, Pilar Mur-Dueñas, and Enrique Lafuente-Millán (eds.). 2010. *Constructing interpersonality: Multiple perspectives on written academic genres.* Newcastle upon Tyne: Cambridge Scholars Publishing.

Manchón, Rosa M. (ed.). 2009. *Writing in foreign language contexts: Learning, teaching, and research.* Bristol, UK: Multilingual Matters.

Martín Martín, Pedro. 2002. A genre-based investigation of abstract writing in English and Spanish. *Revista Canaria de Estudios Ingleses* 44. 47–64.

Matsuda, Paul K., Christina Ortmeier-Hooper, and Xiaoye You (eds.). 2006. *The politics of second language writing.* West Lafayette, IN: Parlor Press.

Mauranen, Anna. 1993. *Cultural differences in academic rhetoric.* Frankfurt: Peter Lang.

Mauranen, Anna and Maria Metsa-Ketela (eds.). 2006. English as a Lingua Franca. *Nordic Journal of English Studies* 5(2). 1–8.

Min, Hui-Tzu. 2011. Participating in academic publishing in the Inner Circle: A Taiwan perspective. Plenary talk, Symposium on Second Language Writing. Taipei, Taiwan, June 9–11.

Møller, Janus Spindler and J. Normann Jørgensen. 2009. From language to languaging: Changing relations between humans and linguistic features. *Acta Linguistica Hafniensia* 41. 143–66.

Moreno, Ana and Lorena Suárez. 2010. Academic book reviews in English and Spanish: is 'giving reasons for critical comments' a universal politeness strategy? In Rosa Lorés-Sanz, Pilar Mur-Dueñas, & Enrique Lafuente-Millán (eds.), *Constructing interpersonality: Multiple perspectives on written academic genres*, 117–136. Newcastle upon Tyne: Cambridge Scholars Publishing.

Mur-Dueñas, Pilar. 2010. Attitude markers in business management research articles: a cross-cultural corpus-driven approach. *International Journal of Applied Linguistics* 19. 50–72.

Okamura, Akiko. 2006. Two types of strategies used by Japanese scientists, when writing research articles in English. *System* 34(1). 68–79.

Olsson, Anna and Vera Sheridan. 2012. A case study of Swedish scholars' experiences with and perceptions of the use of English in academic publishing. *Written Communication* 29(1). 33–54.

Ordóñez-Matamoros, Hector, Susan Cozzens, and Margarita García. 2010. International co-authorship and research team performance in Columbia. *Review of Policy Research* 27(4). 415–431.

Ozturk, Ismet. 2007. The textual organisation of research article introductions in applied linguistics: variability within a single discipline. *English for Specific Purposes* 26(1). 25–38.

Paasi, Anssi. 2005. Globalisation, academic capitalism, and the uneven geographies of international journal publishing spaces. *Environment and Planning A* 37. 769i–789.

Pérez-Llantada, Carmen, Ramón Plo, and Gibson Ferguson. 2011. "You don't say what you know, only what you can": The perceptions and practices of senior Spanish academics regarding research dissemination in English. *English for Specific Purposes* 30(1). 18–30.

Peterson, Margarethe and Philip Shaw. 2002. Language and disciplinary differences in a biliterate context. *World Englishes* 21(3). 357–374.

Salager-Meyer, Francoise. 2012. The open access movement or "edemocracy": its birth, rise, problems and solutions. *Iberica* 12. 55–74.

Salager-Meyer, Francoise, María Angeles Alcáraz Ariza, and Nahirana Zambrano. 2003. The scimitar, the dagger and the glove: intercultural differences in the rhetoric of criticism in Spanish, French and English Medical Discourse (1930–1995). *English for Specific Purposes* 22. 223–247.

Shi, Ling. 2002. How Western-trained Chinese TESOL professionals publish in their home environment. *TESOL Quarterly* 36(4). 625–634.

Silva, Tony and Paul K. Matsuda (eds.). 2000. *On second language writing*. London: Routledge.

Simpson, Steve. 2013. Systems of writing response: A Brazilian student's experiences writing for publication in an environmental studies doctoral program. *Research in the Teaching of English* 48(2). 228–249.

St. John, Maggie Jo. 1987. Writing processes of Spanish scientists publishing in English. *English for Specific Purposes* 60(2). 113–120.

Swales, John. 1987. Utilizing the literature in teaching the research paper. *TESOL Quarterly* 21. 41–68.

Swales, John. 1988. Language and scientific communication: the case of the reprint request. *Scientometrics* 13. 93–101.

Swales, John. 1990. *Genre analysis: English in academic and research settings*. Cambridge: Cambridge University Press.

Swales, John. 1997. English as 'Tyrannosaurus rex'. *World Englishes* 16(3). 373–382.

Swales, John. 1998. *Other floors, other voices: a textography of a small university building*. Mahwah: NJ: Lawrence Erlbaum.

Swales, John. 2004. *Research genres*. Oxford: Oxford University Press.

Swales, John and Christine Feak. 2000. *English in today's research world: a writing guide*. Ann Arbor: University of Michigan Press.

Swales, John and Christine Feak. 2012. *Academic writing for graduate students: essential tasks and skills*, 3rd ed. Ann Arbor: University of Michigan Press.

Tardy, Christine. 2004. The role of English in scientific communication: *lingua franca* or *Tyrannosaurus rex*? *Journal of English for Academic Purposes* 3(3). 247–269.

Tardy, Christine. 2005. 'It's like a story': rhetorical knowledge development in advanced academic literacy. *Journal of English for Academic Purposes* 4(4). 325–338.

Tardy, Christine and Paul K. Matsuda. 2009. The construction of author voice by editorial board members. *Written Communication* 26(1). 32–52.

Tietze, Susanne and Penny Dick. 2009. Hegemonic practices and knowledge production in the management academy: an English language perspective. *Scandinavian Journal of Management* 25. 119–123.

Uzuner, Sedef. 2008. Multilingual scholars' participation in core/global academic communities: a literature review. *Journal of English for Academic Purposes* 7. 250–263.

Ventola, Eija and Anna Mauranen (eds.). 1996. *Academic writing: intercultural and textual issues*. Amsterdam: Benjamins.

Wenger, Etienne. 1998. *Communities of practice: learning, meaning, and identity*. New York: Cambridge University Press.

Yakhontova, Tatyana. 2006. Cultural and disciplinary variation in academic discourse: the issue of influencing factors. *Journal of English for Academic Purposes* 5(2). 153–167.

Yang, Yingli. 2013. Exploring linguistic and cultural variations in the use of hedges in English and Chinese scientific discourse. *Journal of Pragmatics* 50. 23–36.

Yang, Ruying and Desmond Allison. 2003. Research articles in applied linguistics: moving from results to conclusions. *English for Specific Purposes* 22. 365–385.

Susan Parks
10 Workplace writing: From text to context

1 Introduction

In this chapter, I discuss how within applied linguistics, especially since the 1990s, the interest in workplace writing with respect to business communication and other professional and workplace genres has shifted from a primarily materials-led (St. John 1996) to a research-led endeavour. At its most general level, workplace writing refers to writing done in a non-academic as opposed to an academic (or school) setting. However, it should be noted that academic or scholarly writing, even if produced on-the-job, is outside the scope of the present chapter. In addition, the term *workplace writing* will be used to refer to both the processes of text production and textual products. I will first situate the research on workplace writing within the broader domain of mainstream and second/foreign language research on writing. Following this, I will categorize and review relevant research on workplace writing related to applied linguistics. I will also delineate several areas for future research.

2 Workplace writing: A historical perspective

To understand current trends in research on workplace writing within applied linguistics, it is first necessary to consider how approaches to writing as an object of study emerged more generally both within mainstream and second/foreign language contexts.

2.1 Text production: Writing as a socially situated phenomenon

During the 1970s and 1980s, research on writing shifted from a focus on the analysis of product to an interest in cognitive processes in terms of how writers actually produced texts (see Chapter 12, this *Handbook*). Within this research paradigm, particular importance was accorded to the strategies used by writers during the composing process, especially in terms of differences between novice and expert writers, as well as within L2 research, the role of language proficiency (see Chapters 2 and 12). Amongst the critiques levied against what has since come to be referred to as the process approach to writing, one pertained to the limited importance accorded to social context in terms of how texts were produced and how writers developed competency in writing over time. Within the cognitive based perspective, the locus of control was perceived as residing within the individual. Techniques such as oral protocol analysis which required writers to compose in laboratory conditions were viewed as obscuring the processes of text production which might be evidenced in authentic contexts. To respond to these perceived inadequacies, attention turned to and has increasingly focused on exploring text production in socially situated contexts, both academic and workplace. To better situate the forthcoming discussion of workplace writing involving second/foreign language employees, an overview of two particularly significant areas of inquiry will be briefly focused on.

The first pertains to the interest given to delineating the processes of text production within workplace settings. In contrast to the cognitively oriented studies, research on workplace writing has revealed how text production is frequently a complex process which involves both overt and covert forms of collaboration (Couture and Rymer 1991; Paré 1991; Winsor 1989; Witte 1992). Overt collaboration refers to the way colleagues may variously interact with each other in function of their roles (for example, feedback given by a supervisor). Covert collaboration refers to the way previously produced texts may be consulted and used by employees within the institution (often referred to as document cycling, Paradis, Dobrin, and Miller 1985) as well as the way in which talk may mediate various aspects of text production (Paré 1991; Pettinari 1988; Selzer 1983; Spilka 1990).

Another important area of socially situated research pertains to the school work transition. Certain studies have highlighted the difficulties which new employees or interns have experienced as they move from academic to workplace settings as well as the way in which overt and covert forms of collaboration can variously facilitate or constrain the development of relevant workplace writing skills (Couture and Rymer 1991; Dias and Paré 2000; Schryer 1993). In terms of explaining the writing practices in place, a key concept evoked is that of the organizational culture, defined by Odell (1985) as the "internalized values, attitudes, knowledge, and ways of acting that are shared by other members" (p. 250). As discussed by Doheny-Farina (1986), the degree to which a collaborative approach to writing is used may itself be an indication of the extent to which power is shared within the organizational hierarchy.

Within a constructivist perspective, to write is, as Miller (1979) states, "to understand the conditions for one's own participation – the concepts, values, traditions style which permit identification with that community and determine the success or failure of communication" (p. 617). Accordingly, research on situated writing reveals that writers are sensitive to the rhetorical contexts in which their texts are produced. Studies show that stylistic choices made by employees in workplace settings are related to their perceptions of such factors as audience, persona (how writers wish readers to perceive them), and accuracy of information (Odell, Goswami, Herrington, and Quick 1983); organizational culture in terms of attitudes and values, prior actions or circumstances, and agency procedures (Odell 1985); the status of the employee (Winsor 1996) and multiple audiences (Paré 1991). Employees skilled in writing are adept at accommodating to a variety of personal, organizational and genre constraints during composing (Miller and Selzer 1985; Paré 1991; Winsor 1989).

2.2 Explanatory frameworks

To make sense of socially situated writing, both academic and workplace, an array of constructs and theoretical frameworks have been invoked. Of these, one line of theorizing pertains to socially oriented constructivist and constructionist perspectives which draw on the work of such scholars as Bakhtin (literature), Geertz (anthropology), Kuhn and Rorty (philosophers), and Vygotsky (psychologist). In terms of the construal of reality by particular groups within a given institutional or workplace setting, the constructs of interpretive community (Fish 1980) and, in particular, discourse community (have figured prominently. Also of note in this regard is the use of Neo-Vygotskian frames of reference, specifically Activity Theory and Lave and Wenger's (1991; Wenger 1999) conception of communities of practice in terms of legitimate peripheral participation.

However, within a conception of socially situated writing as it emerged in the 1980s, another major theoretical influence was the redefining of genre in terms of social action rather than as a set of formal features. As articulated by Miller (1984), "... a rhetorically sound definition of genre must be centered not on substance or the form of substance but on the action it is used to accomplish" (p. 151). A central notion underpinning the typified rhetorical action is how the members of the discourse community internalize the goals or exigency (Miller 1984) particular to the activity in which they are engaged. Although as discussed by Miller (1994), the perception of discourse communities as "vague, comforting and sentimental" (p. 72) tends to undermine the role of individual agency and the nature of change, subsequent theorizing has emphasized conceptions of genre as dynamic structures and sites of contention and change (Schryer 1993).

As will be seen below, workplace writing within applied linguistics has drawn on both the mainstream socially situated frames of reference as well as the type of genre analysis, which tends to be foregrounded in the work of researchers such as Swales and Bhatia who are more closely aligned with the traditions within applied linguistics.

3 Research perspectives on workplace writing within applied linguistics

This section will focus on workplace writing research which is more closely aligned with applied linguistics. The objective here is to provide a comprehensive view of this research both in terms of textual products and text production processes.

3.1 Workplace writing: Foregrounding textual products

As in academic contexts, a major thrust of research involving workplace and pro-fessional genres has involved genre analysis. In this regard, I will make a distinc-tion between those studies involving genre analysis within one specific setting and those aimed at crosslinguistic comparisons.

3.1.1 Genre analysis: The role of social context

Although within applied linguistics the relationship between genres as textual products and the social contexts in which they are produced has been duly ac-knowledged, most of the studies conducted under the genre analysis banner have nonetheless largely focused on the analysis of textual features (Bhatia 1993; Bhatia and Gotti 2006). What is of note, however, are those studies which more recently have begun to fuse traditional genre analysis with the insights provided by onsite investigations of text production processes or expert informants. Examples of such studies include those conducted by Flowerdew and Wan (2006, 2010) and Hafner (2013).

In the Flowerdew and Wan (2006) study, the researchers analyzed macro and micro level features of a corpus of 25 authentic tax computation letters written by tax accountants within an accounting firm in Hong Kong. Although within this workplace, most of the exchanges amongst employees were in Cantonese, all writ-ten communication was in English. In the context of this study, onsite observation and interviews with the employees enabled the researchers to better understand certain aspects of the text production process. Thus, for example, in terms of the mode of delivery, the decision to fax was based on the need to have a quick re-sponse whereas mailing was preferred for those letters when a more thorough re-flective response on the part of the client would be necessary. In a second related study which was also carried out in the Hong Kong business community, Flower-dew and Wan (2010) focused on the production of audit reports. Like the tax com-putation letters, the audit reports were highly formulaic genres with the exception of certain parts which required more original writing. As these parts proved highly challenging, they would frequently have to be revised by an English-speaking tech-nical manager. In terms of exploring the social context, a study by Hafner (2013), which focuses on the analysis of the barrister's opinion genre in the Hong Kong legal profession, provides an interesting alternative to onsite investigations. In this particular instance, to gain insight into how the textual product was shaped by social practice, five barristers were first asked to write an opinion in response to a simulated set of instructions and then interviewed to share their perspectives on the process of text production as specialist informants. Although the textual prod-uct sufficed to identify the move structure, the interviews provided for a more com-plete understanding of how intertextual and interdiscursive features mediated textualization processes at both macro and micro levels. Amongst other things, the study brought to light the need for barristers to adapt their writing for a dual audience: the instructing solicitor and the lay client. More generally, due to the important role played by the solicitor with respect to the provision of documents and other information, the production of the opinion genre could more aptly be described as co-constructed. The understanding gained from this genre analysis served to inform the design of an online genre-based resource for Hong Kong law students (Hafner 2008).

3.1.2 Genre analysis: Crosslinguistic perspectives

The interest in crosslinguistic perspectives on writing largely originated with Kaplan's (1966) attempts to characterize textual differences in terms of broad rhetorical patterns of discourse organization particular to a given culture. With the re-envisioning of the notion of genre as previously discussed, this broad focus has given way to more fine-grained comparisons of specific genres produced in different cultural settings (Connor, Nagelhout, and Rozyeki 2008). In addition to studies of academic writing, this line of inquiry has also extended to the analysis of workplace and professional genres. Examples of such research are illustrated by the following studies conducted by Vergaro (2004), van Mulken and van der Meer (2005), and Koskela (2006).

A study by Vergaro (2004) analyzed a corpus of 43 Italian and 26 English sales promotion letters. Although at the macro level, the type of moves were the same, cultural differences emerged with respect to the frequency in the Italian letters of a subject line and less detailed propositional content moves with respect to the sales promotion content. As explained by Vergaro, such differences can be attributed to the Italian preference for a reader-responsible rhetoric and to the American preference for a writer-responsible rhetoric. The more schematic approach evidenced in the Italian letters reflects the expectation that readers play a greater role in inferencing to deduce meaning whereas the more detailed approach in the American letters relates to writers' efforts to make the information more explicit and immediately obvious. Analysis of mood and modality at the micro-level also revealed cultural differences, especially with respect to the Italian preference for a high level of deference as evidenced by the widespread use of negative politeness strategies. By contrast, American writers privileged positive politeness strategies so as to emphasize solidarity.

With the advent of the Internet, genres associated with this medium have also been investigated in an attempt to identify how cultural influences might variously mediate text production. One such study is that by van Mulken and van der Meer (2005) which analyzed American and Dutch company replies to customer inquiries. In order to obtain a relevant corpus, an email inquiry was sent to 40 different

American and Dutch companies, which included both Old producers, i.e. companies with a long tradition, and to New producers, i.e. companies with relatively young producers. Results showed that there were no differences in terms of the move structure and only minor differences as pertained to paper-based counterparts. Based on this analysis, the researchers conclude that the differences thus obtained pertain to register due to the channel choice and are not evidence of a new genre. In terms of preferences, it was shown that American producers were more apt to express gratitude whereas Dutch producers were more inclined to apologize for declining a request.

A study by Koskela (2006) used genre analysis to investigate changes in bureaucratic language in the context of websites or cybergenres produced by tax authorities in three countries (Finland, Sweden, and the US). More specifically, the study focused on analysing the degree of reader-orientation through an analysis of the use of mood and personal pronouns. Results revealed that of the three countries, the American website proved most reader friendly as evidenced by the use of *you*, a more informal tone and the more prominent use of active, as opposed to passive, declarative sentences. In addition to the influence of web communication practices, the observed textual differences were attributed to historical and cultural factors.

3.2 Workplace writing: Foregrounding socially-situated practice

The research reported on in this section has as a primary objective to investigate text production processes and practices, and for the most part involves onsite investigations. Although genres as text types are generally evoked, the degree to which they may be analysed varies.

3.2.1 Workplace genres and language preference

A certain number of studies have begun to shed light on the nature and patterns of communication amongst employees within workplace settings where English (or other foreign languages) are in evidence. In this regard, a study by Barbara, Celani, Collins and Scott (1996) investigated the types of languages used and the communicative tasks, both written and oral, carried out by business organizations in the Sao Paulo area of Brazil. To gather the information, a survey questionnaire was sent out to business organizations of varying sizes. For the analysis, 214 questionnaires were used based on a return rate of approximately 16 %. Although all respondents, not surprisingly, used Portuguese, nearly 75 % also used English either internally or externally, thus providing evidence of the status of English as an international language for business communication. Of note is the fact that in organizations where English (or any other foreign language) was in evidence, most were using these languages for one document type only. Of the document types written in English, reports, proposals, prospectuses and projects were the most widely used. The study also showed that industrial, as opposed to non-industrial businesses, were more inclined to use English.

A study by Louhiala-Salminen (1996) provides insight into the use of English for business communication in Finland during the early 1990s. The study involved analysis of 395 survey questionnaires (representing a return rate of 40%) and follow-up interviews with ten respondents. Although 90% of respondents reported the need to use English for work purposes, what was more surprising was the frequency of use (50% stating daily use, 25% weekly or more often). In contrast to the widespread claim amongst business educators as to the increasing prevalence of telephone and face-to-face communication, respondents reported a 50% split in terms of the need for oral and written English language skills. This study also drew attention to the emerging influence of the nature in which technology was influencing both the mode of communication and change in written genres. More specifically, the study showed that correspondence by fax, as opposed to mail or the then emerging use of emails, had become the preferred means for sending English language messages. Beyond this, however, Louhiala-Salminen also demonstrated that the more informal style typical of communication by fax stood in contrast to the more formal genre of the business letter still widely advocated in business textbooks. As revealed in the interviews, what mattered for respondents in a business context was "efficiency", which at the level of fax writing could translate into messages of varying quality, including a drop in language accuracy.

A study by Chew (2005) provides insight into the dynamics of language use within the Hong Kong business context and was specifically undertaken in response to demands within the business community for employees with better English skills. Aimed more specifically at delineating the needs of the banking community, Chew's study involved 16 employees who held a variety of junior to mid-management level positions within four different banking institutions, three local and one international. Of note is that 14 of the study participants were relatively new entrants with work experience ranging from one-and-a-half months to three years. Data for the study were obtained by means of individual interviews and questionnaires. The main finding pertains to the language divide which revealed that almost all written tasks were carried out in English while most oral tasks involved Cantonese. As within this context much of the source information gathered from contact with colleagues or clients was in Cantonese, there was a need to translate into English – either verbatim or in the form of summaries – in order to produce various types of written documents (e.g., memos, minutes, reports, rules and regulations for bank customers). However, the need to use English to gather information through written sources was also important, especially if the research content was international or involved international companies. Although employees indicated an interest in language training, the preference was for short courses due presumably to long working hours as well as employers' reluctance to invest in employee training programs.

In contrast to the preceding studies, Nickerson's (1998) study demonstrated how corporate culture, specifically as pertains to the role of the head office, impacted on the degree to which documents would be written in English. The study which mainly targeted employees in management positions was based on responses obtained from 107 companies (a return rate of 35 %). As revealed by the survey, the majority of subsidiaries sent regular, often daily reports in English, to the Head Office. As there were few native English speakers employed, these reports were considered to be mainly written by Dutch employees. Even though internally within a subsidiary most of the users of the document were Dutch, if the content of the document, including memos, was required by the Head Office, it would be written directly in English; in other words, such documents would not be first written in Dutch with summaries translated into English and sent to the Head Office. The study also showed that within the organizational hierarchy, the presence of a native English speaker who held a position of power would also impact on the use of English as the language of communication. As noted by Nickerson, such individuals were generally "not required to learn Dutch, and their influence on the communication patterns in English may, therefore, be seen as an extension of that Head Office, i.e., Dutch employees are required to keep them informed because of their seniority, and to do so they must communicate with them in English. In this case, the needs (or requirements) of one powerful native speaker individual are likely to outweigh the interest of the non-native majority." (p. 291).

Although the study by Nickerson evokes how choice of language relates to corporate structure, the way in which such preferences are historically embedded in relations of power is more thoroughly explored by LeBlanc (2006). In his study, LeBlanc examined from an ethnosociolinguistic perspective (Blanchot 2003) why and for what purposes Francophone employees elected to use English rather than French in an office of the Canadian federal public service. Within this context, it is important to note that the study took place in New Brunswick, a province where English and French are both considered as the official languages and in a workplace officially designated as bilingual by the Canadian Government. As revealed by previous studies, English, despite legislation, still tends to be the main language of the workplace for both Anglophones and Francophones. Although one reason for this pertains to the need to communicate with unilingual Anglophones, LeBlanc sought to go beyond this factor to investigate how Francophones themselves perceived the use of French within their workplace yet opted to use English even in instances when French could have been an option. Drawing on ethnographic procedures, the study took place over a 14-month period which involved onsite observations and interviews with approximately 30 employees. A first point of note was the perception by Francophones that the English language was more apt for communication pertaining to business and administration. A second finding pertained to a lack of confidence with respect to their ability to write French of a sufficiently high quality. On the one hand, this sense of inadequacy seemed to be fuelled by comparisons with the French norm as reflected in the work of the official translators who, if a French translation was required, would translate the documents they had written in English.

3.2.2 Text production processes within bilingual/multilingual contexts

A few studies have begun to investigate text production processes, highlighting how different languages are implicated. A study by Louhiala-Salminen (2002) documents the discourse practices of a Finnish manager in a Finnish subsidiary of a multinational corporation in the computer industry. To this end, the participant of the study was observed during a one-day onsite visit which included data gathering in the form of observation notes, tape-recording of exchanges, and the collection of written documents (i.e., emails). Based on an analysis of the "discoursal episodes", the study highlighted the intertwined, intertextual nature of written and oral activities. In terms of language, most of the writing and reading activities were in English whereas most of the direct speech situations were in Finnish (face-to-face or on the phone). With respect to the more informal style which appeared to characterize both the oral exchanges and emails, Louhiala-Salminen underscored the importance of corporate culture, which was confirmed through interviews with the participant and his colleagues.

A study by Cheng and Mok (2008) examined the nature of professional communication within the land surveying department of a Hong Kong civil engineering consultancy firm. Data obtained for the study were of three types: observation notes based on six days of observation on the site, samples of written products, and checklists of daily communicative activities provided by individual land surveyors. To facilitate interpretation of the data, the research team also had access to professionals from the site. As a result of this study, researchers were able to provide an inventory of the different types of written and spoken discourse types engaged in by members of this discourse community. Of note in this regard was that all written communication was in English whereas most spoken discourse was in Cantonese, except when a non-Cantonese speaking person was present. The study also highlighted the intertextual nature of the discourse flow both in terms of the generic aspects of the texts produced and the referential links to both previously encountered and enclosed texts. The multimodal aspect of text production, as pertained to such items as maps, graphs and diagrams was also signalled. The analysis also showed that novices and experts (the more senior land surveyors) differed in terms of their involvement in various discourse processes and products.

For his part, Evans (2012) investigated, in the context of the Hong Kong business community, what he referred to as the "dearth of pedagogically oriented research into email use in the field of ESP" (p. 204). Four complementary methods of data collection were involved: 1. semi-structured interviews with 31 business professionals, 2. genre analysis of a corpus of 50 email chains, 3. case studies based on a professional discourse checklist completed by four participants who recorded the pattern of their activities in half-hourly segments and 4. a one-day onsite observation of one participant. Within this context, although emails could be read in Chinese or English, most were written in English. The study underscored the intertextual nature of the communication process as the email chains were bound up in the ongoing interplay between these exchanges and other written and spoken forms of communication. A further finding pertained to a genre-specific difference as the greater formality of the external as opposed to the internal emails related to the varying audiences and purposes of the exchanges. From a pedagogical point of view, the study highlighted divergences between the writing processes recommended in business textbooks and the observed workplace practices.

3.2.3 School work transitions

Very few studies have focused on how new employees have appropriated or failed to appropriate writing skills on the job or how they make a transition from school to the workplace. One notable exception is the 22-month ethnographic study by Parks (Parks 2000, 2001; Parks and Maguire 1999), which investigated the appropriation of nursing notes and care plans by newly hired French-language nurses in an English-language hospital in the province of Quebec (Canada) where French, not English, was the official language. In order to carry out this study, the researcher obtained permission to accompany nurses during their work on the units; in addition to observation notes and interviews, it was also possible to get copies of the documentation produced and in certain instances audiotape exchanges between a clinical educator, herself a nurse, as she gave feedback to the new nurses. Of particular note in this study is how the appropriation process was mediated through collaboration with colleagues and access to the particular genres the new nurses were required to write. A more detailed analysis of incidental collaboration (Parks 2000), defined as spur-of-the moment requests for help from colleagues, revealed how these exchanges enabled the participants to gain access to genre-specific features at three levels: linguistic, rhetorical and informational. In the case of the care plans (Parks 2001), the study also brought to light how the school and workplace versions of this genre differed; these differences were discussed in relation to the notion of motive, whether in terms of a more epistemic function valued within the university setting or the instrumental function more typical of the work setting. In addition to focusing on micro processes, the study also discussed how institutional and disciplinary factors variously mediated the text production processes. Although the genres discussed were highly routinized forms of writing, the study showed that there was nonetheless a learning curve and that even routinized forms of writing, as in the case of the care plans, could be bound up with complex ideological positionings involving issues of professional identity and power.

A study by Cox (2010) documented the case of a Korean ESL student, Min, who during her master's program in speech therapy, was involved in an on-campus internship in a clinic. The study specifically focused on how labelling as an ESL student as internalized by the student herself or as perceived by other university supervisors or co-workers impacted on her professional development. Of note in this regard is that initially the supervisors had not been aware of her linguistic history. Although Min had been recognized as "struggling", the reasons, which up to that point had been attributed to health concerns, were henceforth re-attributed to her ESL status. Despite differing assessments by her two supervisors, Min ended up agreeing to repeat her internship, a turn of events which was extremely unusual in this particular context. During her second internship in the same clinic, it was also observed, among other things, that even though Min had more knowledge about the document production procedures used in the clinic, her fellow students did not consult her. This lack of consultation contrasted with the habit the students had of informally helping each other with their documentation; it was also observed that Min did not take advantage of this resource for her own writing. In contrast to her experiences in the on-campus clinic, Min did not feel identified as a second language writer in any negative ways during a subsequent off-campus internship. In this particular setting, Min came into contact with other successfully practicing second-language speech-language pathologists who in terms of her professional identity "allow[ed] her to envision herself as ultimately finding a place in this profession" (p. 90).

A study by Beer (2000) reports on the challenges related to intercultural communication experienced by three case study students registered in a graduate engineering program in a large research-oriented university in Canada. Drawing on Scollon and Scollon's (1995) notion of the need by the individual for independence and involvement, Beer discusses some of the tensions experienced by these students as they attempted to adapt to the demands of their program of study which included writing for university courses and writing in workplace contexts. As explained by Beer, the varying abilities to adapt their writing were also bound up with their previous experiences in their home countries both in terms of their work and professional experiences and cultural notions of what constituted good writing.

A study by Belcher (1991) reports on an onsite writing course for advanced learners of English with degrees in computer science and engineering who were employed in the research and development division of a large American corporation. In this study, the employees, initially hired for their technical expertise, came very quickly to the "jarring realization" that promotion would depend on their ability "to produce documents that spoke well of them" (p. 105). An analysis of the types of documents produced by the non-native and native-English speaking employees made it possible to pinpoint certain rhetorical differences between the two groups. Of particular note is that in the case of meeting notes and personal progress reports, native-speakers, in addition to reporting facts, also engaged in self-promotion through rapport-building strategies. At another level, it was also noted that within the company the non-natives and natives did not socialize (for example, at lunch time the non-natives sat together and spoke their native languages). Although the social separation may not have been by choice, as observed by Belcher, there were also implications for the development of writing skills as the non-natives were deprived of the oral interaction which could have facilitated the development of sociolinguistic competence. As a teaching strategy, Belcher drew on contrastive analysis in order to sensitize the non-native employees to the various linguistic and rhetorical strategies more typical of the native-speakers' texts.

In reviewing the L2 workplace writing publications, which variously foreground textual products or socially situated practices, a variety of methodological tools are evoked. With respect to the analysis of textual products, the analysis of genre according to the procedures identified by Swales (1990) and Bhatia (1993) predominate. However, other constructs which are variously used include politeness theory (e.g., Flowerdew and Wan 2006), intertextuality (e.g., Cheng and Mok 2008; Flowerdew and Wan 2006; Louhiali-Salminen 2002), and notions from systemic functional grammar (e.g., the analysis of mood in Koskela 2006). Those researchers involved in the analysis of social contexts typically evoke procedures associated with qualitative/ethnographic analysis, including onsite observation, the interviewing of participants and the collection of work-related documents. With respect to work-related documents, one strategy used to better understand how social context and genre production are mutually constitutive is to ask participants to comment on various aspects related to text production processes, the roles of various collaborators and the relationship between readers and writers (Bhatia 2004; Paré and Smart 1994).

However, in terms of the above studies, one strategy which stands apart is that found in Hafner where five barristers were asked to write a barrister's opinion based on a simulated task prepared by a community informant who was a legal academic. In Parks' (2001) study a similar strategy was also used to generate information with respect to differences in the way the nurse participants wrote care plans once they had on-the-job experience as compared to when they were nursing students. Although such a strategy can be revealing, as noted by Parks (2005), care must be taken as, in the context of her study, despite careful instructions context sensitivity was in evidence with respect to the construal of the task, the construal of audience, and the understanding of the case. In order to counter such problems, triangulation with other onsite documents is recommended.

4 Future research

As discussed above, research on workplace writing accords increasing importance to socially situated practice. In the area of genre analysis, although the objective remains formal analysis, onsite investigations or the use of informants has served to refine our understanding of genre-specific rhetorical choices. Other studies, however, have begun to focus more directly on socially-situated practice. In this regard, one line of inquiry has sought to illuminate how, in bilingual/multilingual contexts, language preference is bound up with the writing of specific genres. Other studies have begun to shed light on the text production processes of employees working in bilingual/multilingual contexts or how new employees or interns who work in a second/foreign language develop relevant genre knowledge. Nevertheless, compared to mainstream studies which have tended to deal with monolingual writers, those studies focusing on second/foreign language writers have been slow to emerge. This relative dearth must be viewed on a backdrop where, however, due to globalization and other factors, second/foreign language employees are increasingly present in workplace contexts (Barbara et al. 1996; Belcher 1991; Chew 2005; Louhiala-Salminen 1996) both within North America and throughout the world. Indeed, as remarked by Cox (2010): "Academic writing has proven a rich arena for studying second language writing, but it is time to study second language writing beyond the classroom and into the realm of workplace writing, where most of the world's writing is happening." (p. 92). Although such a call is not new, it underscores the fact that the need for such research is ever present. In terms of future research, the following areas are of particular note.

1. More grounded ethnographic studies are needed to illuminate how second/ foreign language employees or interns appropriate (or fail to appropriate) genre-specific writing skills in workplace contexts. Although even new employees who are native-speakers have difficulty coping with workplace genres and may not be successful (Beaufort 1997; Cross 1990), second/foreign language employees may be particularly vulnerable. Although certain studies have shed light on the intertextual nature of communication and text production processes (Cheng and Mok 2008; Chew 2005; Louhiala-Salminen 2002; Nickerson 1998), attention needs to be given as to how and to what degree novice writers who must cope in a second/foreign language avail themselves of on-the-job resources, both overt and covert, in order to produce texts and develop their competence. In addition, as discussed by Gentil (2011), attention needs to be given as to how bilingual/multilingual writers use their knowledge of various genres in order to perfect or learn new ones.

2. Another area in need of further scrutiny pertains to identity issues. The study by Cox (2010) suggested how labeling as a non-native speaker of English negatively impacted on how Lin's career path unfolded as well as the facilitating role of mentors who were instrumental in helping her develop a more positive

outlook in terms of future success in her chosen career. In Parks' (2001) study, the participants' emerging professional identity was related to the way they positioned themselves rhetorically. The Beer (2000) study drew attention to how international graduate students' identities were implicated in terms of their willingness to engage in (or possibly resist) involvement within the discourse communities encountered during their studies in a Canadian university. Such studies point to research possibilities both in terms of the impact of the second/foreign language identity in regard to professional development as well as the way in which writers accomplish an identity through discourse choices (Ivanič 1998).

3. Research in bilingual/multilingual contexts shows how genre usage tends to be associated with specific language preferences (Barbara et al. 1996; Chew 2005). In particular, English, viewed as the lingua franca, is frequently associated with the use of written genres. Although certain studies discuss this use from a primarily descriptive perspective, LeBlanc's (2006) study draws attention to how such choice may be bound up with socio-political issues related to identity and power. To what degree do employees or others perceive the use of English in such terms? To what degree might employees in certain contexts resist such use or be conscious of how English might threaten the vitality of other languages? For the need to view the use of English in bilingual/multilingual contexts from a critical perspective, also see Pennycook (1997) and Tardy (2013).

4. The focus on workplace writing has increasingly evolved from a largely materials-led movement to one that is more research based. Recommendations for effective practices in workplace language training are indeed drawing on the findings of socially situated practice (Friedenberg et al. 2003). As noted in the above review, researchers involved in doing onsite research frequently claim pedagogical relevance. The Belcher (1991) study provides an intriguing example of an on-the-job writing course. However, to what degree do the resultant pedagogical materials and approaches actually enable the writers to appropriate genre-specific writing competence or empower them to intervene more effectively in their workplaces, especially when high stakes issues such as promotion or continued employment are involved? Such studies appear to be scarce (Hafner and Candlin 2007). Although the degree to which the writing instructor who is not a disciplinary insider has been a topic of frequent debate in regard to academic writing courses, the issue needs to be more closely reexamined with respect to workplace writing (Parks and Maguire 1999). As suggested by Beer (2000), students themselves may not perceive the writing instructor in the same way as an insider specialist audience even when students are advised by the writing instructor to work on disciplinary based assignments.

5. Although a few studies have focused on certain aspects of text production as it pertains to technology, to date such initiatives have been very limited. As

the use of digital technologies continues to expand and diversify, much more attention needs to be given to how both asynchronous (e.g., email) and real-time synchronous tools (e.g., cell phones, Skype or platforms allowing for on-line conferencing such as Elluminate) are transforming workplace practices and more specifically, how the affordances may mediate text production by second/foreign language writers. How might the ability to easily archive documents facilitate document cycling and covertly function as scaffolding for the second/foreign language writer? To what degree is the institutional culture implicated in the way such employees position themselves in regard to their rhetorical stance and the way they may or may not feel obligated to develop new rhetorical strategies?

6. Although there exists a fairly substantive body of research focused on the analysis of workplace genres as textual products, those studies which attempt to illuminate how aspects of the social context mediate linguistic and rhetorical choices are still quite scarce. Analyses of genre which shed light on how individuals negotiate the use of the same genre in crosslinguistic contexts would be particularly welcome (Gentil 2011).

7. Although in terms of examining the social context, the tools of qualitative and ethnographic analysis are frequently evoked, consideration needs to be given to conducting studies which are more specifically guided by sociocultural/socio-constructivist frameworks. One such framework pertains to activity theory which has been increasingly used to explain socially situated approaches to text construction within second/foreign language academic writing contexts (e.g., Haneda 2007; Yasuda 2005). In a similar vein, Lave and Wenger's (1991) community of learning construct with the attendant notion of apprenticeship and legitimate peripheral participation could be an interesting lens through which to view how new employees appropriate writing skills. Although certain studies report on using informants to provide insight into text production processes (Hafner 2013), more systematic discourse-based interviews could prove useful (see, for example, Odell and Goswami 1982). Studies involving the discoursal construction of identity could also draw more extensively on the procedures discussed by Ivanič (1998).

5 Conclusion

Within this chapter, I have discussed how the interest in workplace writing as an object of study first emerged in mainstream research in the 1980s as interest grew in terms of studying text production in authentic writing contexts. Within applied linguistics, as reflected by the present review, the social turn has indeed been negotiated and instantiated. Within genre-based studies, which foreground the analysis of textual products, increasing importance is accorded to onsite observation as a means of refining analyses and explaining why rhetorical choices are made. Although a certain number of studies foreground socially situated practice, those studies which illuminate how employees working in a second/foreign language produce and/or appropriate relevant genre specific knowledge remains sparse. To further respond to the gaps in the research, several lines of inquiry for future research have been evoked.

6 Additional sources

Bargiela-Chiappini, Francesca, Catherine Nickerson, and Brigitte Planken. 2007. *Business discourse*. New York: Palgrave MacMillan.

Bhatia, Vijay. 2010. Interdiscursivity in professional communication. *Discourse & Communication* 21. 32–50.

Dias, Patrick, Aviva Freedman, Peter Medway, and Anthony Paré. 1999. *Worlds apart: Acting and writing in academic and workplace contexts*. Mahwah, NJ: Lawrence Erlbaum.

Gimenez, Julio. 2014. Multi-communication and the business English class: Research meets pedagogy. *English for Specific Purposes* 35. 1–16.

Hafner, Christoph A. 2013. The discursive construction of professional expertise: Appeals to authority in barrister's opinions. *English for Specific Purposes* 32. 131–143.

Lam, Phoenix W. Y., Winnie Cheng, and Kenneth C. C. Kong. 2014. Learning through workplace communication: An evaluation of existing resources in Hong Kong. *English for Specific Purposes* 34. 68–78.

Nickerson, Catherine. 2000. *Playing the corporate language game. An investigation of the genres and discourse strategies in English used by Dutch writers in multinational corporations.* Utrecht studies in language and communication. Amsterdam: Rodopi.

Roberts, Celia. 2005. English in the workplace. In Eli Hinkel (ed.), *Handbook of research in second language teaching and learning*, 117–135. Mahwah, NJ: Lawrence Erlbaum.

Spence, Paul and Gi-Zen Liu. 2013. Engineering English and the high-tech industry: A case study of an English needs analysis of process integration engineers at a semiconductor manufacturing company in Taiwan. *English for Specific Purposes* 32. 97–109.

Warren, Martin. 2013. *"Just spoke to…"*: The types and directionality of intertextuality in professional discourse. *English for Specific Purposes* 32. 12–24.

7 References

Barbara, Leila, M. Antonieta Celani, Heloísa Collins, and Mike Scott. 1996. A survey of communication patterns in the Brazilian context. *English for Specific Purposes* 15. 57–71.

Beaufort, Anne. 1997. Operationalizing the concept of discourse community: A case study of one institutional site of composing. *Research in the Teaching of English* 31. 486–529.

Beer, Ann. 2000. Diplomats in the basement: Graduate engineering students and intercultural communication. In Patrick Dias and Anthony Paré (eds.), *Transitions: Writing in academic and workplace settings*, 61–88. Cresskill, NJ: Hampton Press.

Belcher, Diane. 1991. Nonnative writing in a corporate setting. *The Technical Writing Teacher*. 18. 104–115.

Bhatia, Vijay. 1993. *Analysing genre: Language use in professional settings*. London: Longman.

Bhatia, Vijay. 2004. *Worlds of written discourse: A genre-based view*. Cornwall, UK: Continuum.
Bhatia, Vijay and Maurizio Gotti (eds.). 2006. *Explorations in specialized genres*. Bern: Peter Lang.
Blanchet, Philippe. 2003. Contacts, continuum, hétérogénéité, polynomie, organisation "chaotique", pratiques sociales, interventions…quels modèles? Pour une (socio)linguistique de la "complexité". In Philippe Blanchot & Didier de Robillard (eds.), *Langues, contacts, complexité: approches théoriques en sociolinguistique*, 279–308. Rennes: Presses de l'Université de Rennes.
Cheng, Winnie and Esmond Mok. 2008. Discourse processes and products: Land surveyors in Hong Kong. *English for Specific Purposes* 27. 57–73.
Chew, Kheng-Suan. 2005. An investigation of the English language skills used by new entrants in banks in Hong Kong. *English for Specific Purposes* 24. 423–435.
Connor, Ulla, Ed Nagelhout, and William V. Rozycki (eds.). 2008. *Contrastive rhetoric: Reaching to intercultural rhetoric*. Amsterdam: John Benjamins.
Couture, Barbara and Jone Rymer. 1989. Interactive writing on the job: Definitions and implications of "collaboration". In Myra Kogen (ed.), *Writing in the business professions*, 73–93. Urbana, IL: National Council of Teachers of English.
Couture, Barbara and Jone Rymer. 1991. Discourse interaction between writer and supervisor: A primary collaboration in workplace writing. In Mary Lay and William Karis (eds.), *Collaborative writing in industry: Investigations in theory and practice*, 87–108. Amityville, NY: Baywood.
Cox, Michelle. 2010. Identity, second language writers, and the learning of workplace writing. In Michelle Cox, Jay Jordan, Christina Ortmeier-Hooper, and Gwen Gray Schwartz (eds.), *Reinventing identities in second language writing*, 75–95. Urbana. IL: National Council of Teachers of English.
Cross, Geoffrey. 1990. A Bakhtinian exploration of factors affecting the collaborative writing of an executive letter of an annual report. *Research in the Teaching of English* 24. 173–203.
Dias, Patrick and Anthony Paré (eds.). 2000. *Transitions: Writing in academic and workplace settings*. Cresskill, NJ: Hampton Press.
Doheny-Farina, Stephen. 1986. Writing in an emerging organization: An ethnographic study. *Written Communication* 3. 158–185.
Evans, Stephen. 2012. Designing email tasks for the Business English classroom: Implications from a study of Hong Kong's key industries. *English for Specific Purposes* 31. 202–212.
Fish, Stanley. 1980. *Is there a text in this class?* Harvard, MA: Harvard University Press.
Flowerdew, John and Alina Wan. 2006. Genre analysis of tax computation letters: How and why tax accountants write the way they do. *English for Specific Purposes* 25. 133–153.
Flowerdew, John and Alina Wan. 2010. The linguistic and the contextual in applied genre analysis: The case of the company audit report. *English for Specific Purposes* 29. 78–93.
Friedenberg, Joan, Deborah Kennedy, Anne Loperis, William Martin, and Kay Westerfield. 2003. *Effective practices in workplace language training: Guidelines for providers of workplace English language training services*. Alexandria, VA: TESOL.
Gentil, Guillaume. 2011. A biliteracy agenda for genre research. *Journal of Second Language Writing* 20. 6–23.
Hafner, Christoph. 2008. Designing, implementing and evaluating an online resource for professional legal communication skills. Unpublished doctoral dissertation, Macquarie University Sydney, Australia.
Hafner, Christoph. 2013. A multi-perspective genre analysis of the barrister's opinion: Writing context, generic structure and textualization. *Written Commmunication* 27. 410–441.
Hafner, Christoph and Christopher N. Candlin. 2007. Corpus tools as an affordance to learning in professional legal education. *Journal of English for Academic Purposes* 6. 303–318.
Haneda, Mari. 2007. Modes of engagement in foreign language writing: An activity theoretical perspective. *Canadian Modern Language Review* 64. 297–327.

Ivanič, Roz. 1998. *Writing and identity: The discoursal construction of identity in academic writing*. Amsterdam, Netherlands: John Benjamins.

Kankaanranta, Anne and Leena Louhiala-Salminen. 2010. "English? – Oh, it's just work!": A study of BELF users' perceptions. *English for Specific Purposes* 29. 204–209.

Kaplan, Robert. 1966. Cultural thought patterns in inter-cultural education. *Language Learning* 16. 1–20.

Koskela, Merja. 2006. Writer-oriented authorities on the web. In Vijay Bhatia & Maurizio Gotti (eds.), *Explorations in specialized genres*, 177–199. Bruxelles: Peter Lang.

Lave, Jean and Etienne Wenger. 1991. *Situated learning: Legitimate peripheral* participation. Cambridge, England: Cambridge University Press.

LeBlanc, Matthieu. 2006. Pratiques langagières dans un milieu de travail bilingue de Moncton. Available at http://id.erudit.org/iderudit/1005382ar. DOI: 10.7202/1005382

Louhiala-Salminen, Leena. 1996. The business communication classroom vs reality: What should we teach today? *English for Specific Purposes* 15. 37–51.

Louhiala-Salminen, Leena. 2002. The fly's perspective: Discourse in the daily routine of a business manager. *English for Specific Purposes* 21. 211–231.

Miller, Carolyn. 1979. A humanistic rationale for technical writing. *College English* 40. 610–617.

Miller, Carolyn. 1984. Genre as social action. *Quarterly Journal of Speech* 70. 151–167.

Miller, Carolyn. 1994. Rhetorical community: The cultural basis of genre. In Aviva Freedman and Peter Medway (eds.), *Genre and the new rhetoric*, 67–78. London: Taylor & Francis.

Miller, Carolyn and Jack Selzer. 1985. Special topics of argument in engineering reports. In Lee Odell and Dixie Goswami (eds.), *Writing in nonacademic settings*, 309–341. New York: Guilford.

Nickerson, Catherine. 1998. Corporate culture and the use of written English within British subsidiaries in The Netherlands. *English for Specific Purposes* 17. 281–294

Odell, Lee. 1985. Beyond the text: Relations between writing and social context. In Lee Odell and Dixie Goswami (eds.), *Writing in nonacademic settings*, 231–247. New York: Guilford.

Odell, Lee and Dixie Goswami. 1982. Writing in a non-academic setting. *Research in the Teaching of English* 16. 201–223.

Odell, Lee, Dixie Goswami, Anne Herrington, and Doris Quick. 1983. Studying writing in non-academic settings. In Paul V. Anderson, R. John Brockmann, and Carolyn R. Miller (eds.), *New essays in technical and scientific communication: Research, theory, practice*, 17–40. Farmingdale, NY: Baywood.

Paradis, James, David Dobrin, and Richard Miller. 1985. Writing at Exxon ITD: Notes on the writing environment of an R&D organization. In Lee Odell and Dixie Goswami (eds.), *Writing in nonacademic settings*, 231–247. New York: Guilford.

Paré, Anthony. 1991. Writing in social work: A case study of a discourse community. Unpublished doctoral dissertation. Montreal, McGill University.

Paré, Anthony and Graham Smart. 1994. Observing genres in action: Towards a research methodology. In Aviva Freedman and Peter Medway (eds.), *Genre and the New Rhetoric*. London: Taylor and Francis.

Parks, Susan. 2000. Professional writing and the role of incidental collaboration: Evidence from a medical setting. *Journal of Second Language Writing* 9. 101–122.

Parks, Susan. 2001. Moving from school to the workplace: Disciplinary innovation, border crossings, and the reshaping of a written genre. *Applied Linguistics* 22. 405–438.

Parks, Susan. 2005. Qualitative research as heuristic: Investigating documentation practices in a medical setting. In Paul Kei Matsuda and Tony Silva (eds.), *Second language writing research: Perspectives on the process of knowledge construction*, 135–148. Mahwah, NJ: Lawrence Erlbaum Associates.

Parks, Susan and Mary Maguire. 1999. Coping with on-the-job writing in ESL: A constructivist-semiotic perspective. *Language Learning* 49. 143–175.

Pennycook, Alastair. 1997. Vulgar pragmatism, critical pragmatism, and EAP. *English for Specific Purposes* 16. 253–269.

Pettinari, Catherine Johnson. 1988. *Task, talk and text in the operating room: A study in medical discourse*. Norwood, NJ: Ablex.

Schryer, Catherine. 1993. Records as genre. *Written Communication* 10. 200–234.

Scollon, Ron and Suzanne Wong Scollon. 1995. *Intercultural communication: A discourse approach*. Cambridge, MA and Oxford: Blackwell.

Selzer, Jack. 1983. The composing processes of an engineer. *College Composition and Communication* 34. 178–187.

Smart, Graham. 1992. Exploring the social dimension of a workplace genre and the implications for teaching. *Carleton Papers in Applied Language Studies* 9. 33–46.

Smart, Graham. 1993. Genre as community invention: A central bank's response to its executives' expectations as readers. In Rachel Spilka (ed.), *Writing in the Workplace: New Research Perspectives,* 124–140. Carbondale, IL: Southern Illinois Press.

Spilka, Rachel. 1990. Orality and literacy in the workplace. *Journal of Business and Technical Communication* 4. 44–67.

St. John, Maggie Jo. 1996. Business is booming: Business English in the 1990s. *English for Specific Purposes* 15(1). 3–18.

Swales, John. 1990. *Genre analysis: English in academic and research settings*. Cambridge: Cambridge University Press.

Tardy, Christine. 2013. Writing and language for specific purposes. In Carol A. Chapelle (ed.), *The encylopedia of applied linguistics*. Oxford: Blackwell. DOI: 10.1002/9781405198431.

van Mulken, Margot and Wouter van der Meer. 2005. A genre analysis of American and Dutch company replies to customer inquiries. *English for Specific Purposes* 24. 93–109.

Vergaro, Carla. 2004. Discourse strategies of Italian and English sales promotion letters. *English for Specific Purposes* 23. 181–207

Wenger, Etienne. 1999. *Communities of practice: Learning, meaning and identity*. Cambridge, England: Cambridge University Press.

Winsor, Dorothy. 1989. An engineer's writing and the corporate construction of knowledge. *Written Communication* 6. 270–285.

Winsor, Dorothy. 1996. *Writing like an engineer: A rhetorical education*. Mahwah, NJ: Lawrence Erlbaum.

Witte, Stephen. 1992. Context, text, intertext: Toward a constructivist semiotic of writing. *Written Communication* 9. 237–308.

Yasuda, Sachiko. 2005. Different activities in the same task: An activity theory approach to ESL students' writing processes. *JALT Journal* 27(2). 139–168.

III. Learning writing

William Grabe and Cui Zhang

11 Focus on texts and readers: Linguistic and rhetorical features

Discourse analysis is, one may say, a fuzzy discipline, perhaps more oriented toward chaos theory than toward the kinds of paradigms applied linguists are more accustomed to using. The obvious reason for the fuzziness lies in the huge number of variables implicated in the process of text generation and text recognition .... Discourse analysts will need to struggle along with careful descriptive approaches, dealing with as many of the variables as possible, but recognizing that any presently conceived model will necessarily be incomplete.
(Kaplan and Grabe 2002: 215–216)

The relationship between writing and writing development on the one hand and the study of written discourse analysis (sometimes referred to as text structure analysis) on the other is one that has at times been viewed positively, but at other times as disconnected, or unimportant. At the same time, discourse analysis continues to be a focal area of research for linguistics, applied linguistics, cognitive and educational psychology, and English studies outside of the United States. In this review, we will attempt to provide a map of the territory of discourse analysis as it is practiced today and as it has relevance for writing research and practice. It is not possible to provide an "objective" overview in the sense that such a sprawling field cannot be surveyed comprehensively in a chapter (and perhaps not even in a book). Therefore, we will provide a more selective, and presumably coherent, survey of written discourse analysis. (A survey of spoken discourse analysis would require a separate book or more). The survey will begin with recap of written discourse analysis reported on by Kaplan and Grabe (2002) as a starting point for the twelve years since that publication.

The quotation opening this chapter from Kaplan and Grabe (2002) highlights a central theme running through all research on discourse analysis: It is necessarily partial and particular. Discourse analysis identifies how specific aspects of textual organization is patterned in some way, and presumably reflects some important linkage to the text as a whole and the message conveyed by the text (and the author). Because discourse analysis could examine a very large array of possible variables and patterns, as well as their interactions, it cannot ever fully explain how a text is understood, or interpreted, or created, or improved upon. But a second central theme driving discourse analysis is that it can provide very important insights into how texts are understood, produced, and improved. These two themes also help to explain why discourse analysis can be either qualitative in nature or quantitative (or use mixed method research). Kaplan and Grabe (2002) provided a summary of written discourse analysis from the 1970s to 2000. The summary of these earlier years will provide the foundation for continued research in certain

246 —— William Grabe and Cui Zhang

areas (e.g., organization of discourse patterns, grammar and error correction, genre analysis, stylistics) and extensions into new sub-fields involving corpus linguistics, automated linguistic feature analysis from cognitive psychology, and automated essay scoring. Finally, this survey is oriented by applied linguistics perspectives (rather than rhetoric perspectives, hermeneutics, or semiotics). We are both applied linguists and these are our pathways into understanding discourse analysis. We also apologize beforehand if we leave out major sub-fields, but that is inevitable in a very broad survey.

1 Summary review of discourse analysis studies

In Kaplan and Grabe (2002) the field of written discourse analysis was broken down into five subfields: Linguistic discourse analysis, English studies, discourse analysis in applied linguistics, corpus linguistics, and language use in professional contexts. We will update these fields and add a few new ones in this overview.

1.1 Linguistics discourse analysis

Discourse analysis in linguistics examines texts from several approaches – anthropological linguistics, sociolinguistics, descriptive linguistics, functional linguistics, and systemic linguistics. Anthropological linguistics focuses on the interpretation of the text and the use of language in the real world, although mostly with spoken texts. Sociolinguistics, emerging out of anthropological linguistics, introduced sociological perspectives towards language and communication, such as language used in and across speech communities, dialect variation, register, and discourse. The most well-known approaches to discourse analysis in sociolinguistics (with connections to written texts) include Labov's (1972) model of narrative story structure and Tannen's (1989) theory of involvement. Descriptive linguistics has expanded its early emphasis on analyses of language in actual use to corpus linguistics – the descriptive grammatical analysis of the language based on corpora (Biber, Conrad, and Reppen 1998; Conrad and Biber 2001; Loban 1976). Functional linguistics research has explored how syntactic structures are used for discourse meaning and the way syntactic and discourse features together build the meaning of the text (Givón 1995). Systemic functional approaches to linguistics, developed by Halliday, relate the textual linguistic resources to the extra textual context of use. Historically, systemic approaches have continuously represented a major linguistic orientation toward discourse analysis (Halliday and Hasan 1989; Martin 2000). Of these linguistic approaches, two have remained most influential for written discourse analysis – corpus approaches and systemic approaches.

1.2 Discourse analysis in English studies

As Kaplan and Grabe (2002) summarized it, written discourse analysis in the field of English has been carried out in five sub-fields: literary criticism and semiotics, stylistics, linguistics and rhetoric, rhetorical studies, and composition studies. New criticism emerged in the 1940s and 1950s, focusing on the exploration of specific linguistic features to the understanding of text literariness, and shifting the focus of literary criticism from the author to the text. The subsequent rise of semiotics and reader-response theory shifted the meaning construction of the text to the reader. It also, however, directed the literary criticism away from linguistic discourse analysis.

Stylistics started in the 1950s and 1960s as a new way to apply linguistics to the analysis of English texts. Stylistics most often examined lexico-syntactic features of texts and larger organizational structures to compare specific authors or works of a specific author. In its recent development, this approach has been used to analyze popular literature texts, non-literary texts, and literature analysis for English education, particularly outside the USA (Carter and Nash 1990; Leech and Short 1981 [2007]). Aside from stylistics, the combination of linguistic analyses with the rhetorical situation of the text led to situational studies of texts in various contexts (Vande Kopple 1998, 2002). Finally, the writing and composition studies' use of linguistic approaches to discourse analysis goes back to Hunt (1965) with his analysis of T-units in student writing. Since then, there have been numerous studies of student writing that have used a range of linguistic features, linguistic complexity measures, cohesion measures, and more general structural measures (Grabe and Kaplan 1996). In the past ten years, work involving linguistic measures to analyze student writing, usually associated with genre and discourse function, are evolving rapidly out of corpus linguistics, cognitive approaches to written text, ESP/EAP, and automated essay analyses.

1.3 Discourse analysis in applied linguistics

For applied linguistics, "language as discourse" is a central notion (Kaplan and Grabe 2002). Following the categorization of Kaplan and Grabe (with slight modifications), this section reviews written discourse analysis studies in the following areas: ESL/EFL/EAP/ESP, discourse description, corpus linguistics, and language use in professional contexts.

1.3.1 English as a second/foreign language, English for academic purposes, and English for specific purposes

In the 1960s, ESL/EFL teachers started to notice that patterns of organization of students' first language (L1) seemed to influence their written production in English. Kaplan (1966) attempted to capture these patterns through the notion of contrastive rhetoric. This notion of contrastive rhetoric proposed by Kaplan has generated criticism since its first publication; critiques say that it privileges the writing of native English speakers and lacks cultural and linguistic sensitivity (Matsuda 2001). The debate around Kaplan's notions has continued to the present (See below).

In addition to contrastive rhetoric research, other studies in the ESL/EFL/EAP setting that use discourse analysis explicitly included the work of both Connor and Johns. Connor focused consistently on the use of discourse analysis in writing development, writing assessment, and the use of writing in more advanced settings (Connor 1990, 1996; Connor and Mbaye 2002). Johns consistently focused on the written product of ESL/EFL students with her research on summary writing, coherence, basic writing in university settings, as well as the teaching/learning of genre knowledge in L2 writing (Johns 1997, 2002). (Other work by Johns focused primarily on the socioliterate contexts of student writing development; see Johns 1997).

English for specific purposes (ESP) has had a long tradition of using written discourse analysis for instructional purposes. In its early years, ESP focused on using discourse models for descriptive analyses and instruction (Swales 1981 [2011], 1987, 1990; Trimble 1985). This trend has continued in the past decade through a powerful (and persuasive) focus on genre structure (see below).

1.3.2 Discourse description and genre analyses

Applied linguists have been exploring the discourse organization of spoken and written texts since the 1970s. Early approaches include the "Discourse Bloc" to analyze writing (Kaplan 1972) and systemic approaches to the analysis of written discourse (Coulthard 1977; Hoey 1983). Other developments in discourse analysis involved systematic analyses of lexis, syntactic structure, discourse patterning, and genre types (Bhatia 1993; Hyland 2002). Following Swales, Bhatia (1993) proposed a process-oriented genre analysis, distinguishing moves and strategies in professional writings such as sales promotion letters, job application letters, travel brochures, fund-raising letters, grant proposals, etc. Several discourse studies of professional writing, most following Bhatia's (1993) approach, looked at job application letters. For example, Henry and Roseberry (2001) analyzed 40 application letters collected from multiple sources and identified 11 moves, multiple strategies that realized some of the major moves (e.g., Promoting the Candidate move), and linguistic patterns that indicate move boundaries. Through the analysis of 153 job application letters written by Americans, Belgians, and Finns, Upton and Connor (2001) found differences in the presence/omission of certain move structures as well as differences in linguistic realizations of politeness strategies in the three L1 groups.

In academic writing, Swales' (1981, 1990) move analysis had a huge impact on the discourse analysis of academic research articles and abstracts, conference proposals, posters, manuscript reviews, and grant proposal reviews. In particular, Swales' analyses of IMRD (Introduction, Methods, Results, and Discussion sections) structures in research articles profoundly influenced many areas of written discourse analysis (and continues to be an essential touchstone to this day).

1.3.3 Corpus linguistics

Corpus linguistic descriptions of texts have been reported since the 1980s. Large corpora have been built, like the COBUILD corpus (Sinclair 1987, 1991), the Longman Spoken and Written English Corpus (LSWE), and the International Corpus of Learner English (ICLE) (Granger et al., 2009). With the appearance of publically available corpora, corpus linguistics studies also flourished. However, many of the early studies simply focused on lexico-grammatical aspects of the text. Thus, Flowerdew (1998) called for more "exploitation of the tagging function" on the "semantic or pragmatic discourse level" such as the rhetorical moves of a genre (p. 159) (cf. Biber and colleagues noted above).

1.3.4 Language use in professional contexts

The analysis of texts in professional contexts such as in law and legal settings, news, advertisement, business, science, medicine, and social services has grown tremendously since the 1980s. As Kaplan and Grabe (2002) writes, although discourse analysis in these fields overlaps with many of the previous areas discussed (such as corpus linguistics, EAP, and ESP), it deserves independent comment as it has important practical applications. For example, the Eagleson (1994) and Coulthard (1994) studies cited in Kaplan and Grabe (2002) showed how discourse analysis applied in forensic situations became important evidence to convict the murderer or acquit the defendants. Since 2002, language use and discourse analysis in professional contexts (both spoken and written) has become a major trend in applied linguistics and related fields.

2 Recent trends in written discourse analysis (2002 to present)

In this extended overview of recent trends, we rearrange the above categorization. Partly, this is done to reflect the specific areas in which much of the ongoing work in written discourse analysis is being carried out. Partly, the new categorization reflects the blending and merging of ideas and approaches across categories. It is inevitable today that multiple approaches have combined in several areas (e.g., the multiple explorations combining corpus analysis, descriptive discourse analysis, genre analysis, and writing in disciplinary contexts). Genre analyses, in particular permeates much of the research on written discourse analysis and is no longer a distinct sub-category.

2.1 Systemic linguistics

Systemic linguistics is applied to discourse analysis primarily in three areas: cohesion and cohesive harmony, grammatical metaphor, and genre. Halliday and Hasan (1976) identified five categories of cohesive devices in texts: reference, substitution, ellipsis, conjunction, and lexical cohesion. Since its first appearance, many researchers have conducted studies using this framework, but many early studies simply counted the number of cohesive devices in texts. Halliday and Hasan (1989) argued against the simple counting of cohesion features and proposed a revised theory of cohesive harmony (componential cohesion, organic cohesion, and structural cohesion) to examine the structural cohesion of a text. Tardy and Swales (2008) provide a recent summary discussion of notions of cohesion and coherence.

A second major area of research that grew out of the systemic-functional linguistic theory is grammatical metaphor. Under this notion, the "processes, procedures, and events become nominalized in language, losing their transparency and creating metaphorical objects" (Kaplan and Grabe 2002: 201). This is illustrated in the two sample sentences below:

1. The driver drove the bus too rapidly down the hill, so the brake failed.
2. The driver's over-rapid (reckless) downhill driving of the bus caused break failure.

In the first sentence, the structure of the sentence reflects how events happen in the real world – the driver drove the bus in a manner that caused the brakes to fail. In the second sentence, the language has been transformed (e.g., from verb phrase "(break) failed" to noun phrase "brake failure"), and the events and the processes are no longer transparent. The process of grammatical metaphor is a way to theorize about complex ideas, create new organizations of language, and makes the language more concise, thus it is pervasive in science and technical writing (Halliday 1998; Schleppegrell 2012; Schleppegrell and O'Hallaron 2011).

Throughout much of systemic linguistic approaches to discourse is the assumption that grammatical structures and features reflect functional uses to shape discourse meaning (see Schleppegrell 2012 for recent discussions). This notion of functional meaning making through language is also true of one final major research direction that has been central to systemic-functional linguistics: a theory of genre structuring and its applications for literacy instruction. Generally speaking, genre structures and genre knowledge are related to their context of use (See Martin 1993, 2002; Martin and Rose 2008). In systemic discussions of genre, much more attention has been given to instructional genres and their development in L1 school contexts (in Australia) (Christie and Derewianka 2008). The role of genre from a systemic orientation has also influenced ESP/EAP, either directly or indirectly, from Swales to Bhatia (2004) to Paltridge (2001, 2013) to Hyland (2009) to Nesi and Gardner (2012).

2.2 ESL/EAP/ESP discourse analysis

A number of ongoing issues have shaped discourse analytic approaches in ESL/EAP/ESP contexts in the past decade. These issues include the role of contrastive rhetoric, language use in academic and professional contexts, and uses of discourse analysis in language teaching.

2.2.1 Contrastive rhetoric

Connor (2002) provided a comprehensive synthesis of contrastive rhetoric research over the 35 years since Kaplan's (1966) initial study. In her review, Connor points out that differences in written communication do not simply stem from language or national culture differences, but encompasses much more (e.g., L1 educational background, genre characteristics, disciplinary culture, and mismatched expectations between readers and writers). Since her 2002 review, Connor (2008, 2011) has proposed that contrastive rhetoric be considered as intercultural rhetoric research, which should move its focus from texts to the social contexts in which the texts are constructed. Social context, according to Connor, means not only the large national culture but also small cultures such as classroom and discipline culture. She suggests that the current three most employed research methods to study contrastive rhetoric – text analysis, genre analysis, and corpus analysis – should go beyond linguistic, syntactic, and grammatical analysis of the texts and consider the function of these features as well as the contexts in which the choice of these features are made. For example, she suggests genre analysis be combined with context-sensitive interviews to investigate the reasons behind writers' choices. She has also emphasized the importance of the comparableness of the comparison corpora in corpus-based contrastive analysis and provided a twelve-step research design from formulating research hypothesis to explaining results about the relation between writing cultures. (See also Connor 2011; Kaplan 2000, 2005; Moreno 2014.)

2.2.2 ESP/EAP

In its recent development, ESP has drawn extensively on the Swalesian analysis of various text types and genres (Swales 1990, 2000, 2004; see also Johns 1997, 2002, 2013; Tardy 2009; Thompson 2013). More recently ESP research and instructional applications have expanded greatly, as indicated by major volumes and handbooks devoted to ESP (Belcher, Johns, and Paltridge 2011; Chapelle 2014; Paltridge and Starfield 2013).

Among the many branches of discourse analysis, discourse structure and genre moves in academic and professional writing has received the most attention in the last 25 years, following particularly the work of Bhatia (1993, 2004) and Swales (1990, 2004). In academic writing, Swales's (1981, 1990, 2004) move analysis continues to have a major impact on the discourse analysis of academic research articles and abstracts, conference proposals, posters, manuscript reviews, and grant proposal reviews. Studies modeled after the early move analysis approach have sought to conform/reject/modify the move structure of research articles or sections of the research articles, especially the introduction section (e.g., Samraj's [2002] study of the introduction section in two closely-related disciplines). More recent studies that adopted Swales's (2004) revised move structure have examined conference proposals (Halleck and Connor 2006) and moves in statement of purpose application documents (Samraj and Monk 2008) (see Johns 2013 for commentary on the move-structure research).

Discourse analysis has always been a major feature in both research on and the teaching of ESP. The roles of discourse analysis and genre organization are pervasive in the recent volumes on ESP (Chapelle 2014; Paltridge and Starfield 2013). One of the most frequent topics for ESP research is the structure and variation in the academic research article. One such attempt is illustrated by Chang and Kuo (2004), who examined the effectiveness of using a web-based program to teach computer science graduate students to write academic research articles. The researchers first collected 60 computer science research articles published in a 10-year span and analyzed the move structures as well as the grammatical/linguistic features. Using this information, they developed an online-learning platform and piloted it with 23 graduate students. When writing their own research papers after the learning sessions, the students made qualitative improvements in the move structure and the use of linguistic features in their introduction sections, although not in their data commentary sections. (Several related studies are also noted/described in Flowerdew 2013; Hyland 2006, 2009).

A number of major researchers have focused especially on analyses of multiple advanced academic genres and the development of academic genres by students (instructional genres) in post-secondary contexts (EAP). Hyland (2009, 2011, 2013) has explored this topic through detailed analyses of specific genres and specific texts. Drawing on functional perspectives – that language use reflects purpose, audience relationships, and specific information to convey – writers make specific choices in language to use (novelty features, stance features, engagement features) as well as in specific ways to structure the discourse as a whole. Throughout Hyland's (2009) book, he also shows how close analyses of specific features in very focused corpora allow for useful insights into mood/modality, stance, engagement, identity, authority, theme, text structure, disciplinary variations, and intertextuality. The argument for smaller corpora is that a good part of the corpus can actually be examined by the researcher and an element of semantic interpretation is possible that cannot be easily incorporated into analyses of very large corpora.

Multiple authors have examined the features associated with various academic genres and instructional genres written by students. Feak and Swales (2009) focus specifically on the literature review. Paltridge and Starfield (2007) provide a handbook for thesis and dissertation writing. Hyland (2009) describes a range of academic and instructional discourse and some key features associated with each genre. Nesi and Gardner (2012) use a student writing corpus of over 6.5 million words and stratified across four levels of university study and four disciplinary groupings. They provide extensive analyses to identify a wide range of student instructional genres across disciplines. They combine a multidimensional analysis, various functional linguistic features, and multiple vocabulary analyses to compare not only 13 academic genres, but also compare professional genres with pedagogical genres.

2.2.3 Language teaching and discourse analysis

One of the key issues in applied linguistics is how to take discourse-based insights and turn them into effective resources materials for teaching students (much like Chang and Kuo above). This application has most commonly been considered by researchers in ESP. From an ESP perspective, Feak and Swales (2009, 2011) have developed ways to teach genre structure in advanced research papers to graduate students, focusing on research introductions, the literature review, and other aspects of graduate student writing. A somewhat different approach to teaching writing through genre knowledge is provided by Paltridge (2001, 2013), who suggests the importance of examining genre structure in its social context and addressing the associated communicative activity. Tardy (2006, 2009), also focusing on genre knowledge to improve student writing, similarly approaches the topic from a more contextualized, rhetorical orientation. Cheng (2007, 2008) specifically focuses on the explicit awareness raising and teaching of genre organization using exemplars. Zhang (2013) demonstrates, through a training experiment, how students can be explicitly taught to recognize patterns of discourse organization and use these patterns to structure information synthesis writing tasks. In all of these cases, efforts are made to show how aspects of discourse analysis can make a difference in writing instruction.

2.3 Discourse and language use in professional contexts

Much like research on genre structuring and moves within genres, specific genres make varying uses of specific linguistic features to convey overall discourse interpretations in professional contexts. An interesting example of this patterning within and across genres was carried out by Flowerdew and Wan (2006), who analyzed tax computation letters, one of the "occluded" genres (Swales 1996) that have been understudied. Flowerdew and Wan (2006) examined 25 tax computation letters written by accountants working at an international firm in Hong Kong. Using Swales' (1990) and Bhatia's (1993) move analysis framework, Flowerdew and Wan identified a seven-move structure of the letters and showed politeness strategies achieved through the use of reference, mode, and modality. What is interesting about this study is that the researchers did not limit their analysis to the texts, but they triangulated the textual analysis with observation of the accountants in their usual work environment and interviews with several of them to find out about their writing process and their reasons behind their choice of the lexico-grammatical features in the letters.

A second line of research is exemplified by Hyland and Hyland and Tse, who focus on professional identity construction, knowledge distribution, and disciplinary individuality in professional communities (Hyland 2009, 2011; Hyland and Tse 2009, 2012; Tse and Hyland 2010). Different from the other discourse analysis studies that focused on academic or professional writing such as journal articles, business letters, or travel brochures, Hyland and Tse have examined the discourse of the biographical statements that accompanied journal articles, acknowledgements in graduate students' dissertations, academic homepages of college professors, and journal descriptions. Through the analysis of the move structure, process, sequence, lexical choices, linguistic features, and grammatical structures, Hyland and Tse showcased how academic professionals carefully construct their identity in different disciplines in bio statements and professional homepages, how academic journals promote and situate themselves in academic communities, and how professionals present their individuality while conforming to the community practice in published articles.

Bhatia (1993, 2004) has extended the analyses of written texts beyond the analysis of specific genres and has developed theories that describe genre colonies, genre families, and genre sequences in several professional and academic contexts (see also Nesi & Gardner 2012). This concept of genres working together in symbiotic relationships is powerful in understanding how specific genres are deployed in specific professional contexts. For example, Bhatia describes relationships among various types of reports and focuses on many sub-types of business reports, including audits, technical reports, sales reports, annual reports, progress reports, field reports, etc. These concepts in academic contexts have also been highlighted by Swales (2004), who identifies genre chains, in which one genre depends on the earlier genre, etc. For example, one conference talk leads to a different conference talk, leads to a book chapter, leads to a book. Many variations on this concept come readily to mind. For example, the abstract for a conference leads to a poster presentation, leads to a publication. Or, a book prospectus to a publisher leads to a contract, leads to a book, leads to a book review. Or, a letter requesting an external review of a faculty member, generates a self-statement, a CV, and a set of ancillary documents, leading to a letter of review, leading to a memo for promotion (or not), etc. Research on texts in the real world is just scratching the surface of how texts relate to one another in various ways.

2.4 Stylistics and forensic linguistics

While not popular in most US academic training programs, the study of both stylistics and forensics remains important sub-fields within English language studies and applied linguistics in the UK and elsewhere. Stylistics continues to explore the lexical, syntactic, and organizational features of literary texts whether of a single author, or a comparison across authors, or the development of literary texts across time (Leech and Short 2007; Mahlberg 2014). Many studies of textual style also highlight specific aspects of time reference, reported speech, unusual dialogue, psychological orientation, and dialect variation.

Forensic linguistics similarly looks at language features as they structure discourse in various types of legal, criminal, and evidentiary texts. Forensic linguistics may use various types of texts for their analyses: threat letters, suicide notes, fabricated confessions, blackmail/extortion letters, terrorist threats, ransom notes, e-mails, text messages, and plagiarism. Often analyses center on similarities of texts, unusual patterns within texts, or, in the case of plagiarism, original source versus the style of the writer who has used the plagiarized text (Cotterill 2014; Pecorari 2014). Forensic linguistics provides many real applications of linguistic resources to determine facts about text authorship (see Coulthard and Johnson 2010; Ollson and Luchjenbroers 2013).

2.5 Rhetorical linguistic analyses

Argument and persuasion have long been a tradition in writing and rhetorical research. Much of the research in rhetoric has not made strong use of linguistic features that code argument and persuasion, whether effectively or ineffectively. Miller and Charney (2008) have suggested that textual resources can be an important part of the rhetoric of persuasion. In particular, audience strongly influences how much to say, what to omit, and how to shape a position in writing. Belcher (1994) shows how non-native graduate students have difficulty deciding which sources to cite to show knowledge of a field and write more persuasively. Additional perspectives on rhetorical discourse analysis are offered in Andrus (2014). Taking the next step in this linkage between rhetorical intentions and linguistic features, discourse analysis for argumentative/persuasive genres can combine the rhetorical appeals (ethos, logos, pathos) with linguistic/structural features. This approach is seen in Connor and her colleagues' studies of persuasive genres such as fund-raising letters (Biber, Connor, and Upton 2010; Connor and Galdkov 2004). Linked to this topic is the role of activity theory in exploring genre structuring in response to the wider social/textual context, though activity theory does not focus on the linguistics of the text (see Johns 2002 for chapters on new rhetoric and genre theory).

2.6 Corpus linguistics

It should be evident by now that much contemporary text analyses of written texts are now being carried out using corpora of large numbers of written texts. This is a second nearly pervasive aspect of text analysis in current times. In the past 15 years or so, corpus-linguistic analyses of discourse have seen a few shifts: First, with the emergence of learner corpora, there are more studies that use the ICLE or researcher-constructed learner corpus to compare L2 learners' language/discourse features with that of native speakers (Belz 2004; Luzón 2009). More recently, the extensive explorations of the British Academic Writing in English (BAWE) corpus has greatly expanded ways to work with a large student writing corpus constructed with appropriate corpus construction principles (Nesi 2011; Nesi and Gardner 2012). (See also MICUSP – The Michigan Corpus of Upper-level Student Papers- for a North American version of BAWE). Second, there are more applications of multi-dimensional analysis (Biber 1988) in the analysis of academic and professional writing (Biber 2006; Biber and Conard 2009; Biber, Conrad, and Reppen 1998; Connor and Upton 2003; Conrad and Biber 2001; Gardner and Nesi 2013; Gray 2011). Third, the focus has shifted from simple quantitative counting of lexico/grammatical features to functional analyses of these features, many times in combination with discourse move analyses (Connor and Upton 2004; Gray and Cortes 2011; Hyland 2009; Johns 2013). Fourth, there has been a greatly expanded analysis of writing development of specific learner groups (Doolan 2014; Doolan and Miller 2012; Hinkel 2003; also see following section).

The relevance of error analysis re-emerges as part of the ways that corpus analysis contributes to the discourse analysis of texts. At issue is the extent to which writing errors predict reader assessment of writing quality. It seems that student writing errors play a major role in the reader's/rater's assessment of writing quality. Doolan (2013, 2014; Doolan and Miller 2012) quantitatively and qualitatively analyzed error patterns in generation 1.5, English L1, and English L2 students' essays. They found that errors are a major distinguisher of developmental versus grade appropriate writing abilities. This finding, as much as writing specialists would prefer otherwise, is a finding that also drives much of the automated essay grading algorithms (see below).

In a number of more recent studies, corpus analyses are combined with genre analyses and genre variations. One of the most recent efforts of combining genre analysis and corpus analysis is probably best illustrated by Biber, Connor, and Upton (2010). In their book, *Discourse on the move: Using corpus analysis to describe discourse structure*, corpus based methods are used to identify and describe the discourse organization of professional texts, including academic research articles, professional texts, and university classroom teaching. Studies in the book are based on two approaches: top-down and bottom-up. The three top-down studies in the book employ the more traditional approach to discourse move analysis. First, moves in a text are identified based on qualitative, functional analysis. Then corpus analysis is used to detect linguistic/grammatical features that realize the moves and assist in the identification of move boundaries as well as typical versus less typical move structures in a text. The later chapters of the book employ a bottom-up approach, which begins with the quantitative linguistic analysis of texts that segment the text into sections based on boundaries indicated by the sharp breaks in words used in the text (vocabulary-based discourse units). Interpretation of the discourse function of each unit only comes after the segmentation. Even though it is not clear how well the computer-devised discourse unit segmentations match that of human judgments, this line of research is worth future exploration.

2.7 Automated linguistic analyses from cognitive psychology

A fairly recent addition to corpus analysis and textual quality of writing has been the work of cognitive psychologists and educational psychologists to set up automated text analyses based on principles of discourse processing. The early work was carried out by the cognitive psychology research lab at the University of Memphis under Arthur Graesser, Danielle McNamara, and colleagues. The Automated tool that has emerged for this work is Coh-Metrix. It has been used in well more than 50 studies by now, analyzing both L1 and L2 texts of various types.

Coh-Metrix is a publicly available text analysis tool. It is designed to provide measures of language cohesion, language coherence, language sophistication, use of syntax, and lexical relationships. McNamara and Crossley (McNamara, Crossley, and McCarthy 2010) have shown the usefulness of this text analysis resource in analyzing linguistic features of writing quality and writing proficiency development across grades. Crossley has focused especially on the use of Coh-Metrix with L2 populations and student texts. (For a full explanation of measures and associated references, see Coh-Metrix version 3.0 http://cohmetrix.memphis.edu/cohmetrixpr/cohmetrix3.html). In several studies, Crossley and colleagues have shown how select variables drawn from Coh-Metrix can predict writing proficiency, L2 writing proficiency, text readability, L2 writing similarities across L1s, lexical differences across L1 and L2 writing (Crossley, Greenfield, and McNamara 2008; Crossley and McNamara 2009, 2011).

2.8 Automated essay scoring (AES) systems

A final area in which current linguistic discourse analysis has grown in the past ten years is in the area of automated essay scoring systems. There are now multiple automated approaches to essay scoring and essay diagnostics. Of these, there are three well-known automated essay scoring systems (AES, also called automated writing evaluation (AWE)). The three main corporations promoting AWE products are described briefly in Table 11.1 (adapted from Warschauer and Ware 2006). AES systems attempt to mimic human scoring by being trained to hundreds of samples of human scored essays to "learn" the set of features that contribute to the final score and build a scoring model – most often regression models – to score future essays. Because of this method, most AES systems are prompt-dependent, perhaps with the exception of e-rater V.2, which is a program-level model that can reliably score essays across prompts (Attali and Burstein 2006). The scores given by these AES products are usually comparable to human scorers; the quality of automated feedback, however, is not yet comparable to that provided by trained writing instructors (Warschauer and Ware 2006).

We do not make any specific claims about these projects except to note that a considerable amount of development energy has gone into them. In the cases of Intellimetric and Intelligent Essay Assessor, there is relatively little technical information publicly available and little openly accessible research is available publicly. For this reason, we will focus on the research reported for e-rater (Educational Testing Service).

The e-rater system has undergone many cycles of improvement over the past 15 years. The first version of e-rater used more than 60 features in the scoring process (Attali and Burstein 2006), but the second version is based on a smaller feature set that is believed to reflect the most important attributes of writing. The

Tab. 11.1: Automated Writing Evaluation Software.

Company	Software engine	Evaluation mechanism	Commercial product	Scoring	Feedback
Vantage Learning	Intellimetric	Artificial Intelligence	My Access!	Holistic and component scoring	Limited generic / individualized feedback
Pearson Knowledge Technologies	Intelligent Essay Assessor	Latent Semantic Analysis	WriteToLearn	Holistic and component scoring	Limited individualized feedback
Educational Testing Service	e-rater	Natural Language Processing	Criterion	Holistic scoring	Wide range of individualized feedback

revised feature set for e-rater V.2 includes 10 feature categories: grammar, usage, mechanics, style, organization, development, vocabulary level, word length, and 2 features of prompt-specific vocabulary usage (Attali and Burstein 2006). To score essays, the e-rater compares them along the feature set against the essays that had previously been scored by humans. When only using the first 8 sets of features, e-rater V.2 is able to achieve scoring at program-level (generic scoring) instead of building a separate model for each individual essay prompt. In 1999, e-rater was introduced as one of the two raters to score the essay portion of the Graduate Man-agement Admissions Test (Warschauer and Ware 2006). ETS has been using e-rater in conjunction with human ratings to score the iBT TOEFL independent writing task since 2009 and integrated writing task since 2011 (Attali, Lewis, and Steier 2013; Enright and Quinlan 2010).

The commercial version of the e-rater is called Criterion, a web-based instruc-tional writing tool. With the application of the Natural Language Processing (NLP) technology, Criterion can provide feedback to writing responses that do not have bench mark essays to compare to. The types of feedback include grammar, usage, and mechanics errors, stylistic aspects that need revision (such as over-long sen-tences and overly repetitive words), and the absence of discourse features (e.g., introduction, thesis statement, main ideas, supporting ideas, and conclusion).

Most of the existing research on e-rater has been supported by ETS, but there are some independently published studies on the e-rater's validity. Attali and Burstein (2006) did correlational analyses between e-rater scores and human scores on sixth through twelfth grade essays, GMAT essay responses, and TOEFL essays. Their results showed similar human–e-rater and human–human inter-rater reliabilities for all participant groups on single essays. In addition, there is high reliability between human–e-raters across different essay prompts ($r = .97$). Attali, Bridgeman, and Trapani's (2010) study showed relatively close correlations be-tween the e-rater scores with human rater scores across prompts. Further, there was slightly higher correlation between e-rater scores and other scores (e.g., quan-titative and verbal scores for the GRE General Test) than those of human raters. Attali, Lewis, and Steier, (2013) demonstrate that machine ratings correlate as well with a human rater as do two human raters with each other.

Even though e-rater has been proven to be reliable and valid scoring mecha-nism, many people still argue against the idea of automated essay evaluation. The objections come from the worry that such AES systems could be tricked by clever nonsense essays, or that it could not correctly judge good essays that do not con-form to the linear rhetorical structure, or that it may not correctly judge essays written by ESL students since they are still developing English proficiency. For better or worse, we should certainly expect greater role for AES systems in the coming years.

3 Future developments of discourse analysis

In reviewing the developments in discourse analysis over the past 15 years, it is clear that the role of discourse analysis has evolved considerably. A number of features of close functional discourse analysis are still used regularly, especially with smaller corpora. However, three factors have contributed to a major shift in linguistic discourse analysis. The first factor in this shift involves the growing acceptance of the role of genre to provide functional interpretation in any analysis of texts. The second factor involves the increasing power of technology and automated text analyses to understand many aspects of text structure. The third factor involves the increasing role of corpus analysis in all aspects of discourse analysis. The specific sub-fields of discourse analysis, as they have developed within applied linguistics, clearly demonstrate this shift. At the same time, the specific sub-fields of linguistics discourse analysis have merged in many major research studies, indicating a coalescing of research methods around genre analyses, corpus analyses, and technology tools. This convergence is likely to continue in the coming decade. Such a convergence holds open the promise for many useful applied findings that can lead to more effective analyses of texts and more effective writing instruction.

In the midst of the many advanced innovations outlined in this survey, there is one clear limitation. There is relatively little strong evidence that applications of text analysis lead unequivocally to improved writing instruction, improved writing outcomes, or improved learning of new content from writing tasks. In ten years, we hope that this lacuna will be addressed and the promise of text analysis will provide strong evidence for ways to improve student writing outcomes.

4 Additional sources

Atkinson, Dwight. 1990. Discourse analysis and written discourse conventions. *Annual Review of Applied Linguistics* 11. 57–76.
Bazerman, Charles. 2008. *Handbook of research on writing*. New York: Lawrence Erlbaum.
Connor, Ulla. 1996. *Contrastive rhetoric: Cross-cultural aspects of second language writing*. Cambridge: Cambridge University Press.
English for Specific Purposes.
Gee, James. 2014. *An introduction to discourse analysis: Theory and method* (4th ed.). New York: Routledge.
Hoey, Michael. 2001. *Textual interaction: An introduction to written discourse analysis*. New York, NY: Routledge.
Journal of Enlish for Academic Purposes.
Journal of Second Language Writing.
Paltridge, Brian and Sue Starfield (eds.). 2013. *The handbook for English for specific purposes*. Malden, MA: Wiley-Blackwell.
Written Communication.

5 References

Andrus, Jennifer. 2014. Rhetorical discourse analysis. In Carol Chapelle (ed.), *The international encyclopedia of applied linguistics*. Malden, MA: Blackwell. (Retrieved 4–13–2013) DOI: 10.1002/9781405198431.wbeal1017.

Attali, Yigal, Brent Bridgeman, and Catherine Trapani. 2010. Performance of a generic approach in automated essay scoring. *Journal of Technology, Learning, and Assessment* 10(3). (Retrieved 12–12–2012) from <http://www.jtla.org>.

Attali, Yigal and Jill Burstein. 2006. Automated Essay Scoring with e-rater V.2. *Journal of Technology, Learning, and Assessment (JTLA)* 4(3).

Attali, Yigal, Will Lewis, and Michael Steier. 2013. Scoring with the computer: Alternative procedures for improving the reliability of holistic essay scoring. *Language Testing* 30. 125–141.

BAWE (British Academic Writing in English corpus) (http://www2.warwick.ac.uk/fac/soc/al/research/collect/bawe/)

Belcher, Diane. 1994. The apprenticeship approach to advanced academic literacy: Graduate students and their mentors. *English for Specific Purposes* 13. 23–34.

Belcher, Diane, Ann Johns, and Brian Paltridge (eds.). 2011. *New directions in English for specific purposes research*. Ann Arbor, MI: University of Michigan Press.

Belz, Julie. 2004. Learner corpus analysis and the development of foreign language proficiency. *System* 32. 577–591.

Bhatia, Vijay. 1993. *Analyzing genre: Language use in professional settings*. New York: Longman.

Bhatia, Vijay. 2004. *Worlds of written discourse*. New York, NY: Continuum.

Biber, Douglas. 1988. *Variation across speech and writing*. New York: Cambridge University Press.

Biber, Douglas. 2006. *University language: A corpus-based study of spoken and written registers*. Amsterdam: John Benjamins.

Biber, Douglas and Susan Conrad. 2009. *Register, genre, and style*. New York: Cambridge University Press.

Biber, Douglas, Susan Conrad, and Randi Reppen. 1998. *Corpus linguistics: Investigating language structure and use*. New York: Cambridge University Press.

Biber, Douglas, Ulla Connor, and Thomas Upton. 2010. *Discourse on the move: Using corpus analysis to describe discourse structure*. Philadelphia: John Benjamins.

Carter, Ronald and Walter Nash. 1990. *Seeing through language: A guide to styles in English writing*. Oxford: Blackwell.

Chang, Ching-Fen and Chih-Hua Kuo. 2004. A corpus-based approach to online materials development for writing research articles. *English for Specific Purposes* 30. 222–234.

Chapelle, Carol (ed.). 2014. *The international encyclopedia of applied linguistics*. Malden, MA: Blackwell. DOI: 10.1002/9781405198431.wbeal (Retrieved 4–13–2013)

Cheng, An. 2007. Transferring generic features and recontextualizing genre awareness: understanding writing performance in an ESP genre-based literacy framework. *English for Specific Purposes* 26. 287–307.

Cheng, An. 2008. Analyzing genre exemplars in preparation for writing: The case of an L2 graduate student in the ESP genre-based instructional framework of academic literacy. *Applied Linguistics* 29. 50–71.

Christie, Frances and Beverly Derewianka. 2008. *School discourse*. London: Continuum.

Coh-Metrix version 3.0; http://cohmetrix.memphis.edu/cohmetrixpr/cohmetrix3.html (Retrieved 4–19–2013).

Connor, Ulla. 1990. Linguistic/rhetorical measures for international persuasive student writing. *Research in the Teaching of English* 24. 67–87.

Connor, Ulla. 1996. *Contrastive rhetoric: Cross-cultural aspects of second language writing*. Cambridge: Cambridge University Press.

Connor, Ulla. 2002. *Contrastive rhetoric: Cross-cultural aspects of second-language writing.* Stuttgart: Klett.

Connor, Ulla. 2008. Mapping multidimensional aspects of research: Reaching to intercultural rhetoric. In Ulla Connor, Ulla, Ed Nagelhout, and William Rozycki. (eds.), *Contrastive rhetoric: Reaching to intercultural rhetoric*, 299–315. Philadelphia: John Benjamins.

Connor, Ulla. 2011. *Intercultural rhetoric in the writing classroom.* Ann Arbor, MI: University of Michigan Press.

Connor, Ulla and Kostya Gladkov. 2004. Rhetorical appeals in fundraising direct mail letters. In Ulla Connor and Thomas. A. Upton (eds.), *Discourse in the professions: Perspectives from corpus linguistics*, 257–286. Philadelphia: John Benjamins.

Connor, Ulla and Aymérou Mbaye. 2002. Discourse approaches to writing assessment. *Annual Review of Applied Linguistics* 22. 263–278.

Connor, Ulla and Thomas Upton. 2003. Linguistic dimensions of direct mail letters. In Pepi Leistyna and Charles Meyer (eds.), *Corpus analysis: Language structure and language use*, 71–86. Amsterdam: Editions Rodopi.

Connor, *Ulla and Thomas Upton. 2004. Discourse in the professions: Perspectives from corpus linguistics.* Amsterdam: John Benjamins.

Conrad, Susan and Douglas Biber (eds.). 2001. *Variation in English: Multi-dimensional studies.* London: Longman.

Cotterill, Janet. 2014. Corpus analysis in forensic linguistics. In Carol Chapelle (ed.), *The international encyclopedia of applied linguistics.* Malden, MA: Blackwell. (Retrieved 4–13–2013) DOI: 10.1002/9781405198431.wbeal0238

Coulthard, Malcolm. 1977. *An introduction to discourse analysis.* London: Longman.

Coulthard, Malcolm. 1994. Powerful evidence for the defense: An exercise in forensic discourse analysis. In John Gibbon (ed.), *Language and the law*, 414–427. London: Longman.

Coulthard, Malcolm and Alison Johnson. 2010. *The Routledge handbook of forensic linguistics.* New York: Routledge.

Crossley, Scott, Jerry Greenfield, and Danielle S. McNamara. 2008. Assessing text readability using psycholinguistic indices. *TESOL Quarterly* 42. 475–493.

Crossley, Scott and Danielle S. McNamara. 2009. Computational assessment of lexical differences in L1 and L2 writing. *Journal of Second Language Writing* 18. 119–135.

Crossley, Scott and Danielle S. McNamara. 2011. Shared features of L2 writing: Intergroup homogeneity and text classification. *Journal of Second Language Writing* 20. 271–285.

Doolan, Stephen. 2013. Generation 1.5 writing compared to L1 and L2 writing in first-year composition. *Written Communication* 30. 135–163.

Doolan, Stephen. 2014. Comparing language use in the writing of developmental generation 1.5, L1, and L2 tertiary students. *Written Communication* 31. 215–247.

Doolan, Stephen and Donald Miller. 2012. Generation 1.5 written error patterns: A comparative study. *Journal of Second Language Writing* 21. 1–22.

Eagleson, Robert. 1994. Forensic analysis of personal written texts: A case study. In John Gibbon (ed.), *Language and the law*, 362–373. London: Longman.

Enright, Mary K. and Thomas Quinlan. 2010. Complementing human judgment of essays written by English language learners with e-rater® scoring. *Language Testing* 27. 317–334.

Feak, Christine and John Swales. 2009. *Telling a research story: Writing a literature review.* Ann Arbor, MI: University of Michigan Press.

Feak, Christine and John Swales. 2011. *Creating contexts: Writing introductions across genres.* Ann Arbor, MI: University of Michigan Press.

Flowerdew, John. 2013. English for research publication purposes. In Brian Paltridge and Sue Starfield (eds.), *The handbook of English for specific purposes*, 301–321. Malden, MA: Wiley-Blackwell.

Flowerdew, John and Alina Wan. 2006. Genre analysis of tax computation letters: How and why tax accountants write the way they do. *English for Specific Purposes* 25. 133–153.

Flowerdew, Lynne. 1998. Corpus linguistic techniques applied to text linguistics. *System* 26. 541–552.

Gardner, Sheena and Hilary Nesi. 2013. A classification of genre families in university student writing. *Applied Linguistics* 34. 25–52.

Givón, Talmy. 1995. Coherence in text vs. coherence in mind. In Morton Ann Gernsbacher and Talmy Givón (eds.), *Coherence in spontaneous text*, 59–115. Philadelphia: John Benjamins.

Grabe, William and Robert Kaplan. 1996. *Theory and practice of writing*. London: Longman.

Granger, Sylviane, Estelle Dagneaux, Fanny Meunier, and Magali Paquot. 2009. *International Corpus of Learner English v2*. Presses universitaires de Louvain, Louvain-la-Neuve.

Gray, Bethany. 2011. Exploring academic writing through corpus-linguistics: When discipline only tells part of the story (doctoral dissertation). Retrieved from ProQuest Dissertation and Thesis database. (AAT 3490519)

Gray, Bethany and Viviana Cortes. 2011. Perception vs. evidence: An analysis of this and these in academic prose. *English for Specific Purposes* 30. 31–43.

Halleck, Gene and Ulla Connor. 2006. Rhetorical moves in TESOL conference proposals. *Journal of English for Academic Purposes* 5. 70–86.

Halliday, Michael. 1998. Things and relations: Regrammaticising experience as technical knowledge. In James Martin and Robert Veel (eds.) *Reading science*, 185–235. New York: Routledge.

Halliday, Michael and Ruqaiya Hasan. 1976. *Cohesion in English*. London: Longman.

Halliday, Michael and Ruqaiya Hasan. 1989. *Language, context, and text: Aspects of language in a social semiotic perspective*. Oxford: Oxford University Press.

Henry, Alex and Robert Roseberry. 2001. A narrow-angled corpus analysis of moves and strategies of the genre: 'Letter of Application'. *English for Specific Purposes* 20. 153–167.

Hinkel, Eli. 2003. Simplicity without elegance: Features of sentences in L1 and L2 academic texts. *TESOL Quarterly* 37. 275–301.

Hoey, Michael. 1983. *On the surface of discourse*. London: Allen and Unwin.

Hunt, Kellogg. 1965. *Grammatical structures written at three grade levels*. Urbana, IL: National Council of Teachers of English.

Hyland, Ken. 2002. Genre: Language, context, and literacy. In Mary McGroarty, et al. (eds.) *Annual review of Applied Linguistics, 22. Discourse and dialogue*, 111–133. New York: Cambridge University Press.

Hyland, Ken (ed.). 2006. *Academic discourse across disciplines*. New York: Peter Lang.

Hyland, Ken. 2009. *Academic discourse*. New York: Continuum.

Hyland, Ken. 2011. The presentation of self in scholarly life: identity and marginalization in academic homepages. *English for Specific Purposes* 30. 286–297.

Hyland, Ken. 2013. ESP and writing. In Brian Paltridge and Sue Starfield (eds.), *The handbook of English for special purposes*, 95–113. Malden, MA: Wiley-Blackwell.

Hyland, Ken and Polly Tse. 2009. "The leading journal in its field": Evaluation in journal descriptions. *Discourse Studies* 11. 703–720.

Hyland, Ken and Polly Tse. 2012. 'She has received many honours': Identity construction in article bio statements. *Journal of English for Academic Purposes* 11. 155–165.

Johns, Ann. 1997. *Text, role and context: Developing academic literacies*. New York: Cambridge University Press.

Johns, Ann (ed.). 2002. *Genre in the classroom: Multiple perspectives*. Mahwah, NJ: Erlbaum.

Johns, Ann. 2013. The history if English for specific purposes research. In Brian Paltridge and Sue Starfield (eds.), *The handbook for English for specific purposes*, 5–30. Malden, MA: Wiley-Blackwell.

Kaplan, Robert. 1966. Cultural thought patterns in intercultural education. *Language Learning* 16. 1–20.

Kaplan, Robert. 1972. *The anatomy of rhetoric: Prolegomena to a functional theory of rhetoric.* Philadelphia: Center for Curriculum Development.

Kaplan, Robert. 2000. Contrastive rhetoric and discourse analysis: Who writes what to whom? When? In what circumstances? In Srikant Sarangi and Malcolm Coulthard (eds.), *Discourse and social life*, 82–101. London: Pearson Education.

Kaplan, Robert. 2005. Contrastive rhetoric. In Eli Hinkel (ed.), *Handbook of applied linguistics*, 375–391. Mahwah, NJ: L. Erlbaum.

Kaplan, Robert and William Grabe. 2002. A modern history of written discourse analysis. *Journal of Second Language Writing* 11. 191–223.

Labov, William. 1972. *Language in the inner city.* Philadelphia: University of Pennsylvania Press.

Leech, Geoffrey and Mick Short. 1981. *Style in fiction.* (2nd ed. 2007). New York: Longman Pearson.

Loban, Walter. 1976. *Language development: Kindergarten through grade twelve.* Urbana, IL: National Council of Teachers of English.

Luzón, M. José. 2009. The use of *we* in a learner corpus of reports written by EFL Engineering students. *Journal of English for Academic Purposes* 8. 192–206.

Mahlberg, Michaela. 2014. Corpus analysis of literary texts. In Carol Chapelle (ed.), *The international encyclopedia of applied linguistics.* Malden, MA: Blackwell. (Retrieved 4–13–13) DOI: 10.1002/9781405198431.wbeal0249

Martin, James. 1993. Genre and literacy – modeling context in educational linguistics. *Annual Review of Applied Linguistics* 13. 141–172.

Martin, James. 2000. Design and practice: Enacting functional linguistics. *Annual Review of Applied Linguistics* 20. 116–135.

Martin, James. 2002. Meaning beyond the clause: SFL perspectives. *Annual Review of Applied Linguistics* 22. 52–72.

Martin, James and David Rose. 2008. *Genre relations: Mapping culture.* London: Equinox.

Matsuda, Paul K. 2001. On the origin of contrastive rhetoric: A response to "The Origin of Contrastive Rhetoric Revisited" by H. G. Ying (2000). *International Journal of Applied Linguistics* 11. 257–260.

McNamara, Danielle, Scott Crossley, and Phillip McCarthy. 2010. Linguistic features of writing quality. *Written Communication* 27. 57–86.

Miller, Melissa and Davida Charney. 2008. Persuasion, audience, and argument. In Charles Bazerman (ed.), *Handbook of research on writing*, 583–598. New York: Lawrence Erlbaum.

Moreno, Ana. 2014. Intercultural rhetoric in language for specific purposes. In Carol Chapelle (ed.), *The international encyclopedia of Applied Linguistics.* Malden, MA: Blackwell. (Retrieved 4–13–2013) DOI: 10.1002/9781405198431.wbeal0558

MICUSP (Michigan Corpus of Upper-Level Student Papers). (http://micusp.elicorpora.info)

Nesi, Hilary. 2011. BAWE: An introduction to a new resource. In A. Frankenberg-Garcia, L. Flowerdew, and G. Aston (eds.), *New trends in corpora and language* learning, 212–228. London: Continuum.

Nesi, Hilary and Sheena Gardner. 2012. *Genres across the disciplines: Student writing in higher education.* New York: Cambridge University Press.

Ollson, John and June Luchjenbroers. 2013. *Forensic linguistics.* New York: Continuum.

Paltridge, Brian. 2001. *Genre and the language learning classroom.* Ann Arbor, MI: University of Michigan Press.

Paltridge, Brian. 2013. Genre and English for specific purposes. In Brian Paltridge and Sue Starfield (eds.), *The handbook of English for specific purposes*, 347–366. Malden, MA: Wiley-Blackwell.

Paltridge, Brian and Sue Starfield (eds.). 2007. *Thesis and dissertation writing in a second language: A handbook for supervisors*. New York: Routledge.

Paltridge, Brian and Sue Starfield (eds.). 2013. *The handbook of English for specific purposes*. Malden, MA: Wiley-Blackwell.

Pecorari, Diane. 2014. Plagiarism. In Carol Chapelle (ed.), *The international encyclopedia of Applied Linguistics*. Malden, MA: Blackwell. (Retrieved 4–13–2013) DOI:10.1002/9781405198431.wbeal0914

Samraj, Betty. 2002. Introductions in research articles: Variations across disciplines. *English for Specific Purposes* 21. 1–17.

Samraj, Betty and Lenore Monk. 2008. The statement of purpose in graduate program applications: Genre structure and disciplinary variation. *English for Specific Purposes* 27. 193–211.

Schleppegrell, Mary. 2012. Systemic Functional Linguistics: Exploring meaning in language. In James Paul Gee and Michael Handford (eds.), *The Routledge handbook of discourse analysis,* 21–34. New York: Routledge.

Schleppegrell, Mary and Catherine O'Hallaron. 2011. Teaching academic language in L2 secondary settings. *Annual Review of Applied Linguistics* 31. 3–18.

Sinclair, John. 1987. *Looking up: An account of the COBUILD project in lexical computing*. London: Collins.

Sinclair, John. 1991. *Corpus, concordance, collocation*. Oxford: Oxford University Press.

Swales, John. 1981/2011. *Aspects of article introductions*. Aston ESP Research Reports, No 1. University of Aston, UK. [Reprinted in 2011, University of Michigan Press].

Swales, John. 1987. Utilizing the literatures in teaching the research paper. *TESOL Quarterly* 21. 41–67.

Swales, John. 1990. *Genre analysis: English in academic and research settings*. Cambridge: Cambridge University Press.

Swales, John. 1996. Occluded genres in the academy: The case of the submission letter. In Eija Ventola and Anna Mauranen (eds.), *Academic writing: Intercultural and textual issues*, 45–58. Amsterdam: John Benjamins.

Swales, John. 2000. Languages for specific purposes. In William Grabe, et al. (eds.) *Annual Review of Applied Linguistics* 20. *Applied Linguistics as an emerging discipline*, 59–76. New York: Cambridge University Press.

Swales, John. 2004. *Research genres: Explorations and applications*. New York: Cambridge University Press.

Tannen, Deborah. 1989. *Talking voices*. New York: Cambridge University Press.

Tardy, Christine. 2006. Researching first and second language genre learning: A comparative review and a look ahead. *Journal of Second Language Writing* 15. 79–101.

Tardy, Christine. 2009. *Building genre knowledge*. West Lafayette, IN: Parlor Press.

Tardy, Christine and John Swales. 2008. Form, text organization, genre, coherence, and cohesion. In Charles Bazerman (ed.), *Handbook of research on writing*, 565–581. New York: Lawrence Erlbaum.

Thompson, Paul. 2013. Thesis and dissertation writing. In Brian Paltridge and Sue Starfield (eds.), *The handbook for English for specific purposes*, 283–299. Malden, MA: Wiley-Blackwell.

Trimble, Louis. 1985. *English for science and technology: A discourse approach*. New York: Cambridge University Press.

Tse, Polly and Ken Hyland. 2010. Claiming a territory: relative clauses in journal descriptions. *Journal of Pragmatics* 42. 1880–1889.

Upton, Thomas and Ulla Connor. 2001. Using computerized corpus analysis to investigate the textlinguistic discourse moves of a genre. *English for Specific Purposes* 20. 313–329.

Vande Kopple, William. 1998. Relative clauses in spectroscopic articles in the *Physical Review*, beginnings and 1980. *Written Communication* 15. 170–202.

Vande Kopple, William. 2002. From the dynamic style to the synoptic style in spectroscopic articles in the *Physical Review*. *Written Communication* 19. 227–264.

Warschauer, Mark and Paige Ware. 2006. Automated writing evaluation: Defining the classroom research agenda. *Language Teaching Research* 10. 1–24.

Zhang, Cui. 2013. Effect of instruction on ESL students' synthesis writing. *Journal of Second Language Writing* 22. 51–67.

Julio Roca de Larios, Florentina Nicolás-Conesa, and Yvette Coyle

12 Focus on writers: Processes and strategies

1 Introduction

Second language writing research has shaped its different areas of concern around the three elements that comprise the writing activity: the socio-cultural contexts where writers write and learn to write, the texts writers produce, and the actions writers engage in to produce such texts (e.g., Leki, Cumming, and Silva 2008). These three theoretical orientations are respectively referred to as writing as social-izing, writing as product and writing as process. The present chapter analyses writing as process and examines prominent publications that have focused on the analysis of L2 writing processes and strategies from a variety of perspectives. Studies of feedback, collaborative, or digital writing have been omitted (see chapters 14, 18, 19 and 20, this volume).

The chapter begins by exploring the origins of research into L2 writing process-es and strategies. It then examines the theoretical assumptions guiding conceptual-izations of both constructs, before documenting the research methods used in the field and the insights obtained in current research. It concludes by offering sugges-tions for advancing theory and research on L2 writing processes.

2 Origins and development of research on processes and strategies

The drive behind the process movement was originally cognitive in orientation and emerged in the L1 writing field in the early 80s with the aim of understanding the mental operations writers engage in and sequence while attempting to generate, express and refine ideas to produce a text (Manchón 2001). In the field of L2 writ-ing, researchers have been keen to establish their own research agenda in order to avoid simply appropriating the theoretical assumptions, methodologies and peda-gogical recommendations intended for L1 writing contexts (Silva 1993). The focus, therefore, has been on learners' attentional resources while composing in the L2 as well as on the strategies they deploy for addressing specific problems involved in this endeavour.

These concerns have been explored over the years through different research approaches, ranging from those which have examined L2 writing processes and strategies with analytical tools inspired in L1 writing models, or explored the prob-lem-solving nature of composing and the use of the L1 as a major strategy in the process, to those which have focused on second or foreign language composing

from the communication strategies literature, or as a situated activity to be analyzed from socio-cognitive, socio-cultural or multilingual perspectives. Recent developments also include psycholinguistically oriented studies with experimental
designs.

A first research strand, directly inspired in L1 writing process models, emerged
in the 80s with the aim of providing descriptions of L2 writers' composing processes and strategies with reference to either the *whole* composition process (Raimes
1987) or *one* macro-writing process, i.e., planning (e.g., Jones and Tetroe 1987).
This initial research was subsequently followed by studies that aimed to account
for global composing processes across languages (Armengol-Castells 2001; Woodall 2002) or to explore specific processes, such as planning (e.g., Akyel 1994), formulation (e.g., Chenoweth and Hayes 2001; Zimmermann 2000) or revision (e.g.,
Hall 1990; Takagaki 2003).

At around the same time, Cumming (1989) established the general framework
and analytical categories of another approach to the study of writing processes and
strategies, which, embedded in the problem-solving paradigm in cognitive psychology, opened up a range of research options in the field. These crystallized in a
number studies which (i) made complete or partial use of Cumming's categories
for the exploration of the language learning potential of L2 writing (Swain and
Lapkin 1995), the role of code-switching (Wang 2003) and the analysis of the composition processes of EFL learners in Japan (e.g., Sasaki 2004), or (ii) examined
Cumming's notion of problem-space, which gave rise to a complete research program in Spain (see overview in Manchón, Roca de Larios, and Murphy 2009).

Attempts at studying specific strategies were also made. L1 use in L2 writing
attracted the most attention, with initial small-scale exploratory studies (e.g., Lay
1982) and later with work in which participants were either instructed to plan in
their L1 or L2 before formulating their texts (e.g., Akyel 1994; Friedlander 1990), or
to write their texts in L1 and then translate them into the L2 (Cohen and Brooks-
Carson 2001). More recently, analyses have focused on the use of the L1 as a function of task difficulty (Wang 2003), and on its strategic role in helping L2 writers
access and retrieve lexical items when generating texts (Murphy and Roca de
Larios 2010).

The construct of language learner strategies gave rise to different research
strands which included: (i) the application of Oxford's (1990) taxonomy of strategies (metacognitive, cognitive, compensatory, social and affective) to the study of
L2 writing strategies (e.g., McMullen 2009); (ii) the relationship between writers'
metacognitive strategies (planning, monitoring and evaluation) and their composing processes (e.g., Victori 1999); and (iii) the use of communication strategies by
L2 writers while composing (e.g., Agustín Llach 2010; Navés, Miralpeix, and Celaya
2005; Olsen 1999).

More recent developments include several research programs conducted in the
Netherlands that have explored how conceptual performance can be inhibited by

attention to linguistic matters (see Schoonen, Snellings, Stevenson, and Van Gelderen 2009) or facilitated by training writers in the access and retrieval of L2 words (Van Gelderen, Oostdam, and Van Schooten 2011), and how L1 and L2 writing compares from the perspective of processes and products among university (Van Weijen 2009) and high school students (Tillema 2012).

Mention should also be made of several psycholinguistically oriented studies with experimental designs which have attempted to explore the effects of planning time, the availability of writing assistance (advanced provision of ideas or macrostructure) or previous drafts on the quality and quantity of ideas produced by EFL writers during planning and composing (Ong 2013), on their metacognitive processes (Ong 2014) or on the fluency and lexical complexity of their written texts (Ong and Zhang 2010).

Finally, viewing writing as a situated activity that occurs in specific socio-cultural contexts, some studies have adopted socio-cognitive or socio-cultural perspectives to account for learners' L2 writing processes and strategies. Framed in theories of literacy development (e.g., Riazi 1997) or goal-theories of education (e.g., Cumming 2006), they have provided evidence of the interaction of social and cognitive dimensions in the development of L2 writers' strategic competence. sociocultural studies have made use of the Vygotskian concept of socially mediated learning to look, for example, at the effects of study abroad experiences on EFL writers' strategy use (Sasaki 2009), the impact of social contact with NS peers on the development of strategy use by advanced EAP students (Parks and Raymond 2004), or the strategic mediation of writing by proficient EFL learners (Lei 2008).

3 Main theories informing research

As noted above, research into L2 writing processes and strategies has traditionally drawn on cognitively-oriented L1 writing process models directly inspired in theories of human problem-solving (Ericsson and Simon 1980), theoretical constructs in the field of second language acquisition research related to literacy transfer, and perspectives emerging from research into strategies for language learning and use. The combination of these frameworks has resulted in several cognitive models intended to capture the specifics of L2 writing processes.

The L1 writing model on which most studies have drawn is that of Flower and Hayes (1981). Its adaptation to the second language context has led researchers to consider L2 composing as the complex and recursive interaction of planning, translation and revision processes, which are coordinated by a monitor. In order to engage in those processes, writers access relevant knowledge in their long-term memory (content, lexis, syntax, discourse, etc.) and deploy that knowledge in the context of the task environment. Empirically, this model has enabled a characterization of more and less skilled writers, a distinction that has also been addressed in many studies on L2 writing processes by drawing on Bereiter and Scardamalia's (1987) contrast between knowledge-telling and knowledge-transforming approaches. Writers are assumed to engage in a knowledge-telling approach when content is directly retrieved from long-term memory and organized on the basis of stored associations. In contrast, a knowledge-transforming approach involves a dialectical interaction between content and rhetorical problem spaces: ideas are adjusted, shaped and revised, since they are represented not only as a reflection of the writer's knowledge (content space) but also as a function of their rhetorical function within the text (rhetorical space). One characteristic common to both Flower and Hayes' and Bereiter and Scardamalia's models is that they equate writing with high-level reflective thinking (Galbraith 2009). Consequently, in their application to second language writing it is assumed that the thought processes involved in effective writing are common to L1 and L2, the main difference being related to how the outcome of these processes is linguistically formulated.

This basic tenet of cognitive models of writing is intimately related to the ways in which the transfer of writing processes and strategies from one language to another has been theoretically framed in most studies. This has generally been addressed through recourse to Cummins' (1980) notion of common underlying proficiency (CUP), which holds that once a literacy process such as planning, for example, has been acquired in a language, it does not have to be reacquired in a second language ("Interdependence Hypothesis"). However, this transfer of skills across languages is not unconditioned, since it is also posited that a certain threshold of L2 proficiency and fluency must first be achieved before L1 skills are transferred ("Threshold Hypothesis"). From the perspective of cognitive capacity accounts of writing (e.g. McCutchen 2000), these constraints have specifically been contemplated through the "Inhibition Hypothesis" (Stevenson, Schoonen, and De Glopper 2006), which predicts that the linguistic demands of L2 writing may consume cognitive resources and inhibit writers' attention to such conceptual aspects as the elaboration of content or the production of high-level revisions.

A number of L2 writing process models have attempted to confirm the adaptability of L1 writing models to the L2 context (Wang 2003), elaborate some of the undeveloped macro-processes of L1 models, namely formulation (Zimmermann 2000) or describe the specificity of L2 composition processes (Whalen and Ménard 1995). However, the limitations of these models in accounting for the multiplicity of phenomena involved have recently led some scholars (see Schoonen et al. 2009; Roca de Larios 2013) to posit that explanations might be found in speech production models (e.g., Levelt 1989). Reliance on oral models is justified on the grounds that they are more developed than models of writing, and on the fact that speaking and writing share a number of production processes (see Alamargot and Chanquoy 2001).

Other theoretical approaches also based on oral production but from the perspective of task complexity, namely Robinson's Cognition Hypothesis (2011) and

Skehan's Limited Attentional Capacity model (2009), in combination with Kellogg's (1990) L1 writing-based Interactional and Overload Hypotheses, have been used in studies where writing processes have been analyzed through the experimental manipulation of task conditions (e.g., Ong 2013). Robinson's hypothesis is based on the premise that working memory consists of multiple and noncompeting pools of cognitive resources. Its main tenet is that an increase in task complexity with respect to conceptual demands will lead to more accuracy and complexity in language production, as learners will have to deliberate more and make explicit use of language. At the same time, an increase in procedural demands will lead to less fluency, accuracy and complexity, as learners' attentional resources will be diverted from language-related aspects of the task. The basic assumption of Skehan's model is that humans have a limited information processing capacity consisting of a single pool of resources. More task demands will therefore require more attentional resources, with the result that trade-off effects between fluency, accuracy and complexity will occur. Kellogg's Interaction Hypothesis predicts that planning deteriorates text quality because it may prevent writers from making use of the opportunities that arise in the course of composing through the interaction of planning, translating and reviewing. In contrast, the Overload Hypothesis postulates that planning is beneficial for text quality because it may reduce cognitive demands on writers and allow them to focus mainly on transcribing processes during writing. Finally, other approaches (Tillema 2012; van Weijen 2009) have based their theoretical frameworks on a combination of Hayes' (1996) L1 writing model and a probabilistic model of composing (van den Bergh and Rijlaarsdam 1996).

L2 writing processes place high demands on writers' cognitive resources, which have to be managed by means of effective writing strategies. Consequently, an essential focus of attention within L2 writing process-oriented research has been the analysis of the strategies used by writers. In contrast with the solid theoretical foundations of the models and constructs mentioned above, the term "strategy" is frequently used in L2 writing research but seldom defined or operationalized. Previous reviews (see Manchón et al. 2007) have reported that writing strategies have alternatively been equated with "behaviours" (Armengol-Castells 2001; Raimes 1987), "production processes" (Whalen and Ménard 1995) or, more recently, with "cognitive activities" (Tillema 2012; van Weijen 2009).

The dimension of strategies is also a matter of debate in the field, as these have been understood both as macro-writing processes, and as very specific cognitive operations, i.e., "rhetorical refining" (Sasaki 2000, 2004) or "rehearsing" (Raimes 1987). To the best of our knowledge, Manchón (2001) was the first author to address this terminological and conceptual diversity by suggesting a distinction between a broad and a narrow characterization of writing strategies. Along those lines, writing strategies have recently been conceptualized as goal-oriented clusters of mental actions that may be more or less effective in relation to a specific writing task (see Macaro 2014).

In the cognitive models of writing discussed above, the learning context is viewed as external to the learner, and processes and strategies are regarded as internal mechanisms that interact bi-directionally with that context. Recently, and in consonance with similar orientations in applied linguistics and SLA, there has been a move towards more sociocultural and multilingual approaches to the study of writing. From a sociocultural perspective, the traditional separation between learner-internal cognitive processing mechanisms and the writing context has been replaced by a dynamic, multi-layered and interdependent relationship between the two, whereby viewing processes and strategies as embedded in the local, historical and interactive contexts that provide learners with physical, social and symbolic affordances (Lei 2008). Following the main tenets of Activity Theory (Leontiev 1978), the actions of the individual in the writing activity are thought to be mediated by interrelated factors that include artifacts (e.g., computers, languages), rules (e.g., norms and sanctions), community (e.g., discourse community), and roles (e.g., teachers and writers). Writing strategies are accordingly conceived as "mediated actions which are consciously taken to facilitate writers' practices in communities" (Lei 2008: 220).

In line with this socially-embedded conception of writing strategies, recent multilingual approaches (e.g., Kobayashi and Rinnert 2013) have also moved away from cognitivism by drawing on theories of multicompetence (see Ortega and Carson 2010), genre as a social practice (Gentil 2011) and language and identity (Norton 2000). From a multi-competence perspective, multilingual writers are not conceived as users of independent languages but rather of overlapping systems that interact in intricate ways. The question then is what they can do "with their various knowledge sources and skills when approaching the writing of texts in the different languages that form their repertoires" (Manchón 2013: 112). An important part of these knowledge sources is genre knowledge, which includes text form, rhetorical features, subject matter, and knowledge of writing processes (Tardy 2009). Finally, identity in writing is understood as the way writers make grammatical, lexical and discoursal choices and present themselves in particular texts as a function of individual factors such as language proficiency, perceptions and values, and contextual factors such as audience, task and topic (Kobayashi and Rinnert 2012).

4 Main methods used

Research into writing processes and strategies has used both qualitative and quantitative approaches. Research designs have included both cross-sectional and longitudinal studies, case studies and large-scale studies, and within the latter, both survey and experimental studies (Manchón et al. 2007) conducted in both foreign and second language settings. Most foreign language studies are devoted to English, but others have also focused on French, Russian, German, Arabic, Chinese and Spanish. Participants have mainly been university students, although a few studies have focused on academics (e.g., Flowerdew and Li 2009) high school students (e.g., Lindgren Spellman-Miller and Sullivan 2008; Tillema 2012) and children (e.g., Navés et al. 2005).

Different methods of data collection have been employed, all of which entail their own specific advantages and disadvantages. Methods have included retrospective (stimulated recall, questionnaires, interviews) and introspective (think-aloud) procedures, as well as less intrusive techniques such as text analysis, process logs, observation and computerized tracking. In an attempt to compensate for the drawbacks of the different methods, the use of multiple-data collection procedures has been the norm.

Although information on participants' writing ability in the L2 is plentiful, very few studies report learners' L1 writing ability. When reported, this variable has been assessed on the basis of students' L1 compositions. The standards set in the institution writers are enrolled in or the academic status and writing experience of the participants have also been used as alternative criteria (see Roca de Larios et al. 2002). Writers' command of the L2, in contrast, has been reported via assessment procedures including impressionistic judgments, standardized tests, in-house assessments and institutional ratings, each procedure representing different assumptions of what constitutes proficiency and establishing different cut-off points between proficiency levels that may affect the comparability of findings (Thomas 1994). As for tasks, the majority of studies have opted for short time-compressed compositions (for exceptions, see Lei 2008). Even so, differences can be observed across studies regarding the allocation of time or space for task completion, the range of topics, texts types and specifications used, or the possibility of using aids such as dictionaries, reference materials or glossaries.

5 Main research insights

The research developments and theoretical frameworks discussed above have provided rich insights on writers' composing processes and strategies, as well as on the writer-internal and writer-external variables affecting the former (for reviews, see Leki et al. 2008; Manchón 2013; Manchón et al. 2007; Roca de Larios et al. 2002). In this section, we focus on recent findings produced in four research areas that, to a greater or lesser extent, reveal crucial points of intersection between cognitive skills, personal attitudes and socio-culturally and linguistically diverse contexts (Cumming 2013). These include (i) task-based L2 writing research, (ii) the consideration of writing skill from a developmental perspective, (iii) the activation of processes and strategies across languages, and (iii) the use of the L1 in L2 writing.

5.1 Task-based L2 writing research

Inspired in speech-related task research, a number of studies have focused on possible interfaces between SLA and L2 writing by looking at the relationship between task characteristics (planning time, provision of ideas and macrostructures, availability of previous drafts, etc.) and performance-related measures of written output (accuracy, fluency, complexity, quantity and quality of ideas, cohesion, etc.) which are taken to reveal the allocation of writers' attentional resources. As an illustration, we focus below on studies exploring planning time, one frequently manipulated task characteristic.

In an initial study, Ellis and Yuan (2004) found that their participants in a pre-task planning condition were able to write longer narratives and use a broader range of syntactic structures than writers in an on-line and no planning conditions. Planning supposedly reduced the cognitive demands placed on writers' single pool of resources (Skehan 2009) and allowed them to concentrate on the transcribing process during writing, which led to the production of better quality texts. This separation of planning and transcription processes was in consonance with Kellogg's (1990) "Overload Hypothesis".

These results were not confirmed by Ong and Zhang (2010) in a study intended to measure students' fluency and lexical variety when producing argumentative texts in three conditions of task complexity: extended pre-task planning, pre-task planning and free-writing. The free writing condition was found to result in greater fluency and lexical complexity, since the participants in the planning conditions continued to plan on-line while generating their texts, which negatively affected the quality of their written output. Unlike the previous study, the authors suggest that the processes involved in formulation did not seem to compete in a single pool of resources but in multiple pools, as predicted by Robinson (2011).

The superiority of the free-writing condition became evident in a subsequent study (Ong 2013), which examined the effects of planning time on the quality, quantity and rate of ideas produced in argumentative texts. A significantly greater number of ideas were produced in the no planning time condition compared to the planning time (10 minutes) and extended planning time (20 minutes) conditions, and a trade-off was not found between quantity and quality of ideas, since the latter was not inferior in the no planning condition. This seemed to indicate that the amount and quality of ideas produced by a writer do not necessarily compete for a similar pool of cognitive resources, thus confirming once again Robinson's (2011) hypothesis. Since the poorest quality ideas occurred in the extended planning condition, it was suggested that writers might have experienced difficulties in shifting from planning to transcription, with the result that they had no option but to rely on more on-line planning when transcribing their texts.

The content of this on-line planning processes was clarified in a third study in which Ong (2014) analysed the effects of planning time on five metacognitive processes: generating new ideas, elaborating new ideas, organizing new ideas, thinking of essay structure, and thinking of language aspects of the task. With the proviso that these writing processes were elicited by means of a questionnaire, the data showed that planning conditions only had an effect on the frequency of thinking of language aspects of the task during writing, which was taken by the author as an indication that writers in the extended pre-task and pre-task planning conditions allocated their attentional resources to linguistically oriented on-line planning during the formulation stage. In this respect, Kellogg's Overload Hypothesis failed again to be confirmed. However, the existence of a trade-off effect between the organization of new ideas and the linguistic aspects of the task in the formulation stage meant that the hypothesis could not be totally discarded.

These studies (with the exception of Ong 2014) do not directly contemplate how the features of writing tasks influence writing processes, but they implicitly assume that (i) task conditions impose different sets of demands on the different stages involved in the production of texts, i.e., planning, formulation and monitoring (see Kormos 2011); (ii) writers have to allocate their attentional resources, whether limited or subject to voluntary regulation, to the coordination and management of these processes in order to meet those demands; and (iii) the theoretical interpretation of that allocation of resources from a theoretical perspective is a complex endeavour.

5.2 Writing skill as a continuum of abilities

The incorporation of the notion of writing from L1 writing models into L2 researchers' analytical frames has led to the contemplation of writing skill not only as a dichotomous fixed set of competencies, but also as an evolving continuum of abilities inextricably linked to education and opportunities for learning (Cumming 2012).

Developmental patterns have been reported for flexibility in the coordination of composition processes and the way writers search for lexical or syntactic alternatives in order to upgrade (Manchón et al. 2009) or refine (Sasaki 2004) their linguistic expressions. Alternatively, the development of L2 organizational patterns has been attested by studies showing, for example, that training secondary school learners in genre knowledge may compensate for their word level difficulties (van Gelderen et al. 2011).

The activation of the different components of writers' meta-knowledge has also been explored form a developmental perspective, although results are not uniform. Manchón and Roca de Larios (2011) found that the development of advanced EFL Spanish students' metacognitive knowledge involved multidimensional concerns (ideational, textual and linguistic) which led writers to develop their goals for writing and to improve their writing performance. However, subsequent research in the same context (Nicolás-Conesa, Roca de Larios, and Coyle 2014) indicated that a different cohort of students did not show the same move towards multidimensional concerns but rather a reduction towards bi-dimensional ones, as the students restricted their goals to their immediate academic context and learning needs. Such differences show the situated nature of EFL learners' development of their meta-cognitive knowledge, goals for writing and written performance.

The findings reported above broadly differentiate between skills that are more conducive to acquisition and those which need further experience or instruction. In this respect, writing processes and strategies should be seen as following a course of development known as "hierarchical skill integration" (Schaeffer 1975). From this cognitive perspective, and due to working memory limitations, writers are seen as capable of integrating only the skills they can cope with at any given moment. As the use of new skills becomes fluent or less demanding of cognitive resources, writers will go on to integrate subsequent skills.

From a socio-cultural perspective, in contrast, the development of L2 literacy is not limited to the acquisition of new skills, as priority is also attributed to learners' social experiences and to the contexts in which these experiences occur (Leontiev 1978). In Parks and Raymond's (2004) study, social interaction in the classroom between Chinese university students in Canada and their NS peers allowed the former to reevaluate their strengths and weaknesses, as well as to modify the idealized conceptions they held of their Canadian peers. Sasaki (2009) looked at the development of goals and strategic actions for writing of two groups of Japanese university EFL students over three and a half years. While the stay-at-home group tended not to engage in actions to improve their writing, the study abroad learners developed L2-related imagined communities that motivated them to improve their texts and to use mediating artifacts such as textbooks, dictionaries and teachers. Similarly, Cumming (2012) found that the engagement with literacy and the goals for personal improvement of a group of at-risk ESL high school students differed from those of highly motivated international students enrolled in ESL courses (Cumming 2006). The former initially rejected the support provided by their tutors while the latter made the most of the opportunities offered to them in the course. The findings of these studies indicate that differences in social and learning contexts are crucial for the development of learners' agency in writing.

5.3 Composing processes and strategies across languages

Most of the available research in this line of inquiry has focused on L2 writers who have developed their L2 writing abilities subsequently to their literacy skills in the L1. Consequently, findings have mainly been presented with the intention of showing how writers' L2 writing competence is related to extant L1 writing abilities in terms of similarities and differences.

Cross-linguistic similarities within writers have been reported, for example, in planning strategies (Armengol-Castells 2001), the problems addressed when formulating texts (Manchón et al. 2009), or in revision strategies (Whalen and Ménard 1995). In one of the few studies that have compared the formulation strategies of fully bilingual learners (four NS of Spanish and four NS of English) who were skilled writers in their two languages, Beare and Bourdages (2007) found that each group showed similar strategy preferences across languages. The Spanish NS tended to generate their L1 and L2 texts by means of translation or assignment reading, while their English counterparts relied more on rereading the already written text for further text generation. Similarities across languages have also been reported with less accomplished writers. Stevenson, Schoonen and De Glopper (2006) analyzed the online revisions made by high school students while writing argumentative texts in Dutch (L1) and English (L2). The results showed that, although in the L2 condition the participants made more linguistic revisions below word or below clause level, the frequencies of distant, conceptual revisions above-clause level were similar across languages, probably as a result of their age or lack of writing experience (Schoonen et al. 2009).

As for differences across languages, findings generally reflect the constraining effect that limited L2 vocabulary and grammar imposes on a wide range of composition processes and strategies, such as the difficulty of handling long stretches of L2 text to embody rhetorical procedures already at writers' disposal in their L1 (see Galbraith 2009), the distribution of writing processes during composition and the way this distribution contributes to text quality (Tillema 2012; van Weijen 2009), the difficulty of sustaining formulation processes (Sasaki and Hirose 1996), the use of more fragmentary (Chenoweth and Hayes 2001) and more on-line revisions of form (Lindgren et al. 2008), the greater attention paid to linguistic concerns at the expense of textual or pragmatic ones (Whalen and Ménard 1995), or the difficulties involved in making strong claims in academic writing (Flowerdew and Li 2009). Individual differences have also been reported as a function of what writers value as good writing, whether knowledge of grammar and lexis – in which case linguistic problems become dominant –, or the acquisition of the discourse of an academic community – in which case the dominant concern is related to finding the right evidence to support arguments rather than grammatical correctness.

The above findings should be understood in connection with a conception of multilingualism as composed of isolated and individual language systems. More recent studies, however, have explored the interaction between knowing several languages (L1, L2 and L3) and writing development in non-native languages over time and have offered evidence of the relationship across languages from different perspectives. Kobayashi and Rinnert (2012) adopted a multicompetence perspective and found that multilingual writers' repertoire of L1 and L2 writing knowledge was dynamic and developed, with experience (Hall, Cheng, and Carlson 2006), from two separate systems into a more integrated one. This overlapping system allowed them to make appropriate choices for the texts they were constructing in order to meet the perceived needs of the reader in the specific language used. Kobayashi and Rinnert (2013) made use of three partially related theoretical frameworks (multicompetence, genre as a social practice and identity) to elucidate the paths taken by a multilingual learner in her development from novice to proficient academic writer across three languages. The most noteworthy finding was that the personal and cultural identities developed by the writer "played an essential role in shaping her perceptions of the three languages and in turn affected her text construction and composing process" (p. 25). Canagarajah (2011) used the notions of translanguaging and codemeshing to account for the ability of a multilingual writer to treat her repertoire of languages and symbolic systems as an integrated system by engaging in recontextualization strategies (to assess the appropriateness of the context and prepare it for her multilingual communication purposes), voice strategies (to communicate her own positioning), interactional strategies (to negotiate meaning with readers) and textualization strategies (to develop effective text dimensions).

5.4 The use of L1 in L2 writing

The mother tongue has been found to be strategically used for planning, formulating and revising, as well as for monitoring or controlling the writing process (Manchón et al. 2007). When planning a text, the L1 has been used for organizing and structuring the information to be conveyed (Woodall 2002). Possibly, as a result of faster access to ideas stored in long-term memory and the richer associations between them, L1 use may result in better essays in terms of content and textual organization, both for topics related and unrelated to L1 culture (Friedlander 1990).

When formulating texts, writers have also been found to address text generation problems by means of L1-based strategies that include restructuring, paraphrasing, generation of synonyms, segmentation of the intended meaning into manageable L2 items or backtranslation (Manchón et al. 2007; Wang 2003). At lower levels of L2 proficiency, the L1 has mainly a compensatory function (e.g., Manchón et al. 2007) and writers appear to use it to obtain cognitive stability when writing in the L2 (Woodall 2002). This is reflected in the higher number of borrowings produced by EFL primary school learners at lower rather than higher grades (Navés et al. 2005) or in the fact that translation as an overall composition strategy seems to diminish as L2 proficiency increases (Sasaki 2000). From being a procedure that, in the initial stages of L2 acquisition, may facilitate the exploration of ideas at the writers' intellectual and cognitive levels, it may, if not used skillfully, prevent them from becoming aware of the lack of equivalence between certain categories of words and discourse patterns across languages

As L2 proficiency develops, writers gain greater control over the language and fluency increases. Recent research has shown that advanced EFL learners use the L1 differently as a function of the cognitive difficulty posed by the writing task (Murphy and Roca de Larios 2010). Higher task complexity results in upgrading L1 lexical searches along the lines of the tenets of the Cognition Hypothesis (Robinson 2011), while compensatory L1 lexical searches remain invariable to the cognitive difficulty of the writing task. This adaptation of lexical searches to task demands illustrates how writers at high levels of L2 proficiency may find it helpful to resort to their mother tongue in order to address higher level concerns and engage in deeper processing (Manchón et al. 2009; van Weijen 2009). Proficiency, however, is not the only factor mediating this strategic use of the L1 in L2 writing. Other factors concerning what is valued and promoted in each specific social context may also come into play (Manchón 2013).

Regarding the revision process, the L1 has been found to help writers evaluate their texts (e.g., Wolfersberger 2003), or check the match between expression and intended meaning (Wang 2003; Wolfersberger 2003). Manchón et al. (2000) have reported how writers back-translate the written text, or even the task assignment itself, to check or improve the relevance of the ideas generated, the correspondence between the plans they produce and their implementation, or the solutions generated for the problems addressed during formulation. Finally, the revision process in the writers' L1 has been shown to take place at different levels of concern including ideational, textual or linguistic (Wang 2003; Wolfersberger 2003; Woodall 2002).

Some studies have also shown that the L1 may have a monitoring function which allows writers to (i) sustain the writing process (Cohen and Brooks-Carson 2001; Cumming 1989); (ii) cope with cognitive overload or working memory constraints when task complexity increases (Cohen and Brooks-Carson 2001; Woodall 2002); or (iii) control the writing process through self-instructions and meta-comments (Woodall 2002). In contrast with the use of the L1 for formulation purposes, this monitoring function of the L1 does not seem to decline with increasing L2 proficiency, possibly as a result of writers' personalities being split, as it were, into two personae: writer and reader. Monitoring would be mainly involved in the reader's role and, consequently, the L1 would allow writers to fulfill this role more easily (Manchón 2013).

6 Future developments

Understanding the multifaceted and interactive nature of literacy abilities in general, and of writing abilities in particular, is only possible if attention is paid both to the micro-levels of cognitive skills as well as to socio-cultural practices in relation to macro-societal structures (Cumming 2013). A methodological correlate of this theoretical stance is that research on L2 writing "can and should mix modes of inquiry where appropriate to overcome the limitations of any single mode and to add breadth and depth to a study" (Silva 2005: 12). With these assumptions in mind and having examined the key issues in the literature on L2 writing processes and strategies, in this section we propose some directions for future development in the hope that they will continue to inform theory and research and help us advance current knowledge.

From a cognitive perspective, one of the main limitations of the available research is that most studies framed in L1 writing models have considered writing as a top-down process whereby predetermined content is either instantiated as words on the page or inhibited from being finally written down due to writers' L2 language difficulties. Consequently, very little is known about how thinking is linked moment by moment with the production of text itself or with the externally represented text as it is produced. In addition to recent attempts at furthering our understanding of translation (Fayol, Alamargot and Berninger 2012; Hayes 2012), a theoretical alternative to this state of affairs would involve the consideration that, in addition to knowledge retrieval, effective writing is the outcome of a knowledge constituting process which consists of the development of the writer's internal disposition towards the topic through the synthesis of content guided by the connections stored in an implicit semantic memory system (Galbraith 2009). These connections are sub-symbolic with the result that the writer can only become aware of what s/he wants to say after the content of the different utterances that shape the knowledge being constituted has been formulated, hopefully with minimal interruption. However, as written texts are produced in bursts, which tend to be smaller in the L2 (Chenoweth and Hayes 2001), it follows that the L2 will arguably alter or reduce writers' personal understanding of the topic in hand as well as their motivation to write. Consequently, one crucial issue for future research to look at is the effect of linguistic fluency and linguistic structure on the writer's ability to constitute their thoughts in L2 writing (Galbraith 2009). For this purpose, more empirical research needs to be conducted on how thinking and text production processes interact on-line in L2 writing.

Task-writing research has so far been greatly influenced by research into speaking tasks. This means that it has generally been more concerned with language learning through writing than with the composing process involved in writing as such (Byrnes and Manchón 2014). However, manipulating tasks characteristics and looking only at outcomes is rather simplistic since, as suggested by Manchón (2014), writers may conceptualize the writing task in different ways. Future research will thus have to look at the "internal dimension" of tasks (Manchón 2014) so as to resituate them in the dynamics of language development that is specific to writing. This approach may help researchers reorder the relationship between task conceptualization, task performance and learning outcomes (Manchón 2014) and enable them to add writer's agency into the mix (Macaro 2014).

Future studies should compare the composition processes of individual writers with different motivational, aptitudinal and working memory profiles, so that the complexity of the interaction between these constructs over time is brought to light (Kormos 2012). For this purpose, two theoretical assumptions might be of value. First, the notion of "variability", as depicted in Dynamic Systems Theory (see Verspoor and Smiskova 2012), might be applied in this context to help researchers understand how individual learners' strategic repertoires become unstable when writers select, invent and discard strategies across time in favour of more efficient ones. Secondly, since different tasks may prompt different clusters of strategies, authors should avoid the a-theoretical and de-contextualized elaboration of new taxonomies of strategies because of their limited value for the field (Manchón et al. 2007). Taxonomies should be as fine-grained and task-specific as possible since this specificity seems to be crucial for exploring writers' individual trajectories (Macaro 2014).

A further challenge for researchers is related to the growing awareness in the field that competency in L2 writing should be understood in more complex terms than the skilled/unskilled distinction directly imported from L1 writing models. Recent conceptualizations of writing competencies as developmental, multifaceted and socially-embedded processes necessarily require methodologies that allow researchers to contemplate L2 writing processes and strategies as emerging from the convergence of learners' states of development, personal histories, sociolinguistic and educational contexts and languages at their disposal (Hornberger 2003). These methodologies should involve decisions on the time scale considered for analysis, the number and type of micro and macro variables to be taken into account, the type of tasks used, or the pertinence and theoretical soundness of the analytical procedures used.

In this context, a promising methodological procedure would involve a re-conceptualization of the notion of problem-space, the unit of analysis explicitly or implicitly used in most cognitive studies of L2 writing. This would be based on the view that writers acquire problem-solving representations and strategies from social interaction with peers, teachers, readers and texts and, consequently, that individual writing is also dialogical in nature (Pomerantz and Kearney 2012). This might involve moving the analysis of think-aloud protocols from a mere information-processing perspective to one based on conversational interaction (Deschambault 2012), which may allow researchers to document how L2 writers develop new authorial voices.

The above concerns need to be fully explored across different contexts and populations. Most research has focused on university undergraduates or postgraduates at advanced levels of L2 proficiency and writing ability, which makes the generalizability and potential application of findings limited. There is thus a need to extend the analyses to younger learners and to less proficient writers, as they are both populations with their own goals and writing practices.

7 Acknowledgement

The analysis of research reported in this chapter is part of the work conducted within two research projects financed by the Spanish Ministerio de Economía y Competitividad (research grant FFI2012–35839) and by Fundación Séneca, the research agency of the Autonomous Government of the Region of Murcia, Spain (research grant 19463/PI/14).

8 Additional sources

Bosher, Susan. 1998. The composing process of three Southeast Asian writers at the post-secondary level: An exploratory study. *Journal of Second Language Writing* 7(2). 205–241.

Cumming, Alister. 1990. Metalinguistic and ideational thinking in second language composing. *Written Communication* 7. 482–511.

Kobayashi, Hiroe and Carol Rinnert. 1992. Effects of first language on second language writing: Translation versus direct composition. *Language Learning* 42. 183–215.

Krapels, Alexandra. 1990. An overview of second language writing process research. In Barbara Kroll (ed.), *Second language writing: Research insights for the classroom*, 37–56. New York: Cambridge University Press.

Porte, Graeme. 1997. The etiology of poor second language writing: The influence of perceived teacher preferences on second language revision strategies. *Journal of Second Language Writing* 6. 61–78.

Roca de Larios, Julio, Rosa M. Manchón, and Liz Murphy. 2006. Generating text in native and foreign language writing: A temporal analysis of problemsolving formulation processes. *The Modern Language Journal* 90. 100–114.

Roca de Larios, Julio, Rosa M. Manchón, Liz Murphy, and Javier Marín. 2008. The foreign language writer's strategic behaviour in the allocation of time to writing processes. *Journal of Second Language Writing* 17. 30–47.

Sengupta, Sima. 2000. An investigation into the effects of revision strategy instruction on L2 secondary school learners. *System* 28. 97–113.

Wang, Lurong. 2003. Switching to first language among writers with differing second-language proficiency. *Journal of Second Language Writing* 12. 347–375.

Wang, Wenyu and Qiufang Wen 2002. L1 use in the L2 composing process: An exploratory study of 16 Chinese EFL writers. *Journal of Second Language Writing* 11. 225–246.

9 References

Agustín Llach, María Pilar. 2010. Lexical gap-filling mechanisms in language writing. *System* 38(4). 529–538.

Akyel, Ayse. 1994. First language use in EFL writing: Planning in Turkish vs. planning in English. *International Journal of Applied Linguistics* 4(2). 169–196.

Alamargot, Denis and Lucile Chanquoy. 2001. *Through the models of writing*. Dordrecht: Kluwer Academic Publishers.

Armengol-Castells, Lourdes. 2001. Text-generating strategies of three multilingual writers: a protocol-based study. *Language Awareness.* 10(2–3). 91–106.

Beare, Sophie and Johanne Bourdages. 2007. Skilled writers' generating strategies in L1 and L2: an exploratory study. In Mark Torrance, Luuk van Waes and David Galbraith (eds.), *Writing and cognition: Research and applications*, 151–161. Amsterdam: Elsevier

Bereiter, Carl and Marlene Scardamalia. 1987. *The psychology of written composition*. Hillsdale, NJ: Lawrence Erlbaum Associates.

Byrnes, Heidi and Rosa M. Manchón (eds.). 2014. *Task-based language learning – insights from and for L2 writing*. Amsterdam: John Benjamins.

Canagarajah, Suresh. 2011. Codemeshing in academic writing: Identifying teachable strategies of translanguaging *Modern Language Journal* 95(3). 401–417.

Chenoweth, Ann and John Hayes. 2001. Fluency in writing: Generating text in L1 and L2. *Written Communication* 18(1). 80–98.

Cohen, Andrew and Amanda Brooks-Carson. 2001. Research on direct vs. translated writing: Students' strategies and their results. *Modern Language Journal* 85(2). 169–188.

Cumming, Alister. 1989. Writing Expertise and Second-Language Proficiency. *Language Learning* 39(1). 81–135.

Cumming, Alister (ed.). 2006. *Goals for ESL writing improvement in ESL and university courses*. Amsterdam: John Benjamins.

Cumming, Alister. 2012. Goal theory and second-language writing development, two ways. In Rosa M. Manchón (ed.), *L2 writing development: Multiple perspectives*, 135–164. Boston/ Berlin: Mouton de Gruyter.

Cumming, Alister. 2013. Multiple dimensions of academic language and literacy development. *Language Learning* 63(1). 130–152.

Cummins, Jim. 1980. The cross-lingual dimensions of language proficiency: Implications for bilingual education and the optimal age issue. *TESOL Quarterly* 14(2). 175–187.

Deschambault, Ryan. 2012. Thinking-aloud as talking-in-interaction: Reinterpreting how L2 lexical inferencing gets done. *Language Learning* 62(1). 266–301.

Ellis, Rod and Fangyuan Yuan. 2004. The effects of planning on fluency, complexity and accuracy in second language narrative writing. *Studies in Second Language Acquisition* 26(1). 59–84.

Ericsson, Anders and Simon Herbert. 1980. *Protocol analysis: Verbal reports as data*. Cambridge, MA: MIT Press.

Fayol, Michel, Denis Alamargot, and Virginia Berninger. 2012. *Translation of thought to written text while composing*. New York: Psychology Press.

Flower, Linda and John Hayes. 1981. A cognitive process theory of writing. *College Composition and Communication* 32(4). 365–387.

Flowerdew, John and Yongyan Li. 2009. The globalization of scholarship: Studying Chinese scholars writing for international publication. In Rosa M. Manchón (ed.), *Writing in foreign language contexts: Learning, teaching, and research*, 156–182. Clevedon, UK: Multilingual Matters.

Friedlander, Alexander. 1990. Composing in English: Effects of a first language on writing in English as a second language. In Barbara Kroll (ed.), *Second language writing: Research insights for the classroom*, 109–125. Cambridge: Cambridge University Press.

Galbraith, David. 2009. Cognitive models of writing. *German as a Foreign Language* (2–3). 7–22.

Gentil, Guillaume. 2011. A biliteracy agenda for genre research. *Journal of Second Language Writing* 20(1). 6–23.

Hall, Chris. 1990. Managing the complexity of revising across languages. *TESOL Quarterly* 24(1). 43–60.

Hall, Joan Kelly, An Cheng, and Matthew Carlson T. 2006. Reconceptualizing multicompetence as a theory of language knowledge. *Applied Linguistics* 27(2). 220–240.

Hayes, John R. 1996. A new framework for understanding cognition and affect in writing. In Michael Levy and Sarah Ransdell (eds.), *The science of writing: Theories, methods, individual differences and applications*, 1–27. Mahwah, NJ: Lawrence Erlbaum Associates.

Hayes, John R. 2012. Modeling and remodeling writing. *Written Communication* 29(3). 369–388.

Hornberger, Nancy (ed.). 2003. *Continua of biliteracy: An ecological framework for educational policy, research, and practice in multilingual settings*. Clevendon, UK: Multilingual Matters.

Jones, Stan and Jacqueline Tetroe. 1987. Composing in a second language. In A. Matsuhashi (ed.), *Writing in real time: Modeling production processes*, 34–57. Norwood, NJ: Ablex.

Kellogg, Ronald T. 1990. Effectiveness of prewriting strategies as a function of task demands. *American Journal of Psychology* 103(3). 327–342.

Kobayashi, Hiroe and Carol Rinnert. 2012. Understanding L2 writing development from a multicompetence perspective: Dynamic repertoires of knowledge and text construction. In Rosa M. Manchón, (ed.), *L2 writing development: Multiple perspectives*, 101–134. Walter de Gruyter.

Kobayashi, Hiroe and Carol Rinnert. 2013. L1/L2/L3 writing development: Longitudinal case study of a Japanese multicompetent writer. *Journal of Second Language Writing* 22(1). 4–33.

Kormos, Judit. 2011. Task complexity and linguistic and discourse features of narrative writing performance. *Journal of Second Language Writing* 20(2). 148–161.

Kormos, Judit. 2012. The role of individual differences in L2 writing. *Journal of Second Language Writing* 21(4). 390–403

Lay, Nancy. 1982. Composing processes of adult ESL learners: A case study. *TESOL Quarterly* 16(3). 406–407.

Lei, Xiao. 2008. Exploring a sociocultural approach to writing strategy research: Mediated actions in writing activities. *Journal of Second Language Writing* 17(4). 217–236

Leki, Iona, Alister Cumming and Tony Silva. 2008. *A synthesis of research on second language writing in English: 1980–2005*. New York: Routledge.

Leontiev, Alexei. N. 1978. *Activity. Consciousness. Personality*. Englewood Cliffs, NJ: Prentice Hall.

Levelt, Willem. 1989. *Speaking: From intention to articulation*. Cambridge, MA: MIT Press.

Lindgren, Eva, Kristyan Spelman Miller, and Kirk Sullivan. 2008. Development of fluency and revision in L1 and L2 writing in Swedish high school years eight and nine. *ITL International Journal of Applied Linguistics* 156. 133–151.

Macaro, Ernesto. 2014. Reframing task performance. The relationship between tasks, strategic behavior and linguistic knowledge in writing. In Heidi Byrnes and Rosa M. Manchón (eds.), *Task-based language learning-Insights for and from L2 writing*, 53–78. Amsterdam: John Benjamins.

Manchón, Rosa M. 2001. Trends in the conceptualizations of second language composing strategies: A critical analysis. *International Journal of English Studies* 1(2). 47–70.

Manchón, Rosa M. 2013. Writing. In François Grosjean and Ping Li. *The psycholinguistics of bilingualism*, 100–116. London: Wiley-Blackwell.

Manchón, Rosa M. and Julio Roca de Larios. 2011. Writing to learn in FL contexts: Exploring learners' perceptions of the language learning potential of L2 writing. In Rosa M. Manchón (ed.), *Learning-to-write and writing-to-learn in an additional language*, 181–207. Amsterdam: John Benjamins.

Manchón, Rosa M., Julio Roca de Larios, and Liz Murphy. 2000. An approximation to the study of backtracking in L2 writing. *Learning and Instruction* 10(1). 13–35.

Manchón, Rosa M., Julio Roca de Larios, and Liz Murphy. 2007. A review of writing strategies: Focus on conceptualizations and impact of the first language. In Andrew Cohen and Ernesto Macaro (eds.), *Language learner strategies: Thirty years of research and practice*, 229–250. Oxford, UK: Oxford University Press.

Manchón, Rosa M., Julio Roca de Larios, and Liz Murphy. 2009. The temporal dimension and problem–solving nature of foreign language composing processes. Implications for theory. In Rosa M. Manchón (ed.), *Writing in foreign language contexts: Learning, teaching and research*, 102–124. Clevedon, UK: Multilingual Matters

McCutchen, Deborah. 2000. Knowledge, processing, and working memory: Implications for a theory of writing. *Educational psychologist* 35(1). 13–23.

McMullen, Maram. 2009. Using language learning strategies to improve the writing skills of Saudi EFL students. Will it really work? *System* 37(7). 418–433.

Murphy, Liz and Julio Roca de Larios. 2010. Searching for words: one strategic use of the mother tongue by advanced Spanish EFL writers. *Journal of Second Language Writing* 19(2). 61–81.

Navés, Teresa, Immaculada Miralpeix, and M. Luz Celaya. 2005. Who transfers more … and what? Crosslinguistic influence in relation to school grade and language dominance in EFL. *International Journal of Multilingualism* 2(2). 113–134.

Nicolás Conesa, Florentina, Julio Roca de Larios, and Yvette Coyle. 2014. Development of EFL students' mental models of writing and their effects on performance. *Journal of Second Language Writing* 24(1). 1–19.

Norton, Bonny. 2000. *Identity and language learning*. Harlow, England: Pearson Education.

Olsen, S. 1999. Errors and compensatory strategies: A study of grammar and vocabulary in texts written by Norwegian learners of English. *System* 27(2). 191–205.

Ong, Justina. 2013. Discovery of ideas in second language writing task environment. *System* 41(3). 529–542.

Ong, Justina. 2014. How do planning time and task conditions affect metacognitive processes of L2 writers? *Journal of Second Language Writing* 23. 17–30.

Ong, Justina and Lawrence Zhang. 2010. Effects of task complexity on the fluency and lexical complexity in EFL students' argumentative writing. *Journal of Second Language Writing* 19(4). 218–233.

Ortega, Lourdes and Joan Carson. 2010. Multicompetence, social context, and L2 writing research praxis. In Tony Silva and Paul Kei Matsuda (eds.), *Practicing theory in second language writing*, 48–71. West Lafayette, IN: Parlor Press.

Oxford, Rebecca L. 1990. *Language learning strategies*. Alabama: Heinle and Heinle.

Parks, Susan and Patricia M. Raymond. 2004. Strategy use by nonnative English-Speaking students in an MBA program: Not business as usual! *The Modern Language Journal* 88(3). 374–389.

Pomerantz, Anne and Erin Kearney. 2012. Beyond 'write – talk – revise – (repeat)': Using narrative to understand one multilingual student's interactions around writing. *Journal of Second Language Writing* 21(3). 221–238

Raimes, Ann. 1987. Language proficiency, writing ability, and composing strategies: A study of ESL college student writers. *Language Learning* 37(4). 439–467.

Riazi, Abdolmehdi. 1997. Acquiring disciplinary literacy: A social-cognitive analysis of text production and learning among Iranian graduate students of education. *Journal of Second Language Writing* 6(2). 105–137.

Robinson, Peter. 2011. Task-based language learning: A Review of issues. *Language Learning*, 61(s1). 1–36.

Roca de Larios, Julio. 2013. Second language writing as a psycholinguistic locus for L2 production and learning. *Journal of Second Language Writing* 22(4). 444–445.

Roca de Larios, Julio, Liz Murphy, and Javier Marín. 2002. A critical examination of L2 writing process Research. In Sarah Ransdell and Marie-Laure Barbier (eds.), *New directions for research in L2 writing*, 11–47. Amsterdam: Kluwer Academic Publisher.

Sasaki, Miyuki. 2000. Toward an empirical model of EFL writing processes: An exploratory study. *Journal of Second Language Writing* 9(3). 259–291.

Sasaki, Miyuki. 2004. A multiple-data analysis of the 3.5-year development of EFL student writers. *Language Learning* 54(3). 525–582.

Sasaki, Miyuki. 2009. Changes in EFL students' writing over 3.5 years: A socio-cognitive account. In Rosa M. Manchón (ed.), *Writing in foreign language contexts: Learning, teaching, and researching*, 49–76. Clevedon, UK: Multilingual Matters.

Sasaki, Miyuki and Keiko Hirose. 1996. Explanatory variables for EFL students' expository writing. *Language Learning* 46(1). 137–174.

Schaeffer, Benson. 1975. *Skill integration during cognitive development. Studies in long-term memory*. New York: Wiley.

Schoonen, Robert, Patrick Snellings, Marie Stevenson, and Amos van Gelderen. 2009. Towards a blueprint of the foreign language writer: The linguistic and cognitive demands of foreign language writing. In Rosa M. Manchón (ed.), *Writing in foreign language contexts: Learning, teaching, and research*, 77–101. Clevedon, UK: Multilingual Matters.

Silva, Tony. 1993. Toward an understanding of the distinct nature of second language writing: The ESL research and its implication. *TESOL Quarterly,* 27(4). 657–677.

Silva, Tony. 2005. On the philosophical bases of inquiry in second language writing: Metaphysics, inquiry paradigms, and the intellectual zeitgeist. In Paul Kei Matsuda and Tony Silva (eds.), *Second language writing research: Perspectives on process of knowledge construction*, 3–15. Mahwah, NJ: Lawrence Erlbaum Associates.

Skehan, P. 2009. Modelling second language performance: Integrating complexity, accuracy, fluency, and lexis. *Applied Linguistics* 30(4). 510–532.

Stevenson, Marie, Robert Schoonen, and Kees D. Glopper. 2006. Revising in two languages: A multi-dimensional comparison of online writing revisions in L1 and FL. *Journal of Second Language Writing* 15(3). 201–233.

Swain, Merrill and Sharon Lapkin. 1995. Problems in output and the cognitive processes they generate: A step towards second language learning. *Applied Linguistics* 16(3). 371–391.

Takagaki, Toshiyuki. 2003. The revision patterns and intentions in L1 and L2 by Japanese writers: A case study. *TESL Canada Journal* 21(1). 22–38

Tardy, Christine. 2009. *Building genre knowledge*. West Lafayette, IN: Parlor Press.

Thomas, Margaret. 1994. Assessment of L2 proficiency in second language acquisition research. *Language Learning* 44(2). 307–336.

Tillema, Marion. 2012. *Writing in first and second language: empirical studies on text quality and writing processes*. Utrecht: LOT Dissertation Series.

van den Bergh, Huub and Gert Rijlaarsdam. 1996. The dynamics of composing: Modeling writing process data. In Michael Levy and Sarah Ransdell (eds.), *The science of writing: Theories, methods, individual differences, and applications*, 207–232. Mahwah, NJ: Lawrence Erlbaum.

van Gelderen, Amos, Ron Oostdam, and Erik Van Schooten. 2011. Does foreign language writing benefit from increased lexical fluency? Evidence from a classroom experiment. *Language Learning* 61(1). 281–321.

van Weijen, Daphne. 2009. *Writing processes, text quality, and task effects; Empirical studies in first and second language writing*. Utrecht: LOT Dissertation Series.

Verspoor, Marjorljin and Hana Smiskova. 2012. Foreign language writing development from a dynamic writing-based perspective. In Rosa María Manchón (ed.), *L2 writing development: Multiple perspectives*, 17–46. Berlin/Boston: De Gruyter Mouton.

Victori, Mia. 1999. An analysis of writing knowledge in EFL composing: A case study of two effective and two less effective writers. *System* 27(4). 537–555.

Wang, Lurong. 2003. Switching to first language among writers with differing second-language proficiency. *Journal of Second Language Writing* 12(4). 347–375.

Whalen, Karen and Nathan Ménard. 1995. L1 and L2 writers' strategic and linguistic knowledge: A model of multiple-level discourse processing. *Language Learning,* 45(3). 381–418.

Woodall, Billy R. 2002. Language-switching: Using the first language while writing in a second language. *Journal of Second Language Writing* 11(1). 7–28.

Wolfersberger, Mark. 2003. L1 to L2 writing process and strategy transfer: A look at lower proficiency writers. *TESL-EJ: Teaching English as a Second or Foreign Language,* 7(2). 1–15.

Zimmermann, Rüdiger. 2000. L2 writing subprocesses: A model of formulating and empirical findings. *Learning and Instruction* 10(1). 73–99.

Charlene Polio and Ji-Hyun Park

13 Language development in second language writing

1 Defining language development

A recent edited volume by Rosa Manchón (2012) takes a broad view of writing development. Contributors to the volume examined a variety of features, including vocabulary, morphosyntax, and language chunks, that might change in writers' texts over time. In addition, some of the authors did not examine writers' texts, but instead focused on the writers themselves and studied the development of their goals (Cumming 2012) and genre knowledge (Tardy 2012). Similarly, other longitudinal studies have studied changes in the writing process (e.g., Sasaki 2004) or metacognitive awareness (e.g., Negretti 2012).

This chapter takes a more narrow focus by considering only language development despite Norris and Manchón's (2012) caveat that writing development should not be reduced to linguistic features. Indeed, nonlinguistic areas are important because they probably affect and are affected by linguistic development. Furthermore, there is widespread agreement that language learning, particularly written language learning, is a social phenomenon, even among those who isolate linguistic variables in their research. The interplay of nonlinguistic variables and language cannot be understated. To take a specific example highlighted by Norris and Manchón, Cumming (2012) in a longitudinal study of secondary school at-risk students in Canada, concluded that goals both follow and determine language development. Nevertheless, the reality is that much of the research does focus on only language development and space does not permit providing a broader overview.

In defining language development, we limit this review to studies that examined vocabulary, morphology, syntax, and formulaic language with regard to complexity, accuracy, frequency, and emergence. We include also fluency because fluency is a measure of how quickly one can access and produce linguistic structures and thus is generally measured by number of words produced in a given time.

Defining linguistic features is relatively easy, but defining development is not. We have chosen for this chapter to define it as *change over an extended period of time* leaving open for the moment any specific length of time. *Change* can also be problematic in that it usually means more targetlike production (e.g., greater accuracy) but it can also mean greater complexity or more frequent or fluent use of a structure. Development often coincides with increased writing quality (as judged by evaluators) but it may not. Consider for example the increase in the use a structure to the point of overuse. This would indicate development but not better writing. Development in this chapter is nearly the same as second language (L2) acquisition in the context of writing. The only way it might differ is in the case of change away from a target, as in the case of overuse.

We begin with an historical overview of the origins of the research on writing development, but we note that language development in writing is a relatively new area of inquiry. This is followed by a section on recent studies of language development in writing and then a discussion of methodological issues. We end with directions for future research. At the outset, we should consider why we discuss research that tracks linguistic development or what the ultimate goal of such research is. Ideally, we would like to find commonalities in how learners' language develops, regardless of their L1s and L2s, as they learn to write. Such findings would have implications for measuring linguistic variables in intervention studies as well as for instruction and assessment. Given the influence of nonlinguistic variables, this is likely an unobtainable goal, so instead, we wish here to explore what themes emerge from the wide variety of research on language development, addressed in the last section, and where we might proceed from here.

2 Historical overview of the origins of the research covered

Early studies of second language acquisition attempted to describe language development by charting certain features in learner language such as negation (Schumann 1979), question formation (Meisel, Clahsen, and Pienemann 1981), relative clause development (Gass 1979), and English morphemes (Krashen 1982). Most of these studies focused on oral development with a few exceptions in the area of morpheme-order studies. Dulay, Burt, and Krashen (1982) reviewed four studies comparing writing and speaking and found that the developmental sequences were "virtually identical to those observed in oral production" (p. 211). Larsen-Freeman (1975) examined students' performance across different tasks and found some differences between writing and speaking, but the writing task consisted of filling blanks and not text production. Morpheme-order studies did not endure because of various methodological and theoretical concerns (e.g., Gregg 1984; Huebner 1983) and little further attention was given to writing development.

Other studies attempted to describe language development through a functional approach, specifically looking at how learners expressed certain functions (e.g., Sato 1990) or how they used certain forms (e.g., Duff 1993). A large scale study known as the European Science Foundation study attempted to describe longitudinal development of grammar across several languages in uninstructed contexts (Klein and Perdue 1992). Yet none of these functional studies considered written language. One of the few researchers that has conducted any type of form-function analysis on written language is Kathleen Bardovi-Harlig. She has completed several studies (summarized in Bardovi-Harlig 2000) examining learners' tense-aspect systems with some of the data coming from written narratives. In addition, Sasaki (1990), in a cross-sectional study of Japanese learners of English, examined a progression from topic-comment to subject-predicate structures in students' writing. While these studies help us understand how certain structures work in learner language, they did not isolate any characteristics specific to language development in writing. In fact, in Sasaki's study, she told the students to write as many sentences as possible so that they would not monitor their writing, essentially then making it more like speaking.

In 1998, Wolfe-Quintero, Ingaki, and Kim published a review of studies that used measures of accuracy, complexity, fluency, and lexical development to assess writing development. This marked a turning point for the field of L2 writing in that it was one of the first major works on written language development. They defined language development as "characteristics of a learner's output that reveal some point or stage along a developmental continuum" (p. 2) but this definition raised the issue of what a developmental continuum is; thus, their definition of development is perhaps better explained by describing their methodology. They examined studies that in some way correlated specific measures of accuracy, fluency, grammatical complexity, or lexical complexity with general measures of language or writing proficiency as well as studies that showed change in any of the measures over time. These latter studies included cross-sectional studies, where, for example, students were divided by an in-house placement test, as well as longitudinal studies where students wrote at different points in time. Although advances have been made in using some of the measures to track development, most notably in the area of grammatical and lexical complexity, this synthesis still serves as an important resource.

Finally, much interest has been shown over the years in changing the course of development or in speeding it up through some type of treatment or intervention. This research has focused mostly on linguistic accuracy and much less so on other aspects of writing such as complexity, fluency, or lexical development or on how these subsystems interact. The intervention most often studied was, and probably still is, some type of corrective feedback on language. Although there was an explosion of studies after Truscott (1996) claimed that written error correction was ineffective and possibly harmful, a significant number of studies had been completed prior to 1996 as well. Some of these studies, including Semke (1984), Robb, Ross, and Shortreed (1986), and Kepner (1991), were longitudinal. None of the studies found any differences in accuracy among the groups related to feedback presence or type, but Robb et al. also measured complexity and fluency and found a few differences. Because fluency, accuracy, and complexity are related, examining fluency and complexity are essential if one is going to make claims about the effect of an intervention on development.

These studies suggest that there has been no one dominant theory of language learning drawn from. The early studies of oral language development did quite explicitly situate themselves within specific theories. Schumann (1979), Meisel, Clahsen, and Pienemann (1981), Gass (1979), and Krashen (1982), were all arguing for specific learning mechanisms or factors in SLA. The two early studies of written language development (Bardovi-Harlig 2000 and Sasaki 1990) drew on functional approaches to language, but functional approaches do not necessarily predict stages of development. The work of Wolfe-Quintero et al. (1998) did not draw on any theory but rather used psychometric approaches to validate measures that might indicate development. The section below on recent studies will show that although there is sometimes reference to specific theories of language or language learning, the majority of the studies are not motivated by a specific theory.

3 Recent studies of written language development

This section reports only on research published in 2000 or later. The first section on descriptive studies covers research that focuses on specific grammatical features, specific constructs, specific contexts, and modality differences. In the next section, on theory-based approaches, we include studies conducted within multilingual approaches and dynamic systems theories approaches. Despite being more theory based than the studies in the first section, these studies are descriptive as well. We end with a discussion of experimental intervention studies.

3.1 Descriptive studies

3.1.1 Focus on specific grammatical features

Some studies that examine writing are studies of second language acquisition that use written language as a data source; the extent to which they emphasize the written modality varies. For example, Han (2000) followed two Chinese students in their development of the English passive in their writing. Using a variety of writing tasks completed over two years, she traced the development from pseudo-passive (e.g., *The package have not received.*) to passive. Bardovi-Harlig (2002) collected journals, compositions, essay exams, and narratives from 16 instructed ESL learners over the course of a year. She examined the emergence and subsequent use of *will* vs. *be going to* in the oral and written narratives. She found that *will* emerged first. *Be going to* was less frequent but was used by several students in the formula, *I am going to write about.* Byrnes and Sinicrope (2008) studied the longitudinal development of relative clauses among 23 English learners of German. They showed that development did not follow the pattern predicted by the Keenan and Comrie's (1977) noun phrase accessibility hierarchy, which has been shown to influence oral language acquisition (e.g., Doughty 1991).

Boss (2008) examined 15 Australian students studying German over three years. The focus of her study was German verb morphology. She conducted a detailed study looking at the frequency of different verb forms (*to be*, modals, and regular and irregular lexical verbs) and how they were conjugated in the present, present perfect, and preterite. Although her study was not conducted within a processability framework per se, she was able to compare her findings to those of a study done by Pienemann (1998) on oral language. She found similar results with the exception that past participles of irregular verbs were not acquired as early.

Byrnes (2009) examined grammatical metaphor, or nominalizations, in the writing of English university students studying German. Nominalizations are an important feature in systemic functional linguistics, and complexity in writing is related to their use. Byrnes cited Halliday who said, "Written language tends to display a high degree of grammatical metaphor, and this is perhaps its single most distinctive characteristic" (Halliday 2002: 347). She studied the writing of 14 students over three levels (levels 2–4) of German classes and found a marked increase in nominalization between levels 3 and 4.

These studies differ in the extent to which they emphasize the written modality. Han (2000), for example, did not mention the effect of modality on the acquisition of the passive. Bardovi-Harlig (2002), on the other hand, talked about the importance of using data from more than one modality. She said:

> Examining written and oral production adds depth to the study of formulaic use. Through the study of written texts we see that formulas can be used to increase fluency in different modes, illustrating how some learners may learn discourse structure for compositions. Learners who used going to write may have enjoyed not only a grammatical advantage but also a rhetorical advantage in that the use of the formula at the beginning of a composition or journal entry may have freed planning time for the propositional content of the text (p. 197).

Both Boss (2008) and Brynes and Sinicrope (2008) were able to compare the results of their research to previous studies of oral language. Boss found mostly similar results to work done within a processability approach, but some differences. This is particularly useful information because Pienemann's processability theory has focused on oral language and whether or not it is applicable to writing is an open question (see Polio 2012, for further discussion). Brynes and Sinicrope's study is also important because the noun phrase accessibility hierarchy has been well attested in oral language. If differences in writing are found, this could imply that oral and written language are not produced in the same way.

Byrnes (2009) is unique in that it examines a feature probably not found much in oral language. It emphasizes that writing is not written down speech and that we may not be able to analyze written language in terms of the same features that we might analyze in oral language.

3.1.2 Focus on specific constructs

Some descriptive studies do not focus on one specific feature but on diverse areas of language such as spelling, complexity, fluency, or lexical development. It is interesting, however, that many of the studies come to similar conclusions. Nassaji (2007) followed a six-year old Persian speaker over the course of four years as he learned English spelling. Nassaji classified the spelling errors according to six stages of spelling development and found that although the learner progressed through the stages, he often made errors from both the higher and lower stages and that there was variability even in the use of a single word. Although spelling might be considered to be a minor part of writing, Nassaji drew a conclusion that is echoed in other studies. He stated:

> While these findings provide evidence that the child's spelling behaviour showed a progressive trend, they do not show that one simple behaviour in the early stages of development was always replaced with more sophisticated ones in later stages. Thus, they are not consistent with an invariable stagelike view or the view which proposes that "a child's first step in spelling is to adopt a phonetic spelling strategy" and that children always go forward along their developmental path not backward [...] However, they are consistent with a view that considers development as a variable and multifaceted process and one that involves gradual and continuous changes in frequencies of multiple ways of doing and thinking [...] (p. 92).

Vyatkina (2012) examined development in the writing complexity of English speakers learning German at the university level. She collected data at 19 points over four semesters. Although the data were collected over two years, the student groups changed, so effectively, the study was cross-sectional. Vyatkina also followed two individual students. She measured four types of complexity (general, clausal, coordination and subordination, and lexicogrammatical variety) using six different measures. She correlated changes in scores with time and was able to compare the cohorts' results with those of the two individuals. She found a general increase in most of the measures from both the cross-sectional as well as the longitudinal data. The two individuals followed the overall trend of the cohorts, but they did differ from one another in the paths they took.

Gunnarsson (2012) studied five Swedish students learning French over 30 months using three different types of writing tasks. She examined how fluency, accuracy, and complexity developed and the relationships among the three constructs. With only five participants who wrote very small amounts, the results of this study should be interpreted cautiously, but some of the results were interesting. Although no relationship between fluency and complexity, or between complexity and accuracy was found, there was a trade-off relationship between fluency and accuracy but only for certain, less complex structures. In sum, the relationships were complex and, as with Nassaji (2007) and Vyatkina (2012), the results can be related to dynamic system theory, discussed below.

3.1.3 Focus on specific instructional contexts

In the area of writing development, a relatively large number of studies have examined development within a specific instructional context. Several focus on study abroad students (see Sasaki, this volume) while others document development in a certain type of language course. Serrano, Tragant, and Llanes (2012) and Muñoz (2010) followed students writing abroad. Serrano et al. followed 14 Spanish-speaking learners of English collecting both oral and written language. They collected data at three points: at the beginning of the students' stay, about three months later, and then about five months later. Measures of fluency, syntactic complexity, lexical complexity, and accuracy were used on both the oral and written data. Although there was improvement after five months on all measures in both modalities, except for oral syntactic complexity, improvement in writing did not occur from time 1 to time 2 as it did with speaking. They made the point that in a study abroad context, the two skills did not develop at the same speed. Muñoz (2010) looked at a very different context abroad, which she termed *stay abroad*. She studied two Catalan-Spanish speaking children, 11 and 14-year old siblings, who moved to an English-speaking country with their parents, over a year. She calculated gains in the two children's writing in terms of fluency, structural complexity, lexical diversity, and accuracy. First, like Larsen-Freeman (2006), she noted much intra-learner variability, but unlike Larsen-Freeman, she did not keep the topic or conditions of writing constant. Because of the variability and the lack of control for topic, it's difficult to draw conclusion, but she found more sustained gains in accuracy than in the other measures.

Benevento and Storch (2011) studied 15 high school students in French classes in Australia. They collected three essays written over the course of six months and analyzed the essays for accuracy, complexity, overall quality, and the use of chunks. They found that despite an improvement in overall quality and use of connectors, an increase in clauses per T-unit was not sustained. Furthermore, although instructors emphasized accuracy, there was no improvement. With regard to the use of chunks, there was a decrease. This runs contrary to Verspoor and Smiskova (2012), discussed below, who found an increase in the use of chunks, but such a difference could be due to differences in proficiency level or the different length of the studies. Yasuda (2011) studied 70 Japanese students studying English writing in a genre-based class that focused on email writing. Seventy students wrote from counterbalanced prompts before and after 15 weeks of instruction. The pre- and post-test emails were measured for three global constructs on an analytic scale, as well as lexical diversity, fluency, and lexical sophistication as measured by use of targeted chunks. Students improved on all measures except lexical diversity. Because of different approaches to tracking development, however, cross-study comparisons cannot be made, but we return to some of the conclusions drawn in these studies below.

3.1.4 Focus on modality

We know that students have different competencies in different modalities and that these competencies can be related to their background, instruction, or goals. For example, heritage learners often have weaker written skills compared to their oral skills (e.g., Sohn and Shin 2007). In addition, they have weaker metalinguistic knowledge compared to nonheritage adult learners (Bowles 2011; Montrul and Per-piñán 2011), which could adversely affect editing skills, for example. Yet we know little about the relationship between speaking and writing development from a longitudinal perspective.

Several authors have suggested that writing can be a place for learners to test out structures, so to speak, before using them in oral language. Harklau (2002) in an ethnographic study of ESL learners provided such examples, and Williams (2012) argued that writing may propel oral development. Empirical evidence, how-ever, is limited. Kuiken and Vedder (2012) reviewed six studies that examined grammatical complexity, lexical complexity, and/or accuracy on oral and written tasks. The results showed that students generally performed better on writing for grammatical and lexical complexity, but not accuracy. In some cases, there was no difference. The studies were conducted with foreign language learners, who may have stronger written skills, so these results are not surprising. Nevertheless, only one study (Bulté and Housen 2009), was longitudinal, and they found that develop-ment was not parallel in the two modalities on a variety of lexical measures. One of the few longitudinal studies comparing writing and speaking development was conducted by Weissberg (2000) who followed five adult Spanish speakers learning English over 16 weeks. He collected data using a variety of written and spoken tasks to determine when various morphosyntactic structures appeared. For four of the five participants, most structures appeared first in writing. However, in addi-tion to individual differences, different grammatical structures behaved differently. For example, irregular verb forms appeared first in speaking but regular past ap-peared first in writing.

Finally, the Byrnes and Sinicrope (2008) and Boss (2008) studies discussed above used only written data. Because they studied phenomena that have been well described in the literature, they were able to make comparisons to oral lan-guage. Of course, every study uses different populations, so cross-study compari-sons can be risky, but they allow us to form hypotheses about differences in writing and speaking development.

3.2 Theory-based approaches

3.2.1 Focus on multilingualism

Multilingualism is not a unified theory, but several researchers have argued for a multilingual approach to studying second language learning explaining that learners work between languages and that the two (or more) languages form a system. In other words, there are not two monolingual systems, but one integrated system in which multilinguals can move across languages (see Chapter 17, this volume). This moving among languages has been called *translanguaging* and has been studied in the written context by Suresh Canagarajah (2011a, 2011b). His work focuses less on features of writing discussed above and more so on strategies and the reasons that writers mix codes. His study (Canagarajah 2011a) of a Saudi Arabian student over a semester detailed how she used Arabic in her English writing, and he included some examples of linguistic choices. He found that sometimes she made reasoned choices about including Arabic phrases, choosing what we consider nonidiomatic phrases, and other times she made what she called errors indicating that she did not have control over these features. Canagarajah suggested that her choices became more effective over time.

A related approach is taken by Kobayshi and Rinnert (2012, 2013). Their studies are framed within multicompetence theory. Drawing on Cook's (2003, 2008) work, they developed a model of text construction for multilingual writers. Although their approach is holistic, within their construct of "repertoire of knowledge" (Kobayashi and Rinnert 2012: 104) they include various components including linguistic knowledge of the L1 and L2.

Kobayashi and Rinnert (2012) studied Japanese students writing in English who had studied abroad and returned. Much of their research focused on discourse features of the writing but with regard to language, they also found bidirectional transfer of discourse markers. Kobayashi and Rinnert (2013) presented a 2.5 year case study of a Japanese woman writing in English, Japanese, and Chinese. They looked at linguistic development in Japanese and English by measuring fluency, sentence length, and lexical diversity. One particularly interesting finding was the negative effect of studying in Australia on her Japanese fluency, but although she wrote less fluently, she wrote longer sentences. Her English fluency increased quickly while studying in Australia.

In sum, very few studies of learning to write in more than one language at a time or on bidirectional influence have been conducted, and those that exist are mostly case studies focusing more on process and rhetorical structure. Furthermore, it is impossible to generalize because people write in different languages for different purposes and different audiences. It is difficult to predict what influence such research will have on further studies of writing development at this point.

3.2.2 Dynamic usage-based approaches

Most of the above studies are not explicitly couched in a particular theory of second language acquisition, but we can see that Bardovi-Harlig (2002) takes a usage-based approach by considering form-function relationships and the role of formulaic language. Usage-based acquisition is a somewhat broad term that emphasizes learning through language use and meaning making; there is not an innate language acquisition faculty. Usage-based studies can draw on different linguistic theories such as systemic functional, discourse functional, and cognitive linguistics.

Dynamic systems approaches, a subset of usage-based approaches, have become more popular and brought to the forefront by Diane Larsen-Freeman (e.g., 2006, 2012) in SLA. In 2006, she outlined some of the tenets of a dynamic systems approach. She emphasized both variability within individuals as well as variation among learners. Indeed, variability, which can include different forms for the same meaning, is needed for a system to develop. In addition, learners' environments with regard to input and social aspects of language learning are important influences on development and can causes variation among learners. She stressed the interplay of the different subsystems, which is particularly relevant because many of the studies reviewed here examined only one aspect of writing. In Larsen-Freeman (2006), five Chinese learners of English completed the same task at each data collection point, four times over six months. Participants wrote and then told the story three days later. For the quantitative part of the study she used a range of measures on fluency, accuracy, and complexity and showed a striking difference between individuals and group patterns. She stated, "The messiness is not 'noise', but rather a natural part of dynamically emergent behavior assembled by the individual with a dynamic history of engaging in such tasks, with his or her own self-identified (or jointly identified) target of opportunities for growth" (p. 615).

Two recent studies (Verspoor, Schmid, and Xu 2012, and Verspoor and Smiskova 2012) studied writing development in what the authors call a dynamic usage-based approach, a term combining dynamic system theory and usage-based linguistics. Echoing Larsen-Freeman (2006), they state that there is no innate faculty for acquisition and that learners determine patterns from experience and exposure. Individual differences, in addition to amount and type of exposure, such as aptitude, age, and motivation, will cause differences in the paths learners take toward acquisition. Learning depends on previous stages and the various subsystems are all related (e.g., morphology and the lexicon). More variability occurs while learning and then systems become more stable. Nevertheless, some developmental trends occur.

Verspoor et al. (2012) collected essays from a fairly homogenous group of Dutch students in their first and third year of high school in two types of English programs, two or 15 hours of English a week. They measured 64 variables that were related to some linguistic aspect of writing such as accuracy, clause construction, and the lexicon to determine which variables changed at which stages and which discriminated best between stages. They found that different subsystems developed at different levels of proficiency. Verspoor and Smiskova (2012) followed Dutch learners of English from a low and a high input group for two years with regard to the use of chunks. The high input learners used more chunks over the period of time, but there were not large differences between the two groups. A detailed analysis of the two learners, however, showed different paths with the high input learner's variability decreasing.

Despite some methodological challenges discussed below, dynamic usage-based studies seem helpful for examining variation throughout development. More importantly, they emphasize the complex interplay of the various features of L2 writing that may not develop linearly. In addition, it's quite possible that written language is subject to more individual variability and between subject variation than speaking because of the possibility of drawing on both implicit and explicit knowledge given the slower pace of writing (see Chapter 26, this volume).

3.3 Experimental intervention studies

The studies of specific contexts discussed above did not use control groups and thus cannot be described as experimental studies determining cause and effect, but some researchers have studied the long term effects of some type of curriculum or instruction by employing experimental designs. Alptekin, Ercetin, and Bayyurt (2007) compared the effects of a theme-based syllabus and traditional grammatical syllabus in a Turkish primary school. They found that students who received theme-based instruction outperformed the other group in writing and other language skills after two years of instruction. Short, Fidelman, and Louguit (2012) investigated effects of sheltered instruction over two years, and found that the treatment group outperformed the control group on language proficiency tests. These studies investigated development in writing skill through instruction, but they did not look specifically into specific features or aspects of learner language.

As mentioned earlier, most of the earlier intervention studies focused on improving accuracy through some type of written corrective feedback (WCF) and this is still the case. To give one example, Hartshorn, Evans, Merrill, Sudweeks, Strong-Krause, and Anderson (2010) studied the effects of dynamic WCF. Influenced by skill-acquisition theory, dynamic WCF aims to maximize the individual students' opportunities to learn to write more accurately. Treatment group students were given indirect feedback provided in the form of coded symbol over 15 weeks. Using the tally sheets and error lists, students rewrote their writings until they corrected all their errors. The control group students received traditional process writing instruction. The authors found positive effects of dynamic WCF on accuracy. However, they also found a small negative effect on writing fluency and complexity and no effect on rhetorical competence. This study is noteworthy in that they attempted to investigate effects of instruction on various aspects of language although the aim of the treatment was to promote accuracy.

In sum, longitudinal experimental studies on types of instruction other than corrective feedback are scarce. Although some studies purport to study the effects of instruction over a period of time, they are often descriptive rather than experimental in that no control or comparison group was employed.

4 Methodological issues in studying development

There are a myriad of challenges in studying L2 writing development and most are related to the logistical problems of conducting rigorous longitudinal research. First, we have reported mostly on longitudinal studies here. Most would agree that if we can conduct rigorous longitudinal studies with large sample sizes, this is preferable to cross-sectional studies. But why should they be privileged over short-term studies or cross-sectional studies? As Ortega and Iberri-Shea (2005) stated:

> Indeed, it can be argued that many, if not all, fundamental problems about L2 learning that SLA researchers investigate are in part problems about "time," and that any claims about "learning" (or development, progress, improvement, change, gain, and so on) can be most meaningfully interpreted only within a full longitudinal perspective. It is, therefore, unfortunate that the bulk of disciplinary discussions within the field favors a cross-sectional view of language learning and, as a consequence, discussions about longitudinal research are scarce (p. 26).

Given that many of the studies discussed above have found much individual variation, cross-sectional studies of groups might hide certain patterns of development. A similar point is made by Norris and Manchón (2012) who, in discussing writing development say that "it is only through close and repeated tracking of language and writing phenomena within individuals or groups that the essence of development will be made observable" (p. 228).

With regard to experimental studies, short-term studies can certainly show evidence of learning, but results can be difficult to interpret. No change may mean either that the intervention was ineffective or that it was not long enough. It may also mean that it was not appropriate to the developmental level of the learners or that the measurement used was not fine-grained enough to detect change. Furthermore, an improvement in the intervention group, even with a delayed posttest, could easily be washed out after a certain length of time. Note that we have not stated how long a longitudinal study needs to be. Many of the studies discussed here are about one semester or half a year, which is expected given that if we follow students in a class, it will be a semester long; following students for longer will increase the drop-out rate. One could argue that such studies have some kind of ecological validity from a pedagogical perspective, namely, they can tell us what to expect in one semester of study but, obviously, the longer we follow students, the more we learn. Learning to write is a very long process.

If we agree that longitudinal studies are necessary, we run into problems related to sample size and data elicitation. With regard to sample size, several of the studies discussed above are case studies of only a few learners. While such studies can help us form hypotheses, we cannot know if the results extend to a wider range of participants. Nevertheless, case studies can also provide a bigger picture when they are well conducted and triangulate different sources of data (e.g., Canagarajah 2011a, b). They can also allow us to look at examples of writers with very specific profiles (e.g., Kobayashi and Rinnert 2013) writing in their natural contexts (see also discussion by Norris and Manchón 2012 who argue for the importance of multiple case studies). Thus, if we conduct small case studies, they need to exploit the strengths of qualitative research, namely that they capture the complexity of writing in context and triangulate the data by using data sources other than only writers' texts (e.g., interviews, think-aloud protocols, stimulated recall) as well as a wide variety of text types.

For large scale longitudinal studies, the problem is one of data elicitation. Previous studies have reported effects of tasks, topics, or prompts on students' writing performances. For example, He and Shi (2012) compared prompts requiring general knowledge and specific topical knowledge. They found the participants performed better on the general topic not only in terms of organization and content, but also in length and accuracy. Lu (2011) also confirmed genre effects on writing. He found that Chinese ESL learners wrote with higher syntactic complexity in argumentative essays than in narrative essays. When texts are collected over time, we need to be sure that the tasks are comparable, otherwise, we cannot know if changes are due to development or task differences. This is a major shortcoming of the studies discussed above. Only one of them counterbalanced the topics and tasks, and some of the studies had students writing under conditions that varied greatly from time to time. Thus, the individual variability found within participants is not surprising. Larsen-Freeman (2006) had students do exactly the same task at four different times. Although this may seem unwise because of practice effects, it eliminates the topic and genre problem and can show how different features of writing develop along different paths.

Another serious problem is the lack of validation of the measures used in studying writing development. For some studies, such as those that describe the development of a linguistic feature, this is less of a problem. For studies that purport to measure the effects of an intervention or want to look at progress in certain areas, we often don't know if a lack of change is because of a lack of development or because of an invalid measure. The Wolfe-Quintero et al. (1998) monograph, which was an attempt in a sense to validate measures used in L2 writing has not been updated, and surprisingly, only little progress has been made in validating measures of complexity, accuracy, and fluency (but see Bulté and Housen 2012 for a discussion of complexity measures). One possible reason is that measure validation is not straightforward. Recall that Wolfe-Quintero et al. examined measures for their correlations with other measures of general proficiency, essay quality, or change over time, with last category being the least common because of the lack of longitudinal studies. A measure can be also be validated through correlation with other measures claiming to measure the same construct or through a factor analysis of a variety of measures. In addition, various population variables, particularly proficiency level, will affect which measures are valid.

Two recent studies have attempted to validate accuracy measures in two very different ways. Evans, Hartshorn, Cox, and Martin (2014) correlated three measures of accuracy and found high correlations. They also used Rasch analysis and determined that the measures were reliable and created separation among the students but that the topic and prompt order affected the separation. This caused them to conclude that different accuracy measures might be more appropriate for different contexts. Polio and Shea (2014) used ten different accuracy measures found in L2 writing studies and noted which showed change over the course of a semester for ESL students writing on counterbalanced topics. They found improvement only on holistic measures of language and vocabulary, but no change on other measures such as number of errors, error-free T-units, weighted errors was found with the exception of preposition errors. Using the same data set, Bulté and Housen (2014) examined several measures of complexity and found an increase in some but not others.

We feel that validating measures by looking at change over time is an important endeavor, but we run into logistical problems in that we need to control for topic and genre effects. Furthermore, because of variability and variation, we need to collect data from participants across a wide range of proficiency levels and over extended periods of time. Neither of these tasks is easy. Take for example the Polio and Shea (2014) study. A lack of change over time, however, may not indicate invalid accuracy measures but rather nonlinear development, something several of the studies seems to suggest.

5 Critical reflection on future developments

The above description of research is not exhaustive but, in our opinion, it provides a picture of the types of research being conducted in second language writing development. In terms of future research, we need to seriously consider the methodological issues discussed above and improve quantitative research by controlling for writing task, using a range of measures deemed valid, and using control or comparison groups. Qualitative research can be improved by using a wider range of data sources to complement text analyses.

Despite the methodological challenges, the huge differences in the contexts and foci of the research, and the lack of uniform or clear theoretical perspectives in the studies, two themes clearly emerge. The first is related to intra-learner variability, inter-learner variation, and a lack of linear development. The second is the emphasis on chunks or formulaic sequences. Both of these issues are central to dynamic systems theory approaches. We discussed only three studies that were framed in a dynamic systems approach but several of the studies (Muñoz 2010; Nassaji 2007; Weissberg 2000) not explicitly conducted within a dynamic systems approach showed that different learners take different paths. Nassaji (2007), Sasaki (2004), Vyatkina (2012), and Gunnarsson (2012) all showed a lack of linear development among learners on some measures. All of these studies strengthen the claims of dynamic systems theory.

The emergence of chunks as an issue is not surprising as this topic has been a focus of much recent research in applied linguistics from an SLA perspective (see review in Ellis 2012) and in academic writing research (see review in Hyland 2012). Chunks are central to usage-based approaches and generally learned through exposure. Verspoor et al. (2012) and Verspoor and Smiskova (2012) both discussed the use of chunks, but so do other studies not explicitly stating that they are working in a usage-based framework (e.g., Benevento and Storch 2011; Yasuda 2011). We see this focus on chunks as an important trend in L2 writing research as also evidenced by a recent study by Li and Schmitt (2009).

Given that the emerging themes are related to dynamics systems theory, this might suggest that future research be conducted within this framework. The three studies done within this framework are convincing in terms of showing evidence that the acquisition of writing can be considered a complex system where learners take different paths, show much intralearner variability, do not progress linearly, and progress in different ways on different aspects of writing.

But then what are the implications of research done within this framework? We believe that pedagogical implications are not numerous. Yet, one possible implication is that given that beginners show more variability than more advanced students, we may not want to be concerned with accuracy early on; errors and variability are a normal part of development. There are, however, implications for research. First, short-term changes or lack thereof should be interpreted cautiously given the variation found and the lack of linear development in certain features of writing. Verspoor et al. (2012) found spurts of growth in certain areas and these spurts could be misinterpreted as being caused by instruction, particularly if a study lacks a control group. Second, several features of writing should be examined because of the way that they can interact. An intervention may cause change in one area but not in another. Or, an intervention may cause change in an area that was not intended. For example, Truscott's (1996) criticism of error feedback was that it may cause a decrease in language complexity, a valid concern.

In addition, we need to address why we are conducting research on L2 writing development. With regard to improving teaching, much of the research discussed above has no clear pedagogical implications. The descriptions of development in instructional context might make us reconsider certain practices, but do not give clear answers. For example, Benevento and Storch (2011) found little improvement in accuracy in classes in which accuracy was emphasized. Does this mean that we should emphasize accuracy more or less? Do students need more feedback or is the feedback useless?

The intervention studies, of which there are few, can certainly inform classroom practice, so we need more longitudinal intervention studies. Short-term studies that show effects of an intervention can be redone as longitudinal studies. Van

Beuningen, De Jong, and Kuiken (2012), for example, was a well-designed study that showed an effect for written corrective feedback. A similar study could be conducted over the course of a semester to see if time did or did not wash out any treatment. An even more important avenue of research would be longitudinal intervention studies that focus on linguistic aspects of writing other than accuracy. For example, an intervention could target complexity through task-based writing or explicit instruction. Activities designed to increase vocabulary could also be used over an extended period. Accuracy is only a small part of writing well and many studies have shown little effect for written corrective feedback. Perhaps we need to focus more on complexity and fluency in our interventions.

In sum, much research has occurred since 2000 on language development in writing. Despite writing being such a complex phenomenon, much progress has been made. While we cannot immediately draw teaching implications from much of the research, it can inform us about how we could conduct future intervention studies.

6 Additional sources

Bestgen, Yves and Sylviane Granger. 2014. Quantifying the development of phraseological competence in L2 English writing: An automated approach, *Journal of Second Language Writing* 26. 28–41

Bitchener, John and Ute Knoch. 2009. The contribution of written corrective feedback to language development: A ten month investigation. *Applied Linguistics* 31(2). 193–214.

Bulté, Bram and Alex Housen. 2014. Conceptualizing and measuring short-term changes in L2 writing complexity, *Journal of Second Language Writing* 26. 42–65

Connor-Linton, Jeff and Charlene Polio. 2014. Comparing perspectives on L2 writing: Multiple analyses of a common corpus, *Journal of Second Language Writing* 26. 1–9.

Crossley, Scott and Danielle McNamara. 2014. Does writing development equal writing quality? A computational investigation of syntactic complexity in L2 learners. *Journal of Second Language Writing* 26. 66–79.

Friginal, Eric and Sara Weigle. 2014. Exploring multiple profiles of L2 writing using multi-dimensional analysis, *Journal of Second Language Writing* 26. 80–95.

Housen, Alex, Folkert Kuiken, and Ineke Vedder (eds.). 2012. *Dimensions of L2 performance and proficiency: Complexity, accuracy, and fluency in SLA*. Amsterdam/Philadelphia: John Benjamins.

Ortega, Lourdes and Heidi Byrnes (eds.). 2009. *The longitudinal study of advanced L2 capacities*. Mahwah, NJ: Lawrence Erlbaum.

Polio, Charlene and Mark Shea. 2014. An investigation into current measures of linguistic accuracy in second language writing research. *Journal of Second Language Writing* 26. 10–27.

Spoelman, Marianne and Marjolijn Verspoor. 2010. Dynamic patterns in development of accuracy and complexity: A longitudinal case study in the acquisition of Finnish. *Applied Linguistics* 31(4). 532–553.

Storch, Neomy. 2009. The impact of studying in a second language (L2) medium university on the development of L2 writing. *Journal of Second Language Writing* 18(2). 103–118.

Vyatkina, Nina. 2013. Specific syntactic complexity: Developmental profiling of individuals based on an annotated learner corpus. *The Modern Language Journal* 97(S1). 11–30.

7 References

Alptekin, Cem, Gülcan Ercetin, and Yasemin Bayyurt. 2007. The effectiveness of a theme-based syllabus for young L2 learners. *Journal of Multilingual and Multicultural Development* 28(1). 1–17.

Bardovi-Harlig, Kathleen. 2000. *Tense and aspect in second language acquisition: Form, meaning, and use.* Oxford: Blackwell.

Bardovi-Harlig, Kathleen. 2002. A new starting point? Investigating formulaic use and input in future expression. *Studies in Second Language Acquisition* 24(2). 189–198.

Benevento, Cathleen and Neomy Storch. 2011. Investigating writing development in secondary school learners of French. *Assessing Writing* 16(2). 97–110.

Boss, B. 2008. Exploring the acquisition of German verb morphology by instructed learners. *Australian Review of Applied Linguistics* 31(2). 14–41.

Bulté, Bram and Alex Housen. 2012. Defining and operationalizing L2 complexity. In Alex Housen, Folkert Kuiken, and Ineke Vedder (eds.), *Dimensions of L2 performance and proficiency: Complexity, accuracy, and fluency in SLA*, 21–46. Amsterdam/ Philadelphia: John Benjamins.

Bulté, Bram and Alex Housen. Conceptualizing and measuring short-term changes in L2 writing complexity. *Journal of Second Language Writing* 26(4). 42–65.

Byrnes, Heidi. 2009. Emergent L2 German writing ability in a curricular context: a longitudinal study of grammatical metaphor. *Linguistics and Education* 20(1). 50–66.

Byrnes, Heidi and Castle Sinicrope 2008. Advanced ness and the development of relativization in L2 German: A curriculum-based longitudinal study. In Lourdes Ortega and Heidi. Byrnes (eds.), *The longitudinal study of advanced L2 capacities*, 109–138. New York: Routledge.

Canagarajah, Suresh. 2011a. Codemeshing in academic writing: Identifying teachable strategies in translanguaging. *Modern Language Journal* 95(3). 401–417.

Canagarajah, Suresh. 2011b. Writing to learn and learning to write by shuttling between languages. In Rosa M. Manchón (ed.), *Learning-to-write and writing-to-learn in an additional language*, 111–132. Amsterdam/Philadelphia: John Benjamins.

Cook, Vivian (ed.). 2003. *Effects of the second language on the first.* Clevedon, UK: Multiligual Matters.

Cook, Vivian. 2008. Multi-competence: Black hole or wormhole for second language acquisition research? In ZhaoHong Han (ed.), *Understanding second language process*, 16–26. Clevedon, UK: Multilingual matters.

Cumming, Alister. 2012. Goal theory and second-language writing development, two ways. In Rosa M. Manchón (Ed.), *L2 writing development: Multiple perspectives*, 165–190. Boston/ Berlin: de Gruyter Mouton.

Doughty, Catherine. 1991. Second language instruction does make a difference: Evidence from an empirical study of relativization. *Studies in Second Language Acquisition* 13(4). 431–469.

Duff, Patricia. 1993. Syntax, semantics, and SLA: The convergence of possessive and existential constructions. *Studies in Second Language Acquisition* 15(1). 1–34.

Dulay, Heidi, Marina Burt, and Stephen Krashen. 1982. *Language two.* New York: Oxford University Press.

Ellis, Nick C. 2012. Formulaic language and second language acquisition: Zipf and the phrasal teddy bear. *Annual Review of Applied Linguistics*, 32. 17–44.

Evans, Norman, K. James Hartshorn, Troy Cox, and Teresa Martin. 2014. Measures of written linguistic accuracy: Questions of reliability, validity, and practicality. *Journal of Second Language Writing* 24(2). 33–50.

Gass, Susan. 1979. Language transfer and universal grammatical relations. *Language Learning* 54(1). 1–34.

Gregg, Kevin. 1984. Krashen's monitor and Occam's razor. *Applied Linguistics* 5(2). 79–100.

Gunnarsson, Cecilia. 2012. The development of complexity, accuracy, and fluency in the written production of L2 French. In Alex Housen, Folkert Kuiken, and Ineke Vedder (eds.), *Dimensions of L2 performance and proficiency: Complexity, accuracy, and fluency in SLA*, 247–276. Amsterdam/Philadelphia: John Benjamins.

Halliday, Michael. 2002. Spoken and written modes of meaning. In Jonathan J. Webster (ed.), *On grammar*, 323–351. London: Continuum.

Han, ZhaoHong. 2000. Persistence of the implicit influence of NL: The case of the pseudo-passive. *Applied Linguistics* 21(1). 78–105.

Harklau, Linda. 2002. The role of writing in classroom second language acquisition. *Journal of Second Language Writing* 11(4). 329–350.

Hartshorn, K. James, Norman W. Evans, Paul F. Merrill, Richard R. Sudweeks, Diane Strong-Krause, and Neil J. Anderson 2010. Effects of dynamic corrective feedback on ESL writing accuracy. *TESOL Quarterly* 44(1). 84–109.

He, Ling and Ling Shi. 2012. Topical knowledge and ESL writing. *Language Testing*, 29(3). 443–464.

Huebner, Thom. 1983. A *longitudinal analysis of the acquisition of English*. Ann Arbor, MI: Karoma.

Hyland, Ken. 2012. Bundles in academic discourse. *Annual Review of Applied Linguistics*, 32. 150–169.

Keenan, Edward and Bernard Comrie. 1977. Noun phrase accessibility and Universal Grammar. *Linguistic Inquiry* 8(1). 63–99.

Kepner, Christine Goring. 1991. An experiment in the relationship of types of written feedback to the development of second language writing skills. *Modern Language Journal* 75(3). 305–313.

Klein, Wolfgang and Clive Perdue. 1992. *Utterance structures: Developing grammars again*. Amsterdam/Philadelphia: John Benjamins.

Kobayshi, Hiroe and Carol Rinnert. 2012. Understanding L2 writing development from a multicompetence perspective: Dynamic repertoires of knowledge and text construction. In Rosa M. Manchón (ed.), *L2 writing development: Multiple perspectives*. 101–134. Boston/Berlin: De Gruyter Mouton.

Kobayshi, Hiroe and Carol Rinnert. 2013. L1/ L2/ L3 writing development: Longitudinal case study of a Japanese multicompetent writer. *Journal of Second Language Writing* 22(1). 4–33.

Krashen, Stephen. 1982. *Principles and practice in second language acquisition*. Oxford: Pergamon Press.

Kuiken, Folkert and Ineke Vedder. 2012. Speaking and writing tasks and their effects on second language performance. In Susan Gass and Alison Mackey (eds.), *The Routledge handbook of second language acquisition*, 364–377. London/New York: Routledge.

Larsen-Freeman, Diane. 1975. The acquisition of grammatical morphemes by adult ESL students. *TESOL Quarterly* 9(4). 409–430.

Larsen-Freeman, Diane. 2006. The emergence of complexity, fluency, and accuracy in the oral and written production of five Chinese learners of English. *Applied Linguistics* 27(4). 590–619.

Larsen-Freeman, Diane. 2012. Complexity theory. In Susan Gass and Alison Mackey (eds.), *The Routledge handbook of second language acquisition*, 73–82. London and New York: Routledge.

Li, Jie and Norbert Schmitt. 2009. The acquisition of lexical phrases in academic writing: A longitudinal study. *Journal of Second Language Writing* 18(2). 85–102.

Lu, Xiaofei. 2011. A corpus-based evaluation of syntactic complexity measures as indices of college-level ESL writers' language development. *TESOL Quarterly* 45(1). 36–62.

Manchón, Rosa M. (ed.). 2012. *L2 writing development: Multiple perspectives*. Berlin/Boston: De Gruyter Mouton.

Meisel, Jürgen M., Harald Clahsen and Manfred Pienemann. 1981. On determining developmental stages in natural second language acquisition. *Studies in Second Language Acquisition* 3(2). 109–135.

Montrul, Silvina and Silvia Perpiñán. 2011. Assessing differences and similarities between instructed heritage language learners and L2 learners in their knowledge of Spanish tense-aspect and mood (TAM) morphology. *Heritage Language Journal* (8)1. 90–133.

Muñoz, Carmen. 2010. Staying abroad with the family: A case study of two siblings' second language development during a year's immersion. *ITL. International Journal of Applied Linguistics* 160(1). 24–48.

Nassaji, Hossein. 2007. The development of spelling and orthographic knowledge in English as an L2: A longitudinal case study. *Canadian Journal of Applied Linguistics* 10(1). 77–98.

Negretti, Raffaella. 2012. Metacognition in student academic writing: A longitudinal study of metacognitive awareness and its relation to task perception and evaluation of performance. *Written Communication* 29(2). 142–179.

Norris, John M. and Rosa M. Manchón. 2012. Investigating L2 writing development from multiple perspectives: Issues in theory and research. In Rosa M. Manchón (ed.), *L2 writing development: Multiple perspectives*, 221–244. Boston/Berlin: De Gruyter Mouton.

Ortega, Lourdes and Gina Iberri-Shea. 2005. Longitudinal research in second language acquisition: recent trends and future directions. *Annual Review of Applied Linguistics* 25. 26–45.

Pienemann, Manfred. 1998. Is language teachable? *Applied Linguistics* 10(1). 52–79.

Polio, Charlene. 2012. The relevance of second language acquisition theory to the written error correction debate. *Journal of Second Language Writing* 21(4). 374–389.

Polio, Charlene and Mark C. Shea. 2014. An investigation into current measures of linguistic accuracy in second language writing research. *Journal of Second Language Writing* 26(4). 10–27.

Sasaki, Miyuki. 1990. Topic prominence in Japanese EFL students' existential construction. *Language Learning* 40(3). 337–367.

Sasaki, Miyuki. 2004. A multiple-data analysis of the 3.5 year development of EFL student writers. *Language Learning* 54(3). 525–582.

Sato, Charlene. 1990. *The syntax of conversation in interlanguage development*. Tübingen: Gunter Narr Verlag.

Schumann, John. 1979. The acquisition of English negation by speakers of Spanish: A review of literature. In Roger W. Andersen (ed.), *The acquisition and use of Spanish and English as first and second Languages*, 3–32. Washington, DC: Teachers of English to Speakers of Other Languages.

Semke, Harriet. 1984. The effects of the red pen. *Foreign language Annals,* 17(3). 195–202.

Serrano, Raquel, Elsa Tragant and Angels Llanes. 2012. A longitudinal analysis of the effects of one year abroad. *Canadian Modern Language Review,* 68(2). 138–163.

Short, Deborah J., Caroline G. Fidelman and Mohammed Louguit. 2012. Developing academic language in English language learners through sheltered instruction. *TESOL Quarterly* 46(2). 334–361.

Sohn, Sung-Ock and Sang-Keun Shin. 2007. True beginners, false beginners, and fake beginners: Placement strategies for Korean heritage speakers. *Foreign Language Annals* 40(3). 407–418.

Tardy, Christine. 2012. A rhetorical genre theory perspective on L2 writing development. In Rosa M. Manchón (ed.), *L2 writing development: Multiple perspectives*, 165–190. Boston/Berlin: De Gruyter Mouton.

Truscott, John. 1996. The case against grammar journal correction in L2 writing classes. *Language Learning* 46(2). 327–369.

Verspoor, Marjolijn and Hana Smiskova. 2012. Foreign language writing development from a dynamic usage based perspective. In Rosa M. Manchón (ed.), *L2 writing development: Multiple perspectives*, 17–46. Boston/Berlin: De Gruyter Mouton.

Verspoor, Marjolijn, Monica S. Schmid, and Xiaoyan Xu. 2012. A dynamic usage based perspective on L2 writing. *Journal of Second Language Writing* 21(3). 239–263.

Van Beuningen, Catherine, Nivja H. De Jong, and Folkert Kuiken. 2012. Evidence on the effectiveness of comprehensive error correction in second language writing. Language Learning 62(1). 1–41.

Vyatkina, Nina. 2012. The development of second language writing complexity in groups and individuals: A longitudinal learner corpus study. *The Modern Language Journal* 96(4). 576–598.

Weissberg, Robert. 2000. Developmental relationships in the acquisition of English syntax: writing vs. speech. *Learning and Instruction*, 10(1). 37–53.

Williams, Jessica. 2012. The potential role(s) of writing in second language development. *Journal of Second Language Writing* 21(4). 321–331.

Wolfe-Quintero, Kate, Shinji Ingaki, and Hae-Young Kim. 1998. *Second language development in writing: Measures of fluency, accuracy and complexity*. Honolulu, HI: Second Language Teaching & Curriculum Center, University of Hawai'i.

Yasuda, Sachiko. 2011. Genre-based tasks in foreign language writing: Developing writers' genre awareness, linguistic knowledge, and writing competence. *Journal of Second Language Writing* 20(2). 111–133.

Paige Ware, Richard Kern, and Mark Warschauer
14 The development of digital literacies

Computers and the Internet allow people to participate in new types of communities for work, learning, and play. They provide new ways of representing knowledge, accessing information, and creating new knowledge. They offer new ways for people to represent themselves and new ways to interact with others. They also introduce multimedia dimensions to texts, new language forms, new discourse structures, and new notions of authorship. Consequently, they have spurred scholars to develop views of literacy that go well beyond the ability to read and write paper-based texts.

1 Origins and development of research

The term *digital literacies* refers to reading and writing on electronic devices and the Internet, and broadly includes the knowledge, skills, and practices that people engage with when they read and write in electronic environments. The term is plural because reading and writing can take many different forms and be directed toward many different goals as they are practiced in different social contexts. Composing a digital story involves a different constellation of knowledge, skills, and practices than composing a written narrative. Writing a blog is different from writing a journal, which is in turn different from writing an argumentative essay. Email messages, text messages, and tweets are all electronic forms of writing, but they involve unique genre constraints, and how they are written will vary widely according to audience and purpose. The knowledge, skills, and practices involved in digital literacies are thus wide-ranging and context sensitive. Consequently, it is possible to be quite "digitally literate" in certain ways but not at all in others.

A specific origin of the term digital literacies is difficult to pinpoint, but a rough line can be traced starting in the late 1990s across three fields relevant to second language writers: applied linguistics, literacy studies, and composition studies. First, in the field of applied linguistics, Warschauer (1999) introduced the notion of *electronic literacies* in his book-length ethnography, *Electronic Literacies: Language, Culture, and Power in Online Education*. Shortly thereafter, he refined this construct as composed of four *literacies*: computer literacy, information literacy, multimedia literacy, and computer-mediated communication literacy (Warschauer 2003). *Computer literacy* deals with the physical and operational dimensions of using a computer (familiarity with the interface, managing files, copying and pasting, search techniques, and so on). *Information literacy* has to do with broader issues related to information searches, such as developing good research questions, knowing where to search for information, evaluating search findings, and applying them appropriately. *Multimedia literacy* acknowledges the abilities needed to create texts combining different media and also to read and interpret multimodal texts. Finally, *computer-mediated communication literacy* ranges from the ability to send a situationally appropriate email message to the ability to organize and manage various forms of online communication for the benefit of groups and organizations.

Within literacy studies, a similar approach to literacy as multiple emerged in the late 1990s with the theoretical turn toward *multiliteracies*, a construct forwarded by the New London Group (1996) and taken up by various scholars within the New Literacy Studies tradition (e.g., Cope and Kalantzis 1999; Gee 2000; Street 1995). This approach views literacy as situated in particular cultural and social contexts. Scholars draw primarily on ethnographic research methods to develop in-depth understandings of how various forms of literacy draw differentially on diverse semiotic resources, technological tools, and languages to construct texts that are part of a larger meaning-making fabric of relationships and communicative intentions. Particular lenses within this overarching frame include *new media literacies*, which carries a particular emphasis on participatory learning (e.g., Jenkins 2006) and *cyberliteracy*, which, at least in Gurak's (2001) use of the term, involves consciousness of how computer use affects culture and human behavior.

In composition studies, in the same year as Warschauer introduced the term electronic literacies, Kathleen Welch (1999) developed the notion of "electric rhetoric" (p. 7), which addressed literacy issues specific to computer technology, emphasizing the social construction of literacy, the mediating effects of technology on individual consciousness, and new technology-mediated roles for individuals to express thoughts, identities, and cultures. Stuart Selber (2004) elaborated many of the ideas circulating in composition studies into a conceptual framework involving three categories that express different roles of the computer: functional literacy (computer as tool), critical literacy (computer as cultural artifact), and rhetorical literacy (computer as hypertextual medium). In Selber's model, the categories are not mutually exclusive but serve as vehicles by which students can "exploit the different subjectivities that have become associated with computer technologies" (p. 25). These different subject positions allow students to be users, questioners, and producers of technology.

Across all three fields, a recurring theme is the development of a new theoretical, empirical, and pedagogical framework that helps shift from the former focus on literacy as a stable, conventional phenomenon, to a new conceptualization of *literacies* as multiple, dynamic, dialogic, and situated.

In a framework that accommodates this emerging socio-political stance toward the new literacy education landscape, Warschauer and Ware (2008) proposed three broad frames of literacy: *learning*, *change*, and *power*. The learning and change frames offer insight, respectively, into how technologies can augment and reproduce traditional learning and can radically change what counts as literacy. The power frame addresses additional issues of access and of use within social and economic realities and views literacy as a plural, integrated construct that encompasses all four components of computer literacy, information literacy, multimedia literacy, and computer-mediated literacy. In a power frame, the larger context in which classroom writing occurs is foregrounded as part of the analysis. By bringing the macro context into focus, researchers can trace the social, economic, and even political processes by which literacy education becomes framed institutionally, and then enacted across particular educational contexts and classrooms. Across several of the components of digital literacy laid out, computer literacy has been critiqued for its narrow vocational focus (Sloan 1984), and information literacy has been critiqued for its lack of critical perspective (Luke and Kapitzke 1999) and its insensitivity to cultural difference. The impact of cultural and linguistic diversity on information literacy has recently garnered attention (e.g., Gilton 2007; Patterson 2011). In a later section, this chapter will take up the research that has been done within these domains.

2 Main theories informing research

Over a decade ago, Kern and Warschauer (2000) classified the use of network-based language technologies in language instruction according to three main theoretical approaches: structuralism, cognitivism/constructivism, and social constructionism. Since that time, the rapid increase in using Internet-based and multimedia technologies for communicating through writing and other semiotic modes led Warschauer and Grimes (2007) to add two additional theoretical frames of dialogism and post-structuralism. We briefly review how each has informed views of writing, the role of technology, and the focus within digital literacies (see Table 14.1).

Structuralist theories view writing as an autonomous system that has conventional language structures which are learned through practice and imitation (see Kern and Warschauer 2000). Emphasis is placed on mastery of particular genres with the ultimate goals of correctness in standardized versions of the language. Since technology is viewed as a means for providing immediate and individualized feedback on language structures, the focus within digital literacies is on basic computer literacy to enable students to independently access sites that provide structured practice.

Constructivist approaches emphasize both information literacy as well as basic multimedia literacy, as each enables learners to access rich linguistic input and informational resources. Writing is viewed as a cognitive process in which writers come to understand both the underlying structure of language as well as the needs of readers. Technology offers support for process approaches to writing, in which

Tab. 14.1: Theoretical frameworks.

Theory	View of writing	Role of technology	Focus within digital literacies
Structuralism	Writing as an autonomous system with conventional language structures; emphasis on prescriptive norms and models to be emulated	Provides exercises and explanations of linguistic structure; offers immediate and individualized feedback	Focuses on computer literacy as a means for receiving instruction and completing exercises
Cognitivism/ Constructivism	Writing seen both as a mental process and as a process of moving from writer-based to reader-based prose through a cycle of drafting and revising	Offers variety of options for rich linguistic input; supports process approach to writing; invites learners to analyze their own and others' language	Emphasizes information and multimedia literacy as ways to develop autonomous skills, to reflect on learning, and to access rich information
Social constructionism	Writing as participation in authentic discourse communities; focus on form at the levels of genre, register, and style	Moves writing beyond the classroom to social interaction across many contexts; facilitates the creation of new discourse communities	Centers on computer-mediated literacy; examines participation in different discourse communities (example: wiki; listservs)
Dialogism	Writing as a constant remixing of previous and new utterances; writing as inherently interactive and jointly constructed	Supports the constant exchange of written communication, voicing, and revoicing; refuses to anchor a text in a fixed time-point	Examines computer-mediated literacy and multimedia literacy; seeks potential for building dialogue and repurposing texts (example: blogs)
Post-structuralism	Text is just one layer of semiotic resources; writing carries traces of multivocal and multimodal remixing of signs	Offers endless layering of various semiotic resources and allows for juxtaposition of different artifacts; creates multifaceted texts	Focuses on computer-mediated and multimedia literacy; examines multimodality and layering of semiotic resources (example: social networking)

writers can analyze their own and others' writing and can become more attuned to readers through a cycle of revising and editing.

From a social constructionist perspective, writing is viewed as participation in authentic discourse communities. Technology offers access to discourse communities outside the classroom, and the growth of new discourse communities allows writers to participate in and analyze the development of genre conventions through their own and others' participation patterns over time. Social constructionist approaches retain a focus on socially meaningful writing conventions at the genre, register, and stylistic levels of writing. Examples of technologies that exemplify the social constructionist approach are wikis, which allow multiple authors, and numerous other electronically-mediated discourse communities such as listservs, forums, and social networking sites.

To understand how digital literacies are changing with the increase in Web 2.0 technologies, dialogic and post-structuralist theories are needed (see extended discussion in Warschauer and Grimes 2007). O'Reilly (2005) has described Web 2.0 as a platform for reading and writing, as a support for dynamic and mixable applications, as an efficient system for publishing and delivering content, as a storage center for material that can be used and reused, and as a place where people can participate in forums such as blogs, wikis, and social networks as well as tag content and create their own unique folksonomies. Guth and Thomas (2010) add that the Web 2.0 experience provides users "with a more organic experience of a network environment, in which their contributions have the opportunity to be responded to in turn by others, and thus to grow into a dialogical conversation with participants in an increasingly globalized ... world" (p. 41). They outline the affordances of many media types, from Flickr and YouTube for sharing images and videos to social bookmarking and networking for creating networks of contacts and information.

Each of these five theoretical lenses offers a way to examine digital literacies, but they are not mutually exclusive due to the dynamic interplay between technology mode, context, purpose, and practices. Researchers of digital literacies therefore tend to share discussions and findings that cross theoretical orientations, and the methods they use tend to overlap as well, a point to which we now turn.

3 Main methods of research

Qualitative research, with its emphasis on documenting and describing in rich detail multiple contextual layers and diverse participant perspectives, has been well suited for examining digital literacies. The bulk of empirical work in digital literacies has drawn on a variety of methods within the tradition of qualitative research, including longitudinal and ethnographic inquiry, teacher and action-based research, participatory action research, discourse and semiotic analysis, and cross-case analyses (see also Chapter 23).

The questions pursued in these qualitative research designs can be loosely grouped according to three types of contexts: classroom-based studies, community-based studies, and network-based studies (see Ware and Warschauer 2012). Classroom-based studies examine task design, learner outcomes, sample sizes, instructors' roles, modes of instruction, implementation challenges, and convergences between conventional literacies with digital literacies. Community-based studies examine the possibility of new digital literacy practices to expand on what is traditionally covered in formal learning and ask how different uses of technology offer opportunities for individual agency, for learner identity development, and for the development of new skills. Similarly, network-based studies focus on social identity construction and the exploration of new literacy practices; however, these studies are characterized methodologically by the unique challenges of gaining access to participants who do not share the researcher's physical setting and of tracking new forms of data, and such studies therefore have tended to cross inter-disciplinary boundaries to address these new challenges.

All three domains of research share similar data collection and analysis proce-dures. They rely to varying degrees on triangulating across multiple types of data sources, including field notes of observations and participant observations in class-rooms and community centers; individual and focal group interviews conducted face-to-face and through technology mediation; participant self-report through written products; interactional data archived on discussion boards, blogs, wikis, networking sites, gaming sites, and instant messaging; participant artifacts such as written texts, multimedia productions, and Web sites; and, in a few cases, form-ative and summative assessments of learning. Data analysis typically involves a combination of triangulation: thematic coding of interactional transcripts and other documents; descriptive statistics from surveys; and fine-grained discourse analyses of participant interactions and participant-produced texts.

In addition to these familiar approaches to research, the last ten years of devel-opment in multimodal Internet technologies have generated a renewed interest in capturing both the products of electronic communication and the processes by which texts are produced, exchanged, and consumed. Ware and Warschauer (2012) describe the products of digital communication as both interactional (transcripts of text-based and audio-based asynchronous and synchronous interactions) and generated (Weblogs, wikis, Web sites, and videos). They point to the processes of the production and consumption cycle as involving access, orientation, affiliation, and collaboration, which can be captured through interviews, surveys, observa-tional field notes, participant self-reporting mechanisms, and think-aloud and ret-rospective protocols.

Understanding both the products and processes of digital literacies poses a unique challenge, however, because the line between product and process is in-creasingly blurred. As Leander (2008) has argued, researchers have to retool their data collection and analysis methods to stay committed to tracking information and interaction across both digital and physical spaces. As the distinctions be-tween online and offline, between virtual and real, and between educational and social contexts break down, researchers have begun to grapple with such blurred boundaries by developing novel approaches to qualitative data collection and analysis.

Researchers of telecollaboration have also drawn on various combinations of learners' online asynchronous discussions with peers, face-to-face verbal interactions in the physical classroom, retrospective interviews and surveys, student-generated visual representations, and post-testing of language measures (e.g., Develotte, Guichon, and Kern 2008; Kern 2014; Liaw 2006). Researchers of social networking and gaming have creatively combined the collection and analysis of screen shots of online activities, transcripts of interactions, updates on personal sites, online guidebooks, interviews, and observations (e.g., Black 2008; Leander 2008).

Finally, in addition to this extensive body of qualitative research, there is a growing number of quantitative studies of digital literacies. These include an earlier series of experimental and quasi-experimental comparisons of learning processes outcomes in face-to-face and computer-mediated settings (see summary in Kern and Warschauer 2000), analysis of large-scale test score results from the Program in International Student Assessment to tease out the relationship between print and digital literacy (Naumann 2012), social network analysis to investigate the patterns of digital interactions in a microblogging community of fifth grade English language learners (Zheng and Warschauer 2012), and descriptive and correlational analysis of middle school students' writing on Google Docs (Lawrence, Warschauer, Zheng, and Mullins 2013). Given the ease of computerized analysis of digitized texts, as well as the rapid growth of machine learning techniques for identifying structural and participation patterns, quantitative research of digital literacy practices is certain to expand in the future.

4 Main research insights: Shifts in the development of digital literacies

Digital literacies have obviously been influenced by developments in Internet-based technologies. In this section, we review four major shifts: (1) from a focus on single authorship of written products to collaborative writing processes; (2) from a promotion of cultural contact to the examination of intercultural complexity in online contexts; (3) from an emphasis on classroom-based research to non-classroom, networked contexts; and (4) from linguistic competence with text-based forms of writing to symbolic competence with multiple semiotic modes.

4.1 Single-Authored products to collaborative authorship

Early studies of computer-mediated literacy in second and foreign language writing focused on how student essay writing could be supported, enhanced, or in some cases possibly limited, when technology was integrated. A key recurring theme of this first wave of research was an insistence that the choice of technology does not wield a singular effect but is deeply intertwined with pedagogical, theoretical, and logistical factors (see Kern, Ware, and Warschauer 2004). This theme was first thoroughly illustrated by Warschauer (1999) in showing that the sociocultural context in various settings significantly shaped the nature of online teaching and learning. Contrary to the view that technology itself brings about transformations of learning, Warschauer found that technology tended to reinforce and amplify the effects of whatever instructional orientation teachers already had in place, whether instructors approached second language writing as a form of discipline, liberation, vocation, or apprenticeship. Another key finding of Warschauer's research was how seriously learners took learning new semiotic skills in online media, as compared to completing computer-based instructional exercises.

Another theme of this early work was a focus on the various forms of computer-mediated feedback on student writing. In the late 1990s and early 2000s, classroom-based student writing remained primarily the product of a single author, and the role of technology was to support efficient, motivating, and effective feedback. Ware and Warschauer (2006) synthesized much of this research on feedback delivered electronically. Their synthesis showed that online peer response increase the amount of student writing as well as motivation, in part by decreasing anxiety and by making papers more easily shared and monitored. Second, they concluded that research on the synchronous and asynchronous forums for feedback tends to elicit feedback at the local level of clauses, sentences, and paragraphs, rather on global aspects of idea development and organization. Third, their synthesis documents some evidence that the type of technology shapes the success of feedback delivery and uptake, although such barriers might be alleviated by pedagogical structuring and clarity. Finally, they concluded that researchers examining electronic feedback would likely shift in the near future from a focus on essay writing to "explore questions related to novel forms of writing" (p. 117).

These novel forms of writing have exploded onto the screen in less than a decade, primarily in the shape of blogs and wikis. Early user-friendly software for publishing blogs was introduced in 1999, and at the time of this writing, the tracking engine Technorati is actively tracking over 112 million blogs, although it acknowledges countless other blogs outside those chosen for inclusion in their database. Blogs allow for single or shared ownership and support the posting of texts, images, hyperlinks, videos and comments. They have been described by Herring, Scheidt, Kouper, and Wright (2006) as a *bridging genre* between standard HTML documents (such as personal home pages, which are infrequently updated, asymmetrically broadcast, and composed of multimedia) and asynchronous forms of computer mediated communication (such as online forums, which are constantly updated, involve symmetrical exchange, and are text-based).

In second and foreign language writing instruction, blogs have been researched primarily at the post-secondary level and have been found to support L2 learners in exchanging ideas and writing to audiences outside the classroom (Sykes, Oskoz, and Thorne 2008), developing L2 academic writing skills (Bloch

2007), bolstering confidence in writing (Murray and Hourigan 2008), enhancing motivation for personal expression and collaboration (Lee 2011a), promoting L2 fluency (Fellner and Apple 2006), and developing metalinguistic knowledge of lexical and morphosyntactical errors (Lee 2011b). A few studies have examined the use of blogs in the K-12 context and have found them supportive of elementary school learners' social and academic writing in and out of school (Gebhard, Shin, and Seger 2011) and of adolescent peer interaction across linguistic and geographic contexts (Ware and Rivas 2012).

Wikis are web sites that can be collaboratively written. Any visitor to a wiki can edit or add text, and a history of edits is tracked and archived. The most well-known site, Wikipedia (http://wikipedia.org), is available in 287 languages at the time of this writing. Because wikis inspire knowledge creation and information sharing, language educators have been intrigued by the potential for wiki writing to combine collaborative authoring with more formal modes of interaction, in contrast to the less formal styles of most blogs and social media. In L2 writing research, the primary focus of empirical work, however, has been on student attention to language form when writing in wikis, rather than on their joint creation of information. The results of this focus on form have been mixed. Kessler (2009) and Mak and Coniam (2008) found that students paid little attention to accuracy, while in Elola and Oskoz's (2010) study, students preferred to correct their own errors rather than those of other authors within the wiki. However, a number of researchers have found that students do indeed provide feedback on form, particularly when students are explicitly asked to do so and when they are partnered in smaller groups (Arnold, Ducate, and Kost 2012). In her synthesis of collaborative writing forums, Storch (2012) suggests that in the case of wikis, more research needs to be conducted to explore learners' perspectives and their use of evidence. Gebhard, Shin, and Seger (2011) add that more needs to be learned about how collaborative writing with wikis and blogs is practiced in elementary and secondary schools.

Finally, an important topic in the shift from single-authored products to collaborative authorship is plagiarism. A recent special issue of the *Journal of Second Language Writing* (Polio and Shi 2012) problematizes notions of plagiarism in light of global digital environments where texts are sometimes collaboratively written or hyperlinked to other texts and where different ideological positions held in different cultures can collide. Polio and Shi emphasize the importance of situating writing research within specific cultural and technological contexts since perceptions about appropriation or plagiarism are integrally linked to specific purposes and settings of writing (see also Chapter 15).

4.2 Cultural contact to intercultural complexity

With the ease of linking learners through Internet-based tools such as discussion boards, chat rooms, MOOs, wikis, blogs, and videoconferencing tools, computer-mediated discussions have shifted from single classrooms to multi-site collaborations. This area of research is characterized less by a clear shift, but rather by increasing *complexity* as researchers learn more about how learners write, communicate, and co-exist in a multi-faceted, multilingual digital world. Because of the large amount of research on cultural contact online, we narrow our focus in this section to classroom-based projects that focus on language use, genre differentiation, or intercultural awareness.

Early online language and culture exchanges, often known as telecollaboration, tended to focus on language development. Using second language acquisition (SLA) theory as a lens, they examined how bilingual partnerships might foster opportunities for negotiation of meaning in real-time interactions. Researchers found that learners made more written requests for clarification and elaboration in MOOs (Kötter 2003), that they used translation and paraphrase as frequent strategies (Schwienhorst 2002), and that they developed metalinguistic awareness of grammatical forms through chat-based corrective feedback (O'Rourke 2005). Other studies emphasized that, unless teachers explicitly structured assignments around the provision of form-focused feedback, students attended mostly to communicative meaning and vocabulary, both in online chatting forums as well as in asynchronous interactions (Sotillo 2005; Ware and O'Dowd 2008). In short, feedback on language form can occur in telecollaborative exchanges, particularly when integrated as an explicit course expectation, but little is known about the long- or short-term impact on acquisition of these forms or on ideal feedback activities.

In turning to a research focus on genre, a host of issues are at stake for researchers of writing. Are new, stable, genres emerging online? How might L2 learners and multilingual writers take part in the various genres available in online communities within and outside the classroom? How might writing teachers rethink their own craft in a plurilingual, multi-faceted digital world? A decade ago, Kramsch and Thorne (2002) ignited discussion on these questions with their analysis of students participating in a French-American email exchange who seemed unable to establish common ground. Kramsch and Thorne attributed the communication breakdown to differences in "stylistic conventions of the genre (formal/informal, edited/unedited, literate/orate), and more importantly the whole discourse system to which that genre belonged" (p. 98). Their analysis showed that the American students were writing from a discourse system of trust, whereas their French partners were operating in a genre that emphasized presenting facts in an objective discourse style.

Part of this larger discourse system in which genres are nested is the technology itself, or rather the "cultures of use" (Thorne 2003: 40) that inform technology use – the expectations and values associated with certain uses of technology that influence what genre conventions participants anticipate. As an example, Hanna and de Nooy (2009) illustrated how Anglophone students of French discovered that an online forum of an authentic French newspaper had its own genre and cultural expectations. The researchers suggest that the notion of genre itself be understood within cultural norms and practices. This mutually constitutive interaction between genre and culture is informed by the technology medium in which writing takes place.

Internet-mediated genres, then, might be better characterized by what Thorne (2010) has termed "digital vernacular texts and contexts" (p. 157) that occur across a wide range of formal and informal contexts, each inflected by preferred discursive and rhetorical features. Pasfield-Neofitou's (2011) examination of Australian learners of Japanese participating in various social networking sites such as Facebook and Mixi, which she refers to as *domains*, could be seen as an exploration of digital vernacular texts and contexts. She emphasizes that some domains are more heavily inflected with cultural and generic conventions, such that learners perceive themselves as "foreigners" or "non-native" (p. 105) speakers. In her discussion, Pasfield-Neofitou suggests that such self-identification as a foreigner online can have both negative and positive aspects. Several of the benefits she outlined included opportunities for the learners of Japanese in her study to participate in a virtual communities, to be immersed in authentic cultural symbols and resources, and to witness how native speakers of the language used it across different domains. Although less prevalent, some negative consequences of openly identifying as non-native speakers are worth mentioning: active ostracizing by the native speakers online and limited tolerance for language variation.

4.3 Classrooms to networked contexts

A third shift influenced by the development of Web 2.0 technologies puts into stark relief the differences between the research domains of classroom and non-classroom contexts. Questions are pursued about the role of formal instruction in a plurilingual digital world, in which the lines between standard varieties of languages and digital vernaculars (Thorne 2010), between online and offline worlds (Leander 2008), and between face-to-face and virtual communication, are blurring. Questions about the focus of research are explored, as classroom-based studies maintain an interest in information literacy, computer-mediated literacy, and multimedia literacy, but to date little attention has been paid to the development of information literacy in non-classroom contexts, where computer-mediated and multimedia literacy have instead been highlighted. Against this backdrop, we review research within each domain as well as research that works to bridge the two.

Within classroom-based studies that are focused on information literacy, much of the research is not specific to language learners, but rather explores underlying questions about how new technologies might require different skills for online navigation and reading and for searching and consuming information on the Internet (see discussion in Ware and Warschauer 2012). Promising approaches to information literacy have also been documented, in which information literacy skills receive fuller attention and can include linguistic grounding and structuring through WebQuests (Sox and Rubinstein-Avila 2009) and more student-centered and process-oriented classroom instruction that emphasizes the student's role as an active agent in creating, producing, and exchanging texts (Warschauer 2006).

When moving from the classroom into the "wild" of networked contexts, as Thorne (2010) suggests, researchers have begun to create bridges between formal learning contexts and less conventionalized venues for learning. For example, Sykes developed a virtual game, Croquelandia, designed to help learners develop Spanish pragmatic skills, and used both observational, survey, and outcome data to determine its usefulness as a classroom tool (Thorne, Black, and Sykes 2009). Helm, Guth, and Farrah (2012) reported on a project in which a group of English language students in Palestine and Italy who took part in an online exchange project called the Soliya Connect Program as part of their formal post-secondary coursework. Unlike other telecollaborative projects that are developed by the course instructors, the online exchange components of weekly synchronous audio-video group discussions were led by Soliya-trained facilitators, with the course instructors working with students to reflect on their experiences. In each of these two approaches to classroom-based learning, resources that had been developed and deployed outside of conventional contexts were used to create bridges between the classroom and the wider networked environment.

Such bridges are likely to form the next wave of research on digital literacies. In building links between classrooms and resources within networked contexts beyond the classroom, researchers can draw on a rich foundation of network-based studies (for extended reviews, see Thorne, Black, and Sykes 2009). This body of work often comes from ethnographies documenting how users participate within and across different domains. Black's (2008) three-year study followed six English language learners who participated in online fanfiction communities, in which they provided peer feedback on one another's multilingual fiction writing. Also using a case study approach, Yi (2010) documented how two adolescent multilingual writers used a range of technologies to engage in networked communities outside of the classroom to negotiate "literate and transcultural" (p. 319) identities. Thorne (2008) reports on interactions within the online gaming context of *World of Warcraft* and documented multilingual interactions that provided reciprocity, attention to linguistic form, motivating factors, and positive bonds. Harnessing these types of encounters for analysis and critique, both on their own terms as legitimate sites of writing, as well as on terms that are more conventionalized for enhancing classroom writing instruction, will likely move work on digital literacies forward in novel ways in the coming years.

4.4 Text-based writing to multimodal production

An important component of digital literacies is understanding the contribution of multimedia. Early in the development of multimedia language environments, instructors and researchers developed new pedagogical materials that they then used for instruction. The primary focus in this phase was on developing students' reading comprehension (e.g., Chun and Plass 1997) of foreign language texts. Attention was given to how multiple points of visual and aural input might supplement print to strengthen students' meaning representations. Now, however, with the availability of many low-cost, multimedia-authoring tools, literacy education has seen a shift from teacher production of multimedia to student authorship of their own multimodal documents, as we will illustrate in this section.

Kress (2003) defines multimodal texts as "texts made up of elements of modes which are based on different logics" (p. 46). That is to say, they are texts that integrate writing, speech, images, color, sound, animation, and that therefore combine logics of time and space. One example of multimodal authoring is digital storytelling, which involves the use of video, photographs, drawings, animation, voice, text, and music to develop filmic narratives. Digital stories can take the form of autobiographical narratives, poems, raps, reports, interviews, social commentary, or re-adaptations of stories or movies.

In the area of writing research, Hull and Nelson (2005) draw on Peircian semiotic theory as well as Labovian narrative theory to study the respective logics of modalities and how they function synergistically in digital storytelling. They are particularly interested in the blendings between new and old textual forms, and find that digital stories have much more in common with traditional narratives than they do with associative digital forms like hypertext.

Drawing on Kress's (2003) notions of transformation, transduction, and synaesthesia, Nelson (2006) argues for developing broader semiotic approaches to L2 composition and identifies a number of benefits of multimedia authoring including awareness of how the meaning potential of textual elements changes with each reuse in new contexts, recognition of how linguistic and visual affordances interact and contribute to meaning, and experience with new forms of authorship. Drawbacks he noted in his study included genericization of expression and over-accommodation of audience. Extending this line of work, Nelson and Kern (2012) argue for a relational pedagogy focused on relationships between forms, contexts, and meanings whose aim is not just the learning of conventions and competences but the development of a meta-communicative ability (i.e., an ability to reflect on signifying practices, and specifically on processes of textualization and contextualization).

Multimodal authoring presents us with new questions about what writing is, what literature is, perhaps even what language is. What is not new is that language proficiency has always been developed through a strategic sensitivity to how language is always enmeshed within a broader web of signification and action. As we look to the future of multimodal authoring, our task will be to attend to how learners integrate the spoken word, written text, visual impressions and images, social conventions, memories, feelings, and more to make and remake language for their specific purposes and interests.

As our attention is being drawn toward what learners do with these new forms of authoring, we will also need to critically examine our own stances toward these new productions. Conventionally, in our roles as instructors and researchers, we have had a stake in what counts as literacy for particular contexts and audiences, and in our respective fields, we will likely begin to develop a new language for understanding, interpreting, and evaluating these multimodal texts. How we choose to order and weigh in on this complexity is a high-stakes exercise for instructors and researchers who are pushing the boundaries of conventional literacy into the new terrain of digital literacies. In the final section, we examine some of the many challenges that await us in this process.

5 Future developments

A number of areas are in need of further research: ethical and methodological issues around new research designs, conceptual and analytical issues pertaining to how digital literacies are defined and researched, identity issues related to multilingual writers' at the intersection of technology and textual and multimodal production, pedagogical issues concerning the roles of instructors, and assessment issues that develop around the different dimensions of digital literacies.

Ethical issues about research designs require attention, as questions about online identity verification, informed consent, and privacy differ across contexts and therefore make standardized guidelines difficult to develop. These issues are particularly acute in non-classroom contexts, where participants in a focal interaction may not agree to have their discourse studied. In addition to the ethical challenges they present, such issues pose logistical barriers for researchers working at universities with differing levels of restriction regarding research within the digital domain, particularly when minors are involved (see discussion in Leander 2008). Such logistical issues are one aspect of other methodological concerns we have already discussed in this chapter, including the challenges of managing a large corpus of data, the theoretical choices informing which data are analyzed, and the growing call to develop research designs that integrate analyses across multiple contextual layers (Warschauer 2010; Warschauer and Ware 2008).

As research expands to include issues across multiple layers, research designs will likely begin to involve more collaborative research teams. Qualitative research has often been carried out by individual researchers who, to varying degrees, involve participants in inquiry and analysis. This model is particularly dominant in ethnographic work that requires intensive embedding with participants in order to develop an emic perspective (Black 2008; Lam 2004, 2009). However, a shift toward more interconnectivity among students in writing classrooms has seen a rise in international collaborations between two or more researchers who use their classroom-based work to bring several perspectives to bear on the research design and analysis (Belz and Mueller-Hartmann 2003; Helm, Guth, and Farrah 2012). Other creative collaborative research designs are emerging, some of which expand on qualitative research to include mixed methods (Ware and Rivas 2012), to utilize learner corpus analysis (Vyatkina 2012), and to link to larger economic and social concerns within the "context of power and politics" (Warschauer 2010: 137). Such collaborative efforts are of increasing importance in light of greater global connectivity, as researchers work to capture not just the particulars of local contexts and uses, but also to gain an understanding of how such activities are nested in and influenced by diverse social and economic conditions.

Another challenge for researchers is tackling persistent conceptual questions about how constructs such as digital literacies play out at different levels of analysis. Lamy and Goodfellow (2010) suggest that multi-layered analyses should occur across three levels of micro-, meso-, and macro-analysis. The micro-level refers to classroom interactions and practices, and the meso-level examines school and institutional factors. At the macro-level, the discourse frames established by entities at the societal, national, and supranational level are analyzed for the ways in which discussion of new technologies take place. Lamy and Goodfellow conclude that new technologies may form an "educational culture" (p. 130) rather than merely a pedagogical option, and therefore merit critique using a cultural-historic analytical lens in order to move across all three micro-, meso-, and macro-layers.

The shift toward multimodal textual production and consumption also poses analytical challenges. Researchers must discern which data to analyze and which tools to use in grappling with the amount of data available. Collecting and archiving vast amounts of data – in the form of interviews, surveys, text-based, audio-based, and video-based online interactions, screen shots, videos, self-reports, and assessments – has become much more efficient in recent years. In their discussion of multimodal interactions between language learners, Dooly and Hauck (2012) raise several considerations: which mode – textual, visual, verbal, gestural, physical, or musical – comes to the fore when analyzing multiple data sources; which learners become the focal participants; which roles researchers play and the degree to which researchers acknowledge their own presence; and finally, which transcription, notation, and analytical systems get adopted, adapted, or created in analyzing this wealth of data.

Identity issues will likely play a stronger role as multilingual writers establish their presence in a variety of online forums, communities, and sites of activity. In their collection of empirical pieces and first-person essays about second language writing and identity, Cox, Jordan, Ortmeier-Hooper, and Schwartz (2010) trace a long tradition of theoretical work on identity as it relates, in particular, to composition theory. They argue that the more recent shift toward second language writers' identity of the last 20 years has been strongly influenced by critical theoretical frameworks, such that identity issues are intertwined with those of power, access, community, politics, and cultural hybridity. Such frameworks that acknowledge the sociocultural and sociopolitical aspects of multilingual writers' identities are also found in recent empirical work across many fields, including composition studies, applied linguistics, and education, in which the intersection of technology and identity is foregrounded (Lam 2004, 2009; Yi 2010).

Pedagogically, the role of instructors needs to be further developed in relation to a shift toward digital literacies. Instructors must understand, develop, and train to engage with new goals and approaches to and targets for their writing instruction. The framework of digital literacies has replaced what might have once been viewed as a relatively stable target – proficiency in writing in a standard form of a given language – with a much more nuanced target – applying context-sensitive knowledge and skills of particular literacy practices across a wide range of contexts and genres. Almost ten years ago, in a synthesis of network-based language technologies, the importance of the teacher in "discerning, explaining, and reflecting upon culturally contingent patterns of interaction with their students" was highlighted (Kern, Ware, and Warschauer 2004). Ware and Kramsch (2005), in highlighting the importance of teachers' taking an intercultural stance, argued that instructors must help learners to see culture as a part of discourse from a "decentered perspective that goes beyond comprehending the surface meaning of words to discovering the logic of their interlocutors' utterances" (p. 203). In Thorne's (2010) call for researchers to examine interactions that take place outside of the classroom, "in the wild" (p. 144) of Internet-based domains of social interactivity such as gaming and social networking, he offers pedagogical suggestions for instructors to invite students to observe, collect, explore, analyze, create, and participate in these out-of-classroom environments.

Each of these various angles on the instructor's role shares a focus on the instructor as someone who helps students use language appropriately by developing metalinguistic awareness of the language and by viewing language within its contextual and situational framing. And yet, even if the instructor is viewed in a central role as a facilitator of a stream of online interaction, reflection, and analytical engagement, a clearer set of parameters will likely need to be developed to handle questions about tasks and sequencing, mediation and structuring, and outcomes and assessments.

Finally, issues related to assessment of new digital literacies form a largely underexplored area for substantive development. At the macro level, several countries and international professional organizations have begun larger initiatives to grapple with the new literacy landscape. In the US, for example, the International Society for Technology in Education (ISTE) has a database of online assignments that correlate with digital literacy skills (www.iste.org/standards.aspx). The professional organization Teaching English to Speakers of Other Languages (TESOL) recently published its first volume dedicated to establishing a set of common technology standards for language learners and teachers as a guiding framework (Healey, Hanson-Smith, Hubbard, Ioannou-Georgiou, Kessler, and Ware 2011). In a synthesis of national efforts in Norway, Australia, the United States, and Hong Kong at assessing digital competence, Erstad (2011) argues that these assessments are at an early phase and that educational policymakers and proponents of digital literacy need to be "more in touch with studying knowledge practices, and how digital media create conditions for change and transition within such practices" (p. 108).

When examining the new types of products that multilingual writers create within a digital literacies framework, questions of which products to assess, with which lenses, by which criteria, and for which reasons, remain largely negotiated by stakeholders across many levels. In his book-length examination of the interaction between writing assessments and technology, Neal (2011) urges educators to be actively engaged stakeholders in the development of new writing assessment technologies while we are still at the front end of the curve, lest we get left behind as "conscientious objectors or reluctant accomplices" (p. 9) of the decisions made by those without our field expertise. He proposes two frameworks to guide how writing instructors might proceed as productive contributors: a validity framework currently in use among writing assessment specialists and a framework that analyzes the connections between course outcomes and technological affordances.

As this developmental trajectory of digital literacies continues, the issues we have touched upon in this chapter will continue to explore what it means to write, respond, communicate, consume, and engage in a digital world. These issues have already entered the field of research on digital literacies to shape discussions about theory, pedagogy, and methodology. Over a decade ago, for example, Lemke (1998) highlighted the emerging distinction between a curricular learning paradigm, in which students receive knowledge within conventional structures, and an interactive learning paradigm, in which they engage actively with the creation, consumption, and critique of knowledge. More recently, Wesch (2007) distinguished between the linking of information that had been the focus of early Web-based technologies to the linking of people that characterizes Web 2.0 interactive technologies, a shift that provides an overarching frame for movements within digital literacies from static to interactive views of writing, from single authorship to multivoiced texts, and from essay writing to multimodal textual production. Such thematic labels provide useful heuristics for researchers interested in following and contributing to a field that continues to offer much room for exploration.

6 Additional sources

Barton, David and Carmen Lee. 2013. *Language online: investigating digital texts and practices.* New York: Routledge.

Coiro, Julie, Michelle Knobel, Colin Lankshear, and Donald Leu (eds.). 2008. *Handbook of research on new literacies.* Mahwah, NJ: Erlbaum.

DePew, Kelvin and Susan Miller. 2005. Studying L2 writers' digital writing: An argument for post-critical methods. *Computers & Composition* 22. 259–278.

Dudeney, Gavin, Nicky Hockly, and Mark Pegrum. 2013. *Digital literacies. Research and resources in language teaching.* London and New York: Routledge.

Evans, Michael (ed.). 2008. *Foreign language learning with digital technology.* New York: Bloomsbury Publishing.

Ito, Mizuko (ed.). 2009. *Hanging out, messing around, and geeking out.* Cambridge, MA: The MIT Press.

Miller, Suzanne and Mary McVee (eds.). 2012. *Multimodal composing in classrooms: learning and teaching for the digital world.* New York: Routledge.

Pegrum, Mark. 2014. *Mobile learning: Language, literacies, and cultures.* New York: Palgrave Macmillan.

Selfe, Cynthia. 1999. *Technology and literacy in the 21st century.* Carbondale, IL: Southern Illinois University Press.

Warschauer, Mark. 2011. *Learning in the cloud: How (and why) to transform schools with digital media.* New York: Teachers College Press.

7 References

Arnold, Nike, Lara Ducate, and Claudia Kost. 2012. Collaboration or cooperation? Analyzing group dynamics and revision processes in wikis. *CALICO Journal* 29(3). 431–448.

Belz, Julie and Andreas Müller-Hartmann. 2003. Teachers as intercultural learners: Negotiating German-American telecollaboration along the institutional fault line. *Modern Language Journal* 87(1). 71–89.

Black, Rebecca. 2008. *Adolescents and online fan fiction.* New York, NY: Peter Lang.

Bloch, Joel. 2007. Abdullah's blogging: A generation 1.5 student enters the blogosphere. *Language Learning & Technology* 11(2). 128–141.

Chun, Dorothy and Jan L. Plass. 1997. Research on text comprehension in multimedia environments. *Language Learning & Technology* 1(1). 60–81.

Cope, Bill and Mary Kalantzis. 1999. *Multiliteracies: Literacy learning and the design of social futures.* New York: Routledge.

Cox, Michelle, Jay Jordan, Christina Ortmeier-Hooper, and Gwen Schwartz. 2010. "Introduction." In *Reinventing identities in second language writing*, 15–28. Urbana, IL: National Council of Teachers of English.

Develotte, Christine, Nicolas Guichon, and Richard Kern. 2008. "Allo Berkeley? Ici Lyon ... Vous nous voyez bien?" Etude d'un dispositif de formation en ligne synchrone francoaméricain à travers les discours de ses usagers. *ALSIC* 11(2). 129–156.

Dooly, Melinda and Mirjam Hauck. 2012. Researching multimodal communicative competence in video and audio telecollaborative encounters. In Melinda Dooly and Robert O'Dowd (eds.) *Researching online interaction and exchange in foreign language education: Methods and issues*, 135–162. Bern: Peter Lang.

Elola, Iodia and Ana Oskoz. 2010. Collaborative writing: Fostering foreign language and writing conventions development. *Language Learning & Technology* 14(3). 51–71.

Erstad, Ola. 2011. Citizens navigating in literate worlds: The case of digital literacy. In Michael Thomas (Ed.), *Deconstructing digital natives*, 99–118. New York: Routledge.

Fellner, Terry and Matthew Apple. 2006. Developing writing fluency and lexical complexity with blogs. *The JALT/CALL Journal* 2(1). 15–26.

Gebhard, Meg, Don Shin, and Wendy Seger. 2011. Blogging and emergent L2 literacy development in an urban elementary school: A functional perspective. *CALICO Journal* 28(2). 278–307.

Gee, James. 2000. Teenagers in new times: A new literacy studies perspective. *Journal of Adolescent & Adult Literacy* 43(5). 412–420.

Gilton, Donna. 2007. Culture shock in the library: Implications for information literacy instruction. *Research Strategies* 20. 424–432

Gurak, Laura. 2001. *Cyberliteracy: Navigating the Internet with awareness*. New Haven: Yale University Press.

Guth, Sarah and Michael Thomas. 2010. Telecollaboration with Web 2.0 tools. In Sarah Guth and Francesca Helm (eds.), *Telecollaboration 2.0: Language, literacies, and intercultural learning in the 21st century*, 39–68. Bern: Peter Lang.

Hanna, Barbara and Juliana de Nooy. 2009. *Learning language and culture via public internet discussion forums*. Basingstoke, UK: Palgrave Macmillan

Healey, Deborah, Elizabeth Hanson-Smith, Philip Hubbard, Sophie Ioannou-Georgiou, Gregg Kessler, and Paige Ware. 2011. *TESOL technology standards: Description, implementation, integration*. Alexandria, VA: TESOL.

Helm, Francesca, Sarah Guth, and Mohammed Farrah. 2012. Promoting dialogue or hegemonic practice? Power issues in telecollaboration. *Language Learning & Technology* 16(2). 103–127.

Herring, Susan, Lois A. Scheidt, Inna Kouper, and Elijah Wright. 2006. A longitudinal content analysis of weblogs: 2003–2004. In M. Tremayne (Ed.), *Blogging, citizenship, and the future of media*, 3–20. London: Routledge.

Hull, Glynda and Mark Nelson. 2005. Locating the semiotic power of multimodality. *Written Communication* 22(2). 224–261.

Jenkins, Henry. 2006. *Convergence culture: Where old and new media collide*. New York: New York University Press.

Kern, Richard. 2014. Technology as pharmakon: The promise and perils of the Internet for foreign language education. *Modern Language Journal* 98(1). 330–347.

Kern, Richard, Paige Ware, and Mark Warschauer. 2004. Crossing frontiers: New directions in online pedagogy and research. *Annual Review of Applied Linguistics* 24. 243–260.

Kern, Richard and Mark. 2000. Theory and practice of network-based language teaching. In Mark Warschauer and Richard Kern (eds.), *Network-based language teaching: Concepts and practice*, 1–19. New York: Cambridge University Press.

Kessler, Greg. 2009. Student-initiated attention to form in wiki-based collaborative writing. *Language Learning & Technology* 13(1). 79–95.

Kötter, Markus. 2003. Negotiation of meaning and codeswitching in online tandems. *Language Learning & Technology* 7(2). 145–172.

Kramsch, Claire and Steven Thorne. 2002. Foreign language learning as global communicative practice. In David Block and Deborah Cameron (eds.), *Globalization and language teaching*, 83–100. London: Routledge.

Kress, Gunther. 2003. *Literacy in the new media age*. London: Routledge.

Lam, Wan Shun Eva. 2004. Second language socialization in a bilingual chat room: Global and local considerations. *Language Learning & Technology* 8(3). 44–65.

Lam, Wan Shun Eva. 2009. Multiliteracies on instant messaging in negotiating local, translocal, and transnational affiliations: A case of an adolescent immigrant. *Reading Research Quarterly* 44(4). 377–397. dx.doi.org/10.1598/RRQ.44.4.5

Lamy, Marie-Noëlle and Robin Goodfellow. 2010. Telecollaboration and learning 2.0. In Sarah Guth and Francesca Helm (eds.), *Telecollaboration 2.0: Language, literacies, and intercultural learning in the 21st century*, 107–138. Bern: Peter Lang.

Lawrence, Joshua, Mark Warschauer, Binbin Zheng, and Diana Mullins. 2013. Research in digital literacy: Tools to support learning across the disciplines. In *Adolescent literacy in the era of the common core: From research into practice*, 117–129. Cambridge, MA: Harvard Education Press.

Leander, Kevin. 2008. Toward and connective ethnography of online/offline literacy networks. In Julie Coiro, Michelle Knobel, Colin Lankshear, & Donald Leu (eds.), *Handbook of research on new literacies*, 33–65. Mahwah, NJ: Erlbaum.

Lee, Lina. 2011a. Blogging: Promoting learner autonomy and intercultural competence through study abroad. *Language Learning & Technology* 15(3). 87–109.

Lee, Lina. 2011b. Focus on form through peer feedback in a Spanish-American telecollaborative exchange. *Language Awareness* 20(4). 343–357.

Lemke, Jay. 1998. Metamedia literacy: Transforming meanings and media. In David Reinking, Michael McKenna, Linda Labbo, and Ronald Kieffer (eds.), *Handbook of literacy and technology: Transformations in a post-typographic world,* 283–301. Hillsdale, NJ: Erlbaum.

Liaw, Meei-ling. 2006. E-learning and the development of intercultural competence. *Language Learning & Technology* 10(3). 49–64.

Luke, Allan and Cushla Kapitzke. 1999. Literacies and libraries – Archives and cybraries. *Pedagogy, Culture & Society* 7. 467–491.

Mak, Barley and David Coniam. 2008. Using wikis to enhance and develop writing skills among secondary school students in Hong Kong. *System* 36(3). 437–455.

Murray, Lim and Tríona Hourigan. 2008. Blogs for specific purposes: Expressivist or socio-cognitivist approach? *ReCALL* 20(1). 83–98.

Naumann, Johanes. 2012. The interplay of navigation and text processing in digital reading performance. Paper presented at the American Educational Research Association Annual Meeting, British Columbia.

Neal, Michael. 2011. *Writing assessment and the revolution in digital texts and technologies.* New York: Teachers College Press.

Nelson, Mark. 2006. Mode, meaning, and synaesthesia in multimedia L2 writing. *Language Learning & Technology* 10(2). 56–76.

Nelson, Mark and Richard Kern. 2012. Language teaching and learning in the *Postlinguistic Condition?* In Lubna Alsagoff, Sandra McKay, Guangwai Hu, and Willy Renandya (eds.), *Principles and practices for teaching English as an international language,* 47–66. New York: Routledge.

New London Group. 1996. A pedagogy of multiliteracies: Design social futures. *Harvard Educational Review* 66. 60–92.

O'Reilly, Tim. 2005. *What is Web 2.0?* Retrieved May 10, 2012, from http://oreilly.com/web2/archive/what-is-web-20.html

O'Rourke, Breffni. 2005. Form-focused interaction in online tandem learning. *CALICO Journal* 22(3). 433–466.

Pasfield-Neofitou, Sarah. 2011. Online domains of language use: Second language learners' experiences of virtual community and foreignness. *Language Learning & Technology* 15(2). 92–108.

Patterson, David. 2011. *Becoming Researchers: Community College ESL Students, Information Literacy, and the Library.* Unpublished doctoral dissertation, University of California, Berkeley.

Schwienhorst, Klaus. 2002. Evaluating tandem language learning in the MOO: Discourse repair strategies in a bilingual Internet project. *Computer-Assisted Language Learning* 15(2). 135–146.

Selber, Stuart. 2004. *Multiliteracies for a digital age.* Carbondale: Southern Illinois University Press.

Sloan, Douglas. 1984. *The computer in education: A critical perspective.* New York: Teachers College Press.

Sotillo, Susana. 2000. Discourse functions and syntactic complexity in synchronous and asynchronous communication. *Language Learning & Technology* 4(1). 82–119.

Sox, Amanda and Eliane Rubinstein-Ávila. 2009. WebQuests for English-language learners: Essential elements for design. *Journal of Adolescent & Adult Literacy* 53(1). 38–48.

Storch, Neomy. 2012. Collaborative writing as a site for L2 learning in face-to-face and online modes. In Greg Kessler, Ana Oskoz and Idoia Elola (eds.), *Technology across writing contexts and tasks,* 113–130. San Marcos, TX: CALICO.

Street, Brian. 1995. *Social literacies: Critical approaches to literacy in development, ethnography, and education*. London: Longman.

Sykes, Julie, Ana Oskoz, and Steven Thorne. 2008. Web 2.0 Synthetic immersive environments and mobile resources for language education. *CALICO Journal* 25(3). 528–546.

Thorne, Steven. 2003. Artifacts and cultures-of-use in intercultural communication. *Language Learning & Technology* 7(2). 38–67.

Thorne, Steven. 2008. Transcultural communication in open Internet environments and massively multiplayer online games. In Sally Magnan (ed.), *Mediating discourse online*, 305–327. Amsterdam: John Benjamins.

Thorne, Steven. 2010. The 'intercultural turn' and language learning in the crucible of new media. In Sarah Guth and Francesca Helm (eds.), *Telecollaboration 2.0: Language, literacies, and intercultural learning in the 21st century*, 139–164. Bern: Peter Lang.

Thorne, Steven, Rebecca Black, and Julie Sykes. 2009. Second language use, socialization, and learning in Internet interest communities and online gaming. *The Modern Language Journal* 93. 802–821.

Vyatkina, Nina. 2012. Applying the methodology of learner corpus analysis to telecollaborative discourse. In Melinda Dooly and Robert O'Dowd (eds.) *Researching online interaction and exchange in foreign language education: Methods and issues*, 267–303. Bern: Peter Lang.

Ware, Paige and Claire Kramsch. 2005. Toward an intercultural stance: Teaching German and English through telecollaboration. *Modern Language Journal* 89(2). 190–205.

Ware, Paige and Robert O'Dowd. 2008. Peer feedback on language form in telecollaboration. *Language Learning & Technology* 12(1). 43–63.

Ware, Paige and Brenna Rivas. 2012. Mixed methods research on online language exchanges. In Melinda Dooly and Robert O'Dowd (eds.) *Researching online interaction and exchange in foreign language education: Methods and issues*, 107–131. Bern: Peter Lang.

Ware, Paige and Warschauer, Mark. 2006. Electronic feedback and second language writing. In Ken Hyland and Fiona Hyland (eds.), *Feedback in second language writing: Contexts and issues*, 105–122. Cambridge, UK: Cambridge University Press.

Ware, Paige and Mark Warschauer. 2012. Qualitative research on information and communication technology. In Carol Chapelle (ed.), *The encyclopedia of Applied Linguistics* 8, 4787–4792. Hoboken, NJ: Wiley Blackwell.

Warschauer, Mark. 1999. *Electronic literacies: Language, culture, and power in online education*. Mahwah, NJ: Lawrence Erlbaum Associates.

Warschauer, Mark. 2003. *Technology and social inclusion: Rethinking the digital divide*. Cambridge: MIT Press.

Warschauer, Mark. 2006. *Laptops and literacy*. New York: Teachers College Press.

Warschauer, Mark. 2010. Digital literacy studies: Progress and prospects. In Mike Baynham and Mastin Prinsloo (eds.), *The future of literacy studies*, 123–140. Houndmills, Basingstoke, UK: Palgrave Macmillan.

Warschauer, Mark and Douglas Grimes. 2007. Audience, authorship, and artifact: The emergent semiotics of Web 2.0. *Annual Review of Applied Linguistics* 27. 1–23.

Warschauer, Mark and Paige Ware. 2008. Learning, change and power: Competing frames of technology and literacy. In Julie Coiro, Michelle Knobel, Colin Lankshear, and Donald Leu (eds.), *Handbook of research on new literacies*, 215–240. New York: Lawrence Erlbaum.

Welch, Kathleen. 1999. *Electric rhetoric: Classical rhetoric, oralism, and a new literacy*. Cambridge, MA: MIT Press.

Wesch, Michael. 2007. *Web 2.0: The machine is us/ing us* [Video]. Retrieved May 15, 2012, from http://www.youtube.com/watch?v=6gmP4nk0EOE

Yi, Youngjoo. 2010. Identity matters: Theories that help explore adolescent multilingual writers and their identities. Michelle Cox, Jay Jordan, Christina Ortmeier-Hooper, and Gwen Schwartz (eds.), *Reinventing identities in second language writing*. 303–323. Urbana, IL: National Council of Teachers of English.

Zheng, Binbin and Mark Warschauer. 2012. *Blogging to learn: Participation and literacy among linguistically diverse fifth-grade students*. Paper presented at the American Educational Research Association Annual Meeting, Vancouver, British Columbia, Canada.

Diane Pecorari

15 Writing from sources, plagiarism and textual borrowing

The three elements treated in this chapter – writing from sources, plagiarism and textual borrowing – are inextricably intertwined, and are central concerns in second- and foreign-language writing, an area which has traditionally placed a strong emphasis on *academic* writing. Virtually all written academic genres are characterised by a high degree of intertextuality; the value of a new work is established in part by describing the existing works on related topics and the questions they leave unanswered, which the new work attempts to address. Framing a new work in the context of the existing literature requires the writer to read what others have done, and then to make connections between the current work and earlier ones. Thus source use – incorporating content and language from earlier texts in the creation of a new one – is a standard and indeed unavoidable practice for academic writers. This chapter describes how research into this topic has developed, summarises current knowledge about it, and identifies important issues for the future.

Plagiarism is typically defined as presenting language or ideas which are derived from another work as if they were one's own. While a definition like this can be problematised, it does illustrate that plagiarism is fundamentally a specific form of writing from sources. Although plagiarism has many manifestations, and (as discussed below) a significant amount of disagreement exists as to which forms of source use constitute plagiarism, it has several general characteristics. First, it involves a relationship between one or more sources and a work which makes use of them. Further, that relationship is not adequately signalled. This may mean, for example, that language which is repeated from the source is not be identified as quotation, or that ideas from an earlier work are retold in the new one without indications in the form of the conventional mechanisms of citation. Because academic conventions demand that writers identify their sources, this lack of transparency means that the intertextual relationships involved in plagiarism are unconventional, and indeed norm-breaking. Importantly, though, while a failure to adhere to academic conventions is implied in the word plagiarism, the norm-breaking effect may come about inadvertently rather than as the result of conscious intention on the part of the writer.

In recognition of the fact that plagiarism may be understood to imply intentional deception, a number of alternative terms have been proposed to indicate inappropriate use of sources without deceptive intent. These include *textual borrowing* (e.g. Barks and Watts 2001; Keck 2006; Pennycook 1996; Petrić 2012) and *transgressive intertextuality* (e.g. Abasi, Akbari, and Graves 2006; Borg 2009; Chandrasoma, Thompson, and Pennycook 2004; Thompson 2005). *Patchwriting* was first coined by Rebecca Howard (1995), working within the first-language (L1) composition tradition, to describe a technique of merging borrowed chunks from multiple sources and making superficial changes to them. This term has been widely adopted in the L2 writing literature, often with a broadened meaning to indicate any intertextual relationship which is inappropriate but which is not caused by the intention to cheat. Patchwriting is used in this somewhat broader sense by Pecorari (2008), who contrasts it with *prototypical plagiarism*, a deceptive act, using the umbrella term *textual plagiarism* to signify any text characterised by inappropriately signalled intertextual relationships, setting the writer's intention aside.

Plagiarism and textual borrowing are thus closely related, specific forms of writing from sources. However, as this chapter will show, the tendency in the L2 writing literature has been to approach plagiarism in isolation; it is only recently that it has begun to be examined within the broader context of source use and writing from sources.

1 Historical overview

Aspects of writing from sources in a second language have been intensively investigated in the English for academic purposes (EAP) tradition. An early, pedagogically motivated concern with verb forms (e.g. Hanania and Akhtar 1985; Tarone, Dwyer, Gillette, and Icke 1998) led to an emphasis on reporting verbs[1], particularly in conjunction with their rhetorical functions (Een 1982; Hawes and Thomas 1997; Oster 1981; Shaw 1992). A broader interest in the formal aspects of citation (Swales 1981) emerged, with features such as the positioning of the reference (i.e., integral versus non-integral: Swales 1990) and the choice to paraphrase, quote, etc. (Dubois 1988; Salager-Meyer 1999) being investigated. Models for categorising the semantics of the reporting verb have been developed (Hunston 1993; Thompson and Ye 1991).

An overarching trend has been a growing recognition of the interaction among these factors; for example, not only is there an association between reporting verb form and rhetorical function (for example, whether an idea is presented as new or given information), those tendencies may be shaped by the semantics of the verb (Pecorari 2013a), and those choices in turn are revealing of the writer's stance toward the reported proposition (Hunston 1993). Further, citation has been used as a lens through which to examine differences in writing across academic disciplines (Hyland 2002) and it is increasingly clear that such variation is not arbitrary but rather that formal aspects of citation are reflective of the practices, values and approaches to knowledge construction which themselves vary across subject boundaries (Charles 2006a, 2006b).

---

1 Reporting verbs are verbs used to attribute language or ideas to a source, such as *reports*, *states*, *argues*: Stilton *argues* that the moon is made of green cheese. See also section 2.3 of this chapter.

Researchers in second-language writing came relatively late to the study of source use; citation has a longer history as a topic of inquiry in at least two other research disciplines, the sociology of science and bibliometrics, stretching back to studies such as Burton and Kebler's (1960) on the "half-life" of citations. However, despite Swales' (1986) insightful observation that citation research in applied linguistics has been largely uninformed by that in other areas, and his call for greater cross-disciplinary contact, very little work – with Harwood (2004) and White (2004) as notable exceptions – has attempted to fill the gap.

Thus the body of research on citation developed with an emphasis on producing descriptions of the forms and functions of references to sources in academic discourse. It is possible that the proliferation of research on this topic is due at least in part to the exceptionally neat match between this discoursal feature and the core competences of the L2 writing expert. Citation, possibly more than any other feature of academic discourse, offers the writer a range of formal and lexical choices and each choice serves as a vehicle for conveying the content of the reported proposition, and positioning it in relation to the larger citing text. Citation is, in other words, precisely at the intersection of form and content, where the expertise of the L2 writing specialist is maximally useful.

As the brief review above suggests, the early work on writing from sources was, like much other research within the EAP tradition, aimed at producing descriptions of the conventional features of academic genres, and of the variation in features across academic disciplines, in the belief that such descriptions may guide teacher practice and serve as a benchmark for learner production. More directly pedagogical and learner-oriented studies were slower to emerge. These include Campbell's (1990) and Borg's (2000) descriptions of learners' source use practices, Dong's (1996) work on students learning academic source use conventions and Groom's (2000) pedagogically focused model for describing the rhetorical effect of citation choices.

Plagiarism, by contrast, crept onto the L2 writing research agenda by stealth, garnering brief mentions within case studies (Currie 1998) or being used as an example of the sort of mismatch between expectations and performance which arise when L2 users must produce academic writing in English (Matalene 1985). Early mentions of the topic in the literature frequently featured the often repeated idea that cultural differences may provide an explanation for plagiarism in the work of L2 writers (Evans and Youmans 2000; Shi 2006), an idea which still attracts considerable controversy and debate (for a fuller discussion of the relationship between culture and plagiarism, see Pecorari 2016; Pecorari and Petrić 2014).

Despite the regularity with which plagiarism emerged as an issue in investigations of L2 writing more broadly, and considerable discussion of the phenomenon, the first empirical work with a focus primarily on plagiarism was Deckert's (1993) questionnaire survey of attitudes among students in Hong Kong, and subsequent investigations of the topic were also concerned with writers' and teachers' attitudes and perceptions (Chandrasegaren 2000; Crocker and Shaw 2002). A systematic mapping of the incidence of textual plagiarism in the work of L2 writers came a decade after Deckert's study (Pecorari 2003).

Like citation, plagiarism has been investigated within several research traditions, including educational science and ethics. The development of the topic within the L2 writing research tradition has included a strong tendency to suspend the widespread association between textual plagiarism and an intentional flouting of academic conventions. As a result, the body of research on textual borrowing can be considered broadly identical with that on plagiarism within L2 writing research. However, even when believed to be non-deceptive, plagiarism is generally viewed as something to avoid or prevent, not least of all because of the consequences for the academic writer in whose work it is detected. A recurring theme in the literature has thus been identifying the causes of non-deceptive plagiarism.

An early assumption guiding much of this work was a belief that the likely causes lay in the student's status as a second-language writer. One possible explanation was a knowledge gap: (some) L2 writers have not had the mantra "use your own words" inculcated in them from an early age as pupils in Anglophone schools have. Instead, their writing strategies may be driven by other culturally influenced factors. More recently, this idea has been called into question, at least in its most simplistic form (i.e., an assertion that plagiarism is acceptable in some cultures). The accuracy of these assertions has been questioned (e.g. Ha 2005; Liu 2005; Wheeler 2009) and the relationship between culture and plagiarism is likely to be more complex they indicate (Bloch 2008).

A further trend has been an interest in investigating whether the perceptions of the academic establishment are in fact as stable as they once were assumed to be. Several studies have shown that individual teachers (and others in gatekeeping roles) hold widely differing views on the sorts of intertextual practices which should be condoned or disallowed (Borg 2009; Crocker and Shaw 2002; Pecorari and Shaw 2012). These differences suggest a need for a re-examination of students' supposed divergences from academic norms.

2 Theory and research

The work on appropriate and inappropriate use of sources has, in common with much other research on L2 writing, been largely oriented toward pedagogical applications and therefore driven by practice to a greater extent than theory, and as a result has been eclectic in its choice of theory and methodology. Nonetheless, some common themes can be teased out.

2.1 Theoretical perspectives on plagiarism and source use

An important theoretical underpinning for much of the research on source use and plagiarism has been intertextuality. In this respect the L2 writing literature distinguishes itself from other literature bases which have addressed plagiarism as a violation of ethical principles, and from a view that the boundary between the permissible and the plagiaristic is fairly clear and rule-governed. Second-language writing studies (e.g., Groom 2000; Petrić 2012; Thompson 2005) have drawn on scholars such as Bakhtin (1981) and Kristeva (1980) who view language as inherently dialogic and thus intertextual. By virtue of being informed by this perspective, the body of research on source use and plagiarism in the writing of second-language users has tended to be sensitive to complexities and nuances.

An influential approach has been Fairclough's (1992) distinction between *manifest* and *constitutive* intertextuality. Manifest intertextuality is the direct text-to-text relationships of which quotation, paraphrase and other forms of academic citation are examples. Constitutive intertextuality on the other hand is the less direct set of relationships and influences which result in similarities among texts from the same genre, produced by members of the same community, etc.

Fleshing out the mechanisms of constitutive intertextuality is Hoey's (2005) notion of lexical priming, the idea that our exposure to language creates for each language user a mental reservoir of patterns which translate into the tendency to prefer one form (word, structure, etc.) over another. According to Hoey, if texts within the same genre share certain features and resemble each other, it is because the writers who produced them have been exposed to other, similar texts and are thus more likely (i.e., primed) to reproduce those features.

At different levels, then, Fairclough and Hoey provide support for the understanding that all discourse is socially constructed; conventions for source use, determinations about what is conventional and acceptable, the reader's expectations and the standards against which writers' performance is judged are constructed by the community of readers and writers. Such communities are characterised by a shared set of practices (Lave and Wenger 1991) and by shared forms of communication (Swales 1990) which are used in the service of achieving the community's objectives. In Swales' now classic definition, a discourse community has the following characteristics:

- A discourse community has a broadly agreed set of common public goals (1990: 24)
- A discourse community has mechanisms of intercommunication among its members (1990: 25)
- A discourse community uses its participatory mechanisms primarily to provide information and feedback (1990: 26)
- A discourse community utilizes and hence possesses one or more genres in the communicative furtherance of its aims (1990: 26)

- In addition to owning genres, a discourse community has acquired some specific lexis (1990: 26)
- A discourse community has a threshold level of members with a suitable degree of relevant content and discoursal expertise (1990: 27)

Swales' criteria encompass both macro- and micro-level aspects of communication, thus confirming the importance of both the generic features of academic writing (among which reference to sources is prominent) and the lexico-syntactic forms (e.g., reporting verbs) which are used to realise them. By making explicit the connection between the goals and aims of the community and its discoursal practices, this definition also highlights the potential for differences among academic disciplines, and suggests (as has since been demonstrated) that variation across academic areas is not arbitrary (Becher and Trowler 2001). The discourse community has also been a fundamental notion underlying studies of cross-disciplinary understandings of plagiarism (Borg 2009).

2.2 Methods of inquiry

Given that source use and plagiarism are situated at the intersection of textual relationships and writers' practices, it is only natural that a range of methods have been used to investigate this topic. Two broad methodological tendencies can be distinguished: the first makes use of surveys, questionnaires and other instruments to gather the views and perceptions of key actors (typically student writers, their teachers and/or other gatekeepers); and the second involves textual analysis. In the latter category, the techniques of both corpus linguistics and discourse analysis have been used, as well as comparisons of texts and the sources they draw on.

Corpus methods have been used in a number of studies to investigate formal features such as the frequency with which writers choose to paraphrase or quote, or to use integral or non-integral citations (in Swales' terms; i.e., citations in which the author's name is or is not an element in the reporting sentence); or the structure of the clause in which the reference appears (e.g., Charles 2006b; Hunston 1995; Hyland 2002; Thompson 2000).

In any corpus investigation, the composition of the corpus is an important consideration, and in researching source use an important issue to address in compilation is insuring a sufficiently large number of references to sources. One purpose of corpus studies is to provide learners and teachers with descriptions of conventional practice, so the corpus must consist of texts from which valid lessons can be drawn. As a result, corpora used in investigations of source use are frequently purpose-compiled, in order to retain a focus on academic writing, and are relatively small (by the standards of corpus linguistics). A tension exists between selecting texts which can be considered good models of writing and texts which are similar to those which L2 writers need to produce. Corpora have included published research articles (Hyland 1999), theses produced by L1 writers (Charles 2006a, 2006b) and assignments which have been awarded high marks (Ädel and Römer 2012; Swales 2014).

Many studies of source use have been interested in the rhetorical functions which references to sources in various forms create (e.g. Petrić 2007), and this has involved close textual analysis. Shaw (1992), for example, showed that the choice of verb form (tense, aspect and voice) is contingent upon the writer's need to place a claim at the beginning of a sentence or later, thus positioning it as given or new information. Groom (2000) described how formal choices such as the use of an integral or a non-integral citation shift the balance of authority between the writer of a text and the authors it cites.

In studies of textual plagiarism, the idea that the writer has accounted transparently for all aspects of source use is not a valid starting assumption. As a result, in such studies, textual analysis may include comparisons of the text under investigation with its sources, either in ordinary assessment writing tasks (Davis 2013; Pecorari 2003; Weigle and Parker 2012) or on tasks designed to facilitate comparison by ensuring the writers draw on a limited and known selection of sources (Campbell 1990; Shi 2004).

Understanding what motivates a writer to make certain choices in using sources (e.g., where to include citations, which sources to cite, etc.) has been a focus of a number of investigations. One approach, and the most direct one, is to ask writers about their source use practices, usually in an interview setting (Flowerdew and Li 2007; Harwood 2009; Petrić and Harwood 2013), although other methods such as think-aloud protocols have been used (Hirvela and Du 2013). In order to capture responses to specific source use practices, interviews are frequently text-based, with respondents asked to comment on examples (Harwood 2008; Pecorari and Shaw 2012). The views of writers (frequently students) and readers (frequently their teachers) are sometimes triangulated (Pecorari 2003; Petrić 2004).

Surveys and questionnaires may be used to ask about the attitudes toward source use, knowledge about principles for source use and/or comments on specific examples of source use (Deckert 1993; Hu and Lei 2012; Roig 1997, 2001; Wheeler 2009). These instruments may take the form of paired examples (i.e., an extract from a source and an example of how a writer used the source) or of a set of descriptions of behaviours (e.g., "copying a few words without quotation marks"), asking respondents to rank their acceptability.

Methodological problems in researching attitudes toward intertextual relationships are considerable. Interviews and textual analyses using authentic writing produce rich data but findings may not be representative of other, similar writers. The advantages of a survey approach are primarily that the investigation may encompass larger numbers of participants, and that the same questions or prompts are used, making responses more fully comparable. However, there are also inherent difficulties in such approaches. If questions are asked in abstract forms (e.g.

"Is it acceptable to copy short phrases from a source?") the reliability of the answers depends on the extent to which all respondents associated the abstract descriptions with similar acts: does everyone interpret "short phrases" the same way? When respondents are asked to comment on concrete examples of source use, it is possible that relevant details of the intertextual relationships may not have been noticed by a respondent. To circumvent methodological difficulties, a number of researchers have used mixed methods, sometimes in the context of a case study approach (Li 2013; Li and Casanave 2012; Thompson, Morton, and Storch 2013).

2.3 Current knowledge on the topic

The body of research into this area has resulted in detailed descriptions of the ways in which academic texts of various types make use of and cite sources, and in a lexicon for categorising the choices writers can make as they incorporate sources into their work. A basic choice is whether to quote or paraphrase the cited work, and some researchers have drawn finer-grained distinctions, e.g. between block quotations and those which appear within the running text (Hyland 1999) or 'non-citational' references to schools of research (Tadros 1993). References may be integral, when the name of the author is a syntactic component of the reporting sentence, or non-integral, when it is relegated to a parenthetical reference or footnote (Swales 1990) and despite the fact that referencing systems involving endnotes and footnotes obviate the necessity for integral citations, some writers nonetheless choose to use them (Harwood 2008).

Integral citations frequently require the use of reporting verbs, and these vary considerably in their semantics, and thus on the impact they have on the larger text. Typologies allow verbs to be categorised according to their semantic features. A prominent early typology was that of Thompson and Ye (1991), which considers several aspects (and which has since been widely adopted and adapted: Charles 2006a, 2006b; Hunston 1993).

One is whether the act ascribed to the cited researcher is one of cognition, communication, or engaging in a research process (as exemplified in (a)–(c) below, respectively). Another is what the verb suggests about the cited author's degree commitment to and the writer's stance toward the reported proposition. Thus in (b) below, Smith is shown to believe that the assertion is true, whereas (a) does not reveal whether Smith agrees with it. In (d) there is a strong implication that that the writer believes that Smith is correct in the assertion, while both (a) and (b) withhold the writer's attitude toward the claim.

a) *Smith considers the claim that the moon is made of green cheese.*
b) *Smith asserts that the moon is made of green cheese.*
c) *Smith tested the composition of the moon.*
d) *Smith confirms that the moon is made of green cheese.*

The tense and aspect of the reporting verb have also been a topic of investigation. It has long been understood that the most common choices for reporting verbs – simple present, present perfect and simple past – carry somewhat different connotations in reporting than they do in general discourse (Oster 1981). This has been shown to depend in part on an interaction among verb form and the purpose served by the citation (e.g., making a specific point or putting forward a generalisation; Shaw 1992) and on the semantics of the verb itself (Charles 2006b).

Unsurprisingly, there is considerable variation across academic disciplines. The disciplines traditionally described as *soft* (those in the humanities and social sciences) tend to use more citation overall than engineering and science (i.e., *hard*) fields (Ädel and Garretson 2006; Hyland 1999). They are also much more likely to use signalled quotation; students in the hard areas use quotation sparingly (Ädel and Garretson 2006) and this is reflective of a stronger tendency still to avoid quotation in published writing (though, perhaps because of the highly unconventional nature of direct quotation, writers in the hard fields are more likely to repeat verbatim from their sources without signalling it as quotation; Pecorari 2006). Interestingly, this tendency is one which has become entrenched over time, at least for writers in the field of medicine, who, according to a diachronic study, have moved from a conservative use of quotations in the mid-nineteenth century to virtually abandoning them (Salager-Meyer 1999).

However, other differences across disciplines are less clear. Hyland (1999) found a preference for non-integral citations in all of the subjects studied except philosophy, and the other seven fields in that study ranged in their use of integral citations from about 10 % to 35 %, with the hard fields tending to have fewer than the soft ones. However, in undergraduate writing, integral citations were found to be more frequent in four of six subject areas (Ädel and Garretson 2006) while one study of PhD theses found that writers in politics and materials science used integral citations with approximately the same frequency, and both used them more frequently than non-integral citations (Charles 2006b). Another study of theses (Thompson 2000) found that only 32% of citations in Agricultural Botany were integral while 63% were in Agricultural Economics.

Similarly, there is some evidence that the choice of reporting verb is subject to disciplinary variation. Hyland reports "an enormous variation between disciplines ... suggest[ing] that writers in different fields almost draw on completely different sets of items" (1999: 349). However, he also finds that, out of over 400 reporting verbs identified, seven alone accounted for over a quarter of all citations, and four – *suggest*, *argue*, *show* and *report* – were among the most frequent reporting verbs in three to five fields each. Charles' (2006b) study of two disciplines found only partial confirmation for these results.

It seems likely, therefore, that in addition to variation across subject areas, there are differences between student and published research writing. Less clear is what the pedagogical implications of such differences are, given that the objectives of assessment writing are not identical with those of research articles. It is also possible that some apparent disagreement in findings may be due to corpus composition, and specifically how narrowly or broadly a "discipline" is defined, and the distribution of texts within it, i.e., factors such as whether they come from one or many journals, and were produced by a smaller or larger number of authors. In an interview study of academics' reasons for citing, Harwood (2009) found not only disciplinary variation in the reasons given but *intra*-disciplinary variation which he suggested was due to the individual proclivities of the participants. In short, before confident conclusions can be drawn about the role of academic discipline in influencing source use, more will have to be known about other sources of variation.

At the descriptive end, the occurrence of textual plagiarism has been identified repeatedly in the work of second-language writers. It has been documented in numerous studies of the broader development of L2 writers (Ballard and Clanchy 1991; Cadman 1997; Currie 1998; Leki and Carson 1997; Pennycook 1996; St. John 1987; Shaw 1991; Spack 1997), and case studies of student source use have also identified it frequently (Flowerdew and Li 2007; Li and Casanave 2012; Petrić 2004; Shi 2008). These frequent reports in the literature suggest that it is not a rare or exceptional occurrence, an idea which is confirmed by a study of theses and dissertations, which found source use which might be considered to be plagiarism in all seventeen texts examined (Pecorari 2003).

However, it is difficult to read this literature and not conclude that textual plagiarism frequently has causes which are unrelated to an attempt to deceive. Evidence for this is necessarily circumstantial, but there is such a preponderance of it that it must be taken seriously. First, participants in these studies made a free choice to take part in an investigation of the writing process, and in many cases were forthcoming about the ways they had used sources, and that behaviour is not consistent with the idea that they believed they had engaged in an illicit act.

Secondly, in interviews, surveys and questionnaires, writers have described a constellation of factors which provide alternative explanations for inappropriate source use. One set of factors has to do with knowing what is expected, permissible and inappropriate. Writers may possess declarative knowledge about plagiarism as they have read about it in university policies, but be unable to translate that knowledge into practice when writing from sources (Li and Casanave 2012). They also struggle to align the guidance they are given about source use (generally presented as straightforward rules) with the inherent complexity of identifying all of one's intellectual debts so that they can be acknowledged (Pecorari 2003). Admonitions to cite one's sources presuppose that writers know what sources they have drawn on, but avoiding plagiarism is not the L2 writer's only (or indeed primary) objective, and writers who are under pressures of time and task cannot always identify the source of their knowledge or ideas on a topic (Petrić 2004). Distinguishing between ideas which need to be attributed to a source and those which are common knowledge is also a source of difficulty (Shi 2008). Disciplinary constraints, such as the unconventionality of quotation in hard fields, make the task more difficult by constraining the degrees of freedom available to the writer (Pecorari 2006).

Finding linguistically accurate and idiomatic ways of expressing ideas is challenging for second-language writers, and appropriating language from published sources is one strategy for meeting the challenge. Flowerdew and Li (2007) interviewed L2 writers who used this strategy and who expressed a belief that it was appropriate, as long as they steered clear of taking credit for other authors' research findings, and this view was confirmed by some of the academics interviewed in another study (Pecorari and Shaw 2012). Patchwriting, as described by Howard (1995), involves making superficial changes to language which has largely been copied from a source, and this act of processing language appears to be sufficient to make some writers regard the result as legitimately their own. Wheeler (2009: 25) asked Japanese students to respond to examples of more and less wholesale copying and found that a text which used a patchwriting strategy was condemned less strongly than one which copied the original exactly.

As noted above, the role of culture as a cause of textual plagiarism has attracted considerable debate. Claims for culture as an explanatory factor are typically based on the idea that (some) L2 writers do not share the understanding of plagiarism that their teachers or L1 classmates do. Supposed differences in cultural values such as placing great importance on a polished finished product (Sherman 1992), or a different orientation toward ownership of intellectual property and collaboration, are frequently named as contributing factors.

To date the empirical evidence supporting a cultural explanation is based on student responses to attitude surveys and interviews. Shi (2006) interviewed L1 and L2 English speakers and found some differences between them (for example, a belief that words are individually owned or shared) which might explain plagiarism. Chandrasegaran surveyed students in Singapore and found that their responses to scenarios involving copying of various sorts indicated that their "understanding of plagiarism clearly deviates from the norm in Western academic cultures" (2000: 102).

However, the idea that plagiarism is not the unacceptable act in all cultures that it is in the Anglophone world has been disputed. Alternative perspectives to the cultural explanation have emerged, and the accuracy of these assertions has been questioned, often by insiders from the cultures said to be tolerant of plagiarism, who report precisely the opposite: that students in their cultures are indeed taught to regard plagiarism as wrong (Ha 2006; Liu 2005). Some empirical findings call the cultural explanation into question as well (Evans and Youmans 2000; Wheeler 2009).

The role of culture in textual plagiarism has thus not been fully resolved, but there is a growing recognition that, to the extent that it plays a role, the relationship is more complex than previously thought, not dependent soley on discrete deficits in L2 writers' knowledge or cultural values which ill prepare them for Anglophone expectations of source use. The degree to which writing assignments are used as a form of assessment varies from country to country (Hayes and Introna 2005, 2006), and a lack of extensive experience of assessment writing tasks (and a concomitant lack of instruction for and feedback on them) must impact writers' performance at a number of levels. Less experienced writers will not have heard the repeated admonitions to "cite your sources" and "use your own words" which are so familiar to some from early school days. Relatively inexperienced writers are presumably also less likely to be familiar with the phraseology of academic texts, and therefore more likely to use published works as a phrase bank from which idiomatic expressions can be mined (Flowerdew and Li 2007). They are also less likely to be in possession of a strong writerly voice and a sense of authority over their own texts, another factor which has been linked to textual plagiarism (Angélil-Carter 2000; Cadman 1997). In short, some L2 writers come from backgrounds which have not prepared them optimally for source-based writing and to the extent that the educational system must be regarded as a cultural artefact, culture is implicated, but the relationship is indirect and complex.

The causes – cultural and otherwise – for textual plagiarism suggested in the literature as presented thus far can be encapsulated by pointing out that academic texts are complex and that learning to produce them is equally so; writers who are doubly challenged by having to learn academic discourse in a language which is not their first must draw on all of the resources available, and textual borrowing is one of them. In this view textual borrowing may also be a strategy which can be dispensed with when the writer's linguistic and discoursal skills have matured sufficiently, and this is very much in line with Howard's (1995) suggestion that patchwriting is a feature of the writer's developmental stage.

A further element in explaining textual plagiarism is less related to the writers' development and more to the context in which L2 writers work. There is mounting evidence that teachers and other gatekeepers themselves vary in terms of which source use practices they consider to be plagiarism or otherwise unacceptable (Crocker and Shaw 2002; Pecorari and Shaw 2012; Roig 2001; Sutherland-Smith 2005). This variation is to some extent related to differences in practices across academic disciplines (Borg 2009; Jamieson 2008) but is also due to individual variation. It seems likely as a result that the guidance provided to L2 writers about using sources is equally varied, with a predictable effect on their performance.

3 Future developments

A considerable body of research has, as noted above, provided descriptions of source use in various contexts. A challenge for the future is applying the findings to help second-language learners master this important feature of academic writing. An assumption of descriptive research has been that L2 writers and their teachers need to know what the texts of skilled and established writers look like, in order learn to produce something similar. Yet clearly the lessons for novice writers cannot be couched in prescriptive terms, with guidelines for (for example) the percentage of integral citations which a thesis or research article should have.

Because formal choices for source use are closely related to rhetorical purpose, and because identifying and achieving that purpose is the responsibility of the writer, a viable alternative to prescriptions is consciousness-raising: making writers aware of the formal choices available to them, and of the likely impact on the text of choosing one option instead of another. To facilitate these choices, and given the difficulty of identifying patterns in source use in broad disciplinary lines, it is important that L2 writers have a sense of the textual features which are common in their own research areas. On recent approach to this is to teach writers to compile and interrogate small corpora of texts in the writer's research area (Charles 2012; Lee and Swales 2006). This and other approaches to applying research findings to the development of L2 writers are an important potential contribution of the field.

Potential exists as well for L2 and L1 writing studies to inform each other to a greater extent. As noted famously by Bourdieu and Passeron (1965), all writers, regardless of their native speaker status, come to academic discourse as novices. Many of the difficulties with writing from sources vex both L2 and L1 writers. L1 writers wrestle with understanding how to triangulate simplistic rules for citation, the complexity of acknowledging intellectual debts and the difficulty of finding the nuanced forms of language to express those relationships in a new and unfamiliar discourse (Blum 2010). Patchwriting is a common strategy for L1 writers, even if the quantitative patterns of their textual borrowing are not those of L2 writers (Howard, Rodrigue, and Serviss 2010; Shi 2004). Greater mutual influence between the L1 and L2 writing traditions would be of great mutual benefit.

A third important area for future work is shaping connections among all the research on source use – that is, the research on citation and other legitimate, acknowledged forms of source use, and that on plagiarism and textual borrowing. Although numerous causes have been implicated in non-deceptive plagiarism, the desire to achieve a polished form of expression in the face of linguistic and discoursal challenges is a prominent one. In this sense the objectives of these two branches of research – citation and plagiarism – are in opposition to each other on one point. In one area, research has been aimed at describing the forms of language used in reporting sources. This has had pedagogical spinoffs in the form of materials which highlight or catalogue frequently recurring multi-word units (for example, *a growing body of evidence suggests that ...* and *More recently, Smith has argued that ...*) which are useful for referring to sources (Morely's *Academic Phrasebank*; Swales and Feak 2000). At the same time research into plagiarism has treated the phenomenon of L2 writers copying language from sources as a problem.

This is of course not to suggest that there is no distinction to be made between plagiarism and formulaic language. However, at the points at which they intersect several questions with pedagogical importance remain unresolved. Given that gate-keepers are not in agreement about the extent of phraseological borrowing which is legitimate, what advice can best be given to novice writers? What are the benefits of repetition as a learning strategy? Which aspects of citation and source use are inherently formulaic and which demand novelty? Unifying these thus far dichoto-mised areas of inquiry – source use and plagiarism – would be an important first step in finding answers to these and related questions.

4 Additional sources

Buranen, Lise and Alice M. Roy. 1999. *Perspectives on plagiarism and intellectual property in a postmodern world*. Albany: State University of New York Press.

Blum, Susan. 2010. *My word! Plagiarism and college culture*. Ithaca NY: Cornell University.

Charles, Maggie. 2006a. The construction of stance in reporting clauses: A cross-disciplinary study of theses. *Applied Linguistics* 27. 492–518.

Harwood, Nigel and Bojana Petrić. 2012. Performance in the citing behavior of two student writers. *Written Communication* 29. 55–103.

Howard, Rebecca Moore. 1999. *Standing in the shadow of giants*. Stamford CT: Ablex.

Pecorari, Diane. 2008. *Academic writing and plagiarism: A linguistic analysis*. London: Continuum.

Pecorari, Diane and Bojana Petrić. 2014. Plagiarism in second-language writing. *Language Teaching* 47. 1–34.

Sutherland-Smith, Wendy. 2008. *Plagiarism, the Internet and student learning: Improving academic integrity*. New York: Routledge.

Swales, John. 1990. *Genre analysis: English in academic and research settings*. Cambridge: Cambridge University Press.

Thompson, Geoff and Yiyun Ye. 1991. Evaluation in the reporting verbs used in academic papers. *Applied Linguistics* 12. 365–382.

5 References

Abasi, Ali R., Nahal Akbari, and Barbara Graves, B. 2006. Discourse appropriation, construction of identities, and the complex issue of plagiarism: ESL students writing in graduate school. *Journal of Second Language Writing* 15. 102–117.

Ädel, Annelie and Gregory Garretson. 2006. Citation Practices across the Disciplines: The Case of Proficient Student Writing. In Carmen Pérez-Llantada, Ramón Pló Alastrué, and Claus-Peter Neumann (eds.), *Academic and professional communication in the 21st century: Genres, rhetoric and the construction of disciplinary knowledge. Proceedings of the 5th International AELFE Conference.*

Ädel, Annelie and Ute Römer. 2012. Research on advanced student writing across disciplines and levels: Introducing the *Michigan Corpus of Upper-level Student Papers. International Journal of Corpus Linguistics* 17. 3–34.

Angélil-Carter, Shelley. 2000. *Stolen language? Plagiarism in writing*. Harlow: Longman

Bakhtin, Mikhael M. 1981. Discourse in the novel. In Michael Holquist (ed.), *The dialogic imagination: Four essays by M. M. Bakhtin*, 254–422 (Caryl Emerson & Michael Holquist, Trans.). Austin, TX: University of Texas Press.

Ballard, Brigid and John Clanchy. 1991. Assessment by misconception: Cultural influences and intellectual traditions. In Liz Hamp-Lyons (ed.), *Assessing writing in academic contexts*, 19–35. Norwood, NJ: Ablex.

Barks, Debbie and Patricia Watts. 2001 Textual borrowing strategies for graduate-level ESL writers. In Diane Belcher and Alan Hirvela (eds.), *Linking literacies: Perspectives on L2 reading-writing connections*, 246–267. Ann Arbor, MI: University of Michigan Press.

Becher, Tony and Paul R. Trowler. 2001. *Academic tribes and territories: Intellectual enquiry and the cultures of disciplines*. 2nd ed. Buckingham: Open University Press and the Society for Research in Higher Education.

Bloch, Joel. 2008. Plagiarism across cultures: Is there a difference? In Caroline Eisner and Marta Vicinus (eds.), *Originality, imitation and plagiarism: Teaching writing in the digital age*, 219–230. Ann Arbor: University of Michigan Press.

Blum, Susan. 2010. *My word! Plagiarism and College Culture*. Ithaca NY: Cornell University.

Borg, Erik. 2000. Citation practices in academic writing. In Paul Thompson (ed.) *Patterns and perspectives: Insights into EAP writing practice*, 27–40. Reading: Centre for Applied Language Studies, University of Reading.

Borg, Erik. 2009. Local plagiarisms. *Assessment & Evaluation in Higher Education* 34. 415–426.

Bourdieu, Pierre and Jean-Claude Passeron. 1965. Introduction: Langage et rapport au langage dans la situation pédagogique. In Pierre Bourdieu, Jean-Claude Passeron, and M. de Saint Martin (eds.), *Rapport pédagogique et communication*. Paris: Mouton.

Burton, Robert E. and R. W. Kebler. 1960. The "half-life" of some scientific and technical literatures. *American Documentation* 11(1). 18–22.

Cadman, Kate. 1997. Thesis writing for international students: A question of identity? *English for Specific Purposes* 16. 3–14.

Campbell, Cherry. 1990. Writing with others' words: Using background reading text in academic compositions. In Barbara Kroll (ed.), *Second language writing: Research insights for the classroom*, 211–230. Cambridge: Cambridge University Press.

Chandrasegaran, Antonia. 2000. Cultures in contact in academic writing: Students' perceptions of plagiarism. *Asian Journal of English Language Teaching* 10. 91–113.

Chandrasoma, Ranamukalage, Celia Thompson, and Alastair Pennycook. 2004. Beyond plagiarism: Transgressive and nontransgressive intertextuality. *Journal of Language, Identity and Education* 3. 171–193.

Charles, Maggie. 2006a. The construction of stance in reporting clauses: A cross-disciplinary study of theses. *Applied Linguistics* 27. 492–518.

Charles, Maggie. 2006b. Phraseological patterns in reporting clauses used in citation: A corpus-based study of theses in two disciplines. *English for Specific Purposes* 25. 310–331.

Charles, Maggie. 2012. "Proper vocabulary and juicy collocations": EAP students evaluate do-it-yourself corpus-building. *English for Specific Purposes* 31. 93–102.

Crocker, Jean and Philip Shaw. 2002. Research student and supervisor evaluation of intertextuality practices. *Hermes Journal of Linguistics* 28. 39–58.

Currie, Pat. 1998. Staying out of trouble: Apparent plagiarism and academic survival. *Journal of Second Language Writing* 7. 1–18.

Davis, Mary. 2013. The development of source use by international postgraduate students. *Journal of English for Academic Purposes* 12. 125–135.

Deckert, Glenn. 1993. Perspectives on plagiarism from ESL students in Hong Kong. *Journal of Second Language Writing* 2. 131–148.

Dong, Yu Ren. 1996. Learning how to use citations for knowledge transformation: Non-native doctoral students' dissertation writing in science. *Research in the Teaching of English* 30. 428–457.

Dubois, Betty Lou. 1988. Citation in biomedical journal articles. *English for Specific Purposes* 7. 181–193.

Een, John. 1982. Tense usage in the reporting of past research in geotechnical writing. *Minnesota Working Papers in ESL.* Minneapolis, MN: University of Minnesota.

Evans, Faun Bernbach and Madeleine Youmans. 2000. ESL writers discuss plagiarism: the social construction of ideologies. *Journal of Education* 182. 49–65.

Fairclough, Norman. 1992. *Discourse and social change.* Cambridge: Polity Press.

Flowerdew, John and Yongyan Li. 2007. Language re-use among Chinese apprentice scientists writing for publication. *Applied Linguistics* 28. 440–465.

Groom, Nicholas. 2000. Attribution and averral revisited: Three perspectives on manifest intertextuality in academic writing. In Paul Thompson (ed.) *Patterns and perspectives: Insights into EAP writing practice*, 15–25. Reading: Centre for Applied Language Studies, University of Reading.

Ha, Phan Le. 2006. Plagiarism and overseas students: stereotypes again? *ELT Journal* 60. 76–78.

Hanania, Edith and Karima Akhtar. 1985. Verb form and rhetorical function in science writing: A study of MS theses in biology, chemistry, and physics. *The ESP Journal* 4. 49–58.

Harwood, Nigel. 2004. Citation analysis: A multidisciplinary perspective on academic literacy. In Mike Baynham, Alice Deignan and Goodith White (eds.). *Applied linguistics at the interface*, 79–89. Sheffield: British Association for Applied Linguistics and Equinox.

Harwood, Nigel. 2008. Citers' use of citees' names: Findings from a qualitative interview-based study. *Journal of the American Society for Information Science and Technology* 59. 1007–1011.

Harwood, Nigel. 2009. An interview-based study of the functions of citations in academic writing across two disciplines. *Journal of Pragmatics* 41. 497–518.

Hawes, Thomas and Sarah Thomas. 1997. Tense choices in citations. *Research in the Teaching of English* 31. 393–414.

Hayes, Niall and Lucas Introna. 2005. Cultural values, plagiarism, and fairness: When plagiarism gets in the way of learning. *Ethics and Behavior* 15. 213–231.

Hayes, Niall and Lucas Introna. 2006. Systems for the production of plagiarists? The implications arising from the use of plagiarism detection systems in UK universities for Asian learners. *Journal of Academic Ethics* 3. 55–73.

Hirvela, Alan and Qian Du. 2013. "Why am I paraphrasing?": Undergraduate ESL writers' engagement with source-based academic writing and reading. *Journal of English for Academic Purposes* 12. 87–98.

Hoey, Michael. 2005. *Lexical priming: A new theory of words and language.* London: Routledge.

Howard, Rebecca Moore. 1995. Plagiarisms, authorships, and the academic death penalty. *College English* 57. 788–806.

Howard, Rebecca Moore, Tricia Serviss, and Tanya K. Rodrigue. 2010. Writing from sources, writing from sentences. *Writing and Pedagogy* 2. 177–192.

Hu, Guangwei and Jun Lei. 2012. Investigating Chinese university students' knowledge of and attitudes toward plagiarism from an integrated perspective. *Language Learning* 62. 813–850.

Hunston, Susan. 1993. Professional conflict: Disagreement in academic discourse. In Mona Baker, Gill Francis, and Elena Tognini-Bonelli (eds.), *Text and technology: In honour of John Sinclair*, 115–134. Philadelphia: John Benjamins.

Hunston, Susan. 1995. A corpus study of some English verbs of attribution. *Functions of Language* 2. 133–158.

Hyland, Ken. 1999. Academic attribution: Citation and the construction of disciplinary knowledge. *Applied linguistics* 20. 341–367.

Hyland, Ken. 2002. Activity and evaluation: Reporting practices in academic writing. In John Flowerdew (ed.), *Academic discourse*, 115–130. Harlow: Longman.

Jamieson, Sandra. 2008. One size does not fit all: Plagiarism across the curriculum. In Rebecca Moore Howard and Amy E. Robillard (eds.), *Pluralizing plagiarism: Identities, contexts, pedagogies*, 77–91. Portsmouth, NH: Heinemann.

Keck, Casey. 2006. The use of paraphrase in summary writing: A comparison of L1 and L2 writers. *Journal of Second Language Writing* 15. 261–278.

Kristeva, Julia. 1980. *Desire in language: A semiotic approach to literature and art.* New York: Columbia University Press.

Lave, Jean and Etienne Wenger. 1991. *Situated learning: Legitimate peripheral participation.* Cambridge: Cambridge University Press.

Lee, David and John Swales. 2006. A corpus-based EAP course for NNS doctoral students: Moving from available specialized corpora to self-compiled corpora. *English for Specific Purposes* 25. 56–75.

Leki, Ilona and Joan Carson. 1997. "Completely different worlds": EAP and the writing experiences of ESL students in university courses. *TESOL Quarterly* 31. 39–69.

Li, Yongyan. 2013. Three ESL students writing a policy paper assignment: An activity-analytic perspective. *Journal of English for Academic Purposes* 12. 73–86.

Li, Yongyan and Christine Pearson Casanave. 2012. Two first-year students' strategies for writing from sources: Patchwriting or plagiarism? *Journal of Second Language Writing* 21. 165–180.

Liu, Dilin. 2005. Plagiarism in ESOL students: Is cultural conditioning truly the major culprit? *ELT Journal* 59. 234–241.

Matalene, Carolyn. 1985. Contrastive rhetoric: An American writing teacher in China. *College English* 47. 789–808.

Morley, J. (n.d.). Academic Phrasebank. http://www.phrasebank.manchester.ac.uk/

Oster, Sandra. 1981. The use of tenses in reporting past literature. In Larry E. Selinker, Elaine Tarone and Victor Hanzeli (eds.), *English for academic and technical purposes: Studies in honor of Louis Trimble*, 76–90. Rowley, MA: Newbury House.

Pecorari, Diane. 2003. Good and original: Plagiarism and patchwriting in academic second-language writing. *Journal of Second Language Writing* 12. 317–345.

Pecorari, Diane. 2006. Visible and occluded citation features in postgraduate second-language writing. *English for Specific Purposes* 25. 4–29.

Pecorari, Diane. 2013a. Additional reasons for the correlation of voice, tense and sentence function. In Nils-Lennart Johannesson, Gunnel Melchers and Beyza Björkman (eds.), *Of butterflies and birds, of dialects and genres: Essays in honour of Philip Shaw* 104, 153–167. Stockholm: Acta Universitatis Stockholmiensis.

Pecorari, Diane. 2013b. *Teaching to avoid plagiarism: How to promote good source use.* Open University Press.

Pecorari, Diane. 2016. Intertextuality and plagiarism. In Ken Hyland and Philip Shaw (eds.), *The Routledge handbook of English for academic purposes*. London: Routledge.

Pecorari, Diane and Bojana Petrić. 2014. Plagiarism in second-language writing. *Language Teaching* 47. 1–34.

Pecorari, Diane and Philip Shaw. 2012. Types of student intertextuality and faculty attitudes. *Journal of Second Language Writing* 21. 149–164.

Pennycook, Alastair. 1996. Borrowing others' words: Text, ownership, memory, and plagiarism. *TESOL Quarterly* 30. 201–230.

Petrić, Bojana. 2004. A pedagogical perspective on plagiarism. *NovELTy* 11. 4–18.

Petrić, Bojana. 2007. Rhetorical functions of citations in high- and low-rated master's theses. *Journal of English for Academic Purposes* 6. 238–253.

Petrić, Bojana. 2012. Legitimate textual borrowing: Direct quotation in L2 student writing. *Journal of Second Language Writing* 21. 102–117.

Petrić, Bojana and Nigel Harwood. 2013. Task requirements, task representation, and self-reported citation functions: An exploratory study of a successful L2 student's writing. *Journal of English for Academic Purposes* 12. 110–124.

Roig, Miguel. 1997. Can undergraduate students determine whether text has been plagiarized? *The Psychological Record* 47. 113–122.

Roig, Miguel. 2001. Plagiarism and paraphrasing criteria of college and university professors. *Ethics and Behavior* 11. 307–323.

Salager-Meyer, Françoise. 1999. Referential behavior in scientific writing: A diachronic study (1810–1995). *English for Specific Purposes* 18. 279–305.

St. John, Maggie Jo. 1987. Writing processes of Spanish scientists publishing in English. *English for Specific Purposes* 6. 113–120.

Shaw, Philip. 1991. Science research students' composing processes. *English for Specific Purposes* 10. 189–206.

Shaw, Philip. 1992. Reasons for the correlation of voice, tense and sentence function in reporting verbs. *Applied Linguistics* 13. 302–317.

Sherman, Jane. 1992. Your own thoughts in your own words. *ELT Journal* 46. 190–198.

Shi, Ling. 2004. Textual borrowing in second-language writing. *Written Communication* 21. 171–200.

Shi, Ling. 2006. Cultural backgrounds and textual appropriation. *Language Awareness* 15. 264–282.

Shi, Ling. 2008. Textual appropriation and citing behaviors of university undergraduates. *Applied Linguistics* 31. 1–24.

Spack, Ruth. 1997. The acquisition of academic literacy in a second language: A longitudinal case study. *Written Communication* 14. 3–62.

Sutherland-Smith, Wendy. 2005. Pandora's box: Academic perceptions of student plagiarism in writing. *Journal of English for Academic Purposes* 4. 83–95.

Swales, John. 1981. *Aspects of article introductions*. Birmingham: Language Studies Unit, Aston University.

Swales, John. 1986. Citation analysis and discourse analysis. *Applied Linguistics* 7. 39–56.

Swales, John. 1990. *Genre analysis: English in academic and research settings*. Cambridge: Cambridge University Press.

Swales, John. 2014. Variation in citational practice in a corpus of student biology papers: From parenthetical plonking to intertextual storytelling. *Written Communication* 31. 118–41.

Swales, John and Christine B. Feak. 2000. *English in today's research world: A writing guide*. Ann Arbor: University of Michigan Press.

Tadros, Angele. 1993. The pragmatics of text averral and attribution in academic texts. In Michael Hoey (ed.), *Data, description, discourse*, 98–114. London: Harper Collins.

Tarone, Elaine, Sharon Dwyer, Susan Gillette, and Vincent Icke. 1998. On the use of the passive and active voice in astrophysics journal papers: With extensions to other languages and other fields. *English for Specific Purposes* 17. 113–132.

Thompson, Celia. 2005. "Authority is everything": A study of the politics of textual ownership and knowledge in the formation of student writer identities. *International Journal for Educational Integrity*, 1. http://ojs.ml.unisa.edu.au/index.php/IJEI/article/view/18

Thompson, Celia, Janne Morton, and Neomy Storch. 2013. Where from, who, why and how? A study of the use of sources by first year L2 university students. *Journal of English for Academic Purposes* 12. 99–109.

Thompson, Geoff and Yiyun Ye. 1991. Evaluation in the reporting verbs used in academic papers. *Applied Linguistics* 12. 365–382.

Thompson, Paul. 2000. Citation practices in PhD theses. In Lou Burnard & Tony McEnery (eds.), *Rethinking language pedagogy: Papers from the Third International Conference on Teaching and Language Corpora*, 91–101. Frankfurt: Peter Lang.

Weigle, Sara Cushing and Keisha Parker. 2012. Source text borrowing in an integrated reading/ writing assessment. *Journal of Second Language Writing* 21. 118–133.

Wheeler, Greg. 2009. Plagiarism in the Japanese universities: Truly a cultural matter? *Journal of Second Language Writing* 18. 17–29.

White, Howard. 2004. Citation analysis and discourse analysis revisited. *Applied Linguistics* 25. 89–116.

Christine Tardy
16 Voice and identity

An understanding of writing as a social practice has influenced many aspects of L2 writing scholarship, giving rise to an interest in theoretical concepts like discourse community, genre, and situated learning as well as pedagogical practices such as teacher feedback and peer collaboration. Yet, writing is not purely social but is also influenced – often simultaneously – by many aspects of the individual writer. People write within social contexts, to and with others, influenced by these settings and dynamics; at the same time, they bring their own individual histories, agendas, and sense of self to their writing, all of which are developed within their social environments. Two concepts that have been particularly useful in understanding this mediation of the social and the individual are identity and voice. In many ways, identity and voice could each warrant a separate chapter in this volume, outlining their histories and contributions to the field of second language writing. But while joining them into a single discussion risks restricting the depth of discussion for each concept, it also offers an opportunity to explore some the relationships between them.

1 Historical overview

Though scholarship in second language writing is still relatively young – dating variously to the 1940s or 1960s (Matsuda 2003) – an interest in identity and voice within the field is even more recent, beginning roughly in the mid-1990s. At this time, the interest in identity, as a theoretical concept, reflected trends in the related fields of applied linguistics and second language studies. Bonny Norton's work is particularly noteworthy, as she urged second language acquisition researchers to move beyond dichotomies of individuals and the social structures within which they learn (Peirce 1995). Drawing on social theory and case study research, she developed a theory of social identity relevant to second language learning. Her work convincingly demonstrated learners' identities to be historically and spatially situated, multidimensional, and dynamic – all concepts common to theories of social identity in the social sciences.

Around the same time that Norton's work was attracting attention in second language studies more generally, L2 writing scholars were also beginning to explore how issues of identity played out for second language writers. While not using the same terminology or theoretical foundations as Norton, Severino (1993) and Blanton (1994), for example, highlighted the role of identity in shaping students' choices and when writing within academic discourse communities. A few years later, Roz Ivanič's (1998) book *Writing and identity: The discoursal construc-*

tion of identity in academic writing outlined a theory of identity tied specifically to academic writing. Although the case studies which Ivanič drew upon in this research involved non-traditional adult L1 writers, her theoretical work has been inclusive of multiple populations of learners and thus has been influential in L2 writing research. Like Norton, Ivanič describes identity as fundamentally social, and her theoretical framework interweaves social constructionist and social interactionist perspectives, outlining four aspects of writer identity: the autobiographical self, discoursal self, self as author, and possibilities for self-hood. She further explores the discoursal construction of writer identity, drawing on vocabulary offered by Mikhail Bakhtin to understand the intertextual nature of discourse: "voice(s), multivoiced(ness), othervoiced(ness), doublevoiced(ness), reinvoice(d), populate(d) with, interanimate(d) (ion), ventriloquate(d) (ion), dialogic(al (ism), overtones, reaccentuate (ion)." (Ivanic 1998: 50) Since the publication of *Writing and Identity*, issues of identity and self-representation have taken on a more central role in L2 writing scholarship, being addressed in journal articles (e.g., Ortmeier-Hooper 2008; Ouelette 2008), books (e.g., Casanave 2002; Hyland 2012), and edited collections (e.g., Cox, Jordan, Ortmeier-Hooper, and Schwartz 2010).

Identity encompasses many aspects of writing, including voice – a somewhat slippery and often ill-defined concept that has long been of interest in L1 composition studies. In the 1990s, L2 writing scholars began to explore the implications and applications of voice more specifically for second language writing. Ramanathan and Kaplan's (1996) analysis of *voice* and *audience* in 10 college composition textbooks argued that these terms drew on cultural assumptions that can easily exclude L2 writers. Later, examining in more depth the notion of voice as a culturally biased concept, Ramanathan and Atkinson (1999) looked to the use of the term in L1 composition studies following the work of Peter Elbow (1994, 1999). Elbow's characterizations of voice has been termed "expressivist" because of his emphasis on the expressive and individual characteristics of a writer's voice, extending the metaphoric use of one's spoken voice and its individual qualities to one's written expression. Though the notion of voice as individual style enjoyed a great deal of popularity in scholarship on L1 writers (see Bowden 1999, for a critique of its use), some argued that voice was far more problematic when applied to the culturally and linguistically diverse population of L2 writers. In their critique, Ramanathan and Atkinson pointed specifically to the expressivist description of voice as "the expression of a 'unique inner self'" (p. 51), a definition grounded in a particular conception of individualism. Given the variable range of how individuality is conceived across cultures, however, the authors noted that asking students to adopt a "personal voice" may be at odds with their sense of self.

Ramanathan and Atkinson's (1999) article is noteworthy not only for its provocative argument against the application of voice (i.e., the expressivist notion of personal or individual voice) to L2 writing but also for prompting discussion of the term amongst L2 writing professionals. Just a few years later, in 2001, the *Journal of Second Language Writing* (*JSLW*) devoted a special issue to the concept (Belcher and Hirvela 2001), in which scholars probed the relevance of voice for L2 writers and, perhaps more importantly, offered new definitions and theoretical orientations. Departing largely from the individualistic grounding of Elbow's use of voice, these researchers adopted social constructionist frameworks, highlighting the social, rather than individual, nature of voice. Matsuda (2001) most explicitly articulated this departure from an individual conception of voice to one that is grounded in discourse and, hence, social rather than individualistic. The definition of voice offered by Matsuda – "the amalgamative effect of the use of discursive and non-discursive features that language users choose, deliberately or otherwise, from socially available yet every-changing repertoires" (p. 40) – highlighted voice as an *effect* that results from choices made by writers.

It may be fair to say that the 2001 *JSLW* special issue on voice, along with Ivanič's (1998) work, marked the start of renewed interest in identity and voice in L2 writing. While identity was a primary focus of just five articles in the *Journal of Second Language Writing* from 1990 to 1999, 13 articles focused on issues of identity from 2000 to 2009. These more recent publications frequently looked to work by Ivanič (1998), Ivanič and Camps (2001), Bakhtin (1981, 1986), and Goffman (1981) as theoretical lenses. With its new, decidedly social, orientation, contemporary scholarship in this area has considered how identity and voice work with – rather than in opposition to – other social constructs, such as discourse, community, discipline, and genre.

2 Influential theoretical frameworks of identity and voice

Much work on identity in language studies draws on social constructionism, defining identity as created through social interaction rather than as a psychological construct inherent to an individual. From a social constructionist perspective, we see ourselves, at least in part, through the ways that others see us. Identity, therefore, is understood as always socially situated, changing in relation to the contexts and interactions that we move among. Symbolic interactionist perspectives on identity, especially the work of sociologist Erving Goffman, have often complemented social constructionist perspectives, as in the work of Ivanič (1998) and Hyland (2012). Goffman prioritized identity's performative aspects, offering a metaphor of human behavior as a theatrical performance in which an individual is both a performer and character. In developing her multidimensional theory of writer identity, Ivanič (1998) draws heavily on Goffman, distinguishing the writer-as-performer from the writer-as-character. She notes that writers must negotiate their possible positioning using the discourses available to them. Goffman's (1968) concept of stigma has also been extended to second language writing, though not uncontroversially (see Casanave 2008). Flowerdew (2008) posits that stigma – various deviations from the perceived "normal" – is relevant to the situation of L2 academic writers whose departures from standard English "may be perceived as indicative of some negative characteristic such as laziness, lack of education, low intelligence, etc." (p. 80)

From sociocultural theory, L2 writing scholars have adopted the notions of intertextuality and multivoicedness in understanding how identities are constructed by authors through their texts as they draw on and weave together the oral and written texts encountered over time – bringing us more specifically to the theoretical grounding of the concept of *voice*. The work of Bakhtin (1981, 1986) and Voloshinov (1973) has been employed at times as an explicit contrast to the more individualistic or expressivist orientations to written voice that many associate with Peter Elbow's work. Prior (2001) outlines distinctions between personal and social voices, but ultimately argues that, when language is viewed as "neither inside nor outside, but *between* people" (p. 59, emphasis in original), voice too becomes *both* personal and social. Matsuda (2011) has similarly argued for what he terms a social constructivist approach to written voice, one that sees "individual and social voice to be mutually constitutive and inevitable" (Matsuda and Jeffery 2012: 151). In the introduction to their edited collection on voice and stance, Sancho Guinda and Hyland (2012) emphasize the broad range of ways in which voice has been conceptualized within applied linguistics more broadly. They note the language which the authors in their collection use to describe voice, clearly situating it in a social constructivist framework: it is *crafted, constructed, built, carved, created, found, projected, expressed, adopted,* and *taken on,* to give just a few examples.

When identity (and voice) are considered from a social perspective, they also draw upon linguistic and rhetorical theories of discourse. James Paul Gee's (1989) theoretical work is of importance here, particularly his articulation of discourse as an "identity kit," a particular way of "acting-interacting-thinking-valuing-talking-(sometimes writing-reading) in the 'appropriate way' with the 'appropriate' props at the 'appropriate' times in the 'appropriate' places" (Gee 2010: 34). In other words, adopting or performing a discourse is essentially putting on an identity – discourse is, then, identity work, and identity is, in turn, thoroughly social.

Other theoretical frameworks that have informed current identity and voice scholarship include Bourdieu's notion of habitus, Lave and Wenger's (1991) metaphorical concept of communities of practice, and systemic functional linguistics (SFL). Developing a theoretical framework for understanding the process of becoming a disciplinary expert, Dressen-Hammouda (2008) invokes habitus to define disciplinary identity as "an ensemble of socio-historical regularities and norms that practitioners embody as a result of specializing within their disciplines" (p. 235). Yi (2010) turns to community of practice to understand identity construction through writers' interactions in multiple social constellations, including online communities. She describes identity as a "nexus of multimembership" (p. 310) that is developed through the negotiation of these various social alignments across time and space. Finally, a growing body of work in SFL has examined voice through the lens of APPRAISAL theory (Martin and White 2005), which outlines a linguistic system for realizing evaluative meaning choices (Hood 2012).

3 Methods for researching identity and voice

A fairly wide range of methods has been employed in the study of voice and identity, varying in line with the theoretical foundations and definitions adopted. Qualitative research, often in the form of case studies or ethnographies, has been particularly common for exploring questions regarding identity construction over time and in different contexts. When identity is understood to be multiple and unstable, qualitative research that focuses on individuals can allow researchers to study its contextualized, contested, and contingent nature. Case studies, for instance, follow individual writers in academic contexts, using interviews, observations, and text analyses to understand how identities are constructed and re-constructed (e.g., Casanave 2002; Harklau 2000; Ivanič 1998; Ortmeier-Hooper 2008). Other qualitative studies have adopted the use of surveys or oral interviews, particularly in the investigation of written voice. Semi-structured and discourse-based interviews, for example, have been used to analyze readers' impressions of authors (Matsuda and Tardy 2007; Tardy 2012), of a text's voice (Jeffery 2011), or of the perceptions of the very concept of voice (Petrić 2010). Written surveys have been used to identify discursive and non-discursive features that readers draw on when constructing the voice of an author (Tardy and Matsuda 2009). A combination of interviews and written surveys has also been used to study the identity labels used by or assigned to L2 writers (Chiang and Schmida 1999; Costino and Hyon 2007).

While many qualitative studies include writers' texts as one form of collected data, text analysis is also a prominent method on its own for studying identity and voice through lexicogrammatical features. Using corpus linguistics, Hyland (2010, 2012), for example, has examined how identities are built through discourse and linked to social contexts and interactions. Hyland analyzes academic texts in terms of features such as self-mention, keywords, hedging, and metadiscourse and rhetorical features such as move structures. Studying a corpus of texts allows researchers to identify recurring features that construct identity within specific communities such as academic disciplines or more specific research areas (Gea-Valor 2010; Hyland 2012; Thompson 2012), while analyzing individuals' texts in comparison with a corpus of disciplinary texts can highlight the ways in which writers express their individuality within – or along the edges of – community-sanctioned boundaries (Hyland 2010).

Taking a textual orientation to voice, a smaller cluster of studies has attempted to quantitatively measure the relationship between the nature or "intensity" of written voice and writing quality. One such study by Helms-Park and Stapleton (2003) examined the writing of 63 undergraduate students who used English as a second language, scoring their texts with an analytic rubric measuring writing quality and an instrument rating the texts' "voice intensity" (consisting of text features that demonstrate assertiveness, self-identification, reiteration of a central point, and authorial presence and autonomy of thought). Building on this work, Zhao and Llosa (2008) compared holistic scores of writing quality with scores of voice intensity (using Helms-Park and Stapleton's [2003] scale) on 42 papers written by English L1 writers for the New York State Regents Examination in English Language Arts. Notably, these two studies diverged in their findings, with the former failing to identify a significant correlation between writing quality and voice intensity but the latter identifying a positive significant correlation. While Zhao and Llosa (2008) attribute the difference to the language backgrounds of the writers, it is also possible that the quantitative measures used may lack validity and/or reliability. The difficulty of quantifying dynamic and contingent constructs like identity and voice may be one reason why so few quantitative studies in this area exist.

Other, less common, methods for studying identity and voice include document analysis and autobiography. Regarding the former, an example can be found in Matsuda and Jeffery's (2012) study of how voice is operationalized in writing outcomes statements and assessment rubrics at the secondary and postsecondary levels. The use of autobiography as a way to explore voice can be found in a number of edited collections which include chapters in which authors offer introspective autobiographical sketches of their own identities as writers and professionals (e.g., Belcher and Connor 2001; Casanave and Vandrick 2003; Cox et al. 2010; see also Shen 1989). While this approach is often not considered a traditional research method, such papers have provided unique insights and contributed valuable perspectives.

4 Themes from research findings

Research into identity and voice in second language writing has led to several important, often interrelated insights, discussed here through prominent themes.

1. Identities are constructed within institutional and social discursive spaces. Most recent scholarship on identity begins with the premise that identities are unstable and contingent, and they explore the social spaces of identity construction to understand it as a dynamic processes. Harklau's (2000) ethnographic case study followed three refugee students in the US as they transitioned from high school to college classrooms, showing how the identity label of "ESOL student" was various-ly constructed in these different spaces: "good students" in one context and "prob-lem students" in another. Harklau's study is particularly compelling in the ways in which it reveals how individual teachers adopt societal and institutional dis-courses that lead them to position students in particular ways, ultimately influenc-ing writers' own self-conceptions and their actions, which in turn (re-)construct their identities. Starfield's (2002) textual-ethnographic study of two university stu-dents' writing in South Africa also highlights the importance of social context. In this study, readers constructed a White, native English speaking student as a credi-ble authority through textual features in his writing, while they constructed a Black student using English as an additional language (EAL) as a plagiarist due to certain features of his writing. These differing identity constructions and evaluations, Star-field carefully demonstrates, are not tied simply to the texts, but are inherently linked to the sociopolitical contexts in which those texts are composed and read, including the writers' social relations and access to discourses – in short, their cultural capital and habitus. Other studies have demonstrated how L2 writers' iden-tities are constructed in transnational interactions, paying particular attention to power negotiations and racial ideologies (Liu 2011; Liu and Tannacito 2013). It should perhaps be emphasized that identity construction is not simply something that individuals are *subjected to* but rather something that they too play an agent-ive role in. The studies by Harklau (2000) and Casanave (2002), for example, show that individuals do resist, reimagine, and reconstruct their identities as well.

2. The labels ascribed to second language writers are often limiting and not reflec-tive of students' self-perceptions of identity. Identity labels are important in sec-ond language writing for several reasons. Perhaps most obviously, students are represented through labels in institutional policies and structures. Courses for L2 writers, for instance, may be described as being for "non-native English speakers," "multilingual writers," "international students," or "ESL student," and each of these labels may attract different student populations. Ortmeier-Hooper's (2008) study of three immigrant college students in the US highlighted the disconnect that students may feel with the identity labels ascribed to them. For many early- or late-arriving immigrant students, for example, the term "ESL" brings to mind special pull-out or supplementary classes in middle school or secondary school, often per-ceived as remedial. The students in Ortmeier-Hooper's research specifically de-scribed themselves as "not ESL" and resisted attempts to be defined by static and monolithic terms. Findings from Costino and Hyon's (2007) interview study with nine US college students also painted a complicated picture of identity labels, es-tablishing no clear links between these labels, language ability, and residency sta-tus. The students did have specific associations with terms like ESL, English lan-guage learner, bilingual, and multilingual, but those associations were uniquely related to their individual experiences. Drawing on a similar finding from their study of 20 US college writers, Chiang and Schmida (1999) too noted the inadequacy of identity categories based on false linguistic or cultural boundaries. Studies like these demonstrate a need for L2 writing teachers and researchers to be critical of the labels they employ, both personally and institutionally. As Shuck (2010) argues, the discourses we engage in and reinforce through such markers construct student writers in particular ways – in doing so, we create identities for them that may suit teachers and institutions rather than students themselves.

3. A popular conception of voice as individual expression is common among writers and teachers. Despite a general move in scholarship toward social constructionist and social constructivist orientations to voice, in which voice is both social *and* individual, several studies have demonstrated that an expressivist view of voice as a unique property of the writer – that is, constructed and controlled solely *by* the writer – remains prevalent. Through interviews with master's degree students in Central Europe, Petrić (2010) found that the most frequent conceptions of voice were individualistic, including voice expression of opinion, authorial presence, and personal experience. Similarly, the secondary school teachers interviewed in Jeffery's (2010) study took a primarily expressivist view of voice, associating it with authorial presence, resonance, and authenticity. Jeffery (2011) and Matsuda and Jeffery (2012) further highlight how such views of voice are also echoed in assessment rubrics, where the presence of a "strong" or "authentic" voice is often associated with higher quality ratings. This view of voice as a textual characteristic that can be present or absent differs from conceptions of voice as social and dialogic and therefore found in any text. It may be the case that social views of voice are too complex for most forms of assessment since, as Jeffery (2011) notes, they are not easily measurable.

4. Voice, as an "amalgamative effect," is constructed through a range of discursive and non-discursive features that become relevant to readers in particular social contexts and actions. Several text analysis studies have investigated how particular discursive choices that writers make work to construct voice. Research has examined features such as metadiscourse, citation patterns, or hedges and boosters (Hyland 2000) as resources that signal and construct a writer's relationship with his or her readers, influencing readers' impressions of the author through such discursive resources. As Starfield and Ravelli (2006) demonstrate, even a writer's choices for chapter titles, numbering, layout, and font demonstrate writers' alignments with particular research traditions and epistemologies.

Matsuda's (2001) definition of voice as an impression formed by readers based on discursive and non-discursive features has prompted studies that have directly studied reader responses to texts, such as in a simulated blind peer review (Matsuda and Tardy 2007) and a survey study of journal reviewers (Tardy and Matsuda 2009). These studies have shown that linguistic and rhetorical features, content, disciplinary positioning, and document formatting all contribute to the impressions that readers build. At the same time, such impressions do not seem to be formed predictably, as they are further influenced by the relationship or relative status between writer and reader; the personal history, values, and expectations of the reader; and the social context in which the reading occurs (e.g., to read for grading, for peer review, etc.).

5. Identity and voice interact with genre and discourse. As the above studies suggest, identity and voice (in the sense of Matsuda's [2001] definition) are tied to their discursive (textual and non-textual) contexts, constructed within and through discourses. For the study of writing, this suggests an important link between the constructs of identity and voice and those of genre and discourse. As an example, features of text – such as the use of *I* or the use of APA documentation style – will construct writers differently when used in a professional memoir, a student research paper, and a lab report. In Hyland's (2008) words, writers choose from "culturally available resources" when they write, and these choices align writers with disciplines (or, presumably, other social groups or communities of practice). Such options – that is, what is "culturally available" – are socially determined. Disciplines, for instance, develop norms and preferences that reflect their values and practices and become typified through the community's genres. Hyland's (2005, 2008, 2010, 2012) studies of texts across disciplines (and often within genres) provide numerous examples of how writers convey voice in their academic texts, working within disciplinary norms to represent themselves and their positions.

Taking a case study approach, Dressen-Hammouda's (2008) research further contributes to an understanding of the relationships between genre, discourse, identity, and voice. Tracing a geology student's writing (in both his native French and additional language of English) from the third year of his undergraduate studies through to the final year of his doctoral work, Dressen-Hammouda found that the writer's texts demonstrated increasingly sophisticated textual cues that signal a disciplinary insider-ness to expert peers. This work, in combination with Hyland's, suggests that as L2 writers acquire greater disciplinary, discourse, and genre knowledge, they may also build their proficiency in self-representation.

6. The relationship between features of writers' (constructed) identities and readers' assessment of writing quality is influenced by many social factors. Research in this area has taken up various related but somewhat distinct threads. One line of inquiry has studied how specific features of author identity might relate to readers' assessments of the authors' texts. Haswell and Haswell (1996), for instance, studied the relationship between an author's sex, a reader's sex, and the reader's and author's relative status. Their study of writing instructors and undergraduate student writers found, for example, that readers' knowledge that an author was female in general increased their amount of positive critique; however, they also found that female teachers gave lower assessments to female student-authors, and female student-readers gave higher assessments to male student-authors. A study by Rubin and Williams-James (1997) looked at the effect of ethnicity, race, and language background on teachers' assessments of writing, finding that the teachers did not rate papers perceived to be by non-native English writers lower than those perceived to be by native-English writers. Roberts and Cimasko (2008) compared teachers' assessments of an English-language paper attributed to either a Chinese L1 writer or to a Spanish L1 writer and did not find a significant difference in assessment. Finally, Tardy (2012) studied the assessments and reactions of teacher-readers of student papers with and without knowledge of the authors' identities (as displayed through a short autobiographical video of the author). Qualitative data analysis suggested such knowledge did influence some readers' assessments (and their construction of author voice) but not in the same ways for all readers. In sum, studies in this line of inquiry generally have found that although some relationships between assessment and various aspects of writer identity exist, those relationships are neither simple, static, nor predictable.

5 Research implications

Recent research into both identity and voice in second language writing has, in a sense, a de-stabilizing effect. When identity is complicated as contingent and dynamic, or when identity labels are problematized as monolithic and constraining, many aspects of our research categories, institutional structures, and pedagogical practices are thrown into question. Research in this area, then, challenges the field to examine representations (Harklau 2000) of L2 writers and, where appropriate, to search for alternative representations or disrupt dominant discourses.

Similarly, research findings suggest a complexity to the notion of voice that raises questions about its validity as a feature of assessment and its suitability for teaching. Yet, research has convincingly shown that identities *are* constructed for and by L2 writers, that readers do form impressions and assign voice to authors and their texts, so the question remains as to whether and how identity and voice can be taught. Given the (albeit scant) research into genre, disciplinary identity, and voice, it would seem that advanced L2 writers could benefit from an exploration of self-representation in writing, including gaining familiarity with the disciplinary resources available for such representation.

6 Future developments in identity, voice, and second language writing

Because the study of identity and voice in L2 writing is still relatively new, much remains to be studied in these areas. Most studies of identity in L2 writing remain

relatively short-term, either as snapshots at one point and space in time or as semester-long case studies. Few studies have followed writers over extended periods
of time looking specifically at issues of identity. This type of longitudinal study has
the value of looking not just at how identities change over time and across spaces
but also how such changes interact more specifically with L2 writing development.
A mixed-method approach to such research – for example, examining identity construction through ethnographic methods while exploring writing development
through text analysis – could provide important insights into how identities and
their constructions change as writers become more proficient in particular domains
and/or genres of writing.

Similarly, more research into the relationship between genre/discourse acquisition and identity/voice has potential to contribute to the field's understanding of
academic literacy development. While findings from several studies suggest an important link, only Dressen-Hammouda's (2008) study explores this relationship directly. Additional research with writers at different stages of development (e.g., in
high school, university, graduate school, and professional domains) and perhaps
even spanning these stages) can help build a more detailed understanding of the
role that identity plays in such development, and vice versa.

As may be clear from the discussion throughout this chapter, research to date
has primarily examined voice and identity within a single language – for example, multilinguals writing in English as an additional language or writers composing in their native language. Much could be learned, however, from studies that
examine identity and voice in the multiple languages in which writers compose.
Canagarajah (2006), for example, demonstrated how one Sri Lankan academic's
discursive strategies of self-representation differed across languages (English and
Tamil) and audiences (local versus international). Taking a similarly fluid view of
multilingual competence, Kobayashi and Rinnert (2013) found that the writer they
studied expressed her written voice in both similar and different ways across her
three languages. Additional studies that explore how multilinguals draw on multiple linguistic and cultural resources for identity construction, and the extent to
which they may draw on resources *across* languages, could better inform our understanding of the relationships between identity and language.

Though several of the studies reviewed here have explored identity within instructional contexts, surprisingly few studies of voice are situated in classrooms.
Instead, voice has primarily been researched in contexts of assessment, published
writing, or thesis writing. Future research that examines how instructors construct
voice through the writing of their own students could help broaden an understanding of the influences on voice construction when there is an existing relationship
between the reader and writer. In addition, classroom-based studies of voice may
help to shed more light on pedagogical techniques that aid students in developing
control over their written identities.

There is also the issue of the application of research findings. Scholarship has
demonstrated the influence of dominant discourses and ideologies on identity con-

struction and spoken to the importance of critical awareness of these issues for teachers, administrators, and researchers working with L2 writers. Nevertheless, practitioners may wonder what alternative practices are available for resisting such discourses. Action research that explores new models for identity construction on the part of teachers and administrators – even researchers – would be a valuable contribution to the field.

As well, it should be noted that many studies on identity and voice that are influential in second language writing actually examine L1 writers and/or texts rather than L2 writers (e.g., Hyland 2008; Ivanič 1998; Matsuda 2001; Matsuda and Tardy 2007). There is, therefore, a need for more research on identity and voice that looks specifically at multilingual writers and their texts. Ideally, such studies will also bring in the perspectives of the readers (multilingual and monolingual) who construct identities and voices for these writers. Such work will be important in understanding more about how identities and voices are constructed in the transnational contexts that are increasingly common in today's globalized world.

7 Additional sources

Ball, Arnetha and Pamela Ellis. 2008. Identity and the writing of culturally and linguistically diverse students. In Charles Bazerman (ed.), *Handbook of research on writing: History, society, school, individual, text*, 499–513. Mahwah, NJ: Lawrence Erlbaum Associates.

Bowden, Darsie. 1995. The rise of a metaphor: "Voice" in composition pedagogy. *Rhetoric Review* 14. 173–188.

Burgess, Aamy and Roz Ivanič. 2010. Writing and being written: Issues of identity across timescales. *Written Communication* 27. 228–255.

DiPardo, Anne, Barbara Storms, and Makenzie Selland. 2011. Seeing voices: Assessing writerly stance in the NWP Analytic Writing Continuum. *Assessing Writing* 16. 170–188.

Elbow, Peter. 2007. Voice in writing again: Embracing contraries. *College English* 70. 168–188.

Joseph, John. 2004. *Language and identity: National, ethnic, religious.* Houndmills: Palgrave Macmillan.

Moje, Elizabeth and Allan Luke. 2009. Literacy and identity: Examining the metaphors in history and contemporary research. *Reading Research Quarterly* 44. 415–437.

Morita, Naoko. 2004. Negotiating participation and identity in second language academic communities. *TESOL Quarterly* 38. 573–603.

Norton, Bonny. 2000. *Identity and language learning: Gender, ethnicity, and educational change.* Harlow, UK: Longman/Pearson.

Sperling, Melanie and Deborah Appleman. 2011. Voice in the context of literacy studies. *Reading Research Quarterly* 46. 70–84.

Stapleton, Paul. 2002. Critiquing voice as a viable pedagogical tool in L2 writing: Returning the spotlight to ideas. *Journal of Second Language Writing* 11. 177–190.

Tardy, Christine M. 2012. Current conceptions of voice. In Ken Hyland and Carmen Sancho Guinda (eds.), *Stance and voice in written academic genres*, 34–48. New York: Palgrave Macmillan.

8 References

Bakhtin, Mikhail M. 1981. *The dialogic imagination: Four essays* (M. Holquist, Ed., C. Emerson, and M. Holquist, Trans.). Austin, TX: University of Texas Press.

Bakhtin, Mikhail M. 1986. *Speech genres and other late essays* (C. Emerson and M. Holquist, Eds. and Trans.). Austin, TX: University of Texas Press.

Belcher, Diane and Ulla Connor (eds.). 2001. *Reflections on multiliterate lives*. Clevedon, UK: Multilingual Matters.

Belcher, Diane and Alan Hirvela. 2001. Voice in L2 writing [Special issue]. *Journal of Second Language Writing* 10(1). 83–106.

Blanton, Linda. 1994. Discourse, artifacts, and the Ozarks: Understanding academic literacy. *Journal of Second Language Writing* 3. 1–16.

Bowden, Darsie. 1999. *The mythology of voice*. Portsmouth, NH: Boynton/Cook.

Canagarajah, Suresh. 2006. Toward a writing pedagogy of shuttling between languages: Learning from multilingual writers. *College English* 68. 589–604.

Casanave, Christine P. 2002. *Writing games: Multicultural case studies of academic literacy practices in higher education*. Mahwah, NJ: Lawrence Erlbaum Associates.

Casanave, Christine P. 2008. The stigmatizing effect of Goffman's stigma label: A response to John Flowerdew. *Journal of English for Academic Purposes* 7. 264–267.

Casanave, Christine. P. and Stephanie Vandrick (eds.). 2003. *Writing for scholarly publication: Behind the scenes in language education*. Mahwah, NJ: Lawrence Erlbaum Associates.

Chiang, Yuet-Sim and Mary Schmida. 1999. Language identity and language ownership: Linguistic conflicts of first-year university writing students. In Linda Harklau, Kay M. Losey and Meryl Siegal (eds.), *Generation 1.5 meets college composition: Issues in the teaching of writing to US-educated learners of ESL*, 81–96. Mahwah, NJ: Lawrence Erlbaum Associates.

Costino, Kimberly and Sunny Hyon. 2007. "A class for students like me": Reconsidering relationships among identity labels, residency status, and students' preferences for mainstream or multilingual composition. *Journal of Second Language Writing* 16. 63–81.

Cox, Michelle, Jay Jordan, Christina Ortmeier-Hooper and Gwen Schwartz (eds.). 2010. *Reinventing identities in second language writing*. Urbana, IL: NCTE.

Dressen-Hammouda, Dacia. 2008. From novice to disciplinary expert: Disciplinary identituipy and genre mastery. *English for Specific Purposes* 27. 233–252.

Elbow, Peter. 1994. Introduction. In Peter Elbow (ed.), *Landmark essays on voice and writing*, 168–188. Mahwah, NJ: Lawrence Erlbaum Associates.

Elbow, Peter. 1999. Individualism and the teaching of writing: Response to Vai Ramanathan and Dwight Atkinson. *Journal of Second Language Writing* 8. 327–338.

Flowerdew, John. 2008. Scholarly writers who use English as an additional language: What can Goffman's "*Stigma*" tell us? *Journal of English for Academic Purposes* 7. 77–86.

Gea-Valor, Maria-Luisa. 2010. The emergence of the author's voice in book reviewing: A contrastive study of academic discourse vs. non-academic discourse. In Rosa Lorés-Sanz, Pilar Mur-Dueñas, and Enrique Lafuente-Millán (eds.), *Constructing interpersonality: Multiple perspectives on written academic genres*, 117–135. Newcastle upon Tyne: Cambridge Scholars Publishing.

Gee, James Paul. 1989. Literacy, discourse, and linguistics: Introduction. *Journal of Education* 171. 5–17.

Gee, James Paul. 2010. *An introduction to discourse analysis: Theory and method* (3rd ed.). New York: Routledge.

Goffman, Erving. 1968. *Stigma: Notes on the management of spoiled identity*. Harmondsworth/Englewood Cliffs, NJ: Pelican/Prentice Hall. (Original edition, 1963).

Goffman, Erving. 1981. *Forms of talk*. Philadelphia: University of Pennsylvania Press.

Harklau, Linda. 2000. From the "good kids" to the "worst": Representations of English language learners across educational settings. *TESOL Quarterly* 34. 35–67.

Haswell, Richard and Janis T. Haswell. 1996. Gender bias and critique of student writing. *Assessing Writing* 3. 31–83.

Helms-Park, Rena and Paul Stapleton. 2003. Questioning the importance of individualized voice in undergraduate L2 argumentative writing: An empirical study with pedagogical implications. *Journal of Second Language Writing* 12. 245–265.

Hood, Susan. 2012. Voice and stance as APPRAISAL: Persuading and positioning in research writing across intellectual fields. In Ken Hyland and Carmen Sancho Guinda (eds.), *Stance and voice in written academic genres*, 51–68. New York: Palgrave Macmillan.

Hyland, Ken. 2000. *Disciplinary discourses: Social interactions in academic writing*. New York: Longman.

Hyland, Ken. 2005. Stance and engagement: A model of interaction in academic discourse. *Discourse Studies* 7(2). 172–192.

Hyland, Ken. 2008. Disciplinary voices: Interactions in research writing. *English Text Construction* 1. 5–22.

Hyland, Ken. 2010. Community and individuality: Performing identity in applied linguistics. *Written Communication* 27. 159–188.

Hyland, Ken. 2012. *Disciplinary identities: Individuality and community in academic discourse*. Cambridge: Cambridge University Press.

Ivanič, Roz. 1998. *Writing and identity: The discoursal construction of identity in academic writing*. Amsterdam: John Benjamins Press.

Ivanič, Roz and David Camps. 2001. I am how I sound: Voice as self-representation in L2 writing. *Journal of Second Language Writing* 10. 3–33.

Jeffery, Jill. 2011. Subjectivity, intentionality, and manufactured moves: Teachers' perceptions of voice in the evaluation of secondary students' writing. *Research in the Teaching of English* 46. 92–127.

Kobayashi, Hiroe and Carol Rinnert. 2013. L1/L2/L3 writing development: Longitudinal case study of a Japanese multicompetent student writer. *Journal of Second Language Writing* 22. 4–33.

Lave, Jean and Etienne Wenger. 1991. *Situated learning: Legitimate peripheral participation*. Cambridge: Cambridge University Press.

Liu, Yichun. 2011. Power perceptions and negotiations in a cross-national email writing activity. *Journal of Second Language Writing* 20. 257–270.

Liu, Pei-Hsun Emma and Dan Tannacito. 2013. Resistance by L2 writers: The role of racial and language ideology in imagined community and identity investment. *Journal of Second Language Writing* 22. 355–373.

Martin, James R. and Peter White. 2005. *The languages of evaluation: Appraisal in English*. London: Palgrave Macmillan.

Matsuda, Paul Kei. 2001. Voice in Japanese written discourse: Implications for second language writing. *Journal of Second Language Writing* 10(1). 35–53.

Matsuda, Paul Kei. 2003. Second language writing in the twentieth century: A situated historical perspective. In Barbara Kroll (ed.), *Exploring the dynamics of second language writing*, 15–34. New York: Cambridge University Press.

Matsuda, Paul Kei. 2011. *Conceptions of voice in writing assessment rubrics*. Paper presented at the American Association for Applied Linguistics, Chicago, IL.

Matsuda, Paul Kei and Jill Jeffery. 2012. Voice in student essays. In Ken Hyland and Carmen Sancho Guinda (eds.), *Stance and voice in written academic genres*, 151–165. New York: Palgrave Macmillan.

Matsuda, Paul Kei and Christine M. Tardy. 2007. Voice in academic writing: The rhetorical construction of author identity in blind manuscript review. *English for Specific Purposes* 26. 235–249.

Ortmeier-Hooper, Christina. 2008. "English may be my second language, but I'm not ESL." *College Composition and Communication* 59. 389–419.

Ouelette, Mark. 2008. Weaving strands of writer identity: Self as author and the NNES "plagiarist." *Journal of Second Language Writing* 22. 255–273.

Peirce, Bonny. 1995. Social identity, investment, and language learning. *TESOL Quarterly* 29. 9–31.

Petrić, Bojana. 2010. Students' conceptions of voice in academic writing. In Rosa Lorés-Sanz, Pilar Mur-Dueñas, and Enrique Lafuente-Millán (eds.), *Constructing interpersonality: Multiple perspectives on written academic genres*, 324–336. Newcastle upon Tyne: Cambridge Scholars Publishing.

Prior, Paul. 2001. Voices in text, mind, and society: Sociohistoric accounts of discourse acquisition and use. *Journal of Second Language Writing* 10(1). 55–81.

Ramanathan, Vai and Dwight Atkinson. 1999. Individualism, academic writing, and ESL writers. *Journal of Second Language Writing* 8. 45–75.

Ramanathan, Vai and Robert Kaplan. 1996. Audience and voice in current L1 composition texts: Some implications for ESL students writers. *Journal of Second Language Writing* 5. 21–34.

Roberts, Felicia and Tony Cimasko. 2008. Evaluating ESL: Making sense of university professors' responses to second language writing. *Journal of Second Language Writing* 17. 125–143.

Rubin, Donald and Melanie Williams-James. 1997. The impact of writer nationality on mainstream teachers' judgments of composition quality. *Journal of Second Language Writing* 6. 139–153.

Sancho Guinda, Carmen and Ken Hyland. 2012. Introduction: A context-sensitive approach to stance and voice. In Ken Hyland and Carmen Sancho Guinda (eds.), *Stance and voice in written academic genres*, 1–11. New York: Palgrave Macmillan.

Severino, Carol. 1993. The sociopolitical implications of response to second language writing. *Journal of Second Language Writing* 2. 181–201.

Shen, Fan. 1989. The classroom and the wider culture: Identity as a key to learning English composition. *College Composition and Communication* 40. 459–466.

Shuck, Gail. 2010. Language identity, agency, and context: The shifting meanings of *multilingual*. In Michelle Cox, Jay Jordan, Christina Ortmeier-Hooper, and Gwen Schwartz (eds.), *Reinventing identities in second language writing*, 117–138. Urbana, IL: NCTE.

Starfield, Sue. 2002. "I'm a second-language English speaker": Negotiating writer identity and authority in Sociology One. *Journal of Language, Identity and Education* 1. 121–140.

Starfield, Sue and Louise Ravelli. 2006. 'The writing of this thesis was a process that I could not explore with the positivistic detachment of the classical sociologist': Self and structure in New Humanities research theses. *Journal of English for Academic Purposes* 5. 222–243.

Tardy, Christine M. 2012. Voice construction, assessment, and extra-textual identity. *Research in the Teaching of English* 47. 64–99.

Tardy, Christine M. and Paul Kei Matsuda. 2009. The construction of author voice by editorial board members. *Written Communication* 26. 32–52.

Thompson, Paul. 2012. Achieving a voice of authority in PhD theses. In Carmen Sancho Guinda and Ken Hyland (eds.), *Stance and voice in written academic genres*, 119–133. New York: Palgrave Macmillan.

Voloshinov, Valentin. 1973. *Marxism and the philosophy of language* (Ladislav Matejka and I. R. Titunik, Trans.). Cambridge, MA: Harvard University Press.

Yi, Youngjoo. 2010. Identity matters: Theories that help explore adolescent multilingual writers and their identities. In Michelle Cox, Jay Jordan, Christina Ortmeier-Hooper and Gwen Schwartz (eds.), *Reinventing identities in second language writing*, 303–323. Urbana, IL: NCTE.

Zhao, Cecilia and Lorena Llosa. 2008. Voice in high-stakes L1 academic writing assessment: Implications for L2 writing instruction. *Assessing Writing* 13. 153–170.

Carol Rinnert and Hiroe Kobayashi

17 Multicompetence and multilingual writing

Multicompetence and multilingual writing constitute a relatively new research area in the field of second language writing. *Multicompetence* refers to the theoretical framework developed by Cook (1992, 2002) and widely adopted by researchers in a variety of disciplines. It conceptualizes the individual bilingual or multilingual language user as having a compound state of linguistic knowledge that is different from the combined knowledge of two or more monolingual language users. The term *multilingual writing* refers to the ability to write in two or more languages, so is intended to subsume bilingual writing ability or biliteracy. The study of multilingual writing involves comparison of writing by the same writers in more than one language. In this chapter, we review key issues for researchers and multilingual writers focusing on how writing ability develops across languages.

1 Historical background: From crosslinguistic influence to multicompetence in SLA and L2 writing

The study of multilingualism, meaning the ability to use three or more languages, has become a recent focus of intense interest among researchers (e.g., Aronin and Hufeisen 2009; De Angelis 2007). Although multilingualism (as distinct from bilingualism) has only recently emerged as a field in its own right, its roots can be traced to a variety of fields, most notably second language acquisition (SLA), bilingualism, and contrastive rhetoric (CR).

Two partially overlapping research threads can be considered to underlie current thinking about multilingual writing: (1) how languages interact or influence each other in the process of L2 development, and (2) how developing L2 writer knowledge can be characterized/understood. As for the first trend, *cross-linguistic influence (CLI)*, also referred to as *transfer*, in the process of learning new languages has long been a concern of researchers in SLA and bilingualism, exemplified by studies of assessment of bilingual writing in Canadian immersion programs (e.g., Genesee 1987). In the specific field of L2 writing research, contrastive rhetoric (and later intercultural rhetoric) has attempted to identify cross-linguistic influence on rhetorical features (e.g., Connor 1996), a main concern of this chapter.

For SLA researchers there has been an evolution from characterizing cross-linguistic influence as largely negative, to recognizing its positive effects as being much more frequent and a key to successful language acquisition (Ringbom 2007). In terms of directionality, transfer or CLI can occur from L1 to L2 (*forward transfer*), from L2 to L1 (*reverse transfer*), from L2 to L3 or L3 to L2 (*lateral transfer*), or bi- or multi-directionally (Jarvis and Pavlenko 2007).

Researchers in bilingualism have also investigated cross-linguistic influences by distinguishing different language skills and by attempting to identify and evaluate the relative importance of factors affecting transfer/CLI, as seen in a recent special issue of the *International Journal of Bilingualism* devoted to transfer among bilinguals and L2 users (Treffers-Daller and Sakel 2012). Such factors include perceived similarities between languages (psychotypology, Kellerman 1986), proficiency level and recency of use (Williams and Hammarberg 1998), attrition (e.g., Pavlenko 2003), and context of use (e.g., Grosjean 2013).

In the research on bi/multilingual writing, most of the studies of CLI or transfer have specifically focused on sentence-level or word-level linguistic features (e.g., Kang 2005; Sagasta Errasti 2003). However, a relatively long tradition of research in contrastive rhetoric, beginning with Kaplan (1966), has investigated cross-cultural differences in discourse-level text features. These have included organization of information (e.g., inductive vs. deductive); connections between paragraphs (e.g., explicit vs. implicit); and the use and evaluation of culturally preferred L1 rhetorical features in L2 writing (Hinds 1987; Kobayashi and Rinnert 1996; Kubota 1998a, 1998b). In particular, the issue of inductive (specific ideas leading toward a main point at the end) versus deductive (a main point stated at the beginning, followed by specific ideas to support it) movement of ideas has attracted researchers' attention. East Asian student writers, particularly Japanese, were found to employ an inductive approach more frequently than a deductive one (Kobayashi 1984), and their frequent use of this pattern in L2 writing was considered to be the result of L1 rhetorical transfer. Nevertheless, attributing L1 transfer to L2 writing solely to a cultural factor has been critically disputed because it reflects a view of rhetorical patterns as static and fixed (Matsuda 1997).

Most recently, CR has moved in two new directions that parallel current trends in SLA and bi/multilingualism research. The first, *intercultural rhetoric* (Connor 2011), recognizes "writing as social action" in particular contexts. It focuses on negotiation and accommodation by writers and readers from diverse linguistic backgrounds, not "assimilation by non-native speakers" (p. 7). It also recognizes the importance of English as a Lingua Franca (ELF) among communicators with a variety of L1s. The second, *critical contrastive rhetoric* (Kubota 2010), raises awareness of the fluidity and changing nature of cultural preferences in rhetorical patterns. It also emphasizes the importance of often-conflicting social and political forces influencing such cultural preferences, along with the agency of the writer who may choose to follow and/or resist the dominant patterns. These concerns with social contexts of writing and writer agency relate directly to the discussion of text construction and writer empowerment in Section II below.

As for the second trend mentioned above, representations of developing speaker/writer knowledge have provided means of understanding the individual bi/multilingual speaker/writer; they have also constituted conceptual models for learners to aspire to. Grosjean (1989) was one of the first to warn researchers that a bilingual is not two monolinguals in one, and in the last 20 years, the tide seems to have turned away from using monolingual models or norms for comparison with bilingual and L2 learners, in studies of both bilingualism (Grosjean 2013) and SLA (Ortega 2009). Similarly, a recent contingency of researchers has been arguing that it is necessary to recognize that multilingual knowledge is not the same as bilingual knowledge (e.g., Aronin and Singleton 2012).

One widely accepted approach to characterizing the knowledge of bi/multilingual writers is the theory of multicompetence, proposed by Cook (1992). This theory, which we follow in this chapter, views the knowledge of bi/multilinguals as qualitatively different from that of monolinguals and posits overlapping or merged L1/L2 conceptual knowledge across multiple language systems. A proposal for modifying or expanding multicompetence theory argues that L1 and L2 are not static or fixed abstract systems, but fluid repertoires of experientially based knowledge that continue to grow and change with no end point (Hall, Cheng, and Carlson 2006). Although this view has been criticized for its terminological vagueness and main reliance on research with monolingual speakers of various dialects and registers of the same language (Jarvis and Pavlenko 2007), it has succeeded in drawing attention to the dynamic nature of language knowledge. This characteristic is particularly relevant to the development of writing abilities, which have to be cultivated and practiced and are always changing with experience throughout each writer's lifetime.

In recent years, researchers have advocated taking a multicompetence approach to L2 writing research, mainly in order to overcome the monolingual bias that has dominated the field. In particular, Ortega and Carson (2010) point out the need to apply a multicompetence perspective that is grounded in particular social contexts and recognizes the importance of the writer's "agency, power, and identity" (p. 50). They identify four priorities for research on multilingual writing development: within-writer design, comparable cross-linguistic analytic measures, expanded scope of inquiry with diverse populations and contexts, and multilingual (rather than monolingual) writing evaluators.

At the same time, empirical studies on multilingual writing have begun to adopt a multicompetence perspective. For instance, in their research on composing processes by bilingual writers with lower and higher L2 proficiency levels, Manchón, Roca de Larios, and Murphy (2009) draw on multicompetence theory to interpret their findings regarding strategic use of L1 as well as similarities and differences across L1 Spanish and L2 English writing processes. Other research has taken a multicompetence perspective as a basis (e.g., De Angelis and Jessner 2012; Kobayashi and Rinnert 2013). Many current studies of multilingual writing development have conceptual foundations that are compatible with multicompetence, but carry different labels. These include a "biliteracy genre approach" (e.g., Gentil 2011); "focus on multilingualism" (Cenoz and Gorter 2011); writer identity and "voice" in bi/multilingual writing (Casanave 1998; Hirvela and Belcher 2001; Ivanič

1998); and "translanguaging" and "translingual" approaches (Canagarajah 2011a; Horner, NeCamp, and Donahue 2011). Such studies that focus on discourse-level concerns, rather than purely linguistic ones, provide a primary basis for the following discussion of current issues in the field.

2 Current research/issues: Text construction and writer empowerment

With an increased interest in multilingual writers, a number of studies have investigated the development of their writing in two or three languages (e.g., Cenoz and Gorter 2011; De Angelis and Jessner 2012). While these studies have focused mainly on linguistic level features (e.g., sentential or lexical, or both), research to explore the text construction process of multilingual writers has been scarce. Thus, we would like to focus on discourse-level production to shed light on how multilingual writers shape their text at a macro-level across languages. This section presents a review of relevant research under two basic headings: multilingual text construction and writer empowerment.

2.1 L1/L2/L3 text construction

Drawing on the theory of multicompetence, studies have begun to examine multilingual writing at a rhetorical/discourse level (Kobayashi and Rinnert 2013; Soltero-González, Escamilla, and Hopewell 2012). Through a series of studies by the authors of this chapter (Kobayashi and Rinnert 2008, 2012, 2013; Rinnert and Kobayashi 2009), a model has been developed to explicate the L1/L2/L3 text construction of multilingual writers. As shown in the schematic representation in Figure 17.1, this model comprises three inter-related components: repertoire of knowledge; individual and situational factors affecting writers' decisions; and written output. The first component, repertoire of knowledge, includes L1, L2, and L3 writing knowledge, genre knowledge and disciplinary knowledge, which writers rely upon when they construct text. This component, together with individual and situational factors (i.e., perceptions, language proficiency, audience, and topics) affects writers' decisions on how they frame their writing overall and what specific text features they employ. The third component shows written output produced on the basis of such writers' decisions. To what extent L1, L2, and L3 text features are merged or overlap depends on the first two components. That is, the kinds of knowledge writers have acquired and what decisions they make in constructing text, affected by internal and external factors, determines the written output.

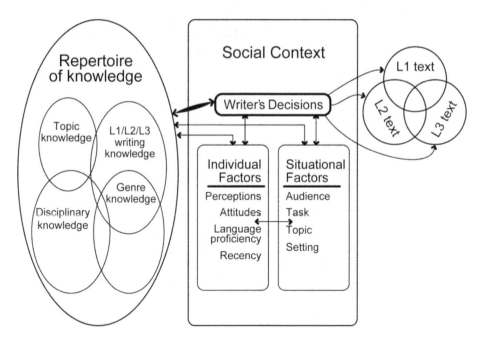

Fig. 17.1: Model of text construction.

2.1.1 Writing knowledge

Figure 17.2 shows sources and kinds of writing-related knowledge. The main sources of knowledge include both explicit and implicit writing instruction (i.e., reading) and writing experience across L1, L2, and L3, in addition to the acquisition of
linguistic features of each language. Knowledge acquired through these sources
ranges from writing conventions (e.g., use of punctuation), rhetorical features (e.g.,
structure/organization), and meta-knowledge (e.g., reader expectations), to disciplinary writing conventions (e.g., ways of writing research reports) and linguistic
knowledge (e.g., grammatical and lexical choices). What writing knowledge multilingual writers have accumulated in the repertoire of knowledge is crucial when
they construct text across languages.

Writing knowledge can be characterized by the following three features; the
first two are related to the nature of the knowledge, and the third concerns its
acquisition.

1. Writing knowledge is locally situated across languages. As revealed by contrastive rhetoric research on cross-cultural differences in discourse-level organizational features, writing knowledge provided could differ according to educational
contexts. For example, among Turkish students writing in L1 and L2 (English),
Uysal (2008) found the frequent use of *specification*, a macro-level rhetorical pattern that includes a preview statement of supporting reasons (Kubota 1998a). In
contrast, such preview statements were not frequently used in the introductions of

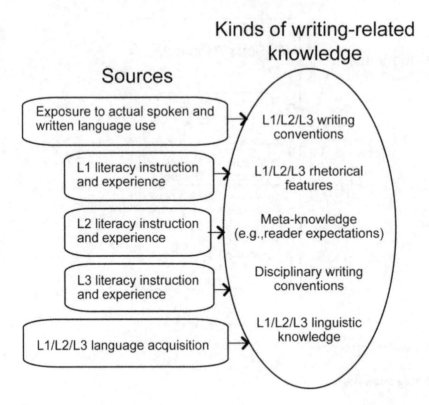

Fig. 17.2: Sources and kinds of writing knowledge.

argumentation essays by Japanese student writers (Kubota 1998b), and opinion writing in Chinese and Japanese textbooks demonstrated little use of this pattern (Kubota and Shi 2005). Kubota and Shi pointed out that there is a "culturally situated interpretation of deduction" (p. 97), which implies that the ways writers orient readers vary according to educational contexts, even when writers develop ideas in a deductive style. As this example illustrates, writing knowledge could differ in terms of conceptions of some text features across languages (Hinkel 1999).

2. Writing knowledge varies within a particular educational context. In the Japanese educational context, for example, along with the recent change toward increasingly greater use of a deductive pattern in L1 and L2 writing (Hirose 2003; Kubota and Shi 2005), diversity has been found in current writing instruction. In pre-university level L1 writing training, some high schools and teachers emphasize exposition, with the structure of raising a problem in the introduction and discussing it through comparison and contrast in the body, while others stress argumentation, focusing on the structure of an opinion statement followed by supporting reasons (Kobayashi and Rinnert 2008). Furthermore, a traditional Japanese pattern called *ki-sho-ten-ketsu* (introduction-continuation-change-conclusion) is also taught by some teachers. Thus, it is possible that each educational context provides

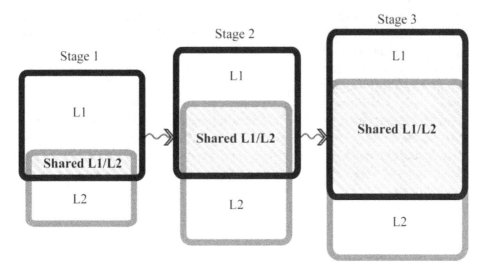

Fig. 17.3: Evolving repertoire of writing knowledge.

either a combination of somewhat traditional and somewhat newly implemented writing instruction, or just one of these, with differing emphasis and focus (Li 2002). This difference could cause difficulties, particularly for less experienced ESL and EFL writers who tend to rely on writing knowledge they receive in L1 instruction when they write in L2 (Yang, Baba, and Cumming 2004).

3. Acquisition of writing knowledge is developmental; as students progress from being novice to more experienced writers by receiving an increasing amount of writing instruction and practice across languages, their repertoire of knowledge expands (Kobayashi and Rinnert 2012). At the same time, interrelations among L1, L2, and L3 writing knowledge also change. Figure 17.3 shows a schematized representation of three stages in the evolution of the writing knowledge of Japanese EFL writers. As they are exposed to L1 and L2 knowledge and training, particularly when similar text features recur in both languages, knowledge about text features begins to overlap. In the case of novice writers, the degree of such overlaps between L1 and L2 writing is rather small because they generally receive more writing knowledge and training in L1 than L2; however, as writers gain more writing knowledge and experience in L2, this overlap becomes larger. Finally, the most highly experienced writers (graduate students and professionals) have a much greater degree of overlap, which contains a variety of text features applicable to both L1 and L2 writing.

This overlap or "bidirectional transfer" has been observed in recent research (e.g., Kobayashi and Rinnert 2012; Rinnert and Kobayashi 2009; Manchón and Roca de Larios 2007). For example, Soltero-González, Escamilla, and Hopewell (2012) demonstrated the parallel structure of narrative writing (i.e., introduction, conclusion, a main idea supported by details) by a Spanish-English speaking child to illustrate how emerging bilinguals write across languages. Earlier, Berman (1994) found that the effects of L1 (Icelandic) and L2 (English) writing instruction were equally influential on the persuasive writing of secondary school students who had received essay-writing classes in either of the two languages, attributing this result to similarity in writing instruction in Icelandic and English. Berman's finding corresponds to those of Hirose (2003) and Rinnert and Kobayashi (2009) that a majority of Japanese undergraduate students wrote argumentation essays similarly across L1 (Japanese) and L2 (English) by including an initial position statement, a macro-level rhetorical pattern (stating reasons), and a summary statement in the conclusion. It appears that similarity of L1 and L2 text features, along with writing instruction, reinforces the tendency for writers to increase the number of shared or overlapping text features across languages.

Compared with those undergraduate students' L1 and L2 argumentation essays, the more advanced Japanese writers with long overseas experience and disciplinary knowledge demonstrated sophisticated knowledge of introduction components, such as *focus* (especially clarification), and used a variety of argumentation sub-discourse types,[1] including *recommendation* and *exploration* as well as *justification* (see note 1 for definitions), which were all equally applied to either language (Kobayashi and Rinnert 2012: 127). At the same time, they tended to be sensitive to audience needs and chose L1 and L2 text features selectively to meet the expectations of local audiences, such as the use of *specific summary* (mentioning the main supporting points) for English conclusions and the use of *general summary* (with no mention of specific points) in Japanese.

While research on interrelations among multiple languages, particularly regarding discourse-level features (e.g., Canagarajah 2011a, 2011b) is limited, one longitudinal study of a multicompetent writer, Natsu (a pseudonym), writing in L1 (Japanese), L2 (English), and L3 (Chinese) provided support for the dynamic nature of writing knowledge and merged systems of knowledge (Kobayashi and Rinnert 2013). By analyzing both elicited and naturally occurring data – including written essays, pausing behavior and interviews, and observations – the study revealed that her repertoire of writing knowledge developed over time from separate L1 and L2 systems to a merged L1, L2, and L3 system. For example, Natsu selected *exposition* to frame her first L1 essay, viewing it as a preferred Japanese discourse type, whereas later she chose the *argumentation* subtype as a core pattern for all three essays, also consistently employing a paragraph structure with topic sentences. At

---

1 The three argumentation subtypes identified are defined as follows: *justification* presents a position and supports it with clear reasons and evidence, with optional counterargument plus refutation; *recommendation* states a position, supports it, identifies potential problems and suggests a solution, and *exploration* identifies issues related to a topic and (1) explores them from different perspectives to reach a position, or (2) puts forward a position and then explicates the thought underlying it (Kobayashi and Rinnert 2012: 114).

the same time, she incorporated language-specific text features for her perceived local audiences, for instance, implicit expression of opinion and a 4-character idiom in Chinese and explicit opinion stating in English. Thus, commonalities and distinctiveness co-existed in the textual aspects of her writing, and it was found that her past writing experience and perceptions affected her text construction.

Based on their research findings, Kobayashi and Rinnert (2012) argued that when writing knowledge overlaps among L1, L2, and L3, there is no cross-language transfer occurring in any direction. They suggested a reconsideration of the notion of transfer particularly for more experienced multilingual writers who tend to rely on a merged system of writing knowledge across languages, rather than transferring writing features from one language to another.

2.1.2 Factors affecting individual writers' choice of text features

Reflecting the recognized importance of the writer's agency (Kubota 2010; Matsuda 1997), individual writers' decisions take a central role in the text construction model shown in Figure 17.1; writers do not simply construct L1, L2, or L3 text based on writing knowledge they have acquired, but make decisions, consciously or unconsciously, about what features to choose from their repertoire of knowledge when they write. In this decision-making process, individual and social factors affect the writers in complex ways, often two or three factors interacting with each other. The factors identified in L2 writing research include such individual factors as perceptions, language proficiency (as distinguished from writing expertise, Manchón 2013: 101), attitudes, and recency (i.e., writing experience acquired recently), and such social factors as task, topic, and setting (e.g., FL or SL, and real or experimental settings) (Kobayashi and Rinnert 2012; Rinnert and Kobayashi 2009; Uysal 2009).

Among the individual factors, writers' perceptions can be considered the most influential, as shown in Natsu's case above. For example, some novice and experienced writers explicitly rejected the L2 logical structure of opinion and support reasons because they viewed it as "too formulaic," while some others employed it in both L1 and L2 writing (Rinnert and Kobayashi 2009). Another influential factor, language proficiency, intersects with other factors including kinds of task and writers' ability to deal with such features. Taking the example of counterargument and refutation, it was found that most of the novice JFL (Japanese as a foreign language) student participants in North America who reportedly had knowledge about this feature from their L1 literary training did not include a counterargument in their L2 Japanese argumentation essay; only three out of 12 writers (25%) did so (Rinnert, Kobayashi, and Katayama 2010). Apparently, this feature was difficult for them to formulate with limited linguistic ability. Among social factors, writers' awareness of local audience greatly affects multilingual writers' text construction.

For example, in three research papers written by a Sri Lankan bilingual professional (Canagarajah 2011b), the author combined different discourse styles according to audience and context. In particular, he created L1 Tamil and L2 English texts for a local audience by adopting an informal style and implicit theme development, while he produced L2 text for an international audience by employing a more formal, explicit style throughout, but still retaining such locally preferred features as referring to civic concerns and including no preview statement of the article structure. Although creating a hybrid text might have been the author's strategic choice, his awareness of different audience expectations was definitely one strong factor influencing his text construction of the three papers.

2.1.3 Gap between writing knowledge and written performance

In the text construction process, writers make a number of decisions on what text features to choose in order to achieve the goal of their writing. While time constraints and lack of topic knowledge affect the writers' decisions, they are sometimes unable to accomplish their goals due to a gap between knowledge they have and skills to apply it to actual writing performance. The case of Japanese university EFL writers with some overseas experience (Rinnert and Kobayashi 2009), for instance, illustrates this gap. While they had a relatively high level of language proficiency (converted TOEFL average: 537 points, Kobayashi and Rinnert 2012) and knowledge about counterarguments, they did not include this feature in their English writing as frequently as their L1 counterparts (30 % for L2; 60 % for L1 writers). In their case, it appears that even if they had knowledge, they had not internalized it yet, due to lack of experience applying it to their L2 writing, which subsequently led to avoidance of employing the feature. According to DeKeyser (2007), skills can be acquired through repeated practice; knowledge becomes proceduralized and then the "procedural knowledge" can be automatized through extensive practice. This suggests that in order to bridge the gap between writing knowledge and performance, student writers need extensive practice applying knowledge in L1 or L2 writing, or both.

In summary, as shown in Figure 17.1, the macro-level model of text construction highlights the central place of the writer's decision-making in choosing text features from the overlapping repertoire of writing knowledge. Although the model can help to clarify multilingual writing development, it is based on the text construction of multilingual writers in rather few educational contexts, mainly in Asia and North American English settings, writing in a limited number of genres, mainly timed essay writing. More research is needed to expand its scope to include other contexts, including diverse regions and non-academic settings, as well as a wide variety of genres.

2.2 Writer empowerment

As explained above, earlier views of monolingualism as normal, or even ideal, and bi/multilingualism as deficient have largely been discredited (Ortega 2009). In line with this change in thinking, it is increasingly being recognized that bi/multilingual writers gain certain advantages over monolingual writers. That is, learning to write in more than one language can empower a writer in L1, as well as L2 and L3. In relation to the development of multilingual writing ability, two factors are closely related to empowerment: the writer's individual history and writer agency. When writers acquire more knowledge and experience along their own learning trajectories, they gain more resources and the ability to apply learned concepts and skills effectively across languages, sometimes in new and innovative ways. Advantages enjoyed by multilingual writers include the following four key processes.

First, as implied by the earlier discussion of merged knowledge and bi-directional transfer, a major positive resource for multilingual writers is a core of shared underlying knowledge, which they can draw on when writing in different languages (Kecskes and Papp 2000). This may begin at a very early age (Verhoeven 1994). For example, many elementary school Spanish/English bilingual children in the US who first learned literacy in Spanish through a whole-language approach were found to be writing in English in different contexts and peer interactions before receiving any instruction in English literacy (Hudelson 2005). The use of underlying knowledge across languages was also observed among professional francophone writers in Canada; regardless of their L2 English linguistic proficiency, they were able to apply their knowledge of discourse organization and content and exert greater control in the L2 composing process than those with lesser L1 writing expertise (Cumming 1989). As discussed earlier, when the core, overlapping portion of developing multilingual writers' repertoire of knowledge grows larger, it gives the writers expanded resources to draw on for their writing in each language.

A second advantage for multilingual writers is the possibility to sharpen awareness of potential differences in dominant rhetorical patterns and reader expectations across languages. As implied in the discussion above, one main source of such audience awareness is exposure to authentic L2 interaction and texts. Like Sasaki (2011), Kobayashi and Rinnert (2012) found that this exposure can occur in an SL context when students go abroad, as evidenced by the intermediate and advanced Japanese EFL writers. Moreover, it can involve exposure to written texts in an FL context, as seen among approximately one-third of the North American JFL writers. Nevertheless, it is clear that simple exposure is not enough, given that not all writers who are exposed to such differences develop sensitivity to them.

To understand the reasons why some writers develop such sensitivities and others do not, it appears necessary to untangle complicated identity-related concerns. These may have to do with self-perceptions and motivations, as detailed in Haneda (2007), who documented very different individual learning trajectories among JFL writers in Canada. In particular, she found varying degrees of audience awareness, ranging from heightened sensitivity toward subtle differences in Japanese rhetorical features on the part of a Japanese studies major, to almost total obliviousness about such concerns on the part of a heritage student, who relied heavily on translation from English when writing in Japanese. More longitudinal case studies in a variety of learning contexts are needed to explore the multiplicity of ways that multilingual writers develop such sensitivities.

A third benefit for multilingual writers concerns the strategic use of more than one language in constructing texts across languages at both product and process levels. For example, Cenoz and Gorter (2011) documented that lexical and phrasal borrowings occur in all directions in the L1/L2 Basque and Spanish, and L3 English, texts of high school students in Spain, showing how such multidirectional transfer can be used to achieve both compensatory and stylistic effects in each of the three languages. This strategic advantage can also extend to the use of multiple languages during the composing process, as shown by think-aloud studies of composing processes by bi/multilingual writers. In particular, such studies have revealed how L1 can play a positive role in planning, generating, and revising text in L2 (Manchón et al. 2009), depending on sometimes-complex interactions among such factors as L2 proficiency and task demands. For example, Woodall (2002) found that L1 use during L2 English, Spanish, and Japanese writing facilitated the L2 writing process for higher proficiency writers in closely related languages for cognitively demanding tasks.

Moreover, it is likely that L2 use could contribute positively during L1 and L3 composing, at least for some multilingual writers. For instance, the analysis of pausing behavior by Natsu revealed that L2 English words and phrases frequently came up in her mind (about 20 % of the time) while she was engaged in time-constrained writing in L1 Japanese, mainly because of the recent extensive practice she had been doing to prepare for an English writing test. Whereas she reportedly had to suppress some of the English phrases, she sometimes was able to use them as the basis for her Japanese formulations (Kobayashi and Rinnert 2013).

A final advantage for multilingual writers is the enhanced possibility for creating innovations that transcend single languages. These may include both hybrid (or merged) concepts that combine knowledge from L1 and L2 and fall somewhere in between the two languages, and more recently hypothesized innovative concepts that are not associated with any prior language system, termed the "original concept scenario" (Bassetti and Cook 2011: 174–175). Some evidence of both hybrid and original text features has been found in various kinds of multilingual writing. For example, both kinds of innovations can be identified in the code-mixing and creative spellings of high school students' informal e-mail writing combining three languages: Basque, Spanish, and English reported by Cenoz and Gorter (2011), as well as in the codemeshing[2] and creative use of phrases by a multilingual writer

---

2 In codemeshing, languages are treated "as part of a single integrated system" (Canagarajah 2011a: 403).

with a Saudi Arabian background (Canagarajah 2013). Hybrid and original discourse-level text features also appear to be involved in the ways highly experienced multilingual writers negotiate conflicting identities in relation to their perceptions of local audience expectations (Canagarajah 2011a), as discussed earlier.

One explanation of how writers might go about developing such innovations, both hybrid and original, is suggested by a recent proposal to reconceptualize writing transfer (DePalma and Ringer 2011), which argues a need to expand the notion of transfer of learning beyond a static view of "use" and "reuse" of prior knowledge to a more dynamic view of "adaptive transfer" that stresses the agency of the individual writer. This conception recognizes that individual writers draw on their own past experiences and (changing) perceptions to transform knowledge in new ways in new contexts. This vision of adaptive transfer closely corresponds to the conceptualization of merged writing knowledge and refined notion of transfer proposed by Kobayashi and Rinnert (2012). Whatever the mechanism that may underlie the production of hybrid and original text features, they clearly expand the creative possibilities available to multilingual writers as they construct texts, regardless of the language they are using. In sum, the four processes discussed here can empower multilingual writers by providing a richer repertoire of resources than what is available to monolingual writers.

3 Future perspectives: Toward multilingual or translingual practices

This overview of past and current research on how multilingual writing ability develops highlights the new directions current researchers and teachers are moving: away from monolingual norms and toward multilingual or translingual practices (Canagarajah 2013). This final section briefly considers some of the implications for researchers and teachers, focusing on future research directions, methodological concerns, and pedagogical applications.

3.1 Future research directions: Diversification and theoretical challenges

To date, most research on rhetorical aspects of multilingual writing has focused rather narrowly on a limited population of developing writers, and on a small number of genres and languages, mainly university students writing L1/L2 argumentation or exposition essays in English and in Japanese, Chinese, or Spanish. As Ortega and Carson (2010) point out, there is a need to expand the inquiry to include diverse populations and types of writing. Possible directions for widening the scope of investigation include the following.

1. *Different populations*: A few studies have begun to look at multilingual writers of different ages and backgrounds, both inside and outside classrooms, including elementary (Buckwalter and Lo 2002; McCarthey, Guo, and Cummins 2005) and secondary school level (Sagasta Errasti 2003; Yi 2010). Such populations should be investigated in other languages and social contexts.

2. *Diverse genres*: A biliteracy approach could be applied to different genres in a variety of academic disciplines and non-academic areas, focusing on MA and doctoral thesis, research article, and/or professional report writing. For example, using such an approach, Gentil (2005) examined how L1 French speaking graduate students in an English-speaking university took different approaches to developing their disciplinary genre knowledge in their L2 while attempting to maintain and advance their ability to write about their research in their L1. Similarly, in the medical field, Parks (2001) examined how nurses educated in an L1 French university nursing department developed expertise in a specific written L2 English genre (care plans) in an Anglophone hospital by reshaping their L1 university based knowledge to meet the expectations of the context.

3. *Roles of multiple languages in text construction*: More research is needed to elucidate the different roles of L1/L2/L3 in composing processes and also how linguistic, cognitive, and social factors are likely to affect interactions among languages in multilingual writing (Manchón 2013). In addition, studies of multilingual text construction (e.g., Canagarajah 2011b) could be expanded to other languages and extended from two languages to three or more by the same multicompetent writer.

On a theoretical level, one challenge for researchers is to apply patterns based on individual, localized findings, which cannot be generalized to other individuals or contexts, to building coherent theory. In addition to multicompetence as discussed in this chapter, another theoretical basis may lie in complex systems theory (Larsen-Freeman 2006), which postulates a non-linear trajectory of language development that fits the findings reported in this chapter regarding the writing development of both individuals and groups. Recent studies based on this theory have found complex interactions among lexical and grammatical constructions in the writing of large groups of L2 writers at different phases of development (Verspoor, Schmid, and Xu 2012) and have identified variability and variation in the usage of lexical chunks by individual developing writers over time (Verspoor and Smiskova 2012); such approaches could be extended to include text features at other discourse levels.

Another challenge is finding ways to integrate influences of social context at various levels on the development of multilingual writing development, as suggested by Hudelson's (2005) critical reanalysis of the study of Spanish/English bilingual elementary school children's writing, cited earlier. Without invalidating the original interpretation of the findings as demonstrating the writers' control of their own literacy, she shows the need to add other, less neutral perspectives, especially considering both the wider social context in which English predominates and issues of power related to the hegemony of English. This concern about unequal power relations among languages is echoed by researchers in such fields as language and identity (e.g., Norton and McKinney 2011), critical contrastive rhetoric (e.g., Kubota 2010), and translingual practice (e.g., Canagarajah 2013), and points to the need for future research incorporating macro- and micro-level aspects of social context.

3.2 Methodological concerns: Multiple data sources and crosslingual comparison

One methodological concern that merits close attention when investigating multilingual writing is research design. As detailed above, comparing the same individual's writing across two or more languages has become a standard method for research in multilingual writing development. As illustrated in this chapter, other new approaches that are increasingly being adopted involve triangulating data from multiple sources, including ethnographic, textual, and process data, rather than relying exclusively on analysis of written products. In addition, combining case studies and cross-sectional studies (e.g., Kobayashi and Rinnert 2013; Verspoor and Smiskova 2012) can be a promising way to connect the findings of small-scale, in-depth studies with those of larger, more generalizable ones.

A second concern that represents a serious challenge for multilingual writing research involves the identification of comparable analytic measures across languages, as noted by Ortega and Carson (2010). In order to compare text features in different languages, particularly those with radically different sentence structure and writing systems, it is necessary to find "etic" features that are non-language-specific, including both linguistic and other analytic categories. Efforts to identify commonalities and distinctive features in writing across languages (as depicted in Figure 17.1) should be extended to include all levels of text, ranging from individual orthographic characters, lexical items and sentences, to larger organizational structure and content units, as well as visual or iconic components that have become more frequent with the spread of electronic media. Whatever the type and level of analytic measures, care must be taken to clarify operational definitions and provide enough examples to make the categories clear and the study replicable. As suggested by Brice (2005), the reliability of the analysis of qualitative research should be judged on the basis of how well the findings are grounded in data in the report and how clearly the procedures, categories, and findings are described using evidence from the data (p. 173).

3.3 Pedagogical applications: Translingual and individualized approaches

Current research in the field of multilingual writing development implies two main practical applications: taking advantage of the multilingual writers' knowledge of multiple languages to enhance their learning (e.g., Soltero-González et al. 2012), and recognizing individual differences, starting from what each writers knows, rather than assuming homogeneity in their writing development (De Angelis and Jessner 2012; Negretti 2012). To this end, several specific pedagogical approaches can be suggested.

First, instead of insisting on exclusive use of L2 in the classroom, a more flexible approach can be taken, especially in FL or SL settings with students who have the same or similar L1 backgrounds. For example, as suggested by Cenoz and Gorter (2011), the recently proposed concept of "translanguaging" can be applied to emphasize the use of resources possessed by multilingual learners. In this conception, the ability to "shuttle between languages" (Canagarajah 2011a: 401), both inside and outside the classroom, is considered to reinforce each language involved and could lead to effective instruction (Horner et al. 2011). Combined use of L1 and L2 appears to be particularly appropriate when teaching difficult text features, such as counterargument and refutation. If student writers have already learned about the feature through L1 writing instruction, they should be reminded that they can make use of this (declarative) knowledge in their L2 writing as well. What they likely have yet to acquire, however, is procedural knowledge, that is, how to make counterarguments and refute them persuasively to support their own side. In FL contexts, practice making opposing arguments could be given in L1, for example, through such oral activities as mini-debate in pairs or groups, while in SL contexts, where students with diverse language background are studying, the same activities would be given in L2. Once having developed familiarity with making counterarguments, students become capable of applying the knowledge to their L2 writing with some ease.

Second, specific tasks can be designed to elicit information about what knowledge, instruction, and experience each writer brings to the L2 writing class. These could include mini-tests of meta-knowledge about writing conventions; writing background questionnaires; and writing prompts asking about past writing classes, other kinds of writing experiences, perceptions of "good" writing in L1/L2, and/or perceived audience expectations. For example, Negretti (2012) used reflective journals both to probe and develop students' task perceptions, metacognitive knowledge of strategic choices, and control over their academic writing. Similarly, Yasuda (2011) monitored writers' reflections on sequenced L2 e-mail task instruction that raised inexperienced writers' knowledge of language choices and consideration for audience, as well as significantly improving their ability and confidence in e-mail writing in L2; for some students, this knowledge was reportedly transferred to their L1 e-mail writing as well.

In short, the findings of current research on multilingual writing development suggest the importance of encouraging multilingual writers to make connections between L1 and L2 writing knowledge, along with the necessity of recognizing each writer's unique learning history. Of course, the proposals offered here could not be applied in every learning context and would have to be adapted to each local setting to address the specific needs of developing multilingual writers. Nevertheless, the perspective provided by multicompetence theory to recognize the positive and productive nature of multilingual knowledge should help to inform research and teaching practices that can contribute to developing multilingual writing ability.

4 Additional sources

Cook, Vivian (ed.). 2003. *Effects of the second language on the first*. Clevedon, UK: Multilingual Matters.

Cook, Vivian and Benedetta Bassetti (eds.). 2011. *Language and bilingual cognition*. New York: Psychology Press.

Grosjean, François and Ping Li (eds.). 2013. *The psycholinguistics of bilingualism*. Oxford: Blackwell Publishing.

Kobayashi, Hiroe. 2005. Rhetorical decisions in L1 and L2 writing: How do novice writers differ? *Language and Culture Study* (Hiroshima University, Integrated Arts and Sciences) 31. 43–73.

Kroll, Judith and Natasha Tokowicz. 2005. Models of bilingual representation and processing: Looking back and to the future. In Judith Kroll and Annette D. Groot (eds.), *Handbook of bilingualism: Psycholinguistic approaches*, 531–553. Oxford: Oxford University Press.

Manchón, Rosa. M. (ed.). 2009. *Writing in foreign language contexts: Learning, teaching, and research*. Clevedon, UK: Multilingual Matters.

Manchón, Rosa. M. (ed.). 2012. *L2 writing development: Multiple perspectives*. Berlin: De Gruyter Mouton.

Pavelenko, Anita and Scott Jarvis. 2002. Bidirectional transfer. *Applied Linguistics* 23. 190–214.

Silva, Tony and Paul K. Matsuda (eds.). 2010. *Practicing theory in second language writing*. West Lafayette, IN: Parlor Press.

Verhoeven, Ludo T. 1994. Transfer in bilingual development: The linguistic interdependence hypothesis revisited. *Language Learning* 4(3). 381–415.

5 References

Aronin, Larissa and Britta Hufeisen (eds.). 2009. *The exploration of multilingualism: Development of research on L3, multilingualism and multiple language acquisition*. Amsterdam: John Benjamins.

Aronin, Larissa and David Singleton. 2012. *Multilingualism*. Amsterdam: John Benjamins.

Bassetti, Benedetta and Vivian Cook. 2011. Relating language and cognition: The second language user. In Vivian Cook and Benedetta Bassetti (eds.), *Language and bilingual cognition*, 143–190. New York: Psychology Press.

Berman, Robert. 1994. Learners' transfer of writing skills between languages. *TESL Canada Journal* 12. 29–46.

Brice, Colleen. 2005. Coding data in qualitative research on L2 writing: Issues and implications. In Paul Kei Matsuda and Tony Silva (eds.), *Second language writing research: Perspectives on the process of knowledge construction*, 159–175. Mahwah, NJ: Lawrence Erlbaum Associates.

Buckwalter, Jan K. and Yi-Hsuan Gloria Lo. 2002. Emergent biliteracy in Chinese and English. *Journal of Second Language Writing* 11. 269–293.

Canagarajah, A. Suresh. 2011a. Codemeshing in academic writing: Identifying teachable strategies of translanguaging. *Modern Language Journal* 95. 401–417. DOI: 10.1111/j.1540-4781.2011.01207.x

Canagarajah, A. Suresh. 2011b. Writing to learn and learning to write by shuttling between languages. In Rosa M. Manchón (ed.), *Learning-to-write and writing-to-learn in an additional language*, 111–132. Amsterdam: John Benjamins Publishing.

Canagarajah, A. Suresh. 2013. *Translingual practice: Global Englishes and cosmopolitan relations*. London: Routledge.

Casanave, Christine P. 1998. Transitions: The balancing act of bilingual academics. *Journal of Second Language Writing* 7. 175–203.

Cenoz, Jasone and Durk Gorter. 2011. Focus on multilingualism: A study of trilingual writing. *The Modern Language Journal* 95(3). 356–369.

Connor, Ulla. 1996. *Contrastive rhetoric: Cross-cultural aspects of second-language writing*. Cambridge: Cambridge University Press.

Connor, Ulla. 2011. *Intercultural rhetoric in the writing classroom*. Ann Arbor: The University of Michigan Press.

Cook, Vivian. 1992. Evidence for multicompetence. *Language Learning* 42. 557–591.

Cook, Vivian. 2002. Background to the L2 user. In Vivian Cook (ed.), *Portraits of the L2 user*, 1–28. Clevedon, UK: Multilingual Matters Ltd.

Cumming, Alister. 1989. Writing expertise and second-language proficiency. *Language Learning* 39(1). 81–141.

De Angelis, Gessica. 2007. *Third or additional language acquisition*. Clevedon, UK: Multilingual Matters.

De Angelis, Gessica and Ulrike Jessner. 2012. Writing across languages in a bilingual context: A dynamic systems theory approach. In Rosa M. Manchón (ed.), *L2 writing development: Multiple perspectives*, 47–68. Berlin/Boston: De Gruyter Mouton.

DeKeyser, Robert M. 2007. Study abroad as foreign language practice. In Robert M. DeKeyser (ed.), *Practicing in a second language: Perspectives from applied linguistics and cognitive psychology*, 208–226. New York: Cambridge University Press.

DePalma, Michael-John and Jeffrey M. Ringer. 2011. Toward a theory of adaptive transfer: Expanding disciplinary discussions of "transfer" in second-language writing and composition studies. *Journal of Second Language Writing* 20. 134–147.

Genesee, Fred. 1987. *Learning through two languages: Studies of immersion and bilingual education*. Cambridge, MA: Newbury House.

Gentil, Guillaume. 2005. Commitments to academic biliteracy: Case studies of francophone university writers. *Written Communication* 22. 421–471.

Gentil, Guillaume. 2011. A biliteracy agenda for genre research. *Journal of Second Language Writing* 20. 6–23.

Grosjean, François. 1989. Neurolinguists, beware! The bilingual is not two monolinguals in one person. *Brain and Language* 36. 3–15.

Grosjean, François. 2013. Bilingualism: A short introduction. In François Grosjean and Ping Li (eds.), *The psycholinguistics of bilingualism*, 5–25. Oxford: Blackwell Publishing.

Hall, Joan Kelly, An Cheng and Matthew Carlson. 2006. Reconceptualizing multicompetence as a theory of language knowledge. *Applied Linguistics* 27(2). 220–240.

Haneda, Mari. 2007. Modes of engagement in foreign language writing: An activity theoretical perspective. *The Canadian Modern Language Review* 64. 301–332.

Hinds, John. 1987. Reader versus writer responsibility: A new typology. In Ulla Connor and Robert B. Kaplan (eds.), *Writing across languages: Analysis of L2 text*, 141–152. Reading, MA: Addison-Wesley.

Hinkel, Eli. 1999. *Culture in second language teaching and learning.* Cambridge: Cambridge University Press.

Hirose, Keiko. 2003. Comparing L1 and L2 organizational patterns in the argumentative writing of Japanese EFL students. *Journal of Second Language Writing* 12(2). 181–209.

Hirvela, Alan and Diane Belcher. 2001. Coming back to voice: The multiple voices and identities of mature multilingual writers. *Journal of Second Language Writing* 10. 83–106.

Horner, Bruce, Samantha NeCamp, and Christiane Donahue. 2011. Toward a multilingual composition scholarship: From English only to a translingual norm. *College Composition and Communication* 63. 269 300.

Hudelson, Sarah. 2005. Taking on English writing in a bilingual program: Revisiting, reexamining, reconceptualizing the data. In Paul Kei Matsuda and Tony Silva (eds.), *Second language writing research: Perspectives on the process of knowledge construction*, 207–220. Mahwah, NJ.: Lawrence Erlbaum Associates.

Ivanič, Roz. 1998. *Writing and identity: The discoursal construction of identity in academic writing.* Amsterdam: John Benjamins Publishing Company.

Jarvis, Scott and Aneta Pavlenko. 2007. *Crosslinguistic influence in language and cognition.* London: Routledge.

Kang, Jennifer Y. 2005. Written narratives as an index of L2 competence in Korean EFL learners. *Journal of Second Language Writing* 14. 259–279.

Kaplan, Robert. B. 1966. Cultural thought patterns in intercultural education. *Language Learning* 16(1). 1–21.

Kecskes, Istvan and Tünde Papp. 2000. *Foreign language and mother tongue.* Mahwah, NJ: Lawrence Erlbaum Associates.

Kellerman, Eric. 1986. An eye for an eye: Crosslinguistic constraints on the development of the L2 lexicon. In Eric Kellerman and Michael Sharwood-Smith (eds.), *Crosslinguistic influence in second language acquisition*, 35–48. New York: Pergamon.

Kobayashi, Hiroe. 1984. *Rhetorical patterns in English and Japanese.* Unpublished doctoral dissertation, Teachers College, Columbia University, New York.

Kobayashi, Hiroe and Carol Rinnert. 1996. Factors affecting composition evaluation in an EFL context: Cultural rhetorical pattern and readers' background. *Language Learning* 46(3). 91–116.

Kobayashi, Hiroe and Carol Rinnert. 2008. Task response and text construction across L1 and L2 writing. In Rosa M. Manchon and Pieter de Haan (eds.), Writing in foreign language contexts: Research insights. Special issue of the *Journal of Second Language Writing* 17, 7–29.

Kobayashi, Hiroe and Carol Rinnert. 2012. Understanding L2 writing development from a multicompetence perspective: Dynamic repertoires of knowledge and text construction. In Rosa M. Manchón (ed.), *L2 writing development: Multiple perspectives*, 101–134. Berlin: De Gruyter Mouton.

Kobayashi, Hiroe and Carol Rinnert. 2013. L1/L2/L3 writing development: Longitudinal case study of a Japanese multicompetent writer. *Journal of Second Language Writing* 22. 4–31.

Kubota, Ryuko. 1998a. An investigation of Japanese and English L1 essay organization: Differences and similarities. *The Canadian Modern Language Review* 1(1). 475–507.

Kubota, Ryuko. 1998b. An investigation of L1-L2 transfer in writing among Japanese university students: Implications for contrastive rhetoric. *Journal of Second Language Writing* 7(1). 69–100.

Kubota, Ryuko. 2010. Critical approaches to theory in second language writing: A case of critical contrastive rhetoric. In Tony Silva and Paul K. Matsuda (eds.), *Practicing theory in second language writing*, 191–208. West Lafayette, IN: Parlor Press.

Kubota, Ryuko and Ling Shi. 2005. Instruction and reading samples for opinion writing in L1 junior high school textbooks in China and Japan. *Journal of Asian Pacific Communication* 15. 97–123.

Larsen-Freeman, Diane. 2006. The emergence of complexity, fluency, and accuracy in the oral and written production of five Chinese learners of English. *Applied Linguistics* 27(4). 590–619.

Li, Xiaoming. 2002. "Track (dis)connecting": Chinese high school and university writing in a time of change. In David Foster and David R. Russell (eds.), *Writing and learning in cross-national perspective: Transitions from secondary to higher education*, 49–87. Mahwah, NJ: Lawrence Erlbaum.

Manchón, Rosa M. 2013. Writing. In Francois Grosjean and Ping Li (eds.), *The psycholinguistics of bilingualism*, 100–115. Oxford: Blackwell Publishing.

Manchón, Rosa M. and Julio Roca de Larios. 2007. On the temporal nature of planning in L1 and L2 composing: A study of foreign language writers. *Language Learning* 57. 549–593.

Manchón, Rosa M., Julio Roca de Larios, and Liz Murphy. 2009. The temporal dimension and problem-solving nature of foreign language composing processes. Implications for theory. In Rosa M. Manchón (ed.), *Writing in foreign language contexts: Learning, teaching, and research*, 102–129. Clevedon, UK: Multilingual Matters.

Matsuda, Paul K. 1997. Contrastive rhetoric in context: A dynamic model of L2 writing. *Journal of Second Language Writing* 6. 45–60.

McCarthey, Sarah J., Yi-Huey Guo, and Sunday Cummins. 2005. Understanding changes in elementary Mandarin students' L1 and L2 writing. *Journal of Second Language Writing* 14(2). 71–104.

Negretti, Raffaella. 2012. Metacognition in student academic writing: A longitudinal study of metacognitive awareness and its relation to task perception and evaluation of performance. *Written Communication* 29. 142–179. DOI:10.1177/0741088312438529

Norton, Bonny and Carolyne McKinney. 2011. An identity approach to second language acquisition. In Dwight Atkinson (ed.), *Alternative approaches to second language acquisition*, 73–94. London: Routledge.

Ortega, Lourdes. 2009. *Understanding second language acquisition*. London: Hodder Education.

Ortega, Lourdes and Joan Carson. 2010. Multicompetence, social context, and L2 writing research praxis. In Tony Silva and Paul K. Matsuda (eds.), *Practicing theory in second language writing*, 48–71. West Lafayette, IN: Parlor Press.

Parks, Susan. 2001. Moving from school to workplace: Disciplinary innovation, border crossings, and the reshaping of a written genre. *Applied Linguistics* 22. 405–438.

Pavlenko, Aneta. 2003. "I feel clumsy speaking Russian": L2 influence on L1 in narratives in narratives of Russian users of English. In Vivian Cook (ed.), *Effects of the second language on the first*, 32–61. Clevedon, UK: Multilingual Matters.

Ringbom, Håkan. 2007. *Cross-linguistic similarity in foreign language learning*. Clevedon, UK: Multilingual Matters.

Rinnert, Carol and Hiroe Kobayashi. 2009. Situated writing practices in foreign language settings: The role of previous experience and instruction. In Rosa M. Manchón (ed.), *Writing in foreign language contexts: Learning, teaching, and research*, 23–48. Clevedon, UK: Multilingual Matters.

Rinnert, Carol, Hiroe Kobayashi, and Akemi Katayama. 2010. Argumentation text construction by North American JFL writers: Transfer or non-transfer? Paper presented at Annual Meeting of American Association of Applied Linguistics, Sheraton Hotel, Atlanta, GA, 6–9 March.

Sagasta Errasti, María Pilar. 2003. Acquiring writing skills in a third language: The positive effects of bilingualism. *International Journal of Bilingualism* 7(1). 27–42.

Sasaki, Miyuki. 2011. Effects of varying lengths of study-abroad experiences on Japanese EFL students' L2 writing ability and motivation: A longitudinal study. *TESOL Quarterly* 45(1). 81–105.

Soltero-González, Lucinda, Kathy Escamillaa, and Susan Hopewell. 2012. Changing teachers' perceptions about the writing abilities of emerging bilingual students: Towards a holistic bilingual perspective on writing assessment. *International Journal of Bilingual Education and Bilingualism* 15. 71–94. DOI:10.1080/13670050.2011.604712

Treffers-Daller, Jeanine and Jeanette Sakel (eds.). 2012. *New perspectives on transfer among bilinguals and L2 users, Special Issue of International Journal of Bilingualism* 16(1).

Uysal, Hacer Hande. 2008. Tracing the culture behind writing: Rhetorical patterns and bidirectional transfer in L1 and L2 essays of Turkish writers in relation to educational context. *Journal of Second Language Writing* 17(3). 183–207.

Verhoeven, Ludo T. 1994. Transfer in bilingual development: The linguistic interdependence hypothesis revisited. *Language Learning* 4(3). 381–415.

Verspoor, Marjolijn and Hana Smiskova. 2012. Foreign language writing development from a dynamic usage based perspective. In Rosa M. Manchón (ed.), *L2 writing development: Multiple perspectives*, 17–46. Berlin/Boston: de Gruyter Mouton.

Verspoor, Marjolijn, Monika S. Schmid, and Xiaoyan Xu. 2012. A dynamic usage based perspective on L2 writing. *Journal of Second Language Writing* 21. 239–263.

Williams, Sarah and Bjorn Hammarberg. 1998. Language switches in L3 production: Implications for a polyglot speaking model. *Applied Linguistics* 19. 295–333.

Woodall, Billy R. 2002. Language-switching: Using the first language while writing in a second language. *Journal of Second Language Writing* 11. 7–28.

Yang, Luxin, Kyoko Baba, and Alister Cumming. 2004. Activity systems for ESL writing improvement: Case studies of three Chinese and three Japanese adult learners of English. In Dorte Albrechtsen, Kristen Haastrup and Birgit Henriksen (eds.), *Writing and vocabulary in foreign language acquisition, Special Issue of Angles on the English-Speaking World* 4, 13–33.

Yasuda, Sachiko. 2011. Genre-based tasks in foreign language writing: Developing writers' genre awareness, linguistic knowledge, and writing competence. *Journal of Second Language Writing* 20. 111–133.

Yi, Youngjoo. 2010. Adolescent multilingual writers' transitions across in- and out-of-school writing contexts. *Journal of Second Language Writing* 19. 17–32.

Neomy Storch
18 Collaborative writing

1 Introduction

Collaborative and cooperative learning have a long history in mainstream education (see review in Johnson and Johnson 1990). The focus of this chapter, however, is on collaboration in the production of a written text. A simple definition of collaborative writing is that it is the production of a text by two or more writers. A more comprehensive definition of collaborative writing builds on the work of Ede and Lunsford (1990) and highlights the distinguishing traits of this activity in terms of process, product and the notion of text ownership (see Storch 2013). In terms of process, collaborative writing involves substantial interaction between the co-authors throughout the composing process. This distinguishes collaborative writing from peer planning or peer response activities, where the interaction occurs only in the pre- or post-writing stages respectively. In terms of product, collaborative writing results in the creation of a single text that cannot be easily reduced to the contribution of each author (Stahl 2006). The third and perhaps the most important trait of collaborative writing is the sense of a shared ownership of the text produced, with all co-authors sharing in the decision-making and responsibility for the entire text. This trait distinguishes collaborative writing from group projects, where each author may have a responsibility to produce one section of the project report. This division of labour would best be described as a cooperative writing activity where authors co-contribute rather than co-construct a written text.

The next section provides a rationale for implementing collaborative writing in L2 contexts. It draws on social constructionist theories of learning but focuses mainly on the work of Swain and the evolution of Swain's thinking on the importance of producing language for language learning. The chapter then reviews extant empirical studies on collaborative L2 writing. This review discusses and critically evaluates three main strands in this body of research. The chapter concludes with a discussion of the pedagogical applications of collaborative writing and of areas requiring additional research.

2 Historical context: The rationale for collaborative writing

Collaborative writing is relatively well established in the discipline of composition studies. It is grounded in social constructionist theories of learning, in the work of scholars such as Dewey ([1938] 1974), Freiri (1970) and Vygotsky (1978). The core assumption underlying social constructivism is that knowledge and human cognitive development are socially constructed by members of the community (Dewey 1938; Vygotsky 1978). Extending this argument to the development of literacy, Freiri (1970) claimed that literacy is best taught in social contexts, with students actively involved in creating knowledge. Composition scholars (e.g., Bruffee 1984; Dale 1994) see collaborative writing as a way of promoting the development of writing skills, by exposing students to different ideas and providing them with a better sense of an audience.

In the field of second language (L2) writing, the arguments in support of collaborative writing are in terms of language learning and align with Manchón's (2011) notion of writing-to-learn. Manchón distinguishes between learning-to-write and writing-to-learn (see Chapter 2, this volume). In the former, writing activities aim to promote improved writing abilities; in the latter, writing is used as a vehicle to promote the learning of content or of language. On the basis of this dichotomy, the arguments in support of collaborative writing in first language (L1) composition classes are in terms of learning-to-write; whereas in L2 contexts, collaborative writing is perceived as an activity that provides opportunities to learn the L2 (writing-to-learn language). Thus, theoretical support for collaborative L2 writing rests on theories of second language acquisition (SLA), and particularly the work of Swain, discussed in what follows.

Specifically, the impetus for collaborative L2 writing can be traced to the early work of Swain (1985, 1993, 1995) on the need to push learners to produce output. In her Output Hypothesis, Swain (1985, 1993) argued that merely exposing learners to comprehensible input is insufficient to promote L2 learning. Rather it is the act of producing language that is more likely to make learners process language more deeply and promote learning. In her 1995 work Swain identifies three main functions of output. The first function is that of noticing gaps or holes in one's L2 knowledge when attempting to produce language. The second function of output is hypothesis testing. Producing output is a means for testing different ways of expressing ideas. The third function of output is a metalinguistic one, encouraging reflections on the language produced. These processes are all key processes in L2 learning from a cognitive perspective of SLA (Ellis 1994; Schmidt 1990).

It should be noted that although the Output Hypothesis referred to both speaking and writing, Swain's own research often employed collaborative writing tasks and investigated the nature of the talk that the tasks elicited (e.g., Kowal and Swain 1994; Swain 1998). The aim of this research was to provide evidence of the cognitive processes that occurred during output promoting tasks. For example, Kowal and Swain's (1994) study was conducted with French immersion students collaborating on a dictogloss task (reconstructing a text based on notes taken from a dictation). The study found evidence of learners noticing gaps in their interlanguage as they reconstructed the text and resolved these gaps.

The unit of analysis used to code the pair or small group talk data in these studies was the Language Related Episode (LRE). These LREs were defined as instances in the data where learners deliberated about language use, be it lexis, grammar or mechanics (punctuation, spelling). Later Swain and Lapkin (1998) refined the definition of LREs to include instances where learners self- or other-correct. Thus LREs were defined as instances in the conversation where learners "talk about the language they are producing, question their language use, or correct themselves or others" (p. 326). LREs have since been used by many researchers to analyse learners' interaction (e.g., Adams 2006; Basterrechea and García-Mayo 2013; Fortune and Thorp 2001; García-Mayo 2002; Kuiken and Vedder 2002; Leeser 2004; Niu 2009; Storch 2001a).

Research on collaborative writing began in earnest from 2000 onwards. However, it is important to note that the theories informing this research were no longer restricted to cognitive theories of SLA. Sociocultural theoretical perspectives were adopted to provide a rationale for collaborative writing and to analyse the interactions that took place during collaborative writing. This change can be attributable to the influence that Vygotsky's (1978) sociocultural theory, promoted by scholars such as Lantolf (2000), Lantolf and Appel (1994) and Donato (1994), had on SLA researchers. This alternative theoretical perspective is reflected in Swain's (2000, 2006, 2010) reconceptualization of the Output Hypothesis.

The reconceptualised Output Hypothesis was broadened to reflect that producing language, whether speaking or writing, was a communicative and a cognitive activity. The term output was abandoned and the importance of the dialogue that occurs in problem-solving task was emphasized. The term used to describe this dialogue is collaborative dialogue (Swain 2000). From a sociocultural theoretical perspective, dialogue that occurs during a problem solving task is a cognitive activity. It is via dialogue that a more able member of the society (the expert) can provide the novice with the appropriate level of assistance that enables knowledge to be co-constructed and eventually to be internalised by the novice. LREs identified in the collaborative dialogues are viewed as instances where learners verbalise their thinking or their deliberations. Verbalised thinking becomes an artefact that can be further explored. The term that Swain (2006, 2010) felt best captured this process is *languaging*.

In any problem solving task, be it in mathematics or language related, languaging is one way to gain new knowledge or consolidate existing knowledge. However, whereas in mathematics, languaging is articulating thinking about mathematical concepts or models, in language related tasks, learners language about language. They language on how best to express intended meaning. In solitary writing, languaging is generally sub-vocal, speech directed to oneself (private speech). In collaborative writing, languaging is externalised and this externalisation confers a number of advantages over solitary writing. For instance, deliberations during collaborative writing can encourage learners to pool their linguistic knowledge in a process termed *collective scaffolding* (Donato 1994; Storch 2002, 2009).

Again, although Swain promoted the use of oral and writing problem solving tasks, many of her studies employed writing tasks, and particularly collaborative writing (e.g., Brooks and Swain 2009; Watanabe and Swain 2007). Many scholars have in fact argued that writing is superior to speaking in terms of generating languaging. Writing gives learners time to pay attention to language use, to draw on their explicit knowledge of language, and to heed any feedback they may receive (Cumming 1990; Harklau 2002; Williams 2008, 2012; see also Chapter 26). Furthermore, writing seems to encourage a greater focus on accuracy. Schoonen, Snellings, Stevenson and van Gelderen (2009) suggest that writing demands higher standards of accuracy than speaking because we tend to be less tolerant of errors in written language than in spoken language. Empirical studies comparing attention to language promoted by speaking and writing activities (e.g., Adams 2006; Adams and Ross-Feldman 2008) provide evidence that writing promotes more languaging than speaking. Furthermore Niu (2009) found that writing also focuses attention on discourse features in addition to lexical and grammatical forms, such attention is absent in speaking tasks.

Drawing on the above discussion, we can conclude that tasks which require language learners to write may confer greater language learning opportunities than tasks which require learners to speak. Writing completed collaboratively may provide more such opportunities than solitary writing. In collaborative writing both the languaging that the composing generates and the written text are available for further exploration. Furthermore, feedback in collaborative writing is available immediately and throughout the writing process (Hirvela 1999; Storch 2002, 2009). In solitary writing the feedback from the teacher or peers (in peer response activities) tends to be given once the writing activity has been completed.

The body of empirical research on collaborative L2 writing is still relatively small. Much of this research has been conducted with ESL, EFL or immersion students (in Canada). An overview of this research is provided in the next section.

3 Overview of research on collaborative L2 writing

Three distinct strands can be identified in research on collaborative L2 writing. The first strand includes studies that examine the factors that are likely to encourage languaging. The second includes studies that investigate whether the languaging that takes place during collaborative writing leads to language learning gains and the effect of such languaging on the text produced. The third strand is of studies investigating collaborative writing mediated by technology, and in particular the use of wikis. Each of these strands of research is discussed in turn, noting the theoretical approach informing the studies, the research design employed, and the main findings of the studies within these strands.

3.1 Factors affecting the volume of languaging in collaborative writing

Factors that that may affect the volume of languaging when learners engage in collaborative writing include: the type of task, the L2 proficiency of the learners assigned to work together as a pair, and the kind of relationships these learners form when working together. The unit of analysis used in all these studies to operationalize languaging is the LRE.

3.1.1 Tasks

A range of writing tasks has been employed in studies on collaborative writing. These tasks can be distinguished in terms of whether they are meaning focused or grammar focused. A meaning focused collaborative writing task, such as a composition, data commentary report and jigsaw, requires the writers to compose a text based on a prompt (verbal or pictorial). A grammar focused task such as a dictogloss[1], the most frequently used task in research on L2 collaborative writing, encourages a focus on form. The dictogloss is generally seeded with specific grammatical structures and aims to encourage learners to use these structures when reconstructing a text based on the notes taken from the dictation listening activity (see Wajnryb 1990).

A number of researchers have investigated the efficacy of various collaborative writing tasks. Comparison between tasks is based on the quantity and type of LREs evident in recorded pair interaction.

Studies comparing meaning focused and grammar focused tasks (e.g., editing, text reconstruction) have shown, not surprisingly, that the grammar based tasks elicit a higher number of LREs than the meaning based tasks, and that most of these LREs deal with morphosyntax. These studies have been conducted predominantly with adult learners in EFL (e.g., Alegría de la Colina & García-Mayo 2007; García-Mayo 2002) and ESL settings (e.g., Storch 2001a). However, the study by Swain and Lapkin (2001), conducted in a French immersion program with adolescent L2 learners, found no significant differences in the quantity and type of LREs generated by a jigsaw (meaning-based task) and a dictogloss. The researchers sug-

---

1 A number of researchers have used text editing and text reconstruction tasks in their research on collaborative writing (e.g., Alegría de la Colina and García-Mayo 2007; Storch 2008). In the editing and text reconstruction tasks, students are given the text to work on rather than required to compose a text. Given the definition of collaborative writing used in this chapter, these two types of tasks are not included in the discussion. The dictogloss, on the other hand, is included because students compose a text based on notes taken from a dictation, and are not required to replicate the text that they had listened to (see Fortune 2005), but to produce a grammatically accurate text which retains the gist of the dictated text.

gested that because both tasks were preceded by a mini grammar lesson, this may have encouraged the learners to focus on grammatical accuracy in both types of tasks.

Research on whether some meaning focused tasks are superior to others in eliciting languaging is scarce. One of the few studies to do so is by Storch and Wigglesworth (2007). The study, conducted with adult highly proficient ESL students, compared the attention to language elicited by a data commentary report and an argumentative essay. The study found that both tasks generated a similar number of LREs. Most of these LREs were lexical, attributable to the meaning focused nature of both tasks, but also perhaps to the high L2 proficiency of the participants.

3.1.2 L2 proficiency

Another factor that may affect the quantity and the resolution of LREs is the L2 proficiency of the learners who form the pairs. In this strand of research we note a shift from early research (Leeser 2004) that adopted a cognitive perspective and a quantitative research design to later studies (e.g., Storch and Aldosari 2013; Watanabe and Swain 2007) that adopted a sociocultural theoretical perspective and included a qualitative dimension in their research design.

One of the earliest studies to consider the impact of proficiency pairing on attention to language in collaborative writing tasks was by Leeser (2004). The 42 participants in this study (learners of L2 Spanish) were assigned to pairs of similar proficiency (eight high-high and nine low-low pairs) and mixed proficiency (four pairs) and asked to complete a dictogloss task. Leeser reported that L2 proficiency had an impact on the number of LREs produced: the high-high pairs produced the greatest number of LREs followed in descending order by the high-low and low-low pairs. The focus of the LREs also seemed to be affected by L2 proficiency: the high-high pairs focused mainly on grammatical forms; the low-low pairs mainly on lexis. Although most LREs were correctly resolved across all proficiency pairings, the highest proportion of unresolved LREs was found in the data of the low-low pairs, suggesting that languaging may not be as successful among low proficiency pairs. Based on these findings, Leeser concluded that collaborative writing may be suitable only for high proficiency learners.

Storch and Aldosari (2013) built on Leeser's study but adopted a sociocultural theoretical perspective, considering not only the quantity of LREs that similar and mixed proficiency pairs produced, but also the quality of the interaction that these learners engaged in. The study also used a meaning based task rather than a dictogloss. The study, conducted with 30 EFL learners in Saudi Arabia, had five pairs in each proficiency pairing: high-high, low-low and high-low. Analysis of LREs generated by the task revealed similar results to those reported by Leeser; with the highest number of LREs found in the data of high-high pairs; the lowest in low-low pairs. However, a closer look at the nature of interaction in mixed and equal proficiency pairs showed that in mixed proficiency pairs, the low proficiency learner was often passive, contributing very little to the interaction and decision making (see also Watanabe and Swain 2007). In contrast, when low proficiency learners were paired with fellow low proficiency learners, they were more involved in the collaborative writing activity, and there was more evidence of collective scaffolding in the data of these pairs. The researchers concluded that it is not just the L2 proficiency of members of the pair but the type of relationship they form that is an important consideration when deciding on how best to assign learners to collaborative writing activities.

3.1.3 Dyadic relationships

The relationships that learners form when working on collaborative writing tasks has been the focus of investigation of a small number of studies. These studies, informed by sociocultural theoretical perspectives, focus on the behavior of the learners and the possible affective factors that may explain their behavior, rather than only on the number of LREs produced. The data collected in such studies goes beyond recorded pair talk, and tends to include retrospective interviews with the learners.

Storch (2002) was one of the first studies to consider the nature of the relationships learners form when writing in pairs. This longitudinal study was classroom based. It was conducted in a university level ESL credit-bearing subject and focused on the data of ten pairs over an entire semester. Storch observed that the ten pairs of learners in her study formed different types of relationships and that such relationships, once established, tended to persist, regardless of task or passage of time. More importantly, the relationships learners formed had an impact on the language learning opportunities that collaborative writing tasks afforded. Analysing the data of the pair talk qualitatively, Storch established a model of dyadic interaction. The model has two intersecting continua: equality and mutuality. Equality, the horizontal continuum, reflects the learners' level of contribution and control over the task. Mutuality, the vertical continuum, reflects the learners' level of engagement with each other's contribution. The two intersecting continua form four quadrants, representing four distinct patterns of pair relations.

In Quadrant 1, both equality and mutuality are relatively high and the relationship is labelled collaborative. That is, both members of the pair contribute to the task and engage with each other's suggestion, often pooling their linguistic resources (collective scaffolding) in resolving deliberations about language. In Quadrant 2, equality is high, but mutuality is low. The pattern is labelled dominant/dominant or cooperative (Storch 2001b). Both members of the pair contribute to the task, but

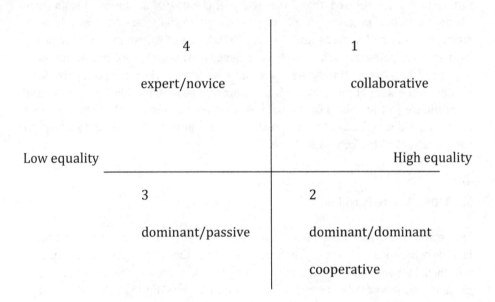

High mutuality

4	1
expert/novice	collaborative

Low equality ————————————————— High equality

3	2
dominant/passive	dominant/dominant
	cooperative

Low Mutuality

Fig. 18.1: A model of dyadic interaction (Storch 2002, 2009).

do not engage with each other's contributions. In Quadrant 3, both equality and mutuality are low. One member of the pair takes or is afforded control of the task; the other member contributes very little to the task. Hence the pattern is labelled dominant/passive. In Quadrant 4, the pattern is labelled expert/novice and reflects a tutor/tutee relationship. In such pairs, one learner takes a leading role but at the same time provides the kind of support and encouragement usually provided by the teacher.

Different patterns of dyadic interaction have since been reported in a number of studies in different contexts. For example, Ives (2004) found evidence of collaborative, expert/novice, and expert/passive patterns of interaction in a primary L2 class where grade 6 learners were paired with native English speaking children. In the Storch and Aldosari (2013) study, mentioned earlier, there was more evidence of collaboration in pairs of equal proficiency (high-high and low-low) than in pairs where learners had different proficiency (high-low). Kim and McDonough (2008), in a study conducted in South Korea with learners of Korean as a second language, also reported different patterns of pair interaction depending on whether the learner worked with an interlocutor of the same or of a higher L2 proficiency. What these studies also show quite clearly is that simply assigning students to work in pairs does not guarantee collaboration.

The research discussed thus far suggests that the L2 proficiency level of members of the pair may explain why certain relationships are formed, but proficiency is not the sole reason to explain why learners form different patterns of interaction. Using interview data, supplemented by discourse analysis of pair talk, Storch (2004) found that it was the learners' goals and attitudes towards the activity which ultimately determined whether the learners collaborated or not. Collaboration occurred when both members of the pair shared goals and viewed the activity and the contribution of each member as valuable. A discourse analysis of the talk of collaborative pairs showed frequent use of first person plural pronouns (we, our), reflecting the sense of a joint ownership of the text. In contrast, in the case of pairs who formed a dominant/dominant or dominant/passive relationship, the use of first person pronouns predominated, suggesting that the task was viewed as an individual responsibility.

Discourse analysis of collaborative talk also shows that such talk is rich in language learning opportunities. That is, when learners collaborate they deliberate about language use: they provide suggestions, counter-suggestions, explanations, and feedback to each other. A number of studies (e.g., Kim and McDonough 2008; Storch 2002, 2009; Storch and Aldosari 2013; Tan, Wigglesworth, and Storch 2010; Watanabe and Swain 2007) have reported more evidence of such languaging in the data of pairs who collaborated than in non-collaborative pairs.

3.2 Evidence of language learning and impact on the accuracy of the text produced

There are two approaches used in the small body of research that has attempted to investigate whether learners gain from engaging in collaborative writing. One approach is the use of a pre- and post-test research design, generally following a single treatment condition (i.e., engaging in a collaborative writing activity). The findings of these studies are mixed. Whereas some of these studies show that collaborative writing leads to language learning gains (e.g., Kim 2008; Watanabe and Swain 2007); others (e.g., Kuiken and Vedder 2002; Shehadeh 2011) show no such evidence of gain.

Kim's study (2008), for example, compared the effects of languaging directed to oneself (individual think aloud) and collaborative dialogue on L2 vocabulary learning. In the study, 32 Korean L2 learners completed a dictogloss task, with half of the participants completing the task in pairs and the other half alone while thinking aloud. The study found that learners who worked in pairs had higher scores on both immediate and delayed vocabulary post-tests than those who worked individually. Analysis of talk showed that pair work conferred an advantage over individual work because during pair work learners were able to pool their knowledge and resolve (usually correctly) their deliberations about language use. However, Kuiken and Vedder (2002), in a study conducted with 34 Dutch high school EFL learners, using a similar task (dictogloss) and research design (pairs versus individuals, but without the think aloud) found that the pairs did not outperform the individual learners on the post and delayed post-test.

A number of reasons may explain these mixed results. One of the major shortcomings of studies that employ a pre- and post-test research design is that the post-test may not relate to what learners focused on during the collaborative writing activities. In an open ended collaborative writing task, such as a composition or jigsaw, it is difficult to predict which language structures or lexical items the learners will focus on during the writing activity (see for example Storch 2009; Swain and Lapkin 2001). Even more structured tasks, such as a dictogloss, elicit attention to a range of structures beyond those seeded in the task (e.g., Kuiken and Vedder 2002; Leeser 2004).

One way to address this shortcoming is to design dyad specific post-tests. In such a research design, the post-test includes only those lexical and grammatical forms that the learners deliberated about during the collaborative writing activity. For example, Swain (1998) investigated whether French immersion students remembered the linguistic targets of their LREs. One week after carrying out collaborative activities, the learners completed dyad-specific post-tests. Swain reported that learners' retention of the LREs varied according to how they had resolved the LREs. Most (79%) of the LREs that had been correctly resolved in the learners' collaborative dialogue were retained, whereas only 40% of the unresolved LREs and 29% of the incorrectly resolved LREs were correct on the post-test. Similarly, Swain and Lapkin (1998, 2001) used post-tests that included only items that were found in the pair talk (LREs). In both studies, the researchers found a positive relationship between the number of LREs produced by each pair of learners and their scores on a post-test.

Another way to gauge the effects of collaborative writing on language learning is to trace the impact of languaging episodes (LREs) on subsequent individual language use. Brooks and Swain's (2009) study found such evidence of language learning in a study that compared the impact of languaging to that of teacher feedback. The small-scale study (2 pairs of adult ESL learners) required students to complete a writing task collaboratively, process feedback (reformulation) received from the researcher, and then participate in a recall session with the researcher about the feedback. The learners were then asked to revise the originally produced texts individually and this formed the post-test. The researchers traced amendments made to the revised text to the source of knowledge (peers, the reformulations, and interactions with the researcher in the recall session). They found that the most effective source of expertise was the peers. A very high proportion of the solutions to language problems that the learners discussed and resolved during the co-authoring session were maintained in the post-test. In contrast, some of the language errors, which were reformulated, discussed with peers and with the researcher, reappeared in the post-tests. The researchers suggest that peers may provide each other with more developmentally appropriate assistance than an expert because peer feedback is given in immediate response to the learner's own identified need.

Storch (2002), in the study mentioned previously, also investigated the effect of languaging on subsequent writing but unlike other studies took into consideration the relationship learners formed when working in pairs. In the study, each writing task was completed twice: once in pairs and then in the following week individually. The two versions of each task were very similar. Evidence of learning was instances where the language item deliberated about in the pair talk was used in the subsequent individual writing. Storch found evidence of learning but mainly in the case of collaborative pairs (and to a lesser extent in expert/novice pairs). Very little such evidence was found in the case of the non-collaborative pairs (expert/novice and dominant/dominant). Watanabe and Swain (2007), using a pre- and post-test design, also found greater evidence of learning in the data of pairs who collaborated than in those who exhibited a non-collaborative orientation. Thus the impact of collaborative writing on learning may be related to patterns of interaction: when learners engage with each other's contributions and co-construct knowledge, this knowledge is more likely to be appropriated and retained.

Variations in level of engagement in LRE resolutions have been noted by a number of researchers. Kuiken and Vedder (2002), for example, in the study discussed above, noted that their learners' level of engagement in resolving LREs varied greatly. Some LRE resolutions elicited limited noticing (simply mentioning the structure with emphasis); others elicited elaborate noticing, where learners considered alternative suggestions. Fortune and Thorp (2001), in presenting their detailed taxonomy of coding LREs, warn researchers that merely counting LREs, although valuable, fails to capture the complexity of the interactions. They argue that researchers need to consider the quality of engagement with language items evident in such episodes. In a related study, Fortune (2005) compared the quality of engagement that dictogloss tasks elicited of advanced ESL learners (compared to the intermediate learners in the earlier study with Thorp) and observed that the advanced learners' engagement was more sustained. Fortune hypothesized that sustained engagement is more likely to lead to language learning. The findings reported by Storch (2008), using a grammar task (text reconstruction), and by Qi and Lapkin (2001), examining the effect of learners' engagement with feedback on their writing, suggest tentatively that extensive languaging leads to learning more so than limited languaging. Clearly more research is needed in order to examine whether the level of engagement in LRE resolution is related to language gains, but such research needs to be mindful of the type of language items. Lower order items (e.g., subject-verb agreement) are less likely to elicit sustained engagement than more complex items which require form-meaning mapping (Fortune 2005; Storch 2008; Storch and Wigglesworth 2010).

Several studies have further investigated the benefits of collaborative writing by comparing the texts produced by learners composing collaboratively with those produced by learners working individually. Overall, texts produced collaboratively tend to be more grammatically accurate than individually produced texts (e.g., Basterrechea and García-Mayo 2013; Fernández Dobao 2012; Malmqvist 2005; Storch 2005; Storch and Wigglesworth 2007; Wigglesworth and Storch 2009). For example, Fernández Dobao (2012), whose study compared the texts produced by small groups (of 4 students), by pairs, and by individuals in an intermediate Spanish L2 class, found that those produced by the small groups were the most accurate, whereas those produced by the learners individually, the least accurate. Analysis of the group and pair talk showed that there were more LREs in the group than in the pair talk data. Fernández Dobao suggests that collaborative writing undertaken in small groups may be preferable to pairs because when working in small groups, learners have more resources to draw on than in the case of pairs. However, as Malmqvist's (2005) study showed, not all groups necessarily work well. Malmqvist observed some learners' reluctance to contribute and engage with each other's contributions. These results are particularly interesting in view of the research on collaborative writing undertaken in groups in the computer mediated environment, discussed in the next section.

3.3 Collaborative on line writing: Wiki collaborative writing tasks

In the past 20 years, the field of computer-mediated interaction has greatly diversified in scope. In particular, diversifications in Web 2.0 applications have extended the way in which information can be created and shared. Web 2.0 applications include blogs, wikis and Google Docs as well as various social networking sites, such as Facebook (Myers 2010). However, it is the wiki, a collaboratively produced web page, which has to-date received the most research attention.

Writing collaboratively using wikis is said to provide a number of potential language learning advantages (Ducate, Lormica, and Moreno 2011; Zorko 2009). Unlike other forms of asynchronous online collaborations (e.g., chats), wikis allow all group members to have equal access to the most recent version of the document, and to amend the text rather than just comment on the text (as in the case of blogs). The time lag between the postings is said to enable the learners to develop a considered response to other students' postings. Wikis also contain discussion spaces. These discussion spaces are where learners can engage in languaging: articulate concerns or uncertainties, comment on any posting or any amendments to an existing page. Wikis, which are designed for multiple users, can be used for longitudinal group writing projects, and thus resemble the type of group projects implemented outside the writing class (see Leki 2001; Strauss and U 2007) and indeed the workplace (see Bremner 2010; Ede and Lunsford 1990). As such, using Manchón's (2011) distinction between writing-to-learn and learning-to-write, wiki collaborative writing could potentially provide L2 learners with an opportunity to learn language but also train learners to write outside the language class and with new and rapidly evolving tools.

There has been a growing awareness of the educational possibilities of wikis in L2 classes, with some reports on how wikis can be incorporated into L2 classes (e.g., Ducate et al. 2011; Kost 2011; Kuteeva 2011), and how they can be assessed (Elola and Oskoz 2011). However, research to date on the nature of interactions that wikis engender is quite limited. Most of this research has focused on the nature of learners' contributions to the wikis and to each other's postings, adopting a qualitative approach in their research design. This body of research shows that, as in the case of face-to-face pair and small group writing, simply assigning students to work on a wiki project does not guarantee collaboration.

A number of studies have reported some reluctance by learners to contribute and to engage with each other's contributions (Kessler 2009; Lund 2008; Mak and Coniam 2008). Research on wikis with L1 students (e.g., Elgort, Smith, and Toland 2008; Wheeler, Yeomans, and Wheeler 2008) reported similar findings also showing that learners seem resistant to having their contributions amended by other group members. However, Kessler and Bikowski's (2010) study shows that over time, as learners become more comfortable with this technology, and with working with each other, the frequency and nature of their contributions changes. They become more willing not only to contribute but also to co-construct. Rather than deletions and replacement of entire texts, there is evidence of additions to and elaborations on the contributions of others. Thus it may be that in the online environment, collaboration takes time to evolve.

Studies on whether wikis encourage languaging; that is, whether wiki collaborative writing activities encourage learners to provide each other with feedback on language, have produced mixed results. Some (e.g., Kessler 2009; Lund 2008; Mak and Coniam 2008) found very few instances of learners correcting their own or their peers' linguistic errors. Furthermore, when such editing did occur, it tended to be on fairly superficial aspects of language (e.g., font size, spelling). Grammatical errors were often ignored despite the instruction to produce a grammatically correct wiki text. Interviews with the participants revealed that the absence of editing was not related to knowledge of grammatical rules (Kessler 2009). In contrast, other researchers (e.g., Arnold, Ducate, and Kost 2009; Kost 2011; Lee 2010) reported that learners provided each other with feedback on language use in wiki projects.

One explanation for these mixed findings may be the implementation conditions and the nature of the tasks used. Whereas Kessler (2009), for example, had the entire group of students (40) working on the wiki site, Arnold et al. (2009) and Lee (2010) used smaller group sizes (4–5 per group), and Kost (2011) used pairs. Furthermore, whereas in Kessler's study the learners worked autonomously, in Lee's study, the instructor played a key role. The instructor assigned students to groups, ensuring that each group had a highly proficient L2 learner. The instructor also constantly offered students hints about effective forms of feedback. It is not clear, however, whether the more highly proficient L2 learner dominated the interactions, as was shown in mixed proficiency pairs in face-to-face collaborative writing activities (see Storch and Aldosari 2013).

Task type may also be a factor. Kessler (2009) used a meaning focused task (reflective writing) whereas in Lee's (2010) study, the tasks had an explicit focus on form (requiring students to use specific grammatical structures). As research on face-to-face collaboration has shown (e.g., Alegría de la Colina and García-Mayo 2007; Storch 2001a), the use of grammar focused tasks encourages a greater focus on form than more meaning focused writing tasks.

A range of affective factors, such as learners' perceptions, goals and attitudes may also explain learners' reluctance to edit each other's postings for accuracy. Mak and Coniam (2008) attributed this behaviour to learners' reluctance to cause their peers to lose face. However, a more commonly given reason by learners in interviews (e.g., Elola and Oskoz 2010; Kessler 2009) is that they perceived the wiki writing activity as a meaning focused rather than language focused activity. They were also more tolerant of errors in the wikis, claiming that the errors did not impede comprehension. This high level of error tolerance in wiki pages suggests that interaction in the creation of wiki texts are perhaps akin to speaking rather than to writing (see Schoonen et al 2009 above).

4 Conclusion: What lies ahead in terms of applications and research

There is now sufficient theoretical and emerging empirical evidence to support the implementation of collaborative writing activities in L2 classes, with both adult and adolescent learners of intermediate L2 proficiency. In implementing such tasks, careful attention needs to be paid to task choice and implementation conditions as well as the aims of the activity.

Given developments in Web 2.0 technology, we are likely to see more uses of collaborative writing activities in L2 classes which utilise this technology. Research on wikis implemented with L2 students has shown that if the aim of these activities is to provide learners with opportunities to learn language, then we need to develop strategies to encourage languaging in this new environment. One such strategy is a blended approach, combining face-to-face and web based communication. Zorko (2009), for example, reported that students chose to deliberate about their projects and about language use in face-to-face meetings and via emails, preferring the immediate (and more familiar) forms of communication to the asynchronous wiki form of communication. Another blended option is to supplement wikis with synchronous audio applications (see Elola and Oskoz 2010), thus combining, as in face-to-face collaboration, oral and written language output. Future research needs to investigate how to best implement such blended approaches and the impact they have on the amount and nature of languaging.

Languaging, whether it occurs in the face-to-face or computer mediated environments, offers opportunities for language learning. Whether such opportunities result in learning gains need more extensive research. In face-to-face collaboration, investigations on language learning gains following collaborative writing have been to date quite limited in number and scope. One of the greatest weaknesses in the studies to date is their research design. A single instance of a collaborative writing activity is unlikely to have a noticeable impact on learners' performance or indeed on language learning. The longitudinal nature of wiki projects and the fact that wiki sites keep records of learners' contributions provide researchers with access to a potentially rich data source to investigate the impact of collaboration on language learning. Yet to date, there has been no research on whether collaborative writing on wiki projects and the feedback that L2 learners provide each other (even if limited) leads to language learning. Such research could utilise the research designs employed in face-to-face collaborative writing, tracing the use of suggestions made during the wiki interactions in subsequent language use.

Collaborative writing, in face-to-face or computer mediated mode, involves interaction between humans; humans who come to participate in the activity with their own goals and learning preferences as well as their own language learning histories. These affective factors will influence how learners behave in collaborative writing activities, and this behaviour may have ramifications for language learning outcomes. As a number of studies have shown, not all face-to-face pair work qualifies as collaborative, and it is collaboration which creates the conditions conducive to language learning rather than pair work per se (Storch 2002, 2009; Storch and Aldosari 2013; Watanabe and Swain 2007). Similarly, assigning learners to work together on a wiki does not guarantee that they will collaborate on the production of such a wiki. To date, research on wiki collaborative activities has considered the quality of learners' contributions to the jointly produced text and the reasons that may explain reluctance to contribute, but few if any have considered the nature of the relationships learners form when working on wiki projects. Although such studies are now beginning to emerge (e.g., Li and Zhu 2011), clearly more such studies are needed.

A greater awareness and understanding of the nature of collaboration and the range of factors that impact on the potential of collaborative writing for learning, is important in order to enhance the language learning opportunities that collaborative writing activities can offer learners in the L2 writing class. However such greater insights can only be gained from research that goes beyond a quantitative analysis of learners' interaction when engaging in collaborative writing. Qualitative, longitudinal, classroom based research is needed, so that the human dimension of interaction is brought to the fore.

5 Additional sources

Bradley, Linda, Berner Lindströma, and Hans Rystedt. 2010. Rationalities of collaboration for language learning in a wiki. *ReCALL* 22. 247–265.

Daiute Colette and Bridget Dalton. 1993. Collaboration between children learning to write: Can novices be masters? *Cognition and instruction* 10. 281–333

Grant, Lyndsay. 2009. 'I don't care do ur own page!' A case study of using wikis for collaborative work in a UK secondary school. *Learning, Media and Technology* 32. 105–117.

Gutiérrez, Xavier. 2008. What does metalinguistic activity in learners' interaction during a collaborative L2 writing task look like? *The Modern Language Journal* 92. 519–537.

Li, Mimi. 2012. Use of wikis in second/foreign language classes: A literature review. *CALL-EJ* 13. 17–35.

Oskoz, Ana and Idoia Elola. 2012. Understanding the impact of social tools in the FL writing classroom: Activity theory at work. In Greg. Kessler, Ana Oskoz, and Idoia Elola (eds.), *Technology across writing contexts and tasks*, 131–153. San Marcos, Texas: CALICO.

Storch, Neomy. 2012. Collaborative writing as a site for L2 learning in face-to-face and online mode. In Greg Kessler, Ana Oskoz, and Idoia Elola (eds.), *Technology across writing contexts and tasks*, 113–130. San Marcos, Texas: CALICO.

Storch, Neomy and Ali Aldosari 2010. Learners' use of first language (Arabic) in pair work in an EFL class. *Language Teaching Research* 14. 355–375.

Swain, Merrill, Lindsay Brooks, and Agustina Tocalli-Beller. 2002. Peer-peer dialogue as a means of second language learning. *Annual Review of Applied Linguistics* 22. 171–185.

Wigglesworth, Gillian and Neomy Storch. 2012. What role for collaboration in writing and writing feedback. *Journal of Second Language Writing* 21. 364–374.

6 References

Adams, Rebecca. 2006. L2 tasks and orientation to form: A role for modality? *International Journal of Applied Linguistics* 152. 7–34.

Adams, Rebecca and Lauren Ross-Feldman. 2008. Does writing influence learner attention to form? The speaking-writing connection in second language and academic literacy development. In Diane Belcher and Alan Hirvela (eds.), *The oral/literate connection: Perspectives on L2 speaking, writing, and other media interactions*, 210–225. Ann Arbor: University of Michigan Press.

Alegría de la Colina, Ana and María Pilar García-Mayo. 2007. Attention to form across collaborative tasks by low-proficiency learners in an EFL setting. In María Pilar García-Mayo (ed.), *Investigating tasks in formal language learning*, 91–116. Clevedon, UK: Multilingual Matters.

Arnold, Nike, Lara Ducate, and Claudia Kost. 2009. Collaborative writing in wikis: Insights from a culture project in a German class. In Lara Lomicka and Gillian Lord (eds.), *The next generation: social networking and online collaboration in foreign language learning*, 115–144. San Marcos, TX: CALICO.

Basterrechea, María and María Pilar García-Mayo. 2013. Language-related episodes during collaborative tasks. A comparison of CLIL and EFL learners. In Kim McDonough and Alison Makey (eds.), *Second language interaction in diverse educational contexts*, 25–44. Amsterdam: John Benjamins.

Bremner, Stephen. 2010. Collaborative writing: Building a bridge between the textbook and the workplace. *English for Specific Purposes* 29. 121–132.

- Student-teacher conferences addressing students' reactions to and motivations in using teacher feedback (Conrad and Goldstein 1999; Lee and Schallert 2008a, 2008b);
- Retrospective student interviews to discuss their texts and the written feedback (e.g. Clements 2008; Goldstein and Kohls 2009; Hyland and Hyland 2006; Lee and Schallert 2008a; Nurmukhamedov and Kim 2010; Séror 2009);
- Stimulated recall (Nurmukhamedov and Kim 2010) and member checking (Chi 1999; Wang and Li 2011).

Studies that look at individual students' revisions in response to their teachers' feedback have used a case study design within either mixed methods (Conrad and Goldstein 1999; Hyland 1998; Goldstein 2006; Goldstein and Kohls 2009) or qualitative methods (Kumar and Kumar 2010; Lee and Schallert 2008a, 2008b; Tardy 2006). Quantitative analyses include comparing the relative frequencies of types of comments and foci of feedback each student received (Conrad and Goldstein 1999; Goldstein 2006; Goldstein and Kohls 2009), the extent to which each student used the feedback (Conrad and Goldstein 1999; Goldstein 2006; Goldstein and Kohls 2009; Hyland 1998), or the degree to which they successfully revised in response to the feedback or different comment types (Conrad and Goldstein 1999; Goldstein 2006; Goldstein and Kohls 2009). Quantitative analyses were also undertaken to compare comment types to each other in terms of how successfully students revised in response to each type (Conrad and Goldstein 1999; Goldstein 2006; Goldstein and Kohls 2009) or how much useable feedback students received (Goldstein 2006; Goldstein and Kohls 2009; Hyland 1998).

Some of the above studies also used qualitative analyses to examine what students did and did not revise in response to feedback and what students revised on their own (Conrad and Goldstein 1999; Goldstein 2006; Goldstein and Kohls 2009), students' reasons for how they used the feedback (Conrad and Goldstein 1999; Goldstein 2006; Goldstein and Kohls 2009; Hyland 1998), the differential nature of the feedback received by different students (Goldstein and Kohls 2009), or how each student revised in response to the teacher's feedback (Conrad and Goldstein 1999; Goldstein and Kohls 2009; Hyland 1998; Lee and Schallert 2008a, 2008b).

All of these case studies triangulated multiple sources of data to understand the contextual, institutional, personal, and interpersonal factors that influenced how individual students used teacher feedback and their reasons for doing so. These data sources included:

- Class observations (Conrad and Goldstein 1999; Lee and Schallert 2008a, 2008b; Hyland 1998);
- Class lessons, materials, and email exchanges (Goldstein 2006; Goldstein and Kohls 2009);
- Retrospective student interviews to discuss how students used their teachers' feedback and why (Goldstein 2006; Goldstein and Kohls 2009; Hyland 1998; Lee and Schallert 2008a, 2008b; Tardy 2006);

- Think aloud protocols while students revised (Kumar and Kumar 2010);
- Student interviews to discuss their revision practices (Lee and Schallert 2008a, 2008b; Goldstein and Kohls 2009);
- Teacher-student conferences within which students discussed their revisions (Conrad and Goldstein 1999; Lee and Schallert 2008a, 2008b);
- Collection and description of artifacts such as grading policies (Goldstein 2006; Goldstein and Kohls 2009) and
- Member checking with the study participants to corroborate understandings and analyses (Hyland 1998).

While studies of students' perceptions of and attitudes towards teacher feedback began in the mid-eighties, it is only recently that researchers have investigated teachers' perceptions of and philosophies about their responding practices. Only one study (Montgomery and Baker 2007) used quantitative methods, in this case, likert scales, to ascertain teachers' perceptions of their feedback. The other studies have employed qualitative methods, including
- Interviews of individual teachers (e.g., Diab 2005; Goldstein 2006; Hyland and Hyland 2006);
- Think aloud protocols as teachers responded to their students' texts (Hyland and Hyland 2006);
- Teacher annotations of their feedback (Goldstein 2006; Goldstein and Kohls 2009), and teacher diaries (Goldstein 2006; Goldstein and Kohls 2009).

Additionally, some studies have used mixed methods to both assess the beliefs and preferences of large numbers of teachers through surveys and a smaller number of individual teachers through interviews (Ferris, Liu, and Rabie 2011; Ferris, Brown, Liu, and Stine 2011; Lee 2008b) and case studies (Ferris 2014; Ferris, Liu and Rabie 2011; Ferris, Brown, Liu, and Stine 2011;) or through open ended questionnaires (Lee 2009). In addition, several of these studies used case studies, within which teachers' beliefs and perceptions were examined along with either students' beliefs and perceptions (Diab 2005; Goldstein and Kohls 2009; Hyland and Hyland 2006; Séror 2009) or along with teacher feedback and student revision (Goldstein and Kohls 2009; Hyland and Hyland 2006; Séror 2009). Case studies have also focused on individual teachers' feedback to individual students. Among these are studies where teachers researched their own feedback practices, combining discourse analyses of the comments with quantitative measures of the frequency of occurrence for different foci, pragmatic intent and/or linguistic shape (Best 2004; Conrad and Goldstein 2009), or undertook critical discourse analyses of the comments to assess the teacher's stance towards individual students (Severino 1993) comment or carried out action research to analyze and modify the teacher's own feedback practices (Best 2004). In other case studies, the researchers looked at the feedback practices of teachers other than themselves (Goldstein 2006; Goldstein and Kohls

2009; Hyland 1998, 2001; Hyland and Hyland 2001, 2006) within which discourse analyses of the teachers' feedback were undertaken to examine the interpersonal features of the feedback and the pragmatic intent of the feedback.

Some research has also compared what teachers say they do and what they indicate as there responding preferences and philosophies to what they actually do when they respond to their students' texts. To make these comparisons, researchers have coded both the areas of teacher feedback focus and qualitatively analyzed the nature, quality, and appropriateness of the teacher's feedback (Goldstein and Kohls 2009), or constructed narratives about the teachers' responding practices based, in part, on analyses of the teachers' response to their students' papers (Ferris, Liu, and Rabie 2011; Ferris, Brown, Liu, and Stine 2011).

Case studies have also looked at the feedback to and the revisions of individual students, using coding schemes developed through grounded theory for the particular sets of texts and comments being analyzed (Conrad and Goldstein 1999; Goldstein 2006; Goldstein and Kohls 2009; Hyland 1998, 2001; Hyland and Hyland 2001, 2006). In addition, to both understand the relationship between comment type and revision success, and understand individual factors that underlie successful and less successful revision, a few studies have used qualitative comparative analyses of student drafts written before and after feedback as well as student cover notes and interviews and conferences with the students (Conrad and Goldstein 1999; Goldstein 2006; Goldstein and Kohls 2009).

4 Main research findings

4.1 Participants and contexts

Before detailing the research findings, it is important to note the contexts and student populations on which the research has focused:
- Secondary students in Hong Kong;
- Pre-matriculated university students in sheltered second language writing courses in the United States, New Zealand, Canada, Brazil, Hong Kong, Puerto Rico, and Japan;
- Matriculated undergraduates in sheltered second language writing courses in the United States, Brazil, Yemen, Turkey, Thailand, Hong Kong, and Korea;
- Matriculated graduate students in sheltered second language writing courses in the United States;
- Second language writers in mainstream writing courses in the United States;
- Second language writers in graduate disciplinary courses in the United States, Australia, and Argentina;
- Second language writers in undergraduate disciplinary courses in Canada.

While the research has been carried out in diverse settings with diverse student populations, the majority of the research has concentrated on countries where English is the dominant language, with most of these studies in the United States, and while there are numerous studies in countries where English is an additional language, there is no concentration of studies in any one of these countries. In addition, most research has focused on sheltered second language writing classes for pre-matriculated and matriculated students, largely at the undergraduate level, with few studies examining sheltered classes for graduate students or students in undergraduate or graduate disciplinary classes or classes for secondary students.

4.2 Findings: Teacher feedback on content and rhetorical aspects of second language writing

How do teachers feel about giving feedback and the effectiveness of their feedback? While teachers believe that giving written feedback is important (Ferris, Liu, and Rabie 2011), they have both positive and negative attitudes towards written feedback. Some enjoy giving feedback and feel stimulated and challenged intellectually as they interact with their students through their texts and revisions (Ferris, Liu, and Rabie 2011). Others express concerns regarding
- How long it takes to give feedback (Diab 2005; Clement 2008; Lee 2011; Ferris Liu, and Rabie 2011)
- How time constraints affect being able to give quality feedback (Ferris, Liu, and Rabie 2011; Goldstein and Kohls 2009)
- The work involved in giving feedback (Ferris, Liu, and Rabie 2011; Lee and Schallert 2008b)
- The poor quality of the texts to which teachers need to give feedback (Ferris, Liu, and Rabie 2011)
- The degree to which students pay attention to and utilize teacher feedback (Ferris, Liu, and Rabie 2011; Goldstein 2006; Goldstein and Kohls 2009)
- How capable students are in using teacher feedback (Ferris, Liu, and Rabie 2011)
- Whether teacher feedback actually helps students to improve (Ferris, Liu, and Rabie 2011)
- The factors teachers need to take into account so their feedback will be understood, appropriate, and usable (Conrad and Goldstein 1999; Ferris, Liu, and Rabie 2011; Goldstein 2006; Goldstein and Kohls 2009)
- Their ability to give feedback that is not overly directive (Ferris, Liu, and Rabie 2011) or that avoids appropriating the student's text (Conrad and Goldstein 1999; Goldstein 2006)
- The need to find an appropriate balance between negative and positive feedback (Clement 2008; Ferris, Liu, and Rabie 2011).

What do we know about the nature of teacher written feedback? There has been a continued although not extensive focus comparing how frequently teachers respond to sentence level issues versus content and discourse level issues. In both earlier studies (Zamel 1985) and in recent ones (Diab 2005; Goldstein and Kohls 2009; Lee 2008a, 2008b; Montgomery and Baker 2007; Séror 2009), and in second language settings (Diab 2005; Goldstein and Kohls 2009; Montgomery and Baker 2007; Séror 2009; Zamel 1985) and foreign language settings (Lee 2008a, 2008b) teachers have focused more on error correction and sentence level issues. Some reasons for doing so include student expectations (Diab 2005; Lee 2008a, 2008b) or institutional and parental expectations (Lee 2008a, 2008b). In some instances teachers have done so, even when the teacher believed that the focus had been on content and discourse level issues and despite many discoursal and content issues in need of feedback and revision (Goldstein 2006; Goldstein and Kohls 2009). Likewise, studies that show teachers' substantial attention to the content and rhetorical aspects of their students' texts have been carried out both recently and earlier (Cohen and Cavalcanti 1990; Conrad and Goldstein 1999; Hyland and Hyland 2006; Leki 2006) and in both foreign (Cohen and Cavalcanti 1990) and second language contexts (Conrad and Goldstein 1999; Hyland and Hyland 2006; Leki 2006).

There has also been interest in the characteristics and pragmatic intent of teachers' written commentary. Studies have consistently revealed that teachers most frequently phrase their comments in the form of statements, followed by questions, and least frequently as imperatives (Best 2004; Ferris 1997). Studies for praise are mixed, showing that teachers may offer more praise than criticism (Hyland and Hyland 2006) or that teachers might not offer praise (Cohen and Cavalcanti 1990). In addition, teachers have frequently mitigated or hedged their feedback (Best 2010; Hyland and Hyland 2001), often to soften a comment that criticizes some aspect of the student's text (Clement 2008; Hyland and Hyland 2001; Hyland and Hyland 2006).

A few studies have also looked at whether or not the shape, wording, focus or content of the comment affects student revision. Some studies suggest that certain aspects of comment form may play a role (Ferris 1997; Nurmukhamedov and Kim 2010; Sugita 2006). In contrast, Conrad and Goldstein (1999) found that the type of problem identified as needing revision, rather than comment form, was strongly related to how successful the students' revisions were.

Variability in a teacher's feedback practices is commonplace and can be affected by the time in the semester (Best 2004; Clement 2008; Ferris, Pezone, Tade, and Tinti 1997; Hyland and Hyland 2001), student proficiency levels (Ferris, Pezone, Tade, and Tinti 1997; Montgomery and Baker 2007), and teachers taking into account individual student needs and their perceptions of individual students (Clement 2008; Hyland and Hyland 2006; Goldstein and Kohls 2009; Lee and Schallert 2008a, 2008b).

Problems with teacher written feedback are also an important consideration. Studies that looked at feedback to students in disciplinary classes (Séror 2009) or in mainstream composition classes (Ferris, Brown, Liu, and Stine 2011; Ferris, Liu, and Rabie 2011) found that some teachers did not differentiate among second language learners, largely not varying their feedback in relation to individual student needs, preferences, and texts. Furthermore, some feedback was unclear and not text specific (Ferris, Liu, and Rabie 2011), and was difficult for students to understand (Séror 2009). Teachers also focused largely on sentence level issues (Ferris, Brown, Liu, and Stine 2011; Séror 2009), and those who focused largely on errors communicated resentment towards having second language writers in their class (Ferris Brown, Liu and Stine 2011) or rarely offered feedback on the students' ideas or explicit advice for how to improve their texts (Séror 2009).

Studies focused on classes designed solely for second language writers have also uncovered the following problematic feedback practices:

- Comments repeated verbatim from draft to draft (Goldstein 2006; Goldstein and Kohls 2009)
- Feedback only on or largely on sentence level issues (e.g. Diab 2005; Goldstein and Kohls 2009; Lee 2008a, 2008b; Montgomery and Baker 2007)
- Unclear and inconsistent feedback (Zamel 1985)
- Feedback that appropriated students' texts (Zamel 1985)
- Feedback that lacked strategies for revision (Zamel 1985; Goldstein and Kohls 2009)
- Feedback that dealt with only some of the issues in need of revision (Cohen and Cavalcanti 1990; Goldstein 2006; Goldstein and Kohls 2009) or failed to address the main issues needing revision (Goldstein 2006; Goldstein and Conrad 1999; Goldstein and Kohls 2009)
- Feedback that was not responsive to students' needs and that made students dependent on their teachers (Lee 2008a, 2008b)
- Unhelpful feedback that resulted from the teacher not understanding the reasons for the problem in the student's text (Goldstein 2006; Goldstein and Conrad 1999; Goldstein and Kohls 2009)
- Unhelpful or inappropriate feedback as a result of teachers attributing negative and sometimes inaccurate motives to students composing and revision processes (Goldstein 2006; Goldstein and Kohls 2009; Lee and Schallert 2008a, 2008b)
- Feedback dealing with issues too indirectly (Goldstein and Kohls 2009; Hyland and Hyland 2001, 2006).

There are also instances of mismatches between what teachers believe they do when giving written feedback and what they actually do (Ferris, Liu, and Rabie 2011; Goldstein 2006; Goldstein and Kohls 2009; Montgomery and Baker 2007) and mismatches between the stance the teacher wished to adopt in her feedback and what she actually did (Hyland and Hyland 2001).

In addition to the quality of the feedback, we can also examine how teachers monitor their students' use of their feedback. In Ferris, Liu, and Rabie (2011), only a third of the teachers reported looking at their feedback in terms of its effectiveness, and more than a third never held students accountable for using their feedback or for reflecting on how feedback helped them and sharing these reflections with their teachers.

Qualitative data from case studies and from mixed methods studies help explain teachers' responding practices. In some cases, teachers' feedback reflects their philosophies about their roles (Hyland and Hyland 2001; Lee 2011). In other cases, teachers may tailor their feedback because of experiences with previous students or the same student in a previous class (Goldstein 2006; Goldstein and Kohls 2009; Hyland and Hyland 2001, 2006), or what they perceive to be student (Diab 2005; Lee 2011), institutional and curricular (Lee 2011; Clement 2008), or parental expectations (Lee 2011). Feedback may also be affected by teachers' discomfort with responding to certain types of problems (Hyland and Hyland 2006) or lack of knowledge about the students' content (Conrad and Goldstein 1999; Goldstein 2006; Goldstein and Kohls 2009). Teachers may feel overwhelmed by the work load involved (Clement 2008), focusing on areas they feel are easier to comment on (Goldstein 2006; Goldstein and Kohls 2009; Lee and Schallert 2008a, 2008b). Less optimal feedback practices also arise because of a lack of institutional support (Lee 2008; Ferris, Liu, and Rabie 2011; Séror 2009), a lack of teacher training (Lee 2008b; Ferris, Liu, and Rabie 2011), institutional devaluation of responding to student work (Séror 2009), large classes (Lee 2008; Séror 2009; Ferris, Liu, and Rabie 2011), heavy teaching loads (Séror 2009; Ferris, Liu, and Rabie 2011), unstable and part time status necessitating working on several campuses and/or ongoing pursuit of employment opportunities (Ferris, Liu, and Rabie 2011; Lee and Schallert 2008b), and the need to use feedback to justify grades (Clement 2008; Séror 2009).

4.3 Students reactions to, preferences for, and ways of using teacher written feedback

Studies have consistently shown that second language writers demonstrate a range of reactions to, attitudes towards, and perceptions of teacher written feedback. Although some students find teacher written commentary helpful (e.g. Clement 2008; Cohen 1990; Hyland 1998; Telceker and Ackan 2010) and motivating (Clement 2008; Hyland and Hyland 2006), and some students pay close attention to feedback (Diab 2005; Leki 2006), students find some commentary confusing (e.g. Chapin and Terdal 1993; Conrad and Goldstein 1999; Ferris 1995; Goldstein 2006) or illegible (Lee 2008a; Mahfoodh 2011) and vary in terms of how much they feel they have understood of their teachers' commentary (e.g. Brice 1995; Ferris 1995; Lee 2008b; Nasif, Biswas and Hilbig 2004). They also report using teacher written feedback without understanding the reasons behind it (Goldstein and Kohls 2009; Hyland 1998) and that even when they do understand a comment, students may have difficulty figuring out a strategy for revising (Chapin and Terdal 1993; Cohen 1991; Conrad and Goldstein 1999; Goldstein 2006; Goldstein and Kohls 2009).

Studies have also considered student reactions to the form, focus, quantity, and emotional content of teacher written feedback. Students have reported a preference for constructive criticism (Clement 2008; Hyland and Hyland 2006; Mahfoodh 2011), or for criticism that is softened by praise (Clement 2008). Sometimes students find praise disingenuous (Nasif, Biswas and Hilbig 2004) but others welcome it (Clement 2008; Mahfoodh 2011). Students have also expressed negative reactions to their teachers' feedback (Clement 2008; Lee 2008b; Wang and Li 2011) affecting their confidence in their abilities and/ or those of their teacher.

Students also find comments phrased as questions, imperatives, and declaratives more or less difficulty to understand (Sugita 2006) and report feeling confused by feedback offered in the form of symbols, circles, check marks, abbreviations, and underlinings (Mahfoodh 2011; Séror 2009). The results for hedged or mitigated comments are also mixed: Students in Hyland and Hyland (2001, 2006) and Conrad and Goldstein (1999) had difficulty understanding mitigated comments while Ferris (1997) and Ferris, Harroun and Jordan (1997) found little relationship between student revision and the presence or absence of hedges. In general, students show a preference for longer comments, especially those that explain specific problems and make specific suggestions (Cohen 1987; Ferris 1995). Students also welcome concrete feedback that provides suggestions for how to improve the draft (Clement 2008; Séror 2009) and have indicated feeling confused when feedback isn't specific enough (Nasif, Biswas and Hilbig 2004). In terms of what students want feedback on, some want comments that focus on content and organization (Clement 2008). Regarding quantity of feedback, while some students feel satisfied with the amount of feedback received (Leki 2006), some students report not receiving enough overall feedback, or enough feedback on certain aspects of their writing (Leki 2006; Mahfoodh 2011) or receiving too much feedback on an aspect of their writing (Séror 2009).

Studies have also looked at how students use their teachers' feedback. Students differ in terms of how open they are to revising with their teachers' feedback (e.g. Conrad and Goldstein 1999; Enginarlar 1993; Goldstein and Kohls 2009; Radecki and Swales 1988) and how much of their teachers' feedback they actually use (e.g. Clement 2008; Conrad and Goldstein 1999; Ferris 1997; Goldstein 2006; Lee and Schallert 2008a, 2008b; Nurmukhamedov and Kim 2010). In addition, some students make critical decisions about which feedback they will use and why (Chi 1999; Conrad and Goldstein 1999; Kumar and Kumar 2010; Mahfoodh 2011; Tardy 2006). Student expectations regarding teacher written feedback also vary: Some expect teachers to provide feedback and support for all aspects of their writing, while others see themselves as partners with their teachers, or go beyond teacher feedback to avail themselves of all possible resources for strengthening their writing (Wang and Li 2011). Students also vary in terms of whether or not they approach the teacher in response to feedback they feel is unclear or when they are uncertain how to revise in response to a comment (Goldstein and Kohls 2009; Nasif Biswas and Hilbig 2004).

In addition to the nature of the feedback, other factors that negatively affect how successfully and the extent to which students revise in response to their teachers' feedback include:

1. Individual student factors including ability level (Ferris 1997), lack of content knowledge (Conrad and Goldstein 1999; Tedick 1990), developmental readiness to enact the feedback (Conrad and Goldstein 1999), an unwillingness to critically examine one's point of view (Conrad and Goldstein 1999), lack of time to do the revisions (Conrad and Goldstein 1999; Goldstein 2006; Goldstein and Kohls 2009), feeling that the teacher's feedback is incorrect (Goldstein and Kohls 2009) or unreasonable (Anglada 1995), a lack of motivation (Goldstein 2006), resistance to revision (Enginarlar 1993; Radecki and Swales 1988), a distrust of the teacher's content or language knowledge (Lee and Schallert 2008a, 2008b), and mismatches between the teachers' responding behaviors and the students' needs and desires (Hyland 1998, 2000);

2. Curricular and programmatic factors, such as writing assignments that are not reading responsible leading to a demotivation to revise (Conrad and Goldstein 1999), contextual factors that negatively affect individual students such as being enrolled simultaneously in credit bearing degree courses and a second language writing course (Goldstein 2006; Goldstein and Kohls 2009), grading policies leading to leaving substantial revising until final drafts because the teacher only grades final drafts (Goldstein 2006; Goldstein and Kohls 2009), and a lack of appropriate courses resulting in students being misplaced and thus not able to understand the teacher's feedback (Lee and Schallert 2008b);

3. Individual students' perceptions of and reactions to the teacher and the students' relationship with the teacher (Goldstein 2006; Goldstein and Kohls 2009; Lee and Schallert 2008a, 2008b).

Case studies further illuminate how students use teacher feedback as well as the interactions among personal, contextual, and interpersonal factors that differentially affect students' expectations about their teacher's feedback and how students work with their teacher's feedback and the reasons underlying how they do so. For example, looking at one student's revision processes, Tardy (2006) showed how the process of developing as a writer involved the student's strategic appropriation of a more expert writer's feedback while overtime taking more and more ownership of his texts. In another case (Goldstein 2006; Goldstein and Kohls 2009), one student made conscious, strategic decisions to not revise or to do so minimally in response to her teacher's feedback on early drafts, because of the interaction of a constellation of factors: She was overwhelmed by the work demands of her disciplinary classes, she had nothing to lose as the writing teacher only graded her final drafts, and she had difficulty revising in response to feedback that contained no strategies or instruction for revision.

5 Pedagogical implications

The research on comment form suggests that students can experience difficulty in either understanding their teachers' feedback or enacting this feedback as a result of how the comment is worded, what the comment focuses on, whether or not the comment contains a strategy for revising, and/or their reactions to and attitudes toward their teacher's feedback.

It is not clear whether or not students across settings revise equally effectively in response to questions, statements, or imperatives. Nonetheless, because students may have difficulty going beyond the locutionary meaning to understanding the pragmatic intent of questions and statements in particular, teachers could help their students by explicitly discussing and exemplifying the pragmatic intent of comments worded as statements and questions. Likewise, there are contradictory results about whether or not teachers' use of mitigating devices, such as hedges, leads to student confusion. Teachers should consider explicitly discussing that mitigating devices are usually not intended to suggest that a revision is just something to think about but not enact. In addition, the research suggests that because students have varied reactions to praise and criticism, teachers should use these judiciously, tailoring how and how often to use praise and criticism to the needs and reactions of individual students. Some research has shown that comments that do not include a revision strategy can affect students' ability to effectively revise, which can be remedied by providing commentary that contains information about how to enact a revision, coupled with class discussions that focus on different types of rhetorical issues and possible strategies for revision (Goldstein 2004, 2005). Lastly, students have evidenced difficulty revising for certain types of rhetorical issues, suggesting that commentary needs to be fine-tuned to student developmental readiness. Additionally, student learning and revision can be supported by class discussions that both examine particular rhetorical goals and how to accomplish these and tie these discussions to strategies for enacting feedback on these issues. In sum, students can greatly benefit from explicit class discussions about the nature of the teacher's feedback, how to make sense of it, coupled with discussions of what poses difficulty for them. In addition, students can attach revise and resubmit letters to their revised drafts, within which they detail what they revised and how and with what they are having difficulty, allowing teachers to understand their revision processes and to offer help, and to also make any needed changes to their feedback practices if they are not effective (Goldstein 2005, 2006).

How students work with their teachers' feedback goes considerably beyond the nature of the feedback they receive. Students bring past experiences, attitudes towards particular teachers and particular pedagogies, and specific expectations to how they use teacher feedback; in addition, how they do so takes place within a web of factors that can affect their willingness, motivation, or time availability for composing and revision. Thus, teachers would best be able to support their students in using feedback effectively by understanding what these webs of factors are for each student. Methods for doing so include (1) student autobiographies regarding their prior writing, feedback, and revision experiences, and their reactions to particular types of feedback; (2) revision diaries and revise and resubmit letters, providing the means for students to communicate with teachers about their revisions, and (3) mechanisms for students to document competing activities outside of the writing class and to discuss how to coordinate these demands on their time outside their writing course with the specific demands of composing and revising. Fundamentally, helping students to best be able to use teacher feedback requires teachers to establish opportunities for communication so they can understand what besides the nature of their comments is playing a role in how each student uses their feedback (Goldstein 2005; 2006).

The research also points to factors that affect how teachers give feedback in general, and how they give feedback to individual students, and that some of these factors also materially affect teachers' lives. Some of these pose difficult issues for teachers, program administrators, and the programs and their institutions alike and give rise to the following suggestions:
- Teachers should be provided or have appropriate training to work with second language writers, whether they are in dedicated second language writing classes, in mainstream writing classes, or in disciplinary classes;
- Programs and institutions should avoid overloading students and diminishing the impact of needed writing instruction;
- Teachers should be supported in terms of appropriate class sizes, sufficient resources and materials, and a manageable number of classes taught;
- Programs should have ongoing discussions regarding what they value in terms of teacher feedback to help students become more effective writers;
- Teachers need support for coping with and changing the expectations of writing programs in settings where an undue focus on accuracy and exams dictate overwhelming attention to sentence level accuracy;
- Program administrators and institutions need to work to ameliorate difficult and sometimes unethical working conditions that negatively impact teachers and their students.

In sum, teachers, administrators, and institutions and their programs must be cognizant of these issues and must work towards creating ethical working conditions, adequate teacher training, and pedagogically sound curricula that include fostering sound feedback practices and the well being of students and teachers alike.

Finally, the research attests to instances of problematic responding practices and instances of sub- optimal relationships between teachers and students that affect how teachers position their students and the nature of their feedback. We need to consider what we bring as teachers to the process of reading and responding, as these will affect how we respond. Teacher factors that affect feedback practices include teacher personality, pedagogical beliefs about how to comment, attitudes towards specific student characteristics, attitudes toward individual students, attitudes towards or knowledge about the content about which students are writing, expectations for students at a particular level, and expectations of particular students. Awareness of these factors should lead to careful examinations of our commentary, both its form and content, to ensure we treat students equitably and to make sure our feedback is effective.

6 Research: Current state and future directions

In my 2001 examination of the research about teacher written feedback on rhetorical and content issues and student revision (Goldstein 2001), I looked at how the research could be strengthened and I delineated a set of questions that future research needed to address. While I would not claim that my article spurred this, I am still happy to report that 15 years later most researchers have provided more complete research reports, a number of researchers have incorporated sounder ways to carry out research, and the field has begun to address a number of essential questions. First, almost all research reports now provide the full details of the context, participants, texts, data collection methods, and data analyses, allowing readers to best understand the study being reported, as well as evaluate its soundness, and allowing us to compare across studies. In looking at research designs, many researchers are moving away from quantitative approaches where teacher feedback, student revisions, or student reactions to feedback are aggregated to instead employing qualitative and mixed methods. Quantitative research approaches where data is aggregated do not allow us to see how individual teachers respond, how they respond differently to different students or to different genres, or different levels, and so forth, nor how individual students use their teachers' feedback and why. Some of the quantitative research has also been plagued by confounding variables: For example, students at different levels or who have different teachers have been combined when analyzing the effectiveness of their revisions in response to particular types of comments or their reactions to teacher feedback, two or more teachers' feedback has been combined in analyzing how teachers give feedback, or essays written at different times in the semester or across semesters, or different genres have been combined for analyses of teacher feedback, student reactions, or student revision. In essence, much of the quantitative research, by focusing on aggregated groups of students, teachers, and/or essays, ends up missing the richness and complexity of the processes of teacher feedback and student revision.

Unlike quantitative approaches where data is aggregated, qualitative and mixed methods studies have almost always avoided confounding variables. Additionally, the collection of data through surveys that are not aggregated, interviews, protocol analyses, student-teacher conferences, teacher and student journals, teacher annotations of their feedback and student annotations of their revisions, and through examinations of and comparisons of individual texts, feedback, and revisions allows us to develop an understanding of (1) why teachers respond the ways that they do, (2) what underlies student perceptions of and attitudes toward specific aspects of teacher feedback, (3) why students use their teachers' feedback in the ways that they do, and (4) how a variety of factors that influence this process interact and affect the processes of composing, feedback and revision.

In 2001, I also mentioned the problems with separating areas of inquiry, where, for example, a study might focus only on students' attitudes towards the feedback without actually looking at the feedback, or focus on teacher feedback without looking at what students did with this feedback. Since that time, more and more qualitative and mixed methods studies are looking either at the whole picture – so, as mentioned above, we can see the whole process, or at all of the aspects of part of the process, such as students' attitudes toward feedback and the feedback itself. There has also been a welcome movement away from imposing coding schemes adapted from other studies towards using grounded theory so that analyses and coding schemes for such analyses arise naturally from the actual texts, feedback, and revisions.

Looking to the future, a number of questions still remain, some of which I delineated in 2001. Two of these questions have hardly been addressed or have not been addressed at all:

- How are the roles teachers adopt such as editor, audience, expert, peer, or gatekeeper reflected in their comments? How do students' perceptions of their teachers' role(s) as reflected in their teachers' feedback affect how students perceive, react to, and use this feedback?
- What roles do teacher commentary and student revision in response to this commentary play in helping students become more effective writers over time? What factors influence this growth and in what ways?

Teachers may adopt stances when they give feedback which may be informed by, for example, the pedagogical ethos of the context within which they work, the institutional work conditions, and/or how they perceive the student, including how these perceptions are influenced by how a student uses the teacher's feedback. In turn, students may react to these stances and/or may form perceptions about the teacher's capabilities on the basis of certain characteristics, such as nonnative speaker status, and may also be influenced by contextual factors. Their reactions to their teachers' feedback practices and what these communicate and to the contextual variables that affect them may then influence how they use their teachers' feedback, which in turn can influence how the teacher gives feedback. However, only a very few studies have looked at these very critical, central processes and their roles in feedback and revision. In addition, almost all of the research to date has focused on feedback and revision within one semester, with some only looking at one paper or a portion of papers, and others at all of the writing, feedback, and revision that took place in that semester. To understand the contextual factors, interpersonal relationships, and feedback practices that either interfere with or foster student writing growth, we need minimally to look at all of the texts and revisions students produce and all of the feedback teachers give within a course. However, we also need to go beyond one course, to trace how and why learning from feedback and revision from one course is or is not sustained over time. We know virtually nothing about the long-term effects of feedback and revision, as, to the best of my knowledge, Tardy (2006) is the only longitudinal study that goes beyond a single semester of feedback and revision.

To the questions above I would add the following questions needing further investigation:

- What do teachers choose to comment on or not comment on and why? What factors – contextual, philosophical, pedagogical, and interpersonal – play a role in these choices?
- How is teacher commentary influenced by the ways in which teachers are educated about teacher feedback and by their experiences of giving feedback over time?
- What role does what teachers do and do not comment on play in students strengthening their writing at the discourse level in the immediate and over time?
- What are the range of factors that affect how teachers give feedback and how do these operate within and across different settings?
- What are the range of factors that affect how students use their teacher's feedback and how successfully they do so, and how do these operate within and across different settings and contexts and across different students?
- How do different teachers within and across different settings and different student populations define what constitutes effective texts and effective revision and what affects these definitions?
- How and why do comment shape and type of problem addressed affect how students use their teachers' feedback and how effectively they do so? How do individual student factors and contextual factors mediate this process?
- When, why, and in what ways do teachers offer feedback tailored to different students? When, how, and why is such differentiation warranted and helpful, and when, why, and how is such differentiation not warranted and potentially ineffective or even harmful?
- How, when, and why do students assert agency or not do so in making decisions about what of their teacher's feedback to use and how and in also undertaking revision independent of teacher feedback?

I raise these questions because, in reviewing the body of research reported in this paper, it is clear that there is a lack of both depth and breadth. These questions have not been thoroughly addressed within any one particular context or across contexts, so presently we have only preliminary answers and we don't have the ability to compare answers within any one context or across contexts. In addition, many contexts remain largely unexamined, with for example, almost no research in FL contexts and within these, across different program types, institutions, and teachers and student populations. It is the compilation of results from studies within and across contexts that address the above questions that will allow us to answer them fully. I also raise these questions because they are fundamental to our being able to understand the complex, reciprocal, interacting processes of feedback and revision and their roles in student learning and the contextual, interpersonal, and comment factors that influence these processes. In summarizing, researchers may find the following chart helpful to see what can be examined, how and why:

Tab. 19.1: Looking to the future: A research approach. The whole "picture" across different settings/students/teachers, immediate and longitudinal effects of all sources of feedback and revision.

WHAT TO EXAMINE	HOW: Case Studies and Qualitative and Mixed Methods	WHY
Student Agency	Interviews, Questionnaires, Annotations of Revisions and Composing, Annotation of Teacher Comments, Think Aloud Protocols, Stimulated Recall, Student Texts, Revisions	(How) do students use teacher feedback and why? What are other sources of revision and how/when do students use them and why? How/When do students use all sources for revision relative to each other and why?
Student Individual Differences	Learner Profiles and Histories, Interviews, Questionnaires	How do individual student characteristics such as motivation and trust influence how (if) students use teacher feedback and why?
Student Developmental Readiness	Texts, Revisions, Comments, Interviews, Annotations of Revisions, Annotation of Teacher Comments, Think Aloud Protocols, Stimulated Recall, Classroom Observation	(How) does students' content/language/rhetorical readiness influence how they use feedback and how they revise?
Teacher Ideologies and Teacher Histories	Interviews, Classroom Observations, Annotations of Feedback, Think Aloud Protocols, Stimulated Recall	How do teacher ideologies influence how they give feedback, what they give feedback on, and what they do not give feedback on? How do teachers' content knowledge vis a vis students' content influence teacher feedback? How do teachers' prior experiences with giving feedback influence their current practices?

Tab. 19.1 (continued)

WHAT TO EXAMINE	HOW: Case Studies and Qualitative and Mixed Methods	WHY
Teacher Pedagogy	Classroom Observations, Materials, Lesson Plans, Syllabi and Curriculum Documents, Textbooks, Interviews, Grading Policies	How does what gets "taught" and how influence student texts and student revisions? What is the relationship between teacher pedagogy and teacher feedback practices?
Interaction: Attitudes and Positioning	Classroom, Office Hour, Email and Conference Interactions, Interviews, Annotations of Feedback, Annotations of Revisions, Think Aloud Protocols, Stimulated Recall	How do teachers and students current and previous experiences with each other and attitudes towards each other influence teacher feedback and student revision with teacher feedback?
Context	Institutional Curricula, Institutional Assessment, Institutional Guidelines for Feedback, Interviews Regarding Students' Current Histories (course loads, jobs, etc.), Class Observations, Interviews	How do contextual factors, such as assessment practices affect how (if) students revise? How do contextual factors, such as departmental criteria for feedback, affect how teachers give feedback and on what teachers do and do not give feedback?
Student Texts and Student Revisions: Immediate and Longitudinal	All Student Texts, All Student Revisions, All Teacher Feedback, Interviews, Students' Annotations of Revisions, Teachers' Annotations of Feedback	What role does feedback play in students' immediate revisions, students' future texts, and students' future revisions? What other sources play a role in student texts and student revisions?
Teacher Comments	Teachers' feedback, Students' Revisions, Interviews, Annotations, Think Aloud Protocols, Stimulated Recall, Patterns (Larger N Sending Us Back Into Case Studies)	Are there identifiable, separable characteristics of "quality" feedback, that is, feedback that is comprehensible, usable, and productive?

7 Conclusion

The research investigating teacher written feedback to second language writers has grown in multiple ways since Zamel's 1985 study. The field has moved towards encompassing a broad range of questions that address not only self reports, but how second language writers actually use teacher written feedback and what influences how they do so, the nature of teacher feedback and factors that influence this, and the complex interrelationships and interactions of student, teacher, interpersonal, and contextual factors and how these influence the processes of teachers giving feedback and students using this feedback. Researchers have also moved towards more fully specified reports that allow us to better understand studies and their findings, critically evaluate the research, and compare across studies. Methodologically, there has been a sustained movement away from quantitative designs and a movement towards mixed method and qualitative methods that allow us a more complete and more complex understanding of the processes of feedback and revision. Pedagogically, a shift towards more qualitative work, along with the findings of the research to date, have shown that the form and nature of teacher feedback alone does not account for how successfully students revise with this feedback, leading to the need for teachers to consider all of the possible influences and how they interact and how this might influence their feedback practices, their pedagogies, and their communications with their students. The research has also given rise to an understanding that feedback and revision can be an inherently political process, within which teachers, teacher educators, and program administrators need to consider political, philosophical, curricular and interpersonal influences on teachers' ability and willingness to give feedback that helps students revise and grow as writers, and that influence students ability and willingness to work with their teachers' feedback. In sum, the more complex picture that is emerging for researchers and teachers alike suggests that it is an exciting time to be carrying out research into teacher written feedback and second language student revision, and I look forward to the continued expansion of our understandings as more research is undertaken across varied contexts.

8 Additional sources

Cooper, David. 2009. *Situating teacher written feedback in an EAP classroom: How context influences responding practices*. MA Thesis, Carleton University.

Hamp-Lyons, Liz. 2006. Feedback in portfolio-based writing courses. In Ken Hyland and Fiona Hyland (eds.), *Feedback in second language writing*, 140–161. Cambridge, England: Cambridge University Press.

Harran, Marcelle. 2011. What higher education students do with teacher feedback: Feedback practice implications. *Southern African Linguistics and Applied Language Studies* 29. 419–434.

Hyland, Fiona. 2000. ESL writers: Giving more autonomy to students. *Language Teaching Research* 4. 33–54.

Lee, Melanie. 2009. Rhetorical roulette: Does writing-faculty overload disable effective response to student writing? *TETYC*, December. 165–178.

Reid, Joy. 1994. Responding to ESL students' texts: The myths of appropriation. *TESOL Quarterly* 28. 273–294.

Séror, Jérémie. 2011. Alternative sources of feedback and second language writing development in university content courses. *The Canadian Journal of Applied Linguistics* 14. 118–143.

Treglia, Maria. 2008. Feedback on feedback: Exploring student responses to teachers' written commentary. *Journal of Basic Writing* 27. 105–138.

Zhao, Huahui. 2010. Investigating learner's use and understanding of peer and teacher feedback on writing: A comparative study in a Chinese English writing classroom. *Assessing Writing* 15. 3–17.

Zhu, Wei. 2004. Faculty views on the importance of writing, the nature of academic writing, and teaching and responding to writing in the disciplines. *Journal of Second Language Writing* 13. 29–48.

9 References

Anglada, Liliana. 1995. *On-line writing center responses and advanced ESL students' writing: An analysis of comments, students' attitudes and textual revisions*. Texas: Tech University dissertation.

Best, Karen. 2004. Transformation through research-based reflection: A self-study of written feedback practice. *TESOL Journal* 2(4). 492–509.

Brice, Colleen. 1995. *ESL writers' reactions to teacher commentary: A case study*. ERIC Document Reproduction Service No. ED394312.

Chapin, Ruth and Marjorie Terdal. 1990. *Responding to our response: Students' strategies for responding to teacher written comments*. ERIC Document Reproduction Service No. ED328 098.

Chi, Feng-Ming. 1999. *The writer, the teacher, and the text: Examples from Taiwanese EFL college students*. ERIC Document Reproduction Service No. Ed442272.

Clements, Peter. 2008. Instructors' written comments on students' compositions in an intensive English program: International standards, local pressures. *Bulletin of Faculty of Education, Shizuoka University, Kyoka Kyoiku Series* 39. 199–212.

Conrad, Susan and Lynn Goldstein. 1999. ESL student revision after teacher-written comments: Text, contexts, and individuals. *Journal of Second Language Writing* 8. 147–179.

Cohen, Andrew. 1987. Student processing of feedback on their compositions. In Anita Wendon and Joan Rubin (eds.), *Learner strategies in language learning*, 57–69. Englewood Cliffs, NJ: Prentice-Hall.

Cohen, Andrew. 1991. Feedback on writing: The use of verbal report. *Studies in Second Language Acquisition* 13. 133–159.

Cohen, Andrew and Marilda Cavalcanti. 1990. Feedback on compositions: Teacher and student verbal reports. In Barbara Kroll (ed.) *Second language writing research: Insights for the classroom*, 155–177. Cambridge: Cambridge University Press.

Diab, Rula. 2005. Teachers' and students' beliefs about responding to ESL Writing: A case study. *TESL Canada Journal* 23. 28–43.

Enginarlar, Hüsnü. 1993. Student response to teacher feedback in EFL writing. *System* 21. 192–203.

Faigley, Lester and Stephen Witte. 1981. Analyzing revision. *College Composition and Communication* 32. 400–414.

Ferris, Dana. 1995. Student reactions to teacher response in multiple-draft composition classrooms. *TESOL Quarterly* 29. 33–53.

Ferris, Dana. 1997. The influence of teacher commentary on student revision. *TESOL Quarterly* 31. 315–339.

Ferris, Dana. 2014. Response to student writing: Teachers' philosophies and practices. *Assessing Writing* 19. 6–23.

Ferris, Dana, Rich Harroun, and Tina Jordan. 1997. *How teacher response affects revision*. Paper presented at the 31st annual TESOL convention, Orlando, FL.

Ferris, Dana, Jeffrey Brown, Hsiang Liu and Eugenia M. Stine. 2011. Responding to L2 students in college writing classes: Teacher perspectives. *TESOL Quarterly* 45. 207–234.

Ferris, Dana, Hsiang Liu and Brigitte Rabie. 2011. "The Job of Teaching Writing": Teaching views of responding to student writing. *Writing & Pedagogy* 3. 39–77.

Ferris, Dana, Susan Pezone, Cathy R. Tade and Sharee Tinti. 1997. Teacher commentary on student writing: Descriptions and implications. *Journal of Second Language Writing* 6. 155–182.

Goldstein, Lynn. 2001. For Kyla: What does the research say about responding to student writers. In Tony Silva and Paul K. Matsuda (eds.), *On second language writing*, 73–89. Mahwah, NJ: Lawrence Erlbaum Associates.

Goldstein, Lynn. 2004. Questions and answers about teacher written commentary and student revision: Teachers and students working together. *Journal of Second Language Writing* 13. 63–80.

Goldstein, Lynn. 2005. *Teacher written commentary in second language writing classrooms.* Ann Arbor: University of Michigan Press.

Goldstein, Lynn. 2006. Feedback and revision in second language writing: Contextual, teacher, and student variables. In Ken Hyland and Fiona Hyland (eds.), *Feedback in second language writing*, 185–205. Cambridge, England: Cambridge University Press.

Goldstein, Lynn and Robert Kohls. 2009. Teachers and students miscommunicating through feedback and revision: Lessons learned. Paper presented at the International TESOL Convention, Denver, CO.

Goldstein, Lynn. 2010. Finding "theory" in the particular: An "autobiography" of what I learned and how about teacher feedback. In Tony Silva and Paul K. Matsuda (eds.), *Practicing theory in second language writing*, 72–89. West Lafayette, IN: Parlor Press.

Hedgcock, John and Natalie Lefkowitz. 1994. Feedback on feedback: Assessing learner receptivity to teacher response in L2 composing. *Journal of Second Language Writing* 3. 141–163.

Hyland, Fiona. 1998. The impact of teacher written feedback on individual writers. *Journal of Second Language Writing* 7. 255–286.

Hyland, Fiona. 2000. ESL writers and feedback: Giving more autonomy to students. *Language Teaching Research* 4. 33–54.

Hyland, Fiona. 2001. Dealing with plagiarism when giving feedback. *ELT Journal* 55. 375–381.

Hyland, Fiona and Ken Hyland. 2001. Sugaring the pill: Praise and criticism in written feedback. *Journal of Second Language Writing* 10. 185–212.

Hyland, Ken and Fiona Hyland. 2006. Interpersonal aspects of response: Constructing and interpreting teacher written feedback. In Ken Hyland and Fiona Hyland (eds.), *Feedback in second language writing*, 206–224. Cambridge, England: Cambridge University Press.

Kumar, Vijay and Margaret Kumar. 2009. Recursiveness and noticing in written feedback: Insights from concurrent think aloud protocols. *European Journal of Social Sciences* 12. 97–103.

Lee, Icy. 2008a. Student reactions to teacher feedback in two Hong Kong secondary classrooms. *Journal of Second Language Writing* 17. 144–164.

Lee, Icy. 2008b. Understanding teachers' written feedback practices in Hong Kong secondary classrooms. *Journal of Second Language Writing* 17. 69–85.

Lee, Icy. 2009. Feedback revolution: What gets in the way? *ELT Journal* 65. 1–12.

Lee, Icy. 2011. Working smarter, not working harder: Revisiting teacher feedback in the L2 writing classroom. *Canadian Modern Language Review* 67. 377–399.

Lee, Given and Diane Schallert. 2008a. Meeting in the margins: Effects of the teacher–student relationship on revision processes of EFL college students taking a composition course. *Journal of Second Language Writing* 17. 165–182.

Lee, Given and Diane Schallert. 2008b. Constructing trust between teacher and students through feedback and revision cycles in an EFL writing classroom. *Written Communication* 25. 506–537.

Leki, Ilona. 2006. "You cannot ignore": L2 graduate students' response to discipline-based written feedback. In Ken Hyland and Fiona Hyland (eds.), *Feedback in second language writing*, 266–285. Cambridge: Cambridge University Press.

Mahfoodh, Omer. 2011. A qualitative case study of EFL students' affective reactions to and perceptions of their teachers' written feedback. *English Language Teaching* 4. 14–25.

Montgomery, Julie and Wendy Baker. 2007. Teacher-written feedback: Student perceptions, teacher self-assessment and actual teacher performance. *Journal of Second Language Writing* 16. 82–99.

Nazif, Ahmed, Debasish Biswas, and Rosangela Hilbig. 2004. Towards an understanding of student perceptions of feedback. *Carleton Papers in Applied Language Studies* 21(22). 166–192.

Nurmukhamedov, Ulugbek and Soo Hyon Kim. 2009. "Would you perhaps consider ... ": Hedged comments in ESL writing. *ELT Journal* 64. 272–282.

Radecki, Patricia and John Swales. 1988. ESL student reaction to written comments on their written work. *System* 16. 355–365.

Saito, Hiroko. 1994. Teachers' practices and students' preferences for feedback on second language writing: A case study of adult ESL learners. *TESL Canada Journal* 11. 46–70.

Séror, Jérémie. 2009. Institutional forces and L2 writing feedback in higher education. *Canadian Modern Language Review* 66. 203–232.

Severino, Carol. 1993. The sociopolitical implications of response to second language and second dialect writing. *Journal of Second Language Writing* 2. 181–201.

Sugita, Yoshihito. 2006. The impact of teachers' comment types on students' revision. *ELT Journal* 60. 34–41.

Tardy, Christine. 2006. Appropriation, ownership, and agency: Negotiating teacher feedback in academic settings. In Ken Hyland and Fiona Hyland (eds.), *Feedback in second language writing*, 60–78. Cambridge, England: Cambridge University Press.

Tedick, Diane. 1990. ESL writing assessment: Subject-matter knowledge and its impact on performance. *English for Specific Purposes* 9. 123–143.

Telçeker, Hürmüz and Sumru Akcan. 2010. The effect of oral and written teacher feedback on students' revisions in a process-oriented EFL writing class. *TESL Reporter* 43. 31–49.

Wang, Ting and Linda Li. 2011. "Tell me what to do" vs. "guide me through it": Feedback experiences of international doctoral students. *Active Learning in Higher Education* 12. 101–112.

Zacharias, Nugrahenny. 2007. Teacher and student attitudes toward teacher feedback. *RELC Journal* 38. 38–52.

Zamel, Vivian. 1985. Responding to student writing. *TESOL Quarterly* 19. 75–101.

IV. Teaching and assessing writing

Fiona Hyland, Florentina Nicolás-Conesa, and Lourdes Cerezo

20 Key issues of debate about feedback on writing

1 Introduction and historical background

Response to students' writing remains a crucial concern in second language (L2) writing scholarship and studies with this focus have increased considerably over the past decade. One major factor which brought the role of feedback to prominence was the popularity of the process approach to writing in North American L1 composition classes from the 1970s onwards. This approach built on Flower and Hayes's (1981) cognitive theory of writing, which emphasized the need for writers to produce multiple drafts, encouraging teachers to provide feedback and suggest revisions on drafts during the process of writing itself. Following Flower and Hayes, many studies often used think-aloud protocols to try to uncover both the thinking and learning processes learners used while revising in response to teacher feedback (e.g. Sachs and Polio 2007) and teachers' decision-making processes when providing feedback (e.g. Hyland 1998).

Theories of reader response on the dialogic nature of writing and the role of the reader in giving meaning to texts have also influenced feedback practices, supporting the use of multiple feedback sources to include real, rather than imagined readers. Socio-cultural theories of learning have provided further justification for using peer and collaborative feedback and have also highlighted its crucial dialogic role in scaffolding learning. From a socio-cultural perspective, Vygotskian theory has also been used to justify the use of feedback as a way of helping L2 writers extend their writing competence and knowledge of the L2 with the assistance of more competent teachers or peers or through the pooling of resources among peers with similar language skills (Liu and Hansen 2002).

Genre theories about the nature of writing and writing pedagogy have also gained prominence over the last twenty years (see Chapter 3, this *Handbook*). These theories have placed increasing importance on feedback as a way to assist students' entry to new discourse communities. Feedback on academic or professional writing skills from 'expert' members of the community is seen as a way of helping students master new literary practices and develop genre knowledge (Li 2006). There are approaches that draw on Lave and Wenger's (1991) concept of the 'community of practice' and consider the role that feedback plays in students' academic acculturation and their identity formation in terms of their academic literacy practices (Casanave and Li 2008; Firth and Martens 2008; Lee 2007).

As for the effects of feedback, developments in the understanding of second language acquisition (SLA) have made researchers re-examine how teachers respond to student writing and made them consider how feedback may contribute to developing both writing skills and language proficiency. As a result, the study of written corrective feedback (WCF) has been approached from two main perspectives: L2 writing and SLA. From the former perspective, the ultimate goal of WCF is to help L2 writers develop their editing, revision, and overall writing skills, which is why the focus of the feedback is not only on language errors, but also on other dimensions such as content or organization. Feedback from this perspective is associated with what has become known as the *learning-to-write dimension* (LW) of L2 writing (Manchón 2011a). From an SLA angle, the ultimate goal of providing feedback to L2 users is to help them enhance their interlanguage and therefore research efforts address the language learning that may derive from processing different forms of WCF. This function of feedback is hence associated with the *writing-to-learn language dimension* (WLL) of L2 writing (Manchón 2011a, see also Chapter 2 this *Handbook*).

In terms of instructional contexts, the LW dimension of L2 writing is generally associated with L2 composition classes, while the WLL dimension is primarily related to SL and FL learning contexts. Globally, these developments fully exploit the formative aspects of feedback and its learning potential for both writing development and language learning.

Significant developments in the understanding of the expanding role of technology in learning in the last decade (see Chapter 14 on electronic literacies) have had a profound impact on feedback practices and delivery modes. There is now greater emphasis on exploiting and researching the potential and possibilities of computer-mediated (CM) feedback (Burston 2001; Milton 2006; Tuzi 2004; Ware and Warschauer 2006). While initially technology was seen as a way of relieving teachers of the burden of providing feedback through the use of automated feedback systems, many researchers now regard it as important for synchronous (i.e. real time) and asynchronous (i.e. delayed) CM response with both teachers and peers. CM settings also allow students access to a variety of online resources, including corpora, which can enhance the quality and accuracy of peer feedback, and provide resources for writers to reflect on and improve their own writing, thus offering a powerful means for autonomous writing development.

The above discussion suggests that feedback continues to be an evolving and rich area for L2 writing research and practice. This chapter focuses on key areas of debate and discussion in feedback research, the debate on the value of WCF and its links to SLA research, the expansion of contexts for research on feedback, and the role of CM feedback.

2 Key issues and debates in responding to students' writing

2.1 The effects of corrective feedback

2.1.1 Written corrective feedback and SLA

An area of growing importance in feedback research has centred on the effect of WCF on the development of L2 competences. This involves looking at L2 writing-SLA interfaces (see Chapter 26), where L2 writing is viewed as both a way of understanding the learners' acquisition process and a means of enhancing language learning through the potential of feedback processing for consciousness-raising and 'noticing' of features of the L2 (Belcher 2012).

In the last ten to fifteen years a considerable body of SLA-oriented L2 writing research has been carried out in an attempt to establish (i) whether writing practice can be conducive to the development of the L2 system itself as well as helping develop learners' writing abilities; and (ii) whether providing different types of feedback on L2 written output can contribute not only to better (more fluent) writing but also to more effective (e.g. more accurate and more complex) L2 use[1]. A large part of this research has tried to elucidate whether L2 writers, after processing a particular type of feedback, incorporate the corrections in their revised texts (known as *uptake* in the WCF literature). Some of this research involves short-term studies. Others have opted for more longitudinal designs involving (i) larger time lapses between the writing episodes and most importantly (ii) the composition of new texts instead of writing multiple drafts of the same text, claiming that *learning* (not *uptake*) might only be demonstrated by incorporating corrections in totally new texts (i.e., demonstrating that errors that had been made in earlier texts and on which feedback had been provided are not made again in subsequent writings). Manchón (2011b) has referred to these two sides of feedback as "feedback for accuracy" and "feedback for "acquisition"", respectively. Regarding the latter, the difference between the notions of *uptake* and *learning/acquisition* is linked to the difference between the two types of knowledge that language learners tap into in any act of (oral or written) communication – the difference between explicit and implicit knowledge. When writing and also when revising one's own writing after having received feedback, both types of knowledge are called upon by the writer, but it is claimed that real acquisition takes place only when feedback processing leads to the development of implicit L2 knowledge (Ortega 2012: 410. See also Chapter 26). In this respect, recent SLA developments suggest that corrective feedback (CF)

---

1 See Bitchener and Ferris (2012) for a comprehensive review of research on written corrective feedback and SLA.

which focuses on form has great potential for L2 learning and that explicit knowledge about language provided by feedback can accelerate the acquisition of implicit knowledge (as reviewed in Bitchener 2012 and Polio 2012).

A related aspect of current debates refers to L2 learner readiness for feedback processing. Studies have focused heavily on the nature of the feedback provided to L2 writers (direct/indirect, focused/unfocused) without enough consideration as to whether the learners were prepared to uptake it – i.e., whether their L2 developmental stage allowed them to understand and integrate it into their existing L2 knowledge. Learner-readiness clearly links learners' L2 level proficiency to the complexity of the linguistic issue(s) targeted in the feedback and the more or less direct nature of the feedback provided by the teacher. The ways that these three elements interrelate and contribute to the advancement of our understanding of the relationship between WCF and SLA has not been sufficiently researched.

2.1.2 The error correction debate

As mentioned above, the potential value of WCF has been an area of intense discussion and debate in L2 writing research for the last three decades, especially regarding the effects of WCF as error correction. Basically there are two camps: those who believe written correction on error can help learners improve their drafts and their longer-term writing ability (e.g. Bitchener 2008; Bitchener and Ferris 2012; Bitchener and Knoch 2008; Chandler 2003, 2009; Ellis et al. 2008; Ferris 1999, 2004, 2006, 2010) and those who have argued against this (e.g. Truscott 1996, 1999, 2004, 2007, 2009; Truscott and Hsu 2008). Scholars in the latter group claim that error correction should be avoided since it is both demotivating to writers and ineffective in terms of improving either students' subsequent writing or language proficiency (Kepner1991;Polio,Fleck,andLeder1998;Robb,Ross,andShortreed1986;Sheppard1992; Truscott 1996).

Recent studies adopting both experimental and quasi-experimental designs have provided support for the argument that learners' writing accuracy can be improved when provided with WCF (e.g., Bitchener, Young, and Cameron 2005; Ellis et al. 2008; Sheen 2004, 2007; Sheen, Wright, and Moldawa 2009), and that such improvement can have a long-term effect (Bitchener and Knoch 2009a, b).

Along these lines, the results of feedback studies on revised and new texts represent an ongoing debate about learning since some researchers hold the view that the revision of errors is not a measure of learning (Truscott and Hsu 2008), while others consider revision as indicative of short-term learning and as a necessary step for long-term acquisition (e.g. Van Beuningen 2011). In both cases, there has been a tendency to focus only on the cognitive aspects of WCF, particularly the effectiveness of specific WCF strategies on L2 learners' use of target forms (usually rule-based structures) in revision and subsequent writing (e.g., Bitchener and

Knoch 2009a; Ellis et al. 2008; Sheen 2007). In this respect, Bruton (2009) has pointed out that a weakness of many studies is that they draw conclusions on the lack of effectiveness of WCF in revision or subsequent writing by using global error rates instead of tracking the progression of specific errors, which may hide language improvement. Furthermore, WCF cannot (i) account for improved accuracy in errors that were not previously corrected; nor can we (ii) attribute improvements in writing accuracy to the unique effects of feedback over time without considering the influence of other possible sources of learning inside or outside the L2 classroom. These problems highlight an unresolved issue in feedback research design and interpretation of findings.

Disciplinary debates over the past twenty years have also considered the effectiveness of error correction for different types of errors. Until recently, research on WCF did not really reflect what happens in classrooms where teachers engage in multiple ways with student writing (Van Beuningen 2010; Van Beuningen, De Jong, and Kuiken 2012). Many previous studies focused on one or two language features, such as articles or verb tenses, while in reality writing teachers tend to give comprehensive CF on all features rather than on a few selected language errors (Bruton 2009). The investigation of specific errors builds on earlier work by Ferris (1999) and Ferris and Roberts (2001), who argued that errors which occur in a "rule-governed way" – such as noun endings, articles, or subject-verb agreement – could be classified as "treatable," and feedback on these errors together with teaching of the rules could improve students' language accuracy. Ferris suggested that errors such as word choice and word order could be labeled as "untreatable" as there was no set of rules that students could use to avoid or correct such types of errors (1999: 6). It was proposed that these errors might need to be treated less directly in terms of feedback, for example, by the teacher simply underlining the problematic feature and getting students to correct it for themselves.

This approach suggested to some practitioners that WCF can be effective, but that teachers might need to be selective in their feedback strategies according to the types of errors their students make. As a result, another issue of debate relates to whether explicit direct feedback or implicit, indirect feedback is more effective for developing implicit knowledge of the language. Panova and Lyster (2002) have suggested that explicit feedback (i.e. complete correction) may help learners master new forms while less explicit correction, including metalinguistic explanation which forces learners to reflect on and engage with the feedback, may be more useful for deeper processing of familiar forms. Some recent studies also show that focused and explicit feedback most effectively prompts accuracy in students' writing (Farrokhi and Sattarpour 2011; Falhasiri et al. 2011). In contrast, other studies (Bitchener and Ferris 2012; Shintani and Ellis 2013) found that less explicit feedback consisting of metalinguistic explanation was more effective in terms of accuracy improvements in writing completed immediately after the treatment, suggesting that such feedback helped develop learners' explicit knowledge of the target structure (articles), although the effect was not lasting. Since there is conflicting evidence on this issue, Bitchener and Ferris (2012) suggest that more research is needed on the long-term impact of indirect and direct error correction. For instance, Ellis et al. (2008: 355) argue that the most effective choice of WCF may depend on the stage of proficiency the learners have reached. However, they also consider it unlikely that teachers will have enough knowledge of their individual learners' language level to be able to make reasoned decisions about whether to correct directly or indirectly. In addition, the effectiveness of feedback may also vary as a result of students' motivational differences in distinct learning contexts (ESL versus EFL) (Hedgcock and Lefkowitz 1994).

2.2 EFL feedback in primary and secondary educational contexts

Research on feedback has mostly focused on ESL university students following a writing-to-learn dimension of L2 writing, while little attention has been paid to the writing development of EFL students in primary and secondary schools (Belcher 2012), although there are some exceptions that we will review next.

Regarding primary school contexts, Coyle and Roca de Larios (2014) conducted a study with EFL students in Spain comparing the effects of two types of feedback (i.e. direct error correction and model texts) on learners' self-reported noticing and revisions of written texts when engaged in collaborative tasks during four weeks. The qualitative and quantitative analyses showed that students' noticing, which was mainly lexical, was influenced by feedback. More interestingly, direct error correction (DEC) resulted in more revisions of grammar and more acceptable output in the revised texts in comparison with the use of models. Accordingly, it was proposed that DEC could have an impact on the development of L2 learners' written accuracy across short periods of time as had also been shown in the case of university students in L2 contexts (Sachs and Polio 2007).

As for secondary schools, Lee is one of the few researchers investigating teachers' feedback practices and students' use of feedback in EFL secondary schools (Lee 2007, 2008a, b). Her research shows that teacher feedback at the secondary level in Hong Kong tends to focus mainly on assessment of learning rather than assessment for learning, and that there is an over-emphasis on written products and error correction, even when students are not concerned about the accuracy of their written production. Lee argues for greater use of feedback for formative purposes in the secondary classroom and indicates that teachers need to consider their students' expectations and perceptions. Other studies by Lee (2011a, b), also in Hong Kong, focused on innovations in writing assessment and showed significant changes in instructional and assessment practices as well as improvements in students' motivation to write in English through the implementation of assessment for learning (AfL) principles and more formative assessment (Lee 2011a, b).

2.3 Feedback in disciplinary contexts

An important research strand has explored the use of writing to develop expertise in a given content area within different disciplines at the university level. Research in disciplinary contexts focuses on both EAP writing tutors' feedback for the development of writing competences (a learning-to-write approach) and for learning disciplinary knowledge (a writing-to-learn-content approach. See Chapter 2 this volume), the focus then being on participating in the communication and discussion of disciplinary knowledge (Wingate 2012).

Hyland's research (2013) suggested that supervisors do not focus on writing practices and conventions of the disciplinary community because they question the effectiveness of their feedback in helping students deal with these issues. Teachers assume that students may eventually learn adequate disciplinary writing practices by themselves. These assumptions may be over-optimistic and disciplinary feedback may actually be very helpful for students. Paré (2011) conducted a longitudinal study of feedback from academic advisors in the humanities and sciences and suggested that feedback worked at two levels. Firstly, feedback helped students enhance and refine their disciplinary knowledge and understanding through writing. Secondly, teachers' feedback also helped learners master discourse practices specific to their discipline. However, like Hyland, Paré noted that supervisors often found these discipline-specific practices difficult to articulate and impart to their students due to their implicit nature.

2.4 The role of technology and computer-mediated feedback

The emergence of new technological tools for the provision of WCF offers great potential for teachers' provision and students' processing of feedback. For instance, corpora can be used to provide feedback in two main ways: firstly, students can use corpora during the writing process itself to follow links and self-edit their writing and, secondly, teacher feedback can be linked to a concordance file, showing the students how the word or phrase is used in a relevant corpus. In this respect, Milton's (2006) *Mark My Words* allows teachers to insert comments in any language in a student's electronic file and then link the comments to other online resources, including corpus data so that learners can see how words are used in authentic contexts.

Online tools allow teachers to support their annotations with authentic language data thus enabling students to make their own decisions about revising their texts, based on both the feedback and the authentic data. This possibility encourages a reflective, active response and engagement with teacher feedback which offers potential for raising students' awareness of genre-specific conventions, developing their independent learning skills, and improving their written products.

Similarly, claims have been made that computer-mediated communication (CMC) has the potential to empower students and make writing classes more collaborative. Students take a more active and autonomous role when seeking feedback because they are able to take the initiative in discussion and raise questions when they arise (Warschauer, Turbee and Roberts 1996). Student conferencing via CMC is also said to be more "student centred", encouraging more student participation due to the increased opportunities for student-student interaction, with the teacher acting as a facilitator rather than a teacher (Warschauer 2002). Other researchers argue that using CMC can give students a greater sense of writing for an audience and a greater sense of community which may empower and motivate less proficient students (Ware 2004; Warschauer 2002) by offering them a less threatening environment to write and receive reader comments on their work.

Additionally, some researchers argue that CMC can lead to better writing products and more focused and complex revisions (Tuzi 2004). There have been suggestions that it can assist students in appropriating new vocabulary and language forms of academic discourse by increasing their opportunities to notice these features (Lai and Zhao 2006) through its facilitation of both teacher and peer interaction and scaffolding (Zheng, Warschauer, and Farkas 2013). However, CMC may be most beneficial when combined with face-to-face peer and teacher feedback activities rather than as a replacement for them (Hyland and Hyland 2006). Similarly, online tools offer the most potential for response when they are used for a clear purpose and as an integral part of a well-structured curriculum (Hyland and Hyland 2006; Phinney and Khouri 1993; Warschauer 1999).

Another aspect of research on feedback and technology focuses on the learning potential of software which can scan student texts and give scores and evaluative comments on their writing. Computer-generated marking offers automated scores based on organizational, grammatical, and mechanical aspects of writing (Burston 2001; Xi 2010). However, researchers point out that automated writing evaluation (AWE) tools do not eliminate the teacher's role, but support it, since the records which are generated allow teachers to track students' progress over time and get a detailed picture of individual students' weaknesses and their revisions (Francis 2011). In addition, the use of computers allows the provision of CF immediately after having made the error. This immediacy in the provision of feedback is known as the priming effect (Ellis 2012; Polio 2012). It is argued that this priming effect can help to increase the effectiveness of feedback by being immediately provided, noticed and used. Therefore, such feedback can be better adapted to the learners' intended meaning, as is also in the case of oral recasts.

Online tools also offer generic feedback on problem areas and possible strategies for revision, plus tailored suggestions for improving particular aspects of a student's writing. Research on one such system, Criterion (Li, Link, and Hegelheimer 2015) has found that its use led to increased revisions and helped improve the language accuracy of students' final drafts, but the extent to which students used it successfully depended on a range of factors, including proficiency level.

Despite these advantages and the growing technological sophistication of such methods of response, computer-generated feedback systems have also been heavily criticised for being unreliable and not flexible enough to deal with individual student problems related to the content and quality of the writing. It has also been suggested that such programmes may encourage the development of formulaic writing because they tend to treat writing as a set of sub-skills, with a stress on grammatical accuracy, rather than viewing writing as a real communicative act (Ware and Warschauer 2006). Although there is some resistance from teachers, these programmes are likely to be an area for future development and research given the current technological advances that make these tools more reader-friendly and more appropriate from a pragmatic and communicative point of view.

3 Main research methods used

Globally considered, most of WCF research has been conducted with university students in ESL settings and, to a lesser extent, in EFL contexts. Descriptive and mostly interventionist studies have been carried out to measure the effects of WCF on learners' linguistic accuracy including inter- and intra-subject designs so as to compare the effectiveness of different types of feedback across time and/or across tasks. Nevertheless, there is enormous variation in the feedback treatments, operationalization and measurement of variables, procedures of data collection and analysis.

Feedback treatments (the independent variable in many studies) have included direct and indirect feedback; metalinguistic CF; error reformulation; model texts; focused and/or unfocused correction; feedback on form and content or just on form. Studies also differ in the measurement of the dependent variable (often operationally defined as linguistic accuracy) including distinct types of global accuracy measures (error per words/T-units; normalized errors), the calculation of the percentage of correct usage of a given target form in obligatory contexts; the computation of complexity, accuracy and fluency (CAF) measures, or the qualitative comparison of changes from original to revised texts.

Other differences in the design of studies are related to the length of time. There are both cross-sectional and longitudinal studies which differ in the duration of the treatment (from a few days or several weeks to one academic year). In particular, there is a predominance of studies involving short-term or "one shot" feedback treatments carried out in experimental, quasi-experimental, and non-naturalistic settings. Thus, some cross-sectional studies have investigated the effects of various types of unfocused feedback to improve linguistic accuracy in revised texts (e.g. Ashwell 2000; Fatham and Whalley 1990; Ferris 1997; Ferris and Roberts 2001), while other focused studies (e.g. Bitchener 2008; Bitchener and Knoch 2008; Ellis et al. 2008; Sheen 2007, 2010) and an unfocused one (Van Beuningen 2011) have researched the impact of feedback in new pieces of writing. It is not surprising that the findings and conclusions of short-term studies carried out in experimental conditions may substantially differ from those conducted in longer-term naturalistic conditions.

Guénette (2007) has pointed out that some studies lack control groups to contrast their results with different WCF treatments, or the control group may not be comparable to the feedback groups due to (i) initial differences in learners' L2 proficiency level; (ii) different amounts of writing practice; or (iii) time provided for the accomplishment of tasks in comparison with the feedback groups. In addition, some studies compared the effects of different types of feedback using distinct classroom activities for the control and experimental groups. Along the same lines, Ferris (2004) highlighted that the results of WCF studies are not comparable due to substantial differences in (i) the types of tasks used (i.e., journal entries versus essays); (ii) the requirement or not to revise essays after receiving feedback; (iii) the person who gives feedback (i.e., teacher or researcher); (iv) the typology of errors; (v) the use of pre-test measures; or (vi) the instruments to measure post-test results.

With respect to data collection, there is variation across studies regarding who provides the feedback (teacher and/or researcher), or data collection instruments, including various types of students' texts (journal entries, essays), grammar tests, progress charts, or interviews. As for data analysis, in some studies inter and/or intra-rater reliabilities have been reported while in others there are no reliability scores. Descriptive and/or inferential analyses have been used as well as qualitative analyses.

The mixed findings in WCF research reported in earlier sections can in part be explained by the above-mentioned variation in research contexts, designs and writer-internal and external variables in focus.

Writer-internal variables include L2 proficiency level (Ellis et al. 2008) or learners' engagement with feedback as a result of students' goals, perceptions, beliefs and understanding of feedback (Storch and Wigglesworth 2010b). Learners' proficiency level is an important variable that has not been always tightly controlled in empirical research. Truscott (2007) also highlighted the existence of writer-internal variables and descriptive measures of written production that may have been overlooked in some WCF studies. For instance, reported improvement in students' writing ability may hide the existence of avoidance strategies, as indicated by a decrease in complexity (Frantzen 1995; Sheppard 1992) or a lack of increase in fluency over a period of time (Frantzen 1995). Writer-external variables such as the complexity of the writing task (e.g. Kuiken and Vedder 2008) have also been reported to have an influence on the quality of the written production, which may in turn influence the effects of CF.

As highlighted by Hyland and Hyland (2006), it is difficult to make comparisons across studies when research designs (sometimes flawed) and contexts can vary so widely with possible impacts on findings. As a whole, the comparison and, especially, the generalizability of findings across studies are complicated by the fact that most of the research on WCF has been carried out with university students in ESL contexts and only a few studies have been conducted in EFL settings.

4 Future developments

This chapter has shown that response to writing remains a highly important area of research. In this section, we shall explore what remains to be done to advance knowledge on WCF (namely, expanding the scope of research, developing links with L1 feedback research, and studying the role of individual differences in writing), and how research should be conducted (i.e. research methodology concerns).

4.1 Expanding the scope of research

Issues that have been debated and researched for some time, such as the value and role of WCF, remain as important areas for debate and discussion, while other aspects, such as the role of technology and the links between SLA and feedback studies, are more recent and developing areas for investigation. There is a need for more research focusing on the interface between L2 writing and SLA and on other contexts for the investigation of feedback, including EFL schools and disciplinary contexts.

4.1.1 Interface between L2 writing and SLA

As suggested above, an issue of paramount importance at the interface of SLA and L2 writing is the elucidation of whether or not the explicit knowledge that L2 writers supposedly acquire as a result of feedback processing can be converted into implicit knowledge.

More studies are also needed both on whether learners process the feedback received and whether they do it successfully (by incorporating it into their revised or new texts), and on the interplay of a number of variables, including (i) feedback-related variables (nature of the feedback provided and the frequency with which it is provided); (ii) learner-related variables (L2 proficiency level) and; (iii) language-related variables (namely, the complexity of the linguistic items on which the feedback is provided and whether the focus of the feedback is a treatable (rule-governed) or a non-treatable L2 aspect) (Bitchener 2012). From a more sociocultural perspective, further studies need to examine a range of variables that may affect feedback processing in collaborative writing conditions, variables such as personality, confidence in L2 ability, experience, and individual learning goals that may affect how dyad members process the feedback received. Important developments can be expected if these future studies employ qualitative as well as quantitative research approaches and are longitudinal in nature. A further issue that needs to be scrutinized is learner readiness in relation to the processing of WCF. In particular, the interplay of the following two types of factors should be carefully examined to determine whether learners are or not ready to uptake the WCF and integrate it into their evolving L2 knowledge and, if so, to what extent it can be expected to be integrated: (i) linguistic issues such as the complexity of the L2 item on which WCF is provided (e.g., in grammar, treatable versus non-treatable items); and (ii) learner issues such as L2 ability, level of confidence in that ability, and level of engagement with the CF processing task. Along these lines, Kormos (2012) suggests that more research should be carried out into how individual differences may influence the degree of effectiveness of WCF depending on learners' different cognitive and motivational strengths.

Two other elements of the L2 writing and WCF processing research that are under-researched relate to teachers and tasks. WCF research should not only analyze the type of feedback teachers provide or which linguistic issues they focus on. It should also explicate the nature of teacher and learner classroom social dynamics and how this relationship between the two agents affects the feedback provided by the former and the use made of it by the latter.

Although feedback is an essential part of a writing teacher's repertoire, many teachers learn how to provide effective feedback only through trial and error. Teacher training programmes and research could focus on this important aspect of the writing class and link it more systematically to teachers' knowledge of SLA theories so as to enhance the provision of tailored WCF for different students and learning contexts. Another related issue for future L2 research is to investigate what kinds of responding practices can facilitate the development of the capacity of L2 students to reflect on their own academic performance and evaluate their writing, balancing support with scaffolding to help students become autonomous writers. This research is needed at both the undergraduate and graduate levels, especially in terms of thesis writing. It has been suggested that writing teachers should focus on making their feedback practices more "sustainable". According to Carless et al. (2010), sustainable feedback practices can help students develop the self-regulation strategies which are necessary to enhance their performance. These practices involve self-assessment and peer feedback as well as teacher feedback so as to raise students' awareness of expected standards and criteria that could in turn increase their ability to self-monitor their writing, set goals, and plan for improvement. With this purpose, an integrated feedback system could be created that combined both teacher and peer feedback and utilised online resources for students' independent use and development.

Finally, future research should consider making use of more authentic, "multi-stage writing tasks [that] encourage learners to identify their respective problems in their attempt to produce output, to seek for solutions from relevant input provided to them, and to utilize them in their subsequent production" (Hanaoka and Izumi 2012: 344). In the case of collaborative writing, tasks should be designed in such ways that the collaboration required offers learners the benefit of greater attention to form (e.g., by *languaging* about the L2 hypotheses tested during writing and while processing WCF) and deeper engagement with writing (Wigglesworth and Storch 2012). Aside from varying the degree of complexity of the writing task, new studies should also consider the use of non-academic writing tasks demanded of L2 learners in contexts other than schools or universities, such as the workplace (Karlsson 2009). As Ortega (2012: 412) suggests, whatever the writing tasks asked of L2 learners, these must be "valued, intrinsically interesting, and engendering a sense of ownership."

4.2 Developing links with L1 feedback research

There is also a need for closer links with research on feedback in L1 contexts, especially at the tertiary levels, where both L1 and L2 students experience similar problems in writing in a new discourse community. In this respect, there is a considerable body of research investigating effective feedback practices in higher education generally outside the L2 context. For example, Nicol and Macfarlane-Dick (2006) outline a number of principles for effective feedback at the tertiary level, including practices designed to facilitate self-assessment and reflection.

4.3 Individual differences in writing

Research on individual differences in writing is an area for future investigation that needs longitudinal qualitative studies focusing on how to engage with feedback in different contexts, tracing development over a period of time and investigating the role of feedback in more depth. The investigation of learners' individual differences could involve various factors such as their previous learning experience and language background, motivational factors, L2 proficiency, L1/L2 writing ability, age, learners' own perceptions and understandings of the tasks, previous writing experiences, learning and/or writing goals as well as their writing and feedback strategies.

Much of the previous research on WCF has drawn direct links between the teacher's feedback and the students' subsequent revisions without taking into account what students bring to the feedback situation that could explain their reactions to teachers' WCF and their processing. Developments in research on responding to students' writing point to the need for more sociocultural research.

Given the sociocognitive nature of WCF, "a full account of corrective feedback requires a sociocognitive orientation that combines the cognitive, social, and psychological dimensions" (Ellis 2010:152). Such research will help improve our understanding of how different modes and sources of feedback can effectively work together to support the development of L2 writers.

4.4 Methodological concerns

Students need to engage purposefully with feedback over a period of time if it is to achieve its full learning potential, but there are few studies which investigate how best this can be achieved. Learners are capable of using a variety of strategies and resources to consciously and actively engage with feedback and improve their writing products and processes (Hyland 2003). However, many research designs fail to fully account for learners' active involvement in their own writing development and its longer-term potential looking at how it affects writing processes, revising practices, self-evaluation and learners' accuracy. Feedback to facilitate engagement should be investigated over time rather than being a one-shot treatment, as it has often been done in previous studies. There is also need for more naturalistic research designs focusing on the learner's role in interpreting and using feedback in real-life contexts, as well as more studies involving in-depth, contextualized accounts of students' use of WCF (Ferris et al. 2013). The above-mentioned problems in research designs should be controlled in future studies as well as the influence of writer-internal and external variables so as to isolate the influence of WCF on learners' accuracy.

In addition, more complex qualitative or mixed method designs rather than global accuracy measures are needed to trace and understand learners' accuracy development across time (Bruton 2009) as well as to explain how and when feedback is effective (Storch and Wigglesworth 2010b) in different learning contexts. In this respect, more studies on WCF need to be conducted in EFL settings in order to compare the effects of distinct types of feedback with those obtained in ESL contexts.

5 Conclusion

This chapter has offered an overview of theoretical and empirical developments in research on responding to students' writing as well as suggestions for fruitful research avenues to be explored. Further research could shed light on how different modes and sources of feedback can best contribute to the overall development of L2 learners as independent reflective writers in a wide variety of contexts. Instead of seeing the various forms of feedback in terms of dichotomies (i.e. either face to face or computer-mediated, either focusing on form or content), the future may offer us the chance to design feedback systems which make use of different sources of feedback such as peers and teachers and different delivery systems to make full use of the various resources available. This approach will ensure that writing teachers can fully utilise feedback's potential for scaffolding and learning in the myriad of writing contexts in which it is given.

6 Acknowledgement

The analysis of research reported in this chapter is part of the work conducted within two research projects financed by the Spanish Ministerio de Economía y Competitividad (research grant FF12012-35839) and by Fundación Séneca, the research agency of the Autonomous Government of the Region of Murcia, Spain (research grant 19463/PI/14).

7 Additional sources

Bruton, Anthony. 2009. Improving accuracy is not the only reason for writing, and even if it were ... *System* 37(4). 600–613.
Bruton, Anthony. 2010. Another reply to Truscott on error correction: Improved situated designs over statistics. *System* 38(3). 491–498.
Evans, Norman, James Hartshorn, Rob McCollum, and Mark Wolfersberger. 2011. Contextualizing corrective feedback in second language writing pedagogy. *Language Teaching Research* 14(4). 445–463.
Ferris, Dana. 2002. *Treatment of error in second language student writing*. Ann Arbor, MI: University of Michigan Press.
Hyland, Fiona. 2011. The language learning potential of form-focused feedback on writing: Students' and teachers' perceptions. In Rosa M. Manchón (ed.), *Learning-to-write and writing-to-learn in an additional language*, 159–179. Amsterdam: John Benjamins.
Manchón, Rosa M. and Julio Roca de Larios. 2007. Writing-to-learn in instructed language learning contexts. In Eval Alcón and Pilar Safont (eds.), *Intercultural language use and language learning*, 101–121. Dorchert: Springer.
Storch, Neomy and Gillian Wigglesworth. 2010a. Learners' processing, uptake, and retention of corrective feedback on writing. *Studies in Second Language Acquisition* 32. 303–334.
Truscott, John. 2010. Some thoughts on Anthony Bruton's critique of the correction debate. *System* 38(2). 329–335.
Xu, Cuiqin. 2009. Overgeneralization from a narrow focus: A response to Ellis et al. (2008) and Bitchener (2008). *Journal of Second Language Writing* 18(4). 270–275.

8 References

Ashwell, Tim. 2000. Patterns of teacher response to student writing in a multiple-draft composition: Is content feedback followed by form feedback the best method? *Journal of Second Language Writing* 9. 227–257.

Belcher, Diane. 2012. Considering what we know and need to know about second language writing. *Applied Linguistics Review* 3. 131–150.

Bitchener, John. 2008. Evidence in support of written corrective feedback. *Journal of Second Language Writing* 17. 102–118.

Bitchener, John. 2012. A reflection on the 'language learning potential' of written CF. *Journal of Second Language Writing* 21. 348–363.

Bitchener, John and Dana Ferris. 2012. *Written corrective feedback in second language acquisition and writing*. New York: Routledge.

Bitchener, John and Ute Knoch. 2008. The value of written corrective feedback for migrant and international students. *Language Teaching Research* 12. 409–431.

Bitchener, John and Ute Knoch. 2009a. The contribution of written corrective feedback to language development: A ten month investigation. *Applied Linguistics* 31. 193–214.

Bitchener, John and Ute Knoch. 2009b. The relative effectiveness of different types of direct written corrective feedback. *System* 37. 322–329.

Bitchener, John, Stuart Young, and Denise Cameron. 2005. The effect of different types of corrective feedback on ESL student writing. *Journal of Second Language Writing* 14. 191–205.

Bruton, Anthony. 2009. Designing research into the effects of grammar correction in L2 writing: Not so straightforward. *Journal of Second language Writing* 18. 136–140.

Burston, Jack. 2001. Computer-mediated feedback in composition correction. *CALICO Journal* 19. 37–50.

Carless, Dave, Diane Salter, Min Yang, and Joy Lam. 2010. Developing sustainable feedback practices. *Studies in Higher Education* 30. 1–13.

Casanave, Christine and Xiaoming Li (eds.). 2008. *Learning the literacy practices of graduate school*. Michigan: University of Michigan Press.

Chandler, Jean. 2003. The efficacy of various kinds of error correction for improvement of the accuracy and fluency of L2 student writing. *Journal of Second Language Writing* 12. 267–296.

Chandler, Jean. 2009. Response to Truscott. *Journal of Second Language Writing* 18. 57–58.

Coyle, Yvette and Julio Roca de Larios. 2014. Exploring the role played by error correction and models on children's reported noticing and output production in a L2 writing task. *Studies in Second Language Acquisition* 36. 451–485

Ellis, Nick. 2012. Frequency-based accounts of second language acquisition. In Susan M. Gass and Alison Mackey (eds.), *The Routledge handbook of second language acquisition*, 193–210. New York: Routledge.

Ellis, Rod. 2010. Cognitive, social, and psychological dimensions of corrective feedback. In Rob Batstone (ed.), *Sociocognitive perspectives on language use and language learning*, 151–165. Oxford: Oxford University Press.

Ellis, Rod, Younghee Sheen, Mihoko Murakami, and Hide Takashima. 2008. The effects of focused and unfocused written corrective feedback in an English as a foreign language context. *System* 36. 353–371.

Farrokhi, Farahman and Simin Sattarpour. 2011. The effects of focused and unfocused written corrective feedback on grammatical accuracy of Iranian EFL learners. *Theory and Practice in Language Studies* 1. 1797–1803.

Falhasiri, Mohammad, Mansoor Tavakoli, Fatemeh Hasiri, and Ali Mohammadzadeh. 2011. The effectiveness of explicit and implicit corrective feedback on interlingual and intralingual errors: A case of error analysis of students' composition. *English Language Teaching* 4. 251–264.

Fatham, Ann and Elizabeth Whalley. 1990. Teacher response to student writing: Focus on form versus content. In Barbara Kroll (ed.), *Second language writing: Research insights for the classroom*, 178–190. Cambridge: Cambridge University Press.

Ferris, Dana. 1997. The influence of teacher commentary on student revision. *TESOL Quarterly* 29. 315–339.

Ferris, Dana. 1999. The case for grammar correction in L2 writing classes: A response to Truscott (1996). *Journal of Second Language Writing* 8. 1–10.

Ferris, Dana. 2004. The "Grammar Correction" Debate in L2 Writing: Where are we, and where do we go from here? (And what do we do in the meantime ...?). *Journal of Second Language Writing* 13. 49–62.

Ferris, Dana. 2006. Does error feedback help student writers? New evidence on the short- and long-term effects of written error correction. In Ken Hyland and Fiona Hyland (eds.), *Feedback in second language writing: Contexts and issues*, 81–104. Cambridge: Cambridge University Press.

Ferris, Dana. 2010. Second language writing research and writing corrective feedback in SLA: Intersections and practical applications. *Studies in Second Language Acquisition* 32. 181–201.

Ferris, Dana and Barrie Roberts. 2001. Error feedback in L2 writing classes: How explicit does it need to be? *Journal of Second Language Writing* 10. 161–184.

Ferris, Dana, Hsiang Liu, Aparna Sinha, and Manuel Senna. 2013. Written corrective feedback for individual L2 writers. *Journal of Second Language Writing* 22. 307–329.

Firth, Ann and Erika Martens. 2008. Transforming supervisors? A critique of post-liberal approaches to research supervision. *Teaching in Higher Education* 13. 279–289.

Flower, Linda and John Hayes. 1981. Cognitive process theory of writing. *College Composition and Communication* 32. 365–387.

Francis, Melissa. 2011. But will it improve their writing? The use of verbal, peer and written feedback as formative assessments. *Journal of Classroom Research in Literacy* 4. 15–23.

Frantzen, Diana. 1995. The effects of grammar supplementation on written accuracy in an intermediate Spanish content course. *The Modern Language Journal* 79. 329–344.

Guénette, Danielle. 2007. Is feedback pedagogically correct? Research design issues in studies of feedback in writing. *Journal of Second Language Writing* 16. 40–53.

Hanaoka, Osamu and Shinichi Izumi. 2012. Noticing and uptake: Addressing pre-articulated covert problems in L2 writing. *Journal of Second Language Writing* 21. 332–347.

Hedgcock, John S. and Natalie Lefkowitz. 1994. Feedback on feedback: Assessing learner receptivity to teacher response in L2 composing. *Journal of Second Language Writing* 3. 141–163.

Hyland, Fiona. 1998. The impact of teacher written feedback on individual writers. *Journal of Second Language Writing* 7. 255–286.

Hyland, Fiona. 2003. Focusing on form: student engagement with teacher feedback. *System* 31. 217–230.

Hyland, Ken. 2013. Faculty feedback: Perceptions and practices in L2 disciplinary writing. *Journal of Second Language Writing* 22. 240–253

Hyland, Ken and Fiona Hyland. 2006. Contexts and issues in feedback on L2 writing: An introduction. In Ken Hyland and Fiona Hyland (eds.), *Feedback in second language writing*, 1–20. New York: Cambridge University Press.

Karlsson, Anna-Malin. 2009. Positioned by Reading and Writing Literacy Practices, Roles, and Genres in Common Occupations. *Written Communication*, 26(1). 53–76.

Kepner, Christine. 1991. An experiment in the relationship of types of written feedback to the development of writing skills. *Modern Language Journal* 75. 305–313.

Kormos, Judit. 2012. The role of individual differences in L2 writing. *Journal of Second Language Writing* 21. 390–403.

Kuiken, Folkert and Ineke Vedder. 2008. Cognitive task complexity and written output in Italian and French as a foreign language. *Journal of Second Language Writing* 17. 48–60.

Lai, Chun and Yong Zhao. 2006. Noticing and text-based chat. *Language Learning & Technology* 10. 102–120.

Lave, Jean and Etienne Wenger. 1991. *Situated learning: Legitimate peripheral participation*. Cambridge: Cambridge University Press.

Lee, Icy. 2007. Feedback in Hong Kong secondary writing classrooms: Assessment for learning or assessment of learning? *Assessing Writing* 12. 180–198.

Lee, Icy. 2008a. Understanding teachers' written feedback practices in Hong Kong secondary classrooms. *Journal of Second Language Writing* 17. 69–85.

Lee, Icy. 2008b. Student reactions to teacher feedback in two Hong Kong secondary classrooms. *Journal of Second Language Writing* 17. 144–164.

Lee, Icy. 2011a. Bringing innovation to EFL writing through a focus on assessment for learning. *Innovation in Language Learning and Teaching* 5. 19–33.

Lee, Icy. 2011b. Formative assessment in EFL writing: An exploratory case study. *Changing English* 18. 99–111.

Li, Jinrong, Stephanie Link, and Volker Hegelheimer. 2015. Rethinking the role of automated writing evaluation (AWE) feedback in ESL writing instruction. *Journal of Second Language Writing*. 1–18.

Li, Yongyan. 2006 Negotiating knowledge contribution to multiple discourse communities: A doctoral student of computer science writing for publication. *Journal of Second Language Writing* 15. 159–178.

Liu, Jun and Jette Hansen. 2002. *Peer response in second language writing classrooms*. Ann Arbor: The University of Michigan Press.

Manchón, Rosa M. (ed.). 2011a. *Learning-to-write and writing-to-learn in an additional language*. Amsterdam: John Benjamins.

Manchón, Rosa M. 2011b. The language learning potential of writing in foreign language contexts: Lessons from research. In M. Reichelt and Tony Chimasko (eds.), *Foreign language writing. Research insights*, 44–64. West Lafayette, IN: Parlour Press.

Milton, John. 2006. Resource-rich web-based feedback: Helping learners become independent writers. In Ken Hyland and Fiona Hyland (eds.), *Feedback in second language writing*, 123–39. New York: Cambridge University Press.

Nicol, David and Debra Macfarlane-Dick. 2006. Formative assessment and self-regulated learning: A model and seven principles of good feedback practice. *Studies in Higher Education* 31. 199–218.

Ortega, Lourdes. 2012. Exploring L2 writing-SLA interfaces. *Journal of Second Language Writing* 21. 404–415.

Panova, Iliana and Roy Lyster. 2002. Patterns of corrective feedback and uptake in an adult ESL classroom. *TESOL Quarterly* 36. 573–595.

Paré, Anthony. 2011. Speaking and writing: Supervisory feedback and the dissertation. In Lynn McAlpine and Cheryl Amundsen (eds.), *Doctoral education: Research-based strategies for doctoral students, supervisors and administrators*, 59–70. New York: Springer.

Phinney, Marianne and Sandra Khouri, 1993. Computers, revision, and ESL writers: The role of experience. *Journal of Second Language Writing* 2. 257–277.

Polio, Charlene. 2012. The relevance of second language acquisition theory to the written error correction debate. *Journal of Second Language Writing* 21. 375–389.

Polio, Charlene, Catherine Fleck, and Nevin Leder. 1998. "If I only had more time:" ESL learners' changes in linguistic accuracy on essay revisions. *Journal of Second Language Writing* 7(1). 43–68.

Robb, Thomas, Steven Ross, and Ian Shortreed. 1986. Salience of feedback on error and its effect on EFL writing quality. *TESOL Quarterly* 20. 83–93.

Sachs, Rebecca and Charlene Polio. 2007. Learners' uses of two types of written feedback on a L2 writing revision task. *Studies in Second Language Acquisition* 29. 67–100.

Sheen, Young Hee. 2004. Corrective feedback and learner uptake in communicative classrooms across instructional settings. *Language Teaching Research* 8. 263–300.

Sheen, Young Hee. 2007. The effect of focused written corrective feedback and language aptitude on ESL learners' acquisition of articles. *TESOL Quarterly* 41. 255–284.

Sheen, Young Hee. 2010. Differential effects of oral and written corrective feedback in the ESL classroom. *Studies in Second Language Acquisition* 32. 203–234.

Sheen, Young Hee, David Wright, and Ana Moldawa. 2009. Differential effects of focused and unfocused written correction on the accurate use of grammatical forms by adult ESL learners. *System* 37. 556–569.

Sheppard, Ken. 1992. Two feedback types: Do they make a difference? *RELC Journal* 23. 104–110.

Shintani, Natsuko and Rod Ellis. 2013. The comparative effect of direct written corrective feedback and metalinguistic explanation on learners' explicit and implicit knowledge of the English indefinite article. *Journal of Second Language Writing* 22. 286–306.

Storch, Neomy and Gillian Wigglesworth. 2010b. Students' engagement with feedback on writing: the role of learner agency/beliefs. In Rob Batstone (ed.), *Sociocognitive perspectives on language use and language learning*, 166–185. Oxford: Oxford University Press.

Truscott, John. 1996. The case against grammar correction in L2 writing classes. *Language Learning* 46. 327–369.

Truscott, John. 1999. The case for "the case against grammar correction in L2 writing classes": A response to Ferris. *Journal of Second Language Writing* 8. 111–122.

Truscott, John. 2004. Evidence and conjecture on the effects of correction: A response to Chandler. *Journal of Second Language Writing* 13. 337–343.

Truscott, John. 2007. The effect of error correction on learners' ability to write accurately. *Journal of Second Language Writing* 16. 255–272.

Truscott, John. 2009. Arguments and appearances: a response to Chandler. *Journal of Second Language Writing* 18. 59–60.

Truscott, John and Angela Yi-ping Hsu. 2008. Error correction, revision, and learning. *Journal of Second Language Writing* 17. 292–305.

Tuzi, Frank. 2004. The impact of e-feedback on the revisions of L2 writers in an academic writing course. *Computers and Composition* 21. 217–235.

Van Beuningen, Catherine. 2010. Corrective feedback in L2 writing: theoretical perspectives, empirical insights, and future directions. *International Journal of English Studies* 10. 1–27.

Van Beuningen, Catherine. 2011. The effectiveness of comprehensive corrective feedback in second language writing. (Doctoral dissertation). Retrieved from Universiteit van Amsterdam Digital Academic Repository.

Van Beuningen, Catherine, Nivja H. De Jong, and Folkert Kuiken. 2012. Evidence on the effectiveness of comprehensive error correction in second language writing. *Language Learning* 62. 1–41.

Ware, Paige D. 2004. Confidence and competition online: ESL student perspectives on web-based discussions in the classroom. *Computers and Composition* 21. 451–468.

Ware, Paige and Mark Warschauer. 2006. Electronic feedback and second language writing. In Ken Hyland and Fiona Hyland (eds.), *Feedback and second language writing*, 105–122. New York: Cambridge University Press.

Warschauer, Mark. 1999. *Electronic literacies: Language, culture, and power in online education.* Mahwah, NJ: Erlbaum.

Warschauer, Mark. 2002. Networking into academic discourse. *Journal of English for Academic Purposes* 1. 45–58.

Warschauer, Mark, Lonnie Turbee, and Bruce Roberts. 1996. Computer learning networks and student empowerment. *System* 24. 1–14.

Wigglesworth, Gillian and Neomy Storch. 2012. What role for collaboration in writing and writing feedback. *Journal of Second Language Writing* 21. 364–374.

Wingate, Ursula. 2012. Using academic literacies and genre-based models for academic writing instruction: A 'literacy' journey. *Journal of English for Academic Purposes* 11. 26–37.

Xi, Xiaoming. 2010. Automated scoring and feedback systems: Where are we and where are we heading? *Language Testing* 27(3). 291–300.

Zheng, Binbin, Mark Warschauer, and George Farkas. 2013. Digital writing and diversity: The effects of school laptop programs on literacy processes and outcomes. *Journal of Educational Computing Research* 48(3). 267–299.

Carol Severino and Jane Cogie

21 Writing centers and second and foreign language writers

1 What is a writing center?

A writing center has been articulated as both a place and a philosophy. It is a place for writers to work on their writing – a place where ideally any writer of any level of writing experience can get help and support at any stage of the writing process with any aspect of any writing project – be it academic, professional, or personal – in the native or a second language. As a philosophy, particularly in the US with writing in English, a writing center has been conceptualized as an embodiment of collaborative learning (Harris 1988; Lunsford 1991) and of writing as a process. In terms of collaboration, the tutor as the more able peer – that is, with more experience with academic writing in English (Bruffee 1984; Trimbur 1987) – assists students with their writing processes and written products – with students contributing their greater knowledge of the assignment, the subject matter, and the course context. The fact that tutors do not formally evaluate and grade student work facilitates the development of the collaborative, complementary, and mutually beneficial relationship between tutors and students. Based on Vygotsky's theory that learning begins as social and becomes individual (1986), the writer internalizes the tutor's questions about the developing draft – for example, about purpose, clarity, and audience needs – and becomes a more independent writer.

In the tutor's and student's process of co-constructing knowledge about and for writing, the tutor learns as much from the student – about the writing process and the student's subject matter – as the student does about his or her own writing from the tutor. Thus, the writing center is a site for learning as much for the tutor as for the student. In fact, many in the international writing center community consider the center's professionalizing of tutors to be almost as important as the empowering of student writers.

After explaining the history of writing centers and how they have served second language writers, this chapter will examine two significant issues in the writing center literature on tutoring second language writers: how directive or non-directive tutoring should be and whether higher-order concerns (abbreviated as HOCs) such as content, organization and argument should always be addressed before lower-order concerns (abbreviated as LOCs) such as syntax, vocabulary, and grammar.

2 What is the history of writing centers?

Although the classroom-based laboratory method that has influenced writing center pedagogy developed in the late 1800s (Carino 1995, 1996) and US writing centers have existed as places separate from classrooms since the 1930s, they rapidly expanded as a result of the US Civil Rights Movement in the 1960s and 1970s when colleges opened their doors to more sectors of the population, thus democratizing a system of higher education that tended to serve mainly middle class and upper middle class white students. In fact, writing centers arose to complement classroom instruction – to assist both students and their classroom teachers (Bruffee 1984).

Writing centers have for the most part shed their remedial ethos, although besides being committed to all writers in a college, they are specifically committed to helping underprepared writers succeed and thus helping the college in its equity mission educate and retain underrepresented minority students. Writing centers have become standard features of most of the 3,500 US college campuses, serving all types of writers. Often the most multicultural spaces on campus, writing centers are contact zones (Severino 2002) where multiple cultures, disciplines, rhetorics, and languages meet.

Writing centers are becoming increasingly popular outside the US, as shown by the development of The European Writing Centers Association, The Middle-East and North African Writing Centers Association and centers in Asia, South Africa, and many Latin American countries, some of which help with both native language and second language writing. In addition, foreign language writing centers in the US are also growing – with Spanish Writing Centers at approximately 20 colleges, and French and German Writing Centers at several colleges. Dickinson College in Pennsylvania, for example, has a Multilingual Writing Center where students can go for help on their essays in Arabic, French, German, Hebrew, Italian, Japanese, Portuguese, Russian, and Spanish.

3 How writing centers have served second language writers

Over the last few decades in the US, writing centers have developed a close, reciprocal relationship with second language writers, often the majority of their clients or appointments, especially when the writing center is the college's de facto ESL Program, frequently the case in smaller or in resource-poor institutions. Like first-language writers, second language writers learn from tutors more efficient strategies for approaching their writing tasks, but more than for native speakers of the target language, a writing center becomes a place to learn language and metalanguage in the process of developing writing skills (Nakamaru 2010; Severino and Deifell 2011; Williams 2002). The intensive one-to-one talk about writing that brings linguistic features to the learner's conscious awareness (Schmidt 1990) – conversation about and conversation that leads to writing – furthers second language learning.

Second language writers themselves see the writing center as a place to learn from their tutors both the rhetorical and the linguistic dimensions of writing. However, not every writing center director has been willing to give both the rhetorical and the linguistic dimensions of writing equal attention. Influenced by first-language composition pedagogy and by the desire to avoid the stigma of the writing center as "fix-it shop" (North 1984) and the perception of tutors as contributing too much to a writer's paper, they prefer to train tutors mainly to focus on ideas, organization, and argument, leaving both first and second language writers to edit and correct language on their own. Yet non-native speakers often lack the intuitions to tell whether a phrase "sounds right" or is semantically, syntactically, or grammatically correct, and their errors in word choice and syntax often have a greater chance of impeding communication than the typical language errors of native speakers. As we will demonstrate later in this essay, the failure of certain sectors of the writing center community to fully recognize and develop the writing center as a site for language learning as well as a site for learning writing has resulted in the controversies about tutoring strategies and tutoring focus.

Therefore, writing center practice and scholarship have been characterized by tensions between rhetorical and linguistic concerns and between non-directive and directive tutoring styles. Since the impact of Judith Powers's 1993 article urging a different and more directive role for tutors with second language writers, tutors are often trained to see themselves as cultural and rhetorical informants, explaining to second language writers, if needed, the target culture's rhetorical principles and writing assignments, for example, the notion of writer vs. reader responsibility (Hinds 1987) – which often helps international student second language writers write more successfully in a US writer-responsible academic context.

However, more of the writing center community is gradually coming to realize that with increasing enrollment of multilingual writers, tutors must also be trained as language informants (Myers 2003) so they can better address the linguistic issues in students' drafts. Tutors must learn to explain puzzling or difficult aspects of the second language's syntactic, lexical, or grammatical systems, so that if needed, they can work with students to compare and contrast those features with the corresponding features of the students' first languages. Relying solely on their native speaker intuitions, that is, acting only as what Ryan and Zimmerelli (2010) call "native informants" can only go so far to help tutors help second language writers. The lack of an explanation besides "It just doesn't sound right" or "I don't know why that's an error – it just is" can frustrate and fail to advance some second language learners. When tutors learn about and gain confidence addressing the language levels of discourse, that is, syntax, vocabulary, and grammar, they will be less likely to avoid addressing them.

4 Writing center research and second language writers

Even though writing centers are natural sources of cultural and linguistic issues to investigate and second language writing data to collect and analyze (Severino 1994), and even though writing center publications, master's theses, and dissertations have seen a recent increase in empirically oriented studies culminating in the first all-empirical issue of *Writing Center Journal* (Fitzgerald 2012), writing centers have continued to serve mainly as teaching sites for a number of reasons related to institutional and disciplinary politics. Because writing centers are generally not located in or associated with Applied Linguistics programs (Williams 2006), the disciplinary division of labor, in which Applied Linguistics has had the responsibility for second language acquisition (Matsuda 1999), means that few writing center directors and tutors have been trained to do linguistically and empirically oriented language-based research on second language writing and writers.

Most of the literature, including the empirical research, on second language writers by writing center directors and tutors is meant to improve the writing center as a teaching site that better serves that population. Such literature consists of "how-to" discussions for tutors on how to better help second language writers, for example, the ESL sections of tutor training manuals like the *Longman* (Gillespie and Lerner) or *Bedford Guides* (Ryan and Zemmerelli) or Bruce and Rafoth's collections *ESL Writers* (2004, 2009). Other literature closely examines second language writing issues that have arisen because second language writers' expressed needs for efficiently communicated, tutor-taught language and language rules are viewed as challenging the collaborative and process concepts upon which writing centers are based. A process-oriented pedagogy of non-directive tutoring that addresses global levels of discourse such as argument, organization, and development rather than the direct teaching of language as product is thought to be too based on working with native speakers of English (Matsuda 2012), also a criticism leveled against composition pedagogy in general (Silva, Leki, and Carson 1997). Other writing center scholars see less potential pedagogical conflict between writing center philosophy and addressing the needs of second language writers. They stress that writing centers have always been multicultural and multilingual and that writing center literature has always realized the tutor's need for flexibility – to change roles and stances, for example, from more student-centered to more teacher-centered (McAndrew and Reigstad 2001; Severino 1992) or from more of a peer to more of a tutor (Trimbur 1987), depending on the student, the situation, and the particular rhetorical and linguistic problems discussed in the tutorial. With some second language writers, the nature of the collaboration may more often be hierarchical rather than dialogic (Ede and Lunsford 1990), but it is still collaborative.

The potential challenges to collaboration and process caused by meeting second language writers' particular needs have contributed to two related issues that this chapter will examine:

1. To what extent the tutoring of second language writers is and should be direct-ive or non-directive (Thonus 2004; Williams 2004), including whether tutors should edit and proofread second language writing (Cogie et al. 1999; Myers 2003) in both face-to-face and online contexts (Breuch and Clemens 2009; Bruce and Rafoth 2009). What are the optimal conversational dynamics – the ideal balance – in tutoring second language writers? When should the tutor ask questions to draw the student out, and when should the tutor simply "tell" the student as does a teacher, for example, how to phrase an idea more effec-tively and conventionally?
2. To what extent the focus of tutorials with second language writers should be global, local, somewhere in between, or all of the above. If all levels are ad-dressed, should they be addressed in a particular sequence or all at once? If they should be addressed in a sequence, what is the order – higher order to lower order concerns or lower order to higher order concerns?

We will examine each of these issues in detail by reviewing and critiquing the literature and then draw from these discussions to speculate about the future of writing center pedagogy and research with second language writers.

5 The debate between non-directive and directive tutoring styles: L1

Significant increases in international student enrollment in US universities in the 1990s heightened a debate already underway on how to balance collaborative learning with the guidance needed by writers with differing writing abilities and backgrounds. For some, particularly before Powers (1993) had questioned the non-directive style's adequacy for L2 writers, the debate posed non-directive/directive tutoring styles as mutually exclusive options (Ashton-Jones 1988; Brooks 1991) rather than as a continuum along which the tutor's role is adjusted to the particular student's needs (Clark 2001). When viewed in its purest form, non-directive tutor-ing has been considered a student-centered, hands-off, writing process-based ap-proach, requiring tutors as peers to withhold direct input, build the students' confi-dence, and involve them in practicing and acquiring more productive writing strat-egies. Directive tutoring, on the other hand, has been characterized as a product-driven, tutor-centered approach, like the hierarchical approach of classroom teach-ers, focused on correcting students' texts and delivering the academic, sometimes domain-specific knowledge necessary for meeting institutional standards (Shamoon and Burns 1995). An example of directive tutoring when a tutor believes that a writer's draft has an organizational problem would be, "You should move this par-agraph over here to build on the connection between these two ideas." Non-directive tutoring might involve asking the student, "Why did you place that paragraph here?" or "Tell me the relationship between the ideas in this paragraph and that one," to enable the writer to discover for him/herself that the paragraphs should be re-ordered. Directive tutoring as a betrayal of the writing center's student-centered mission was questioned early on by authors arguing the value of a more direct approach with writers lacking the knowledge to correct their own writing issues (Clark 1998). And the case for a directive role for writing tutors was supported by a limited number of empirical studies that analyzed the tutor-student interaction in actual sessions (Cogie 2002; Davis et al. 1988; Porter 1991; Severino 1992; Thonus 1999b; Wolcott 1989). Overall, these studies confirm the contrast cited in tutor training guides between the role of peer tutors and the role of classroom teachers (Gillespie and Lerner 2000), with findings indicating that students interrupt tutors more than teachers (Davis et al. 1988) and tutor-student conferences are "far less routinized, 'scripted,' and predictable" than are classroom teacher-student conferences (Thonus 1999: 226). Yet the research also confirms a spectrum of tutor-student interactions, including some that are more associated with the teacher-student dynamic, such as a greater number of topic initiations by tutors than students and at least some "scripted" tutor discourse with use of classroom teacher management discourse patterns (Davis et al. 1988; Porter 1991).

6 Directiveness refocused: Response to L2 student differences

Following the appearance of Judith Powers' 1993 article and other ESL-related articles published that same year (Harris and Silva, Kennedy, Severino, and Thonus 1993), the axis of the directive/non-directive debate began to shift from endorsement of the non-directive style for all tutees to recognition of a more directive and flexible tutoring style as valuable for meeting L2 student needs. The prime differences cited by Powers – the L2 students' status as language learners and their lack of cultural information and of unconscious knowledge of their target language – all affect the L2 learner's ability to respond to Socratic questioning, a staple strategy in L1 sessions (Blau and Hall 2002). To this preliminary articulation of differences, more specific points on L2 students' backgrounds were added, such as the rule-based orientation from students' past EFL experiences (Harris and Silva 1993), the greater authority granted – and often expected of – teacher/tutors by L2 students (Harris and Silva 1993; Thonus 2004), and their cultures' contrastive rhetoric and emphasis on the active role of the reader (Severino 1993). These authors, however, emphasize not just the differences but also the similarities between L1 and L2 students' needs. For instance, Powers notes that, like L1 students, L2 students often benefit from non-directive tutoring strategies for the idea generation stage of the

writing process, and Severino emphasizes that, while contrastive rhetoric can account for differences in L2 writers' essay organization, such as a non-linear development of ideas, the cause may simply be the writer's confusion about the essay's
focus (1993), also an issue with L1 writers.

This increased clarity concerning L2 writers' needs and the cultural and language differences driving those needs are not the only factors that prompted a
more fine-tuned definition of what directiveness might productively mean in the
L2 context. Added to those factors are findings on the negative consequences of
the pressure non-directive tutor training can place on tutors, including session time
wasted by tutors using open-ended questions even when the L2 tutee, regardless
of the amount of wait time the tutor provides, has no way of producing a correct
response without tutor input (Blau and Hall 2002; Thonus 2004). The distorting
impact that the hands-off mandate can have is confirmed by the findings of several
survey studies, such as the findings that the tutors perceived themselves as less
directive than did their tutees (Clark 2001) and that tutors' directives were perceived as negative by tutors but as the tutors' "right and duty" by the students
(Thonus 2001).

With the aim of countering both blanket allegiance to the non-directive style
and blanket rejection of the collaborative potential of a directive style, a number
of writing center researchers forwarded theories of language learning useful to analyzing the tutor and L2 student interaction and the likelihood of that interaction
promoting language learning. These theories include Long's interaction hypothesis
(Ritter 2000; Williams 2002), Lyster and Ranta's negotiation of form and meaning
(Lyster and Ranta 1997; Severino and Williams 2004), and sociocultural theory as
it posits the social context – in this case, the tutor-student dynamic – as playing a
constitutive role in language learning (Vygotsky 1986; Williams 2002). Indeed,
these and other language acquisition theories, given their focus on the learning
resulting from interactions between language learners and their teachers, have
been central to the design of empirical studies on the structure of L2 language
learners' writing center sessions. By highlighting the complex variables that shape
any interaction – whether directive or non-directive – and the influence of those
variables on the interaction's outcome, this research exposes the false dichotomy
in any simple opposition between these two tutoring styles. The debate, then, as
redefined by writing center discussions of language acquisition theory (e.g., Myers
2003; Nakamura 2010) and empirical studies (e.g., Severino and Deifell 2011; Thonus 2004; Williams 2004) is no longer whether a tutor should use a non-directive
or directive style but what combination of styles is actually used in writing center
tutoring sessions and what combination of styles most fosters the tutor's role as
cultural and language informant and helps L2 students' progress as language
learners and writers (Myers 2003). In response to these multiple factors, a more
empirically based definition of tutors' and students' roles and their benefits has
become more central to concept-driven discussions of the writing center work.

7 Beyond the directive/non-directive debate: Research on tutor-L2 tutee interaction

In the interest of determining what happens in L2 writing center sessions, that is, the structure of interactions that actually take place and the extent to which those interactions promote or block learning, a small, though increasing number of researchers have focused on analyzing the "what is" of L2 tutoring sessions (Thonus 2004). Many of these studies, as is noted in overviews of writing center research (Babcock and Thonus 2012; Severino and Williams 2004), have taken the form of discourse analyses of tutor-L2 tutee interactions. One consequence of the analyses of data collected in these studies has been recognition of the different possible interpretations of directive tutoring behaviors, including, more recently, the potentially collaborative aspects of these behaviors. A number of discourse analyses of tutor-student interactions confirm an even greater dominance by tutors in work with L2 students as compared to the degree of dominance in work with L1 students, such as in the length of turns taken, the number of topic nominations and shifts in topics, and the number of interruptions (Thonus 2004). Yet in discussions of the findings, the difficulty of defining "dominance" by single characteristics is recognized. For instance, Taylor (2007) recognized that, while the two to three times greater number of words spoken by the tutors in her study than by their L2 students could be interpreted as signifying the tutors' dominance, it could also be interpreted as collaborative since the tutors' greater number of words involved recasts of the L2 learners' ideas (Taylor 2007, in Babcock and Thonus 2012, p. 104).

Another case that supports a more nuanced interpretation of the direct tutoring style comes in Williams' (2004) discussion of the results of her mainly descriptive study of the relationship between tutor-L2 tutee interactions and the L2 tutees' subsequent revisions. For example, successful revisions, particularly small-scale revisions at the sentence-level, were linked to extended negotiations by the L2 writers with the tutor and also to direct advice from tutors. As Williams concludes, there is no simple yes/no response to the question of whether tutors should "provide information to writers rather than elicit it" (p. 195). These and other studies on the structure of tutor-student interactions and, in the case of Williams, on the interactions associated with certain successful post-session student revisions, confirm the need, when assessing writing center work, not simply to separate out specific variables, such as how many words were spoken or how many open-ended questions were asked, but also to consider the interaction of these variables of both tutor and student as they are informed by theories of second language learning.

8 Language-related L2 session challenges and implications for tutoring style

The many variables affecting tutor-student interactions and tutors' decisions to be direct can be further complicated by language choices facing tutors in their interactions with L2 tutees. A prime example of tension related to language use is the conflict between the pressure to be polite according to the tutor's role as peer and institutional representative and the need to be direct to be comprehended by L2 speakers (Thonus 1999b). By using polite language, such as *"Wouldn't it be a good idea to write that down?"* versus *"Write that down"* (Brown and Levinson, as quoted in Thonus 1999b: 259), tutors can avoid committing a face threatening act. However, they can also, in the process, fall short of the other two goals of tutoring: comprehensibility and effectiveness. And, given cultural differences in politeness formulae, tutees can be confused by tutors upholding the writing center's collaborative ethos by withholding an answer or avoiding openly stating a directive. Indeed, L2 tutees may perceive such a strategy as impolite (Thonus 1999b: 259). Further complicating tutors' language choices can be the cultural differences in standards of politeness and ways in which dominance is expressed. For the L2 participant tutees in Bell and Youmans' study (2006), the pattern of critique immediately following praise, typical in US teachers' responses, was interpreted by the L2 tutees as contradictory and even lacking in politeness. For instance, one L2 tutee in the study was confused by her tutor's praise of her introduction since it was followed immediately by the tutor's requests for clarification on the introduction's relationship to another section of the essay (p. 41). Thus, not only do tutors face a conflict in the simultaneous demand to be non-directive to achieve politeness and yet to be direct to be comprehended; given culture-specific mitigation devices, they also face the difficulty of not knowing how their acts of politeness might be misinterpreted. Other empirical research and articles focusing on language learning theory cite additional language/status issues that can affect the tutee's and tutor's understanding of each other, such as is evidenced in Japanese tutees' silence when interacting with their tutors without the aid of honorific designations used to define the status of speakers in Japan (Moujtahid 1996). Bell and Youmans (2006), citing Powers (1993) and Weigle and Nelson (2004), confirm in more general terms the problem some L2 students may have when interacting with someone of greater status, given their lacking in English "a schema for the notion of collaboration" (p. 40).

With increasing recognition of factors affecting L2 tutees' participation and of the limits of prescribed tutoring styles for achieving that participation, tutor training guides have a greater opportunity and challenge to provide tutors, the majority of whom have little knowledge of applied linguistics, with the information needed to be responsive to their L2 – and L1 – tutees. Some training guides still implicitly endorse a non-directive style, such as Gillespie and Lerner's *Longman's Guide to*

Peer Tutoring in characterizing tutors as "asking questions" and editors as "giving advice" (4). Yet most current guides, including *Longman's* (2009), advocate too some version of "informed flexibility" (Blau, Hall, and Strauss 1998) for deciding the best tutoring style to use, defining an effective tutor as "respond[ing] to a writer's preparation and needs, the context of the assignment, and [his or her] sense of sound tutoring practice in order to best help the writer improve" (p. 125).

9 The global/local debate

The debate about which levels of discourse should be prioritized in a tutorial and in what order these levels should be addressed in many ways parallels the debate about how directly to tutor. Although the global/local distinction serves as useful meta-discourse for either analyzing what happens in a tutorial, posing the global levels (content, focus, organization, argument, development, purpose and audience, also called Higher Order Concerns or HOCs) **against** the local (various levels of language, mechanics, and punctuation also called Lower or Later Order Concerns or LOCs) has become another false dichotomy akin to that of directive vs. non-directive tutoring. The line between HOCs and LOCs becomes so blurred it is hard to distinguish them from one another. Especially in lower proficiency second (and first) language writing, supposedly lower level language problems can so impede communication and comprehension that they therefore affect the higher levels of focus, purpose, content and argument. A thesis statement or topic sentence that is garbled because of problematic syntax and vocabulary is flawed at both global and local levels. Take, for example, the topic sentence "Internet has not very inclined population." "Inclined," the wrong word, would technically be classified as an LOC because vocabulary is a language concern. However, because the thought is crucial to the paper and is not understandable (inclined towards what?), the word choice error becomes an HOC.

The HOCs/LOCs distinction, which places HOCs before LOCs in priority, first appeared in Reigstad and McAndrew's 1984 tutor-training pamphlet and then again in their more developed tutoring manual in 2001. Although in the ESL chapter of the 2001 manual, they acknowledge that tutoring procedures developed for monolingual native speakers of English will "perhaps require a substantial modification" (p. 97), they still recommend the HOCs/LOCs hierarchy for ESL writers: "ESL writing often seems plagued by miscues at all levels. Tutors need to be reminded to maintain a hierarchy of concerns, HOCs before LOCs" (p. 98).

Like the directive/non-directive distinction, the global/local or HOCs/LOCs contrast first arose mainly in relation to tutoring monolingual English speakers. The writing center community wanted to ensure that tutors were not strong-armed by students (or did not follow their own inclinations) to edit or proofread for language errors, especially when the paper had much larger/global problems, for example, when it did not fulfill the assignment because it summarized rather than analyzed the course readings. The rationale was that it did not make sense to work on the language of a passage that might be deleted in the next draft. Nakamaru (2010) points out how a tutorial's focus on language was oversimplified (language = grammar) and stigmatized (working on language = proofreading) even though these attitudes are counterproductive for the development of second language writing and writers: "Attention to language is often presented as editing or proofreading and is almost always equated with 'grammar,' despite the fact that having access to and being able to effectively use English words and phrases (i.e. lexical knowledge/skills) is crucial to creating meaningful written texts in English" (p. 95). She argues that the false HOCs/LOCs or content vs. grammar dichotomy, which ignores the level of vocabulary in between, has distorted the tutoring of second language writers.

Another reason that the HOCs/LOCs dichotomy has thrived is that in order to shed their remedial image, writing centers have established themselves as places for the generation, exchange, and development of global level ideas rather than "fix-it shops" that tune up students' language and correct their punctuation (North 1984). Thus, following McAndrew and Reigstad (1984; 2001), most tutoring manuals and how-to oriented articles (Caposella 1998; Gillespie and Lerner 2000, 2009; Harris 1986; Harris & Silva 1993; Ryan and Zimmerelli 2003, 2010; Severino 2009) took on "HOCs before LOCs" as a maxim or slogan for tutor training. Some of the versions of the maxim are stronger (Caposella 1998; Gillespie and Lerner 2009), while others are weaker. The weaker versions are characterized by conditional language such as "unless language obscures meaning" and the terms "global error" vs. "local error" (Harris and Silva 1993), or they are forwarded as one of many antidotes to the over-direct tutor appropriation of the student's text (Severino 2009). When a tutor trained with a strong version of the maxim attends to LOCs before or instead of HOCs, he or she may feel the same guilt as when s/he directively rather than non-directively arrives at solutions to an L2 writer's rhetorical and linguistic problems (Blau and Hall 2002).

One of the strongest articulations of the HOCs before LOCs for second language writers maxim was one of the eight Myths in the chapter "Working with ESL Writers" in both editions of *The Allyn and Bacon* (now *Longman*) *Guide to Peer Tutoring*. The gist of these Myths was that the belief that having to significantly change procedures to work with second language writers was untrue. According to co-editor Paula Gillespie, *The Guide*'s intent was to ensure that new tutors, especially undergraduates, as well as new writing center directors, saw the similarities between native and non-native speakers as well as the differences between them. Thinking solely of differences between the two groups, a naïve undergraduate tutor might get bogged down in correcting and explaining every article and preposition error when the L2 writer's draft did not fulfill the assignment, for example, if the assignment asked for an argument and the student had constructed a narrative instead.

In such a case, a tutor would have inadvertently contributed to the student's not fulfilling the assignment requirements and deprived the tutee of the chance to learn more about the differences between narrative and argument (P. Gillespie, personal communication, February 3, 2013).

In their turning point article questioning LOCs before LOCs, Blau and Hall (2002) took issue with Myth 5: "I need to clean up the grammar in NNS writers' papers before we can get to higher order concerns." In explaining this Myth, Gillespie and Lerner "urge [tutors] not to give into the easy inclination to tackle LOCs before HOCs" (p. 123). In response, Blau and Hall expressed for the first time in print what many second language writers already knew and what many tutors had already discovered – that language for many NNS writers IS a Higher Order Concern. Using empirical data from recorded tutoring sessions with second language writers, they also noted the logic of interweaving HOCs and LOCs or working line by line from LOCs to HOCs when such a strategy is needed for the first step of discovering and clarifying what the student is saying – even before discussing revisions. However, in the second edition of *The Guide* (2009). the same Myth with the same urging in the same language appears in the ESL chapter, without recognizing Blau and Hall's HOC vs. LOC critique, though the editors had adjusted Myth 8's prescriptiveness on directive vs. non-directive tutoring to incorporate Blau and Hall's "informed flexibility." According to Gillespie, the next edition of *The Guide* if there is one will take Blau and Hall's critique into account (personal communication, February 3, 2013).

Numerous logical arguments like Blau and Hall's (2002) contradict the maxim and support the practice of addressing LOCs before HOCs, LOCs only, or LOCs and HOCs at the same time depending on the situation. For example, during a face-to-face session, minor errors such as singular-plural, subject verb or pronoun/antecedent agreement, and tenses can be addressed in passing while the student or the tutor is reading the draft aloud for the tutor to gain a sense of the paper's content and argument before discussing its HOCs. One could argue that the above language features are not crucial, especially in relation to higher order problems but that their cumulative effect – "error density" – often causes readers to struggle or misunderstand the content, and causing incomprehension or misunderstanding would be the highest of higher order concerns. Indeed, it can require more effort for the tutor and student to ignore or postpone addressing these errors than it does to address them before or while addressing the content and argument. With such a correct-in-passing strategy, the tutor points, the student notices and corrects, or if the student cannot, the tutor does and briefly reminds the student of the rule.

Or the draft could be part of a dissertation chapter on a highly technical topic such as plasma physics where the tutor may not need to comment on content or organization; nor would the student necessarily want such comments from a tutor who never even took high school physics. Instead, the student may need feedback on transitions and tenses, that is, on LOCs only. Blau and Hall (2002) dispute the common writing center argument that since the material might be discarded, it is not worth clarifying or correcting. They say that students will be learning more about language, syntax, and grammar from that material even if it does not appear in the final draft, an argument that Nakamaru also makes (2010). In other words, this second purpose for the second language writing tutorial – to learn language – may change the recommended tutoring procedures of starting high on the "ladder of concerns" and descending. Transcripts and observations of what tutors actually do – the "what is" of a tutorial (Thonus 2004) – reveal that they are indeed, in Blau and Hall's words, interweaving HOCs and LOCs, that is, addressing them at the same time. One sentence that the tutor and student read might spark a brief correction of a verb form. The next sentence might spark a discussion of key ideas related to the assignment task, for example, differences between socialism and capitalism.

Language issues and how to help with language and meaning making were much more the focus of the second than the first edition of the Bruce and Rafoth how-to collection *ESL Writers: A Guide for Writing Center Tutors* (2004; 2009). Over half the chapters focus on language and language learning, including a chapter called "Editing Line by Line" (Linville) and a chapter on when to use definite (the), indefinite (a, an), or no article in English (Deckert). The fact that editing and articles are now recognized as important enough issues to warrant entire chapters constitutes a significant change in the writing center literature. Conference presentations are also challenging the hierarchy, for example, a conference presentation called "HOCs and LOCs on the ROCKS" (Severino, Rafoth & Gillespie 2010) that demonstrated the dichotomy to be false.

Hence, "informed flexibility" (Blau, Hall, and Strauss 1998) rather than a "one-size fits all" approach seems to be the solution to the HOCs before LOCs dispute as well as the directive/non-directive dispute. Some tutoring sessions will focus only on LOCs; or on LOCs before or at the same time as HOCs; or on some LOCs that interfere with communication and are therefore HOCs. The focus depends on the situation: on the student's proficiency level (Blau and Hall 2002), on what kind of help the student has requested and the student's perceived needs, and on the tutor's diagnosis of the draft in relation to the assignment. Tutoring is thus more situationally and rhetorically based than rule-based. Such a conceptualization of tutoring may mean increased tutor training and directors trusting tutors more to make these challenging decisions based on the situation rather than on maxims. The usefulness of what seems to be a second false dichotomy and overgeneralization about the priority of HOCs will continue to be questioned by second language writing center research, for example, research that posits the neglected language level vocabulary and word choice as a Middle Order Concern that radiates up and down to higher and lower levels of discourse (Nakamaru 2010; Severino and Deifell 2011).

Subsequent editions of tutoring manuals and collections have been modified in the direction of flexibility and attention to language. *The Bedford Guide*'s last two editions (2003; 2010) include an insert from the *Washington Post* called "A Towering Language Barrier" showing how the direct translation of the Korean sentence "Last night, I ate rice instead of bread" is "Yesterday evening in rice instead of bread ate." The differences in syntax and grammar illustrate the obstacles that Korean students and therefore their tutors face when they write English. But why not go a step further to teach the tutor that while Korean is an SOV language, English is SVO and that while Korean has post-positions, English has prepositions? The guide could also discuss errors from first language transfer. Research reports (Cogie 2006; Nakamaru 2010; Severino and Deifell 2011) pointing out that tutors do address language issues, and recommending best practices for addressing them will continue to change the guides' and how-to collections' recommended practices. Advice about second language tutoring needs to be based on actual practice and research findings rather than on prescriptions developed with monolingual native speakers in mind.

10 The future of writing center work

From the above discussion of the false dichotomies of directive/non-directive tutoring and global/local issues especially in relation to second language writers, we can expect that less ink will be spilled on research and pedagogy that takes one side or another, as writing centers slowly increase their focus on tutoring as a vehicle for second language learning, looking to Applied Linguistics and Second Language Acquisition for theoretical and research guidance. There is often a lag between published scholarship and practice. Tutoring practice is often more informed directly by tutor training manuals, which are in turn informed by both "what is" research and "what should be" thinking. We predict that more writing center scholarship will be devoted to "both-and" points of view based on empirical research on tutoring sessions that interweave directive and non-directive strategies and global and local discourse levels. Based on our knowledge of the state of the art in writing center work, we also predict an increased research and scholarship focus on changing and comparative writing center demographics, and the kinds of tutoring interactions associated with revision and improvement on future drafts in both face-to-face and online tutoring. Below are the kinds of realities and issues that future writing center researchers may find valuable to focus on.

1) Cultural, linguistic, and disciplinary diversity are the hallmark of a writing center, and both principal groups in the center – tutors and students – have varied increasingly by language background. Most research on second language writers in the writing center has been done with international students although studies by Thonus (2003) and Williams (2004) involved tutors and/or students who were resident bilinguals, sometimes called Generation 1.5 in the US (Roberge, Siegal and

Harklau 2009). The second language skill profile of resident bilinguals is that they have oral and listening skills that international students lack, yet sometimes they lack the reading and writing skills and the grammatical knowledge of international students (Cummins 1980). As more and more resident bilinguals obtain the skills and opportunities to achieve a higher education and proceed through the K-12 pipeline, their numbers in universities and therefore in writing centers as both tutors and students will also increase. Because of local demographics, some universities, for example, St. John's in New York, have a writing center staff composed of many resident bilinguals. Likewise, the number of international students who become tutors is increasing, although not as rapidly as the number of international students who use the writing center.

Questions relevant to address these ongoing changes in tutors' and tutees' language backgrounds include, how does a session between two international students compare to one between a native speaker and a non-native speaker? To a session between between two resident bilinguals? To one between an international tutor and a resident bilingual student? To one between a resident bilingual tutor and an international student? When tutors are from the majority of the world's population that speaks English as an additional rather than as a native language, how is the global/local balance of issues affected? For example, would less attention be paid to articles and prepositions since neither party uses articles and prepositions in all the ways in which most native speakers do, but according to their particular versions of World English? Also, how do such dynamics play out in non-US writing centers, especially in EFL writing centers around the world in which many tutors will also be second language writers? What role do the native language and translation play in EFL writing centers? More importantly, how do the missions and philosophies of non-US writing centers differ from the collaborative, reciprocal, and process-oriented mission described above? How does the country's first language writing pedagogy affect that of its second language, both in the writing center and in the classroom?

2) Increasingly, writing centers, like other units and departments of the university, have been asked to assess their success with student writers, for example, via the common writing center survey with general questions about how students' tutoring sessions went, whether they used the global and local feedback if both were given, and whether they would return to the writing center. Although undoubtedly these types of customer satisfaction surveys result in helpful information, more fine-grained results are needed about what students do with the feedback they are given after they leave the center. To what extent do second language writers understand and then use the oral and written (e.g. online) feedback to make changes in their drafts? How successful are these changes in terms of reader comprehension and improved assignment fulfillment? What kinds of tutor feedback and tutorial interactions result in textual changes in general and in more successful changes

in particular? Such writing center-based feedback/revision research, although extremely useful, is rare in the profession except for Williams' study (2004). L2 revision research that demonstrates long-term improvement in both learning to write and writing to learn language (Manchón 2011) as a result of participating in writing center sessions will continue to strengthen the links between writing centers and Applied Linguistics/Second Language Acquisition and further emphasize writing centers as sites for continued second language learning.

11 Additional sources

International Writing Centers Association: writingcenters.org

Lerner, Neal. 2009. *The idea of a writing laboratory*. Carbondale, IL: Southern Illinois University Press.

McKinney, Jackie Grutsch. 2013. *Peripheral visions for writing centers*. Boulder: University Press of Colorado.

Murphy, Christina and Joe Law (eds.). 1995. *Landmark essays on writing centers*. Davis, CA: Hermagoras Press.

Rafoth, Ben. 2015. *Multilingual writers and writing centers*. Boulder: University Press of Colorado.

Reynolds, Dudley W. 2009. *One on one with second language writers: A guide for writing tutors, teachers, and consultants*. Ann Arbor, MI: University of Michigan Press.

Praxis: A Writing Center Journal: http://www.praxisuwc.com/

Schendel, Ellen and William J. Macauley, Jr. 2012. *Building writing center assessments that matter*. Boulder: University Press of Colorado.

Writing Center Journal http://writingcenterjournal.org/

WLN: A Journal of Writing Center Scholarship https://wlnjournal.org

12 References

Agar, Michael. 1985. Institutional discourse. *Text-Interdisciplinary Journal for the Study of Discourse* 5(3). 147–168.

Ashton-Jones, Evelyn. 1988. Asking the right question: a heuristic for tutors. *Writing Center Journal* 9(1). 29–36.

Babcock, Rebecca and Terese Thonus. 2012. *Researching the writing center: Toward an evidence-based practice*. New York: Peter Lang.

Bell, Diana and Madeleine Youmans. 2006. Politeness and praise: rhetorical issues in ESL (L2) writing center conferences, *Writing Center Journal* 26(2). 31–47.

Bergman, Linda, Robert Cedillo, Chloe de los Reyes, Magnus Gustafsson, and Carol Haviland. 2009. Being a linguistic foreigner: Learning from international tutoring. In Shanti Bruce and Ben Rafoth (eds.), *ESL writers: A guide for writing center tutors* (2nd ed.), 195–207. Portsmouth, NH: Boynton/Cook.

Blau, Susan, John Hall, and Tracy Strauss. 1998. Exploring the tutor/client conversation: A linguistic analysis. *Writing Center Journal* 19(1). 18–49.

Blau, Susan and John Hall. 2002. Guilt-free tutoring: Rethinking how we tutor non-native-English-speaking students. *Writing Center Journal* 23(1). 23–44.

Brooks, Jeff. 1991. Minimalist tutoring: Making students do all the work. *Writing Lab Newsletter* 15(6). 1–4.

Bruce, Shanti and Ben Rafoth (eds.). 2004. *ESL writers: A guide for writing center tutors*. Portsmouth, NH: Boynton/Cook.

Bruce, Shanti and Ben Rafoth (eds.). 2009. *ESL writers: A guide for writing center tutors*. 2nd edition. Portsmouth, NH: Boynton/Cook.

Bruffee, Kenneth. 1984. Peer tutoring and the "conversation of mankind". In Gray Olson (ed.), *Writing centers: Theory and administration*, 3–15. Urbana, IL: National Council of Teachers of English.

Caposella, Toni-Lee. 1998. *The Harcourt Brace guide to peer tutoring*. Fort Worth, TX: Harcourt Brace.

Carino, Peter. 1995. Early writing centers: Toward a history. *Writing Center Journal* 15(2). 103–116.

Carino, Peter. 1996. Open admissions and the construction of writing center history: A tale of three models. *Writing Center Journal* 17(2). 30–49.

Clark, Irene. 1988. Collaboration and ethics in writing center pedagogy. *Writing Center Journal* 9(1). 3–12.

Clark, Irene. 2001. Perspectives on the directive/non-directive continuum in the writing center. *Writing Center Journal* 21(3). 33–58.

Cogie, Jane, Sharon Lorinskas, and Kim Strain. 1999. Avoiding the proofreading trap: The value of the error-correction process. *Writing Center Journal* 19(2). 6–32.

Cogie, Jane. 2002. Peer tutoring: Keeping the contradictions productive. In Jane Nelson and Kathy Evertz (eds.), *The politics of writing centers*, 37–49. Portsmouth, NH: Boynton/Cook.

Cogie, Jane. 2006. ESL student participation in writing center sessions. *Writing Center Journal* 26(2). 49–66.

Cummins, Jim. 1980. The entry and exit fallacy in bilingual education. *NABE Journal* 4(3). 25–59.

Davis, Kevin, Nancy Hayward, Kathleen Hunter, and David Wallace. 1988. The function of talk in the writing conference: A study of tutorial conversation. *Writing Center Journal* 9(1). 45–51.

Deckert, Sharon. 2009. A(n)/The/0 article about articles. In Shanti Bruce and Ben Rafoth (eds.), *ESL writers: A guide for writing center tutors*, 105–115. Portsmouth, NH: Boynton/Cook.

Ede, Lisa and Andrea Lunsford. 1990. *Singular texts/plural authors: Perspectives on collaborative writing*. Carbondale, IL: Southern Illinois University Press.

Fitzgerald, Lauren. 2012. Writing center scholarship: A "big cross-disciplinary tent." In Kelly Ritter and Paul Matsuda (eds.), *Exploring composition studies: Sites, issues and perspectives*, 73–88. Logan: Utah State University Press.

Gillespie, Paula and Neal Lerner. 2000. *The Allyn and Bacon guide to peer tutoring*. New York: Longman.

Gillespie, Paula and Neal Lerner. 2009. *The Longman guide to peer tutoring*. 2nd edition. New York: Longman.

Goldstein, Lynn and Susan Conrad. 1990. Student input and negotiation of meaning in ESL writing conferences. *TESOL Quarterly* 24(3). 443–60.

Harris, M. 1997. Cultural conflicts in the writing center: Expectations and assumptions of ESL students. In Carol Severino, Juan Guerra and Johnatella Butler (eds.), *Writing in multicultural settings*, 220–233. NY: MLA.

Harris, Muriel. 1988. The concept of a writing center. SLATE: Support for the learning and teaching of English. National Council of Teachers of English. Writingcenters.org/resources/writing-center-concept/

Harris, Muriel. 1986. *Tutoring one-to-one: The writing center conference*. Urbana, IL: NCTE.

Harris, Muriel and Tony Silva. 1993. Tutoring ESL students: Issues and options. *College Composition and Communication* 44(4). 525–537.

Hinds, John. 1987. Writer versus reader responsibility: A new typology. In Ulla Connor and Robert Kaplan (eds.), *Writing across languages: Analysis of L2 text*, 141–152. Reading, MA: Addison-Wesley.

Jones, Rodney, Angel Garralda, David C. S. Li, and Graham Lock. 2006. Interactional dynamics in on-line and face-to-face peer-tutoring for second language writers. *Journal of Second Language Writing* 15(1). 1–23.

Kennedy, Barbara. 1993. Non-native English speakers in first-year composition classrooms with native speakers: Can writing center tutors help? *Writing Center Journal* 13. 27–38.

Kim, YunJung. 2007. A discourse analysis of writing tutorials with reference to the dominance in nonnative tutors and nonnative tutees. *Seoul National University Working Papers in English Linguistics and Language* 6. 14–34.

Linville, Cynthia. 2009. Editing line by line. In Shanti Bruce and Ben Rafoth (eds.), *ESL writers: A guide for writing center tutors*, 116–131. Portsmouth, NH: Boynton/Cook.

Long, Michael. 1996. The role of the linguistic environment in second language acquisition. In William Ritchie and Tej Bhatia (eds.), *The new handbook of second language acquisition*, 413–68. San Diego: Academic Press.

Lunsford, Andrea. 1991. Collaboration, control, and the writing center. *Writing Center Journal* 12(1). 3–11.

Lyster, Roy and Leila Ranta. 1997. Corrective feedback and learner uptake: Negotiation of form in communicative classrooms. *Studies in Second Language Acquisition* 19. 37–66.

Manchón, Rosa M. (ed.). 2011. *Learning-to-write and writing-to-learn in an additional language.* Amsterdam: John Benjamins.

Matsuda, Paul K. 1999. Composition Studies and ESL Writing: A disciplinary division of labor. *College Composition and Communication* 50(4). 699–721.

Matsuda, Paul K. 2012. Teaching composition in the multilingual world: Second language writing in Composition Studies. In Kelly Ritter and Paul K. Matsuda (eds.), *Exploring composition studies: Sites, issues, and perspectives*, 36–51. Logan: Utah State University Press.

McAndrew, Donald and Thomas Reigstad. 2001. *Tutoring writing: A practical guide for conferences.* Portsmouth, NH: Boynton/Cook.

Myers, Sharon. 2003. Reassessing the ‚proofreading trap’: ESL tutoring and writing center instruction. *Writing Center Journal* 24(1). 51–70.

Nakamuru, Sarah. 2010. Lexical issues in writing center tutorials with international and US-educated multi-cultural writers. *Journal of Second Language Writing* 19(2). 95–113.

North, Stephen. 1984. The idea of a writing center. *College English* 46(5). 433–46.

Powers, Judith. 1993. Rethinking writing center conferencing strategies for the ESL writer. *Writing Center Journal* 13(2). 39–47.

Rafoth, Ben. 2004. Responding online. In Ben Rafoth and Shanti Bruce (eds.), *ESL Writers: A guide for writing center tutors* (2nd ed.), 149–160. NY: Boynton/Cook: Heinemann.

Reigstad, Thomas and Donald McAndrew. 1984. *Training tutors for writing conferences.* Urbana, IL: NCTE.

Ritter, Jennifer. 2000. Recent developments in assisting ESL writers. In Ben Rafoth (ed.), *A tutor's guide: Helping writers one to one*, 102–110. Portsmouth, NH: Boynton/Cook.

Roberge, Mark, Meryl Siegal, and Linda Harklau (eds.). 2009. *Generation 1.5 in college composition: Teaching academic writing to US-educated learners of ESL.* New York: Routeledge.

Ryan, Leigh and Lisa Zimmerelli. 2010. *The Bedford guide for writing tutors.* 2nd edition. NY: Bedford/St. Martin's.

Ryan, Leiigh and Lisa Zimmerelli. 2003. *The Bedford guide for writing tutors.* NY: Bedford/St. Martin's.

Schmidt, Richard. 1990. The role of consciousness in second language learning. *Applied Linguistics* 11. 129–158.

Severino, Carol. 2009. Avoiding appropriation. In Shanti Bruce and Ben Rafoth (eds.), *ESL Writers: A guide for writing center tutors*, 51–65. NY: Boynton/Cook: Heinemann.

Severino, Carol, Ben Rafoth and Paula Gillespie. 2010. HOCs and LOCs on the ROCKS. IWCA@CCCC. Louisville, KY.

Severino, Carol. 1992. Rhetorically analyzing collaboration(s). *Writing Center Journal* 13(1). 52–64.

Severino, Carol. 1993. The "doodles" in context: Qualifying claims about contrastive rhetoric. *Writing Center Journal* 14(1). 42–62.

Severino, Carol. 1994. The Writing Center as site for cross-language research. *Writing Center Journal* 15(91). 51–62.

Severino, Carol. 2002. Writing centers as linguistic contact zones and borderlands. In Janice Wolff (ed.), *Professing in the contact zone*, 230–239. Urbana, NCTE.

Severino, Carol and Jessica Williams. 2004. Second language writers and the writing center. Introduction to special issue of *Journal of Second Language Writing* 13. 165–172.

Severino, Carol and Elizabeth Deifell. 2011. Empowering L2 tutoring: A case study of a second language writer's vocabulary learning. *Writing Center Journal* 31(1). 25–54.

Shamoon, Linda and Deborah Burns. 1995. Critique of pure tutoring. *Writing Center Journal* 15(2). 134–152.

Silva, Tony, Ilona Leki, and Joan Carson. 1997. Broadening the perspective of mainstream composition studies: Some thoughts from the disciplinary margins. *Written Communication* 14(3). 398–428.

Taylor, V. G. 2007. *The balance of rhetoric and linguistics: A study of second language writing center tutorials.* (Doctoral dissertation, Purdue University) ProQuest Dissertations and Theses, 3340684.

Thonus, Terese. 2003. Serving generation 1.5 learners in the university writing center. *TESOL Journal* 12(2). 17–24.

Thonus, Terese. 1993. Tutors as teachers: Assisting ESL/EFL students in the writing center, *Writing Center Journal* 13(2). 13–27.

Thonus, Terese. 1999a. Dominance in academic writing tutorials: Gender, language proficiency, and the offering of suggestions. *Discourse & Society* 10(2). 225–248.

Thonus, Terese. 1999b. How to communicate politely and be a tutor too: NS-NNS interaction and writing center practice. *Text* 19(2). 253–279.

Thonus, Terese. 2001. Triangulation in the writing center: Tutor, tutee, and instructor perceptions of the tutor's role. *Writing Center Journal* 21(3). 59–82

Thonus, Terese. 2004. What are the differences? Tutor interactions with first- and second language writers. *Journal of Second Language Writing* 13(3). 227–242.

Trimbur, John. 1987. Peer tutoring: A contradiction in terms? *Writing Center Journal* 7(2). 21–29.

Vygotsky, Lev S. 1986. *Thought and Language.* Boston: MIT.

Wolcott, Willa. 1989. Talking it over: A qualitative study of writing center conferencing. *Writing Center Journal* 9(2). 15–29.

Weigle, Sara and Gayle Nelson. 2004. Novice tutors & their ESL tutees: Three case studies of tutor roles and perceptions of tutorial success. *Journal of Second Language Writing* 13(3). 203–225.

Williams, Jessica. 2002. Undergraduate second language writers in the writing center. *Journal of Basic Writing* 21(1). 16–34.

Williams, Jessica. 2006. The role(s) of writing centers in second language writing instruction. In Paul Matsuda, Christina Ortmeier-Hooper and Xiaoye You (eds.), *The politics of second language writing*, 109–126. West Lafayette, IN: Parlor Press.

Williams, Jessica. 2004. Tutoring and revision: second language writers in the writing center. *Journal of Second Language Writing* 13(3). 173–201.

Sara Cushing Weigle
22 Second language writing assessment

In a world where global communication is instantaneous and more and more people connect to each other through writing, the ability to write in a second language has never been more important. Providing effective writing instruction requires appropriate assessment as well. In this chapter I first discuss writing assessment as it has been conceptualized by the disciplines of applied linguistics and composition, and then provide a historical overview of second language writing assessment, a discussion of current research trends, and a view towards the future.

1 Second language writing assessment – two perspectives

The ability to write in a second language requires both proficiency in that language and composing skills (e.g., Cumming 1989; Weigle 2002). Thus scholars concerned with second language writing ability come from the disciplines of applied linguistics/second language acquisition studies and rhetoric/composition. Similarly, second language (L2) writing assessment stands at the intersection of two related but distinct disciplines: language assessment (including the assessment of second language writing) and composition (including second language composition). These disciplines have long histories that have diverged and intersected at various points (Cumming 2009; Matsuda 2005), and have at times taken quite different perspectives on the goals of writing assessment. This divergence is evidenced by how scholars in the two fields define writing.

For example, in his chapter on testing writing in a popular language testing book, Hughes (1989) wrote: "In language testing, we are not normally interested in whether students are creative, imaginative, or even intelligent, have wide general knowledge, or have good reasons for the opinions they happen to have. For that reason we should not set tasks which measure those abilities" (p. 82). In contrast, White (1994), in a classic text on first language writing assessment in a US context, stated almost the opposite: "We want student writers to reveal how they think and express what they know" (p. 16). It is no wonder, then, that scholars of second language writing assessment, coming from these different perspectives, often demonstrate conflicting notions of what the construct of writing is, what types of writing are valued, and the degree to which writing assessment should focus on originality, voice, syntactic structure, or the avoidance of errors.

Tracing the history of L2 writing assessment thus requires some knowledge of developments in both composition and language assessment and some understanding of the differences in population and emphasis. In this section of the chapter, I outline some differences and provide a brief historical overview of each field.

One source of the differences in perspective between language assessment and composition stem from the fact that the two disciplines have traditionally focused on different learner populations. Composition specialists working with second language issues are primarily concerned with L2 students in writing classes in English language contexts, frequently alongside native speaking peers. This is a population that is rapidly increasing in the United States and other English-speaking countries. For example, in 2009, approximately 21 % of children ages 5 to 17 in the US (approximately 11.2 million) spoke a language other than English at home (Aud et al. 2011); of these, 2.7 million, or 5 % of the total school population, spoke English with difficulty. In addition, there were close to 765,000 international students (3.7 % of total enrollment) enrolled in colleges and universities in 2011–12 (IIE 2012). This figure does not include US residents who speak a language other than English at home, as such statistics are surprisingly difficult to come by (Kanno and Cromley 2013).

In contrast, scholars coming from a second language assessment perspective have traditionally been concerned with students in diverse countries whose main focus is learning a second language, frequently with an emphasis on spoken language and/or grammar and reading. For many such students and their instructors, writing is primarily a way of displaying, practicing, and adding to their linguistic knowledge rather than an end in itself. Only when students reach an advanced level of proficiency does writing tend to take a more central place in instruction and thus in assessment.

The population of learners studying English in non-English speaking countries is also quite large; in fact, second language writers in these contexts vastly outnumber those in composition or language arts courses in the US or other English-speaking countries. For example, approximately 13 million college students in China took the College English Test in 2006, a requirement for university students in China (Zheng and Cheng 2008). In many European countries, a foreign language such as English is a compulsory subject on secondary school leaving examinations.

Because the learning goals of these populations differ, there is also a difference in how the construct of writing is defined and assessed. For example, the 6-trait writing rubric, commonly used in middle and secondary schools in the US and developed with a primarily monolingual population in mind, comprises ideas, organization, voice, word choice, sentence fluency, and conventions (Arter et al. 1994). In contrast, the IELTS (International English Language Testing System), a major English language test for students wishing to study in the UK or Australia, and thus specifically developed to assess second language writing, includes the categories of task response or task achievement, coherence and cohesion, lexical resource, and grammatical range and accuracy (Shaw and Weir 2007: 163). One difference between these two ways of conceptualizing the construct of writing is that the former emphasizes authorial identity in terms of ideas and voice, whereas the latter tends to emphasize the communicative effect and linguistic characteristics of the written response.

Furthermore, in L2 assessment, writing is often tested as one part of a larger language proficiency test, in which reading, listening, and speaking are also assessed. As such, linguistic skills and knowledge (e.g., vocabulary, sentence structure, morphology) are a main focus, and rhetorical skills only become more relevant at higher levels of proficiency. In fact, some language testing specialists suggest that writing should not even be considered a skill *per se*, but rather as a specific type of "language use activity" (Bachman and Palmer 2010), that requires a certain level of language ability along with a more general strategic competence that allows one to martial linguistic and other cognitive resources to produce discourse appropriate for a given situation (Bachman and Palmer 1996, 2010).

In recent years, there has been a convergence of these two traditions, driven in part by the increase in numbers of L2 students in educational settings alongside native speakers, both in primary/secondary education and in post-secondary education. For many such students, both writing to learn and learning to write are equally pressing goals, and for their teachers, knowing how to diagnose student language and writing needs, assess individual growth in writing, and use assessments for programmatic evaluation requires an understanding of writing theory and second language acquisition, and how these relate to assessment.

2 Second language writing assessment – historical overview

It is possible to trace the roots of writing assessment back to ancient China and Rome (see Cumming 2009, for a research timeline), but for this article I begin in the mid-twentieth century. In the US in the 1950s and 60, the influence of measurement theory on both L1 and L2 writing assessment was particularly felt in an emphasis on reliability of scoring and the minimization of measurement error (Behizadeh and Engelhard 2011). This emphasis led to the widespread practice of using so-called objective tests of grammar and usage to assess writing, since the rating of essays was considered less reliable and more prone to measurement error. The use of these indirect tests of writing was consistent with the predominant emphasis on writing as form in research on composition (Yancey 1999). At the same time, the field of language testing was influenced by scholars such as Lado (1961), who advocated discrete items to test language knowledge, and Carroll (1961), whose influential grid of aspects of language (orthography/phonology, morphology, syntax, lexis) and skills (reading, writing, speaking, listening) dominated language testing in the US for many years. Both Lado and Carroll were advocates of using compositions to test writing for second language learners, but the dominant peda-gogical tradition of grammar-translation or audio-lingual methods of teaching lan-guage, which did not emphasize writing, combined with the expense and feasibili-ty issues of large-scale writing tests, convinced many test developers that direct testing of second language writing was problematic.

Starting in the 1970s, trends in language teaching and writing instruction led to parallel trends in assessment. In second language pedagogy, the notion of com-municative language teaching (Johnson and Morrow 1981) began to dominate the field, with a shift in the goals of instruction from mastery of discrete forms and rules to the ability to communicate in the language. This movement led to ideas about communicative language testing (Carroll 1980; Morrow 1979) and models of communicative competence, starting with the work of Hymes (1972) and continuing with the influential models of Canale and Swain (1980) and Bachman (1990). McNamara (2000) notes that the theory of communicative competence "represen-ted a profound shift from a psychological perspective on language, which sees language as an internal phenomenon, to a sociological one, focusing on the exter-nal, social, functions of language" (p. 17).

One important component of this development was an increased focus on ana-lyzing real-word language use situations that examinees would be likely to encoun-ter. For example, the Occupational English Test, a test for health professionals in Australia (MacNamara 1990) was developed in part through surveying profession-als in clinical settings about the language tasks that were required in for their jobs. In the case of academic writing, this focus led to careful study of the writing tasks that university students faced across a variety of disciplines, including but certain-ly not limited to composition courses (Ginther and Grant 1996; Horowitz 1986; Kroll 1979).

While second language pedagogy and assessment were becoming more fo-cused on real-world language use, the world of composition was experiencing a similar trend, moving away from focusing the formal aspects of written texts to the cognitive processes engaged in by writers, with seminal works by Emig (1971) and Hayes and Flower (1980), among others. This movement had a profound influence on second language writing instruction (e.g., Raimes 1985; Zamel 1983) but little influence on the practice of writing assessment (Behizadeh and Engelhard 2011).

During this period, more writing specialists (e.g., White 1985, for L1, and Ja-cobs, Zinkgraf, Wormuth, Hartfield, and Hughey 1981, for L2) advocated successful-ly to replace indirect tests of writing with direct ones: typically, timed essays based on a prompt and scored on a holistic scale. Research on writing assessment in both L1 and L2 also began to expand around this time. Huot (1990a, 1990b) published important review articles that provided an excellent overview of L1 writing assess-ment. At about the same time, Hamp-Lyons (1991) published the first major edited volume on second language writing assessment. An international study by Purves (1992) surveyed writing instruction and achievement in 14 countries which demon-strated great variability in standards and practices across the countries surveyed.

Beginning in the 1990s, a more sociocultural view of writing began to emerge in composition studies. Many scholars in both first and second language writing advocated portfolio assessment for both large-scale and classroom assessment (e.g., Calfee and Perfumo 1996; Hamp-Lyons and Condon 2000; Yancey 1992), citing, among other things, the ability of portfolios to support literacy learning by prompting students to write more, be more reflective about their writing, and assess their own writing more accurately (Dunn, Luke, and Nassar 2013). The push for portfolios came primarily from teachers rather than educational measurement specialists (Behizadeh and Engelhard 2011; Hamp-Lyons 2002).

Since the 1990s, an important development in writing assessment has been the emergence of new measurement models for scaling performances that involve human judgments. These models stem from an understanding that variability is an intrinsic characteristic of complex activities, including both writing and the evaluation of writing; rather than focusing on reducing measurement error, then, the goal of such models is to understand and map this variability (Deville and Chalhoub-Deville 2006: 16). One model that has been used with increasing frequency is multifaceted Rasch modeling (Linacre and Wright 2002), which provides a mechanism for incorporating information about rater behavior (severity and consistency), task difficulty, and other facets of an assessment situation in estimating student ability along a scale. MFRM has been used to research rater behavior in particular (e.g., Eckes 2008; Lumley 2005; Weigle 1998).

A more recent phenomenon of importance to writing assessment is the development of natural language processing and corpus analysis tools. Corpus linguistics has allowed for a greater understanding of the features of different genres of writing (see, for example, Biber 1988; Biber, Connor, and Upton 2007; Swales 1990, 2004). Large corpora such as Michigan Corpus of Academic Spoken English (MICASE http://quod.lib.umich.edu/m/micase/), the British Academic Written English Corpus (BAWE: http://www2.warwick.ac.uk/fac/soc/al/research/collect/bawe/) and the International Corpus of Learner English (ICLE: http://www.uclouvain.be/en-cecl-icle.html) have provided opportunities to investigate various aspects of language use such as vocabulary, syntactic complexity, and discourse moves in successful writing. This research can inform both instruction and assessment by providing empirical evidence of how successful writers use linguistic resources in different genres and on different task types. A natural extension of these tools has been the development of automated tools for scoring and providing feedback on writing. I discuss this issue again in the last section of this chapter.

3 Current research trends

Second language writing assessment as an area of research inquiry has expanded substantially in the past 30 years. Most of this research has been done in the context of large-scale assessment, rather than classroom assessment (Leki, Cumming, and Silva 2008). As such, it has focused on writing assessment as a measurement issue (Behizadeh and Engelhard 2011) rather than use of assessment to enhance writing instruction or the effects of assessment on instruction. This research has tended to focus on factors related to the writing task, the scoring process, and features of the written text and the relationships between these factors and test scores (Barkaoui 2007a), with less emphasis on factors related to test-takers themselves. In this section I review the major findings in each of these areas.

3.1 Task

A central component in writing assessment is the task: i.e., the topic or prompt, along with additional instructions as to length, audience, time allotment, and other factors that may affect performance. Scholars have investigated task-related questions involving reliability (e.g., do students perform equally well on two different task types?) and validity (e.g., does the task elicit writing that is representative of writing in other domains?). Features of the writing task that have been explored include topic (e.g., general vs. discipline-specific, familiarity to test-takers), cognitive demands, discourse mode (e.g., argument or narrative), rhetorical context (audience and purpose), and input (e.g., a reading or listening text). Reviews of this literature (Barkaoui 2007a; Shaw and Weir 2007; Weigle 2002) note that task characteristics can affect the processes that test takers employ, the rhetorical and linguistic features of the texts they produce, and the perceptions of raters, and thus ultimately the scores that are awarded. The research suggests that there is not a simple relationship between task characteristics and scores, but rather that different task types can elicit different rhetorical strategies and linguistic choices, which may in turn influence raters' judgments of the written product. Nevertheless, the literature on tasks does propose certain "best practices" related to writing task: tasks should:
- be engaging to both writers and raters,
- elicit writing that can be scored reliably
- elicit writing that is relevant to the construct of interest
- not be biased in favor of or against any particular group of test-taker,
- allow test-takers from a wide range of proficiency levels to demonstrate their writing ability (Weigle 2002; White 1994).

An important trend related to tasks in large-scale second language writing assessment is the inclusion of integrated tasks (reading and writing, or sometimes reading, listening and writing) to simulate the "content-responsible" (Leki and Carson 1997) writing that characterizes much of academic writing. The inclusion of integrated tasks on the TOEFL iBT since 2005 reflects this trend and is also the driver of much research on such tasks. Research on integrated tasks, particularly in comparison with independent tasks, has demonstrated that rating on both integrated and independent tasks can be equally reliable (Gebril 2009), but scores across the two task types may differ (Plakans 2008). Furthermore, writing processes may differ across the two task types (Guo 2011; Plakans 2008). Since academic writing is typically based on reading, including both integrated and independent writing on a large-scale test may serve to broaden the construct being assessed (Cumming et al. 2005; Guo 2011).

Although integrated tasks are considered in many ways superior to independent tasks, one issue of interest with regard to such tasks is that of textual borrowing, as students may use words and phrases from the source texts in inappropriate ways in their essays. From a composition perspective, the ability of students to incorporate and appropriately reference the ideas and words of others in their writing is an important academic skill; for example, Hyland (2009) argues that assessments should explicitly address source use as a component of the writing construct. From a language testing perspective, on the other hand, concerns about textual borrowing center more on the degree to which borrowing of source text language may make it difficult for raters to accurately evaluate the candidate's language ability (Weigle and Parker 2012). The extent to which students borrow language from source texts has been investigated recently by Cumming et al. (2005), and Plakans and Gebril (2012).

Other task factors relate to test administration, include time allotment, whether to give a choice of tasks, and transcription mode (handwriting or word processing). The limited research on time allotment has been reviewed by Weigle (2002) and Shaw and Weir (2007) and does not conclusively demonstrate an advantage for longer time periods. Shaw and Weir (2007: 64) conclude that "there should be sufficient time available for candidates to produce a situationally and interactionally authentic written product appropriate to level;" as an example, in the Cambridge suite of examinations, students at higher levels of proficiency are expected to write between 240 and 700 words in one and a half to two hours, while low proficiency examinees write 25 to 100 words of continuous text in a much shorter timeframe.

The issue of giving students a choice in prompts has provoked both theoretical discussions and empirical research (see Lee 2008 for a review). Research on test-taker choice suggests that students prefer having a choice of topics and tend to choose topics they feel are most familiar (Polio and Glew 1996). However, there is no clear consensus about the effects of choice on writing performance, with most studies showing little or no difference in overall performance whether or not a choice is given (Lee and Anderson 2007; Powers and Fowles 1998).

Another task-related question is whether the mode of transcription – handwriting or computer – makes a difference either in terms of writing process or essay scores. The growth in access to computers over the past twenty years means that early research on this topic must be evaluated in light of more recent developments; however, some of this research is relevant to computer-based writing assessments. First, research shows that students who are used to writing on the computer tend to write better and revise more when typing rather than writing by hand, and this tends to be reflected in higher scores. Some research suggests that raters tend to give higher scores to handwritten essays than to the same essays typed on a computer (Brown 2003, cited in Shaw and Weir 2007; Powers, Fowles, Farnum, and Ramsey 1994). A further consideration is that low proficiency students who have low computer skills may be particularly affected by a computer test, performing worse than they would if they wrote their essays by hand.

3.2 Scoring

Turning to research on the scoring process, scoring involves one or more raters evaluating the written product using a rating scale or rubric. Research on scoring thus typically involves investigating aspects of the rating process or features of the rating scale. In the past 30 years, a substantial amount of research on rater processes has been conducted, investigating what raters actually attend to when they score L2 writing, and on characteristics that influence rater behavior, including training, rating and teaching experience, first language and professional background. Research on rater background has largely focused on raters as a source of measurement error, with the goal of improving rater selection and training to reliability. Research on rater processes, however, tends to have a validity focus – that is, the goal of such research is to determine whether the aspects of writing that are the intended focus of the assessment are those that raters attend to in assigning scores.

Summarizing the literature on raters, Barkaoui (2007a: 105) states: "rater factors – such as personality, cultural, linguistic, and education background, and rating experience – influence rater decision-making behavior, interpretations and expectations concerning task requirements and scoring criteria, reaction to ESL/EFL essays, severity (inter-rater reliability) and self-consistency (intra-rater reliability)." Shaw and Weir (2007) divide rater characteristics into three categories: physical/ physiological (e.g., age, sex, short- or long-term ailments or disabilities), psychological (e.g., personality, cognitive style, emotional state), and experiential (e.g., education, experience). Numerous studies have investigated the role of these characteristics individually or in combination. For example, Mendelsohn and Cumming (1987) compared ratings of ESL and engineering faculty on ESL student papers; and Kobayashi and Rinnert (1996) investigated the role of the rater's native language in evaluating Japanese student writing. Eckes (2008) identified six different rater types among raters of German essays, depending on the degree to which aspects of global impression, task realization, or linguistic realization were given priority.

Of all the rater variables that could be studied, variables related to rater experience have tended to receive the most attention in part because these variables can be most easily addressed through rater recruitment and training (Shaw and Weir

2007). One important experiential variable is the extent to which raters are familiar with second language writing and/or the rhetorical conventions of the first languages of writers. This research, summarized by Shaw and Weir (2007), suggests that raters who are more familiar with second language writing and writers may be more sympathetic to such writing than raters who are not.

A second important experiential variable is the academic discipline of the rater, particularly given that the goal of many international writing tests is to evaluate readiness for academic study in English. One line of this research compares ESL/EFL specialists with English composition specialists, or one or both of these specialties with content area specialists. Collectively this research suggests that disciplinary faculty are more concerned with content than with language, audience is a notion that is more important to English composition teachers than to other specialists, and ESL/EFL specialists are more attuned to grammar and cohesion than are faculty in other areas (Shaw and Weir 2007).

A recent innovation in terms of raters is the use of automated scoring technology to score second language writing, as noted above. While this phenomenon has engendered a great deal of controversy among composition scholars, it has been somewhat less controversial among second language testing experts, possibly because of their traditional concerns with the language proficiency component of second language writing ability rather than the writing skills component, as discussed earlier. Perhaps the most well-known application of automated scoring for second language writing is *e-rater*, used along with human raters to score writing on the TOEFL (see Enright and Quinlan 2010 for a recent description of how e-rater is used).

Along with the rater, the rating scale used to score writing has also been the subject of some inquiry. One question that arises frequently is whether raters should use a holistic scale, giving a single score to each essay, or an analytic or multi-trait scale, rating different aspects of writing. Some scholars (e.g., Bacha 2001; Hamp-Lyons 1991) generally support analytic scales, particularly for diagnostic purposes or classroom use, but for decision-making purposes such as admission or placement, where ultimately a single cut-score must be used, there is no clear evidence that one type of scale or another leads to more valid decisions. One recent study (Barkaoui 2007b) found that inter-rater agreement was higher on a holistic scale than an analytic one but that raters used similar decision-making processes using both rubrics.

The rating scale can be seen as the *de facto* definition of the writing construct being measured (McNamara 1996; Weigle 2002). However, the content of rating scales has received surprisingly little attention in the literature, even though, as Schoonen (2005) notes, the focus of the scoring procedures determines which aspects of the written product influence the raters to assign specific scores. Fulcher (2003) distinguishes between intuitively and empirically designed rating scales. Intuitively designed scales are typically based on pre-existing scales or expert opinions of what characterizes different levels of writing ability or language proficiency. Empirically designed scales, on the other hand, are created by generalizing from characteristics of actual student samples at different levels (see, e.g., Turner and Upshur 2002)

The number of scale points and specificity of the descriptors are issues that need to be addressed in practice. Lim (2011) writes: "Ideally, a rating scale would be precise enough to allow raters to focus on the same aspects of writing to the same degree, and thus arrive at the same scores. But the fact is that writing and reading are both complex phenomena that cannot be easily reduced to a single set of criteria. Lumley (2006) observes that a rating scale cannot possibly describe every feature of a composition that raters might notice. Rather, raters notice many things and then attempt to channel those observations into the wording of the rating scale. The rating scale thus only needs to provide enough detail for raters to do this channeling reliably."

3.3 Textual features

Research on task and scoring typically has as its focus identifying and reducing sources of measurement error, while the written text itself should be the focus of the assessment. Several researchers have looked at the relationship between various surface textual features and essay scores. Syntactic features that have been found to be associated with higher scores include passive voice (Connor 1990; Ferris 1994; Grant and Ginther 2000), subordination (Grant and Ginther 2000), nominalizations (Connor 1990), and connectives (Connor 1990). These studies have not always yielded consistent results, however, in part because the study of individual textual features may not be as useful as studying how writers use different features in combination (Jarvis, Grant, Bikowski, and Ferris 2003). In addition, some research suggests that lexical variables such as lexical diversity and word frequency may be even more closely related to essay scores than syntactic variables (Crossley and McNamara 2011; Engber 1995; Grant and Ginther 2000; Jarvis 2002; Nation 1988). Discoursal features have also been the focus of research on L2 texts, which may affect how raters score such texts. In a recent review of the literature in this area, Hinkel (2010) provides a lengthy list of differences between L2 texts and texts written by L1 writers of similar backgrounds. These differences include, among others, the organization and structure of discourse moves and thesis statements, the use of personal opinions and/or emotional appeals rather than factual data in support of an idea, and the degree to which the readers' background knowledge is taken into consideration in writing.

3.4 Test takers

Research on test-takers is the least developed area, although scholars (Hamp-Lyons 1990; Leki 2001; Rea-Dickins 1997) have long called for such research. Barkaoui

(2007a) identified only two studies dealing with "how examinees choose, read, and interpret writing tasks" (p. 103) and five on test-taker background characteristics (primarily native language) and their effects on essay features or essay scores.

Few studies have investigated test-taker perceptions of writing tests (Hamp-Lyons 1997, being a notable exception). However, research is beginning to emerge regarding perceptions of L2 testing in general. For example, Huhta, Kalaja, and Pitkänen-Huhta (2006) discuss the various roles and identities students construct for themselves when faced with preparing for and taking a high-stakes school-leaving test. In another recent study, Cheng and DeLuca (2011) elicited written reports of test takers perceptions of a testing event. Specific themes that emerged from their analysis specifically related to writing included lack of sufficient time to complete complex writing tasks, the problem of unfamiliarity with a writing topic, and lack of clarity about how their written responses would be evaluated.

The role of student beliefs regarding plagiarism and textual borrowing is an area that is becoming more important, particularly with the increased use of integrated writing assessment tasks. Studies of student beliefs about plagiarism (e.g., Pittam, Elander, Lusher, Fox, and Payne 2009) suggest that students have a great deal of uncertainty about the boundaries between quotation, referencing, and plagiarism; this may be particularly the case in a timed writing test. In fact, a recent exploratory study (Weigle and Montee 2012) suggests that test raters do not necessarily agree on the acceptability of textual borrowing in testing situations; thus, it is likely that students may be even more uncertain about this issue. This is an area where further research is needed.

4 Future directions

In a review of the literature on second language writing assessment, Cumming (2009) describes five recurring themes that had emerged since the early 20th century. These themes were:
1. Broadening of the contexts to which assessment has been applied.
2. Concerns for the validity of assessments, particularly scoring methods and the evidence and arguments to support inferences made from writing assessments.
3. Congruence and conflict between the purposes of assessment and of education in general.
4. Debates over appropriate or variable standards of writing quality.
5. An expanding repertoire of research methods and technologies to improve and validate L2 writing tests. (p. 95).

In this section of the chapter I will discuss what may lie ahead in each of these areas.

4.1 Broadening of the contexts to which assessment has been applied

The majority of research on L2 writing assessment has focused on English writing at universities; research is more limited in the areas of foreign language writing assessment, assessment in primary and secondary schools, workplace writing assessment, and classroom assessment of writing. An area of growing interest is the relationship between oral language proficiency and literacy development in young learners, where there are gaps in both theoretical and empirical research (Jang, Wagner, and Stille 2011). With regards to classroom writing assessment, an area of continued controversy is the usefulness of different types of feedback for second language writers (see Ferris 2002; Hyland and Hyland 2006; Leki, Silva, and Cumming 2008, for thorough reviews of this topic). Meta-analytic studies may provide more conclusive guidance in this area. For example, Biber, Nekrasova, and Horn (2011) found that teacher feedback was associated with improvements in writing for both L1 and L2 students, and that, particularly for L2 writers, focus on both content and language use was more effective than focus on language only. Furthermore, comments were found to be more useful than error correction.

Writing in the disciplines is also an important area of concern. Hirvela (2011) provides an up-to-date review on writing to learn in content areas, but research on how scholars in different disciplines evaluate writing has not progressed much beyond notions of error gravity and acceptability of non-native language forms. The majority of research in this area has been conducted using impromptu test essays, which do not necessarily represent the genres in which students are expected to write. More needs to be known about how disciplinary faculty assess L2 writing in the context of their own disciplines.

An emerging area in writing instruction is the development of new digital media tools and genres such as blogs and wikis, which may be useful in second language writing instruction as they allow students to develop an authorial voice, write for authentic purposes, and learn to write collaboratively (Warschauer 2010). It may be possible to make use of these socially constructed media forms in assessment, but to my knowledge this has not been attempted on a large scale. This is an area that will certainly expand rapidly over the next decades.

4.2 Concerns for the validity of assessment

Validity of writing assessments have long been an issue of concern, but how validity is conceptualized has changed over the past several decades. Many recent discussions of validity in language testing (e.g., Bachman 2005; Chapelle, Enright, and Jamieson 2008; Kane 2002;) conceptualize validation as an attempt to articulate the inferential steps that are made between a test performance and interpretation of test scores and to seek evidence in support of these inferences. For example, when student essays are scored on a writing test, the inference is made that the scores are accurate representations of some important quality of the writing. Behind this inference lies the assumption that the scoring rubric accurately reflects the construct and that the raters base their scores on the rubric. A process of validation would involve gathering evidence to test these two assumptions. Chapelle et al. (2008) represents a fully articulated validity framework for the TOEFL.

A complementary approach to investigating test validity is the socio-cognitive framework developed by Weir (2005) and specified more fully in Shaw and Weir (2007). This framework expands on traditional notions of construct, content, and criterion validity to encompass a broader view of the factors that lead to valid interpretations and uses of test scores. The factors that directly impact performance on a particular writing task include *context validity*, which includes aspects of the task and administrative setting, along with the linguistic demands of the task input and output, and *cognitive validity*, which covers the cognitive processes involved in completing the task. *Scoring validity* includes the factors such as rater and scale characteristics, rater training and conditions that influence the scores given to the responses. Finally, test developers must consider *consequential validity*, or washback on students and impact on society; and *criterion-related validity*, or comparisons with external standards or variations of the same test. Shaw & Weir use this framework as a guide to compiling validity evidence for widely used writing tests produced by Cambridge ESOL, including the IELTS.

Both of these frameworks recognize that test validation is an ongoing concern that requires collection of a variety of different kinds of evidence to support a validity argument. This evidence includes both traditional reliability and content validity concerns along with consideration of the impacts of assessments on individuals and on society at large. These frameworks will continue to be useful for validating the uses of writing tests for a variety of purposes.

4.3 Congruence and conflict between the purposes of assessment and education in general

Much has been written about the dangers of "teaching to the test" in composition (e.g., Au 2007; Winn and Behizadeh 2011) and in L2 writing (e.g., Hamp-Lyons 2007; Leki, Cumming, and Silva 2008). Scholars argue that single-shot approaches to assessment, particularly the timed impromptu essay, narrow the construct of writing unacceptably and place too much emphasis on assessment for the sake of accountability rather than assessment in the service of learning. For example, Hillocks (2002, cited in Au 2007) found that, in states with poorly designed writing assessment systems, pedagogy was adapted to a "technical, mechanical, five-paragraph essay form" (Au 2007: 264). Au further points out that high-stakes testing is associated with lower achievement for lower-income students and students of color, a group that includes many L2 writers.

As Shohamy (2011) argues, high-stakes testing frequently serves to support a political agenda, and specifically in the case of language, an ideology of monolingualism, despite evidence that multilingual speakers continue to use their primary language in support of academic and social goals. Multilingual students who are tested on standardized tests and expected to achieve native-like proficiency in the dominant language run the risk of being further marginalized, given the length of time it takes to achieve academic literacy in a second language. The issue of how writing tests are used to further political agendas vis-à-vis their use to further student learning in important areas is certainly an issue that will continue to be important in the foreseeable future, (see, for example, Inoue and Poe 2012 for a recent edited volume on the effects of writing assessment on minorities).

4.4 Debates over appropriate or variable standards of writing quality

A perennial debate in writing assessment is the degree to which sentence-level errors made by students in the process of acquiring English can or should be penalized in standardized writing tests or in writing courses. Some instructors feel that they need to hold students accountable to the same standards, while others feel that they need to take into account the longer time it takes to acquire a second language (see Ferris, Brown, Liu, and Stine 2011, for a recent survey of teachers' perspectives on ESL students). Given the increase in non-native writers in education, this issue will continue to be at the forefront of discussions. Interestingly, some research suggests that ESL errors may not be as stigmatized as errors associated with low-prestige dialects of English such as African-American English (Johnson and VanBrackle 2012). This result may be due to racial discrimination (conscious or unconscious) or, more benignly, a deliberate attempt to prepare students for the "real world" of employment, where command of standard language is expected. However, it is clear that writing is typically associated with more prestige than speaking (Leith 1997), and thus deviations from a standard prestige form of the language are usually less acceptable in writing than in speaking.

4.5 An expanding repertoire of research methods and technologies to improve and validate L2 writing tests

It is becoming increasingly clear in writing assessment research that both quantitative and qualitative research methods will be important in validating and improving assessments. To further explore the effects of rater and task-related variables, quantitative research methods include powerful statistical tools such as including generalizability theory (e.g., Huang 2012), structural equation modeling (e.g., Schoonen 2005), and multi-faceted Rasch measurement (e.g., Eckes 2008; Schaefer 2008), which allow researchers to study the effects of several variables such as task and rater in a single design. Meta-analytic studies (e.g., Biber, Nekrasova, and Horn 2011) allow researchers to synthesize existing literature on specific variables to identify both patterns and inconsistencies in research methods and findings, and make generalizations with more confidence than a single study can provide. These methods are certain to become more widely used in writing assessment research in the years to come.

On a more micro level, writers' processes can be explored through the analysis of keystrokes: for example, pauses between sentences may represent text planning processes, while pauses between and within words may represent dysfluencies in text production (Deane, Quinlan, and Kostin 2011); relating these keystroke measures to test scores may provide insight into the relationship between cognitive processes and test performance. Similarly, the use of eye-tracking software can be helpful in investigating the processes involved in reading for integrated writing tasks (e.g., Bax 2013).

Natural language processing tools such as syntactic parsers and part-of-speech taggers, along with the availability of large corpora of written texts, are certain to have a great influence on writing assessment in the future in terms of identifying features of texts that are associated with different scores or that develop over time and improving automated essay scoring tools.

Research of this nature, conducted systematically across topics, proficiency levels, and native language groups, could be helpful to inform and improve automated scoring algorithms such as those used by e-rater and other commercially available products. Ideally, such research could also feed back into rating scale development and rater training to provide stronger connections between the rating scale and the writing construct.

In addition to these technological tools, which lend themselves to quantitative research, investigations of the social impact of tests and of test-taker perceptions require more qualitative research, including techniques such as think-aloud protocols of writers and raters, ethnographic studies of classrooms, and in-depth interviews of writers, teachers, and raters, to understand the contexts in which tests are administered, taken, and scored. For example, much of the literature on automated scoring of writing has tended to focus on the technical aspects of the algorithms and demonstrations of reliability and usability. This research needs to be complemented by qualitative research that explores questions such as whether and in what ways test-takers adjust their writing process and teachers change their methods to accommodate computer scoring of writing, and whether human raters change how they score writing if they know that their scores will be compared to automated scores.

5 Conclusion

In conclusion, just as writing in a second language is a complex, multi-faceted process, assessing second language writing is equally complex. The increased importance of writing in an era of globalization, and the rising number of second language learners in writing courses, from beginning language learners in monolingual settings to advanced graduate students in multilingual settings, makes it imperative to continue seeking ways to assess writing that are authentic, fair, and feasible. The consequences of assessment may be far-reaching, and thus teachers, researchers, and policy makers must be cognizant of the factors that enhance or detract from test validity and fairness as they seek to assess student writing accurately.

6 Additional sources

Crusan, Deborah. 2010. *Assessment in the second language writing classroom*. Michigan: University of Michigan Press.

Cumming, Alister. 2002. Assessing L2 writing: Alternative constructs and ethical dilemmas. *Assessing Writing* 8(2). 73–83.

Cumming, Alister. 2013. Assessing integrated writing tasks for academic purposes: Promises and perils. *Language Assessment Quarterly* 10(1). 1–8.

Elliot, Norbert and David Williamson. 2013. Special issue: Assessing writing with automated scoring systems. *Assessing Writing* 18(1).

Hamp-Lyons, Liz and Barbara Kroll. 1997. *TOEFL 2000: Writing: Composition, community, and assessment*. Princeton, NJ: Educational Testing Service.

Kroll, Barbara and Joy Reid. 1994. Guidelines for designing writing prompts: Clarifications, caveats, and cautions. *Journal of Second Language Writing* 3(3). 231–255.

Lim, Gad. 2011. The development and maintenance of rating quality in performance writing assessment: A longitudinal study of new and experienced raters. *Language Testing* 28(4). 543–560.

Weigle, Sara. 2006. Investing in assessment: Designing tests to promote positive washback. In Paul Matsuda, Christina Ortmeier-Hooper and Xiaoye You (eds.), *Politics of second language writing: In search of the Promised Land*, 222–244. West Lafayette, IN: Parlor Press.

Weigle, Sara. 2007. Teaching writing teachers about assessment. *Journal of Second Language Writing* 16(3). 194–209.

White, Edward. 2007. *Assigning, responding, evaluating: A writing teacher's guide*. (4th edition). Bedford/St. Martin's.

7 References

Arter, Judit, Vicki Spandel, Ruth Culham, and Jim Pollard. 1994. The impact of training students to be self-assessors of writing. Paper presented at the Annual Meeting of the American Educational Research Association, New Orleans, LA, 4–8, April. Retrieved from ERIC database (ED370975).

Au, Wayne. 2007. High-stakes testing and curricular control: A qualitative metasynthesis. *Educational Researcher* 36(5). 258–267.

Aud, Susan, William Hussar, Grace Kena, Kevin Bianco, Lauren Frohlich, Jana Kemp, and Kim Tahan. 2011. The condition of education 2011 (NCES 2011–033). US Department of Education, National Center for Education Statistics. Washington, DC: US Government Printing Office.

Bacha, Nahla. 2001. Writing evaluation: what can analytic versus holistic essay scoring tell us? *System* 29(3). 371–383.

Bachman, Lyle. 1990. *Fundamental considerations in language testing.* Oxford: Oxford University Press.

Bachman, Lyle. 2005. Building and supporting a case for test use. *Language Assessment Quarterly: An International Journal* 2(1). 1–34.

Bachman, Lyle and Adrian Palmer. 1996. *Language testing in practice: Designing and developing useful language tests* (Vol. 1). Oxford: Oxford University Press.

Bachman, Lyle and Adrian Palmer. 2010. *Language assessment in practice: Developing language assessments and justifying their use in the real world.* Oxford: Oxford University Press.

Barkaoui, Khaled. 2007a. Participants, texts and processes in ESL/EFL Essay Tests: A Narrative Review of the Literature. *Canadian Modern Language Review* 64(1). 99–134.

Barkaoui, Khaled. 2007b. Rating scale impact on EFL essay marking: A mixed-method study. *Assessing Writing* 12(2). 86–107.

Bax, Stephen. 2013. The cognitive processing of candidates during reading tests: Evidence from eye-tracking. *Language Testing* 30. 441–465

Behizadeh, Nadia and George Engelhard. 2011. Historical view of the influences of measurement and writing theories on the practice of writing assessment in the United States. *Assessing Writing* 16(3). 189–211.

Biber, Douglas. 1988. *Variation across speech and writing.* Cambridge: Cambridge University Press.

Biber, Douglas, Ulla Connor, and Thomas Upton. 2007. *Discourse on the move.* Amsterdam: John Benjamins.

Biber, Douglas, Tatiana Nekrasova, and Brad Horn. 2011. *The Effectiveness of feedback for L1-English and L2-Writing development: A Meta-Analysis.* ETS Research Report RR-11-05). Princeton, NJ: ETS.

Calfee, Robert and Pamela Perfumo (eds.). 1996. *Writing portfolios in the classroom: Policy and practice, promise and peril.* London: Routledge.

Canale, Michael and Merril Swain. 1980. Theoretical bases of communicative approaches to second language teaching and testing. *Applied Linguistics* 1. 1–47.

Carroll, Brendan. 1980. *Testing communicative performance: An interim study.* Exeter, UK: Pergamon.

Chapelle, Carol, Mary Enright, and Joan Jamieson. 2008. *Building a validity argument for the Test of English as a foreign language.* London: Routledge.

Cheng, Liying and Christopher DeLuca. 2011. Voices from test-takers: Further evidence for language assessment validation and Use. *Educational Assessment* 16(2). 104–122.

Connor, Ulla. 1990. Linguistic/rhetorical measures for international persuasive student writing. *Research in the Teaching of English.* 67–87.

Carroll, John. 1961. Fundamental considerations in testing for English language proficiency of foreign students. *Testing the English proficiency of foreign students.* 30–40.

Crossley, Scott and DanielleMcNamara. 2011. Understanding expert ratings of essay quality: Coh-Metrix analyses of first and second language writing. *International Journal of Continuing Engineering Education and Life Long Learning* 21(2). 170–191.

Cumming, Alister. 1989. Writing expertise and second-language proficiency. *Language learning* 39(1). 81–135.

Cumming, Alister. 2009. Assessing academic writing in foreign and second languages. *Language Teaching* 42(01). 95–107.

Cumming, Alister, Robert Kantor, Kyoko Baba, Usman Erdosy, Keanre Eouanzoui, and Mark James. 2005. Differences in written discourse in independent and integrated prototype tasks for next generation TOEFL. *Assessing Writing* 10(1). 5–43.

Deane, Paul, Thomas Quinlan, and Irene Kostin. 2011. *Automated scoring within a developmental, cognitive model of writing proficiency*. ETS Research Report Series: 11–16. Princeton, NJ: ETS.

Deville, Craig and Micheline Chalhoub-Deville. 2006. Old and new thoughts on test score variability. In Micheline Chalhoub-Deville, Carol A. Chapelle, and Patricia A. Duff (eds.), *Inference and generalizability in applied linguistics: Multiple perspectives*, 9–25. Amsterdam: John Benjamins.

Dunn Jr, J., Carrie Luke, and David Nassar. 2013. Valuing the resources of infrastructure: Beyond from-scratch and off-the-shelf technology options for electronic portfolio assessment in first-year writing. *Computers and Composition* 30. 61–73.

Eckes, Thomas. 2008. Rater types in writing performance assessments: A classification approach to rater variability. *Language Testing* 25(2). 155–185.

Emig, Janet. 1971. *The composing processes of twelfth graders*. Urbana, Illinois: The National Council of Teachers of English.

Engber, Cheryl. 1995. The relationship of lexical proficiency to the quality of ESL compositions. *Journal of Second Language Writing* 4(2). 139–155.

Enright, Mary and Thomas Quinlan. 2010. Using e-rater® to score essays written by English language learners: A complement to human judgement. *Language Testing* 27(3). 317–334.

Ferris, Dana. 1994. Lexical and syntactic features of ESL writing by students at different levels of L2 proficiency. *TESOL Quarterly* 28(2). 414–420.

Ferris, Dana. 2002. *Treatment of error in second language student writing*. Ann Arbor, MI: University of Michigan Press.

Ferris, Dana, Jeffrey Brown, Hsiang Liu, and M. Eguenia. 2011. Responding to L2 students in college writing classes: Teacher perspectives. *TESOL Quarterly* 45(2). 207–234.

Fulcher, Glenn. 2003. *Testing second language speaking*. Harlow, UK: Pearson Education.

Gebril, Atta. 2009. Score generalizability of academic writing tasks: Does one test method fit it all? *Language Testing* 26(4). 507–531.

Ginther, April and Leslie Grant. 1996. *A review of the academic needs of native English-speaking college students in the United States*. Educational Testing Service. TOEFL Monograph Series MS-1.

Grant, Leslie and April Ginther. 2000. Using computer-tagged linguistic features to describe L2 writing differences. *Journal of Second Language Writing* 9. 123–145.

Guo, Liang. 2011. Product and process in TOEFL iBT independent and integrated writing tasks: a validation study. Unpublished doctoral dissertation, Georgia State University.

Hamp-Lyons, Liz. 1990. Second language writing: Assessment issues. In Barbara Kroll (ed.) *Second language writing: Research insights for the classroom*, 69–87. Cambridge: CUP.

Hamp-Lyons, Liz. 1991. *Assessing second language writing in academic contexts*. Norwood, NJ: Ablex.

Hamp-Lyons, Liz. 1991. Scoring procedures for ESL contexts. In Liz Hamp-Lyons (ed.), *Assessing second language writing in academic contexts*. Norwood, NJ: Ablex.

Hamp-Lyons, Liz. 1997. Exploring bias in essay tests. In Carol Severino, Juan Guerra, and Johnnella Butler (eds.), *Writing in multicultural settings* (Vol. 5), 51–66. New York: Modern Language Association of America.

Hamp-Lyons, Liz. 2002. The scope of writing assessment. *Assessing writing* 8(1). 5–16.

Hamp-Lyons, Liz and William Condon. 2000. *Assessing the portfolio: Principles for practice, theory, and research*. Hampton Press.

Hayes, John and Linda Flower. 1980. Identifying the organization of writing processes. In Lee Gregg and Erwin Steinberg (eds.), *Cognitive processes in writing*, 31–50. Hillsdale, NJ: Lawrence Erlbaum Associates.

Hinkel, Eli. 2011. What research on second language writing tells us and what it doesn't. In Eli Hinkel (ed.), *Handbook of Research in Second Language Teaching and Learning* 2, 523–538. New York: Routledge.

Hirvela, Alan. 2011. Writing to learn in content areas: Research insights. In Rosa M. Manchón. *Learning-to-write and writing-to-learn in an additional language*, 37–59. Amsterdam: John Benjamins.

Horowitz, Daniel. 1986. What professors actually require: Academic tasks for the ESL classroom. *TESOL Quarterly* 20(3). 445–462.

Huang, Jinyan. 2012. Using generalizability theory to examine the accuracy and validity of large-scale ESL writing assessment. *Assessing Writing* 17(3). 123–139.

Hughes, Arthur. 1989. *Testing for language teachers*. Cambridge/New York: Cambridge University Press.

Huhta, Ari, Paula Kalaja, and Anne Pitkänen-Huhta. 2006. Discursive construction of a high-stakes test: The many faces of a test-taker. *Language Testing* 23(3). 326–350.

Huot, Brian. 1990a. The literature of direct writing assessment: major concerns and prevailing trends. *Review of Educational Research* 60(2). 237–263.

Huot, Brian. 1990b. Reliability, validity, and holistic scoring: What we know and what we need to know. *College Composition and Communication* 41(2). 201–213.

Hyland, Theresa. 2009. Drawing a line in the sand: Identifying the borderzone between self and other in EL1 and EL2 citation practices. *Assessing Writing* 14(1). 62–74.

Hyland, Ken and Fiona Hyland. 2006. *Feedback in second language writing: Contexts and issues*. Cambridge: Cambridge University Press.

Hymes, Dell. 1972. On communicative competence. In J. B. Pride and Janet Holmes (eds.), *Sociolinguistics: Selected readings*, 269–293. Harmondsworth: Penguin.

Institute for International Education. 2012. Fast Facts. Retrieved 4/1/2013 from http://www.opendoors.iienetwork.org/

Inoue, Asao and Mya Poe (eds.). 2012. *Race and writing assessment. Studies in composition and rhetoric. Volume 7.* New York: Peter Lang.

Jacobs, Holly, Stephen Zinkgraf, Deanna Wormuth, V. Faye Hartfield, and Jane Hughey. 1981. *Testing ESL composition: A practical approach*. Rowley, MA: Newbury House.

Jang, Eunice, Maryam Wagner, and Saskia Stille. 2011. Issues and challenges in using English proficiency descriptor scales for assessing school-aged English language learners. University of Cambridge ESOL Examination *Editorial notes* 15(4). 8.

Jarvis, Scott. 2002. Short texts, best-fitting curves and new measures of lexical diversity. *Language Testing* 19. 57–84

Jarvis, Scott, Leslie Grant, Dawn Bikowski, and Dana Ferris. 2003. Exploring multiple profiles of highly rated learner compositions. *Journal of Second Language Writing* 12(4). 377–403.

Johnson, David and Lewis VanBrackle. 2012. Linguistic discrimination in writing assessment: How raters react to African American "errors," ESL errors, and standard English errors on a state-mandated writing exam. *Assessing Writing* 17(1). 35–54.

Johnson, Keith and Keith Morrow. 1981. *Communication in the classroom: Applications and methods for a communicative approach*. New York: Longman.

Kane, Michael. 2002. Validating high-stakes testing programs. *Educational Measurement: Issues and Practices* 21(1). 31–41.

Kanno, Yasuko and Jennifer Cromley. 2013. English language learners' access to and attainment in postsecondary education. *TESOL Quarterly* 41(1). 89–121.

Knoch, Ute. 2009. Diagnostic assessment of writing: A comparison of two rating scales. *Language Testing* 26(2). 275–304.

Kobayashi, Hiroe and Carol Rinnert. 1996. Factors affecting composition evaluation in an EFL context: Cultural rhetorical pattern and readers' background. *Language Learning* 46(3). 397–433.

Kroll, Barbara. 1979. A survey of the writing needs of foreign and American College Freshmen. *English Language Teaching Journal* 33(3). 219–227.

Lado, Robert. 1961. *Language testing: The construction and use of foreign language tests. A teacher's book.* London: Longman.

Lee, H. K. 2008. The relationship between writers' perceptions and their performance on a field-specific writing test. *Assessing Writing*, 13(2). 93–110.

Lee, Hee-Kyung and Carolyn Anderson. 2007. Validity and topic generality of a writing performance test. *Language testing* 24(3). 307–330.

Leith, Dick. 1997. *"A" Social History of English.* (2nd edition). London: Routledge.

Leki, Ilona. 2001. Hearing voices: L2 students' experiences in L2 writing courses. In Tony Silva and Paul K, Matsuda (eds.), *On second language writing*, 17–28. Mahwah, NJ: Lawrence Erlbaum.

Leki, Ilona and Joan G. Carson. 1994. Students' perceptions of EAP writing instruction and writing needs across the disciplines. TESOL Quarterly 28(1). 81–101.

Leki, Ilona, Alister Cumming, and Tony Silva. 2008. *A synthesis of research on second language writing in English.* New York: Routledge.

Lim, Gad. 2011. Meeting multiple validation requirements in rating scale development. Paper presented at AAAL, Ann Arbor, Michigan.

Linacre, John and Benjamin Wright. 2002. Construction of measures from many-facet data. *Journal of Applied Measurement* 3(4). 486–512.

Lumley, Tom. 2005. *Assessing second language writing: The rater's perspective* (Vol. 3). Frankfurt am Main: Peter Lang.

Matsuda, Paul. 2005. Historical inquiry in second language writing. In Paul Matsuda and Tony Silva (eds.). *Second language writing research: Perspectives on the process of knowledge construction*, 33–46. Mahwah, NJ: Lawrence Erlbaum.

McNamara, Tim. 1996. *Measuring second language performance.* London: Longman.

McNamara, Tim. 2000. *Language testing*: OUP Oxford.

Mendelsohn, David and Alister Cumming. 1987. Professor's ratings of language use and rhetorical organizations in ESL compositions. *TESL Canada Journal* 5(1). 09–26.

Morrow, Keith. 1979. Communicative language testing: Revolution or evolution. In Christopher Brumfit and Keith Johnson (eds.), *The communicative approach to language teaching*, 143–157. Oxford: Oxford University Press.

Nation, Paul. 1988. *Word lists.* Victoria: University of Wellington Press.

Pittam, Gail, James Elander, Joane Lusher, Pauline Fox, and Nicola Payne. 2009. Student beliefs and attitudes about authorial identity in academic writing. [Article]. *Studies in Higher Education* 34(2). 153–170.

Plakans, Lia. 2008. Comparing composing processes in writing-only and reading-to-write test tasks. *Assessing Writing* 13(2). 111–129.

Plakans, Lia and Atta Gebril. 2012. A close investigation into source use in integrated second language writing tasks. *Assessing Writing* 17(1). 18–34.

Polio, Charlene and Margo Glew. 1996. ESL writing assessment prompts: How students choose. *Journal of Second Language Writing* 5(1). 35–49.

Powers, Donald, Mary Fowles, M., Marisa Farnum, and Paul Ramsey. 1994. Will they think less of my handwritten essay if others word process theirs? Effects on essay scores of intermingling handwritten and word-processed essays. *Journal of Educational Measurement* 31(3). 220–233.

Powers, Donald and Mary Fowles. 1998. Test takers' judgments about GRE writing test prompts. ETS Research Report 98–36. Princeton, NJ: Educational Testing Service.

Purves, Alan. 1992. *The IEA study of written composition II: Education and performance in fourteen countries.* Oxford, UK: Pergamon Press.

Raimes, Ann. 1985. What unskilled ESL students do as they write: A classroom study of composing. *TESOL Quarterly* 19(2). 229–258.

Rea-Dickins, Pauline. 1997. So, why do we need relationships with stakeholders in language testing? A view from the UK. *Language Testing* 14(3). 304–314.

Schaefer, Edward. 2008. Rater bias patterns in an EFL writing assessment. *Language Testing* 25(4). 465–493.

Schoonen, Rob. 2005. Generalizability of writing scores: an application of structural equation modeling. *Language Testing* 22(1). 1–30.

Shaw, Stuart and Cyril Weir. 2007. *Examining writing: Research and practice in assessing second language writing* (Vol. 26). Cambridge: Cambridge University Press.

Shohamy, Elana. 2011. Assessing multilingual competencies: Adopting construct valid assessment policies. *The Modern Language Journal* 95(3). 418–429.

Swales, John. 1990. *Genre analysis: English in academic and research settings*. Cambridge: Cambridge University Press.

Swales, John. 2004. Research Genres: Exploration and Application. Cambridge: Cambridge University Press

Turner, Carolyn and John Upshur. 2002. Rating scales derived from student samples: Effects of the scale maker and the student sample on scale content and student scores. *TESOL Quarterly* 36(1). 49–70.

Ware, Paige. 2011. Computer-Generated feedback on student writing. *TESOL Quarterly* 45(4). 769–774.

Warschauer, Mark. 2010. Invited commentary: new tools for teaching writing. *Language Learning and Technology* 14(1). 3–8.

Weigle, Sara. 1998. Using FACETS to model rater training effects. *Language Testing* 15(2). 263–287.

Weigle, Sara. 2002. *Assessing Writing*. Cambridge: Cambridge University Press

Weigle, Sara. 2012. English language learners and automated scoring of essays: Critical considerations. *Assessing Writing* 18(1). 85–99.

Weigle, Sara and Megan Montee. 2012. Raters' perceptions of textual borrowing in integrated writing tasks. In Marion Tillema, Elke Van Steendam, Gert Rijlaarsdam and Huub van den Bergh (eds.) *Measuring writing: Recent insights into theory, methodology and practices*, 117–151. Bingley, UK: Emerald Books.

Weigle, Sara and Keisha Parker, 2012. Source text writing in an integrated reading/writing assessment. *Journal of Second Language Writing* 21(2). 118–133.

Weir, Cyril. 2005. *Language testing and validation*. Houndmills, Basingstoke: Palgrave Macmillan.

White, Edward. 1985. *Teaching and assessing writing: Recent advances in understanding, evaluating and improving student performance* (1st ed.). San Francisco: Jossey-Bass.

White, Edward. 1994. *Teaching and assessing writing: Recent advances in understanding, evaluating and improving student performance* (2nd ed.). San Francisco: Jossey-Bass.

Yancey, Kathleen. 1992. *Portfolios in the writing classroom: An introduction*. Urbana, IL: National Council of Teachers of English.

Yancey, Kathleen. 1999. Looking back as we look forward: Historicizing writing assessment. *College Composition and Communication* 50(3). 483–503.

Zamel, Vivian. 1983. The composing processes of advanced ESL students: Six case studies. *TESOL Quarterly* 17. 165–187.

Zheng, Ying and Liying Cheng. 2008. College English Test (CET) in China. *Language Testing* 25(3). 408–417.

V. Researching writing

Christine Pearson Casanave
23 Qualitative inquiry in L2 writing

1 Introduction

In this chapter I review how qualitative L2 writing research has been conducted. The emphasis is on English as a second or foreign language (ESL/EFL) because much L2 writing research concerns English. Given the extent of this work and the fact that the division between qualitative and quantitative studies is often fuzzy, I cannot be comprehensive in my coverage, but will use my discussion of particular studies to exemplify several types of qualitative work.

Throughout the history of L2 writing, research has built on work in first language writing, even though English language learners have often been neglected in L1 studies (Matsuda 1998). Although a good case has been made for distinctions in language proficiency, rhetorical conventions, and needs (Silva 1993), a separate treatment of L2 writing runs the risk of distancing two subfields that really ought to be brought together or at least expanded into a symbiotic model (Matsuda 1998). Some of what I discuss will thus inevitably pertain to both L1 and L2 writing.

1.1 What is qualitative inquiry in L2 writing?

Interest in qualitative inquiry in L2 writing is growing. Many researchers appreciate its descriptive and explanatory goals, understanding the limitations of experimental and interventionist approaches in writing research. Given the complexity of qualitative inquiry and continued debates about its status (e.g., Atkinson and Delamont 2006; St. Pierre and Roulston 2006) and about the philosophical assumptions underlying writing research (Silva 2005), it is challenging to characterize it accurately. From its earliest incarnations, L2 writing research has drawn on data that can be both quantified and described qualitatively such as observations, questionnaires, interviews, think-aloud techniques, and some kinds of text analysis. Although used widely, holistic descriptions and narratives – qualitative in essence – have sometimes been wrongly maligned as unscientific and therefore unworthy as legitimate L2 writing research. What criteria, then, characterize qualitative inquiry in L2 writing?

In his review of trends in qualitative research in language teaching, Richards (2009: 149) proposed the following criteria: The study must be locally situated under natural conditions; participant-oriented; holistic rather than a study of isolated aspects of a phenomenon; and inductive, resulting from immersion in a setting. I add the importance of transparency of researcher roles, of time spent in a setting with participants, of an interpretive not just fact-finding stance, of particularity, and of connectivity to readers (e.g., through clarity and relevance of detail). These criteria do not exclude the use of numbers, and many studies adopt a mixed method approach (not covered in this review). However, I distinguish between ethnography and other naturalistic techniques: Ethnography by its very nature tends to follow the criteria laid out for qualitative inquiry, but is steeped in anthropological traditions that include long-term immersion and observation in particular (cultural) settings and fundamentally interpretive stances. Many qualitative studies are not fully ethnographic in this sense because they focus on limited aspects of a question.

In the remainder of this chapter I review some early qualitative work in L2 writing. In section 3, I summarize some exemplary studies of different types. I conclude by looking at several areas of potential change and growth in coming years.

2 Historical and theoretical background

Multiple kinds of qualitative research always exist concurrently, making it difficult to pinpoint precisely when qualitative inquiry in L2 writing began. One way is to situate its beginning in L1 composition and rhetoric – often a model for later L2 studies. In general we can identify a shift from early empirical and theoretical interest in cognitive and expressive processes, to growing (and continued) emphasis on the dynamic socially influenced nature of writing: genre theory (Bazerman 1994; Bhatia 1993; Swales 1990); "situated" approaches (Atkinson 2005; Barton, Hamilton, and Ivanič 2000); and Vygotskian-influenced sociocultural theories such as Legitimate Peripheral Participation (LPP), Communities of Practice (Lave and Wenger 1991; Wenger 1998), and activity theory (Engeström 1999). I review just a few representative examples of some of the earlier work.

2.1 The shift from product to process

In the 1970s and 1980s, studies of writing processes, not products, by L1 composition scholars (Emig 1971, 1977; Flower and Hayes 1981) quickly influenced early L2 writing research, especially through the work of Zamel (1982, 1983). Emig (1971) used a case study approach and think-aloud protocols – transcripts made from writers' audiorecorded thought processes as they wrote – to study the composing processes of twelfth-grade students. She later argued for doing writing research beyond the positivistic paradigm, which she did not find suitable for many kinds of writing research (Emig 1982). A decade after Emig's original study, Flower and Hayes (1981) also used think-aloud techniques, but with data from expert L1 adult writers. From the resulting transcripts (protocols) they constructed a still influential theory of the composing process that identified the nonlinear, recursive, and discovery-oriented nature of L1 composing.

Inspired by this and other L1 work, Zamel (1982, 1983) studied the composing processes of advanced ESL writers. She believed that these writers would compose similarly to L1 writers as described by Flower and Hayes, but reasoned that the think-aloud technique might distract them from the work of composing. She thus opted to interview her students about their composing (1982) or to observe them closely as they composed an essay from readings, followed by retrospective interviews (1983). She identified discovery-oriented processes like those for L1 writers. However, what is striking by current standards about these early studies is what is missing. There is little attention to conceptual frameworks beyond the assumed cognitive process model, and many details are absent that today would be considered essential in a qualitative research report. For instance, we know little about Zamel herself, almost nothing about how the data were collected and analyzed, and little about individual writers. Additionally, from the mid-1980s on, the rather uniform model of writing processes, which implied that all expert writers follow the same processes regardless of goal or personal style, was challenged (Horowitz 1986; Reid 1984).

A second type of early study concerns L2 writers' cognitive and linguistic development as reported in early journal writing studies in multilingual classrooms (Peyton and Staton 1993, among others; see the review in Casanave 2011). Dialogue journal research used the ongoing written dialogues between teachers and young L1 and L2 students to show how linguistic and cognitive development resulted from regular writing (sometimes quantified; Reed 1993; Staton 1993) and, using more holistic analyses, to highlight diversity among older L2 writers (Lucas 1992). In these studies, the dialogue journal activity was both a pedagogical tool and a source of written data for analysis that could show the cognitive and expressive benefits of regular uninstructed writing.

Another influential and still interesting process-oriented study of L2 literacy development is Edelsky's (1982, 1986) year-long investigation of children's writing in a bilingual program, with data collected from ongoing classroom activities. Using a whole-language framework that presumes that language develops through learners' engagement in natural, meaningful activities rather than from piecemeal instruction, Edelsky displayed drawings and text-based images made by children in English and Spanish. We see few studies of young children's development of bilingual literacy, but this one is a nice example of both a linguistic and contextual analysis with evidence from images so common to young children's developing literacy. Maturation over time is indeed obvious.

This early work revealed the connection between writing and learning. But a methodological dilemma still exists today – that of figuring out ways to "see" the invisible cognitive processes of learning, thinking, and composing without altering the process itself.

2.2 A sociocognitive-sociocultural-contextual shift

In the 1980s and early 1990s, influenced by Western scholars in anthropology, education, and sociolinguistics (e.g., Gee 1990; Heath 1983; Street 1984) and by a social turn in SLA (Atkinson 2002; Block 2003; Firth and Wagner 1997), some writing researchers began to shift attention away from cognitive processes and linguistic development to work that was more situated in writers' homes, schools, and communities (Schultz 2006).

One example is Johns's (1991) qualitative study of Luc, a Vietnamese biology student who passed all his science courses in an American university, but could not pass his English competency exam. From this semester-long, multi-data, naturalistic study, Johns raised important questions about the form and purpose of written competency exams. But Prior's early and still exemplary work (1991, 1994, 1995a, 1995b) represents perhaps the most complexly situated studies of L1 and L2 academic writing. Using frameworks inspired by sociohistoric views of disciplinary writing, Prior observed seminars over full semesters in a US university and followed the trajectories of particular pieces of writing as they evolved through interactions among particular students, professors, and texts. These studies demonstrate the inherent contextual complexity of disciplinary writing.

However, in the earliest issues of the L2 writing field's flagship journal, the *Journal of Second Language Writing*, we do not see many exclusively qualitative studies that are fully contextualized or theorized in ways they would be later. Works that are labeled "naturalistic case studies" (e.g., Cumming 1992) were naturalistic in the sense that no tasks were imposed. Other early studies also featured some techniques usually considered qualitative, such as observations and interviews, which were then treated quantitatively through coding and counting (e.g., Nelson and Murphy 1992; Pennington and So 1993). Some focused case studies began to appear (e.g., Currie 1993; Severino 1993) that fit more closely within a social-contextual framework. In general, as studies of writers and teachers shifted toward the social, findings reflected increased diversity and complexity in our understanding of L2 writers, writing processes, and pedagogy.

In short, some early studies lack the holism, detail, transparency, and theoretical grounding of later qualitative work. Nevertheless, Prior (1991: 304) concluded what has now become a commonplace understanding of L1 and L2 academic writing (e.g., Ramanathan and Atkinson 1999), namely that "written, academic assignments are complex and socially situated," and are interpreted by writers in complex ways through interactions with people, tasks, and personal goals.

3 Types of qualitative inquiry in L2 writing

My groupings in this section suggest different focuses: studies of writers' development; studies emphasizing writers' interactions with others; text-oriented studies; and studies involving digital literacy practices. Within these groupings, some are long term and others quite short. Overlaps and other possible groupings will be evident. I discuss just a few examples of each type.

3.1 Studies of writer development

Studies of development, including ethnographies, are quite rare in L2 writing research, mostly because they are so time-consuming and labor intensive. Other than Blanton (1998), who traveled to Morocco to do her work, the examples below were carried out by researchers who conducted research in their own universities and who produced book-length reports or major journal articles (cf. long-term work on literacy practices and identities done in the UK, e.g., Barton and Hamilton 1998, Ivanic 1998).

I include Blanton (1998, reissued in 2007) because her book-length study of the literacy learning experiences of young multilingual Moroccan children is a rare study of L2 children's literacy learning in a field full of studies of university students (see Belcher 2012: 139–141 on younger learners). Though not heavily theorized, the study provides novelistic, richly detailed, and contextualized examples of ethnographic-style research in one international school in Morocco. Blanton spent a year there, living with teachers and students, and documenting the English language reading and writing activities of some very young children from numerous countries, all of whom were already bi-or multilingual (French, Arabic, others). Among other descriptive data, she provided enough visual examples of several children's lettered drawings, arranged chronologically over the school year, so that we can see change over time in the "writing." The visual record of literacy development is powerful.

Another developmental study (Mlynarczyk 1998) was framed with theories of "inner speech" and expressive language, inspired by Vygotsky and Britton, and of reflection (Schön 1983). Mlynarczyk studied the journal writing of two US university ESL writing classes for a semester, hoping to help focal students improve their English and their abilities to use writing to reflect on readings and on self. The book includes rich details about herself, the context of the school and classes, her five focal students from different countries, and their journal writing. Her data were classically qualitative – a field log; students' weekly journal entries and her responses; recordings, transcriptions, and field notes of class segments and student conferences; and retrospective interviews with the students, analyzed descriptively and holistically. Mlynarczyk concluded by revising her stereotyped assumptions about journal writing, gender, and cultural background and by confirming the potential of journal writing as a pedagogical tool.

A small group of L1 and L2 adult students struggling with their US college writing assignments were featured in Sternglass (1997). She followed their academic development throughout their undergraduate study (six years) to show how complex reasoning and learning were aided by writing. Sternglass was an insider to this project, and knew the students well, but had a limited data set that included primarily notes from interviews and conversations (rather than recordings) and samples of students' writing. She showed the central role that writing played in the students' academic lives and, importantly, the many personal factors outside the conventional academic context that influenced their progress (cf. Leki 2007).

Two other book-length studies of US university students that adopted social and situated frameworks are Leki's (2007) case studies of undergraduate ESL students and Tardy's (2009) genre-framed case studies of graduate students, both documenting how students dealt with writing requirements in their writing and subject matter classes. Leki's project investigated whether ESL writing courses actually served the purpose of aiding students with their subject matter writing. Leki followed four students for five years from their ESL classes into their disciplinary programs as they tried to make sense of very diverse writing assignments. With data that included observations, interviews with students and instructors, email, documents, recordings from writing center conferences, and journal entries, she documented not only writing experiences but also broader personal and social contexts of the students' academic literacy practices. Data excerpts are extensive, lending credibility to her finding that writing tasks varied widely across disciplines, differed greatly from ESL writing requirements, and were handled by students in strategically different ways. For her part, Tardy (2009) used a version of genre theory in which social, community, and textual aspects of disciplinary knowledge building were highlighted. From observations, interviews, text analyses, and professors' feedback over one to two years she revealed four L2 graduate students' conflicted relations with and gradual mastery of various disciplinary genres. Numerous text excerpts, in addition to interview data and her own transparent role, are especially valuable in this genre-based project, which like Leki's raises questions about the function of writing classes.

Other case studies of writer development include Spack's (1997) study of "Yuko," Gentil's (2005) study of three bilingual Francophone academics in Canada, and some of my own work. Spack's case study of a single writer followed Yuko, a fearful Japanese undergraduate student in Spack's US ESL class, into her subject matter classes, where Yuko was struggling to survive. Over a three-year period Spack talked to Yuko regularly, collected assignments and syllabuses from subject matter classes, and looked at drafts of her papers and at teachers' comments and evaluations. Spack's main focus was on Yuko as an evolving reader-writer who eventually found a way to take some ownership of her writing and develop some strategic confidence, as can be seen in numerous interview and essay excerpts. Spack did not frame her study theoretically, but used her insider local knowledge at her own university to trace and explicate Yuko's development as a writer of English.

In a rare study of biliteracy, Gentil (2005), bilingual in French and English, examined the choices over two and half years made by three French-speaking university students in Québec to write in English or French. His study is heavily theorized (a model of biliteracy, Bourdieu's critical literacy, and philosophical hermeneutics) and data-rich. Excerpts from interviews and texts are presented in both

French and English to show individual students' diverse responses to pressures to write in English yet remain committed to French.

Some of my own work has focused on longitudinal qualitative case studies of particular writers in the US and Japan. I have focused on writers' understandings and activities as they wrote high stakes pieces over time such as graduate core course assignments (Casanave 1995), doctoral dissertations (Casanave 2010), or early career-building publications (Casanave 1998). In all cases, I came to know the participants well, read drafts of their writing, and employed thematic analyses of frequent interviews and emails to learn about the writers as people – their attitudes, struggles, strategies, and decisions. In addition to drawing on work from writing in the disciplines, I used frameworks that were social and participatory (e.g., Lave and Wenger 1991; Wenger 1998), a common choice for qualitative inquiry in the 1990s and 2000s. I attempted to tell compelling stories of individual writers' journeys without pretending to uncover fixed truths. Finally, I was transparent about my role in the various projects. However, our shared language was always English, a potential weakness of qualitative inquiry in L2 scholarship.

In all cases, the advantage of longitudinal qualitative studies of L2 writers is that we come to know deeply the contexts, the participants, and their practices in ways that reveal change over time from a multitude of data sources and perspectives. The time required for these projects, as well as the insider expertise, make such work challenging in L2 writing research, but all the more valuable when done well.

3.2 Studies of writers' interactions with others

Some qualitative case studies of L2 writers feature interactions with others, such as professors, mentors, and reviewers or editors. Texts are always present in these studies but not always analyzed. These studies highlight the negotiated and interactive nature of undergraduate, graduate, and professional writing. They raise questions about the roles of mentors, professors, and editors in helping L2 writers complete high stakes work and about the dominance of English in academic and research writing.

In a well-known study of mentoring, Belcher (1994), for example, used a framework of LPP (Lave and Wenger 1991) in her naturalistic case study of three doctoral students in her 10-week long dissertation writing class (two males from China, one female from Korea). She investigated the connection between different mentoring experiences and success in dissertation writing. She met with each student weekly to discuss their drafts and their advisors' responses and also met twice with the advisors. The Korean female, with a supportive, involved female mentor, was the only successful dissertation writer of the three. Belcher described the relationship as "dialogic," in contrast to the more hierarchical relationship between the two Chinese students and their male advisors (p. 31). The less successful students differed from their advisors in how they understood the research community, research goals, and expectations of readers. Similar to the findings of Blakeslee (1997) and Li (2012), the novices were not always given responsibilities to develop their own ways of fully participating in their research communities.

A welcomed development is that research is increasingly conducted by bilingual researchers, often in non-Anglophone settings. I discuss briefly a series of case studies by Y. Li that document the difficult, interactive struggles by mainland Chinese scientists to fulfill requirements to write from sources and publish in English. The first project (2005) was long term, and subsequent case studies (Li. 2006a, 2006b, 2007, 2012) have followed the earlier pattern of bilingual data collection including multiple written, oral, and electronic data sources from individual participants from different science fields. Drawing on frames of disciplinary writing, expert-novice, mentoring, and activity theory, Li has combined interviews in Chinese with text analyses, allowing readers to see how the Chinese scientists interact with colleagues, professors, and source material to produce texts for publication in English. In some cases, the novice scientists' texts revealed instances of inappropriate textual borrowing. In the 2012 study, Li was interested in a professor's responses to passages from two "extreme cases" of copying based on plagiarism software analyses she did of the students' writing (40–44 % overlap) (p. 62). From text-based interviews with the professor using original and revised copies of student drafts, Li learned that the professor routinely rewrote his students' papers without providing instruction in writing for publication.

Space prevents me from discussing some other important studies of L2 writers' interactions with others as they write for publication, such as Blakeslee's (1997) study of a difficult mentoring relationship between an Algerian graduate student in physics and his professor and the work by Lillis and Curry (2006, 2010) with European scholars and their literacy brokers publishing in English and local languages. These studies confirm other findings, that in spite of interactions with professors and literacy brokers, pressure to publish scholarly writing in English causes great hardship for many international scholars.

To conclude this section, I note that few studies have been done of L2 writers learning to write in languages other than English. This paucity is regrettable because it contributes to accusations of ethnocentrism in L2 writing research. Haneda's (2004, 2005) research on several Canadian university students learning to write in Japanese can be seen as a model for future qualitative studies on nonEnglish literacy acquisition, as can her study of two adolescent Japanese sojourners' outside-of school literacy activities in both English and Japanese (Haneda and Monobe 2009). Jia's (2009) study of adolescent heritage students' acquisition of Mandarin, and McCarthey, Guo, and Cummins's (2005) two-year study of five elementary school children learning English and Mandarin are other examples. In these studies, the researchers used multiple oral and written data sources over time, revealing that interactions with others (teachers, parents, tutors) played a large role in the students' attitudes and activities.

3.3 Text-oriented qualitative studies

In both L1 and L2 writing research, analyses of texts are common, whether of students' developing texts and academic identities (Ivanic 1998), or the polished writing of professionals (Hyland 2000, 2009). However, exclusively text-oriented qualitative studies are rare.

One such study concerns the construction of arguments from an intercultural rhetoric perspective – Bloch's (2004) analysis of the blog postings of Chinese students. Bloch wished to demonstrate "how non-native English speakers can take control of the discourse on the Internet for their own purposes even when having to write in a second language" (p. 68). He analyzed 153 L2 English Usenet postings on responses of international Chinese students to a CBS (US) report by Connie Chung about potential Chinese spies among Chinese international students. Bloch reviewed all postings for themes and categories, several of which reflected the possible influence of traditional Chinese rhetorical strategies. Following the requirements of well-done qualitative inquiry, Bloch described the context for the postings in some detail, including the controversy over reporter Connie Chung's stance. He also displayed numerous excerpts from the students' postings – twenty-nine excerpts in all.

I conclude this section with brief mention of Sun and Chang's (2012) semester-long case study of the blog posts of seven TESOL graduate students in Taiwan, because it points toward a future of increased bilingual and text-based online research in L2 writing. In this study, the authors analyzed 168 postings the students made as part of a required assignment. The authors coded for the topics students blogged about, and for evidence of accumulation of knowledge and of identities as academic writers. Important for a study of bilingual digital literacy practices (see next section) is that given the choice whether to post in Chinese or English, the students posted in Chinese 67 % of the time.

Future work on L2 writing will surely include more bilingual electronic data than in the past. It is also evident that text-oriented data do not always have to be treated quantitatively but can lend themselves to more naturalistic and holistic treatment.

3.4 Digital literacies

Studies of L2 writers' digital literacy experiences are growing increasingly common, and point the way toward future research, especially of young Internet-savvy L2 writers. Most of this work focuses on English language activities, but several studies of adolescent online practices include writing in L1s as well. Much of it explores the benefits of digital literacy activities for second language acquisition and EAP (e.g., Chun 2012) and identity (McLean 2010, 2012). I review a few of these to demonstrate what kinds of work have been done.

As an insider to the Chinese immigrant community, Lam (2000, 2004, 2006) was naturally drawn to research that would allow her some insider and bilingual status. Her well-known 2000 study of "Almon," a Hong Kong immigrant teenager in California, showed how an unhappy teenager recreated his identity by using extensive English writing to forge Internet connections with other young people around the world about his favorite topic, Japanese pop culture. In her 2004 and 2006 articles, Lam continued her investigations of the literacy practices of several Hong Kong immigrant adolescents and the theme of refashioning identities via networked communication. Lam calls her approach a "multisite or connective ethnographic methodology" in which she was a participant in the urban high school site and also on the electronic sites over many months. Her data consisted of participant observation with field notes, multiple interviews with each student, and document analysis (Lam 2006: 176), analyzed inductively. Lam's work has alerted us to the growing importance of understanding L2 students' multiple textual identities created electronically.

In another example of adolescents' out-of-school digital literacy activities, Black (2005, 2009) focused exclusively on a fan fiction website. In the 2005 study, she spent a year looking at postings on a Japanese *anime* site where many L2 adolescent girls living in the United States contributed their fiction in English. In a later project, framed with theories of globalization, she joined a site and for three years spent many hours a week participating. In typical literacy activities on this site, members both contributed stories and reviewed the contributions of others. Unusual (but bound to become more common) is Black's exclusively online connections with her three case study students (three girls, from the Philippines, mainland China, and a Taiwanese girl living in Canada). Having never met her participants in person, she calls this work an "online form of ethnographic research" (Black 2009: 405).

Finally, some important work on adolescents' digital literacies has been conducted by Yi in the United States within a multimedia social framework (Barton and Hamilton 1998; Cope and Kalantzis 2000). Yi, a bilingual insider, traced the Korean and English digital literacy activities of a group of Korean immigrant adolescents over a year or more (2005, 2007, 2008, 2009, 2010; Yi and Hirvela 2010) to learn how they used both languages in their out-of-school digital activities. She found incredible productivity in both languages, including diaries, poems, stories, chat, and "relay writing." Her data included regular interviews over many months in English and Korean, visits to the website, field notes, and close observation of postings. Typical of complex qualitative research, she searched for key words and themes in all these data, and regularly checked her interpretations with the focal participants. She was transparent about her multiple roles with the teenagers, as appropriate in carefully done qualitative reporting. Educators who work with L2 adolescents will be impressed by the variety and creativity of writing done by these students.

4 Looking ahead

Qualitative inquiry in L2 writing and literacy studies holds great promise in helping scholars understand the intricacies of people's L2 literacy practices – texts, contexts, people, and activities. The importance of situatedness, complexity, and credibility – established from time in field, multiple data sources, and participants' perspectives – will continue. It is likely that case study, longitudinal work, and narrative research will be well suited to such inquiry in the future. My main worry is that the pressure on novice scholars to publish quickly in English, in prestigious high-impact journals, will result in work that privileges speed and superficiality over depth. That said, I comment below on several specific areas of potential change and development.

4.1 (Re)Defining writing

A fundamental imperative for the future is the need to reconsider what we mean by "writing" to encompass literacy and multimodality more broadly, in and out of school. Some time ago, Luke (2000: 81) noted that traditional print literacy skills no longer serve us in a world inundated with global information and electronic multimodal networks. Gee (2008) as well has influenced our views of discourse with his concept of big D discourses – those that include attitudes, beliefs, ideologies, and practices, as has the work of Street (1995). L2 writers' visual, print, and electronic text-based literacy practices will be the focus of inquiry and help us redefine what we mean by "writing" (Cope and Kalantzis 2012; Hawisher, Selfe, Guo, and Liu 2006; Kress 2003).

However, will our conceptualizations of writing and literacy include all electronic interactions, from video gaming skills (Gee 2003) to brief text messaging to construction of elaborate web sites? What are the consequences for individual's learning, identities, and relationships with schools, workplaces, and professions if sustained work on single writing projects gives way to increasingly fragmented multimedia piece work? Our definition of L2 writing will continue to evolve, in part as a result of future qualitative inquiry that addresses these questions.

4.2 Relevance

With more international scholars participating in qualitative inquiry in L2 writing and literacy studies, the ever-present issue of relevance continues to grow in importance. How can scholars in (say) Taiwan or Japan make their work on L2 writers relevant to readers worldwide, usually meaning readers of English dominant journals? Gatekeepers such as journal editors and reviewers also need to ask how scholars from English dominant countries can make their work relevant to readers in important non Anglophone venues. This means reflecting critically on the relevance and ideological implications of English language scholarship worldwide (Alsagoff, McKay, Hu, and Renandya 2012; Canagarajah 2002; Lillis and Curry 2010), and finding ways to encourage studies of writing in languages other than English. Moreover, qualitative scholarship in L2 writing needs to consider the relevance of specific settings, stories, participants, and tasks (always part of well-done qualitative work) to something beyond the particulars, including connections to appropriate theories.

4.3 Types of research

Investigations of L2 writing and literacy will continue to benefit from qualitative projects such as individual case studies and narratives of diverse literacy practices (Barkhuizen 2011), and from text analyses that show change over time. However, short-term qualitative and mixed methods studies may turn out to be more practical than longitudinal in-depth studies. Such studies are arguably easier and quicker, bypassing the complex and intensive fieldwork (Atkinson and Delamont 2006) that is so fundamental to good qualitative inquiry.

Effort and commitment by novice and established scholars are thus needed in coming years to produce complex, high-quality fully qualitative work, including longitudinal studies. One shift we are likely to see as case studies accumulate is toward more meta- and cross-case analyses, in particular ones that are socially and culturally contextualized and politically and ideologically sensitive (Purcell-Gates 2007; Purcell-Gates, Perry, and Briseño 2011).

Qualitative inquiry may also be done increasingly in digital form only. Physical co-presence of researchers and L2 participants may become an option, not a requirement. Black's (2005, 2009) case studies of fan fiction writers discussed above are examples of one direction such qualitative inquiry might take, as are textual analyses of blog postings (e.g., Bloch 2004; Sun and Chang 2012, above) and qualitative corpus analyses of writing (Hyland 2000) and studies of (professional) email communication (e.g., Jensen 2009). Many studies, however, will continue to combine digital data with in-person interviews and observations of writers (e.g., Liu 2011). Some cautions are in order about issues of unequal access to technology, evidence of real benefit to writers (MacArthur 2006), and our undue infatuation with the latest electronic fads.

Finally, as past work has shown, some of the best insights into L2 literacy practices come from richly detailed longitudinal studies of writers. We may see further autobiographical and autoethnographic studies (Canagarajah 2012), narratives (Casanave 2005; Pomerantz and Kearney 2012), and first person commentaries by scholars on their writing-related activities and development (Belcher and Connor 2001; Casanave and Vandrick 2003; Connor 1999).

4.4 Types of participants, researchers, and contexts

Following models such as Yi's (above), more qualitative studies will likely be done of youth learning to write in L1s and L2s in and out of school, often with the aid of visuals (drawing, digital media) (Belcher 2012; Black 2009; Choi 2009; Christianakis 2011; Haneda and Monobe 2009; Lam and Rosario-Ramos 2009; Sze, Chapman, and Shi 2009). However, because of the convenience of the university setting and pressure to publish, many important studies of L2 literacy practices will continue to be situated in university life, in both Anglophone and non-Anglophone contexts, including studies of L2 graduate student writers (Belcher and Hirvela 2005, 2010; Casanave 2010; Paltridge and Woodrow 2012) and of L2 scholars writing for publication (Flowerdew and Li 2007, 2009; Lillis and Curry 2010). Moreover, researchers will increasingly need to be bilingual or to work on multilingual teams and to be active multiliterates who can conduct in-depth interviews, observations, and text-analyses in more than one language (Cho 2010; Fránquiz and Salinas 2011; Gentil 2011; Li, X. 1996; Li, Y. 2012; Manchón 2009, 2011, 2012; Manchón, Roca de Larios, and Murphy 2009; Yi 2010).

Interest will also grow in within-context diversity as writers traditionally labeled L1 and L2 pursue the same activities in heterogeneous settings. Additionally, reflecting Atkinson and Delamont's (2006) critiques of the ethnocentrism of qualitative inquiry in the United States, L2 writing scholars are likely to increase their attention to non-school contexts, professional writing, and issues that have political import beyond the US context.

4.5 The demise of monolingual-monocultural assumptions

Monolingual approaches (i.e., English) still linger in L2 qualitative inquiry but are gradually giving way to a less ethnocentric and more diverse perspective on global English (Alsagoff, McKay, Hu, and Renandya 2012) and on writing in languages other than English (Flowerdew and Li 2009; Lillis and Curry 2010). At the same time, greater attention is being given to English that is learned outside English-dominant settings as well as in North America, the United Kingdom, Australia, and New Zealand (Alsagoff, et al. 2011; Jin and Cortazzi 2011; Lillis and Curry 2010; Manchón 2009). Moreover, in coming years populations of writers that we study will be increasingly diverse, such that it might be difficult to separate them into tidy L1-L2 categories. This trend will affect both quantitative and qualitative studies of writing-literacy. However, problems of translation and representation remain, as do those of the credibility of participants' and researchers' accounts (hence the need for multiple data sources in multiple languages).

4.6 Improved standards for qualitative inquiry

We can also expect improved standards for qualitative inquiry in L2 writing. Compared to many earlier studies, recent work tends to be more transparent and precise about methods, theoretical assumptions, descriptive details, and researcher positionality. Although few multi-year ethnographies of writing and writers are being done (they are just too time-consuming when pressure to publish quickly is so intense), in order to truly understand the development and attitudes of L2 writers, researchers will benefit from conducting complex long-term studies of individual writers that can be judged by the thoroughness and credibility of the researching and reporting. The status of replication studies in qualitative writing research will also continue to be discussed (e.g., Casanave 2012; Porte and Richards 2012), and debates will likely continue as to the meaning of "rigor" in qualitative studies. These debates are not likely to be resolved anytime soon. It is possible that separate strands of qualitative L2 writing research will follow either a more holistic (narrative, descriptive, anthropological) path or one that lends itself more to mixed methods, including statistical analysis of interview and textual data. Additionally, as reliance on web sources grows, it is also likely that more full displays and electronic storage of participants' writing and online work in their L1s and L2s will be provided, as will original interview and written data in languages other than English.

Finally, theoretical and conceptual framing will increase in importance. It is the connections between empirical work and conceptual framing (as well as to other empirical work) that, in addition to cross-case analyses, allow generalizing across qualitative studies. One question concerns the extent to which researchers provide only lip-service to complex theoretical underpinnings, as has sometimes happened with references to various sociocultural theories, including Vygotskian concepts (Smagorinsky 2011) and concepts related to "communities of practice" (Wenger 1998). Nevertheless, qualitative inquiry in L2 writing will be increasingly embedded in historical, social, and cultural milieu that emphasize writing's dynamic and changing nature. Future scholars will need to attend to this shift both theoretically and empirically.

5 Additional sources

Casanave, Christine Pearson. 2002. *Writing games: Multicultural case studies of academic literacy practices in higher education*. Mahwah, NJ: Lawrence Erlbaum Associates.
Duff, Patricia A. 2008. *Case study research in applied linguistics*. New York: Lawrence Erlbaum Associates.
Heigham, Juanita and Robert Croker (eds.). 2009. *Qualitative research in applied linguistics: A practical introduction*. London: Palgrave MacMillan.
Hesse-Biber, Sharlene N. and Patricia Leavy. 2011. *The practice of qualitative research* (2nd ed.). Thousand Oaks, CA: Sage Publications.

Matsuda, Paul Kei and Tony Silva (eds.). 2005. *Second language writing research: Perspectives on the process of knowledge construction.* Mahwah, NJ: Lawrence Erlbaum Associates.

Paltridge, Brian. 1997. *Genre, frames, and writing in research settings.* Amsterdam: John Benjamins.

Riessman, Catherine K. 2011. What's different about narrative inquiry? Cases, categories and contexts. In David Silverman (ed.), *Qualitative research* (3rd ed.), 310–330. Thousand Oaks, CA: Sage.

Silva, Tony and Paul Kei Matsuda (eds.). 2010. *Practicing theory in second language writing.* West Lafayette, IN: Parlor Press.

Stake, Robert E. 2005. Qualitative case studies. In Norman K. Denzin and Yvonna S. Lincoln (eds.), *The Sage handbook of qualitative Research* (3rd ed.), 443–446. Thousand Oaks, CA: Sage Publications.

Temple, Bogusia and Alys Young. 2004. Qualitative research and translation dilemmas. *Qualitative Research* 4. 161–178.

6 References

Alsagoff, Lubna, Sandra L. McKay, Guangwei Hu, and Willy A. Renandya (eds.). 2012. *Principles and practices for teaching English as an international language.* London: Routledge.

Atkinson, Dwight. 2002. Toward a sociocognitive approach to second language acquisition. *Modern Language Journal* 86. 525–545.

Atkinson, Dwight. 2005. Situated qualitative research and second language writing. In Paul K. Matsuda and Tony Silva (eds.), *Second language writing research: Perspectives on the process of knowledge construction*, 49–64. Mahwah, NJ: Lawrence Erlbaum.

Atkinson, Paul and Sara Delamont. 2006. In the roiling smoke: Qualitative inquiry and contested fields. *International Journal of Qualitative Studies in Education* 19. 747–755.

Barkhuizen, Gary. 2011. Narrative knowledging in TESOL. *TESOL Quarterly* 45. 391–414.

Barton, David and Mary Hamilton. 1998. *Local literacies: Reading and writing in one community.* London: Routledge.

Barton, David, Mary Hamilton, and Roz Ivanič (eds.). 2000. *Situated literacies: Reading and writing in context.* London: Routledge.

Bazerman, Charles. 1994. Systems of genres and the enactment of social intentions. In Aviva Freedman and Peter Medway (eds.), *Genre and the New Rhetoric*, 79–101. London: Taylor and Francis.

Belcher, Diane. 1994. The apprenticeship approach to advanced academic literacy: Graduate students and their mentors. *English for Specific Purposes* 13. 23–34.

Belcher, Diane. 2012. Considering what we know and need to know about second language writing. *Applied Linguistics Review* 3. 131–150.

Belcher, Diane and Ulla Connor (eds.). 2001. *Reflections on multiliterate lives.* Clevedon: Multilingual Matters.

Belcher, Diane and Alan Hirvela. 2005. Writing the qualitative dissertation: What motivates and sustains commitment to a fuzzy genre? *Journal of English for Academic Purposes* 4. 187–205.

Belcher, Diane and Alan Hirvela. 2010. "Do I need a theoretical framework?" Doctoral students' perspectives on the role of theory in dissertation research and writing. In Tony Silva and Paul Kei Matsuda (eds.), *Practicing theory in second language writing*, 263–284. West Lafayette, IN: Parlor Press.

Bhatia, Vijay K. 1993. *Analysing genre: Language use in professional settings.* London: Longman.

Black, Rebecca W. 2005. Access and affiliation: The literacy and composition practices of English-language learners in an online fanfiction community. *Journal of Adolescent and Adult Literacy* 49. 118–128.

Black, Rebecca W. 2009. Online fan fiction, global identities, and imagination. *Research in the Teaching of English* 43. 397–425.

Blakeslee, Ann M. 1997. Activity, context, interaction, and authority: Learning to write scientific papers in situ. *Journal of Business and Technical Communication* 11. 125–169.

Blanton, Linda Lonon. 1998. *Varied voices: On language and literacy learning*. Boston, MA: Heinle and Heinle.

Blanton, Linda Lonon. 2007. *Varied voices: On language and literacy learning*. Mahwah, NJ: Lawrence Erlbaum Associates.

Bloch, Joel. 2004. Second language cyberhetoric: A study of Chinese L2 writers in an online usenet group. *Language, Learning and Technology* 8. 66–82.

Block, David. 2003. *The social turn in second language acquisition*. Washington, DC: Georgetown University Press.

Canagarajah, A. Suresh. 2002. *A geopolitics of academic writing*. Pittsburgh: University of Pittsburgh Press.

Canagarajah, A. Suresh. 2012. Teacher development in a global profession: An autoethnography. *TESOL Quarterly* 46. 258–279.

Casanave, Christine Pearson. 1995. Local interactions: Constructing contexts for composing in a graduate sociology program. In George Braine and Diane Belcher (eds.), *Academic writing in a second language: Essays on research and pedagogy*, 83–110. Norwood, NJ: Ablex.

Casanave, Christine Pearson. 1998. Transitions: The balancing act of bilingual academics. *Journal of Second Language Writing* 7. 175–203.

Casanave, Christine Pearson. 2005. Uses of narrative in L2 writing research. In Paul Kei Matsuda and Tony Silva (eds.), *Second language writing research: Perspectives on the process of knowledge construction*, 17–32. Mahwah, NJ: Lawrence Erlbaum Associates.

Casanave, Christine Pearson. 2010. Taking risks?: A case study of three doctoral students writing qualitative dissertations at an American university in Japan. *Journal of Second Language Writing* 19. 1–16.

Casanave, Christine Pearson. 2011. *Journal writing in second language education*. Ann Arbor: University of Michigan Press.

Casanave, Christine Pearson. 2012. Heading in the wrong direction? A response to Porte and Richards. *Journal of Second Language Writing* 21. 296–297.

Casanave, Christine Pearson and Stephanie Vandrick (eds.). 2003. *Writing for scholarly publication: Behind the scenes in language education*. Mahwah, NJ: Lawrence Erlbaum Associates.

Cho, Sookyung. 2010. Academic biliteracy challenges: Korean scholars in the United States. *Journal of Second Language Writing* 19. 82–94.

Choi, Jayoung. 2009. Asian English language learners' identity construction in an after school literacy site. *Journal of Asian Pacific Communication* 19. 130–161.

Christianakis, Mary. 2011. Children's text development: Drawing, pictures, and writing. *Research in the Teaching of English* 46. 22–54.

Chun, Christian W. 2012. The multimodalities of globalization: Teaching a YouTube video in an EAP classroom. *Research in the Teaching of English* 47. 145–170.

Connor, Ulla. 1999. Learning to write academic prose in a second language: A literacy autobiography. In George Braine (ed.), *Non-native educators in English language teaching*, 29–42. Mahwah, NJ: Lawrence Erlbaum Associates.

Cope, Bill and Mary Kalantzis (eds.). 2000. *Multiliteracies: Literacy learning and the design of social futures*. London: Routledge.

Cope, Bill and Mary Kalantzis. 2012. *Literacies*. Cambridge: Cambridge University Press.

Cumming, Alister. 1992. Instructional routines in ESL composition teaching: A case study of three teachers. *Journal of Second Language Writing* 1. 17–35,

Currie, Pat. 1993. Entering a disciplinary community: Conceptual activities required to write for one introductory university course. *Journal of Second Language Writing* 2. 101–117.

Denzin, Norman K., Yvonna S. Lincoln and Michael D. Giardina. 2006. Disciplining qualitative research. *International Journal of Qualitative Studies in Education* 19. 769–782.

Edelsky, Carole. 1982. Writing in a bilingual program: The relation of L1 and L2 texts. *TESOL Quarterly* 16. 211–228.

Edelsky, Carole. 1986. *Writing in a bilingual program: Había una vez*. Norwood, NJ: Ablex.

Emig, Janet. 1971. *The composing processes of twelfth graders*. Urbana, IL: National Council of Teachers of English.

Emig, Janet. 1977. Writing as a mode of learning. *College Composition and Communication* 28. 122–128.

Emig, Janet. 1982. Inquiry paradigms and writing. *College Composition and Communication* 33. 64–75.

Engeström, Yrjö. 1999. Activity theory and individual and social transformation. In Yrjö Engeström, Reijo Miettinen and Raija-Leena Punamäki (eds.), *Perspectives on Activity Theory*, 19–38. Cambridge, UK: Cambridge University Press.

Firth, Alan and Johannes Wagner. 1997. On discourse, communication, and (some) fundamental concepts in SLA research. *The Modern Language Journal* 81. 285–300.

Flower, Linda and John R. Hayes. 1981. A cognitive process theory of writing. *College Composition and Communication* 32. 365–387.

Flowerdew, John and Yongyan Li. 2007. Language re-use among apprentice scientists writing for publication. *Applied Linguistics* 28. 440–465.

Flowerdew, John and Yongyan Li. 2009. English or Chinese? The trade-off between local and international publication among Chinese academics in the humanities and social sciences. *Journal of Second Language Writing* 18. 1–16.

Fránquiz, María E. and Cinthia S. Salinas. 2011. Newcomers developing English literacy through historical thinking and digitized primary sources. *Journal of Second Language Writing* 20. 196–210.

Gee, James P. 1990. *Social linguistics and literacies: Ideology in discourses*. Brighton, England: Falmer Press.

Gee, James P. 2003. *What video games have to teach us about learning and literacy*. New York: Palgrave/MacMillan.

Gee, James P. 2008. *Social linguistics and literacies: Ideology in discourses*, 3rd ed. New York: Routledge.

Gentil, Guillaume. 2005. Commitments to academic biliteracy: Case studies of Francophone university writers. *Written Communication* 22. 421–471.

Gentil, Guillaume. 2011. A biliteracy agenda for genre research. *Journal of Second Language Writing* 20. 6–23.

Haneda, Mari. 2004. The joint construction of meaning in writing conferences. *Applied Linguistics* 25. 178–219.

Haneda, Mari. 2005. Investing in foreign-language writing: A study of two multicultural learners. *Journal of Language, Identity and Education* 4. 269–290.

Haneda, Mari and Gumiko Monobe. 2009. Bilingual and biliteracy practices: Japanese adolescents living in the United States. *Journal of Asian Pacific Communication* 19. 7–29.

Hawisher, Gail E., Cynthia L. Selfe, Yi-Huey Guo, and Lu Liu. 2006. Globalization and agency: Designing and redesigning the literacies of cyberspace. *College English* 68. 619–636.

Heath, Shirley Brice. 1983. *Ways with words: Language, life, and work in communities and classrooms*. Cambridge, MA: Cambridge University Press.

Horowitz, Daniel. 1986. Process not product: Less than meets the eye. *TESOL Quarterly* 20. 141–144.

Hyland, Ken. 2000. *Disciplinary discourses: Social interactions in academic writing*. London: Longman.

Hyland, Ken. 2009. *Academic discourse*. London: Continuum.

Hyon, Sunny. 1996. Genre in three traditions: Implications for ESL. *TESOL Quarterly* 30. 693–722.

Ivanič, Roz. 1998. *Writing and identity: The discoursal construction of identity in academic writing*. Philadelphia, PA: John Benjamins.

Jensen, Astrid. 2009. Discourse strategies in professional e-mail negotiation: A case study. *English for Specific Purposes* 28. 4–18.

Jia, Li. 2009. Contrasting models in literacy practice among heritage language learners of Mandarin. *Journal of Asian Pacific Communication* 19. 56–75.

Jin, Lixian and Martin Cortazzi (eds.). 2011. *Researching Chinese learners: Skills, perceptions and intercultural adaptations*. New York: Palgrave MacMillan.

Johns, Ann M. 1991. Interpreting an English competency exam: The frustrations of an ESL science student. *Written Communication* 8. 379–401.

Kress, Gunther. 2003. *Literacy in the new media age*. London: Routledge.

Lam, Wan Shun Eva. 2000. L2 literacy and the design of the self: A case study of a teenager writing on the Internet. *TESOL Quarterly* 34. 457–483

Lam, Wan Shun Eva. 2004. Second language socialization in a bilingual chat room: Global and local considerations. *Language Learning and Technology* 8. 44–65.

Lam, Wan Shun Eva. 2006. Re-envisioning language, literacy, and the immigrant subject in new mediascapes. *Pedagogies: An International Journal* 1. 171–195.

Lam, Wan Shun Eva and Enid Rosario-Ramos. 2009. Multilingual literacies in transnational digitally mediated contexts: An exploratory study of immigrant teens in the United States. *Language and Education* 23. 171–190.

Lave, Jean and Etienne Wenger. 1991. *Situated learning: Legitimate peripheral participation*. Cambridge, England: Cambridge University Press.

Leki, Ilona. 2007. *Undergraduates in a second language: Challenges and complexities of academic literacy development*. Mahwah, NJ: Lawrence Erlbaum Associates.

Li, Xiaoming. 1996. *"Good writing" in cross-cultural context*. Albany: SUNY Press.

Li, Yongyan. 2005. Multidimensional enculturation: The case study of an EFL Chinese doctoral student. *Journal of Asian Pacific Communication* 15. 153–170.

Li, Yongyan. 2006a. A doctoral student of physics writing for international publication: A sociopolitically-oriented case study. *English for Specific Purposes* 25. 456–478.

Li, Yongyan. 2006b. Negotiating knowledge contribution to multiple discourse communities: A doctoral student of computer science writing for publication. *Journal of Second Language Writing* 15. 159–178.

Li, Yongyan. 2007. Apprentice scholarly writing in a community of practice: An intraview of an NNES graduate student writing a research article. *TESOL Quarterly* 41. 55–79.

Li, Yongyan. 2012. "I have no time to find out where the sentences came from; I just rebuild them": A biochemistry professor eliminating novices' textual borrowing. *Journal of Second Language Writing* 21. 59–70.

Lillis, Theresa and Mary Jane Curry. 2006. Professional academic writing by multilingual scholars: Interactions with literacy brokers in the production of English-medium texts. *Written Communication* 23. 3–35.

Lillis, Theresa and Mary Jane Curry. 2010. *Academic writing in a global context: The politics and practices of publishing in English*. London: Routledge.

Liu, Yichun. 2011. Power perceptions and negotiations in a cross-national email writing activity. *Journal of Second language Writing* 20. 257–270.

Lucas, Tamara. 1992. Diversity among individuals: Eight students making sense of classroom journal writing. In Denise E. Murray (ed.), *Diversity as resource: Redefining cultural literacy*, 202–232. Alexandria, VA: Teachers of English to Speakers of Other Languages.

Luke, Carmen. 2000. Cyber-schooling and technological change. In Bill Cope and Mary Kalantzis (eds.), *Multiliteracies: Literacy learning and the design of social futures*, 69–91. London: Routledge.

MacArthur, Charles A. 2006. The effects of new technologies on writing and writing processes. In Charles A. MacArthur, Steve Graham, and Jill Fitzgerald (eds.). *Handbook of writing research*, 248–262. New York: The Guilford Press.

Manchón, Rosa M. (ed.). 2009. *Writing in foreign language contexts: Learning, teaching, and research*. Clevedon, UK: Multilingual Matters.

Manchón, Rosa M. (ed.). 2011. *Learning-to-write and writing-to-learn in an additional language*. Amsterdam: John Benjamins.

Manchón, Rosa M. (ed.). 2012. *L2 writing development: Multiple perspectives*. Berlin/Boston: de Gruyter Mouton.

Manchón, Rosa M., Julio Roca de Larios, and Liz Murphy. 2009. The temporal dimension and problem-solving nature of foreign language composing process. In Rosa M. Manchón (ed.), *Writing in foreign language contexts: Learning, teaching, and research*, 102–129. Clevedon, UK: Multilingual Matters.

Matsuda, Paul Kei. 1998. Situating ESL writing in a cross-disciplinary context. *Written Communication* 15. 99–121.

McCarthey, Sarah J., Yi-Huey Guo, and Sunday Cummins. 2005. Understanding changes in elementary Mandarin students' L1 and L2 writings. *Journal of Second Language Writing* 14. 71–104.

McLean, Cheryl A. 2010. A space called Home: An immigrant adolescent's digital literacy practices. *Journal of Adolescent and Adult Literacy* 54. 13–22.

McLean, Cheryl A. 2012. The author's I: Adolescents mediating selfhood through writing. *Pedagogies: An International Journal* 7. 229–245.

Mlynarczyk, Rebecca W. 1998. *Conversations of the mind: The uses of journal writing for second-language learners*. Mahwah, NJ: Lawrence Erlbaum Associates.

Nelson, Gayle L. and John M. Murphy. 1992. An L2 writing group: Task and social dimensions. *Journal of Second Language Writing* 1. 171–193.

Paltridge, Brian and Lindy Woodrow. 2012. Thesis and dissertation writing: Moving beyond the text. In Ramona Tang (ed.), *Academic writing in a second or foreign language: Issues and challenges facing ESL/EFL academic writers in higher education contexts*, 88–104. London: Continuum.

Pennington, Martha and Sufumi So. 1993. Comparing writing process and product across two languages: A study of 6 Singaporean university student writers. *Journal of Second Language Writin*, 2 41–63.

Peyton, Joy Kreeft and Jana Staton (eds.). 1993. *Dialogue journals in the multi-lingual classroom: Building language fluency and writing skills through written interaction*. Norwood, NJ: Ablex.

Pomerantz, Anne and Erin Kearney. 2012. Beyond 'write-talk-revise-(repeat)': Using narrative to understand one multilingual student's interactions around writing. *Journal of Second Language Writing* 22. 221–238.

Porte, Graeme and Keith Richards. 2012. Focus article: Replication in second language writing research. *Journal of Second Language Writing* 21. 284–293.

Prior, Paul. 1991. Contextualizing writing and response in a graduate seminar. *Written Communication* 8. 267–310.

Prior, Paul. 1994. Response, revision, disciplinarity: A microhistory of a dissertation prospectus in sociology. *Written Communication* 11. 483–533.

Prior, Paul. 1995a. Redefining the task: An ethnographic examination of writing and response in graduate seminars. In Diane Belcher and George Braine (eds.), *Academic writing in a second language: Essays on research and pedagogy*, 47–82. Norwood, NJ: Ablex.

Prior, Paul. 1995b. Tracing authoritative and internally persuasive discourses: A case study of response, revision, and disciplinary enculturation. *Research in the Teaching of English* 29. 288–325.

Purcell-Gates, Victoria (ed.). 2007. *Cultural practices of literacy: Case studies of language, literacy, social practice, and power*. Mahwah, NJ: Lawrence Erlbaum Associates.

Purcell-Gates, Victoria, Kristen H. Perry, and Adriana Briseño. 2011. Analyzing literacy practice: Grounded theory to model. *Research in the Teaching of English* 45. 439–458.

Ramanathan, Vai and Dwight Atkinson. 1999. Ethnographic approaches and methods in L2 writing research: A critical guide and review. *Applied Linguistics* 20. 44–70.

Reed, Leslie. 1993. Opening the door to communication in the multilingual/multicultural classroom. In Joy Kreeft Peyton and Jana Staton (eds.), *Dialogue journals in the multi-lingual classroom: Building language fluency and writing skills through written interaction*. 29–46. Norwood, NJ: Ablex.

Reid, Joy. 1984. The radical outliner and the radical brainstormer. *TESOL Quarterly* 18. 529–533.

Richards, Keith. 2009. Trends in qualitative research since 2000. *Language Teaching* 42. 147–180.

Schön, Donald. 1983. *The reflective practitioner: How professionals think in action*. New York: Basic Books.

Schultz, Katherine. 2006. Qualitative research on writing. In Charles A. MacArthur, Steve Graham, and Jill Fitzgerald (eds.), *Handbook of writing research*, 357–373. New York: The Guilford Press.

Schwandt, Thomas A. 2006. Opposition redirected. *International Journal of Qualitative Studies in Education* 19. 803–810.

Severino, Carol. 1993. The sociopolitical implications of response to second language and second dialect writing. *Journal of Second Language Writing* 2. 181–201.

Silva, Tony. 1993. Toward an understanding of the distinct nature of L2 writing: The ESL research and its implications. *TESOL Quarterly* 27. 657–677.

Silva, Tony. 2005. On the philosophical bases of inquiry in second language writing: Metaphysics, inquiry paradigms, and the intellectual zeitgeist. In Paul Kei Matsuda and Tony Silva (eds.), *Second language writing research: Perspectives on the process of knowledge construction*, 3–15. Mahwah, NJ: Lawrence Erlbaum Associates.

Smagorinsky, Peter. 2011. *Vygotsky and literacy research: A methodological framework*. Rotterdam, The Netherlands: Sense Publishers.

Spack, Ruth. 1997. The acquisition of academic literacy in a second language: A longitudinal case study. *Written Communication* 14. 3–62.

Staton, Jana. 1993. Dialogue journals as a means of assisting written language acquisition. In Joy Kreeft Peyton and Jana Staton (eds.), *Dialogue journals in the multi-lingual classroom: Building language fluency and writing skills through written interaction*. 103–122. Norwood, NJ: Ablex.

Sternglass, Marilyn S. 1997. *Time to know them: A longitudinal study of writing and learning at the college level*. Mahwah, NJ: Lawrence Erlbaum Associates.

St. Pierre, Elizabeth Adams and Kathryn Roulston. 2006. The state of qualitative inquiry: A contested science. *International Journal of Qualitative Studies in Education* 19. 673–684.

Street, Brian. 1984. *Literacy in theory and practice*: Cambridge, England: Cambridge University Press.

Street, Brian V. 1995. *Social literacies: Critical approaches to literacy in development, ethnography and education*. London: Longman.

Sun, Yu-Chih and Yu-Jung Chang. 2012. Blogging to learn: Becoming EFL academic writers through collaborative dialogues. *Language Learning and Technology* 16. 43–61.

Swales, John M. 1990. *Genre analysis: English in academic and research settings*. New York: Cambridge University Press.

Sze, Celine, Marilyn Chapman, and Ling Shi. 2009. Functions and genres of ESL children's English writing at home and at school. *Journal of Asian Pacific Communication* 19. 30–55.

Tardy, Christine. 2009. *Building genre knowledge*. West Lafayette, IN: Parlor Press.

Wenger, Etienne. 1998. *Communities of practice: Learning, meaning, and identity*. Cambridge, England: Cambridge University Press.

Yi, Youngjoo. 2005. Asian adolescents' in and out-of-school encounters with English and Korean literacy. *Journal of Asian Pacific Communication* 15. 57–77.

Yi, Youngjoo. 2007. Engaging literacy: A bilterate student's composing practices beyond school. *Journal of Second Language Writing* 16. 23–39.

Yi, Youngjoo. 2008. Relay writing in an adolescent online community. *Journal of Adolescent and Adult Literacy* 51. 670–680.

Yi, Youngjoo. 2009. Adolescent literacy and identity construction among 1.5 generation students: From a transnational perspective. *Journal of Asian Pacific Communication* 19. 100–129.

Yi, Youngjoo. 2010. Adolescent multilingual writers' transitions across in- and-out-of-school writing contexts. *Journal of Second Language Writing.* 19. 17–32.

Yi, Youngjoo and Alan Hirvela. 2010. Technology and "self-sponsored" writing: A case study of a Korean-American adolescent. *Computers and Composition* 27. 94–111.

Zamel, Vivian. 1982. Writing: The process of discovering meaning. *TESOL Quarterly* 16. 195–209.

Zamel, Vivian. 1983. The composing process of advanced ESL students: Six case studies. *TESOL Quarterly.* 17. 165–187.

Rosa M. Manchón

24 Quantitive inquiry in L2 writing

1 Introduction: The nature and place of quantitative inquiry in L2 writing scholarship

My goal in this chapter is to review trends and methods of disciplinary inquiry in representative quantitatively-oriented L2 writing research. Alike the research analyzed in Chapter 23, the bulk of the empirical work to be synthesized corresponds to studies centred on writing in English as a second or foreign language (L2), a limitation that is simply a reflection of where most research efforts have taken place (but see Introduction and Chapter 8). The approach to be taken is to identify main directions in this body of empirical work in terms of purposes of research and prominent items in research agendas, theoretical frameworks informing inquiry, and relevant research methodology considerations. Space limitations do not allow the (more than necessary) assessment of research quality in this domain, an issue I will nevertheless revisit in the concluding remarks. I would also like to note from the outset that the survey will be necessarily selective, although I shall point the reader to further elaborations through citations of representative studies and previous reviews and, when appropriate, through cross-reference to those chapters in this *Handbook* in which the strand in focus is more thoroughly examined.

Two further initial observations are in order. The first is that, as repeatedly mentioned in overviews of the field (cf. Hyland 2010a; Polio 2012), quantitative research approaches and L2 writing have not always gone hand in hand. This can be explained in part by the necessary congruence that must exist between how a given phenomenon is envisioned and theoretically informed in the first place, and how researchers go about investigating it empirically. As Mackey and Gass (2012: 1) aptly put it, "methods are not determined or decided upon devoid of context; research methods are dependent on the theories that they are designed to investigate". L2 writing research is no exception to this rule and the attested traditional preference for qualitative approaches in explorations of central preoccupations in the field should be interpreted simply as a direct consequence of the prevalence of socio-cognitive and socio-cultural theories, especially in North-America, a context in which "dominant current views of L2 writing" are still "fundamentally social and political" (Ortega 2012: 405). Yet, the brief overview of historical developments presented in the next section, together with the more detailed analysis undertaken in parts 3 and 4, will hopefully show that the diversification of theories informing L2 writing research, coupled with the expansion of the diverse facets of the global phenomenon of L2 writing addressed in research agendas, collectively explain important shifts in disciplinary orientations and preoccupations, and, as a result, the wealth of influential work conducted within quantitatively-oriented strands.

The second initial observation pertains to what is meant by "quantitative" in the context of this chapter. This is a needed clarification given that some confusion is observed at times between quantitative research "approaches", quantitative "instruments", quantitative "data", and quantitative "analyses". In effect, the purported minor presence of quantitative research in L2 writing scholarship mentioned above applies solely to the adoption of quantitative "approaches", but by no means to the use of quantitative data, instruments, or analyses in L2 writing empirical inquiry globally considered. To clarify matters, we adopt here a definition of quantitative inquiry as "a research paradigm designed to address questions that hypothesize relationships among variables that are measured frequently in numerical and objective ways" (Newman, Ridenour, Newman, and DeMarco 2003: 170). This contrasts with qualitative inquiry, which corresponds to "a research paradigm designed to address questions of meaning, interpretation, and socially constructed realities" (Newman et al. 2003: 170). As for data coding and analysis, quantitative studies must end up with quantified data, but it is pertinent to note that the data may originally be either quantitative (for instance, test scores or measures of written performance) or qualitative (for example, think-aloud verbalizations or stimulated recalls), the latter, qualitative data, requiring stringent methodological decisions regarding coding and segmentation criteria as a key preliminary step for subsequent quantification (see Manchón, Roca de Larios, and Murphy 2005; Révész 2012). Needless to say, mixed-method studies would make use of both quantitative and qualitative data (see Teddlie and Tashakkori 2003).

Equally relevant is to note that one and the same phenomenon can be conceived of from diverse perspectives and hence be validly inspected through the lens of either quantitative or qualitative approaches, although the intent of the research endeavor, the theories informing it, and the questions being asked will differ considerably in each case. For instance, writing processes and strategies can be (and have indeed been) explored qualitatively, as was the case of Zamel's (1983) exploratory study of the way advanced writers write, Spack's (1994) detailed case study of development in strategy use, Leki's (2005) exploration of strategy development in disciplinary writing or, more recently, Li and Casanave's (2012) investigation of the strategies employed by two L2 writers for writing from sources. Writing processes can nevertheless be (and have often been) inspected through a quantitative lens, as in Roca de Larios et al's (2008) study of the proficiency-dependency of the temporal allocation of attentional resources to diverse cognitive activities, Van Weijen et al's (2009) analysis of potential variations in the execution of cognitive activities throughout the writing process, Beare and Bourdages's (2007) exploration of L1 and L2 writing strategies or, more recently, Ong's (2014) examination of the moderating effect of task-related variables on writing processes. Another telling example would be research on collaborative writing, a more recently added strand in which central concerns have been addressed in qualitative studies (cf. Yang 2014) and in quantitative investigations (e.g. Fernández-Dobao 2012; Kuiken

Table 24.1: Research purposes in quantitative L2 writing inquiry.

Type of research	Research purposes			
	Add to knowledge base	Understand complex phenomena	Measure change	Test new ideas
Descriptive	●	●		
Explanatory-interventionist			●	●

and Vedder 2002 a,b). In sum, the key point I wish to make is that both quantitative and qualitative methodologies ought to be seen as legitimate pathways to knowledge construction in L2 writing research.

With these provisos in mind, the objective of this chapter is to review representative quantitative research seeking to "describe" or "explain" relationships among variables related to L2 writers and/or their texts. Alongside previous reviews (cf. Hyland 2010a, 2010b; Polio 2003, 2012), the analysis is partially structured around research foci and elicitation procedures. However, being inspired by Newman et al.'s reflections (2003), and in order to make sense of the vast amount of available quantitative research in a principled way, I have considered relevant to incorporate the concept of "research purposes" to the analysis, this being a more general organizing principle behind the crucial steps of establishing research questions and, subsequently, of "selecting the appropriate methods to investigate the questions that are derived from that purpose" (p. 169). Purposes are therefore aligned to methods. Out of all the general research purposes listed by Newman et al. (2003), L2 writing quantitative inquiry has chiefly attempted to "add to knowledge base", "understand complex phenomena", "measure change" and "test new ideas". These purposes have guided research in two main types of studies, to be referred to as "descriptive" and "explanatory-interventionist", respectively (see Table 24.1). The former correspond to cross-sectional and longitudinal observational empirical works that have provided rich descriptions of L2 texts and L2 writing processes as a function of a range of writer-internal and writer-external variables. This has been done with the intent of, mainly, adding to the knowledge base (by, for instance, attempting to clarify connections among variables, such as the proficiency-dependency of cognitive activity while writing) and understanding certain dimensions of the complex phenomenon of L2 writing (for instance, by analyzing and quantifying textual features of disciplinary writing). The latter, explanatory-interventionist studies, encompass a range of cross-sectional and, to a lesser extent, longitudinal investigations centered on measuring the effect of pedagogical treatments or experimental interventions of various kinds and duration on writing products and processes. In terms of purposes, researchers have been chiefly concerned with (i) measuring change by means of quantifying treatments effects, and

(ii) testing new ideas, in this case positing relationships among variables and then collecting data in those variables to put the predicted relationships to the empirical test (Newman et al. 2003: 179). This has been done, for instance, in studies examining the effect of training programs on writing strategy deployment, or in those quantifying the effect of manipulating task complexity factors on written performance.

Before embarking on the analysis of both groups of studies, it is relevant to put the development of quantitatively-oriented L2 writing research in historical perspective.

2 Historical development

It should be stated at the outset that quantitative studies of L2 writing processes and products have always been central to L2 writing research, as clearly exemplified in the reviews included in most contributions in Part 2 of this *Handbook* as well as in previous overviews of the field (cf. Hyland 2010a; Leki, Cumming, and Silva 2008; Polio 2003, 2012). It is nevertheless possible to identify a number of key developments that over the years have notably contributed to broadening the scope of quantitative research and to making various strands of quantitative inquiry be at the forefront of L2 writing studies.

The first contributing factor is theoretical in nature and it should be linked to the necessary congruence between theories and methods referred to in the opening section. More precisely, theoretical diversification and theoretical expansion are distinctive characteristics of the short history of L2 writing scholarship (see Chapter 3). Importantly, different theories make different predictions about the phenomenon in focus and investigating some of these predictions empirically requires the employment of quantitative methodologies. A case in point is the study of writing development, an area in which diverse theories (see contributions to Manchón 2012) make different predictions about what develops in L2 writing, how, and why. In fact, having these theoretical predictions is considered a "necessary requisite for principled research" in this domain (Norris and Manchón 2012: 226). As is the case with many other phenomena, both quantitative and qualitative approaches can guide the examination of writing development. Yet, some theoretical predictions are more readily and validly investigated through a quantitative lens. This explains, for instance, the quantitative orientation taken in recent studies on writing development framed in Complex Dynamic Systems (cf. Verspoor and Smiskova 2012), a research strand in which new sophisticated quantitative analyses are needed in order to test the predictions the theory makes about the inherent variability that characterizes writing development. These quantitative analytic procedures will nevertheless differ from those undertaken in, for example, quantitative analyses intended to test the theoretical predictions about the development of "meaning-making capacities" made within the framework of Systemic Functional Linguistics (cf. Byrnes 2009; Ryshina-Pankova and Byrnes 2013).

In addition to theoretical diversification and corresponding implications for research methodologies, the expansion of quantitatively-oriented L2 writing agendas is also a direct consequence of the recognition of the situated nature of L2 writing, which, in turn, has brought about a notable diversification of contexts and populations under study and hence a broader orientation in research agendas in an attempt to uncover the multiplicity of factors involved in learning, practising and teaching writing in diverse geographical and educational settings. Just to provide a telling example, back in 2003 Polio concluded her authoritative review of L2 writing research by pointing to "the dearth of research on writing in a foreign language context" (p. 59). Yet, this area has grown considerably since (see Cimasko and Reichelt 2011; Manchón 2009), a phenomenon that I would suggest cannot be dissociated from two facts. One is that many L2 writing specialists are now based in diverse parts of the world, which contrasts with the clear predominance of US-based scholars in earlier stages in the development of the field. Another contributing fact is an attested growing disciplinary interest in writing in foreign languages other than English, both in the US and in other locations. As a result, the range of phenomena under the spotlight and, consequently, the theories and methods used to investigate those phenomena have gradually become more diverse. In the case of foreign language settings, for instance, it is theoretically and pedagogically relevant to look into the role that L2 writing may play in the language learning experience of FL writers (see Chapter 26), this being a new research preoccupation in the field closely linked to cognitive theories of learning and hence likely to be approached within a quantitative research paradigm.

Together with the development of quantitative studies as the result of the theoretical and/or pedagogical relevance of investigating new dimensions of L2 writing in new locations or with respect to new populations, a further beneficial factor for advancing quantitative research agendas is a direct outcome of the internal dynamics of research preoccupations in areas related to L2 writers and texts that have nevertheless traditionally been approached from a quantitative perspective. As for writers, initial empirical efforts centered on the very act of composing in individual writing conditions with the ultimate aim of contributing to psycholinguistic accounts of language production, in general, and written production, in particular (see Chapter 12 for a fuller analysis). Yet, with the passing of time, important shifts in research orientations have taken place, and these bear relevant implications for research methodology. On the one hand, research foci have widened to include the examination of processes in both individual and collaborative writing conditions (the latter absent in earlier studies of writing processes), as well as the exploration of processes while writing (as traditionally done) and while processing feedback (see chapters 19 and 20). On the other hand, a diversification of items in these new research agendas into writing processes and strategies have resulted from the establishment of closer links between L2 writing studies and SLA acquisition research. This interdisciplinarity explains why the ultimate aim of current SLA-psycholinguistically-oriented studies of writing processes and strategies is more closely aligned to theoretical and pedagogical interests in testing SLA tenets and findings in the written modality (see 4.1. below), in part as a reaction to the scant attention paid to the written mode in theoretical positions and empirical research in language learning studies (see Chapter 26).

Research shifts in quantitative research on written texts have also been greatly influenced by a growing methodological movement intended to refine, innovate or validate research instruments and analytic methods. For instance, Grant and Ginther (2000) examined the effectiveness of computer tagging of written texts. Yang et al. (2014) have recently looked into the issue of reactivity of concurrent protocols, an important methodological concern that have always attracted the attention of writing scholars (see Manchón et al. 2005; Sachs and Polio 2007), and yet additional efforts have gone in the direction of investigating the new light that can be shed on written texts by using new computational tools (especially Co-Metrix) or by applying more sophisticated and powerful statistics (as done, for instance, in Crossley and McNamara's [2009] exploration of new analyses to uncover L1–L2 differences). Similarly, important recent initiatives are motivated by an interest in shedding new light on how to conceptualize and measure central constructs in the analysis of written production (especially analytic measures of text features) in theoretically and empirically valid ways, as recently done, for instance, by Polio and Shea (2014) and Evans, Hartshorn, Cox, and Martin (2014) for linguistic accuracy, Biber, Gray and Poonpon (2011) and Lu (2011) for grammatical complexity, and Latif (2009) for fluency. Finally, over the years some isolated initiatives have tried to validate questionnaires and research instruments, as done, for example, in Cheng's (2004) validation of a writing anxiety scale, Petric and Czárl's (2003) validation of a strategy writing questionnaire, or Snellings, van Gelderen de Glopper's (2004) validation of a test of second language written lexical retrieval.

In short, quantitative inquiry in L2 writing has significantly grown and expanded in diverse directions as a consequence of theory diversification, enlarged contexts and populations under study, and expanded researched agendas with new theoretical, applied, and methodological preoccupations. What follows is a selective review of representative trends in this body of quantitative work, distinguishing, as announced above, between two main groups of studies: descriptive and explanatory-interventionist.

3 Trends and methods in quantitative inquiry: Descriptive studies

Guided by the general purposes of adding to the knowledge base and understanding complex phenomena related to L2 writers and their texts, descriptive studies constitute a general category of cross-sectional and longitudinal investigations that have examined L2 writing products and processes as a function of a range of writer-internal and writer-external variables. Collectively considered, they can be characterized as following "observational/descriptive designs", which Plonsky and Gurzynski-Weiss (2013) characterize as those seeking "to describe a linguistic phenomenon or set of phenomena without attempts at incurring change. These studies do not test the effects or outcomes of a treatment or intervention; they simply look to describe as systematically as possible what is occurring, interpret the occurrence within a larger context and, at times, hypothesize why the incidence is observed" (p. 33). Descriptive quantitative studies have been informed by cognitive theories of language learning, cognitive accounts of L1 and L2 writing, as well as by several linguistic theories and linguistic-oriented approaches, most notably Intercultural Rhetoric (see review in Chapter 3), Genre theories (see chapters 3, 9 and 11), Multi-competence theories (as reviewed in Chapter 17), Systemic Functional Linguistics and Complex Dynamics Systems (see Chapter 13).

Regarding research foci, two main groups of quantitative descriptive studies are to be distinguished: (i) cross-sectional and longitudinal studies of L2 writers' text features, and (ii) cross-sectional investigations of L2 writers' processes and strategies.

3.1 Descriptive studies of text features

Descriptive studies of writers' text features constitute important linguistically- and psycholinguistically-oriented lines of quantitative inquiry that have produced systematic, rigorous descriptions of the frequency of occurrence and/or development of both general and specific characteristics of L2 texts as a function of writer-related or text/genre-related variables. Some prominent recent examples of these linguistic analyses have been framed in Systemic Functional Linguistics (Achugar and Carpenter 2014; Byrnes 2009, 2013), theories of multicompetence (cf. Lindgren and Stevenson 2013; Kobayashi and Rinnert 2012), and Complex Dynamics Systems (cf. Baba and Nitta 2014; Nitta and Baba 2014; Verspoor and Smiskova 2012; Verspoor et al. 2012). To this we should add the abundant genre-oriented investigations of textual features of disciplinary writing, a well-researched and still vibrant domain of interest (see full discussion and key references in chapters 3, 9 and 11).

In terms of populations, descriptive studies have mainly studied university students and, to a much lesser extent, secondary school pupils (cf. Lindgren and Stevenson 2013) or children (cf. Verheyden et al. 2010). They have made use of both cross-sectional and, in a less proportion, longitudinal designs (see detailed review in Chapter 13) and of inter- and intra-subject designs. In inter-subject studies the texts written by L2 writers are compared to those written by L1 writers (cf. Crossley and McNamara 2011; Leedham and Cai 2013; Lindgren, Spelman Miller, and Sullivan 2008), whereas intra-subject studies are those in which participants are asked to write texts in their L1 and L2 and the characteristics of the resulting texts in both languages are then contrasted, as done, for instance, in Lindgren and Stevenson's (2013) study of the expression of interactional meaning by young Swedish EFL writers in their L1 and L2, or Kobayashi and Rinnert's (2008) study of structural features of L1 Japanese and L2 English texts written by Japanese university students.

The dependent variable in descriptive studies is text features, measured either holistically or analytically (frequently in terms of CAF measures, i.e. complexity, accuracy, and fluency), with Co-Metrix being a computational tool widely used in recent studies. A prominent concern in this body of work has been the analysis of (the development) of global and specific textual features of L2 writers' texts (see review in Chapter 13). Important insights have also been obtained in studies that have more narrowly focused on aspects of language use in a given domain, complexity being an area that has raised considerable interest (see Ortega 2003 for a thorough review; Buté and Housen 2014; Crossley and MacNamara 2014; Lu 2011; Vyatkina 2012 for representative studies, and contributions to Vyatkina 2015 for recent developments in this area). Although the bulk of this research has examined textual features of English L2, other languages studied include French L2 (Benevento and Storch 2011; Gunnarson 2012; Kuiken and Vedder 2008), Italian L2 (Kuiken and Vedder 2002b, 2008, 2011) and Dutch L2 (Kuiken and Vedder 2002b). Special mention should also be made of the important advancements provided in research on German L2, such as Byrnes's (2009) and Ryshina-Pankova and Byrnes's (2013) studies of the development of grammatical metaphor in L2 German, or Vyatkina's (2012) longitudinal analysis of multiple dimensions of linguistic complexity in the writing of beginner German L2 learners.

A range of independent variables have been investigated, including writer-related variables (mainly language proficiency and writing expertise), discipline-related variables, task-related variables, and contextual/instructional variables. For example, abundant SLA-oriented research efforts have recently gone into the analysis of the moderating effects of task implementation variables on written products, especially regarding individual vs. collaborative writing conditions (cf. Kim 2008; Wigglesworth and Storch 2009, 2012) and task-modality effects (i.e. oral vs. written performance, cf. Adams 2006; Adams and Ross-Feldman 2008; Genc 2012; Kormos 2014; Kormos and Trebits 2012; Kuiken and Vedder 2011; Niu 2009; Tavakoli 2014; Yu 2009). Regarding contextual/instructional factors, and complementing the abundant qualitative research in the area, a small but growing body of research has explored the influence of previous or current writing experience and instruction on features of university students' written texts (cf. Kobayahi and Rinnert 2008; Leedham and Cai 2013; McDonough, Crawford and De Vleeschauwer 2014). Equally relevant is another expanding strand interested in analyzing the development of textual features as potentially mediated by a stay (or participation in an instructional program) at a given institution abroad (cf. Benevento and Storch 2011; Kobayashi and Rinnert 2012, 2013; Mazgutova and Kormos 2015; Serrano,

Tragant, and Llanes 2012; Storch 2009), at times comparing such development with that of a comparison group of L2 writers who did not enjoy the stay abroad experience (Llanes and Muñoz 2013; Pérez Vidal 2014; Sasaki 2004). These research strands are more fully analyzed in chapters 5, 6, 7 and 12. Similarly, abundant quantitative research efforts have gone into the analysis of text features as a function of feedback provision and processing (as reviewed in chapters 19 and 20) and an expanding body of quantitative studies of digital literacies should also be mentioned (see Chapter 14).

3.2 Descriptive studies of writing processes and strategies

A second main strand of quantitative studies has investigated the task-related and writer-related variables that may impact on the cognitive activity behind textual production, operationalized as writing processes and writing strategies. This research is monographically surveyed in Chapter 12 (see also Chapter 3) and hence only a brief picture of main trends and methodological practices in this domain of inquiry will be provided here.

Studies of writing processes and strategies are essentially cognitive in orientation and hence the main theories informing research are cognitive accounts of L1 writing (especially Flower and Hayes 1980; Hayes 1996, 2012; Kellogg 1996). This research has explored, inter alia, the applicability of tenets of L1 writing models to the case of L2 writing (investigating, for instance, the purported problem-solving and recursive nature of writing in the L2 condition, cf. Manchón, Roca de Larios and Murphy 2009), the bilingual nature of L2 writing (a crucial item in research agendas being the analysis of L1 use in L2 writing, as reviewed in Manchón 2013 and Manchón et al. 2007), and the allocation of attentional resources to macro-writing processes as a function of, for instance, writer-related (cf. Manchón and Roca de Larios 2007; Tillema 2012) or instructional-related (cf. Porte 1996, 1997) variables. As is also the case in descriptive studies of L2 texts, studies of writing processes have also compared cognitive activity in L1 and L2 writing (Beare and Bourdages 2007; Chenoweth and Hayes 2001; Schoonen et al. 2003; Stevenson, Schoonen and De Gloper 2006; Tillema 2012; Thorson 2000; Van Weijen 2008).

Participants in studies of writing processes have been second and foreign language university students (cf. Manchón, Roca de Larios, and Murphy 2009), although some have investigated professional writers (cf. Beare and Bourdages 2007) and secondary school students (cf. Schoonen et al. 2009, 2011; Tillema 2012). Given the nature of these research foci and the fact that the phenomena under the spotlight are not always directly accessible, data collection procedures have included introspective techniques (e.g. think-aloud protocols or stimulated recalls), survey data collection procedures (questionnaires or interviews), text analysis, and computerized tracking, often triangulating data from several sources. Most of this research is cross-sectional in nature. Collectively, the main independent variables in this body of research are task-related variables (time on task, topic familiarity, cognitive task complexity, and stage of the writing process), and writer-related variables (L2 proficiency, writing expertise, and previous/current writing experience and instruction). The dependent variables investigated are strategy deployment, the type and amount of problems experienced while composing, and the allocation of attentional resources to several dimensions of writing (see Chapter 12 for a fuller analysis).

4 Trends and methods in quantitative inquiry: Explanatory-interventionist studies

As mentioned in the opening section, two main purposes have guided explanatory-interventionist research, namely, measuring change by means of quantifying treatments effects (usually through experimental – including pre-, quasi- and true experiments. See Plonsky and Gurzynski-Weiss 2013; Porte 2010), and testing new ideas, in this case positing relationships among variables and then collecting data in those variables to put the predicted relationships to the empirical test (frequently through *ex post facto* designs. See Porte 2010). These general purposes have guided a range of cross-sectional and, to a lesser extent, longitudinal investigations centered on explaining and/or measuring the effect of pedagogical treatments or experimental interventions of various kinds and duration on the actions L2 writers engage in while writing, their resulting texts, and/or their learning, including both advances in the development of writing competence/abilities and (short-term) language learning through writing. In what follows a brief analysis of two representative strands of interventionist studies is presented.

4.1 Experimental manipulations of task-implementation and task-execution conditions

Important advances have been made in two groups of interventionist studies that have tested the effects of task implementation and task execution conditions. The first corresponds to **task complexity studies,** a growing body of research (characterized by the use of both *ex post facto* and experimental designs) that has tested theoretical predictions on the relationship between task complexity factors (and corresponding demands on attentional resources) and features of written performance by both university and secondary school L2 writers. These investigations have for the most part being concerned with testing the theoretical predictions of SLA theories of task complexity, especially the Cognition Hypothesis (cf. Robinson 2011) and the Trade-Off Hypothesis (cf. Skehan 2009). Accordingly, the independent variables investigated correspond to dimensions of task complexity as propounded in the Robinson's and Skehan's theoretical models, including planning time and planning conditions (cf. Ellis and Yuan 2004; Johnson, Mercado, and Acevedo 2012; Ong 2014; Ong and Zhang 2010), reasoning demands (cf. Frear and Bitchener 2015; Kuiken and Vedder 2007, 2008, 2012; Ruiz-Funes 2015; Salimi and Dadashpour 2012), +/- provision of topic, ideas, and macro-structure (cf. Ong 2014; Ong and Zhang 2010), degree of task structure and provision of language support (Alwi, Adams, and Newton 2012), revision conditions (i.e. initial-essay-accessible vs. initial-essay-removed, cf. Ong and Zhang 2010) and familiarity of topic, genre, and/or task type (Ruiz-Funes 2015). As for dependent variables, the main interest has centered on measuring the effects of these experimentally manipulated task complexity factors (as mediated at times by the participants' L2 proficiency level, cf. Ruiz-Funes 2015) on written performance (mainly in terms of CAF measures), and one study (Ong 2014) has investigated task complexity effects on writing processes, operationalized in terms of metacognitive operations and idea generation.

Feedback studies (see also chapters 19 and 20, this *Handbook*), constitute another important line of research within this interventionist strand. Part of this research corresponds to SLA-oriented L2 writing studies framed in both cognitive and SLA sociocultural frameworks whose main focus is the analysis of the potential language learning outcomes that may derive from feedback processing. Accordingly, researchers have explored the manner in which providing learners with (different types of) feedback and prompting them to process it (either individually or collaboratively) has any effects on their learning of L2 grammar and lexis. The participants in these studies include university and high school students (see reviews in chapters 5 and 20).

The standard design is this growing body of work is a three-stage procedure whereby participants are asked to produce a text (in individual or collaborative writing conditions) in stage 1, they are then provided with (various forms of) feedback in stage 2 (at times contrasted with a no feedback condition), and, they are subsequently asked to revise their original texts in stage 3. The designs are varied and include having the same participants writing in two feedback conditions, measuring the effect of the same feedback type in the writing of two groups of participants who differed with respect to some relevant independent variables, or making use of (quasi-)experimental (counter-balanced) designs in order to test the effects of different feedback conditions. The feedback conditions investigated have included the provision of oral/written feedback or focused and/or unfocused feedback with or without metalinguistic explanations (cf. Bitchener 2008; Bitchener and Knoch 2008, 2009; Ellis et al. 2008; Sheen 2007, 2010; Sheen, Wright, and Moldewa 2009, Van Beuningen, De Jong, and Kuiken 2012), reformulation and editing/error correction (cf. Sachs and Polio 2007; Storch and Wigglesworth 2010), and error correction vs. metalinguistic explanation (Shintani and Ellis 2013; Shintani, Ellis and Suzuki 2014). A pre-test/treatment/post-test (at times followed by a delayed post-test) design has been the norm. Measures of learning have included both performance on language tests (pre- and post-treatment), noticing processes while processing feedback, and features of the texts produced before and after the experimental intervention, including both quantitative and qualitative analyses of errors and holistic analytic measures of text features. It is important to mention that, for the most part, these measures of learning targeted short-term learning (or "uptake"), rather than long-term learning (or "retention"), a limitation of research that needs to be addressed in future work. It is relevant to mention that some of these studies employ mixed-method approaches, hence triangulating data sources and analyses.

4.2 Research looking into the effects of instructional treatments

A much more reduced group of cross-sectional and longitudinal experimental studies have measured the effects of pedagogical treatments (with different degrees of experimental control and duration) in real classrooms, including both university and secondary school levels. This small number contrasts with the numerous qualitative investigations focused on the same issue (see, for instance, chapters 4, 5, 6, 8, 19, 20 and 23). As this strand of quantitative works does not represent a homogeneous group, I shall refer to some representative investigations as a way of exemplifying trends and methods. For instance, Zhang (2013) examined (in a pre- and post-tests design) the effect of a one-semester instructional treatment on ESL students' synthesis writing. The treatment condition consisted of five iterations of discourse synthesis instruction, whereas the participants in the control condition engaged in reading and writing practice. Looking into a key dimension of writing competence, Van Gelderen, Oostdam and Schooten (2011) carried out a classroom experimental study with secondary school Dutch students of English in which they measured the effect of training students in lexical retrieval of familiar words. The aim of the study was to "to compare the effect of a writing course including lexical fluency training with the same writing course without such training and to compare both of these groups with a baseline control group in relation to posttest text quality" (p. 8). Along similar lines, in a counterbalanced experimental design with randomized assignment, Snellings, Van Gelderen and De Glopper (2004) implemented a computerized training program for improving fluency of lexical retrieval in a secondary school classroom. They then measured the effects of enhanced lexical retrieval on several aspects of L2 narrative written by their Dutch secondary education students.

Another set of studies have in common an interest in measuring the effects of strategy training, although they lean on the observational/descriptive rather than the interventionist experimental side. Using a within-subject design, Ransdell, Lavelle and Levy (2002) measured the effects of two working memory strategies (one strategy more narrowly associated with skilled writers' behavior and the other associated with less skilled writers) on writing performance (operationalized as writing quality and fluency) in L1 and L2. Other groups of interventionist studies include even less controlled attempts to measure the effects of training students in the use of writing strategies, including revision (Sengupta 2000), or planning and revision (Ching 2002) strategies. The effect of the training was measured in terms of its influence on the participants' mental model of writing (Sengupta 2000; Ching 2002), their self-determination or attribution (Ching 2002), as well as on the quality of the essays produced before and after treatment (Sengupta 2000).

5 Concluding thoughts. Looking ahead

As noted in the Introduction to this *Handbook*, L2 writing research has grown exponentially in the last 25 years. The vitality and dynamism of the field is manifested in the gradual expansion of theoretical frameworks and epistemological paradigms informing research, and in the diversification of theoretical, applied, and, to a lesser extent, methodological preoccupations in research agendas. The development of L2 writing research has also resulted in an enlarged range of research methods, instruments, and analytical techniques, as well as in expanded contexts and populations under study. All these facts together explain why, in line with the arguments presented throughout the chapter, knowledge construction in L2 writing scholarship has been possible with the help of both qualitative and quantitative empirical research.

The review of quantitative inquiry presented is by no means exhaustive but, I hope, it provides a fair picture of those research preoccupations and general methodological practices that have guided quantitative research on crucial dimensions of L2 writing related to writers and their texts. Missing in the analysis, as mentioned at the outset, is an assessment of research quality in the domain. It is precisely in this direction where I would like to situate these concluding remarks.

Admittedly, methodological preoccupations and a disciplinary interest in promoting good research practices in L2 writing research have gradually made their way into disciplinary conversations. As for quantitative research, it is relevant to note that a statistics advisor is part of the *Journal of Second Language Writing* (*JSLW*) editorial team. Equally telling is that a whole issue of the "Disciplinary Dialogues" in the *JSLW* was devoted to the issue of replications (*JSLW*, 21, 3, 2012), and that two recent special issues of the *JSLW* are monographically devoted to crucial concerns in quantitative data coding and analysis of written texts. Hence, one has to be optimistic that methodological rigor will continue being a preoccupation in future research enterprises. After all, progress in quantitative research is ultimately and crucially dependent on "sound research designs, principled data analyses, and transparent reporting practices" (Plonsky 2013: 656). Researchers themselves, journal editors, and reviewers will have a big role to play in this endeavour. In addition, as noted for the field of language learning studies more generally (see Plonsky 2014), perhaps the time has come for PhD writing programs to include a solid foundation in quantitative research methodology. All these efforts together should result in improved research standards. We can perfectly apply Plonsky's (2014: 455) future projection for SLA studies to the field of L2 writing: "If quantitative L2 methods continue towards what is considered best practice by applied statisticians and methodologists in the social sciences, we should find changes and improvements over time in the designs, analyses, and reporting practices in L2 research".

Fundamentally, and also in line with the recent critical methodological research movement in the SLA field (see Plonsky 2014 and references within), some strands of quantitative inquiry into L2 writing have reached a critical point in their development for the field to engage in a critical retrospective analysis of whether or not standards of methodological quality have been applied. Methodological syntheses using meta-analytic procedures would also be welcome future initiatives in L2 writing studies.

Finally, and rather crucially, I would like to add one more piece to the puzzle, and this is the importance of balancing methodological rigor with relevance. By relevance I refer here to both (i) engaging in quantitative research on dimensions of L2 writing that is theoretically and pedagogically relevant, and (ii) aiming at advancing research agendas with studies that are ecologically valid. Space limitations prevent me from developing these issues in full and so I will simply mention what I consider to be two crucial concerns for the future of this domain.

One concern is that, based on the review presented in the chapter (as well as in many other contributions to this *Handbook*), important future developments in what we may generally call quantitative, SLA-oriented L2 writing research can be expected. These are very welcome initiatives that will help strengthen SLA-L2 writing interfaces. However, and here is where the issue of relevance becomes central, this research will succeed in advancing disciplinary conversations in the domain of L2 writing if, and only if, the ultimate purpose of the endeavor is to throw further light on a crucial dimension or facet of the global phenomenon of L2 writing. This would contrast with pseudo-writing studies that may simply use written data to test tenets or shed further light on SLA concerns that have nothing to do with writing itself, however important those concerns may be when seen through a SLA lens.

A second concern is again a word of caution regarding the progress that can be expected from purely quantitative studies in the analysis of many writing phenomena. As an example, cognition in writing is always situated cognition, and hence, at a minimum, the analysis of cognitive activity cannot be and should not be dissociated from writers themselves and everything they bring with them to the act of writing. This applies equally to the writer's involvement in feedback processing or in interpreting task complexity when engaged with writing tasks (see Manchón 2014). Therefore, a sole focus on quantitative data and quantitative analyses can only provide partial answers to the empirical questions we have, whereas a combination of quantitative and qualitative data and analyses in mixed-method studies has many more chances of providing better opportunities for providing principled answers to research problems and questions. Importantly, however, as Tashakkori and Teddlie (2003) remind us, mixed methods are only "marginally mixed" in that the research approach in its origin will be either quantitative or qualitative (along the lines of the characterization of quantitative and qualitative research presented in the opening section). An important point to be remembered when the mixed-method card is invoked.

To conclude, I hope to have convinced readers that quantitatively-oriented empirical efforts should be credited with having played and be currently playing a key role in advancing our understanding of key dimensions of the multi-faceted phenomenon of writing in an additional language. Future progress will nevertheless crucially depend on maintaining, improving, and reflecting critically on the standards of research quality applied and to be applied in the field, and on combining research quality with relevance in future research endeavours. I would also like to think that divergent disciplinary directions, perspectives and epistemologies will peacefully and fruitfully coexist in future developments in L2 writing scholarship.

6 Acknowledgement

The analysis of research reported in this chapter is part of the work conducted within two research projects financed by the Spanish Ministerio de Economía y Competitividad (research grant FF12012-35839) and by Fundación Séneca, the research agency of the Autonomous Government of the Region of Murcia, Spain (research grant 19463/PI/14).

7 Additional sources

Hyland, Ken. 2010a. *Teaching and researching writing*. Harlow, UK: Longman/Pearson Education Limited (3rd edition, 2016, Routledge).
Hyland, Ken. 2010b. Researching writing. In Brian Paltridge and Aek Phakiti (eds.), *Continuum companion to research methods in applied linguistics*, 191–204. London/New York: Continuum.
Mackey, Alison and Susan M. Gass (eds.). 2012. *Research methods in second language acquisition. A practical guide*. Malden, MA: Wiley-Blackwell.
Matsuda, Paul Kei and Tony Silva (eds.). 2005. *Second language writing research: Perspectives on the process of knowledge construction*. Mahwah, NJ: Lawrence Erlbaum.
Plonsky Luke and Laura Gurzynski-Weiss. 2014. Research methods. In Christiane Fäcke (ed.), *Manual of language acquisition*, 31–49. Berlin: de Gruyter Mouton.

Polio, Charlene. 2012. How to research second language writing. In Alison Mackey and Susan M. Gass (eds.), *Research methods in second language acquisition. A practical guide*, 139–157. Malden, MA: Blackwell Publishing Ltd.

Porte, Graeme. 2010. *Appraising research in second language learning. A practical approach to critical analysis of quantitative research*. Amsterdam: John Benjamins.

Rasinger, Sebastian. 2013. *Quantitative research in linguistics*. London/New York: Bloomsbury

Silva, Tony and Paul Kei Matsuda (eds.). 2010. *Practicing theory in second language writing*. West Lafayette, IN: Parlor Press.

Tashakkori, Abbas and Charles Teddle (eds.). 2003. *Handbook of mixed methods in social and behavioural research*. Thousand Oaks, CA: Sage.

8 References

Achugar, Mariana and Brian Carpenter. 2014. Tracking movement toward academic language in multilingual classrooms. *Journal of English for Academic Purposes* 14. 60–71.

Adams, Rebecca. 2006. L2 tasks and orientation to form: A role for modality? *ITL: International Journal of Applied Linguistics* 152. 7–34.

Adams, Rebecca and Lauren Ross-Feldman. 2008. Does writing influence learner attention to form? In Diane Belcher and Alan Hirvela (eds.), *The oral-literate connection*, 243–266. Ann Arbor, MI: The University of Michigan Press.

Alwi, Nik A. N. M., Rebecca Adams, and Jonathan Newton. 2012. Writing to learn via text chat: Task implementation and focus on form. *Journal of Second Language Writing* 21. 23–39.

Baba, Kyoko and Ryo Nitta. 2014. Phase transitions in development of writing fluency from a Complex Dynamic Systems perspective. *Language Learning* 64. 1–35

Beare, Sophie and Johanne Bourdages. 2007. Skilled writers' generating strategies in L1 and L2: An exploratory study. In Mark Torrance, Luuk Van Waes, and David Galbraith (eds.), *Writing and cognition: Research and applications*, 151–161. Amsterdam: Elsevier.

Benevento, Cathleen and Neomy Storch. 2011. Investigating writing development in secondary school learners of French. *Assessing Writing* 16(2). 97–110.

Biber, Douglas, Bethany Gray, and Kornwipa Poonpon. 2011. Should we use characteristics of conversation to measure grammatical complexity in L2 writing development? *TESOL Quarterly* 45. 5–35.

Bitchener, John. 2008. Evidence in support of written corrective feedback. *Journal of Second Language Writing* 17. 102–118.

Bitchener, John and Ute Knoch. 2008. The value of written corrective feedback in migrant and international students. *Language Teaching Research* 12. 409–431.

Bitchener, John and Ute Knoch. 2009. The relative effectiveness of different types of direct written corrective feedback. *System* 37. 322–329.

Bulté, Bram and Alex Housen. 2014. Conceptualizing and measuring short-term changes in L2 writing complexity. *Journal of Second Language Writing* 26. 42–65.

Byrnes, Heidi. 2009. Emergent L2 German writing ability in a curricular context: A longitudinal study of grammatical metaphor. *Linguistics and Education* 20. 50–66.

Byrnes, Heidi (ed). 2013. Writing as meaning-making-Teaching to mean. Special of the *Journal of Second Language Writing* 22.

Byrnes, Heidi. 2014. Linking task and writing for language development: Evidence from a genre-based curricular approach. In Heidi Byrne and Rosa M. Manchón (eds.), *Task-based language learning – Insights from and for L2 writing*, 237–263. Amsterdam: John Benjamins.

Byrnes, Heidi and Rosa M. Manchón. 2014. Task, task performance, and writing development: Advancing the constructs and the research agenda. In Heidi Byrnes and Rosa M. Manchón (eds.), *Task-based language learning: Insights to and from writing*, 267–299. Amsterdam: John Benjamins.

Chenoweth, Ann and John Hayes. 2001. Fluency in writing: Generating text in L1 and L2. *Written Communication* 18. 80–98.

Cheng, Y.-S. 2004. A measure of second language writing anxiety: Scale development and preliminary validation. *Journal of Second Language Writing* 13. 313–335.

Ching, L. Chien. 2002. Strategy and self-regulation instruction as contributors to improving students' cognitive model in an ESL program. *English for Specific Purposes* 21. 261–289.

Cimasko, Tony and Melinda Reichelt. 2011. *Foreign language writing. Research insights*. Parlour Press, West Lafayetter.

Connor-Linton, Jeff and Charlene Polio (eds.). 2014. Comparing perspectives on assessing ESL writing: Multiple analyses of a common corpus. Special issue, *Journal of Second Language Writing* 26.

Crossley, Scott A. and Danielle S. McNamara. 2009. Computational assessment of lexical differences in L1 and L2 writing. *Journal of Second Language Writing* 18. 119–135.

Crossley, Scott. A. and Danielle S. McNamara. 2011. Shared features of L2 writing: Intergroup homogeneity and text classification. *Journal of Second Language Writing* 20. 271–285.

Crossley, Scott. A. and Danielle S. McNamara. 2014. Does writing development equal writing quality? A computational investigation of syntactic complexity in L2 learners. *Journal of Second Language Writing* 26. 66–79.

Ellis, Rod and Fangyuan Yuan. 2004. The effects of planning on fluency, complexity and accuracy in second language narrative writing. *Studies in Second Language Acquisition* 26(1). 59–84.

Ellis, Rod, Younghee Sheen, Mihoko Murakami, and Hide Takashima. 2008. The effects of focused and unfocused written corrective feedback in an English as a foreign language context. *System* 36. 353–371.

Evans, Norman, K. James Hartshorn, Troy Cox, and Teresa Martin de Jel. 2014. Measures of written linguistic accuracy: Questions of reliability, validity, and practicality. *Journal of Second Language Writing* 24. 33–50.

Fernández-Dobao, Ana. 2012. Collaborative writing tasks in the L2 classroom: Comparing group, pair, and individual work. *Journal of Second Language Writing* 21. 40–58.

Flower, Linda and John Hayes. 1981. A cognitive process theory of writing. *College Composition and Communication* 32(4). 365–387.

Frear, Mark and John Bitchener. 2015. The effects of cognitive task complexity on writing complexity. *Journal of Second Language Writing* 30. 45–57.

Genc, Zubeyde Sinem. 2012. Effects of strategic planning on the accuracy of oral and written tasks in the performance of Turkish EFL learners. In Ali Shehadeh and Christine A. Coombe (eds.), *Task-based language teaching in foreign language contexts. Research and implementation*, 67–88. Amsterdam: John Benjamins.

Grant, Leslie and April Ginther. 2000. Using computer-tagged linguistic features to describe L2 writing differences. *Journal of Second Language Writing* 9. 123–145.

Gunnarsson, Cecilia. 2012. The development of complexity, accuracy, and fluency in the written production of L2 French. In Alex Housen, Folkert Kuiken, and Ineke Vedder (eds.). *Dimensions of L2 performance and proficiency: Complexity, accuracy, and fluency in SLA*, 247–276. Amsterdam: John Benjamins.

Hayes, John R. 1996. A new framework for understanding cognition and affect in writing. In Michael Levy and Sarah Ransdell (eds.). *The science of writing: Theories, methods, individual differences and applications*, 1–27. Mahwah, NJ: Lawrence Erlbaum Associates.

Hayes, John. 2012. Modelling and remodeling writing. *Written Communication*. 29. 369–388.

Hyland, Ken. 2010a. *Teaching and researching writing*. Harlow, UK: Longman/Pearson Education Limited (3rd edition, 2016, Routledge).

Hyland, Ken. 2010b. Researching writing. In Brian Paltridge and Aek Phakiti (eds.), *Continuum companion to research methods in applied linguistics*, 191–204. London/New York: Continuum.

Kellogg, Ronald. 1996. A model of working memory in writing. In Michael Levy and Sarah Ransdell (eds.), *The science of writing: Theories, methods, individual differences and applications*, 57–71. Mahwah, NJ: Lawrence Erlbaum Associates.

Kim, Youjin. 2008. The contribution of collaborative and individual tasks to the acquisition of L2 vocabulary. *The Modern Language Journal* 92. 114–130.

Kobayashi, Hiroe and Carol Rinnert. 2012. Understanding L2 writing development from a multicompetence perspective: Dynamic repertoires of knowledge and text construction. In Rosa M. Manchón, (ed.), *L2 writing development: Multiple erspectives*, 101–134. Boston/ Berlin: de Gruyter Mouton.

Johnson, Mark D., Leonardo Mercado, and Anthony Acevedo. 2012. The effect of planning sub-processes on L2 writing fluency, grammatical complexity, and lexical complexity. *Journal of Second Language Writing* 21. 264–282.

Kormos, Judit. 2011. Task complexity and linguistic and discourse features of narrative writing performance. *Journal of Second Language Writing* 20. 148–161.

Kormos, Judit. 2014. Differences across modalities of performance: An investigation of linguistic and discourse complexity in narrative tasks. In Heidi Byrnes and Rosa M. Manchón (eds.), *Task-based language learning: Insights to and from writing*, 193–216. Amsterdam: John Benjamins.

Kormos, Judit and Ana Trebits. 2012. The role of task complexity, modality and aptitude in narrative task performance. *Language Learning* 62. 439–472.

Kuiken, Folkert and Ineke Vedder. 2002a. The effect of interaction in acquiring the grammar of a second language. *International Journal of Educational Research* 37. 343–358.

Kuiken, Folkert and Ineke Vedder. 2002b. Collaborative writing in L2: The effect of group interaction on text quality. In Sarah Ransdell and Marie-Laure Barbier (eds.), *New directions for research in L2 writing*, 169–188. Dordrecht: Kluwer.

Kuiken, Folkert and Ineke Vedder. 2007. Task complexity and measures of linguistic performance in L2 writing. *International Review of Applied Linguistics in Language Teaching* 45. 261–284.

Kuiken, Folkert and Ineke Vedder. 2008. Cognitive task complexity and written output in Italian and French as a foreign language. *Journal of Second Language Writing* 17. 48–60.

Kuiken, Folkert and Ineke Vedder. 2011. Task performance in L2 writing and speaking: The effect of mode. In Peter Robinson (ed.), *Second language task complexity: Researching the Cognition Hypothesis of language learning and performance*, 91–104. Amsterdam: John Benjamins.

Kuiken, Folkert and Ineke Vedder. 2012. Syntactic complexity, lexical variation and accuracy as a function of task complexity and proficiency level in L2 writing and speaking. In Alex Housen, Folkert Kuiken and Ineke Vedder (eds.), *Dimensions of L2 performance and proficiency. Complexity, accuracy and fluency in SLA*, 43–169. Amsterdam: John Benjamins.

Laif, Muhammad. 2009. Toward a new process–based indicator for measuring writing fluency: Evidence from L2 writers' think-aloud protocols. *The Canadian Modern Language Review* 65. 531–558.

Leedham, Maria and Guozhi Cai. 2013. *Besides ... on the other hand*: Using a corpus approach to explore the influence of teaching materials on Chinese students' use of linking adverbials. *Journal of Second Language Writing* 22. 374–389

Leki, Ilona. 2005. Coping strategies of ESL students in writing tasks across the curriculum. *TESOL Quarterly* 29. 235–260.

Leki, Ilona, Alister Cumming, and Tony Silva. 2008. *A synthesis of research on second language writing in English*. New York: Routledge/Taylor and Francis.

Li, Yongyan and Christine Pearson Casanave. 2012. Two first-year students' strategies for writing from sources: Patchwriting or plagiarism? *Journal of Second Language Writing, Volume* 2. 165–180.

Lindgren, Eva and Marie Stevenson. 2013. Interactional resources in the letters of young writers in Swedish and English. *Journal of Second Language Writing* 22. 390–405.

Lindgren, Eva, Kristyan Spelman Miller, and Kirk Sullivan. 2008. Development of fluency and revision in L1 and L2 writing in Swedish high school years eight and nine. *ITL International Journal of Applied Linguistics* 156. 133–151.

Llanes, Àngels and Carmen Muñoz. 2013. Age effects in a study-abroad context: Children and adults studying abroad and at home. *Language Learning* 63. 63–90.

Lu, Xiaofei. 2011. A corpus-based evaluation of syntactic complexity measures as indices of college-level ESL writers' language development. *TESOL Quarterly* 45. 36–62.

Mackey, Alison and Susan M. Gass. 2012. Introduction. In Alison Mackey and Susan M. Gass (eds.), *Research methods in second language acquisition. A practical guide*. Malden, MA: Wiley-Blackwell.

Manchón, Rosa M. (ed.). 2009. *Writing in foreign language contexts: Learning, teaching and research*. Bristol: Multilingual Matters.

Manchón, Rosa M. (ed.). 2012. L2 writing development: Multiple perspectives. Boston/Berlin: de Gruyter-Mouton.

Manchón, Rosa M. 2013. Writing. In François Grosjean and Ping Li. *The psycholinguistics of bilingualism*, 100–116. Malden, MA: Wiley Blackwell.

Manchón, Rosa M. 2014. The internal dimension of tasks. The interaction between task factors and learner factors in bringing about learning through writing. In Heidi Byrnes and Rosa M. Manchón (eds.), *Task-based language learning: Insights to and from writing*, 27–52. Amsterdam: John Benjamins.

Manchón, Rosa M. and Julio Roca de Larios. 2007. On the temporal nature of planning in L1 and L2 composing. *Language Learning* 27. 549–593.

Manchón, Rosa M., Julio Roca de Larios, and Liz Murphy. 2005. Using concurrent protocols to explore L2 writing processes: Methodological issues in the collection and analysis of data. In Paul Kei Matsuda and Tony Silva (eds.), *Second language writing research. Perspectives on the process of knowledge construction*, 191–205. Mahwah, NJ: Lawrence Erlbaum Associates.

Manchón, Rosa M., Julio Roca de Larios, and Liz Murphy. 2007. A review of writing strategies: Focus on conceptualizations and impact of the first language. In Andrew Cohen and Ernesto Macaro (eds.), *Language learner strategies: Thirty years of research and practice*, 229–250. Oxford, UK: Oxford University Press.

Manchón, Rosa M., Julio Roca de Larios, and Liz Murphy. 2009. The temporal dimension and problem-solving nature of foreign language composing. Implications for theory. In Rosa M. Manchón (ed.), *Writing in foreign language contexts: Learning, teaching and research*, 102–129. Bristol: Multilingual Matters.

Mazgutova, Diana and Judit Kormos. 2015. Syntactic and lexical development in an intensive English for Academic Purposes programme. *Journal of Second Language Writing* 29. 3–15.

McDonough, Kim, William J. Crawford, and Jindarat De Vleeschauwer. 2014. Summary writing in a Thai EFL university context. *Journal of Second Language Writing* 24. 20–32.

Newman, Isadore, Carolyn S. Ridenour, Carole Newman, and George M. P. de Marco. 2003. A typology of research purposes and its relationship to mixed methods. In Abbas Tashakkori and Charles Teddlie (eds.), *Handbook of mixed methods in social and behavioral research*, 167–188. Thiusand Oaks, CA: Sage.

Nitta, Ryo and Kyoko Baba. 2014. Task repetition and L2 writing development: A longitudinal study from a dynamic systems perspective. In Heidi Byrnes and Rosa M. Manchón (eds.), *Task-based language learning: Insights to and from writing*, 107–136. Amsterdam: John Benjamins.

Niu, Ruiying. 2009. Effect of task-inherent production modes on EFL learners' focus on form. *Language Awareness* 18. 38402.

Norris, John and Rosa M. Manchón. 2012. Investigating L2 writing development from multiple perspectives: Issues in theory and research. In Rosa M. Manchón (ed.), *L2 writing development: Multiple perspectives*, 221–244. Boston: de Gruyter Mouton.

Ong, Justina. 2014. How do planning time and task conditions affect metacognitive processes of L2 writers? *Journal of Second Language Writing* 23. 17–30.

Ong, Justina and Lawrence Zhang. 2010. Effects of task complexity on the fluency and lexical complexity in EFL students' argumentative writing. *Journal of Second Language Writing* 19(4). 218–233.

Ortega, Lourdes. 2003. Syntactic complexity measures and their relationship to L2 proficiency: A research synthesis of college-level L2 writing. *Applied Linguistics* 24. 492–518.

Ortega, Lourdes. 2012. Epilogue: Exploring L2 writing – SLA interfaces. *Journal of Second Language Writing* 21. 404–415.

Pérez-Vidal, Carmen (ed.). 2014. *Language acquisition in study abroad and formal instruction contexts*. Amsterdam: John Benjamins.

Petric, Bojana and Bernardett Czárl. 2003. Validating a writing strategy questionnaire. *System* 31. 187–215.

Plonsky, Luke. 2013. Study quality in SLA: An assessment of designs, analyses and reporting practices in quantitative L2 research. *Studies in Second Language Acquisition* 35. 655–687.

Plonsky, Luke. 2014. Study quality in quantitative L2 research (1990–2010): A methodological synthesis and call for reform. *The Modern Language Journal* 98. 450–470.

Plonsky Luke and Laura Gurzynski-Weiss. 2014. Research methods. In Christiane Fäcke (ed.), *Manual of language acquisition*, 31–49. Berlin: de Gruyter Mouton.

Polio, Charlene. 2003. Research on second language writing: An overview of what we investigate and how. In Barbara Kroll (ed.), *Exploring the dynamics of second language writing*, 35–65. Cambridge: Cambridge University Press.

Polio, Charlene. 2012. How to research second language writing. In Alison Mackey and Susan M. Gass (eds.), *Research methods in second language acquisition. A practical guide*, 139–157. Malden, MA: Blackwell Publishing Ltd.

Polio, Charlene and Mark C. Shea. 2014. An investigation into current measures of linguistic accuracy in second language writing research. *Journal of Second Language Writing* 26(4). 10–27.

Porte, Graeme. 1996. When writing fails: How academic context and past learning experience shape revision. *System* 24. 107–116.

Porte, Graeme. 1997. The etiology of poor second language writing: The influence of perceived teacher preferences on second language revision strategies. *Journal of Second Language Writing* 6. 61–78.

Porte, Graeme. 2010. *Appraising research in second language learning. A practical approach to critical analysis of quantitative research*. Amsterdam: John Benjamins.

Ransdell, Sarah, Beverly Lavelle, and C. Michael Levy. 2002. The effects of training a good working memory strategy on L1 and L2 writing. In Sarah Ransdell and Marie-Laurie Barbier (eds.), *New directions for research in L2 writing*, 133–144. Dordrecht: Kluwer.

Robinson, Peter. 2011. Second language task complexity, the Cognition Hypothesis, language learning, and performance. In Peter Robinson (ed.), *Second language task complexity. Researching the Cognition Hypothesis of language learning and performance*, 3–37. Amsterdam: John Benjamins.

Roca de Larios, Julio, Rosa M. Manchón, Liz Murphy, and Javier Marín. 2008. The foreign language writer's strategic behaviour in the allocation of time to writing processes. *Journal of Second Language Writing* 17. 30–47.

Ruiz-Funes, Marcela. 2015. Exploring the potential of second/foreign language writing for language learning: The effects of task factors and learner variables. *Journal of Second Language Writing* 28. 1–19.

Ryshina-Pankova, Marianna and Heidi Byrnes. 2013. Writing as learning to know: Tracing knowledge construction in L2 German compositions. *Journal of Second Language Writing* 22. 179–197.

Sachs, Rebecca and Charlene Polio. 2007. Learners' uses of two types of written feedback on an L2 writing revision task. *Studies in Second Language Acquisition* 29. 67–100.

Salimi, Asghar and Soghra Dadashpour. 2012. Task complexity and language production dilemmas. *Procedia* 46. 643–652.

Sasaki, Miyuki. 2004. A multiple-data analysis of the 3.5-year development of EFL student writers. *Language Learning* 54(3). 525–582.

Sengupta, Sima. 2000. An investigation into the effects of revision strategy instruction on L2 secondary school learners. *System* 28. 97–113.

Serrano, Raquel, Elsa Tragant, and Àngels Llanes. 2012. A longitudinal analysis of the effects of one year abroad. *The Canadian Modern Language Review* 68. 138–163.

Schoonen, Rob, Amos van Gelderen, Kees de Gloper, Jan Hulstijn, Annegien Simis, Patrick Snelling, and Marie Stevenson. 2003. First language and second language writing: The role of linguistuc knowledge, speed of processing, and metacognitive knowledge. *Language Learning* 54. 165–202.

Schoonen, Rob, Amos van Gelderen, Reinoud Stoel, Jan Hulstijn, and Kees de Glopper. 2011. Modeling the development of L1 and EFL writing proficiency of secondary-school students. *Language Learning* 61. 3179.

Schoonen, Robert, Patrick Snellings, Marie Stevenson, and Amos Van Gelderen. 2009. Towards a blueprint of the foreign language writer: The linguistic and cognitive demands of foreign language writing. In Rosa M. Manchón (ed.), *Writing in foreign language contexts: Learning, teaching, and research*, 77–101. Clevedon, UK: Multilingual Matters.

Sheen, Young Hee. 2007. The effect of focused written corrective feedback and language aptitude on ESL learners' acquisition of articles. *TESOL Quarterly* 41. 255–284.

Sheen, Young Hee. 2010. Differential effects of oral and written corrective feedback in the ESL classroom. *Studies in Second Language Acquisition* 32. 203–234.

Sheen, Young Hee, David Wright, and Ana Moldawa. 2009. Differential effects of focused and unfocused written correction on the accurate use of grammatical forms by adult ESL learners. *System* 37. 556–569.

Shintani, Natsuko and Rod Ellis. 2013. The comparative effect of direct written corrective feedback and metalinguistic explanation on learners' explicit and implicit knowledge of the English indefinite article. *Journal of Second Language Writing* 22. 286–306.

Shintani, Natsuko, Rod Ellis, and Wataru Suzuki. 2014. Effects of written corrective feedback and revision on learners' accuracy in using two English grammatical structures. *Language Learning* 64. 103–131.

Skehan, Peter. 2009. Modelling second language performance: Integrating complexity, accuracy, fluency, and lexis. *Applied Linguistics* 30. 510–532.

Snellings, Patrick, Amos van Gelderen, and Kees de Glopper. 2004a. Validating a test of second language written lexical retrieval: A new measure of fluency in written language production. *Language Testing* 21. 174–201.

Snellings, Patrick, Amos Van Gelderen, and Kees D. Glopper. 2004b. The effect of enhanced lexical retrieval on L2 writing: A classroom experiment. *Applied Psycholinguistics* 55. 175–200.

Spack, Ruth. 1997. The acquisition of academic literacy in a second language. A longitudinal case study. *Written Communication* 14. 3–62

Stevenson, Marie, Robert Schoonen, and Kees de Glopper. 2006. Revising in two languages: A multi-dimensional comparison of online writing revisions in L1 and FL. *Journal of Second Language Writing* 15(3). 201–233.

Storch, Neomy. 2009. The impact of studying in a second language (L2) medium university on the development of L2 writing. *Journal of Second Language Writing* 18. 103–118.

Storch, Neomy and Gillian Wiglesworth. 2010. Learners' processing, uptake, and retention of corrective feedback on writing. *Studies in Second Language Acquisition* 32. 303–334.

Tavakoli, Parvaneh. 2014. Storyline complexity and syntactic complexity in writing and speaking tasks. In Heidi Byrnes and Rosa M. Manchón (eds.), *Task-based language learning: Insights to and from writing*, 217–236. Amsterdam: John Benjamins.

Teddlie, Charles and Abbas Tashakkori. 2003. Major issues and controversies in the use of mixed methods in the social and behavioral sciences. In Charles Teddlie and Abbas Tashakkori (eds.), *Handbook of mixed methods in social and behavioral research*, 3–50. London: Sage.

Thorson, Helga. 2000. Using the computer to compare foreign and native language writing processes: A statistical and case study approach. *The Modern Language Journal* 84. 155–170.

Tillema, Marion. 2012. *Writing in first and second language: Empirical studies on text quality and writing processes*. Utrecht: LOT Dissertation Series.

Van Beuningen, Catherine, Nivja H. De Jong, and Folkert Kuiken. 2012. Evidence on the effectiveness of comprehensive error correction in second language writing. *Language Learning* 62. 1–41.

Van Gelderen, Amos, Ron Oostdam, and Erik Van Schooten. 2011. Does foreign language writing benefit from increased lexical fluency? Evidence from a classroom experiment. *Language Learning* 61(1). 281–321.

Van Weijen, Daphne. 2008. *Writing processes, text quality, and task effects; Empirical studies in first and second language writing*. Utrecht: LOT Dissertation Series.

Van Weijen, Daphne, Huub van den Bergh, Gert Rijlaarsdam, and Ted Sander. 2009. L1 use during L2 writing: An empirical study of a complex phenomenon. *Journal of Second Language Writing* 18. 235–250.

Verheyden, Lieve, Kris Van den Branden, Gert Rijlaarsdam, Huub Van den Bergh, and Sven De Maeyer. 2010. Written narrations by 8- to 10-year-old Turkish pupils in Flemish primary education: A follow-up of seven text features. *Journal of Research in Reading* 33. 20–38.

Verspoor, Marjolijn and Hana Smiskova. 2012. Foreign language writing development from a dynamic writing-based perspective. In Rosa M. Manchón (ed.), *L2 writing development: Multiple perspectives*, 17–46. Boston/Berlin: de Gruyter Mouton.

Verspoor, Marjolijn, Monika S. Schmid, and Xiaoyan Xu. 2012. A dynamic usage based perspective on L2 writing. *Journal of Second Language Writing* 21. 239–263.

Vyatkina, Nina. 2012. The development of second language writing complexity in groups and individuals: A longitudinal learner corpus study. *The Modern Language Journal* 96(4). 576–598.

Vyatkina, Nina (ed.). 2015. New developments in the study of L2 writing complexity. Special issue of the *Journal of Second Language Writing* 28.

Wigglesworth, Gillian and Neomy Storch. 2009. Pair versus individual writing: Effects of fluency, complexity and accuracy. *Language Testing* 26(3). 45–466.

Wigglesworth, Gillian and Neomy Storch. 2012. Feedback and writing development through collaboration: A socio-cultural approach. In Rosa M. Manchón (ed.), *L2 writing development: Multiple perspectives*, 69–97. Boston/Berlin: De Gruyter Mouton.

Yang, Chengsong, Guangwei Hu, and Lawrence Jun Zhang. 2014. Reactivity of concurrent verbal reporting in second language writing. *Journal of Second Language Writing* 24. 51–70.

Yasuda, Sachico. 2011. Genre-based tasks in foreign language writing: Developing writers' genre awareness, linguistic knowledge, and writing competence. *Journal of Second Language Writing* 20. 111–133.

Yu, Guoxing. 2009. Lexical diversity in writing and speaking task performances. *Applied Linguistics* 31(2). 236–259.

Zamel, Vivian. 1983. The composing processes of advanced ESL students: Six case studies. *TESOL Quarterly* 17. 165–190.

Zhang, Cui. 2013. Effect of instruction on ESL students' synthesis writing. *Journal of Second Language Writing* 22. 51–67.

VI. **Interdisciplinary relations**

Dwight Atkinson

25 Second language writing and culture

"Culture" has had a mixed career in academia over the past half-century. It was first developed as a social science concept by pioneer anthropologist Franz Boas and his students from German sources, starting around the turn of the 20th century. By the 1950s, it had become as central to the social sciences as "gravity [was] to physics, disease to medicine, and evolution to biology" (Kroeber and Kluckhohn 1952: 3). This was followed, starting in the 1970s, by a prolonged period of critique, which the concept is still under. Today, culture is "half-abandoned in anthropological theory" (Mazzerella 2004: 345) – the same may be true in other fields, including second language (L2) writing.

One of the many problems with culture is its definition. Raymond Williams (1983), co-founder of the field known as cultural studies, proclaimed it one of the three most difficult words in English, while anthropologists Kroeber and Kluckhohn (1952) extracted some 160 definitions from the literature in an unsuccessful attempt to develop a single, agreed-upon understanding. Radical definitional differences existed even among Boas' highly influential students: his first, Robert Lowie (1920), defined culture as "that planless hodgepodge, that thing of shreds and patches" (p. 441) on the "diffusionist" principle that cultures were more or less random collections of social practices, beliefs, material technologies, religious rituals, and art forms learned from those living "over the hill" (Eriksen and Nielsen 2001). Edward Sapir (1924/1949), on the other hand, used the word to:

> embrace in a single term those general attitudes, views of life, and specific manifestations of civilization that give a particular people their distinctive place in the world …. [This] conception of culture is apt to crop up particularly in connection with problems of nationality, with attempts to find embodied in the character and civilization of a given people some peculiar excellence, some distinguishing force, that is strikingly its own. Culture thus becomes synonymous with the "spirit" or "genius" of a people, yet not altogether, for whereas these loosely used terms refer rather to a psychological, or pseudo-psychological, background of national civilization, culture includes with this background a series of concrete manifestations which are believed to be peculiarly symptomatic of it (p. 311).

A third influential Boasian, Ruth Benedict (1934, quoted in Salzman 2001: 72), defined a culture as "a more or less consistent pattern of thought and interaction". Kuper (1999) has argued that it was in fact Benedict and Margaret Mead who took the concept in more deterministic directions, as evidenced in Benedict's (1934) statement:

> The life history of the individual is first and foremost an accommodation to the patterns and standards traditionally handed down in his [sic] community. From the moment of his birth the customs into which he is born shape his experience and his behaviour. By the time he can

talk, he is the little creature of his culture, and by the time he is grown and able to take part in its activities, its habits are his habits, its beliefs his beliefs, its impossibilities his impossibilities (p. 3).

Facing definitional indeterminacy, and with certain reservations, I here adopt Benedict's "more or less consistent pattern of thought and interaction" to which "the life history of the individual is first and foremost an accommodation" as representing a view of culture that was adopted historically across many fields, including L2 writing. Something like this, at any rate, has been the main target of the concept's critics.

Culture critique has arisen largely (but not completely) in a particular context: the advent of neo-Marxist and poststructuralist/postmodernist critical theory in Western academia. From literary studies to the social sciences to education, a "restless problematization of the given" (Dean, quoted in Pennycook 2001: 8) has prompted the deep questioning of "modern" concepts used to explain human difference, including race, society, ethnicity, sex/gender, nation, and culture. This critique has yielded many positive results, but also contains its own contradictions. Often embedded within it is a quintessentially modern Marxist narrative of pure oppressed versus pure oppressor – "the one right story" by "the one who knows" (Lather 2001: 184 and 191).

Critical charges against culture, most of them interrelated, include: its deterministic, essentializing character; its complicity with colonialism and discourses of "othering"; its fundamental racism, in that it acts as a covert substitute concept for "race"; and its conflation with categories like nation and ethnicity. The concept has undergone powerful critique in applied linguistics, TESOL, and L2 writing as well. In L2 writing, the area known as contrastive rhetoric (CR) has come in for particularly heavy questioning, but other forms of cultural research have also been placed under the microscope. As a result, cultural influence on L2 writing often seems to have become a topic either to critique or avoid.

This chapter reviews research in and beyond L2 writing studies that bears directly on how culture has been conceptualized in the field. It takes a loosely historical-chronological approach, beginning with CR, moving on to earlier non-CR work, and then introducing current issues in L2 writing research on culture. In each case I give prominence to critical studies, in the belief that they constitute the main engine of development in the field.

1 Historical review

1.1 Contrastive rhetoric

Historical accounts of L2 writing usually note the pioneering contribution of Robert B. Kaplan. In the mid-1960s, before any real sense of L2 writing as a discrete phenomenon existed, Kaplan published an article entitled "Cultural thought patterns in intercultural education" (1966). There he proposed that different cultural thought styles lead to different forms of rhetorical organization in writing, and that to help L2 students write effectively in English these differences must be analyzed and addressed (see Chapter 3). To do so, Kaplan adopted the then-popular method of applied linguistic analysis called contrastive analysis, which compared linguistic structures in particular L1s side-by-side with their target language counterparts, on the principle that structural differences led to learning difficulty. Kaplan adapted this approach to rhetorical analysis, yielding "a contrastive analysis of rhetoric" (p. 15).

Applying this approach, Kaplan made a preliminary analysis of a heterogeneous group of writings in English, including "some 700 foreign student compositions" (p. 6). According to this analysis, writers from Semitic language backgrounds wrote paragraphs featuring "elaborate parallelism", which Kaplan diagrammed as a series of parallel horizontal vectors connected by diagonal dotted lines; Oriental language writers wrote in a vortex-like pattern, which he described as "approach by indirection" (p. 10); and Romance-language and Russian writers organized their texts digressively by English standards, with the former beginning and ending linearly but with "much greater freedom to digress … than in English" (p. 12) in between, and the latter revealing "a series of parallel constructions … and subordinate structures, at least half of which appear to be irrelevant to the central idea of the paragraph" (p. 12). In keeping with contrastive analysis, each native style was described in terms of its divergence from "the rhetoric of the English paragraph" (p. 19), itself diagrammed as a linear vertical vector.

Kaplan's paper has received an enormous amount of attention since it was published, much of it critical. The immediate response, however, was largely positive: researchers took up Kaplan's call to place CR on firmer empirical and theoretical ground. Early examples include John Hinds' work and chapters in Connor and Kaplan (1987), as well as Kaplan's many subsequent publications. Later efforts include Ulla Connor's work, as well as Xiaoming Li's, Anna Mauranen's, and the papers collected in Connor, Nagelhout, and Rozycki (2008). Major proposals and findings include a semi-inductive expository prose structure in some Asian languages (Hinds 1990); differences in Japanese versus English writing regarding "reader versus writer responsibility" for making meaning from written texts (Hinds 1987); genre's mediating effect on prose structure (Connor 1996; Kaplan 1992; Mauranen 1993); and differences in cultural expectations for "good writing" (Li 1996). Connor (e.g., 1996, 2002, 2011) has devoted considerable energy to connecting CR to other domains of applied linguistics and developing reliable research methods.

1.2 Critiques of contrastive rhetoric

It was the critical response to CR, however, which carried the day (see also discussion in Chapter 3). Early critics noted that comparing L1 and L2 texts for signs of cultural difference was problematic, since L2 developmental factors might inter-vene. They further noted the randomness of Kaplan's corpus and the scientific in-accuracy of his "Oriental" language group. Later critics, usually influenced by criti-cal theory, questioned the whole CR enterprise, focusing substantially on its con-ceptualization of culture. This later critique, in my opinion, has largely set the tone for subsequent treatments of culture in L2 writing.

Kubota (1997) can be said to have initiated the later critique of CR by question-ing Kaplan's claim that single languages and cultures have single rhetorics which represent them uniquely. Kubota illustrated this claim using Hinds' (1983a) re-search on the Japanese *ki-sho-ten-ketsu* pattern, which Hinds suggested was a ma-jor (but, contra Kubota, by no means the only – e.g., Hinds 1983b) Japanese exposi-tory prose style. Kubota argued that Hinds thereby essentialized Japanese prose, "dichotomizing us and them and constructing, instead of discovering, cultural dif-ferences" (p. 475).

Pennycook (1998) compared Kaplan's description of "Oriental rhetoric to a 19th-century colonial schoolmaster's claim that Chinese people could not think logical-ly, resulting in circular argumentation. For Pennycook, both descriptions were part of a larger "Orientalist" discourse in which Chinese are portrayed as passive, uno-riginal, rote learners versus active, original, critical-thinking Westerners – a dis-course also pervading the TESOL literature. Kaplan's CR thus participated in a dis-course of colonialism which "reproduces ... the view of the Other as deviant and ... locked in ancient and unchanging modes of thought and action" (p. 189).

In a later series of papers, Kubota (e.g., 2001, 2004) sharpened her critique of CR, as well as other L2 writing and TESOL research on non-Western cultures. Her main arguments *vis-à-vis* culture included: 1. the "discourse of cultural dichotomy" (2001: 24) featured in CR specifically and TESOL generally is part of long-lived Western racist ideology; 2. by treating cultural groups as separate but equal, stan-dard (so-called "liberal") multiculturalism participates in the same racist discourse of cultural difference while ignoring inequality and power differences in intercul-tural relations; and 3. an alternative form of multiculturalism – *critical multicultur-alism* – is superior to liberal multiculturalism because it problematizes cultural power relations, interrogates discourses of difference, and views cultural descrip-tion as constructed through powerful forms of knowledge, or discourses. Critical multiculturalist pedagogy allows students to develop their own English rather than having to assimilate and accommodate to "native-speaker" norms.

Other historical critiques of CR included Leki (1997), Kachru (1997), and Cana-garajah (2002). Matsuda (1997) advocated going beyond the static assumptions and cultural programming of classic CR, instead emphasizing writer agency, context, and writing processes. Casanave (2004) and Atkinson (2012) provided historical reviews of CR research and its critique, and, in Casanave's case, treated its peda-gogical implications.

1.3 Other historical work on L2 writing and culture

Non-CR L2 writing research also took the culture concept on board; much of it was subsequently criticized for this reason. This research and its critique are reviewed here.

Shen (1989) described his efforts to develop an English writing identity after coming to the US from China. His university writing teachers' encouragement to "be yourself" and "just write what *you* think" (p. 460) proved unhelpful, because the individualist ideology behind it was unknown to Shen, who conceptualized himself in terms of a Chinese and Marxist collective self. Only mental tricks like imagining himself climbing out of his Chinese skin and into a Western one, and writing strategies like filling his compositions with "I", helped Shen bridge the gap. He was further challenged by "logical" differences such as starting essays with thesis statements versus building up to the main point, and the "verbal logic" of US composition versus the "pictorial logic" of the nature-oriented *yinjing* style in Chinese.

Carson (1992) reviewed literacy learning research on Japan and China for how it might impact US-based L2 writing instruction, identifying certain culturally variable practices: 1. memorization was a key learning strategy in Japan and China, whereas personal invention and creativity were emphasized in the US; 2. group work was common across cultures but had divergent goals, promoting group solidarity and cooperation in Japan and China versus individual development in the US; 3. education was a moral enterprise in Japan and China versus the US; and 4. skill in close reading and "reading between the lines" might be a mixed blessing especially for Japanese students, because while US academia valued the former it favored reader-responsible prose.

Following up on Carson's review, Carson and Nelson investigated the implications of peer response group work for L2 writers in US universities, focusing especially on Chinese students. Carson and Nelson (1994) reviewed research suggesting that students from "collectivist" (Hui and Triandis 1986) cultures – cultures emphasizing group needs over individual achievement – might find peer response problematic because: 1. its purpose is to promote individual learning, not group harmony; 2. emphasis on group harmony may discourage provision of critical comments; and 3. collectivist approaches to in-group – out-group relations could further mitigate effective peer response. Carson and Nelson (1996, 1998) investigated these issues empirically, focusing on Chinese students but using Mexican students as a comparison group. They concluded that peer response was problematic both cross-culturally, due in part to differences 1. and 2. above, and in general.

Ramanathan and Kaplan (1996) analyzed US university composition textbooks for assumptions they contained about "audience" and "voice". They argued that, as part of a more general inductive approach to teaching writing, neither concept was adequately defined or taught, leaving "students from non-US cultures" (p. 22) at a disadvantage. To alleviate this problem, they suggested teaching discipline-specific writing instead of general composition.

Pennycook (1996) investigated the complexities and contradictions underlying the notion of plagiarism. Tracing the concept of the autonomous author to the historical growth in the West of "creative and possessive individualism" (p. 212), he suggested that the cult of originality which resulted was a very particular (and peculiar) cultural construction – one which, for example, glossed over the socially shared nature of language. Pennycook then discussed Chinese notions of textuality and memorization, often cited as diametrically opposed to expectations for originality in the West. Questioning this view, he argued that originality and memorization could be seen not as opposed, but complexly bound together. Finally, Pennycook reported interviewing Chinese students in Hong Kong who had been accused of plagiarism and finding that the notion itself insufficiently explained the wide range of behaviors and motivations leading students to use others' texts in (normatively defined) illegitimate ways.

Atkinson (1997; see also Fox 1994) critically examined the notion of critical thinking, suggesting that it might be a complex social practice learned implicitly by certain groups rather than a well-defined, teachable set of behaviors. He reviewed research suggesting that some East Asian groups adopted social norms diametrically opposed to a US middle-class emphasis on argument for argument's sake and using language substantially as a knowledge-discovery device.

Ramanathan and Atkinson (1999a) discussed four US composition teaching concepts/practices apparently influenced by a Western ideology of individualism: 1. voice; 2. peer response; 3. critical thinking; and 4. textual ownership. Regarding voice, they reviewed studies suggesting that its "personalist" version – dominant in expressivist approaches to process writing – was a culturally specific (i.e., Western) phenomenon. Ramanathan and Atkinson concluded by suggesting that individualism may also motivate some critics of cultural L2 writing research: They may understand others largely along individualist lines, thus minimizing cultural influence. Ramanathan and Atkinson argued that this possibility made cultural research all the more necessary and important in the field.

Two culture critics addressed by Ramanathan and Atkinson were Vivian Zamel and Ruth Spack. Zamel (1997) had argued that culture-focused L2 writing research led to "a deterministic stance and deficit orientation as to what students can accomplish in English and what their writing instruction should be" (p. 341). She described her experience with her students as confirming that supposed cultural differences in no sense limit what students can learn, and can even stimulate learning. Zamel concluded by calling for a complex "transcultural" understanding of L2 writers – one that did not confine them to predesignated cultural categories, because:

> The reality of cultures is that they are highly unpredictable, "elusive", even chaotic, that they are "fictions people entertain about themselves and about other peoples" (Scheper-Hughes

1995, p. 22). We need to remember that these fictions ... are extensions of who we are ... ; and that what we make of our students and their experiences may very well be an artifact of these influences (p. 350).

For her part, Spack (1997) critiqued the TESOL profession's labeling of what she called "multilingual students". Such labeling marks students as *different* (e.g., "English as a *second* language") and *deficient* (e.g., "*non*-native speakers"), thereby fitting them to L2/cultural norms and disregarding their personal histories and identities. Cultural labels, specifically, "perpetuat[e] cultural myths" (p. 767) – here Spack provided a detailed critique of Carson's (1992) use of sources, and how other researchers took Carson's generalizations at face value. Spack then asserted that "teachers and researchers need to view students as individuals, not as members of a cultural group, in order to understand the complexity of writing in a language they are in the process of acquiring" (p. 772). She concluded by calling on TESOL practitioners to question the power dynamics behind labeling, instead allowing students to "name themselves and thus define and construct their own identities" (p. 773).

Kubota (1999a) questioned dichotomous cultural descriptions in L2 writing research, taking Japanese culture as an example. Her goal was to examine the place of such descriptions in larger circuits of power/knowledge, or *discourses* (Foucault 1980). Discourses not only define and label individuals authoritatively, for example through academic cultural description, but also circulate this "knowledge" back to those same individuals, causing them to internalize and thus be controlled by it. Kubota identified a colonialist discourse of the exotic "Other", which portrayed non-Western cultures as static and "knowledge-conserving", as the particular discourse operating in cultural research on L2 writing. She then: reviewed historical contradictions in this discursive knowledge; argued that it had nonetheless been internalized by many Japanese; reviewed evidence of Japanese educational practices problematizing this discourse; and ended by calling for a critical multiculturalist pedagogy, as described in the previous section.

Harklau (1999) investigated how four immigrant students who had grown up in the US were positioned as cultural "others" in community college/university writing classrooms. For example, the students were assigned writing prompts asking for explicit comparisons of the US and "your country", where their country – in terms of length of residence and/or relevant experience – was the US. Likewise, when the students introduced their hybrid identities into their writings they were discouraged from doing so by their teachers. Generally, there was a mismatch between the students' cultural realities and their ESL teachers' goals.

Finally, some of the authors reviewed in this section published critical responses to one another's' work, as well as rebuttals to those responses: Raimes and Zamel (1997) on Ramanathan and Kaplan (1996) and the latters' (1997) response; Carson (1998) and Nelson (1998) on Spack (1997) and Spack's (1998a, b) responses;

Atkinson (1999a) on Kubota (1999a) and Kubota's (1999b) response; and Atkinson (2002) on Kubota (2001) and Kubota's (2002) response.

2 Current research on L2 writing and culture

Dividing what is historical from what is current is inevitably a personal and arbitrary decision – this is even truer in a new field like L2 writing. In the present case, I use the turn of the 21st century as a rough line of demarcation, with due allowance given to other factors, such as tracing a critique's development over multiple years and papers. Even more personal and arbitrary is any attempt to describe a field's current state, yet that is my task in this section.

Within these limits, the current era of L2 writing can be described as one of cultural critique, response to critique, and/or avoidance or replacement of the culture concept. In the same way culture is now "half-abandoned" (see above) in anthropology, it appears to rest on precarious foundations in L2 writing. Below, I divide my account into subsections on theoretical research of a general nature in and beyond the field, theoretical work on contrastive/intercultural rhetoric specifically, and non-contrastive/intercultural rhetoric research on culture and L2 writing.

2.1 Current theoretical research of a general nature on culture

In this subsection, I review theoretically oriented literature on culture in L2 writing as well as sample from applied linguistics research more widely. If, as suggested above, culture avoidance/replacement is prevalent in L2 writing, then theoretical inspiration must also be sought outside the field.

Atkinson (1999b) analyzed all articles appearing in *TESOL Quarterly* from 1984 to 1998 with the word "culture" in their titles, finding signs of a shift toward critical approaches. He then: 1. summarized major critiques of culture emanating from the social sciences, humanities, and education; 2. attempted to reformulate the culture concept in a way that was sensitive to these critiques; 3. proposed guiding principles for studying culture in TESOL; and 4. concluded by calling for a robust if critically aware notion of culture for TESOL in the 21st century. While not focused on L2 writing specifically, this article was written in direct response to culture critique in the field circa 2000, as described above.

Holliday (1999) developed the notion of "small cultures" as an alternative to the "large culture" concept dominating cultural research in applied linguistics. For Holliday, the small-culture concept avoids essentialism, reification, and "otherization" by treating cohesive groups below the large-culture level as cultures in their own right, or small cultures. Thus, a classroom can be considered a culture, as can a discipline or profession. Small cultures differ from subcultures in not simply being contained within large cultures but potentially spreading across them, as for example hip-hop culture or TESOL professional culture do today. Additionally, small cultures emphasize cultural processes rather than products, envisioning culture as a dynamic site for social construction. Holliday concluded by discussing research methods for studying small cultures.

Atkinson (2003) explored possible uses of the culture concept in a "post-process" approach to L2 writing. First and foremost, he suggested studying US composition classrooms as sites of cultural production – in terms of the particular writing practices they adopt and how these link to larger sociocultural structures and ideologies like capitalism, private ownership, and individualism. Second, he suggested investigating the cultural hybridity and meshing so prominent in the global scene today. Third, he discussed attempts to complexify the culture concept, focusing especially on Holliday's (1999) small cultures.

Nelson and Carson (2006) reviewed culture critique in and beyond L2 writing, with special reference to peer response. They 1. noted a recent tendency across fields either to replace culture with critical/poststructuralist concepts such as identity and discourse or to avoid it altogether; 2. acknowledged that cultural description can lead to essentialism and stereotyping, but only when applied deterministically; and 3. called for qualitative research on peer response groups highlighting the complex, fragmented, and dynamic aspects of culture.

Finally, Pennycook (2007) developed Appadurai's (1996) notion of "transcultural flows" to describe new global cultural practices like hip-hop and the English that often accompanies them:

> I use the term transcultural flows to address the ways that cultural forms move, change, and are reused to fashion identities in diverse contexts. This is not, therefore, merely a question of cultural movement but take-up, appropriation, change, and refashioning. While not ignoring the many detrimental effects of globalization on economies and ecologies across the world … I am interested centrally here on the cultural effects of globalization (p. 6).

Pennycook thus investigated how local and global cultural traditions meet, mix, mesh, and form into something different, as well as what these differences mean in the lives of the practitioners of these new cultural forms.

Theoretical writings on culture dealing directly with contrastive/intercultural rhetoric are reviewed in the next subsection.

2.2 Current theoretical research on contrastive/intercultural rhetoric

Connor (2002) reviewed the state of CR at the start of the 21st century. She described its expansion beyond an original focus on text analysis of student essays to include a variety of genres, writing contexts, analytical methods, and writing processes. Regarding cultural issues, Connor noted the contribution of the culture critics in

helping stimulate new developments in CR, while suggesting that "to ignore cultural differences leads to ... 'discrimination of another sort'" (p. 504). She asserted
that CR treatments of contextual influences on rhetoric had not been as one-dimen-
sional as critics had described: "Researchers have explained ... differences in written communication as often stemming from multiple sources, including L2, national culture, L1 educational background, disciplinary culture, genre characteristics,
and mismatched expectations between readers and writers" (p. 504). Finally, Connor argued that criticism of CR-based pedagogies for enforcing native speaker
norms ignored reader expectations, as in her collaborative research (Connor et al.
1995) on Finnish scientists preparing European Union grant proposals – proposals
judged by norms of standard scientific English.

Connor (2004) proposed a name change for CR, based on new developments
in this research area. She drew on Sarangi's (1995) discussion of culture in intercultural pragmatics, in which he distinguished between *cross-cultural* and *intercultural* research. For Sarangi, cross-cultural research tends to produce idealized and
static portraits of language practices which, while useful in the search for linguistic
universals, fail to honor the complexity and dynamism of language and culture.
Intercultural research, on the other hand, allows for divergence from norms and
the creation of linguistic practices in interaction. Connor called for including *both*
types of research under the new umbrella term "intercultural rhetoric" (IR): 1.
cross-cultural studies comparing pre-existing text types across discrete cultures;
and 2. intercultural studies of the interpretation, negotiation, and modification of
linguistic practices in the spaces between cultures.

On the premise that CR had not yet "engaged with the notion of culture in a
serious, critical way" (p. 280), Atkinson (2004) suggested alternative approaches
to culture which might be useful for the field: 1. postmodernist approaches, which
highlight the fragmented nature of current society/culture; 2. cultural studies approaches, which treat culture as a site of ideological struggle; 3. process approaches, which view cultures as dynamic and ever-evolving; 4. sociocognitive approaches, which treat culture in terms of integrated "mind-body-world" complexes; and
5. Holliday's large-versus-small culture distinction, as described above.

Kubota and Lehner (2004) proposed a "critical contrastive rhetoric", which responds to mainstream CR by: 1. critically questioning "standard average European"
norms of language and culture, because mainstream CR valorizes them, thereby
placing L2 students in inferior positions; 2. critically questioning essentialized versions of language, culture, and identity for their hidden political motives; 3. cele-
brating diversity, including students' natal languages and cultures, in the classroom; 4. insisting that teachers "reflect critically on how classroom dialogue that
underscores cultural difference in rhetoric ... could perpetuate Othering, cultural
stereotyping, and unequal relations of power" (p. 18); 5. examining effects of colonialist and assimilationist discourses on students' natal languages and identities;
6. adopting a postmodernist view of knowledge as constructed, interested, and

partial, and English as globalized, hybrid, and the common property of all its us- ers; and 7. emphasizing student agency and critical exploration of the supposed cultural differences hypothesized by mainstream CR.

Canagarajah (2005) questioned whether a CR model which equated a single culture with a single writing style in a single genre in a single language was valid for multilingual writers who "shuttled between" communities and discourses in their English academic writing. Examining the case of a Sri Lankan sociolinguist writing in English, Canagarajah argued that this author adapted his use of genre conventions to the situated expectations of his audience. Thus, in papers aimed at a local Sri Lankan Tamil audience, the author adopted a more narrative and per- sonal style, whereas his style became "objective" and impersonal when he wrote for international audiences. Canagarajah also suggested, however, that these tend- encies were complexified by the author's strategic choices – for instance, adding a more formal research article-like introduction to a basically narrative and personal account. For Canagarajah, such cases reveal that multilingual academic writers operate agentively and creatively in multiple discourses to produce their own blended identities and rhetorical effects.

Li (2005) argued that mainstream CR research on written cultural norms com- plemented rather than opposed postmodernist research on globalization-induced instability and change because "fluidity is a valid concept only in relation to stabil- ity, just as permeability is a phenomenon that exists only when there are still bor- ders" (p. 128). To support this claim, Li compared two qualitative studies she had conducted of writing in China – one focusing on traditional Chinese values of "good writing" (1996), the other examining changes in secondary/tertiary-level writing pedagogy due to globalization (2000). She concluded that the two studies' findings, while different in focus, were hardly contradictory, and defended CR against "the charge that seeing writing as a cultural phenomenon ... essentializes unique individuals" because this "implies that there is an essential selfinsulated from its context" (p. 128).

Connor (2008) elaborated on her earlier call to rename CR "intercultural rhetoric":

> Contrastive rhetoric has been useful and explanatory. Yet it ... needs to move far beyond such binary distinctions as linear versus nonlinear discourse, Japanese prose versus Finnish prose, inductive versus deductive logic, and collectivist versus individualist norms. Instead, it needs to describe the vast complexities of cultural, social, and educational factors affecting a writing situation. It must attempt to understand why and how individuals behave rather than simply study cultural artifacts and products ... We need to know what went into the processes of writing as well as the historical background and context that affected the writing and the writer (p. 304).

More specifically, Connor proposed three directions for the new IR – their relevance to culture theory and research in L2 writing are as follows: 1. Fairclough's (1992) influential model of discourse, which Connor adopted to broaden the notion of discourse for IR, includes *discourse as social practice*. This involves studying socio-cultural norms and structures in the context of power, inequality, and struggles over representation; 2. Holliday's small-cultures concept enriches IR's notion of culture – Connor summarized a co-authored study (Connor and Mayberry 1996) of a US-based Finnish student whose lack of academic success arose from unfamiliari-ty with US university classroom culture; and 3. Giddens's (1979) model of social "structuration" opposes the idea that societies or cultures simply determine indi-vidual behavior, leading to a situation in which there is no social change. Instead, Giddens hypothesized "virtual" sociocultural norms, institutions, rules, etc. which are realized only in the behavior of individuals, who actively interpret, imperfectly understand or remember, bend, resist, and subvert such norms to their own ends. As a result, the norms are reworked each time they are instantiated in individual behavior, leading to their continual if often incremental development and change.

Li (2008) offered a defense of CR at the moment of its reinvention as IR. Regard-ing culture, she noted that critics of the concept *vis-à-vis* CR came from two differ-ent camps – one that "often fall[s] back on the romantic version of the individual" as a self-enclosed "cognitive universe" (p. 14, partly quoting Geertz 1983: 59), and one that adopts postmodernist and postcolonialist views of "reality as inscribed in power relations" (p. 14). While acknowledging the importance of these critiques, Li pointed out that their preferred vision – a world largely devoid of cultural groups and borders – still presented a limited view, and one not confirmed by her research experience in China. There, cultural tradition and change were co-dependent as well as highly uneven, with education remaining quite traditional in some ways – for example, in the use of "moral propositions" as university entrance exam writing prompts circa 2005. More generally:

> The interconnected world does not necessarily create a homogeneous world culture ... Each culture will select, invent, revise, and create its identity in response to a new reality by incor-porating its unique tradition instead of erasing it. [For example] Although it is not certain when and whether the grand vision of democracy is to be realized in the Middle East, it is certain that when [sic] it does it will demonstrate the distinct Islamic tradition of that area and will not be a copy of democracy as conceived and practiced in the West. A globalized world ... is not going to be a piece of flattened cardboard (p. 16).

In a wide-ranging academic conversation on the move from CR to IR (Matsuda and Atkinson 2008), Matsuda noted that while culture was standardly used to explain text structure in CR, it rarely received focal attention. As a result, claims about cultural influence on text were assumed rather than empirically demonstrated. At-kinson, for his part, presented his view of what "intercultural" could mean for the field: Investigating the "in-between space[s]" across cultures and the social action taking place there (see Bhabha 1994) – similar to Sarangi's (1995) sense of "inter-cultural" as employed by Connor (2004), described above. Matsuda then explored the idea of dropping "cultural" from the "intercultural" in CR/IR's new name, re-sulting in "inter-rhetoric", in which different rhetorics, whether cultural or not, could be directly compared. The authors concluded, however, by agreeing that culture was a vital – perhaps even the crucial – concept for the future success of intercultural rhetoric, a view also taken by Hirvela (2010).

Connor (2011) set out to reformulate the culture concept for IR. After reviewing attempts to rework the concept in other fields, she offered the metaphor of a patch-work coat to describe how she viewed her own cultural background: Her natal Finnish culture was the largest patch, with numerous smaller patches – her experiences living in different parts of the world, her multiple social roles and identities, etc. – superimposed on it; together, they made up a whole. Connor then developed Holliday's (1999) large-versus-small culture distinction in a way which complemented the patchwork metaphor, including a diagram in which national culture, professional-academic (e.g., English teacher) culture, classroom culture, student culture, and youth culture all overlapped in contributing to the culture of particular classrooms. Next, Connor introduced "interaction and accommodation" processes as key to IR "because we are concerned about real-life interactive communication situations that produce natural give-and-take negotiation and accommodation, such as in emails and other business communication" (p. 32). Finally, Connor reviewed Byram's (1997) widely cited framework for intercultural competence, which combines various kinds of attitudes, knowledge, and skills for navigating intercultural situations.

Atkinson (2012) reviewed the history of CR, including its rebranding as IR, over the past decade. Arguing that the field's future depended critically on developing the culture concept, he suggested that no single, ideal definition of culture was likely to emerge. Rather, IR should take its inspiration from a variety of sources, including the historical development of the anthropological culture concept prior to its critique. Boas' original formulation, for instance, based on the idea that cultures are accretions of borrowed practices and objects which are "stable-for-the-moment" but hardly coherent, unchanging wholes (e.g., Eriksen and Nielsen 2001) – best captured in Lowie's (1920) definition of culture as "that planless hodgepodge, that thing of shreds and patches", (p. 441 and also quoted above) – seems to closely reflect the conditions of the current globalized world, while retaining the core truth that people do "live culturally" (Ingold 1994).

Baker (2013) critiqued IR from a Lingua Franca English (LFE) perspective – i.e., one in which English is used throughout the world among those who do not speak it "natively". This view entails that English is the common property of all its users, whose uses of it should therefore be evaluated on their communicative effectiveness, not adherence to native speaker norms. Baker acknowledged that IR had begun to move in this direction, but argued that it had yet to abandon either the idea of discrete cultures or the authority of native-speaker Englishes to which all others must therefore accommodate. In place of norms, LFE foregrounds negotiation, fluidity, variability, and emergence as core characteristics of language behavior in intercultural contexts. Likewise, it views culture from an ideological perspective, asking for whose benefit and for what purpose claims of cultural influence on writing are made, especially in our current culturally mixed and unbounded global situation.

Complementing Baker (2013), Canagarajah (2013) described the "contact zone" nature of LFE interactions, arguing that they often resist cultural interpretation because LFE speakers "co-construct [communicative norms that] … may have nothing to do with the cultural backgrounds they come from" (p. 204). In place of culture, Canagarajah proposed the concept of "cosmopolitanism", signifying that people from different backgrounds can cooperate and communicate without sharing common norms and codes; instead, they develop shared practices in the course of interaction. In addition, people can also "perform" culture by "temporarily tak[ing] on the practices and values of communities they are not always born into (or situated in) to adopt alternative identities" (p. 206). Thus, rather than being a static or predefined entity, culture emerges from "specific interactions" (p. 209) as interactors negotiate and align. To support his argument, Canagarajah presented a sample LFE interaction, which he analyzed to reveal its negotiated and emergent nature.

2.3 Current non-CR/IR L2 writing research

Beyond the studies reviewed so far, relatively little research has appeared in the past decade which engages directly in the ongoing exploration and/or conceptualization of culture in L2 writing. This is not to say that the notion never appears; it continues to figure, for instance, as a putative influence on L2 writing practices – usually from a critical perspective – but is rarely accorded much discussion. A clear example is the plagiarism/textual borrowing literature (e.g., Bloch 2012; Hu and Lei 2012; Shi 2004). Such studies invariably mention the possibility of cultural influence, often involving the assumption that East Asian writers may privilege fidelity to pre-existing texts over originality of ideas and expression, but then typically go on to reject "culturalist" explanations, even when their empirical findings seem to suggest this possibility.

Below, I review the few published L2 writing studies I have located which include, in my view, substantive discussions/complications/critiques of the culture concept.

Questioning the claim that East Asian writers are reluctant to critique others' work in their academic writing, Cheng (2006) examined one Chinese doctoral student's growing critical awareness in a US university EAP class. An active in-class debater, the student was initially surprised to find little open criticism of others' work in published research articles (RAs) in his field – electrical engineering – finally concluding that either indirect criticism or none at all was the dominant strategy (it can be noted in passing that three of the five published RAs analyzed by the student had authors with Chinese surnames). In his own attempts to write RA introductions, however, the student employed both direct and indirect critical evaluation of past literature. Cheng interpreted the student's experience as revealing that, while cultural generalizations are not necessarily invalid, "rhetorical, disciplinary, and instructional influences ... seem more discernable and illuminating" (p. 302) in this case, suggesting "the need for a more nuanced view of the influence of national culture on L2 learners' academic literacy learning in general and their approach to academic criticism in particular" (p. 303).

You (2010) provided a book-length history of English composition in China, beginning with Western colonialism in the 19th century. He documented changing attitudes – from "writing in the [Western colonial] devil's tongue" in order to master that devil's technology in the last third of the 19th century, to using modern Western knowledge to overthrow feudalism and innovate a "new Chinese culture" in the early 20th, to supporting proletarian revolution in the mid-20th century, to joining the global information economy circa 2000. As a result, "the devil's tongue" has now become "our tongue":

> English composition took on both Anglo-American and Chinese rhetorical traditions at the same time. Confucian rhetoric dominated Chinese school writing for two thousand years ... In the early twentieth century, Western scientific rhetoric made its way into both English and Chinese composition and was strengthened in Chinese proletarian rhetoric in the 1950s. This new rhetoric located truth in the external, sensible world: the rhetor needed to convey truth to the audience objectively ... Chinese rhetorical traces never stopped creeping in ... Students were not poor learners of the devil's tongue, but rather they used English to describe their thoughts and feelings for both Chinese and international audiences and to experiment with, in Patricia Bizzell's words, "the textual arts of the contact zone" (168). Schooled with a scientific attitude and subjected to the local cultural signification, students had to adulterate the devil's tongue to signify their intended meanings (pp. 172–173).

Sharma (2012) studied "elite bilingual" Nepali college students' uses of English on Facebook, the social networking site. By using English in this context, the participants innovated new transcultural identities while communicating with college peers and family members for whom Nepali was otherwise the medium of communication. In doing so, the students actively aligned with the globalized media world and its multimodal, English-based norms, while still retaining local currency. Although not described by Sharma in exactly these terms, such innovative transcultural practices can be seen as agentive action for the purpose of differentiate one's socioeconomic group from the masses in order to preserve one's "cultural capital" (Bourdieu 1986). At the same time, however, "culture" gets globalized and complexified.

3 Future prospects for culture in second language writing

I stated above that little work has appeared in recent years which explicitly attempts to develop the culture concept in L2 writing, at least beyond the confines of IR. For someone who continues to believe that culture – properly disciplined and reimagined for the 21st century (Atkinson 1999b, 2003, 2012; Atkinson and Sohn 2013) – has explanatory value in L2 writing, this is disappointing. From a less self-interested perspective, however, there are other ways to view culture's current prospects in the field.

First, it may be that the culture concept has simply outlived its usefulness. In a time of radical cultural mixing and meshing – when one can fashion one's identity from the "cultural supermarket" (Mathews 2000) proffered by global media, effortless travel, international education, mass immigration, etc. – any notion of stable cultural influence may be a thing of the past. This seems to be part of the spirit behind suggestions for alternative concepts, such as Canagarajah's (2013) cosmopolitanism, Pennycook's (2007) transcultural identity performance, and perhaps Holliday's small cultures.

Second, as argued by some critics, the culture concept may be so tainted by its colonialist, racist past that any attempt to use it today amounts to discrimination. Certainly, culture is deeply implicated in "otherization" (Holliday 1999) – it has often been used to mark non-Western groups as different, and thus at least by implication, deficient. The basic ethics of the culture concept can therefore be questioned.

Third, and in my opinion most convincingly, culture has standardly been treated as a top-down, deterministic influence on the life of the individual – "the little creature of his culture" (Benedict 19343). Yet humans are clearly not cultural robots – they adopt an infinite variety of positions and identities *vis-à-vis* the norms (such as they are) of their natal cultures. The growth of identity studies in TESOL, applied linguistics, and to a lesser extent L2 writing has been substantially a response to such top-down concepts as culture, social class, race, and gender. In the words of Du Gay, Evans, and Redman (2000), "identity has achieved its contemporary centrality ... because that to which it is held to refer ... is regarded ... as being more contingent, fragile, and incomplete, and thus more amenable to reconstitution" (p. 2) than top-down notions like culture.

In practice, the three critiques just mentioned are usually combined in some form, amounting to a powerful, multi-perspectival attack on the culture concept. I would merely point out, however, that culture has been variably defined, and any attempt to paint it with a broad brush after nearly 100 years of development by many hands will be insufficient. The future of culture for L2 writing may therefore be in its alternative conceptions, starting, I believe, with the founding notion, as developed by Franz Boas and Robert Lowie, itself.

4 Acknowledgments

I would like to thank Suresh Canagarajah, Guangwei Hu, Gayle Nelson, and Ling Shi for kindly sharing their writings with me.

5 Additional sources

Akbasi, Ali and Nahal Akbari. 2014. What intercultural rhetoric is and isn't: A response to Xiaoming Li. *Journal of Second Language Writing* 25. 114–115.

Atkinson, Dwight. 2015. Writing across cultures: Culture' in second language writing studies. In Farzad Sharifian (ed.), *Routledge handbook of language and culture*, 417–430. London: Routledge.

Atkinson, Dwight and Paul Kei Matsuda. 2013. Intercultural rhetoric – a conversation: The sequel. In Diane Belcher and Gayle Nelson (eds.), *Critical and corpus-based approaches to intercultural rhetoric*, 227–247. Ann Arbor: University of Michigan Press.

Belcher, Diane. 2015. What we need and don't need intercultural rhetoric for: A retrospective and prospective look at an evolving research area. *Journal of Second Language Writing* 25. 59–67.

Canagarajah, Suresh. 2002. *A geopolitics of academic writing*. Pittsburgh: University of Pittsburgh Press.

Connor, Ulla. 2014. Comments on Xiaoming Li's 'Are "cultural differences a mere fiction"?' *Journal of Second Language Writing* 25. 114–115.

Grabe, William and Robert B. Kaplan. 1996. *Theory and practice of writing*. London: Longman.

Kubota, Ryuko. 2014. Conceptual confusions and contradictions: A response to Professor Xiaoming Li. *Journal of Second Language Writing* 25. 118–120.

Li, Xiaoming. 2014. Are "cultural differences a mere fiction"?: Reflections and arguments on contrastive rhetoric. *Journal of Second Language Writing* 25. 104–113.

You, Xiaoye. 2014. A comparative-rhetoric view of contrastive rhetoric. *Journal of Second Language Writing* 25. 116–117

6 References

Appadurai, Arjun. 1996. *Modernity at large: Cultural dimensions of globalization*. Minneapolis: University of Minnesota Press.

Atkinson, Dwight. 1997. A critical approach to critical thinking in TESOL. *TESOL Quarterly* 31. 71–94.

Atkinson, Dwight. 1999a. Comments on Ryuko Kubota's "Japanese culture constructed by discourses: Implications for applied linguistics research and ELT." *TESOL Quarterly* 33. 745–749.

Atkinson, Dwight. 1999b. TESOL and culture. *TESOL Quarterly* 33. 625–654.

Atkinson, Dwight. 2002. Comments on Ryuko Kubota's "Discursive construction of the images of US classrooms". *TESOL Quarterly* 36. 79–84.

Atkinson, Dwight. 2003. Writing and culture in the post-process era. *Journal of Second Language Writing* 12. 49–63.

Atkinson, Dwight. 2004. Contrasting rhetorics/contrasting cultures: Why contrastive rhetoric needs a better conceptualization of culture. *Journal of English for Academic Purposes* 3. 277–289.

Atkinson, Dwight. 2012. Intercultural rhetoric and intercultural communication. In Janet Jackson (ed.), *Routledge handbook of language and intercultural communication*, 116–129. Oxford: Routledge.

Atkinson, D. and Jija Sohn. 2013. Culture from the bottom up. *TESOL Quarterly* 47. 669–693.

Baker, Will. 2013. Interpreting the culture in intercultural rhetoric: A critical perspective from English as a Lingua Franca studies. In Diane Belcher and Gayle Nelson (eds.), *Critical and corpus-based approaches to intercultural rhetoric*, 22–45. Ann Arbor, MI: University of Michigan Press.

Benedict, Ruth. 1934. *Patterns of culture*. Boston: Houghton-Mifflin.

Bhabha, Homi. 1994. *The location of culture.* Oxford: Routledge.

Bloch, Joel. 2012. *Plagiarism, intellectual property and the teaching of L2 writing.* Bristol, England: Multilingual Matters.

Bourdieu, Pierre. 1986. The forms of capital. In John G. Richardson (ed.), *Handbook of theory and research for the sociology of education*, 241–258. New York: Greenwood Press.

Byram, Michael. 1997. *Teaching and assessing intercultural communicative competence.* Clevedon, UK: Multilingual Matters.

Canagarajah, Suresh. 2002. *Critical second language writing.* Ann Arbor, MI: University of Michigan Press.

Canagarajah, Suresh. 2005. Shuttling between discourses: Textual and pedagogical possibilities for periphery scholars. In Giuseppina Cortese and Anna Duszak (eds.), *Identity, community, discourse: English in intercultural settings*, 47–68. Berlin: Peter Lang.

Canagarajah, Suresh. 2013. From intercultural rhetoric to cosmopolitan practice: Addressing new challenges in Lingua Franca English. In Diane Belcher and Gayle Nelson (eds.), *Critical and corpus-based approaches to intercultural rhetoric*, 203–226. Ann Arbor, MI: University of Michigan press.

Carson, Joan. 1992. Becoming biliterate: First language influences. *Journal of Second Language Writing* 1. 37–60.

Carson, Joan. 1998. Cultural backgrounds: What should we know about multilingual students? *TESOL Quarterly* 32. 735–740.

Carson, Joan and Gayle Nelson 1994. Writing groups: Cross-cultural issues. *Journal of Second Language Writing* 3. 17–30.

Carson, Joan and Gayle Nelson. 1996. Chinese students' perceptions of ESL peer response group interaction. *Journal of Second Language Writing* 5. 1–19.

Carson, Joan and Gayle Nelson. 1998. ESL students' perceptions of effectiveness in peer response groups. *Journal of Second Language Writing* 7. 113–131.

Casanave, Christine. 2004. *Controversies in second language writing.* Ann Arbor, MI: University of Michigan Press.

Cheng, An. 2006. Analyzing and enacting academic criticism: The case of an L2 graduate learner of academic writing. *Journal of Second Language Writing* 15. 279–306.

Connor, Ulla. 1996. *Contrastive rhetoric.* Cambridge: Cambridge University Press.

Connor, Ulla. 2002. New directions in contrastive rhetoric. *TESOL Quarterly* 36. 493–510.

Connor, Ulla. 2004. Introduction to the special issue on contrastive rhetoric. *Journal of English for Academic Purposes* 3. 271–276.

Connor, Ulla. 2008. Mapping multidimensional aspects of research: reaching to intercultural rhetoric. In Ulla Connor, Ed Nagelhout, and William Rozycki (eds.), *Contrastive rhetoric: Reaching toward intercultural rhetoric*, 219–315. Amsterdam: John Benjamins.

Connor, Ulla. 2011. *Intercultural rhetoric in the writing classroom.* Ann Arbor, MI: University of Michigan Press.

Connor, Ulla, Tuija Helle, Anna Mauranen, Hakan Ringbom, Sonja Tirkkonen-Condit, and Marjo Yli-Antola, M. 1995. *Tekokkaita EU-projectiehdotuksia* [Successful EU grant proposals]. Helsinki: Tekes.

Connor, Ulla and Robert Kaplan (eds.). 1987. *Writing across languages: Analysis of L2 text.* Reading, MA: Addison-Wesley.

Connor, Ulla and Susan Mayberry. 1996. Learning discipline-specific academic writing: A case study of a Finnish graduate student in the United States. In Eija Ventola and Anna Maurenen (eds.), *Academic writing: Intercultural and textual issues*. 231–253. Amsterdam: John Benjamins.

Connor, Ulla, Ed Nagelhout and William Rozycki. 2008 (eds.). *Contrastive rhetoric: Reaching to intercultural rhetoric.* Amsterdam: John Benjamins.

du Gay, Paul, Jessica Evans, and Paul Redman. 2000. General introduction. In Paul du Gay, Jessica Evans, and Paul Redman (eds.), *Identity: A reader*, 1–6. London: Sage.

Eriksen, Thomas Hylland and Finn Sivert Nielsen. 2001. *A history of anthropology*. London: Pluto Press.

Fairclough, Norman. 1992. *Discourse and social change*. London: Polity Press.

Foucault, Michel. 1980. *Power/knowledge*. New York: Pantheon Books.

Fox, Helen. 1994. *Listening to the world*. Urbana, IL: NCTE.

Geertz, C. 1983. *Local knowledge: Further essays in interpretive anthropology*. New York: Basic Books.

Giddens, Anthony. 1979. *Central problems in social theory: Action, structure, and contradiction in social analysis*. Berkeley, CA: University of California Press.

Harklau, Linda. 1999. Representing culture in the ESL writing classroom. In Eli Hinkel (ed.), *Culture in second language teaching and learning*, 109–130. Cambridge: Cambridge University Press.

Hinds, John. 1983a. Contrastive rhetoric: Japanese and English. *Text* 3. 183–195.

Hinds, John. 1983b. Linguistics and written discourse in English and Japanese: A contrastive study (1978–1982). *Annual Review of Applied Linguistics* 3. 78–84.

Hinds, John. 1987. Reader versus writer responsibility: A new typology. In Ulla Connor and Robert Kaplan (eds.), *Writing across languages: Analysis of L2 text*, 141–152. Reading, MA: Addison-Wesley.

Hinds, John. 1990. Inductive, deductive, quasi-inductive: expository writing in Japanese, Korean, Chinese, and Thai. In Ulla Connor and Ann Johns (eds.), *Coherence in writing: Research and pedagogical perspectives*, 87–109. Alexandria, VA: TESOL.

Hirvela, Alan. 2010. Review of "Contrastive Rhetoric: Reaching to Intercultural Rhetoric". *English for Specific Purposes* 28. 286–288.

Holliday, A. 1999. Small cultures. *Applied Linguistics* 20. 237–264.

Hu, Guangwei and Jun Lei. 2012. Investigating Chinese university students' knowledge of and attitudes toward plagiarism from an integrated perspective. *Language Learning* 62. 813–850.

Hui, C. Harry and Harry C. Triandis. 1986. Individualism-collectivism: A study of cross-cultural researchers. *Journal of Cross-Cultural Psychology* 17. 255–248.

Ingold, Tim. 1994. Introduction to culture. In Tim Ingold (ed.), *Companion encyclopedia of anthropology*, 329–349. London: Routledge.

Kachru, Yamuna. 1997. Cultural meaning and contrastive rhetoric in English education. *World Englishes* 16. 337–350.

Kaplan, Robert. 1966. Cultural thought patterns in intercultural education. *Language Learning* 16. 1–20.

Kaplan, Robert. 1992. Contrastive rhetoric. In William Bright (ed.), *International encyclopedia of applied linguistics*. Oxford: Oxford University Press.

Kroeber, Alfred Louis and Clyde Kluckhohn. 1952. *Culture: A critical review of concepts and definitions*. Cambridge, MA: Peabody Museum of American Archaeology and Ethnology, Harvard University.

Kubota, Ryuko. 1997. A reevaluation of the uniqueness of Japanese written discourse. *Written Communication* 14. 460–480.

Kubota, Ryuko. 1999a. Japanese culture constructed by discourses: Implications for applied linguistics research and ELT. *TESOL Quarterly* 33. 9–35.

Kubota, Ryuko. 1999b. The author responds. *TESOL Quarterly* 33. 749–758.

Kubota, Ryuko. 2001. Discursive constructions of images in US classrooms. *TESOL Quarterly* 35. 9–38.

Kubota, Ryuko. 2002. The author responds: (Un)raveling racism in a nice field like TESOL. *TESOL Quarterly* 36. 84–92.

Kubota, Ryuko. 2004. Critical multiculturalism and second language education. In B. Norton and K. Toohey (eds.), *Critical pedagogies and language learning*, 30–52. Cambridge, UK: Cambridge University Press.

Kubota, Ryuko and Al Lehner. 2004. Toward critical contrastive rhetoric. *Journal of Second Language Writing* 13. 7–27.

Kuper, Adam. 1999. *Culture: The anthropologist's account.* Cambridge, MA: Harvard University Press.

Lather, Patti. 2001. Ten years later, yet again: Critical pedagogy and its complicities. In Kathleen Weiler (ed.), *Feminist engagements: Reading, resisting, and revisioning male theorists in education and cultural studies*, 183–195. New York: Routledge.

Leki, Ilona. 1997. Cross-talk: ESL issues and contrastive rhetoric. In Carol Severino, Juan C. Guerra and Johnnella E. Butler (eds.), *Writing in multi-cultural settings*, 234–244. New York: Modern Language Association of America.

Li, Xiaoming. 1996. *"Good writing" in cross-cultural context.* Albany, NY: State University of New York Press.

Li, Xiaoming. 2000. Track disconnecting: Chinese high school and university writing in a time of change. In D. Foster and D. Russell (eds.), *Writing and learning in cross-national perspective*, 49–87. Urbana, IL: NCTE.

Li, Xiaoming. 2005. Composing culture in a fragmented world: The issue of representation in cross-cultural research. In Paul Matsuda and Tony Silva (eds.), *Second language writing research: Perspectives on the process of knowledge construction*, 121–131. Mahwah, NJ: Lawrence Erlbaum.

Li, Xiaoming. 2008. From contrastive rhetoric to intercultural rhetoric: A search for identity. In Ulla. Connor, Ed Nagelhout and William Rozycki (eds.), *Contrastive rhetoric: Reaching to intercultural rhetoric*, 11–24. Amsterdam: John Benjamins.

Lowie, Robert. 1920. *Primitive society.* New York: Boni and Liveright.

Mathews, Gordon. 2000. *Global culture/individual identity: Searching for home in the cultural supermarket.* London: Routledge.

Matsuda, Paul K. 1997. Contrastive rhetoric in context: a dynamic model of L2 writing. *Journal of Second Language Writing* 6. 45–60.

Matsuda, Paul K. and Dwight Atkinson. 2008. A conversation on contrastive rhetoric. In Ulla Connor, Ed Nagelhout, and William Rozycki (eds.), *Contrastive rhetoric: Reaching to intercultural rhetoric*, 277–298. Amsterdam: John Benjamins.

Mauranen, Anna. 1993. *Cultural differences in academic rhetoric.* Berlin: Peter Lang.

Mazzarella, William. 2004. Culture, globalization, mediation. *Annual Review of Anthropology* 33. 345–367.

Nelson, Gayle. 1998. Comments on Ruth Spack's "The rhetorical construction of multilingual students: Categorizing, classifying, labeling: A fundamental cognitive process." *TESOL Quarterly* 32. 727–732.

Nelson, Gayle and Joan Carson. 2006. Cultural issues in peer response: Revisiting culture. In Ken Hyland and Fiona Hyland (eds.), *Feedback in second language writing: Contexts and issues*, 42–59. Cambridge, UK: Cambridge University Press.

Pennycook, Alastair. 1996. Borrowing other's words: Text, ownership, memory, and plagiarism. *TESOL Quarterly* 30. 201–230.

Pennycook, Alastair. 1998. *English and the discourses of colonialism.* London: Routledge.

Pennycook, Alastair. 2001. *Critical applied linguistics: A critical introduction.* Mahwah, NJ: Lawrence Erlbaum.

Pennycook, Alastair. 2007. *Global Englishes and transcultural flows.* Oxford: Routledge.

Raimes, Ann and Vivian Zamel. 1997. Response to Ramanathan and Kaplan. *Journal of Second Language Writing* 6. 79–81.

Ramanathan, Vai and Dwight Atkinson. 1999a. Individualism, academic writing, and ESL writers. *Journal of Second Language Writing* 8. 45–75.

Ramanathan, Vai and Dwight Atkinson. 1999b. Ethnographic approaches and methods in L2 writing research: A critical guide and review. *Applied Linguistics* 20. 44–70.

Ramanathan, Vai and Robert Kaplan. 1996. Audience and voice in current L1 composition texts: Some implications for ESL student writers. *Journal of Second Language Writing* 5. 21–34.

Ramanathan, Vai and Robert Kaplan. 1997. Response to Raimes and Zamel. *Journal of Second Language Writing* 6. 83–88.

Salzman, Philip Carl. 2001. *Understanding culture: An introduction to anthropological theory*. Prospect Heights, IL: Waveland Press.

Sapir, Edward. 1924/1949. Culture, genuine and spurious. In David G. Mandelbaum (ed.), *Edward Sapir: Selected writings in culture and personality*, 308–331. Berkeley: University of California Press.

Sarangi, Srikant. 1995. Culture. In Verschueren, Jan-Ola, Jef Verschueren and Eline Versluys (eds.), *Handbook of pragmatics*. 1–30. Philadelphia: John Benjamins.

Sharma, Bal Krishna. 2012. Beyond social networking: Performing global Englishes in Facebook by college youth in Nepal. *Journal of Sociolinguistics* 16. 483–509.

Shen, Fan. 1989. The classroom and the wider culture: Identity as a key to learning composition. *College Composition and Communication* 40. 459–466.

Shi, Ling. 2004. Textual borrowing in second-language writing. *Written Discourse* 21. 171–200.

Spack, Ruth. 1997. The rhetorical construction of multilingual students. *TESOL Quarterly* 31. 765–774.

Spack, Ruth. 1998a. The author responds to Nelson. *TESOL Quarterly* 32. 732–735.

Spack, Ruth. 1998b. The author responds to Carson. *TESOL Quarterly* 32. 740–746.

Tannen, D. 1985. Cross-cultural communication. In Teun A. Van Dijk (ed.), *Handbook of discourse analysis*, 203–216. New York: Academic Press.

Williams, Raymond. 1983. *Keywords: A vocabulary of culture and society*. London: Oxford University Press.

You, Xiaoye. 2010. *Writing in the devil's tongue: A history of English composition in China*. Carbondale: Southern Illinois University Press.

Zamel, Vivian. 1997. Toward a model of transculturation. *TESOL Quarterly* 31. 341–352.

Rosa M. Manchón and Jessica Williams

26 L2 writing and SLA studies

1 Introduction: SLA-L2 writing interfaces in historical perspective

In the last decades of the twentieth century, second and foreign language (L2) writing research and pedagogy largely developed separately from the area of second language acquisition (SLA). L2 writing scholarship historically took composition as its base field, which, at the time, had turned away from issues of linguistic accuracy and development, focusing instead on topics such as the development of arguments, text structure, genre, and voice. The field of SLA, in contrast, took linguistics and first language (L1) acquisition as its starting point, prioritizing a focus on both how language develops and how to facilitate and accelerate acquisition.

This lack of cross-fertilization between the fields of SLA and L2 writing is evident in both directions. L2 writing theory, empirical research, and pedagogical thinking have privileged the study of the "writing" component of L2 writing, hence making a priority of the intricacies of the process of teaching and learning writing in an additional language. To a lesser extent, L2 writing preoccupations have also included the study of writing as a vehicle for learning the content areas (see Chapter 2). However, the "L2" dimension of L2 writing has traditionally featured less prominently in L2 writing research agendas, with the very important exception of the role of language in learning to write, as we will see below.

From the perspective of SLA research, attention to "writing" per se (not as a means of data collection) has been almost non-existent until recently. Ortega (2012) has explained this neglect of the written modality as resulting from different disciplinary goals together with divergent ontological and epistemological principles. Importantly, as Cumming (2013) suggests, writing is "highly variable and contingent on education, opportunities for learning, and needs for use" (p. 1. See also Chapter 3, this volume), a characteristic that does not facilitate the generalizability of research findings sought by SLA scholars. In addition, the monitoring activity that characterizes the process of composing leads to the perception that they are "compromised evidence", another fact explaining why "written evidence takes a back seat compared to oral evidence in SLA research programs" (Ortega 2012: 405).

This panorama has nevertheless changed in recent years and important efforts have been put into cross-disciplinarity and the development of SLA-L2 writing interfaces. These initiatives can be seen in a number of books (cf. Bitchener and Ferris 2012; Byrnes and Manchón 2014a; Manchón 2011a, 2012), position papers and special issues in prestigious journals (cf. Bitchener 2012; Ferris 2010; Ortega 2012; Ortega and Carson 2010; Polio 2012; Williams 2012), as well as in a rapidly growing body of empirical studies (to be reviewed in later sections). Collectively, this research has opened a research path in which the spotlight is narrowly focused on the connection between language and writing (see Manchón 2016). Three important areas of overlap include: 1. the development of learners' written language over time; 2. the contribution of general L2 proficiency to writing; and 3. the contribution of writing, writing instruction, and feedback to L2 proficiency.

Issues of writing development are fully discussed in Chapter 13 and hence we will not review this research here, although we will briefly refer to this interface in the concluding section. Instead, in the rest of the chapter we explore the last two of these SLA-L2 writing interfaces, to be referred to as "Interface 1" (the role of language proficiency in developing L2 writing expertise) and "Interface 2" (the role of writing and writing instruction in the acquisition of L2 competencies). The last part of the chapter suggests ways of moving forward in the research agenda on L2 writing-SLA interfaces.

2 Interfaces 1: The role of language in the development of L2 writing expertise

Three dimensions of the linguistic component of L2 writing academic abilities have attracted considerable attention in L2 writing scholarship, (Manchón 2016) namely: (i) the linguistic characteristics of L2 academic texts, whose analysis includes important methodological debates on issues of measurement and analysis (a growing area of concern for L2 specialists. See Connor-Linton and Polio 2014), (ii) the language-related challenges and dilemmas faced by international students and publishing academics as users of additional languages (See Chapter 9 this *Handbook*), and (iii) the connection between the development of language capacities and writing expertise. In what follows we focus on this last issue as an important area of SLA-L2 writing interfaces.

That language proficiency will affect writing is obvious. What is not so obvious is the extent to which L2 proficiency versus other factors, particularly writing expertise in general or in the L1, affects the texts produced in the L2 and the writing process. Also not obvious are the pedagogical implications of the research on the contribution of L2 proficiency to writing.

Cumming (1989) conducted one of the first extensive studies on the relationship between L2 proficiency and writing expertise, and features of learners' texts and their writing strategies. In a fairly small-scale study of Francophone university students writing in English, he found that both L2 proficiency and writing expertise, two psychologically distinct factors, contributed to text quality. He also found that, regarding the composing process, the writing task had more of an effect than L2 proficiency.

Since that study, others have been conducted with larger populations. Thus, Sasaki and Hirose (1996) studied the role of L2 proficiency and L1 writing ability, as well as metaknowledge of English writing on the quality of texts produced and found that L2 proficiency contributed to more than half of variance while the other two factors contributed much smaller amounts. Unlike Cumming, they found that L2 proficiency and L1 writing expertise were not independent. In an even larger study of 281 Dutch adolescents learning English, Schoonen et al. (2003) examined several factors that might affect L2 writing, including L1 writing proficiency, L2 linguistic knowledge, processing speed, and metacognitive knowledge about writing in general and English texts. They found that L2 writing proficiency was highly correlated with L1 writing proficiency, as opposed to L2 knowledge or processing speed, a finding that differed from that of Sasaki and Hirose. In a second study (Schoonen et al. 2011) with 400 secondary school students, the researchers found that various linguistic measures did make a contribution to L2 writing proficiency although the amount of that contribution was, not surprisingly, inconsistent over time.

In a different line of research, Manchón, Roca de Larios, and Murphy (2009) studied 21 Spanish EFL writers (secondary students, university students, and recent university English major graduates) at three levels of proficiency (pre-intermediate, intermediate and advanced). They examined differences in the writing processes and strategies of these students and found that although all participants, regardless of their L2 proficiency, devoted most of their attention resources to language-related concerns, the more proficient writers were able to devote resources to concerns other than language and text length. Put another way, resources were freed up from a focus on linguistic-level problems and could be used for a wider range of concerns. Interestingly, they also found that the kind of linguistic concerns addressed by their L2 writers equally varied as a function of L2 proficiency.

Explorations of the interplay between language proficiency and writing abilities have more recently been framed in theories of multi-competence, and readers are referred to Chapter 17 for further elaboration of this approach.

3 Interfaces 2: The effect of writing and writing instruction on language learning

Another important area of concern in L2 writing-SLA interfaces, and one that has attracted considerable attention in the last few years, can be encapsulated in one basic question: Can the processes involved in writing – planning, composing, reflecting, monitoring, retrieving knowledge, and processing feedback – promote L2 acquisition?

Seen though an SLA lens, within the broad and quite plausible claim that writing can promote language development, lie two potentially conflicting possibilities. Thus, writing can actually lead to a change in linguistic knowledge by encouraging learners to analyze their (possibly inaccurate) implicit L2 knowledge (Bialystok 1994) or, more significantly, by encouraging them to draw repeatedly on explicit knowledge, thereby promoting the restructuring of their L2 knowledge in the opposite direction – from explicit to implicit (N. Ellis 2011). The second potential claim is that writing might, as Cumming (1990) originally suggested, simply encourage retrieval of explicit, analyzed L2 knowledge, perhaps improving the accuracy of output, or causing L2 writers to automatize their explicit knowledge (e.g., DeKeyser 2007), but leaving the developing L2 system qualitatively unchanged.

SLA-oriented L2 writing scholars have moved in two different directions in their attempts to shed light on the issues and question posed above. First, several position papers have delved into the theoretical and empirical foundation of the potential role of writing in L2 learning, with a focus on (i) what is unique about writing (including both the very act of writing and the processing of feedback) that can lead to language-learning outcomes, and (ii) how and why such potential learning outcomes can be supported with SLA theories and with available empirical evidence in various SLA and L2 writing domains (cf. Bitchener 2012; Manchón 2011b; Polio 2012; Williams 2012). Second, several new lines of SLA-oriented L2 writing research have accepted the challenge of "giving empirical substance to the language learning potential of writing" (Ortega 2012, p. 409) by providing new evidence on the potential effects of writing, and processing feedback on writing, on L2 development. This empirical evidence has been sought in explorations of writing processes and products in individual and collaborative writing conditions (see chapters 12 and 18) and in analyses contrasting task performance in speaking and writing (cf. Kormos 2014; Tavakoli 2014). Some other studies have explored whether or not the learning effects that have been found for task-related variables in the oral domain apply to writing, be it task repetition (cf. Nitta and Baba 2014) or task complexity factors (cf. Ruiz-Funes 2015). This SLA-oriented body of empirical research also includes the exploration of the language learning effects of feedback processing, crucially including questions closely related to the explicit/implicit debate alluded to above (cf. Shintani and Ellis 2013).

In an attempt to synthesize these trends in theory and research, our review will start with a brief account of relevant positions regarding what is special about the act of writing that might impact or facilitate specific processes in L2 development. We then focus on relevant theory and research that has shed light on specific processes of L2 acquisition in relation to writing. We will distinguish between indirect effects of writing on learning (including noticing, focus on form, and hypothesis testing monitoring, and responding to feedback) and more direct effects in terms of creating and restructuring L2 knowledge.

Because it is important to situate L2 writing in a pedagogical context, in addition to exploring the impact on L2 development of the act of writing itself, considerations of the role of writing instruction are certainly relevant. However, pedagogical considerations will not be part of the analysis that follows (but see chapters 12,

13, 18, 19 and 20). We simply note that L2 writers usually learn this skill as part of classroom instruction, which goes beyond mere writing practice. Learners are engaged in a variety of pedagogical activities as they prepare to write and revise their writing. As part of their instruction, they are also likely to get feedback from their teacher and their peers. Thus, any future discussion of the role of writing in L2 learning will need to include the role of writing instruction. After all, as Ortega (2012) notes, "It is precisely out of a shared interest in instructional research that the most promising L2 writing-SLA interfaces have been emerging as of late", and she also talks about the "vitality of *instructional interests* in supporting interfaces between the two fields" (p. 405. Emphasis added).

3.1 The act of writing and potential language learning outcomes

Although obvious, it is relevant to remind ourselves that the written modality can be used in a variety of contexts, and so writing does not entail the exact same processes in every case. This is why Manchón (2014a) has recently argued that in any discussion of why and how L2 writing may lead to learning, L2 writing should be made to encompass:

> individual and collaborative writing, in time-constrained and time-unlimited conditions, in both pen-and-paper and computer-mediated environments, totally or partially performed within and/or outside the confines of the language classroom, with and without the availability of (printed or electronic) external sources, and, importantly, with and without the availability of (different types of) feedback provided at different points in the composing process, which may serve different functions (pp. 29–30).

Despite this variability, there are features of the act of writing that differentiate it from other forms of language use (see Ortega 2012 for a full discussion of these characteristics and the implications for present and future research agendas). Perhaps the most obvious is that writing, with perhaps the exception of synchronous, computer-mediated forms of communication, does not take place with the same time pressure as speech. The slower pace of writing has been claimed to allow users to reflect on the linguistic demands of the task, plan on how to meet those demands, draw on different knowledge stores in doing so, and use these resources to edit their output. The second important feature is the permanent record left by writing, which potentially allows cognitive comparison between output and input and facilitates writers' examination and revision of their output (Manchón 2011a; Williams 2012).

The potential learning outcomes that may derive from these characteristics are closely related to (and, we would say, rather relevant to) crucial disciplinary debates in SLA research concerning the acquisition, use and development of implicit and explicit L2 knowledge. Seen from the perspective of writing, if the opportunity to plan, reflect, and edit (which allows, or even encourages, learners to access and retrieve knowledge) is what distinguishes writing from other types of language use, an important question is what kind of knowledge learners would be able to exploit under these conditions that would otherwise be unavailable (or at least less available) to them. There are two possibilities: 1. Additional time may allow learners to access explicit/analyzed knowledge, and the permanent record left by writing may allow them to compare that knowledge to their written output. 2. Additional time may allow learners to access implicit or unanalyzed knowledge for inspection and analysis. Both suggest heightened learner attention to formal aspects of language during writing, which may result in a more complex/and or accurate performance than on tasks in which this access is not available (Housen and Kuiken 2009). In other words, writing may result in better output than speaking. By better, it is usually meant that it may be grammatically more accurate or complex, or lexically more complex or varied. Empirical evidence for these claims comes from studies on task-modality effects (cf. Kormos 2014; Kormos and Trebits 2012; Tavakoli 2014), an area of research in SLA- L2 writing interfaces that we foresee will expand in the near future.

In addition to the pace and permanence of writing, the problem-solving nature of writing has also been adduced as a distinctive characteristic of writing potentially leading to language learning. The basic argument put forward (see Byrnes and Manchón 2014a, 2014b; Manchón 2014a; Manchón and Roca de Larios 2007) is that the deeper linguistic processing associated with the meaning-making activity that characterizes complex forms of writing will prompt L2 users to engage in crucial language learning processes, such as noticing, or metalinguistic reflection/analysis of explicit knowledge, as we will discuss in following sections.

Finally, Ortega (2012) adds a further characteristic of writing to be explored in future discussions, namely, the fact that "writing draws on physical and temporal displacement and mediacy" (p. 410). Her argument is that these two characteristics apply to (i) writing processes ("which are not only slow in pace but also unfold in time that is dauntingly cyclical, recursive, and intermittent", p. 410), (ii) written products (as the written text "becomes physically decoupled from the writer as soon as formulated", p. 410), and (iii) to any response to writing, which is always subsequent to the act of writing and the text on the page or screen.

In what follows we review some of the research that has delved into the learning potential associated with these distinctive characteristics of writing, distinguishing between indirect and direct effects on learning.

3.2 Indirect language learning effects: Writing and noticing processes

Some of the claims for the potential role for output in general rest on the assumption that learners have more control over their output than their input. There is an even stronger case for written production due to the more generous time constraints and enduring record of writing mentioned in the previous section. During both spoken and written output activities, learners may find themselves unable to reach their communicative goals because of their lack of knowledge of the L2. Swain (1998) referred to this as *noticing holes* in their L2 systems and claimed that this process has an impact on noticing future input and shaping intake, a claim that has been supported by empirical studies of written output (e.g., Izumi and Bigelow 2000; Hanaoka and Izumi 2012; Uggen 2012). In writing specifically, learners may have more opportunity to notice holes in their L2, which can be registered only fleetingly in spoken interaction. What is more, whereas in both speaking and writing such holes may prompt learners to scan future input for the forms to fill them, in writing learners often have an opportunity to resolve their communication problems immediately by consulting experts, reference materials, or simply reflecting on their own knowledge during the composing process itself and, importantly, while processing feedback on their own writing.

Cognitive comparison is certainly a major part of processing and responding to feedback in writing (see Chapter 20). There is an ongoing controversy regarding the impact of corrective feedback on language development in general, and more specifically, about the relative effectiveness of different types of feedback. A similar controversy is evident in writing research, specifically, concerning the effects of written corrective feedback on language development (Ferris 2010; Truscott 2007; see also Bitchener 2012; Polio 2012 for reviews). Two of the essential features of writing mentioned above emerge again as important here. Unlike more fleeting oral feedback, written feedback provides a permanent record for learners to compare to their own written production. Response to written corrective feedback can also take place at a slower pace than response to oral negative feedback and thus, offers an opportunity for deliberate reflection. However, written feedback, unlike oral, is delayed long after the act of writing, and this could account for its limited effectiveness (Polio 2012). Most studies of the effect of written corrective feedback have relied on short-term measures, that is, revisions made by learners in the texts on which they received the corrective feedback, what Manchón (2011c) calls "feedback for accuracy." Many researchers have argued that the ability to apply the knowledge acquired from feedback on an earlier writing task to new writing tasks would be more convincing evidence that development has occurred (Polio 2012; Truscott 2007). Manchón calls this "feedback for acquisition".

Of special relevance in this debate are studies that have looked into reformulation, a technique in which L2 writers compare their original work with a new version that has been reformulated by a native speaker. This research has examined what learners notice in written input as reformulation can influence noticing and shape intake by helping learners to *notice the gap* between their own production and the target, a form of processing for which there is empirical validation of effectiveness (cf. Adams 2003; Hanaoka 2007; Qi and Lapkin 2001; Tocalli-Beller and Swain 2005; Ong and Zhang 2010). As a whole, the reformulation studies suggest that the act of writing (which prompts learners to reflect on holes in their knowledge and primes them to focus on specific aspect of future input) combined with the pedagogical technique of reformulation (which provides tailored input and potential resolutions to composing problems) promotes noticing and at least short-term changes in language production. Active participation by the writers in this process appears to be an important factor in noticing and revision and, hence, in bringing about learning through feedback processing (see Bichener 2012). What is not clear from the reformulation studies is whether the language processing associated with making use of feedback in the form of reformulation contributes to the restructuring of the developing L2 system or whether learners simply use the information provided by native speakers to reach their immediate communication goals, or perhaps some of both. Hence, more research is needed before we can have more robust findings on the precise learning outcomes that may derive.

As discussed in Polio and Williams (2009) and Williams (2012) part of these future development would benefit from the insights obtained in vocabulary research regarding lexical acquisition as a function of task conditions. More precisely, within vocabulary research, *the involvement load hypothesis* suggests that certain task characteristics are more likely promote lexical acquisition than others (Laufer and Hulstijn 2001). The specific claim of the hypothesis is that tasks with a high involvement index, that is, high values for *need* (i.e., the need to know a word), *search* (i.e., an attempt to find the right word to match desired meaning), and *evaluation* (i.e., the comparison of word with other candidates for appropriateness) are more likely to promote acquisition. Previous studies have assigned writing tasks the highest involvement index, as compared to, for instance, reading tasks (cf. Keating 2008; Kim 2008). Thus, writing tasks seem to do more than simply focus attention on input needed to solve an immediate communicative problem. They can also potentially move L2 development forward. However, these conclusions require further empirical substantiation.

3.3 Indirect language learning effects: Focus on form and monitoring processes

In early discussions of the importance of output, Swain (1985) made the claim that the encoding demands of output can facilitate acquisition. The term *pushed output* is based on this need to encode form as well as meaning when learners speak or write. In contrast, when learners listen or read, the input may be processed simply for comprehension. For these reasons, it has been claimed that production processes require greater attention to form-meaning connections in the input than comprehension processes, as well as real-time syntactic encoding of those connections in output (Erlam, Loewen and Philp 2009; Swain 1998; Toth 2006). In short, output processes can promote focus on form, a process that has been suggested as facilitative of L2 development.

These observations pertain to output in general. However, the act of writing naturally entails both a greater need and more opportunity for focus on form than does speaking (Schoonen et al. 2009). This opportunity is afforded, in part, by the slower pace of writing, which allows for more deliberate retrieval as well as pre-task and during-task planning. An additional effect may be that learners are more likely to retrieve forms at the leading edge of their L2 development when they have time to do so. The potential connection between time availability and focus on form processes is at the center of two important lines of research, namely, studies of planning, and task-modality effects studies

SLA research on effects of planning has been done within two different models. The first is the limited capacity model (Skehan 1998), which is based on the idea that the brain has limited attentional and processing resources. Therefore, increased planning time is expected to free up these resources to focus on specific aspects of production, such as increased accuracy or the use of a recently acquired form. A competing model, the Cognition Hypothesis (Robinson 2001, 2007, 2011) suggests that there are multiple pools of attentional resources. Within this model, there is no tradeoff among these aspects of production with increased complexity, provided that the complexity increases along resource-directing dimensions. Resource-directing features of task complexity can connect learners' cognitive resources, such as attention and memory, with linguistic resources. Such tasks potentially enhance several aspects of production at the same time, for example, complexity and accuracy. Indeed, increasing complexity in writing tasks along this dimension has been shown to result in better performance, in terms of accuracy, and lexical and syntactic complexity (Kuiken and Vedder 2007, 2008). Just as important is the claim that increasing these resource-directing dimensions can push language development, as evidenced in Ruiz-Funes' (2015) recent study (see also Ong and Zhang 2010).

The studies on the effects of planning specifically on written production have yielded mixed results, however, with some studies showing that learners express themselves with more complex and varied forms in their production when they have time to plan their writing, but others showing little difference on individual measures. Ellis and Yuan (2004, 2005) concluded that the opportunity for pre-task planning was the crucial factor in allowing learners to include new and more complex forms in their production. Ellis (2009) suggests that this opportunity for strategic planning can promote restructuring of the developing L2.

An important question is how learners use additional planning time available in writing tasks. Writing may allow or even encourage the deployment of explicit, or even metalinguistic, L2 knowledge, which may not be available to them while speaking (R. Ellis 2003; Schoonen et al. 2009). Thus, planning through prewriting can help learners produce better writing, and planning in writing, for example through freewriting, might lead to better speaking. However, longer-term studies are needed to determine if the effects of planning persist and ultimately change learners' interlanguage system.

The meaning-making activity of writing may be inherently more focused on form, in contrast to speaking. Schoonen et al. (2009) note that "requirements of adequacy are felt more strongly in written language than spoken language, the latter generally being more tolerant of 'errors' or sloppy wording" (pp. 79–80). In short, writing seems to demand greater level of precision than speech. Yet the results of many of the task-modality studies that have compared written and oral production have been mixed on complexity, variety, and accuracy. Some studies have found higher accuracy in written production than in speaking (Granfeldt 2008; Kormos 2014). Others found no difference (Kuiken and Vedder 2011). Some have found greater lexical variety (Kormos and Trebits 2012); others, none (Kuiken and Vedder 2011); some, greater syntactic complexity (Kuiken and Vedder 2011), and others, again, no difference (Granfeldt 2008). In short, there is a lack of consensus on the impact of modality on task performance, suggesting it is premature to make specific claims for the effects of writing on L2 performance or development.

Since direct comparisons of written and oral production have yet to capture a specific, consistent advantage for writing, the processes involved in writing and writing instruction, rather than written production itself, may provide a better way to observe how focus on form is accomplished. Much of the focus on form literature is closely identified with two processes: negotiated interaction and corrective feedback (see below). There is considerable evidence that the negotiation that often occurs during collaborative pre-writing activities can increase interactional moves thought to facilitate language learning (Kuiken and Vedder 2005; Niu 2009; Storch 1999; Storch and Wigglesworth 2007; Wiggleworth and Storch 2012). These investigations have measured focus on form with Language Related Episodes (LREs), that is, occasions in which learners reflect on and/or discuss language as object (Adams 2006; Niu 2009). Niu (2009), for example, compared the amount of focus on form generated by oral and written collaborative tasks and found that writing tasks generated more LREs, and more turns that focused on form. Interestingly, this effect held, even allowing for the longer time on task for writing.

Monitoring is another form of cognitive comparison in which learners check their production against their current knowledge. They may check against implicit knowledge, what has been referred to as monitoring "by feel," but monitoring is generally thought of a consulting explicit knowledge. DeKeyser (2009) cites monitoring as important for L2 development, claiming it can help bring about "practically useful forms of knowledge, which may eventually become implicit" (2009, p. 132).

DeKeyser's explicitly refers to monitoring in speech, but the benefits may in effect be greater for written production. Since monitoring is a resource-consuming activity, the extra time afforded by writing, as well as its permanent record, can reduce resource consumption, making the cognitive comparison easier. Working memory is an important component of cognitive comparison and differences in working memory may also affect noticing and learners' ability to respond to feedback (cf. Trofimovich, Ammar, and Gatbonton 2007).

Given that most writing occurs without the same time pressure as conversation, one would expect the demand on working memory to be lower in writing processes, including monitoring. Schoonen et al. (2009) describe the written page as a temporary extension of working memory although they caution that limitations on memory remain even in the context of writing. It is probably safe to say that the cognitive window is open somewhat wider and learners have a richer opportunity to test their hypotheses when they write than when they speak. They can make cognitive comparisons between their output and feedback at their own pace.

3.4 Direct language learning effects. Knowledge creation and restructuring

Thus far, the potential role that has been described for writing (and other types of output) is relatively uncontroversial. The more fundamental question for L2 acquisition and for the emerging SLA-oriented L2 writing research is whether L2 knowledge can actually be created as a result of production processes. As noted by Williams (2012), "it has been claimed that a direct influence for output – oral or written – on this first stage in L2 development is not possible" (p. 324). Yet, there is some evidence that some forms of writing and writing instruction can facilitate knowledge creation. This is the case of collaborative writing (see Chapter 18): Learners have been shown to co-construct knowledge, usually documented as increased target-like use, when they participate in scaffolded or collaborative tasks. Together learners may create new knowledge not uniquely held by any one of them prior to the task (Nassaji and Tian 2010; Storch 1999, 2001; Storch and Wigglesworth 2007; Swain and Lapkin 2002; Wigglesworth and Storch 2012). The act of writing is not strictly required in this process; yet, in most of the studies that demonstrate this result, new knowledge creation is prompted by collaborative tasks that involve writing. Indeed, because the permanent record left by writing increases the demand for attention to formal language features, writing tasks seem to be ideal for such co-construction of knowledge.

As discussed in Williams (2012), the creation of this new knowledge might occur in two steps. The first step, reflection, is potentially part of any writing task: Because writing in an off-line activity, learners have the opportunity to consult their knowledge as they compose. The second step is collaboration, which may at times be a more effective way to create new linguistic knowledge than solitary activity because it involves the pooling of knowledge from several sources, as well as interactional moves thought to facilitate language learning. Several studies have directly compared writers working alone and together, and most have found a superior result for the latter, particularly as regards accuracy (Fernández-Dobao 2012; Kuiken and Vedder 2005; Nassaji and Tian 2010; Storch and Wigglesworth 2007).

Yet, as noted in some other recent studies, the nature of LREs in individual writing performance as well as the learning outcomes that may derive is a somewhat uncharted territory in which more research is needed before we can come to any firm conclusions regarding the language learning benefits of writing tasks in individual and collaborative conditions.

Particularly relevant in this context is whether the linguistic processing associated with writing practice – repeated engagement in the act of writing – can lead to changes in the developing system, especially regarding the relationship of implicit and explicit knowledge. The existence of these two separate kinds of L2 knowledge – explicit/analyzed knowledge and implicit/unanalyzed knowledge – is generally accepted, although there is less agreement among SLA scholars on whether they are dichotomous or continuous (DeKeyser 2009; N. Ellis 2005; R. Ellis 2004, 2005; Hulstijn 2005). It is also generally accepted that different types of tasks draw differentially on these two knowledge stores (DeKeyser 2009; R. Ellis 2004). Ellis (2004, 2005) has attempted to define criterial features of the two knowledge sources, as well as how they map onto tasks. At first glance, writing tasks would seem to fall on the explicit side. There is less time pressure and relatively greater, though by no means exclusive, focus on form, than in oral productions tasks. Writing tasks pose sufficient difficulty that learners are likely to use rule knowledge in responding to them. Because writing tasks do also focus on meaning, however, they are by no means at the extreme explicit end of the task taxonomy, as would be, say, an untimed grammaticality judgment task. However, it is evident that writing tasks can encourage or perhaps even require learners to consult their explicit knowledge, as evidenced in some recent research (cf. Manchón and Roca de Larios 2011).

Although the existence of these two knowledge stores is widely assumed, the existence or nature of the interface between these two types of knowledge, in contrast, is subject to considerable debate. It has been claimed that the act of writing prompts learners to consult their explicit knowledge and that collaborative prewriting activities can also encourage analysis of existing implicit knowledge. In other words, the interaction of the two knowledge stores is bidirectional; indeed, any direct role for writing in knowledge creation depends on this claim. The first direction – the claim that implicit knowledge can be analyzed and made explicit – is probably not terribly controversial. More controversial is the other direction: Can the creation, retrieval, or use of explicit knowledge result in a change to the developing L2 system, as claimed by proponents of the strong and weak interface positions (e.g., DeKeyser 2009)? In a recent discussion of the interface, N. Ellis maintains that the bulk of L2 research points to a conclusion that explicit knowledge (often a result of instruction) can promote the development of implicit knowledge. Furthermore, he specifically names output processes and feedback as a pathway for doing so. He notes that during production, "the learner can use explicit knowledge to consciously construct an utterance into working memory ... whose subsequent usage can promote implicit learning" (2011: 44). In an earlier discussion, he elaborated this process in more detail:

> Explicit memories are used as scaffolding in the building of linguistic constructions in working memory. Formulas that express related meanings can be used in processes of construction involving analogic reasoning and conceptual blending in working memory. Drilled patterns, conjugations and declensions, mnemonics, and declarative statements of pedagogic grammar can all contribute in the conscious construction of a desired utterance ... In various ways, explicit memories, and declarative knowledge can partake in utterance building and monitoring. Both the process and the result of this explicit construction process themselves feed into implicit learning (N. Ellis 2005: 328).

Ellis's discussion pertains to the value of output activities in general in promoting the interaction of knowledge sources. However, from his description of the resources that L2 learners assemble for utterance construction, it seems clear that the additional time available during writing, as well as the opportunity for editing, present the ideal context for these processes to occur. We now need future SLA-oriented L2 writing studies that can provide empirical evidence to substantiate these claims and that should look into both individual and collaborative writing.

4 Future developments

We mentioned at the outset three areas of inquiry where writing research can or should overlap with SLA research: how written language develops, the role of general proficiency in writing ability, and the potential role of writing and written feedback in L2 acquisition. While it is this last area that we believe has the most potential to inform writing instruction as well as general language instruction, we believe that carving out a research agenda in each of these areas can inform the SLA and L2 writing fields.

In the area of language development, studies comparing oral and written language might tell us how similar or different the processes are. Yet, as noted in an earlier section, future studies in the general area of task-modality effects should refine their methodological apparatus and, crucially, engage in truly developmental explorations of language development. In addition to the suggestions put forward in Chapter 13, readers are also referred to Norris and Manchón (2012) for specific suggestions as to how move developmental research agendas forward in terms of (i) the whole array of both SLA and L2 writing theories that may inform this research, (ii) the crucial methodological challenges to be faced in future studies attempting to advance the field, and, finally, (iii) the range of pedagogically-relevant concerns that this research should address.

Regarding the second SLA-L2 writing interfaces explored in the chapter, studies on the relationship between proficiency and writing (both text quality and writing process) can add to our knowledge base about L2 writing but general conclusions are difficult to draw because the studies available vary in population, sample size, writing tasks, and proficiency measures used. In addition to these methodological considerations, the pedagogical implications of this research are also open questions to be added to future research agendas.

Basically, the question for future studies is the following: even if there were clear conclusions about the effect of proficiency on text quality and writing processes, what would the implications for pedagogy be? For example, if writers can focus more on higher-order thinking skills once they have achieved a higher level of linguistic proficiency, does that mean that we should withhold writing instruction until they reach this level of proficiency? Additionally, it is also pedagogically relevant to know when learners of different levels might benefit from different types of writing activities. Importantly too, future basic and applied SLA-oriented L2 writing research needs to explore how L2 proficiency and L2 writing expertise develop and interact in those contexts in which instructed learners (especially pre-university L2 users in foreign language settings) are simultaneously developing writing abilities in all the languages of their educational program (i.e. their L1 and all the L2s that may form part of their school curriculum) and their L2 general proficiency. How language and writing develop in content-based instruction and CLIL programs is another area in need of investigation in future research on SLA-L2 writing interfaces.

Finally, with regard to the learning potential of writing and writing activities, we entirely agree with Ortega in her claim that "including a healthier, more imaginative variety of writing tasks in the study of instructional interfaces between L2 writing and SLA is likely to be necessary in order to fuel research into the broad sense of writing engagement" (p. 412). Many of these areas for future exploration are related to issues of task, be it the language learning potential associated with task repetition (see Manchón 2014b), or with task-modality effects on learning processes and products (see Byrnes and Manchon 2014a for a discussion).

As also advanced in an earlier section, future studies of writing as a site for language learning must necessarily explore in greater depth the linguistic processing associated with writing, an area in which a comprehensive research agenda has recently been set up (cf. Byrnes and Manchón 2014b, c; Roca de Larios 2013). Crucial concerns in these future research avenues are related to implicit/explicit interface controversy discussed in various places in the chapter. This applies to the study of writing itself but also, and very importantly, to the study of feedback and the language learning that may derive from feedback processing. Underlying any discussion of SLA and writing, particularly the effect of corrective feedback, is the implicit/explicit interface controversy and an understanding of what writers draw on as they write. The issue requires empirical verification in future studies as well determining what type of knowledge is used in writing and what type of knowledge corrective feedback provides. Examining these issues with the framework of some theories of SLA might be helpful in future studies. In our view, the debate is part of a more encompassing research agenda, one that incorporates "feedback for accuracy" and "feedback for acquisition" dimensions.

We would like to close with Lourdes Ortega's (2012) optimistic vision of what the future holds in developing SLA-L2 writing interfaces:

> Researchers committed to developing interface work grapple with challenging and interesting problem-posing and problem-solving opportunities, including the translation of constructs while maintaining disciplinary integrity, the appropriate choice of methods, and the careful consideration of theoretical traditions originating in the two fields and beyond. [...] Some readers in both fields may even see reason for hope that it will eventually contribute to change in the landscape of both fields, by leaving a trail of valuable intellectual bridges among the relevant L2 writing and SLA research communities (Ortega 2012: 413).

5 Acknowledgement

The analysis of research reported in this chapter is part of the work conducted in two research projects financed by the Spanish Ministerio de Economía y Competitividad (research grant FF12012-35839) and by Fundación Séneca, the Research Agency of the Autonomous Government of the region of Murcia, Spain (research grant 19463/PI/14).

6 Additional sources

Belcher, Diane and Alan Hirvela (eds.). 2008. *The oral-literate connection*. Ann Arbor, MI: University of Michigan Press.

Izumi, Shinichi. 2013. Noticing and L2 development: Theoretical, empirical, and pedagogical issues. In Joara M. Bergsleithner, Sylvia Nagem Frota and Jim K. Yoshuioka (eds.), *Noticing and second language acquisition: Studies in honour of Richard Schmidt*, 25–38. Honolulu: National Foreign Language Resource Center, University of Hawai'i at Manoa.

Kormos, Judit. 2012. The role of individual differences in L2 writing. *Journal of Second Language Writing* 21. 390–403.

Manchón, Rosa M. 2014. Learning and teaching writing in the FL classroom: Fostering writing-to-learn approaches. In Patricia Driscoll, Ernesto Macaro and Ann Swarbrick (eds.), *Debates in modern language education*, 96–107. London: Routledge.

Polio, Charlene. 2012. The acquisition of second language writing. In Susan M. Gass and Alison Mackey (eds.), *The Routledge handbook of second language acquisition*, 319–334. New York: Routledge.

Polio, Charlene and Jessica Williams. 2009. Teaching and testing writing. In Michael Long and Catherine Doughty (eds.), *The handbook of language teaching*, 476–517. Oxford: Blackwell.

Roca de Larios, Julio. 2013. Second language writing as a psycholinguistic locus for L2 production and learning. *Journal of Second Language Writing* 22(4). 444–445.

Williams, Jessica. 2005. *Teaching writing in second and foreign language classrooms*. Boston/New York: McGraw-Hill.

Wolff, Dieter. 2000. Some reflections on the importance of writing in a foreign language. In Ingo Plag and Klaus Schneider (eds.), *Language use, language acquisition and language history*, 213–226. Trier: Wissenschaftlicher Verlag.

Zhang, Lawrence. 2013. Second language writing as and for second language learning. *Journal of Second Language Writing* 22. 446–447.

7 References

Adams, Rebecca. 2003. L2 output, reformulation and noticing: Implications for L2 development. *Language Teaching Research* 7. 347–376.

Bialystok, Ellen. 1994. Representation and ways of knowing: Three issues in second language acquisition. In Nick Ellis (ed.), *Implicit and explicit factors in second language learning: Interdisciplinary perspectives*, 549–569. London: Academic Press.

Bitchener, John. 2012. A reflection on the language learning potential of written corrective feedback. *Journal of Second Language Writing* 21. 348–363.

Bitchener, John and Dana Ferris. 2012. *Written corrective feedback in second language acquisition and writing*. New York: Routledge.

Byrnes, Heidi and Rosa M. Manchón (eds.). 2014a. *Task-based language learning: Insights to and from writing*. Amsterdam: John Benjamins.

Byrnes, Heidi and Rosa M. Manchón. 2014b. Task, task performance, and writing development: Advancing the constructs and the research agenda. In Heidi Byrnes and Rosa M. Manchón (eds.), *Task-based language learning: Insights to and from writing*, 267–299. Amsterdam: John Benjamins.

Byrnes, Heidi and Rosa M. Manchón. 2014c. Task, task performance, and writing development: Advancing the constructs and the research agenda. In Heidi Byrnes and Rosa M. Manchón (eds.), *Task-based language learning: Insights to and from writing*, 267–299. Amsterdam: John Benjamins.

Connor-Linton, Jeff and Charlene Polio (Guest Eds.). 2014. Comparing perspectives on L2 writing: Multiple analyses of a common corpus. *Journal of Second Language Writing* 26.

Cumming, Alister. 1989. Writing expertise and second-language proficiency. *Language Learning* 39. 81–141.

Cumming, Alister. 1990. Metalinguistic and ideational thinking in second language composing. *Written Communication* 7. 482–511.

DeKeyser, Robert. 2007. Introduction: Situating the context of practice. In Robert DeKeyser (ed.), *Practicing in a second language: Perspectives from applied linguistics and cognitive psychology*, 1–18. Cambridge: Cambridge University Press.

DeKeyser, Robert. 2009. Cognitive-psychological processes in second language learning. In Michael Long and Catherine Doughty (eds.), *The handbook of language teaching*, 119–138. Chichester, UK: Blackwell.

Ellis, Nick. 2005. At the interface: Dynamic interactions of explicit and implicit language knowledge. *Studies in Second Language Acquisition* 27. 141–172

Ellis, Nick. 2011. Implicit and explicit SLA and their interface. In Cristina Sanz and Ronald Leow (eds.), *Implicit and explicit language learning*, 35–47. Washington D.C.: Georgetown University Press.

Ellis, Rod. 1993. Second language acquisition and the structural syllabus. *TESOL Quarterly* 27. 91–113.

Ellis, Rod. 2004. The definition and measurement of L2 explicit knowledge. *Language Learning* 54. 227–275.

Ellis, Rod. 2005. Measuring implicit and explicit knowledge of a second language. *Studies in Second Language Acquisition* 27. 305–352.

Ellis, Rod and Fangyuan Yuan. 2004. The effects of planning on fluency, complexity, and accuracy in second language narrative writing. *Studies in Second Language Acquisition* 26. 59–84.

Ellis, Rod and Fangyuan Yuan. 2005. The effects of careful within-task planning on oral and written task performance. In Rod Ellis (ed.), *Planning and task performance in a second language*, 167–192. Amsterdam: John Benjamins.

Erlam, Rod, Shawn Loewen, and Jenefer Philp. 2009. The roles of output-based and input-based instruction in the acquisition of L2 implicit and explicit knowledge. In Rod Ellis, Shawn Loewen, Catherine Elder, Rosemary Erlam, Jenefer Philp, and Hayo Reinders (eds.), *Implicit and explicit knowledge in second language learning, testing and teaching*, 241–261. Clevedon, UK: Multilingual Matters.

Fernández-Dobao, Ana. 2012. Collaborative writing tasks in the L2 classroom: Comparing group, pair, and individual work. *Journal of Second Language Writing* 21. 40–58.

Ferris, Dana. 2010. Second language writing research and written corrective feedback in SLA. Intersections and practical applications. *Studies in Second Language Acquisition* 32. 181–201.

Granfeldt, Jonas. 2008. Speaking and writing in L2 French: Exploring effects on fluency, accuracy and complexity. In Siska Van Daele, Alex Housen, Folkert Kuiken, Michel Pierrard, and Ineke. Vedder (eds.), *Complexity, accuracy and fluency in second language use, learning and teaching*, 87–98. Wetteren: KVAB Universa Press.

Hanaoka, Osamu. 2007. Output, noticing, and learning: An investigation into the role of spontaneous attention to form in a four-stage writing task. *Language Teaching Research* 11. 459–479.

Hanaoka, Osamu and Shinichi Izumi. 2012. Noticing and uptake: Addressing pre-articulated covert problems in L2 writing. *Journal of Second Language Writing* 21. 332–347

Housen, Alex and Folkert Kuiken. (Guest eds.). 2009. Complexity, accuracy and fluency in second language acquisition. *Applied Linguistics* 30.

Hulstijn, Jan. 2005. Theoretical and empirical issues in the study of implicit and explicit second-language learning: Introduction. *Studies in Second Language Acquisition* 27. 129–140.

Izumi, Shinichi and Martha Bigelow. 2000. Does output promote noticing and second language acquisition? *TESOL Quarterly* 34. 239–278.

Keating, Gregory. 2008. Task effectiveness and word learning in a second language. *Language Teaching Research* 16. 365–386.

Kim, YouJin. 2008. The role of task-induced involvement and learner proficiency in L2 vocabulary acquisition. *Language Learning* 58. 285–325.

Kormos, Judit. 2014. Differences across modalities of performance: An investigation of linguistic and discourse complexity in narrative tasks. In Heidi Byrnes and Rosa M. Manchón (eds.), *Task-based language learning: Insights to and from writing*, 193–216. Amsterdam: John Benjamins.

Kormos, Judit and Anna Trebits. 2012. The role of task complexity, modality and aptitude in narrative task performance. *Language Learning* 62. 439–472.

Kuiken, Folkert and Ineke Vedder. 2005. Noticing and the role of interaction in promoting language learning. In Alex Housen and Michel Pierrard (eds.), *Investigations in instructed second language acquisition*, 357–381. Berlin: Mouton deGruyter.

Kuiken, Folkert and Ineke Vedder. 2011. Task performance and linguistic performance in L2 writing and speaking: The effect of mode. In Peter Robinson (ed.), *Second language task complexity: Researching the Cognition Hypothesis of language learning and* performance, 91–104. Amsterdam: John Benjamins.

Laufer, Batia and Jan Hulstijn. 2001. Incidental vocabulary acquisition in a second language: The construct of task-induced involvement. *Applied Linguistics* 22. 1–26.

Manchón, Rosa M. (ed.). 2011a. *Learning-to-write and writing-to-learn in an additional language*. Amsterdam: John Benjamins.

Manchón, Rosa M. 2011b. Writing to learn the language: Issues in theory and research. In Rosa M. Manchón (ed.), *Learning-to-write and writing-to-learn in an additional language*, 61–82. Amsterdam: John Benjamins.

Manchón, Rosa M. 2011c. The language learning potential of writing in foreign language contexts. In Melinda Reichelt and Tony Chimasko (eds.), *Foreign language writing: Research insights*, 44–64. West Lafayette, IN: Parlor Press.

Manchón, Rosa M. (ed.). 2012. *L2 writing development: Multiple perspectives*. Berlin/Boston: De Gruyter Mouton.

Manchón, Rosa M. 2014a. The internal dimension of tasks: The interaction between task factors and learner factors in bringing about learning through writing. In Heidi Byrnes and Rosa M. Manchón (eds.), *Task-based language learning: Insights to and from writing*, 27–52. Amsterdam: John Benjamins.

Manchón, Rosa M. 2014b. The distinctive nature of task repetition in writing. Implications for theory, research, and pedagogy. *ELIA* 14. 13–42. DOI: http://dx.doi.org/10.12795/elia.2014.i14.02

Manchón, Rosa M. 2016. Language and L2 writing: Learning to write and writing to learn in academic contexts In Ken Hyland and Philip Shaw (eds.), *Handbook of English for Academic Purposes*, 139–151. London: Routledge.

Manchón, Rosa M. and Julio Roca de Larios. 2007. Writing-to-learn in instructed language contexts. In Eva Alcón-Soler and Pilar Safont (eds.), *The intercultural speaker. Using and acquiring English in instructed language contexts*, 101–121. Dordrecht: Springer-Verlag.

Manchón, Rosa M., Julio Roca de Larios, and Liz Murphy. 2009. The temporal dimension and problem-solving nature of foreign language composing processes. In Rosa M. Manchón (ed.), *Writing in foreign language contexts. Learning, teaching, and research*, 102–129. Bristol, UK: Multilingual Matters.

Nassaji, Hosssein and Jun Tian. 2010. Collaborative and individual output tasks and their effects on learning English phrasal verbs. *Language Teaching Research* 14. 397–419.

Niu, Ruiying. 2009. Effect of task-inherent production modes on EFL learners' focus on form. *Language Awareness* 18. 384–402.

Norris, John and Rosa M. Manchón. 2012. Investigating L2 writing development from multiple perspectives: Issues in theory and research. In Rosa M. Manchón (ed.), *L2 writing development: Multiple perspectives*, 221–244. New York/Berlin: De Gruyter Mouton.

Ong, Justina and Lawrence Zhang. 2010. Effects of task complexity on the fluency and lexical complexity in EFL students' argumentative writing. *Journal of Second Language Writing* 19. 218–233.

Ortega, Lourdes. 2012. Epilogue: Exploring L2 writing – SLA interfaces. *Journal of Second Language Writing* 21. 404–415.

Ortega, Lourdes and Joan Carson. 2010. Multicompetence, social context, and L2 writing research praxis. In Tony Silva and Paul K. Matsuda (eds.), *Practicing theory in second language writing*, 48–71. West Lafayette, IN: Parlor Press.

François Pichette, Linda de Serres, and Marc Lafontaine. 2012. Sentence reading and writing for second language vocabulary acquisition. *Applied Linguistics* 33. 66–82

Polio, Charlene. 2012. The relevance of second language acquisition theory to the written error correction controversy. *Journal of Second Language Writing* 21. 375–389

Polio, Charlene and Jessica Williams, 2009. Teaching and testing writing. In Michael Long and Catherine Doughty (eds.) *The handbook of language teaching*. 476–517. Oxford: Blackwell.

Qi, Donald and Sharon Lapkin. 2001. Exploring the role of noticing in a three-stage second language writing task. *Journal of Second Language Writing* 10. 277–303.

Robinson, Peter. 2001. Task complexity, task difficulty and task production: Exploring interactions in a componential framework. *Applied Linguistics* 22. 27–57.

Robinson, Peter. 2007. Criteria for classifying and sequencing pedagogical tasks. In M. Pilar García-Mayo (ed.), *Investigating tasks in formal language learning*, 7–26. Clevedon, UK: Multilingual Matters.

Robinson, Peter. 2011. Second language task complexity, the Cognition Hypothesis, language learning, and performance. In Peter Robinson (ed.), *Second language task complexity. Researching the Cognition Hypothesis of language learning and performance*, 3–37. Amsterdam: John Benjamins.

Roca de Larios, Julio. 2013. Second language writing as a psycholinguistic locus for L2 production and learning. *Journal of Second Language Writing* 22(4). 444–445.

Ruiz-Funes, Marcela. 2015. Exploring the potential of second/foreign language writing for language learning: The effects of task factors and learner variables. *Journal of Second Language Writing*, 28. 1–19. DOI: 10.1016/j.jslw.2015.02.001

Sachs, Rebecca and Charlene Polio. 2007. Learners' uses of two types of written feedback on a L2 writing revision task. *Studies in Second Language Acquisition* 29. 67–100.

Sasaki, Miyuki and Keiko Hirose. 1996. Explanatory variables for EFL students' expository writing. *Language Learning* 46(1). 137–174.

Schoonen, Rob, Amos van Gelderen, Kees de Glopper, Jan Hulstijn, Annegien Simis, Patrick Snellings, and Marie Stevenson. 2003. First language and second language writing: The role of linguistic knowledge, speed of processing, and metacognitive knowledge. *Language Learning* 53. 165–202.

Schoonen, Rob, Patrick Snellings, Marie Stevenson, and Amos Van Gelderen, 2009. Towards a blueprint of the foreign language writer: The linguistic and cognitive demands of foreign language writing. In Rosa M. Manchón (ed.), *Writing in foreign language contexts: Learning, teaching, and research*, 77–101. Clevedon, UK: Multilingual Matters.

Schoonen, Rob, Amos van Gelderen, A., Reinoud D. Stoel, Jan Hulstijn, and Kees de Glopper. 2011. Modeling the development of L1 and EFL writing proficiency of secondary school students. *Language Learning* 61. 31–79.

Shintani, Natsuko and Rod Ellis. 2013. The comparative effect of direct written corrective feedback and metalinguistic explanation on learners' explicit and implicit knowledge of the English indefinite article. *Journal of Second Language Writing* 22. 286–306.

Skehan, Peter. 1998. *A cognitive approach to language learning*. Oxford: Oxford University Press.

Storch, Neomy. 1999. Are two heads better than one? Pairwork and grammatical accuracy. *System* 27. 363–374.

Storch, Neomy. 2001. How collaborative is pair work? ESL tertiary students composing in pairs. *Language Teaching Research* 5. 29–53.

Storch, N. and Gillian Wigglesworth. 2007. Writing tasks: The effects of collaboration. In M. Pilar García-Mayo (ed.), *Investigating tasks in formal language learning*, 157–177. Clevedon UK: Multilingual Matters.

Swain, Merrill. 1998. Focus on form through conscious reflection. In Catherine Doughty and Jessica Williams (eds.), *Focus on form in classroom second language acquisition*, 64–81. Cambridge: Cambridge University Press.

Swain, Merrill and Sharon Lapkin. 2002. Talking it through: Two French immersion students' response to reformulation. *International Journal of Educational Research* 3/4. 285–304.

Tavakoli, Parvaneh. 2014. Storyline complexity and syntactic complexity in writing and speaking tasks. In In Heidi Byrnes and Rosa M. Manchón (eds.), *Task-based language learning: Insights to and from writing*, 217–236. Amsterdam: John Benjamins.

Tocalli-Beller, Agustina and Merrill Swain. 2005. Reformulation: the cognitive conflict and L2 learning that it generates. *International Journal of Applied Linguistics* 15. 5–28.

Toth, Paul. 2006. Processing instruction and a role for output in second language acquisition. *Language Learning* 56. 319–385.

Trofimovich, Pavel, Ahlem Ammar, and Elizabeth Gatbonton. 2007. How effective are recasts? The role of attention, memory and analytical ability. In Alison Mackey (ed.), *Conversational interaction in second language acquisition*, 171–195. Oxford: Oxford University Press.

Truscott, John. 2004. Evidence and conjecture on the effects of correction: A response to Chandler. *Journal of Second Language Writing* 13(4). 337–343.

Truscott, John. 2007. The effect of error correction on learners' ability to write accurately. *Journal of Second Language Writing* 16. 255–272.

Truscott, John and Angela Yi-ping Hsu. 2008. Error correction, revision and learning. *Journal of Second Language Writing* 17. 292–305.

Uggen, Maren. 2012. Reinvestigating the noticing function of output. *Language Learning* 62. 506–540.

Wigglesworth, Gillian and Neomy Storch. 2009. Pair versus individual writing: Effects of fluency complexity and accuracy. *Language Testing* 26. 45–466

Wigglesworth, Gillian and Neomy Storch. 2012. What role for pair work in writing and writing feedback? *Journal of Second Language Writing* 21. 364–374.

Williams, Jessica. 2012. The potential role(s) of writing in second language development. *Journal of Second Language Writing* 21. 321–331.

Yang, Luxin and Ling Zhang. 2010. Exploring the role of reformulations and a model text in EFL students' writing performance. *Language Teaching Research* 14. 464–484.

Alan Hirvela and Diane Belcher

27 Reading/writing and speaking/writing connections: The advantages of multimodal pedagogy

In this chapter we explore the integration of three skills of great importance in the development of academic literacy. Though it would be possible to look at the simultaneous integration of all three skills, we have chosen to separate reading-writing and speaking-writing connections in the belief that each set of connections merits its own coverage. Furthermore, it has been the case that these two sets of connections have been treated separately in the L2 writing scholarship, and in this chapter we want to capture the directions in which the scholarship has appeared. However, it may well be that in the multimodal age we live in, future reviews of this kind will have to look across speaking-reading-writing connections, especially in view of the increased tendency toward the multiple integration of skills in the teaching and assessment of second language writing proficiency.

1 Reading-writing connections

1.1 Historical overview

Reading-writing connections in the L2 context have come a long way in a relatively short period of time, from an era of modest interest in the early 1990s to the present when, note Hedgcock and Ferris (2009: 188), "few would argue against the view that reading and writing are inextricably connected". The scholarship has changed from initial efforts to demonstrate the existence and importance of such connections to the current focus on better understanding how those connections play out, especially within two primary domains: *reading-to-write* (where reading is used as input for writing) and *writing-to-read* (where writing is used to deepen knowledge of reading).

Historically speaking, interest in reading-writing connections began with a seminal Tierney and Pearson article in 1983 in which they asserted that reading and writing share similar composing processes and thus should be treated jointly, not separately, a view that was the driving force behind the reading-writing connections work that appeared in the 1980s and remains a useful framework today.

While L1 writing scholars responded favorably to the view put forth by Tierney and Pearson, Grabe (2003: 242) noted that L2 writing specialists were slow to look at such connections within a distinctly L2 framework. That may well have been due to the general lack of the use of reading as what Weigle (2002) calls "stimulus material' for writing tasks. In the 1980s and into the 1990s, L2 writing specialists were far less inclined to focus on source-based writing in ways that are common nowadays.

In the case of L2 reading-writing connections, real interest began in the 1990s, especially with the publication of Joan Carson and Ilona Leki's 1993 edited collection of papers exploring the role of reading in writing classrooms. As other reading-writing connections scholarship appeared in publications and conference presentations, an important link emerged with the field of English for Academic Purposes (EAP), where there is an emphasis on preparing students to meet the academic literacy demands in the content courses they take, particularly surrounding the use of source texts for reading-to-write purposes. However, Grabe (2003: 258) has pointed out that developing such ability is a difficult task for EAP teachers because of the multitude of skills and understandings that students must acquire.

In the current century, where there has been steady interest in L2 reading-writing connections, the challenges noted by Grabe have been a primary motivator of reading-writing connections scholarship. Looking broadly across this domain, Grabe and Zhang (2013b) observe that, in both pedagogy and research, interest centers around source-based writing as enacted mainly in four areas: summary writing, synthesis writing, research paper writing, and plagiarism. In addition to a number of individual papers published in various journals and edited books, this interest is reflected powerfully in special issues of the *Journal of Second Language Writing*, guest-edited by Charlene Polio and Ling Shi (2012a); the *Journal of English for Academic Purposes*, guest-edited by Diane Pecorari and Philip Shaw (2013); and *Reading in a Foreign Language*, guest-edited by Betsy Gilliland and Jeongyeon Park (2015). The allocation of whole issues of these journals to reading-writing connections attests to the importance of this area in the field of second language studies.

Another important historical dimension of reading-writing connections work has been the quest to develop a viable theory which captures the essential dynamics of such connections. Theory in the context of reading-writing connections can be viewed within two broad frameworks: *models* of reading-writing connections and *perspectives* on such connections. Models provide broader frameworks for capturing reading-writing relations, while perspectives are theoretical constructs that help enrich these models. Both are briefly summarized in this section of the chapter, with the caveat that the focus is strictly on reading and writing for academic, not personal, purposes.

Models

Model building for reading-writing connections was initially driven by the work of Shanahan and Lomax (1986, 1988) who, operating in the context of native language writers, identified three models based on the key construct "of how information moves *across* reading and writing" (1988: 199). As depicted in their 1988 work, first was the interactive model, in which "information can transfer *from* reading to writing *and* from writing to reading" (p. 199). Second is the reading-to-writing model, in which "all information or knowledge [is] emanating *from* reading *to* writing" (p. 200). The third model, the writing-to-reading model, "shows writing as an influence on reading, but with no equivalent transfer of knowledge from reading to writing" (p. 200).

The key components of directionality and transfer between reading and writing seen in the Shanahan and Lomax approach are also reflected in what is still the dominant model in the L2 context. This was proposed by Eisterhold (1990), who directly invoked the notion of directionality. In her taxonomy, one option is the *directional model*, in which writing is improved by reading *or* reading is improved by writing. The *nondirectional model* asserts that improvement can occur in both directions at the same time. The *bidirectional model* resembles the nondirectional one, but it places greater emphasis on what it sees as the interdependent nature of the interaction between reading and writing, in which improvement in one skill must therefore involve improvement in the other as well. Eisterhold (1990: 89) saw the directional approach as the most valuable model from which to work. Whether that is still the case is one of the areas of debate in the reading-writing connections field. What does seem clear with respect to directionality, albeit in another mode, is that it is *reading-to-write* that is the center of scholarly attention. However, both Hirvela (2004) and Grabe (2001, 2003, 2009) have asserted that *writing-to-read* deserves greater attention than it has received.

Perspectives

Historically speaking, the first theoretical framework driving reading-writing connections work was the *constructivist* orientation seen in Tierney and Pearson's seminal (1983) article in their composing view of reading and writing. This led to an initial interest in identifying the specific acts at work in the construction of meaning taking place in writing and reading. This reflected a fundamentally cognitive perspective on reading and writing shaped by important insights from the earlier work of Flower and Hayes (1981, 1984), who had presented an elaborate theory depicting the strategic, cognitively-based acts at work in writing and reading.

One notable constructivist effort was by Kucer (1985, 2005), who built on what he called the notion of "text world production," which, as he explained in 1985, consisted of three categories of cognitively-oriented activity: 1. "common information location and retrieval procedures"; 2. "shared cognitive strategies employed to transform background knowledge into text world productivity"; and 3. "the role of context in the production of meaning". Also of particular note was the work of Spivey (1990, 1997), who focused on what she called "textual transformations" occurring during reading and writing; in this vein, she identified and explored three core operations which allow writers to access and utilize input during reading and writing: 1. organizing, 2. selecting, and 3. connecting.

This constructivist orientation dominated reading-writing scholarship in the 1980s and remained strong in the 1990s. Gradually, though, it has generally given way to what Solé, Miras, Castells, Espino, and Minguela (2013) refer to as a *socio-constructivist* view that accounts for the socially mediated acts associated with reading and writing while still interested in the cognitively based subskills that allow for the construction of meaning to occur. Flower (1994: 56), in making a case for what she called a more inclusive social cognitive theory (and that has since morphed into the current socioconstructivist view), invoked three metaphors to capture the activities guiding reading and writing: reproduction, conversation, and negotiation. That is, in addition to reproducing existing meaning, writers (as reader-writers) must account for other variables as well, including the literacy demands and conventions of disciplinary communities. This is where conversation and negotiation take place, as the writers must engage in a process by which they learn about these variables (conversation) and then engage in a balancing act between their own ideas and practices and those expected of them (negotiation). The socioconstructivist approach draws on this framework, especially in exploring what happens in the reading-writing based domain of source-based writing in which students read sources and incorporate them into their writing in one way or another.

With respect to source-based writing, Polio and Shi (2012b: 95) point out that central to academic literacy is students' ability to incorporate source text material into their own writing. Rinnert and Kobayashi (2005: 33), while noting that such skill is necessary for all academic writers, explain that L2 writers face challenges in learning to do so that extend beyond those faced by native language writers. This is where the socioconstructivist perspective plays an important role in current research and teaching, in that there is a focus on what is involved in helping these students engage in Flower's process of reproduction, conversation, and negotiation as they move between their native language literacy practices and those expected of them in the L2 domain.

Looking further at theoretical perspectives, Grabe and Zhang (2013b) comment on the importance of what they call "writing socialization practices," another way of labelling the interest in *academic socialization* that has been dominant in the current century with respect to EAP writing instruction and that is embedded within the socioconstructivist framework. That is, academic literacy practices are situated in different contexts of use as defined by different disciplinary communities, and novice writers must also acquire an understanding of these disciplinary nuances while they develop their reading and writing skills. The academic socialization perspective is especially important in addressing plagiarism-related issues, and here there is an overlap with such source-based writing tasks as summarizing, synthesizing, and paraphrasing, all of which figure heavily in EAP writing research and pedagogy. To aid in this process, Li (2013) has recently explored the addition of an activity system framework that has thus far been used far more extensively in L1 writing scholarship.

1.2 Disciplinary interpretation of the field: Current trends

Reading-writing connections scholarship can be explored within a variety of strands, particularly long-time areas of interest such as summarizing and plagiarism, as noted earlier (Grabe and Zhang 2013b). What has been especially noteworthy with respect to these traditional foci has been the narrowing of interest to the use of citations in various writing contexts (e.g. Harwood 2009; Harwood and Petrić 2012; Pecorari 2006; Petrić 2007, 2012; Petrić and Harwood 2013). Paraphrasing has emerged as another topic of interest (e.g. Hirvela and Du 2013; Keck 2006, 2014; Shi 2012). Collectively, these studies, along with other research on source-based writing, consistently reveal that L2 writers find it difficult to work effectively with sources.

Two newer strands of interest are discussed in the remainder of this section of the chapter: 1. integrated reading-writing assessment and 2. multimodality. These are examined because they represent the most significant areas in which L2 reading-writing scholarship has evolved since what might be called the foundational period of the 1990s.

1.2.1 Integrated reading-writing connections and assessment

One of the most important areas of development in current reading-writing connections scholarship has been the increased focus on the integration of reading and writing for assessment purposes (see also Chapter 22). Research in this area has looked at a) whether the findings support the movement to integrated reading-writing assessment, and b) what happens under these integrated circumstances. There had been some work on this in the past in terms of developing integrated testing approaches (e.g., Feak and Dobson 1996), especially as interest in source-based writing grew, but, as Hamp-Lyons and Kroll (1996: 54) have observed, there was a dearth of research on the effects of integrated reading-writing tasks. That situation has changed dramatically in the current century, and for reasons that reflect two primary directions that will be examined in more detail shortly.

First, major assessment instruments such as the Test of English as a Foreign Language (TOEFL) now favor integrated forms of assessment in order to produce a more meaningful picture of how test takers will perform in authentic academic situations, where language skills are rarely used in isolation. This is particularly true with respect to test takers' ability to read and write about source texts. This has necessitated a close look at whether integrated reading-writing tasks are effective from an assessment perspective. That is, do they work? Second, assessment contexts provide useful sites for exploring the dynamics of the interplay between reading and writing. With these reasons in mind, the focus of this section of the chapter now shifts to examining the two directions just described, with studies most directly related to these directions cited.

With respect to attempts to examine the effectiveness of integrated reading-writing assessment tests, a few studies stand out. Weigle (2004) investigated a test of writing proficiency required of all undergraduate students studying at universities financially supported by the state of Georgia in the United States, with a specific focus on an adjusted version of the examination designed for nonnative speakers of English. Weigle's study found encouraging results for this adapted version of the test. In a recent follow-up study, Weigle and Parker (2012) examined the source text use of students taking the same examination and concluded that such use validated this form of the exam in measuring students' proficiency in academic literacy.

Other work in this area has also provided support for assessing reading and writing together, but with a cautionary note as well. For instance, Plakans (2009a) looked at research participants completing a discourse synthesis task in a reading-to-write university placement examination. She found that this task generally elicited the kinds of reading-writing interaction envisioned in the construction of the examination, thereby validating its use. Support was also found in a study by Gebril (2010) of students at an Egyptian university, in this case by comparing performances on two independent writing tasks (i.e., writing only – no use of source texts) and two reading-to-write tasks where source texts played a major role. On the other hand, in a study of students' use of source texts to write an argumentative essay and investigating the use of a newly designed rubric for scoring such writing at an Egyptian university, Plakans and Gebril (2012) found that the test task was useful from a reading to write perspective, but that scoring of such an assessment was complicated, prompting them to urge writing instructors and writing assessors to proceed cautiously in their development and scoring of integrated reading-writing tasks. Also worth noting with respect to viewing integrated assessment cautiously is a study by Ascensión Delaney (2008), who examined university students' performance in two reading-to-write examination tasks: the writing of a summary and of a response essay, each based on the same source texts. She found that how students engaged in connections between reading and writing differed across the two tasks, thus challenging the view of reading-writing connections as a unitary construct. This study holds important implications for reading-to-write assessments with respect to the kinds of tasks assigned.

Shifting to the other direction noted earlier, where the focus is on the dynamics of reading-writing connections as revealed through integrated reading-writing tasks, Plakans (2008, 2009b, 2010) has looked at integrated reading-writing assessment through various lenses under the umbrella notion of reading-to-write. These studies have produced a mixed picture of such dynamics. In her 2008 study, which focused on composing processes, she examined how both international undergraduate and graduate students at an American university approached a writing only and a reading-to-write assessment task in which they composed an essay in each condition. She concluded that the reading-to-write tasks enabled the test takers to engage in authentic composing processes. Her 2010 study, based on the same participants and research circumstances, but this time investigating task representation, looked at the students' experiences during the two tasks (writing only and reading to write) in the belief that to better understand integrated reading-writing assessment, it is necessary to know how students conceptualize such tasks. Here she found differences among the participants, suggesting a need for teachers and test designers to account for how L2 writers conceptualize the integration of reading and writing. Working from another direction, Plakans (2009b) focused her attention on how participants approached the reading aspect of the integrated assessment. She found differences in the strategy use among high and low scoring test-takers, thus drawing attention to the need to look more closely at the reading dimension of reading-to-write assessments.

While studies are generally showing promising returns on the use of integrated reading-writing tasks in assessment contexts, challenges remain. Weigle (2002), for example, notes that in the common reading-to-write format, those who read in the L2 with difficulty are likely to struggle with the subsequent writing as well. Grabe (2009), meanwhile, expresses a concern about such assessments privileging writing over reading, thus making it difficult to evaluate test takers' reading comprehension skills and generating a need to develop measures by which the reading side of integrated reading-writing tasks can be also assessed.

1.2.2 Multimodality and source text use

Thompson, Morton, and Storch (2013: 100) have pointed out that a major shift has occurred in source text use among students, with electronic texts now dominating over the traditional use of print-based texts, thus signaling a shift to a multimodal world of reading and writing connections. As Bolter (2001) states, we have moved from "the late age of print" to a more inclusive use of sources that draws heavily from the internet in the current period of digital literacy. Bloch (2008) explains that "the shift from reading print texts to reading digital texts not only changes how the information is accessed but also how the texts are read and written". It is these changes, and their impact on reading-writing relationships, that is a significant new frontier in understanding contemporary interactions between reading and writing. That frontier has been explored from various directions.

One of those directions has been students' ability to evaluate the value or credibility of electronic sources. Two studies of note here are by Stapleton (2005) and Radia and Stapleton (2008). In the former, undergraduate students at a university in Japan tended to have difficulty evaluating the reliability of the electronic sources they cited as they completed a reading for writing assignment. According to Stapleton, they lacked the critical literacy skills necessary to use such sources well for reading-to-write purposes. Similar results occurred in the study by Radia and Stapleton (2008), in this case among undergraduate students at a university in Canada. In analyzing the citations in the students' essays, they saw evidence of an "anything goes" environment with respect to the online sources used by the students. That is, the students relied on such sources without an awareness of or sensitivity to the biases that may have shaped how the original sources were written. In both of these studies, there are implications for how students can operate as readers-writers in a digital context.

Also of interest is the issue of how L2 students actually work with electronic texts. Stapleton (2010), for example, compared a Hong Kong graduate student's use of "electronic age" resources on her composing processes compared to more traditional resources. He found that the cognitive demands on the student when using electronic sources were lower than those for traditional print-based sources. Hong Kong was also the site for recent studies by Li (2012) and Li and Casanave (2012). Li (2012) was interested in the search processes and reading approaches used by undergraduates completing end of semester writing assignments. Li found that the participants consulted a variety of search engines while locating sources for these assignments and engaged in a strategic, globally-oriented reading approach (skimming and using key words) as they sought relevant information for their papers. They also relied on screen-based versions of the source texts rather than hard copies as they read them and extracted the material they needed. On the whole, says Li, the students placed a heavy emphasis on efficiency in their use of Web-based sources. Meanwhile, Li and Casanave (2012) investigated the source-based strategies used by two undergraduate students writing in an introductory linguistics course and found that the participants relied heavily on texts located via the Internet and engaged in what they called "partial reading" of them in the search for relevant information to incorporate into their papers. As in Li's 2012 study, the participants sought efficiency in their source text use. Also similar to Li's 2012 study was the finding that the students made efforts to avoid plagiarizing source text material.

The results from these studies regarding students' sensitivity to plagiarism issues, especially while using electronic sources, have been seen in other multimodality research involving source text use. For instance, Davis (2013) investigated this issue by examining how three post-graduate Chinese students at a university in the United Kingdom dealt with both print-based and electronic sources. Of particular note in her study was the fact that the students were more likely to include citations from online sources and to copy that material directly than in the case of print-based sources. Also interesting was the fact that these were attributed portions of copied text, thus avoiding plagiarism issues. Their use of attributions was in contrast to the findings in a study by Sutherland-Smith (2005), who, in a study centered on internet plagiarism, explored the use of internet sources by undergraduate L2 writers at a university in Australia. What she found was that the "ESL students considered the Internet a 'free zone' and not governed by legal proprietary rights" (p. 15).

These results are especially important in light of the findings of another study conducted in Australia, where Thompson, Morton, and Storch (2013) compared source text choices among undergraduate L2 writers. They found that students relied far more on Web-based sources (mainly using Google as their preferred search engine) than print-based sources, thus reinforcing Bolter's (2001) assertion cited earlier about an important shift away from traditional print-based sources. Hence, from a reading-writing connections perspective, it is essential to examine those connections from a multimodal perspective that accounts for electronic sources and not just print texts.

1.3 Future developments

As we move forward with reading-writing connections scholarship, it is important to bear in mind how much higher the stakes are now than in the early days of that scholarship. That students are increasingly assessed via reading-to-write tasks in gate-keeping contexts like the TOEFL, as well as locally-based placement tests, alerts us to the significance attached to being able to move effectively between reading and writing and make connections between the two. As such, there is a need to build on the assessment-related foundation now emerging. Integrated reading-writing assessment is seemingly here to stay, so we must continue to explore students' encounters with reading-writing connections in assessment contexts.

The stakes are also higher now with respect to plagiarism issues (e.g. Pecorari 2008), which provide an important cross-section for the ways in which reading and writing interact as students negotiate source texts and the complexities of academic socialization in circumstances that may be very different than those in their native cultures. Here is where the shift in research to students' use of citations is a significant development, as studies in this area are helping shed light on why students struggle with textual borrowing and engage in what is considered plagiarism. This includes looking at how teachers are actually teaching citation practices and not just at what students do with citations.

Meanwhile, it is clear that reading-writing connections play a major role in contemporary L2 writing instruction, especially within the EAP framework. However, we still know very little about actual EAP classrooms and how L2 writing teachers treat reading-writing connections and related issues tied to academic enculturation and socialization. Here, as suggested in Chapter 2 of this volume, we also need to account for the growing interest in learning to write and writing to learn (Manchón 2011). Writing to learn, in particular, is likely to be a dynamic area of research in coming years, but at present we know very little about reading-writing relations within this context.

In short, this is perhaps an optimum time for examining reading-writing connections, as the steady stream of research on source text use indicates. There are established models for such examinations, as well as a rich theoretical base that has been generated over the past 30 years or so. Useful research methods have also developed. In a sense, then, we are better equipped than ever before to investigate these connections. On the other hand, an updated model of reading-writing connections that accounts for the complexities associated with digital literacy has not yet emerged. Furthermore, in the continued dominance of the reading-to-write direction, there is still too little attention paid to the movement from writing-to-read. Finally, it is interesting to note the focus in the research literature on students. While that focus is understandable, we know very little about how *teachers* understand and treat the connections between reading and writing. Future years will hopefully see a move toward adding teachers and their perspectives and approaches to the reading-writing connections scholarship.

2 Speaking-writing connections

A few years ago we (Belcher and Hirvela 2008) observed that L2 speaking (that is, oral interaction) and writing connections had been even more neglected than L2 reading/writing relationships. We could say the same today; however, the tide is starting to turn, and our claim may actually have been somewhat overstated to begin with. Certainly, explicit attention to speaking/writing connections has not been extensive over the past few decades, but attention to dialogic activities that accompany writing has not been lacking (Weissberg 2006a). Why speaking/writing interfaces have been more implicitly than explicitly addressed in L2 research and pedagogy is a question that the historical development of our own and related fields may shed some light on.

2.1 From the two-way street to the Internet highway: A short history

Approximately three decades ago, Kantor and Rubin (1981) compellingly argued for connecting speaking and writing for literacy learners. They contended that there was much reason to believe that growth in writing and speaking reciprocally affected each other. Around the same time, in L2 English language education, pedagogists, led by Zamel (1976), began to see writing as worthy of far more attention than it had so far been given. Up to that time, L2 writing had been commonly viewed as the handmaiden of language learning – a means of reinforcing grammar and vocabulary learning, as spoken language written down (see Matsuda 2003). Zamel (1982) and others argued that L2 writing should be perceived as not just language practice but as a means of discovering meaning, expressing oneself, and transforming (the writer's) knowledge. L2 writing theorists were following the lead of the expressivists and cognitivists who masterminded the L1 writing process movement, which shifted pedagogical emphasis from the written product to the writer. The 1980s also witnessed rapidly growing interest in the communicative language teaching (CLT) approach (Savignon 1997), which treated all the linguistic modalities (listening, speaking, reading, writing) as resources for building the fluency needed for communicative competence, but, in practice, tended to prioritize speaking. From the CLT perspective, language teachers were not primarily literacy instructors, while from Zamel's (1985) and other L2 compositionists' vantage point, L2 writing teachers should not primarily be language teachers but instead facilitators of writing development. This distancing of L2 writing from language instruction was not conducive to explicit attention to speaking/writing relationships.

Yet speaking/writing connections were forged nonetheless as an integral part of the process approach that L2 writing specialists advocated. This implicit linking of speaking and writing took the form of such scaffolding of composing and revising processes as group pre-writing activities, peer responding, teacher conferencing, and writing center tutorials. The work of social-interaction proponents Bruner (1978) and Bruffee (1999) and the father of sociocultural theory, Vygotsky (1986), provided theoretical impetus for collaborative activities (Weissberg 2006a, 2006b). Such oral interaction was seen as promoting "a natural tutorial phenomenon" (Weissberg: 2006a: 16), or the Vygotskian zone of proximal development, the space between what learners can do when assisted as opposed to unassisted. The rising popularity of socioliterate views, which, as Johns (1997) has observed, view "literacies ... [as] acquired principally through exposure to discourses from a variety of social contexts" (p. 14), also informed a more social approach to conceptualizing writing in general (Ferris and Hedgcock 2014). At the same time, the greater prominence given to writing in the TESOL profession in conjunction with the rising popularity of CLT, with its emphasis on integrated skills through content- and task-based activities (Brown 2001), no doubt encouraged language teachers, especially those in postsecondary intensive ESL language programs, which taught all linguistic modalities, to take a more balanced view of written and spoken communication. Teachers of younger learners in the US were influenced by the whole language movement (Rigg 1991), which advocated a meaning-oriented approach to literacy instruction, with such activities as helping children inscribe, often with their own invented spelling, orally composed narratives.

In the past decade, Rubin, working with Kang (Rubin and Kang 2008), has revisited his earlier conceptualization of speaking/writing relationships, which he had seen, with Kantor (Kantor and Rubin 1981), as bidirectional, but now envisions not as a "two-way street" but a "double helix," always intertwined, with the "focal outcome" continually shifting from speaking to writing and back again (Rubin and Kang 2008: 220). In fact, Prior's research (1998), which is inclusive of both L1 and L2 advanced academic literacy, has long presented speaking and writing as inseparable elements in a stream of multimodal semiotic activity (Prior and Shipka 2003). Weissberg's work (2006a, 2006b), however, has more explicitly foregrounded speaking/writing connections with L2 pedagogy in mind. Like Prior, Weissberg was inspired by Vygotskian sociocultural theory and Bakhtinian dialogism, both of which assert that "even the words and expressions that find their way into our written texts ultimately derive from conversations we have had with others" (Weissberg 2006b: 246). Weissberg's research and teacher-oriented writings provide illustrations and evidence of the efficacy of treating writing and speaking as interconnected, with writing seen, again from a sociocultural perspective, as the textualization of inner speech (internalized social interaction). Weissberg argues not just for the pedagogical necessity of talk as oral discourse but for a variety of dialogical practices, oral and written, such as journaling and peer responding, in the L2 classroom.

Interestingly, second language acquisition (SLA) researchers, after many years of privileging spoken discourse, have become more interested in writing, viewing it as one of the forms of output, along with speaking, that may enhance language learning by promoting noticing, or conscious reflection on what learners know and do not know about language (Chapter 26, this *Handbook*). Also influenced by sociocultural theory, notably its emphasis on the role that talk can play in making "new knowledge available for inspection and discussion" (Williams 2008: 18), SLA researchers, such as Swain and Lapkin (1998), have become intrigued by the advantages of peer-peer interaction, with such collaborative writing activities as dictogloss and story reconstruction, in which peers talk through writing tasks and together scaffold each other's ability to notice and address language issues. Such activities appear to result in more accurate text production and, as indicated by delayed post-tests, internalization of socially constructed knowledge (Williams 2008).

The most powerful catalyst for reconceptualization of and engagement with conjoined oral/literate activities, however, is arguably not the work of theorists, researchers, or pedagogists but the real life development of our digital virtual world. Web 2.0, or social media, in particular, where we consume, produce, and distribute multimodal – aural/graphic, verbal/visual – content, has propelled us into hybrid forms of communication. Some of these, like online chat and blogs, though written, combine features of both spoken and written discourse, while others, like digital storytelling, translate writing into ensembles of speech, music, and still and video images (Hafner and Miller 2011). These new digital genres (and requisite digital literacies), as Bloch (2008) has noted, are not just potential pathways to more formal academic literacies, but also constitute new literacy (and oracy) practices that, in their own right, merit literacy educators' attention.

2.2 Where speaking/writing research is taking us: Current trends

Research relevant to an interest in speaking/writing interactions can be viewed as branching off in three directions: one that is more writing-focused, another more speaking-focused, and a third, multimodality-oriented. These directional foci, or orientations, are not, however, mutually exclusive areas of inquiry or practice, especially from a genre systems (Tardy 2008) or a Bakhtinian intertextual perspective, from which any utterance or genre instantiation (spoken, written, or multimodal) can be seen as preceded by and leading to others.

2.2.1 Focus on speaking-to-write

As mentioned earlier, a number of dialogic L2 classroom activities facilitative of composing and revising processes have been theorized about and investigated. The research that will be briefly surveyed here considers the role of actual face-to-face (F2F) dialogue in L2 writing pedagogy, or talk-write activities. As suggested above, much of this research is informed by the theoretical work of Bruner, Bruffee, and more foundationally, Vygotsky. The preferred research methods include discourse analysis of classroom talk, whether peer-peer, teacher-student, or tutor-tutee, and textual analysis of written products. As Williams (2008) has noted, the findings of this research provide mounting evidence for speaking-to-write as a means of improving writing – both its content, or proposition-density, and its linguistic and rhetorical form – at least, that is, from draft to draft.

The talk in speaking-to-write activities need not be about writing as process or product in order to contribute to writing quality. Those focused on content-based instruction for younger language learners have found talk about content to serve, in effect, as pre-writing heuristics. Patthey-Chavez and Clare (1996), for example, found through analysis of reading lesson transcripts and student portfolios that ideas articulated in bilingual fourth-grade students' "anchoring activit[ies] for the negotiation of joint meaning" (p. 515) resurfaced in their writing. Zwiers (2006) has reported how his use of "proactive action research methods of inquiry to record and reflect upon" (p. 327) interactions in his ESL middle school classroom led to effective scaffolding of students' persuasive writing about history. Classroom activities included historical event role-playing and think-aloud teacher modeling of reading and writing. Developing the ideational dimension needed for academic writing, often through collaborative activities, is considered an essential component in the "teaching/learning cycle" of the Hallidayan systemic functional linguistic (SFL) approach to language/literacy instruction for both younger and older learners (Feez 2002: 65).

In much of the L2 writing research literature, however, far more attention has been given to talk, especially peer talk, about writing itself, rather than about content for writing. Peer responding has become a fixture in many process-oriented L2 writing classes, yet decades of research point to teachers and peer learners themselves often having mixed feelings about the value of spending time and effort on peer response (Ferris and Hedgcock 2014). Recent research, though, suggests what may make peer talk about writing more worthwhile in the eyes of instructors and students (see also chapters 19 and 20).

Medium and mode have been found to make a difference in the effectiveness of peer review. Examining peer response in an EFL context, with the help of textual, questionnaire, video-recording, and interview data, Yang, Badger, and Yu (2006) discovered that Chinese students were more receptive to peer feedback than might be expected given their normally teacher-centered classrooms and what earlier research suggested about the impact of a Confucian cultural background. Compared to teacher feedback, their oral peer negotiation resulted in more meaning-related revision. Use of their mother tongue in peer interactions may have facilitated idea exploration. In another Chinese setting, Hong Kong, Jones, Garralda, Li, and Lock (2006) observed, in their comparison of transcripts of F2F tutoring and logs of analogous online sessions, that response mode mattered. The F2F sessions, always in English, with fellow Cantonese-speaking students, were more hierarchical and accuracy-oriented whereas online sessions with the same peer tutors were more egalitarian and global meaning-focused. While medium (language) and mode (F2F or online) both may well matter in peer responding, Zhu and Mitchell (2012), in their activity-theory-informed study of two ESL university students' peer interactions, advise us to be careful not to assess peer review solely from the perspective of the teacher's assigned task. Students may have their own distinctive motives, as readers or writers, motives that can shape their task representation and resulting task performance.

Research on teacher/student F2F conferences has led to pedagogical implications similar to those of a number of peer response studies: the more collaborative the interaction, the more helpful the feedback for writers (see chapters 19 and 20). The few studies that have focused specifically on teacher/student conference discourse, through analysis of conference transcripts and subsequent student revisions, have found that students who more actively negotiate with the teacher during conferences tend to revise more (Goldstein and Conrad 1990; Patthey-Chavez and Ferris 1997). Ewert's (2009) research, which looked not only at negotiation but also scaffolding in conferences, points toward what is likely to encourage negotiation and substantive revision, namely, limiting discussion to a small number of content-related rhetorical topics. To achieve this, Ewert advises that teachers examine the discourse in their own conferences and proactively invite students to talk.

Writing center tutors at English-medium universities that serve both L1 and L2 writers have long felt challenged by how best to conference with their L2 writer clients (see Chapter 21). According to Thonus's (2004) analysis of a decade of writing center research, writing center tutors, though usually trained to use a Socratic, dialogic interactional style with their tutees, have been found to be more dominant in their interaction with L2 than with L1 writers, engaging in less extensive negotiation sequences, inviting less input, ceding the conversational floor less often. L2 tutees, in turn, have been likely to view the tutor as an authority figure, someone to be listened to rather than to engage in discussion with. Thonus does not argue that L2 tutees should be trained to be more assertive but does, in the same vein as Ewert, suggest that tutors may gain insight into their "frustrations" (p. 240) by analyzing recordings of their own interactions.

While the vast majority of recent talk-write research – whether on content-priming pre-writing activities, peer responding, or teacher and tutor conferencing – in effect encourages continued attempts at engaging L2 writers in talk for or about writing, in the context of much EAP instruction oral proficiency itself may receive scant attention. Leki (2003) found in her multi-year case study of an undergraduate ESL nursing student that she struggled with writing the nursing care plans essential to her program of study and clinical work with patients, with whom she could not easily communicate. While academic writing was supported through instruction, oral communication and professional writing dependent on knowledge gained through it were not.

In EFL settings, limited opportunities for oral interaction can have implications for writing. Professional academics who find oral communication at English-language conferences challenging can also find it challenging to form the collaborative relationships that ideally result from such meetings and may lead to publication in English-medium journals (Pérez-Llantada, Plo, and Ferguson 2011). For EFL students, Sasaki (2011; see also Chapter 7) found in her longitudinal study of Japanese undergraduates that spending time studying abroad meant that relationships with English speakers were formed and, through the Internet, maintained, and this may, in turn, have motivated the returnees' continued improvement of their L2 writing. Further investigation is certainly warranted into how social interaction dependent on oral skills and the supportive relationships that result may contribute to the success of academic and non-academic L2 written communication.

2.2.2 Focus on writing-to-speak

Decidedly less examined empirically than speaking-to-write is writing-to-speak. Rubin and Kang (2008) note that there is considerable theoretical motivation for turning our attention to the role writing can play in speaking. At a very basic level, as literacy/oracy theorists such as Olson and Torrance (1991) have argued, learning to encode enhances "metalinguistic representation of speech" (Rubin and Kang 2008: 214), hence ability to more fully realize word and phonemic boundaries and pronunciations (see also Tarone, Bigelow, and Hansen 2009). At a higher developmental level, written discourse expertise, Rubin and Kang suggest, can heighten "metarhetorical awareness of oral structures" (p. 215). SLA theorists, as mentioned earlier, are growing more interested in the language learning potential of writing, given its slower pace (than speech) and relative permanence (Williams 2012), "greatly supporting noticing of the most aware kind" (Ortega 2012: 140). Finding empirical evidence, however, that such noticing translates into the implicit knowledge that cognitively-oriented SLA researchers assume is needed for knowledge automatization, and the real-time processing of speaking, may prove to be a tall order, Ortega (2012) suggests. Researchers less concerned about implicit knowledge, on the other hand, such as those who are socioculturally-oriented or systemic-functional linguists, and more interested in such higher-order processing as development of metalinguistic knowledge, Ortega points out, may more unproblematically pursue their research agendas, analyzing language-related behaviors and written products. Such research is likely to strengthen the case for writing and language learning, thus writing → speaking, connections. Another of Rubin and Kang's (2008) motivations for more attention to writing-to-speak is the ability of writing to scaffold oral genre performance. More theory-informed than empirically based, their argument, that L2 pedagogists should take greater advantage of writing as a means of scripting and guiding oral interaction, offers insights into the demands of oral genres. Rubin and Kang observe, for example, that the increasingly popular academic genre of the poster presentation, often perceived as a primarily textual graphic display, in fact requires complex oral skills in response to conference attendees' queries, potentially intimidating interactions for L2 (or any) speakers. Advance scripting of content synopses, however, can lessen the challenges of this oral genre. Likewise, in the business world, Rubin and Kang add, the interactional demands of briefings with clients, colleagues, or the public can be made more manageable with scripted talking points. If language/literacy educators hope to promote the "synergy between speaking and writing," Rubin and Kang argue, they will need to become more aware of the "myriad ways in which speaking serves as a teleological end or outcome of writing" (p. 221).

Not fully understanding, however, that although some oral genres may be the "teleological end" of written genres, there are still significant differences between them can have consequences. Successfully orally presenting a written research report, for instance, requires much more than reading it aloud, as Hood and Forey (2005) found in their social semiotic analysis of the language and gestures of conference paper presentations. Accomplished presenters employ an array of complex rhetorical strategies, at times foregrounding interpersonal more than ideational dimensions. Such presentation strategies, rhetorical and linguistic, may be challenging to deploy, or even become conscious of, for L2 speakers, suggest Rowley-Jolivet and Carter-Thomas (2005), who found in their SFL-inspired analysis of the information structure of L1 and L2 scientists' articles and conference presentations that L2 speakers were less likely than L1 speakers to adapt their language use to the processing needs of listeners.

Yet, while written and oral genres can be different in crucial ways, writing, as a process, as noted earlier, can be seen as contributing to the development of the underlying linguistic proficiency needed for L2 oral competence. Not only does writing have the advantage of a slower pace and comparative permanence, but affectively, Williams (2008) has noted, writing, as less immediately public production, may encourage learners to try out new forms, which, in a language classroom, they are more likely to receive supportive feedback on than in out-of-class contexts. Collaborative writing tasks can offer particularly supportive environments for learners (Storch 2013; see also Chapter 18). Fernández-Dobao (2012), for example, found that learners jointly writing in groups of four gave each other immediate oral feedback on language-related issues, often leading to correct resolution, and, ultimately, more accurate texts than those of writers working alone or even in pairs. Storch (2005, 2013) has concluded, based on her own and others' research, that when learners share responsibility for text creation, they may be much more receptive to each other's ideas and output monitoring than they would be in typical peer responding sessions, where there is no joint textual ownership. While so far there is limited evidence of long term language learning as a result of collaborative (or any other) writing, Storch (2013) sees certain research approaches as especially promising, in particular, qualitative longitudinal studies using Vygotskian microgenetic analysis, looking for evidence of local, socially-situated learning in the collaborative writing processes of learners. As for the case for the writing → speaking relationship in general, Williams too (2008) sees reason for optimism, even from a more cognitivist perspective, specifically that of skill acquisition theory (DeKeyser 2007), which suggests that strengthening the form-meaning connection in planned production (as in writing) should increase the likelihood of the automization needed for spontaneous production (in speaking).

2.2.3 Focus on multimodality

Hybrid forms of discourse, such as journaling, especially dialogue journaling, which fall somewhere in the middle of the speaking-writing continuum, are not new (Weissberg 2006a). Computer-mediated communication (CMC), however, especially with the onset of social media, has led to a profusion of new hybrid dialogic written genres, both synchronous and asynchronous, e.g., texting and tweeting. While these new discourse forms share features of both speaking and writing, synchronous CMC genres, such as online chat, with its real-time conversational turn-taking, have been viewed as especially supportive of oral proficiency development (Payne and Whitney 2002), while asynchronous CMC genres, such as blogging, have been seen as bridges from the vernacular to more formal academic, especially argumentative, writing (Bloch 2008). Yet, synchronous CMC can also be seen as facilitative of writing development, capable of increasing the quantity and complexity of L2 text production, and asynchronous CMC can be viewed as supportive of speaking, insofar as it emboldens reticent L2 speakers to participate in class discussion, not just online but in their real-life classes as well (Williams 2008). Rubin and Kang's (2008) double helix metaphor for speaking and writing, as continuously interlinked, seems particularly apt when one considers CMC.

Not only are there new digitally-enabled forms of dialogic text-based communication (see Chapter 14), but also more truly multimodal forms that do not just exhibit features of written and oral discourse but actually are both visual and aural, forms such as video blogging and digital storytelling, and the more synchronous video chat and videoconferencing (Jones and Hafner 2012). Many of these multimodal forms might seem to privilege oral performance over writing, yet the mode privileged is not always so straightforward. Research articles in online journals, for example, may now include video abstracts. Rather than simple oral readings of written abstracts, video abstracts make it possible for authors to transport the viewing audience to the scene of the research and what motivated it (see http:// thesocietypages.org/sociologylens/category/video-abstract/). Clearly, though, such abstracts are still meant to draw viewers to the author's text. Similarly, for students, another genre, digital storytelling, might seem at first glance to unidirectionally lead from written to oral narrative, embellished with music and graphics. However, while students will move from composing and storyboarding to making the video, the video production process itself keeps them immersed in text interpretation, hence involved in a recursive bidirectionality. In their account of a video science documentary course project for English-language students, Hafner and Miller (2011), drawing on data from questionnaires, focus-group interviews, and blog comments, recount how the students progressed from reading relevant research literature, to collaboratively designing and performing experiments, and then re-enacting scripted versions of these for their videos. Such projects can lead to both oral presentations and reflection-based papers as well as inspire a surprising amount of learner autonomy and engagement, as students may aim for a video audience not just of instructor and classmates but anyone with Internet access.

Given the multimodality of digital genres, the notion of discrete linguistic modalities, viewed from a digital literacies perspective, looks less and less meaningful. As Jones (2013) has observed, what matters to the digitally literate is participation in social groups and activities, for which linguistic competencies are necessary by not sufficient enablers. Particularly productive approaches to understanding such phenomena, Jones suggests, can be found in the language-as-social-practice theoretical lens of the new literacies movement (Gee 2008) and such research methods as naturalistic observation and analysis of digital artifacts. While it has been argued that the uniqueness of digital literacies, with their "new forms of representation and interactions" (Hafner, Chik, and Jones 2013: 813), makes them deserving of language specialists' attention (Bloch 2008), equally motivating may be the fact that far from totally distinct from other literacies, academic or otherwise, digital literacies are increasingly inseparable from and transformative of them.

2.3 Looking into the future of speaking and writing connections: Theory, research, and pedagogy

Although this discussion of the future of speaking and writing in L2 educational contexts begins by considering theory, the underlying assumption is not that theory begets research and pedagogy. In fact, when one surveys the work of Weissberg (2006a, 2006b), who has perhaps written more about speaking/writing connections than anyone else in L2 language/literacy education, one sees how closely connected his interest in Vygotskian sociocultural theory (SCT) is to his decades of language teaching and research. Despite being one of the most vocal proponents of this theory (in the L2 speaking/writing literature), Weissberg (2008) has made a point of articulating a number of caveats about importing a theory like SCT, originally meant for and based on research on L1 acquisition and cognitive development. Many L2 learners, especially adult learners, Weissberg reminds us, may not initially develop their L2 as a result of social interaction or perceive inner speech in their L2 as a resource. Weissberg is not warning us away from SCT, but cautioning us against wholesale adoption of it as a theoretical lens for L2 language/literacy learning. While Vygotskian theory can be too uncritically adopted for L2 education, however, Bakhtin's dialogic view of language as "shaped and developed in continuous interaction" with the utterances of others (Bakhtin 1986: 89; see Tardy 2008) has so far received relatively little attention, with some notable exceptions (Hall, Vitanova, and Marchenkova 2005; Prior 1998; Tardy 2008). Increasingly influential is Leonťev's activity theory, an offshoot of SCT that "recognize[es] the social nature of activity, [but] focuses more on the motives of individuals and the connectedness of motives and behaviors" (Zhu and Mitchell 2012: 364). Such an orientation has the potential to encourage a more emic perspective on how students view and do tasks. As multimodality figures more and more prominently in L2 speaking/writing events, the work of new literacies theorists such as Gee (on digital literacy, see Gee and Hayes 2011) and Kress (on social semiotics, see Kress 2010) is likely to be seen as an increasingly valuable resource.

While many L2 speaking/writing pedagogical practices have been inspired by sociocultural theory, finding evidence for the efficacy of connecting speaking with writing remains challenging. A number of researchers have focused on textual analysis, looking primarily at subsequent drafts after student interaction with peers, tutors and teachers. Both L2 writing and SLA researchers have looked to learners' written products for evidence of uptake – of feedback for the former (L2 writing), and of lessons learned from languaging (or talk about language; Swain 2000) for the latter (SLA) – but relatively little attention has been given to long term gains for writers, beyond the delayed post-tests in SLA research. Oral interaction in speaking-to-write has also been relatively neglected, especially with respect to teacher/student conferencing. When the discourse of oral feedback and task interaction is examined, it tends to be analyzed as text, though conversation analysis techniques may be used, rather than as aural or video data, which has the potential to reveal much more about interaction than written transcripts can (Leander and Prior 2004). More aural/video data collection and analysis will also be needed if more attention is to be given to the impact of writing on oral genre performance. When ethnographic research methods have been employed in speaking/writing research, they have tended to be in the form of a limited number of interviews or classroom observations rather than prolonged engagement in multiple contexts. For research on multimodality, more social semiotic analytic techniques will be in order for multimodal creations such as digital stories and documentaries (Hafner and Miller 2011), and more innovative research methods, such as computer tracking, will be needed for analysis of production processes.

There are a number of directions that teachers interested in connecting speaking and writing may want to move in. Considering that genres never exist in isolation in the real world, or even in the real academic world, taking a more genre systems perspective, as Tardy (2008) has advised, could facilitate a more integrated approach to speaking and writing instruction. Writing is, after all, commonly preceded or followed, especially in academia, by use of oral genres, such as lectures or class discussion, and speaking by written genres, such as note-taking or summary-response tasks. When a genre approach is taken, it generally has been in the context of writing instruction and focused on discrete written, rarely oral, genres. More attention to oral genres, as Rubin and Kang (2008) argue, would be a service to learners faced with a sink-or-swim challenge when required to perform such genres as oral presentations and dissertation defenses. Collaborative writing tasks offer an excellent opportunity to connect speaking with writing, but so far in formal writing instruction, most peer collaboration has taken the form of responding, not actual joint writing. Providing learners with more collaborative writing experience may help prepare them for the situated learning of life after school. Collaboration in the form of multimodal tasks would provide guidance and validation for digital literacy practices that will likely become ever more prevalent in students' future lives as workers and global citizens. The goal of all these instructional strategies should be to persuade learners that speaking to others can support not just fluency but also the content and the desire to communicate needed for writing, and writing, as planning and means of form-focused noticing, can contribute the scaffolding and, very likely, the automaticity needed for speaking.

3 Envoi

At the start of this chapter, we noted, almost apologetically, that we had decided to treat reading-writing and speaking-writing connections separately in light of the abundant research literature on each of these relationships. After surveying these rich research strands, we feel, given how much has been learned from viewing two modalities as inter-related, that still more will be gained by examining reading-speaking-writing interactions together. As we all become increasingly aware of the multimodal nature of discourse, online and offline, its seems likely that those interested in the progress of language/literacy learners will also increasingly feel compelled to investigate the affordances and challenges of the multi-directionality of reading, speaking, and writing.

4 Additional sources

August, Diane and Timothy Shanahan (eds.). 2006. *Developing literacy in second-language learners: A Report of the National Literacy Panel on Language Minority Youth and Children.* Mahwah, NJ: Lawrence Erlbaum.

Biber, Douglas. 2006. *University language: A corpus-based study of spoken and written registers.* Amsterdam: John Benjamins.

Bloch, Joel and Mark J. Wilkinson. 2014. *Teaching digital literacies.* Alexandria, VA: TESOL.

Dovey, Teresa. 2010. Facilitating writing from sources: A focus on both process and product. *Journal of English for Academic Purposes* 9. 45–60

Graham, Steve and Michael Hebert. 2010. *Writing to read: Evidence for how writing can improve reading.* Carnegie Corporation, NY: Alliance for Excellent Education.

Lantolf, James and Steven Thorne. 2006. *Sociocultural theory and the genesis of second language development.* Oxford: Oxford University Press.

Rose, David and J. R. Martin. 2012. *Learning to write, learning to read.* Bristol, CT: Equinox.

Schleppegrell, Mary J. and M. Cecilia Colombi (eds.). 2002. *Developing advanced literacy in first and second languages: Meaning with power.* Mahwah, N: Lawrence Erlbaum.

Wertsch, James. 1991. *Voices of the mind: A sociocultural approach to mediated action.* Cambridge, MA: Harvard University Press.

Wolfersberger, Mark Andrew. 2007. *Second language writing from sources: An ethnographic study of an argument writing task.* Auckland: The University of Auckland PhD thesis.

5 References

Ascención Delaney, Yuly. 2008. Investigating the reading-to-write construct. *Journal of English for Academic Purposes* 7. 140–150.

Belcher, Diane and Alan Hirvela. 2008. Introduction. In Diane Belcher and Alan Hirvela (eds.), *The oral-literate connection*, 1–8. Ann Arbor, MI: University of Michigan Press.

Bloch, Joel. 2008. *Technologies in the second language composition classroom.* Ann Arbor: University of Michigan Press.

Bolter, Jay D. 2001 [1991]. *Writing space: Computers, hypertext, and the remediation of print*, 2nd ed. Mahwah, NJ: Lawrence Erlbaum.

Brown, H. Douglas. 2001 [1994]. *Teaching by principles* (2nd ed.). White Plains, NY: Longman.

Bruffee, Kenneth A. 1999 [1993]. *Collaborative learning: Higher education, interdependence, and the authority of knowledge* (2nd ed.). Baltimore, MD: Johns Hopkins University Press.

Bruner, Jerome. 1978. The role of dialog in language acquisition. In A. Sinclair, R. Jarvella, and W. Levelt (eds.), *The child's conception of language*, 241–255. Berlin: Springer-Verlag.

Carson, Joan and Ilona Leki (eds.). 1993. *Reading in the composition classroom: Second language perspectives.* Boston, MA: Heinle and Heinle.

Daley, Elizabeth. 2003. Expanding the concept of literacy. *Educational Review* 38. 33–40.

Davis, Mary. 2013. The development of source use by international postgraduate students. *Journal of English for Academic Purposes* 12. 125–135.

DeKeyser, Robert. 2007. Skill acquisition theory. In Bill VanPatten and Jessica Williams (eds.), *Theories in second language acquisition*, 97–112. Mahwah, NJ: Lawrence Erlbaum.

Eisterhold, Joan G. 1990. Reading-writing connections: Toward a description for second-language learners. In Barbara Kroll (ed.), *Second language writing: Research insights from the classroom*, 88–101. New York: Cambridge University Press.

Ewert, Doreen E. 2009. L2 writing conferences: Investigating teacher talk. *Journal of Second Language Writing* 18. 251–269.

Feak, Christine and Barbara Dobson. 1996. Building on the impromptu: A Source-based academic writing assessment. *College ESL* 6(1). 73–84.

Feez, Susan. 2002. Heritage and innovation in second language education. In Ann Johns (ed.), *Genre in the classroom*, 43–69. Mahwah, NJ: Lawrence Erlbaum.

Fernández-Dobao, Ana. 2012. Collaborative writing tasks in the L2 classroom: Comparing group, pair, and individual work. *Journal of Second Language Writing* 21. 40–58.

Ferris, Dana R. and John S. Hedgcock. 2014 [1998]. *Teaching L2 composition* (3rd ed). New York: Routledge.

Flower, Linda. 1994. *The construction of negotiated meaning: A social cognitive theory of writing.* Carbondale and Edwardsville, IL: Southern Illinois University Press.

Flower, Linda and John Hayes. 1981. A cognitive process theory of writing. *College Composition and Communication* 32. 365–387.

Flower, Linda and John R. Hayes. 1984. Images, plans, and prose: The presentation of meaning in writing. *Written Communication* 1. 120–160.

Gebril, Atta. 2010. Bridging reading-to-write and writing-only assessment tasks together: A generalizability analysis. *Assessing Writing* 15(1) 100–117.

Gee, James P. 2008 [1996]. *Social linguistics and literacies: Ideology in discourses* (3rd edn.). London: Routledge.

Gee, James and Elizabeth Hayes. 2011. *Language and learning in the digital age.* New York: Routledge.

Gilliland, Betsy and Jeongyeon Park (eds.). 2015. Connections between second language reading and writing. Special issue of *Reading in a Foreign Language*.

Goldstein, Lynn and Susan Conrad. 1990. Student input and the negotiation of meaning in ESL writing conferences. *TESOL Quarterly* 24. 443–460.

Grabe, William. 2001. Reading-writing relations: Theoretical perspectives and instructional practices. In Diane Belcher and Alan Hirvela (eds.), *Linking literacies: Perspectives on L2 reading-writing connections*, 15–47. Ann Arbor: University of Michigan Press.

Grabe, William. 2003. Reading and writing relations: Second language perspectives on research and practice. In Barbara Kroll (ed.), *Exploring the dynamics of second language writing*, 242–262. New York: Cambridge University Press.

Grabe, William. 2009. *Reading in a second language: Moving from theory to practice.* New York: Cambridge University Press.

Grabe, William and Cui Zhang. 2013a. Reading and writing together: A critical component of English for Academic Purposes Teaching and Learning. *TESOL Journal* 4(1). 9–24.

Grabe, William and Cui Zhang. 2013b. Second language reading-writing relations. In A. S. Horning and E. W. Kraemer (eds.), *Reconnecting reading and writing*, 108–133. Anderson, SC and Fort Collins, CO: Parlor Press and The WAC Clearinghouse.

Hafner, Christoph, Alice Chik, and Rodney Jones. 2013. Engaging with digital literacies in TESOL. *TESOL Quarterly* 47(4). 812–815.

Hafner, Christoph and Lindsay Miller. 2011. Fostering learner autonomy in English for science: A collaborative digital project in a technological learning environment. *Language Learning and Technology* 15. 68–86.

Hall, Joan Kelly, Gergana Vitanova, and Ludmila Marchenkova (eds.). 2005. *Dialogue with Bakhtin on second and foreign language learning: New perspectives.* Mahwah, NJ: Lawrence Erlbaum.

Hamp-Lyons, Liz and Barbara Kroll. 1996. Issues in ESL writing assessment: An overview. *College English* 6(1). 52–72.

Harwood, Nigel. 2009. An interview-based study of the functions of citations in academic writing across two disciplines. *Journal of Pragmatics* 41. 497–518.

Harwood, Nigel and Bojana Petric. 2012. Performance in the citing behavior of two student writers. *Written Communication* 29. 55–103.

Hedgcock, John and Dana R. Ferris. 2009. *Teaching readers of English: Students, texts, and contexts*. New York: Routledge/Taylor and Francis.

Hirvela, Alan. 2004. *Connecting reading and writing in second language writing instruction*. Ann Arbor: University of Michigan Press.

Hirvela, Alan and Qian Du. 2013. "Why am I paraphrasing?": Undergraduate ESL writers' engagement with source-based academic writing and reading. *Journal of English for Academic Purposes* 12. 87–98.

Hood, Susan and Gail Forey. 2005. Introducing a conference paper: Getting interpersonal with your audience. *Journal of English for Academic Purposes* 4. 291–306.

Johns, Ann. 1997. *Text, role, and context: Developing academic literacies*. New York: Cambridge University Press.

Jones, Rodney. 2013. Research methods in TESOL and digital literacies. *TESOL Quarterly* 47(4). 843–848.

Jones, Rodney, Angel Garralda, David Li, and Gail Lock. 2006. Interactional dynamics in on-line and face-to-face peer tutoring sessions for second language writers. *Journal of Second Language Writing* 15. 1–23.

Jones, Rodney and Christoph Hafner. 2012. *Understanding digital literacies*. London: Routledge.

Kantor, Kenneth and Donald Rubin. 1981. Between speaking and writing: Processes of differentiation. In Barry Kroll and Roberta Vann (eds.), *Exploring speaking-writing relationships: Comparison and contrasts*, 55–81. Urbana, IL: National Council of Teachers of English.

Keck, Casey. 2006. The use of paraphrase in summary writing: A comparison of L1 and L2 writers. *Journal of Second Language Writing* 15. 261–278.

Keck, Casey. 2014. Copying, paraphrasing, and academic writing development: A Re-examination of L1 and L2 summarization practices. *Journal of Second Language Writing* 25. 4–22.

Kress, Gunther. 2010. *Multimodality: A social semiotic approach to contemporary communication*. London: Routledge.

Kucer, Stephen B. 1985. The making of meaning: Reading and writing as parallel processes. *Written Communication* 2. 317–336.

Kucer, Stephen B. 2005 [2001]. *The dimensions of literacy: A conceptual base for teaching reading and writing in school settings* (2nd edn.). Mahwah, NJ: Lawrence Erlbaum.

Leander, Kevin and Paul Prior. 2004. Speaking and writing: How talk and text interact in situated practices. In Charles Bazerman and Paul Prior (eds.), *What writing does and how it does it: An introduction to analyzing texts and textual practices*, 201–238. Mahwah, NJ: Lawrence Erlbaum.

Leki, Ilona. 2003. Living through college literacy: Nursing in a second language. *Written Communication* 20. 81–98.

Li, Yongyan. 2012. Undergraduate students searching and reading Web sources for writing. *Educational Media International* 49. 201–215.

Li, Yongyan and Christine P. Casanave. 2012. Two first-year students' strategies for writing from sources: Patchwriting or plagiarism? *Journal of Second Language Writing* 21. 165–180.

Manchón, Rosa M. (ed.). 2011. *Learning-to-write and writing-to-learn in an additional language*. Amsterdam: John Benjamins.

Matsuda, Paul K. 2003. Second language writing in the twentieth century: A situated historical perspective. In Barbara Kroll (ed.), *Exploring the dynamics of second language writing*, 15–34. New York: Cambridge University Press.

Olson, David and Nancy Torrance. 1991. *Literacy and orality*. Cambridge, UK: Cambridge University Press.

Ortega, Lourdes. 2012. Exploring L2 writing – SLA interfaces. *Journal of Second Language Writing* 21. 404–415.

Patthey-Chavez, G. Genevieve and Lindsay Clare. 1996. Task, talk, and text: The influence of instructional conversation on transitional bilingual writers. *Written Communication* 13. 515–563.

Patthey-Chavez, G. Genevieve and Dana R. Ferris. 1997. Writing conferences and the weaving of multi-voiced texts in college composition. *Research in the Teaching of English* 31. 51–90.

Payne, J. Scott and Paul Whitney. 2002. Developing L2 oral proficiency through synchronous CMC: Output, working memory and interlanguage development. *CALICO Journal* 20. 7–32.

Pecorari, Diane. 2006. Visible and occluded citation features in postgraduate second-language writing. *English for Specific Purposes* 25. 4–29.

Pecorari, Diane. 2008. *Academic writing and plagiarism: A linguistic analysis*. London: Continuum.

Pecorari, Diane and Philip Shaw (eds.). 2013. Source use in L2 academic writing. [Special issue] *Journal of English for Academic Purposes* 12(2).

Pérez-Llantada, Carmen, Ramón Plo, and Gibson Ferguson. 2011. "You don't say what you know, only what you can": The perceptions and practices of senior Spanish academics regarding research dissemination in English. *English for Specific Purposes* 30. 18–30.

Petrić, Bojana. 2007. Rhetorical functions of citations in high-and low-rated master's theses. *Journal of English for Academic Purposes* 6. 238–253.

Petrić, Bojana. 2012. Legitimate textual borrowing: Direct quotations in L2 student writing. *Journal of Second Language Writing* 21. 102–117.

Petrić, Bojana and Nigel Harwood. 2013. Task requirements, task representation, and self-reported citation functions: An exploratory study of a successful L2 student's writing. Journal of *English for Academic Purposes* 12. 110–124.

Plakans, Lia. 2008. Comparing composing processes in writing-only and reading-to-write test tasks. *Assessing Writing* 13(1). 111–129.

Plakans, Lia. 2009a. Discourse synthesis in integrated second language writing assessment. *Language Testing* 26(4). 561–587.

Plakans, Lia. 2009b. The role of reading in integrated L2 writing tasks. *Journal of English for Academic Purposes* 8. 252–266.

Plakans, Lia. 2010. Independent vs. integrated writing tasks: A comparison of task representation. *TESOL Quarterly* 44(1). 185–194.

Plakans, Lia and Atta Gebril. 2012. A close investigation into source use in integrated second language writing tasks. *Assessing Writing* 17(1). 18–34.

Polio, Charlene and Ling Shi (Guest eds.). 2012a. Textual appropriation and source text use in L2 writing. *Journal of Second Language Writing* 21(2).

Polio, Charlene and Ling Shi. 2012b. Perceptions and beliefs about textual appropriation and source use in second language writing. *Journal of Second Language Writing* 21. 95–101.

Prior, Paul 1998. *Writing/disciplinarity: A sociohistoric account of literate activity in the academy*. Mahwah, N.J.: Erlbaum.

Prior, Paul and Jody Shipka. 2003. Chronotopic lamination: Tracing the contours of literate activity. In Charles Bazerman and David Russell (eds.), *Writing selves/Writing societies*, 180–238. Fort Collins, CO: The WAC Clearinghouse and Mind, Culture, and Activity.

Radia, Pavlina, and Paul Stapleton. 2008. Unconventional Internet genres and their impact on second language undergraduate students' writing process. *Internet and Higher Education* 11. 9–17.

Rigg, Pat. 1991. Whole language in TESOL. *TESOL Quarterly* 25. 521–542.

Rinnert, Carol and Hiroe Kobayashi. 2005. Borrowing words and ideas: Insights from Japanese writers. *Journal of Asian Pacific Communication* 15. 31–56.

Rowley-Jolivet, Elizabeth and Shirley Carter-Thomas. 2005. Genre awareness and rhetorical appropriacy: Manipulation of information structure by NS and NNS scientists in the international conference setting. *English for Specific Purposes* 24. 41–64.

Rubin, Donald L. and Okim Kang. 2008. Writing to speak: What goes on across the two-way street. In Diane Belcher and Alan Hirvela (eds.), *The oral-literate connection*, 210–225. Ann Arbor, MI: University of Michigan Press.

Sasaki, Miyuki. 2011. Effects of varying lengths of study-abroad experiences on Japanese EFL students' L2 writing ability and motivation: A longitudinal study. *TESOL Quarterly* 45. 81–105.

Savignon, Sandra J. 1997 [1983]. *Communicative competence: Theory and classroom practice*, 2nd edn. Reading, MA: Addison-Wesley.

Shanahan, Timothy and Richard G. Lomax. 1986. An analysis and comparison of theoretical models of the reading-writing relationship. *Journal of Educational Psychology* 79. 116–123.

Shanahan, Timothy and Richard G. Lomax. 1988. A developmental comparison of three theoretical models of the reading-writing relationship. *Research in the Teaching of English* 22. 196–212.

Shi, Ling. 2012. Rewriting and paraphrasing source texts in second language writing. *Journal of Second Language Writing* 21. 134–148.

Solé, Isabel, Mariana Miras, Núria Castells, Sandra Espino, and Marta Minguela. 2013. Integrating information: An analysis of the processes involved and the products generated in a written synthesis task. *Written Communication* 30. 63–90.

Spivey, Nancy. 1990. Transforming texts: Constructive processes in reading and writing. *Written Communication* 7. 256–287.

Spivey, Nancy. 1997. *The constructivist metaphor: Reading, writing, and the making of meaning*. New York: Academic Press.

Stapleton, Paul. 2005. Using the Web as a research source: Implications for L2 academic writing. *The Modern Language Journal* 89. 177–189.

Stapleton, Paul. 2010. Writing in an electronic age: A case study of L2 composing processes. *Journal of English for Academic Purposes* 9. 295–307.

Storch, Neomy. 2005. Collaborative writing: Product, process, and students' reflections. *Journal of Second Language Writing* 14. 153–173.

Storch, Neomy. 2013. *Collaborative writing in L2 classrooms*. Bristol, UK: Multilingual Matters.

Sutherland-Smith, Wendy. 2005. Internet plagiarism and international students' academic writing. *Journal of Asian Pacific Communication* 15. 15–29.

Swain, Merrill. 2000. The Output Hypothesis and beyond: Mediating acquisition through collaborative dialogue. In James Lantolf (ed.), *Sociocultural theory and second language learning*, 97–114. Oxford, UK: Oxford University Press.

Swain, Merrill and Sharon Lapkin. 1998. Interactions and second language learning: Two adolescent French immersion students working together. *Modern Language Journal* 82. 320–337.

Tardy, Christine. 2008. Multimodality and the teaching of advanced academic writing: A genre systems perspective on speaking-writing connections. In Diane Belcher and Alan Hirvela (eds.), *The oral-literate connection*, 191–208. Ann Arbor, MI: University of Michigan Press.

Tarone, Elaine, Martha Bigelow, and Kit Hansen. 2009. *Literacy and second language oracy*. Oxford: Oxford University Press.

Thompson, Celia, Janne Morton and Neomy Storch. 2013. Where from, who, why, and how? A study of the use of sources by first year L2 university students. *Journal of English for Academic Purposes* 12. 99–109.

Thonus, Terese. 2004. What are the differences?: Tutor interactions with first- and second-language writers. *Journal of Second Language Writing* 13. 227–242.

Tierney, Robert J. and David P. Pearson. 1983. Toward a composing model of reading. *Language Arts* 60. 568–580.

Vygotsky, Lev. 1986. *Thought and language*. Cambridge, MA: MIT Press.

Weigle, Sara C. 2002. *Assessing writing*. Cambridge: Cambridge University Press.

Weigle, Sara C. 2004. Integrating reading and writing in a competency test for non-native speakers of English. *Assessing Writing* 9(1). 27–55.

Weigle, Sara C. and Keisha Parker. 2012. Source text borrowing in an integrated writing assessment. *Journal of Second Language Writing* 21. 118–133.

Weissberg, Robert. 2006a. *Connecting speaking and writing in second language writing instruction*. Ann Arbor, MI: University of Michigan Press.

Weissberg, Robert. 2006b. Scaffolded feedback: Tutorial conversations with advanced L2 writers. In Ken Hyland and Fiona Hyland (eds.), *Feedback in second language writing*, 246–265. New York: Cambridge University Press.

Weissberg, Robert. 2008. Critiquing the Vygotskian approach to L2 literacy. In Diane Belcher and Alan Hirvela (eds.), *The oral-literate connection*, 26–45. Ann Arbor, MI: University of Michigan Press.

Williams, Jessica. 2008. The speaking-writing connection in second language and academic literacy development. In Diane Belcher and Alan Hirvela (eds.), *The oral-literate connection*, 10–25. Ann Arbor, MI: University of Michigan Press.

Williams, Jessica. 2012. The potential role(s) of writing in second language development. *Journal of Second Language Writing* 21. 321–331.

Yang, Miao, Richard Badger, and Zheng Yu. 2006. A comparative study of peer and teacher feedback in a Chinese EFL writing class. *Journal of Second Language Writing* 15. 179–200.

Zamel, Vivian. 1976. Teaching composition in the ESL classroom: What we can learn from research in the teaching of English. *TESOL Quarterly* 10. 67–76.

Zamel, Vivian. 1982. Writing: The process of discovering meaning. *TESOL Quarterly* 16. 195–209.

Zamel, Vivian. 1985. Responding to student writing. *TESOL Quarterly* 19. 79–102.

Zhu, Wei and Deborah A. Mitchell. 2012. Participation in peer response as activity: An examination of peer response stances from an activity theory perspective. *TESOL Quarterly* 46. 362–86.

Zwiers, Jeff. 2006. Integrating academic language, thinking, and content: Learning scaffolds for non-native speakers in the middle grades. *Journal of English for Academic Purposes* 5. 317–332.

Biographical notes

Dwight Atkinson is an applied linguist and second language educator who works at the University of Arizona (Tucson, Arizona, USA). His past research in second/foreign language writing has dealt with practices of individualism in the U. S. first-year university writing classroom, theorizing culture in SLW, theorizing SLW generally, studying SLW ethnographically, early-stage professional development of students in SLW-friendly Ph.D programs, and SLW as an extended, distributed, sociocognitive process. Atkinson also works in the areas of second language acquisition, second language teaching, ESP/EAP, and culture theory.
dwightatki@gmail.com

Diane Belcher, Chair and Professor of Applied Linguistics and ESL at Georgia State, University (USA), has published a number of books, articles and book chapters primarily about advanced academic literacy. Former co-editor of *English for Specific Purposes* and *TESOL Quarterly*, she currently coedits the *Michigan Series on Teaching Multilingual Writers*.
dbelcher1@gsu.edu

Lourdes Cerezo is Associate Professor at the University of Murcia (Spain). She teaches Applied Linguistics at the undergraduate level and Second Language Assessment and Cooperative Language Learning courses for M.A. students. Her research areas include second language writing, error correction and feedback in writing, and second language assessment and language teaching methodology.
lourdesc@um.es

Jane Cogie is emerita Associate Professor of English and Director of the Southern Illinois University Writing Center, USA. Her articles on writing center pedagogy and administration and issues related to tutoring Non-Native English speakers have appeared in *The Writing Center Journal* and *WPA: Writing Program Administrator*, as well as in essay anthologies, including *The Politics of Writing Centers; Marginal Words, Marginal Works: Tutoring the Academy in the Work of Writing Centers;* and *Writing Centers and the New Racism: A Call for Sustainable Dialogue and Change*.
jcogie@siu.edu

Yvette Coyle is Associate Professor in the Faculty of Education at the University of Murcia, Spain, where she teaches EFL courses for future primary school teachers. Her research interests include young language learners, computer-mediated communication and written corrective feedback. Her work has been published in *Studies in Second Language Acquisition, Journal of Second Language Writing* and *ELT Journal* among others.
ycoyle@um.es

Alister Cumming is Professor Emeritus in the Department of Curriculum, Teaching and Learning and formerly (from 1993 to 2013) the Head of the Centre for Educational Research on Languages and Literacies, OISE, University of Toronto, Canada. He has written numerous books and articles on second-language education, language assessment, literacy, and international education policy.
acumming@oise.utoronto.ca

Mary Jane Curry is Associate Professor in the Department of Teaching and Curriculum at the University of Rochester, United States. She is co-author of *Teaching Academic Writing: A Toolkit for*

Higher Education, Academic Writing in a Global Context: The Politics and Practices of Publishing in English, and *A Scholar's Guide to Getting Published in English* and co-editor of several books. She has published on teaching English academic writing, the experiences of immigrant students at the community college, and academic publishing by multilingual scholars and engineers in journals including *Written Communication, TESOL Quarterly, English for Specific Purposes*, and *AILA Review* and contributed numerous book chapters.
mjcurry@warner.rochester.edu

Dana Ferris is Professor at the University of California, Davis, in the United States, and Associate Director for Second Language Writing in the University Writing Program. She has published many books, book chapters and articles in top journals on second language writing and response to student writing. She is the Editor in Chief of the newly launched *Journal of Response to Writing* and she is also Associate Editor of the *Journal of Second Language Writing*.
drferris@ucdavis.edu

Lynn Goldstein is Professor and Program Chair at Middlebury Institute of International Studies at Monterey, in the United States. She has served as a consultant to Educational Testing Service, is on the editorial board of the *Journal of Second Language Writing* and has served on the TESOL publications committee and the TESOL serial publications committee. She has published articles in *TESOL Quarterly, Studies in Second Language Acquisition, The Journal of Second Language Writing,* the *CATESOL Journal* and in various edited volumes and is the author of *Teacher Written Commentary in Second Language Writing Classrooms* (University of Michigan Press).
lgoldstein@miis.edu

Bill Grabe is Vice President for Research and Regents' Professor at Northern Arizona University, in the United States. His continuing research interests remain in the area of second language reading and writing skills development. He has published extensively in these fields and his research and service to applied linguistics was recognized with the lifetime Distinguished Scholarship and Service Award from AAAL (2005).
william.grabe@nau.edu

Alan Hirvela is Professor in the Department of Teaching and Learning at Ohio State University. His research interests and abundant publications focus on second language literacy, academic writing and the relationships between reading and writing. He has held several editorial positions, including those of Assistant Editor for *English for Specific Purposes*, and, together with Diane, co-editor of *TESOL Quarterly*.
Hirvela.1@osu.edu

Fiona Hyland is an honourary Associate Professor in the English Language Education Division in the Faculty of Education at the University of Hong Kong. She has more than thirty years of experience teaching and researching in the areas of applied linguistics and teacher education. She has published widely in both journals and edited volumes in the areas of written feedback and academic writing. She is co-author (with Ken Hyland) of *Feedback in Second Language Writing: Contexts and Issues* (CUP, 2006).
fhyland@hku.hk

Ken Hyland is Professor and Chair of Applied Linguistics and Head of the Centre for Applied English Studies, at The University of Hong Kong. He is well known for his work on academic

discourse and EAP and has published over 200 articles and 25 books on these issues. He is past Editor of both *Applied Linguistics* and *Journal of English for Academic Purposes*.
khyland@hku.hk

Richard Kern is Professor of French and Director of the Berkeley Language Center at the University of California at Berkeley. He teaches courses in French linguistics, language, and foreign language pedagogy. His research interests include language acquisition, literacy, and relationships between language and technology. He has most recently published *Language, Literacy, and Technology* (2015 Cambridge UP) and is currently working with Christine Develotte on an edited volume entitled *Online Multimodal Communication and Intercultural Encounters: Theoretical and Educational Perspectives*.
rkern@berkeley.edu

Hiroe Kobayashi, Professor Emeritus at Hiroshima University, has taught advanced English writing and pragmatics to Japanese and international university students. Her current research interest focuses on development of multilingual writing ability, by analyzing L1/L2 text features and writing processes, and writers' background. She has published articles, co-authored with Carol Rinnert, in international journals, including *Language Learning*, *the Journal of Second Language Writing*, and *the Modern Language Journal*.
hkobaya@hiroshima-u.ac.jp

Icy Lee is Professor and Chair at the Department of Curriculum and Instruction at the Chinese University of Hong Kong. Her research areas include second language writing, error correction and feedback in writing, classroom writing assessment, and teacher development. She has published extensively on these areas in top journals and edited collections. She has served on the editorial boards of *ELT Journal*, *Journal of Second Language Writing, Assessing Writing* and *TESL Canada Journal*. She is currently Associate Editor of the *Journal of Second Language Writing* and Senior Associate Editor of *The Asia-Pacific Education Researcher*.
icylee@cuhk.edu.hk

Theresa Lillis is Professor of English Language and Applied Linguistics at The Open University, in England. Her main research area is writing, especially form a perspective that can be summarized as *the politics of access, location, production and participation*. In addition to her numerous publications, she is co-editor of *Linguistics and Education* and co-convenor of the AILA research network *Academic Publishing and Presenting in a Global Context.*
t.m.lillis@open.ac.uk

Rosa M. Manchón, Professor of Applied Linguistics at the University of Murcia in Spain, has published extensively on L2 writing, especially SLA-oriented L2 writing research, including articles in leading journals, books chapters and edited collections. First with Ilona Leki and then with Chris Tardy, she co-edited the *Journal of Second Language Writing* between 2008 and 2014.
manchon@um.es

Paul Kei Matsuda is Professor of English and Director of Second Language Writing at Arizona State University, in the United States, where he works closely with doctoral students specializing in second language writing. He has founded the Symposium on Second Language Writing and edits the Parlor Press Series on Second Language Writing. He has published widely on the nature, history and definitions of the field of second language writing, writing instruction, identity in writing, writing for publication, and the professional development of second language writing specialists.

Corey McCullough is a doctoral candidate in Composition Studies at the University of New Hampshire, in the Unted States. His scholarly and research interests include second-language writers and writing, particularly in writing center contexts, as well as historical and archival inquiry in the fields of composition, rhetoric, and second-language writing.

Florentina Nicolás-Conesa is Assistant Professor at the University Centre of Defence in the Spanish Air Force Academy in Murcia, Spain. Her research interests include the analysis of writing processes, written products, students' cognition, and L2 learning and teaching. Her doctoral dissertation on "Development of Mental Models of Writing in a Foreign Language Context: Dynamics of Goals and Beliefs" received the best doctoral thesis award by the Spanish Society for Applied Linguistics. She has published her work in the *Journal of Second Language Writing* and in Spanish journals. florinicolas1@yahoo.es

Christina Ortmeier-Hooper is Associate Professor of English at the University of New Hampshire, in the United States. Her research areas reflect her investment in school-university collaborations, writing teacher education, and immigrant adolescent literacy. Along with her monograph, *The ELL Writer: Moving Beyond the Basics in Secondary Schools* (Teachers College Press, 2013), she has edited four collections on second language writing. Her newest book (with Todd Ruecker) is *Linguistically Diverse Immigrant and Resident Writers: Transitions from High School to College* (Routledge, 2016). Her work has also been published in top journals. christina.ortmeier@unh.edu

Ji-Hyun Park is a Ph.D. student in the Second Language Studies program at Michigan State University (USA) with degrees from Seoul National University. She is a Fulbright scholar writing her dissertation on linguistic complexity in L2 writing. parkji36@msu.edu

Susan Parks is Associate Professor at Université Laval in Quebec City, Canada. She teaches in the undergraduate teacher education program for ESL teachers as well as gives graduate courses, including one on second language writing research. Her research mainly focuses on exploring ESL literacy and enculturation processes in school and workplace contexts. Publications of her work are available in a variety of journals, including *Journal of Second Language Writing*, *Canadian Modern Language Review*, *The Modern Language Journal*, *Language Teaching Research*, *The Language Learning Journal*, and *Journal of Language Learning and Technology*. She currently serves on the editorial board of the *Journal of Second Language Writing*. susan.parks@lli.ulaval.ca

Christine Pearson Casanave writes, publishes, and presents on topics in second language writing, scholarly writing for publication, dissertation writing, and doctoral supervising, often focusing on writers and their experiences. She also serves on the editorial boards of several journals, and is currently the book review co-editor (with Yongyan Li) for *Journal of Second Language Writing*. Her current work consists of advising doctoral students (online) at Temple University's Japan campus who are working on qualitative dissertations. She is affiliated with the Middlebury Institute of International at Monterey as Visiting Faculty. casanave@redshift.com

Diane Pecorari is Professor of English Linguistics at Linnaeus University, in Sweden. Her research interests include English medium instruction and questions related to source use and intertextual-

ity in academic writing. Her books include *Teaching to Avoid Plagiarism* (Open University Press, 2013) and, together with Maggie Charles, *Introducing English for Academic Purposes* (Routedge, 2016).
diane.pecorari@mdh.se

Charlene Polio is a Professor in the Department of Linguistics & Germanic, Slavic, Asian, & African Languages at Michigan State University, USA. She is the past editor of *the Annual Review of Applied Linguistics*, and the co-editor of the *Modern Language Journal*. She is particularly interested in the various research methods and measures used in L2 writing as well as the interface between the fields of L2 writing and second language acquisition. She is the co-author with Debra Friedman of *Understanding, Evaluating, and Conducting Second Language Writing Research* (Routledge/Taylor and Francis, 2016). Her most recent work appears in the *Journal of Second Language Writing* and *TESOL Quarterly*.
polio@msu.edu

Melinda Reichelt is Professor of English at the University of Toledo, in the United States, where she directs the ESL writing program. She has published her work in leading journals and is co-author with Tony Silva and Colleen Brice of *Annotated Bibliography of Scholarship in Second Language Writing: 1993–1997* (Ablex, 1999). She co-edited, with Tony Cimasko, *Foreign Language Writing: Principles and Practices* (Parlor Press, 2011).
mreiche@utoledo.edu

Carol Rinnert, Professor Emeritus, Hiroshima City University, has been living in Hiroshima, Japan for almost 30 years. She has taught English writing and linguistics to EFL, ESL, and L1 university students in Japan, the U.S, and Yemen. She is particularly interested in comparing English and Japanese communication styles with a goal of developing intercultural pragmatic competence in speaking and writing. She has published articles with Hiroe Kobayashi in a number of international journals, including the *Journal of Pragmatics*.
rinnert@intl.hiroshima-cu.ac.jp

Julio Roca de Larios is Associate Professor in the Department of Didáctica de la Lengua y la Literatura at the University of Murcia (Spain). His main research interests include second language writing processes and strategies and feedback in writing. He has published extensively on these areas in highly ranked journals and edited books. He currently serves on the editorial board of the *Journal of Second Language Writing*.
jrl@um.es

Miyuki Sasaki is Professor at the Graduate School of Humanities and Social Sciences, Nagoya City University, Japan. Her research interests include second language acquisition, language testing, foreign language education and second language writing. She has published numerous book chapters in edited collections and articles in leading journals in applied linguistics and second language writing.
miyuki.sasaki@gmail.com

Carol Severino is Professor of Rhetoric and Director of the Writing Center and Writing Fellows Program at the University of Iowa, USA. She uses writing center data to investigate issues in second language writing and has published recently in Writing Center Journal and Writing on the Edge. She teaches tutor training courses and the Writing topics course for Iowa's Second

Language Acquisition Ph.D. program. She also teaches travel writing and enjoys writing and publishing travel essays.
carol-severino@uiowa.edu

Tony Silva is Professor in the the Department of English at Purdue University in the United States, where he directs the Graduate Program in Second Language Studies and teaches graduate courses and first year writing courses for international students. With Ilona Leki, he founded and edited the *Journal of Second Language Writing* and with Paul Kei Matsuda he founded the Symposium on Second Language Writing.
tony@purdue.edu

Neomy Storch is a Senior Lecturer in ESL and Applied Linguistics at the University of Melbourne in australia. Her research has focused on issues related to second language (L2) pedagogy and particularly collaborative writing, feedback on L2 writing, and assessing writing development. She has published widely on these topics including a book on collaborative writing (2013) and a co-authored book on corrective feedback (2016).
neomys@unimelb.edu.au

Christine Tardy is Associate Professor in the Department of English of the University of Arizona, in the United States, where she is also Associate Director of the Writing Program. She has published extensively on L2 writing, academic writing, genre theory, and pedagogy and policy and politics of English language instruction. She is Co-Editor of the *Journal of Second Language Writing*.
ctardy@email.arizona.edu

Paige Ware is a Professor in the School of Education and Human Development at Southern Methodist University, in the United States. Her research focuses on the use of multimedia technologies for fostering language and literacy growth among adolescents, as well as on the use of Internet-based communication for promoting intercultural awareness through international and domestic online language and culture partnerships. She was a National Academy of Education/Spencer Post-Doctoral Fellow and the principal investigator of a Department of Education Office of English Language Acquisition (OELA) professional development grant.
pware@mail.smu.edu

Mark Warschauer is Professor of Education at the University of California, Irvine, in the United States, where he directs both the Digital Learning Lab and the Teaching and Learning Research Center. Warschauer is a fellow of the American Educational Research Association and editor-in-chief of AERA Open. His books include *Learning in the Cloud: How (and Why) to Transform Schools with Digital Media* (Teachers College Press), *Laptops and Literacy: Learning in the Wireless Classroom* (Teachers College Press), and *Technology and Social Inclusion: Rethinking the Digital Divide* (MIT Press).
markw@uci.edu

Sarah Weigle is Professor of Applied Linguistics at Georgia State University in the United States. She has published research in the areas of assessment, second language writing, and teacher education, She is the author of *Assessing Writing* (2002, Cambridge University Press) and her work has also been published in journals such as *Assessing Writing, Language Testing, Journal of Second Language Writing,* or *TESOL Quarterly*. Her current research focuses on assessing integrated skills and the use of automated scoring for second language writing.
sweigle@gsu.edu

Shauna Wight is Assistant Professor of English at Southeast Missouri State University, USA, where she teaches courses in TESOL, English Education, and Composition. Her research interests focus on multilingual adolescent writers' transitions to college, pre-college outreach, and school-university collaborations. Her work has appeared in the edited collection, *Linguistically Diverse Immigrant and Resident Writers: Transitions from High School to College.*
ssz27@wildcats.unh.edu

Jessica Williams is the Head of the Department of Linguistics and teaches in the M.A. TESOL program at the University of Illinois at Chicago, USA. She has published articles on variety of topics in second language acquisition, including second language writing, lexical acquisition, and the effect of focus on form. She is the co-editor (with Bill VanPatten) of *Theories in Second Language Acquisition*. She is also the author or co-author of more than a dozen ESL textbooks.
jessicaw@uic.edu

Cui Zhang is Assistant Professor in the Department of English and Theatre at Eastern Kentucky University, in the United States. Her research interests focus on the development of second language writing abilities and on reading-writing interactions and their applications in writing instruction. Her recent journal publications have appeared in *Journal of Second Language Writing, Language Teaching*, and *TESOL Journal*.
Cui.Zhang@nau.edu

Name index

Subject index